Harry,
Hope you enjoy this - thanks so very much for your support
Janis

Rescue! The Companies' Creditors Arrangement Act

Janis P. Sarra, B.A., M.A., LL.B., LL.M., S.J.D.

University of British Columbia Faculty of Law

THOMSON
CARSWELL™

Library and Archives Canada Cataloguing in Publication

Sarra, Janis Pearl, 1954-
Rescue! : the Companies' Creditors Arrangement Act / Janis P. Sarra. — 2007 ed.

Includes text of Companies' Creditors Arrangement Act.
ISBN 978-0-7798-0002-5

1. Canada. Companies' Creditors Arrangement Act. 2. Bankruptcy—Canada. 3. Debtor and creditor—Canada. I. Canada. Companies' Creditors Arrangement Act II. Title.
KE1518.C6S27 2007 346.7107'8 C2007-900016-9
KF1544.S27 2007

Composition: Computer Composition of Canada Inc.

One Corporate Plaza
2075 Kennedy Road
Toronto, Ontario
M1T 3V4

Customer Relations:
Toronto 1-416-609-3800
Elsewhere in Canada/U.S. 1-800-387-5164
Fax 1-416-298-5082
World Wide Web: http://www.carswell.com
E-mail: carswell.orders@thomson.com

ABOUT THE AUTHOR

Janis Sarra, B.A., M.A., LL.B., LL.M., S.J.D. (Toronto)

Dr. Sarra is Associate Dean and Associate Professor of Law, University of British Columbia Faculty of Law, Vancouver, Canada. In 2004, she was awarded the title of Distinguished University Scholar. She is the Director of the National Centre for Business Law at UBC Faculty of Law.

Dr. Sarra teaches corporate law, commercial insolvency law, contract law and law and economics at the UBC Faculty of Law. She was a commercial and labour arbitrator prior to joining the Faculty of Law in 2000, and is a member of the Bar in Ontario. Dr. Sarra is a member of The Insolvency Institute of Canada, the American Bankruptcy Institute, INSOL Academics Forum, the International Insolvency Institute and the Canadian Bar Association. She is a previous member of the Board of Directors for the Canadian Association of Insolvency and Restructuring Professionals and the Board of Directors of the Canadian Insolvency Foundation. She is co-author, with the Honourable L.W. Houlden and the Honourable G.W. Morawetz, of *The 2006 Annotated Bankruptcy and Insolvency Act* (Toronto: Carswell, 2005).

ACKNOWLEDGMENTS

My sincere thanks to The Insolvency Institute of Canada and to the Social Sciences and Humanities Research Council of Canada for research funding for this project.

My heartfelt thanks to the Honourable James Farley, the Honourable Geoffrey Morawetz, Susan Grundy, Jean-Daniel Breton, Patrick McCarthy, Bob Sanderson and the two anonymous academic readers for their comments on a draft of this book. My thanks also to Ronald Davis for assistance on the pension law section of the text.

Given that one audience for this text is young practitioners and law students, my thanks also to UBC law students Bridget Gilbride and Ian Graf for providing comments from that perspective. My thanks to Bettina Ruhstein (Law II) for research support and Karen Higginson for administrative support.

As always, I wish to thank my family for their support, particularly my son Alex and my partner Book, who once again tolerated piles of cases throughout the house over a period of many months.

FOREWORD

As a judge of the Superior Court of Justice for Ontario, I always looked forward to reading whatever Professor Janis Sarra wrote on a multitude of topics; with my retirement that expectation remains. She was always insightful and balanced. This book on the *Companies' Creditors Arrangement Act* follows that excellent tradition. She has produced a very fine and thoughtful work that will be indispensable to those practicing or interested in the field.

Even on its expanded basis, the *CCAA* is a rather skeletal statute. While it is now over 70 years old, there have been significant periods when this statute was basically unutilized. However the past two decades have seen its employment to deal not only with the reorganization of ailing companies, but also to provide an effective mechanism for preserving and maximizing value for creditors and other interested stakeholders even if the corporation were not rehabilitated, but rather, viable parts of the enterprise sold on a going concern basis. The generality and open-endedness of the *CCAA* has proved to be a fertile ground upon which those with a great deal of ingenuity have been able to sow the seeds of imaginative solutions to fit an ever evolving set of economic, financial and operational circumstances.

While the judiciary involved in this type of work in Canada have taken care to write extensively on the topic when able, unfortunately the chaotic time pressures of fast moving cases have required that many decisions be supported by only quickly prepared brief reasons. It is therefore very valuable for the profession and public that Professor Sarra has been able to "tie it all together" in such an able and understandable fashion while appropriately positing points of open debate for consideration.

We are indeed blessed by having Professor Sarra, who has now become a joint author of *Houlden and Morawetz*, provide us with a book of this calibre. I warmly recommend it to you.

Honourable James M. Farley, Q.C.
Senior Counsel to McCarthy Tétrault LLP
(Retired from the Superior Court of Justice
for Ontario)

TABLE OF CONTENTS

TABLE OF CASES

CHAPTER 1

INTRODUCTION AND OVERVIEW OF THE *CCAA*

I. INTRODUCTION

The *Companies' Creditors Arrangement Act (CCAA)* is an extraordinary Canadian statute.[1] Extremely short in length, only 22 provisions, it is one of the enabling tools to allow insolvent companies to restructure. It has been the statute of choice for debtor corporations in every major restructuring in the past quarter century, including national airlines, major steel and forestry companies, telecommunications companies and the national blood delivery system. The statute's full title, *An Act to Facilitate Compromises and Arrangements between Companies and Their Creditors,* precisely describes its purpose; providing a court-supervised process to facilitate the negotiation of compromises and arrangements where companies are experiencing financial distress, in order to allow them to devise a survival strategy that is acceptable to their creditors.

While there is no official database, a recent empirical study by the author has found that there have been 254 cases under the *CCAA*, the overwhelming majority of these in the past 20 years.[2] Of those cases, the majority were privately held companies.

CCAA proceedings can involve a broad range of workout options. The going forward solution to the firm's financial distress depends on the reason for the insolvency, the firm's capital structure, the viability of its business plan and effectiveness of its governance structure. One could broadly categorize financial distress in two ways.

In the first category, the debtor corporation may have used its assets efficiently, but a temporary downturn in the market or unforeseen liquidity crunch has precipitated the insolvency. Similarly, the debt/equity ratio decided on by corporate officers for one type of market may no longer be sustainable with unforeseen capital market changes. In such cases, the best option may be to devise a plan that allows the firm to keep operating for a period, where there is a current or expected future market

---

[1] *Companies' Creditors Arrangement Act,* R.S.C. 1985, c. C-36, as amended (*CCAA*).

[2] Janis Sarra, UBC *CCAA Empirical Study*, data on file with author, funded by the Social Sciences and Humanities Research Council of Canada.

for its output. Hence, it is essential to understand the particular market in which the debtor is operating.

In the second category, the problem is one of governance, such as management's failure to respond adequately or in a timely manner to capital market changes or failure to develop and implement a viable business plan. Financial decisions, such as borrowing on a short-term basis that has negative long-term consequences, or cost overruns on plant expansion can also account for the firm's financial distress. The insolvency has often signalled inefficient use of assets or managerial slack or incompetence. A firm can be inefficient, and the optimal strategy is to continue operating, but to radically change the governance practices to generate value for the firm. The debtor may need to change how it achieves efficiency, including improving productivity, implementing better decision making and oversight structures, and shifting its labour/management relationships from confrontational to co-operative in order to have all stakeholders committed to a long-term survival strategy for the firm. When the firm is economically inefficient and change in governance will not remedy its financial distress, the best outcome may be to liquidate or sell the business as a going concern and release the capital to higher value uses. It avoids the further erosion of capital if losses are projected over the long term.[3] Often there is a combination of governance and market factors that have led to the insolvency.

As with all commercial economies, Canada's statutory framework creates a hierarchy of claims to the corporation's assets. Secured creditors, subject to very limited exceptions, generally have first claim on the assets when a firm is insolvent. In contrast, shareholders' equity claims have little or no value. Hence, during firm financial distress, it is the senior secured creditors that are the parties largely driving the process, although directors and officers may remain in place for a period of time during the negotiations for a going forward business plan. While directors continue to have an obligation to act in the best interests of the corporation, commercial reality dictates that they must be sensitive to the demands of secured creditors or the process will fail and the business will be liquidated. How those interests are thus reconciled with other stakeholders such as employees, trade suppliers, customers and the community as a whole is one of the key challenges for insolvency proceedings.

While the debtor and its advisors need to have a clear understanding of the source of the debtor corporation's financial distress if there is to be a viable workout, this information is not used to assign blame under the *CCAA*. Rather, it provides important information to determine the operational or other changes that may be required to allow the debtor corporation to make its business viable and devise a business plan that can garner the requisite creditor support.

Hence, a *CCAA* restructuring proceeding is a step to avoid bankruptcy. In bankruptcy, the assets of a company vest with a trustee in bankruptcy, who is an insol-

---

[3] Janis Sarra, "Governance and Control: The Role of Debtor-in-Possession Financing under the *CCAA*", in J. Sarra, ed., *Annual Review of Insolvency Law, 2004* (Toronto: Carswell, 2005) 119-172.

vency professional that liquidates the assets and distributes the proceeds among creditors according to the priority of their claims, as set out in the *Bankruptcy and Insolvency Act (BIA)*.[4] The company could still be sold as a going concern, although it is the trustee that has carriage of the process, not the directors and officers. Insolvency and bankruptcy law is aimed at allocating decision and control rights in the financially distressed corporation to ensure optimal use of the assets, whether the ultimate disposition is continuation of the business, sale as a going concern and/ or liquidation.[5]

Where an insolvent corporation's business is viable, the *CCAA* provides an opportunity for the debtor corporation to negotiate a workout with its creditors, either through compromises of the amount of claims owing or timing of payments, refinancing agreements, conversion of debt to equity, or the injection of new equity investment in the firm. Restructuring can result in arrangements that are a hybrid of these strategies, such as liquidation on a going-concern basis or liquidation of part of the business in order to finance restructuring of the rest of the enterprise and dispose of underperforming assets, or a mix of liquidation and going forward business, which the courts have approved in appropriate circumstances.[6] A business is frequently worth more as a going concern than if its assets are liquidated on a piecemeal basis to satisfy creditors' claims.

Where a debtor corporation can restructure, preservation of ongoing value, such as the skilled workforce, supply arrangements, customer base and other goodwill, adds extra value over and above the aggregate value of individual hard assets. Alternatively, sale of the enterprise on a going-concern basis to third parties may be the solution, especially if the new owner brings operational expertise, management skills, liquidity, access to reserve capital, and other benefits to the business. The court-supervised process assists with controlling and allocating the collective action and transaction costs among the firm's diverse creditors, thus ensuring more value is extracted from the firm.[7]

While Canada's insolvency system historically favoured liquidation of firms that were unable to meet their debts as they generally became due, the system has shifted to more of a rehabilitation system, although there continues to be a fair degree of control by senior lenders. Canada's regime shifted towards a rehabilitation model

---

[4] *Bankruptcy and Insolvency Act*, R.S.C. 1985, c. B-3, as amended (*BIA*). The *BIA* also contains restructuring provisions, discussed below.

[5] G. Triantis, "The Interplay Between Liquidation and Reorganization in Bankruptcy, The Role of Screens, Gatekeepers and Guillotines" (1996) 16 Int. Rev. Law & Economics 101 at 103.

[6] *Anvil Range Mining Corp., Re* (2002), 34 C.B.R. (4th) 157 (Ont. C.A.), additional reasons at (2002), 38 C.B.R. (4th) 5 (Ont. C.A.), leave to appeal refused (2003), 2003 CarswellOnt 730 (S.C.C.).

[7] Thomas Jackson, "Translating Assets and Liabilities in the Bankruptcy Forum" and the Hon. Richard Posner, Chief Judge, U.S. Court of Appeals for the Seventh Circuit, "Foreword", both in J.S. Bhandari and L.A. Weiss, eds., *Corporate Bankruptcy: Economic and Legal Perspectives* (Cambridge: Cambridge University Press, 1996) at xi, 53. Lynn LoPucki and George Triantis, "A Systems Approach to Comparing U.S. and Canadian Reorganization of Financially Distressed Companies" in Jacob Ziegel, ed., *Current Developments in International and Comparative Corporate Insolvency Law* (Oxford: Clarendon Press, 1994) at 109.

almost a decade earlier than nations such as the United Kingdom or Germany, which are now moving from liquidation to reorganization as a key focus of the insolvency system. This global context is important, because, as will be seen throughout this book, there is pressure for the system to change once again, given the control shifts in international capital markets in terms of the nature and type of lenders that increasingly dominate capital markets. The most recent changes raise new public policy challenges for an effective restructuring system.

Insolvency law is an indispensable component of commercial economies and regulates governance of the insolvent corporation during the key period of decision-making regarding its future. Insolvency law also plays a broad social and economic role in overall economic planning; the survival of financially distressed firms and the economic activity that they generate are in themselves important objectives of the system.[8] However, rehabilitation of the firm can only occur where a business is viable, and there may be some industries in which current capacity must be rationalized. Globalization pressures make these determinations complex, because the decision is layered with whether there is a national interest in preserving particular types of economic activity within Canada or whether the assets should be put to their highest use elsewhere.

There can also be public policy issues associated with allowing one corporation to shed its debt and reorganize, creating a somewhat competitive advantage over corporations in the same market that were competitive until the debtor went through reorganization, down-sized or took other measures, free of the costs normally imposed on such activities by contractual and regulatory obligations. Workouts that provide an advantage to one party to the detriment of more vulnerable parties can create a downward spiral of economic activity in a particular sector. Arguably, the goal of the insolvency system is to maximize the value of the enterprise overall; and where firms can generate more value for stakeholders on a going-concern basis, the insolvency system should facilitate the debtor corporation's negotiation with creditors for a viable plan of arrangement.[9] Equally, however, one needs to be cognizant of the overall impact on a particular sector where one major corporation has restructured when the entire sector is in a struggle to survive.

1. The *CCAA* in the Context of the Canadian Insolvency System

There are currently three principal insolvency statutes in Canada, which together provide a regime that deals with insolvency of individuals and companies, the *Companies' Creditors Arrangement Act,* the *Bankruptcy and Insolvency Act* and the *Winding-up and Restructuring Act.*[10] Also significant are the arrangement provisions

---

[8] Karen Gross, *Failure and Forgiveness: Rebalancing the Bankruptcy System* (New Haven: Yale University Press, 1997).

[9] Janis Sarra, *Creditor Rights and the Public Interest, Restructuring Insolvent Corporations* (Toronto: University of Toronto Press, 2003).

[10] *Winding-up and Restructuring Act*, R.S.C. 1985, c. W-11, as amended.

of federal, provincial and territorial corporations statutes. Other mechanisms to deal with firm financial distress are receiverships under provincial courts of justice statutes, and remedies that arise out of secured transactions under provincial and territorial personal property security statutes.[11] There are also provincial and territorial statutes that deal with fraudulent conveyances, assignments and preferences, which can be accessed as a means to enforce creditor claims when a firm is in financial distress.[12] The discussion in this part confines itself only to the first four of these options.

The *Bankruptcy and Insolvency Act (BIA)* addresses both individuals and companies, and provides a mechanism for assigning or petitioning financially troubled debtors into bankruptcy and liquidating their assets, as well as providing a series of interim mechanisms such as appointment of receivers to take conservatory and other measures for the protection of creditors.[13]

When a corporation is insolvent, there are remedies available to creditors. The insolvency scheme provides that secured creditors can privately enforce their claims by meeting statutory and common law requirements of demand, reasonable notice and notice of intention to enforce security.[14] Once these are met, the creditor can privately appoint or seek a court appointment of a receiver to realize on the property securing its claims. A creditor falls within the scope of the *BIA* enforcement provisions if the debtor is "insolvent" within the meaning of the statute and the collateral being enforced against by the secured creditor constitutes all or substantially all of a category of the debtor's assets. The *BIA* defines an "insolvent person" as one who has debts exceeding $1,000, is unable to meet obligations or has ceased paying them in the ordinary course of business as they generally become due, or the aggregate of whose property is not, at fair valuation, sufficient, or if disposed of at a fairly conducted sale under legal process would not be sufficient to enable payment of all obligations due and accruing due.[15]

The *BIA* is aimed at bringing uniformity to the administration and liquidation of bankrupt estates in Canada. The underlying principle is that creditors should control administration of the assets of the corporation that has been placed into bankruptcy, because liquidation is for the almost exclusive benefit of the creditors and they are in the best position to determine what is in their interests. The *BIA* sets a hierarchy for the satisfaction of claims.[16]

---

[11] See for example, Ontario *Courts of Justice Act*, R.S.O. 1990, c. C. 43, s. 101; Alberta *Personal Property Security Act*, R.S.A. 2000, c. P-7, s. 66; Nova Scotia *Personal Property Security Act*, S.N.S. 1995-96, c. 13, s. 66.

[12] For a helpful introduction to these other remedies on insolvency, see Kevin McElcheran, *Commercial Insolvency in Canada*, (Toronto: LexisNexis Canada Inc., 2005).

[13] *Bankruptcy and Insolvency Act*, R.S.C. 1985, c. B-3, as amended (*BIA*).

[14] Section 244, *BIA*.

[15] Section 2(1), *BIA*.

[16] This hierarchy interacts with other statutes, such as the *Bank Act*, section 427; see also provincial statutes such as the *Personal Property Security Act*.

In addition to the mechanisms outlined in the *BIA* addressing the realization of property of a debtor and the distribution thereof to the creditors according to their relative rights, the *BIA* also provides a scheme for commercial "proposals", in order to allow an insolvent person or a bankrupt an opportunity to restructure its affairs and become financially viable.[17] As with the *CCAA* process, the proposal process allows a brief reprieve in which the *status quo* is maintained and creditors' realization rights are temporarily suspended. Proposal is defined in the *BIA* as including a proposal for a composition, where creditors agree to accept less than full repayment or an extension of time; and/or a scheme of arrangement in terms of alteration of debt and equity structure.[18] Corporate officers retain control of the corporation's assets and operations, and the trustee that assists with development of the proposal acts in a monitoring and advisory capacity, as opposed to taking over control of the company. The *BIA* proposal proceedings are used for individuals and for all sizes of business, from sole proprietorships to larger corporations. The greatest challenge for using the *BIA* as the tool to rescue a financially distressed company, however, is its "sunset clause"; specifically, failure to negotiate and receive creditor support for, and the sanction of the court of, a proposal within six months results in the company automatically becoming bankrupt. There is no judicial discretion to extend the stay past six months. This is discussed further below.

The second statute is the *Companies' Creditors Arrangement Act (CCAA)*, which allows corporations to negotiate a plan of arrangement or compromise with their creditors, as discussed in the introduction.[19] The *CCAA* is available to debtor corporations that are insolvent or bankrupt and have debts greater than $5 million.[20] Both the *BIA* proposal provisions and the *CCAA* allow for compromise of claims of both secured and unsecured creditors. Any reorganization of the equity of the corporation requires concurrent proceedings under corporations statutes.[21] Section

---

[17] Section 50, *BIA*. The *BIA* provides that a proposal may be made by an insolvent person and a bankrupt, as well as by various persons on behalf of the insolvent person or bankrupt. For ease of reading, the remainder of this text refers only to a proposal being filed by an insolvent person, and the reader should understand that the provisions apply equally to the other situations, unless specifically stated otherwise. Refer also to section 2 of the *BIA* for the definitions of "person", "insolvent person" and "corporation". In effect, the *BIA* applies to a wide category of debtors, whether the debtor is an individual, partnership, corporation, cooperative society, association, etc., excluding banks, insurance companies, trust companies, loan companies and railway companies.

[18] Section 2(1), *BIA*. *Mutual Trust Co.* v. *Scott, Pichelli & Graci Ltd.* (1999), 11 C.B.R. (4th) 54 (Ont. Bktcy.), additional reasons at (1999), 11 C.B.R. (4th) 62 (Ont. Bktcy.).

[19] *Companies' Creditors Arrangement Act*, R.S.C. 1985, c. C-36, as amended (*CCAA*).

[20] Section 2, *CCAA*. The *CCAA* specifies that a debtor company may be a company that is insolvent or bankrupt. The distinction as relates to proceedings in respect of a bankrupt are found in section 11.6 of the *CCAA*. This section provides that a bankrupt can avail itself of the provisions of the *CCAA* only in the situation where the bankruptcy does not result from a failed restructuring proceeding under the *BIA*, and then only with the prior approval of inspectors appointed to the estate. The remainder of the text refers only to a plan of arrangement being filed in respect of an insolvent person, and the reader should understand that the comment applies equally to a bankrupt, unless specifically stated otherwise.

[21] Once Chapter 47 is proclaimed in force, this will no longer be a requirement. *An Act to Establish the Wage Earner Protection Program Act, to amend the Bankruptcy and Insolvency Act and the Companies' Creditors Arrangement Act and to make consequential amendments to other Acts*, S.C. 2005, Chapter 47, Royal Assent November 25, 2005, not yet proclaimed in force as of December 2006.

8 of the *CCAA* specifies that the *Act* has full force and effect notwithstanding anything to the contrary contained in a security interest; hence parties cannot contract out of the *CCAA* provisions.[22] Whereas the *BIA* is highly codified, the *CCAA* is a skeletal statute. The scope and contours of the *CCAA* have been set through the caselaw, with the court acting in a supervisory capacity during the period that parties negotiate a workout strategy and business plan.

The third insolvency statute is the *Winding-up and Restructuring Act (WURA)*, which covers financially distressed financial institutions and certain corporations and allows such persons to be liquidated or restructured.[23] Finally, there is the *Farm Debt Mediation Act*, enacted to help farmers in financial distress by allowing them to seek relief from secured and unsecured debt in particular circumstances.[24]

There are also private workouts that are undertaken without the benefit of any statutory mechanism. An insolvent corporation can restructure its affairs through a private arrangement with its creditors, which may be possible if there are few creditors or it is a closely held company where there is some ability to deal with equity and debt claims for only a few stakeholders. Use of a private workout does not necessarily signal to consumers or trade suppliers that the corporation is in difficulty and may facilitate the retention of key employees and distributors who might otherwise begin diversifying their risk by seeking employment or contracts elsewhere.[25] Generally, private workouts with a few creditors are cheaper and faster than court-supervised processes, in part, precisely because there are fewer creditors and thus fewer transaction costs and collective action problems in the negotiations for a workout.

However, private workouts are rarely a practical solution, except in special circumstances. The characteristics of an efficient restructuring tool include the ability to suspend recourse against the debtor while the discussions are progressing, and the ability to force a minority of creditors to be bound by an agreement acceptable to the majority. Under the *BIA* and the *CCAA*, the debtor need only win the support of a majority in number representing two thirds in value of claims in each class of creditors, present or represented at the meeting, in order to meet the statutory requirements for a proposal or plan; hence the debtor can deal with "holdout creditors", who will not agree to a plan or will agree only if they receive payment in full. This ability to deal with holdout creditors is not possible under a private workout. In other words, the stay under the *BIA* or *CCAA* creates the potential ability to compel creditors to act collectively rather than individually. In many cases of cor-

---

[22] *Hongkong Bank of Canada* v. *Chef Ready Foods Ltd.* (1990), 4 C.B.R. (3d) 311 (B.C. C.A.).

[23] *Winding-up and Restructuring Act*, R.S.C. 1985, c. W-11 (*WURA*). For example, by virtue of section 3(3) of the *Canada Business Corporations Act*, R.S.C. 1985, c. C-44, as amended *(CBCA)*. The *WURA* does not apply to corporations incorporated under the *CBCA*.

[24] *Farm Debt Mediation Act*, S.C. 1997, c. 21. This Act is essentially a voluntary mediation act, but since it has no mechanism to bind creditors who do not agree with a proposed arrangement, its utility is limited.

[25] Janis Sarra, *Creditor Rights and the Public Interest, Restructuring Insolvent Corporations* (Toronto: University of Toronto Press, 2003).

porate insolvency, there are hundreds and sometimes thousands of creditors, and thus a private workout is not possible. Given that creditors are not prevented from seeking to enforce their claims during negotiation for a private workout, debtor corporations often seek the protection of court-supervised processes.[26] For companies with a number of creditors or any complexity in the debt structure, the provisions under both the *BIA* and the *CCAA* that stay creditors' ability to realize on their claims for a period, provide a breathing space to corporations so that they can negotiate a workout plan with creditors.

A less commonly used means of restructuring than the *BIA* or *CCAA* is use of the arrangement provisions under the *Canada Business Corporations Act (CBCA)* and companion provincial and territorial corporations statutes, where at least one corporation in a group of affiliated companies that are trying to restructure is solvent, even if the principal company in the corporate group is itself insolvent.[27] The principal reason for using the *CBCA* or other corporations statutes is to preserve equity for shareholders. A precondition to use of the *BIA* or *CCAA* is that the corporation is insolvent and thus there is little or no equity remaining in the corporation.

In contrast, the arrangement provisions of the *CBCA* require the corporation to be solvent, and thus can be used to try to preserve shareholder equity as well as value for creditors.[28] For example, in *Dome Petroleum*, Dome was insolvent yet the proposed arrangement required amalgamations and debt exchanges, neither easily provided for under the *CCAA*, even if the application had been brought conjointly with a *CBCA* application.[29] Amoco Acquisitions, a solvent corporation, applied to the court under the *CCAA* and received a declaration from the Alberta Court of Queen's Bench that its proposed arrangement was an arrangement pursuant to the *CBCA* and that the court had jurisdiction. It then proceeded to secure the support of creditors and shareholders, and the endorsement of the court to amalgamate with Dome and several other subsidiaries. The Court thus facilitated the plan of arrangement by liberally interpreting the arrangement provisions of the *CBCA,* by finding at least one company solvent within a group of affiliated companies seeking to utilize the corporations statute to effect a restructuring.

As this book goes to press, it is important to note that legislative reform has been proposed. Chapter 47 of the Statutes of Canada, 2005, amending the *CCAA* and the *BIA* and creating a new national wage earner protection program, has been enacted

[26] *Ibid.*

[27] *Canada Business Corporations Act,* R.S.C. 1985, c. C-44, as amended *(CBCA)*. For an example of provincial provisions, see Ontario *Business Corporations Act,* R.S.O. 1990, c. B. 16, section 186; and Alberta *Business Corporations Act*, R.S.A. 2000, c. B-9, s. 192.

[28] See for example, the cases of *Dome Petroleum* and *Unitel Communications* in J. Ziegel and D. Baird, eds., *Case Studies in Recent Canadian Insolvency Reorganizations, In Honour of the Honourable Lloyd W. Houlden* (Toronto: Carswell, 1997).

[29] Simon Scott, "The Acquisition of Dome Petroleum Limited by Amoco Corporation" in Ziegel and Baird, *ibid.* at 300, citing unreported judgment, *Amoco Canada Petroleum Co.* v. *Dome Petroleum Ltd.* (January 28, 1988), Doc. Calgary 8701-20108 (Alta. Q.B.) at 311, 313.

but has not yet been proclaimed in force.[30] Subsequent to the legislation receiving Royal Assent in November 2005, there was a federal election in Canada and the Liberal government was replaced by a Conservative government. The new Government is expected to bring further amendments forward early in 2007 prior to proclaiming Chapter 47 in force.[31] There are references throughout this book to the proposed changes to the *CCAA* under Chapter 47.

2. Policy Objectives of the *CCAA*

The *CCAA* has a broad remedial purpose, permitting compromises or arrangements to be made between an insolvent company and its creditors. The courts have held that the *CCAA* allows the debtor company to avoid bankruptcy, to continue operating, and to find a business strategy that enables it to meet the demands of creditors.[32] The *CCAA* is to be given a large and liberal interpretation so as best to meet its policy objectives.[33]

Canadian courts have held that the *CCAA* is aimed at avoiding, where possible, the devastating social and economic consequences of the cessation of business operations, and at allowing the corporation to carry on business in a manner that causes the least possible harm to employees and the communities in which it operates. There is a public policy interest in allowing for a certain transition period to allow debtors to economically adjust in difficult markets in unsettled times; and the courts have held that co-operation is required if the debtor corporation is to emerge competitive, innovative, and able to withstand temporary adversity.[34] The costs of the process are outweighed by the benefits of potential success and the protection of multiple interests. The Alberta Court in *Fracmaster* held that the objective of the

---

[30] *An Act to Establish the Wage Earner Protection Program Act, to amend the Bankruptcy and Insolvency Act and the Companies' Creditors Arrangement Act and to make consequential amendments to other Acts,* S.C. 2005, Chapter 47, Royal Assent November 25, 2005, not yet proclaimed in force as of December 2006 (Chapter 47). On December 8, 2006, the Government gave notice of further amendments under the *Notice of Ways and Means Motion to introduce an Act to amend the Bankruptcy and Insolvency Act, the Companies' Creditors Arrangement Act, the Wage Earners Protection Act and Chapter 47 of the Statutes of Canada, 2005,* (December 8, 2006, Library of Parliament), which are primarily in the nature of administrative amendments to Chapter 47 to clarify language or align the provisions of the *CCAA* more directly with the companion provisions of the *BIA*. However, the amendments have not yet been tabled as of December 31, 2006.

[31] Current projections are that Chapter 47 may come into force in 2007 (Industry Canada, Policy Branch).

[32] *Multidev Immobilia Inc.* v. *S.A. Just Invest,* (1988), 70 C.B.R. (N.S.) 91, [1988] R.J.Q. 1928 (Que. S.C.); *Meridian Development Inc.* v. *Toronto Dominion Bank* (1984), 52 C.B.R. (N.S.) 109, 32 Alta L.R. (2d) 150 (Alta. Q.B.).

[33] *Nova Metal Products Inc.* v. *Comiskey (Trustee of)* (1990), 1 C.B.R. (3d) 101, (sub nom. *Elan Corp.* v. *Comiskey*) 1 O.R. (3d) 289 (Ont. C.A.); *Citibank Canada* v. *Chase Manhattan Bank of Canada* (1991), 5 C.B.R. (3d) 165 (Ont. Gen. Div.).

[34] *Algoma Steel Inc., Re* (2001), 2001 CarswellOnt 4640, [2002] O.J. No. 66, 30 C.B.R. (4th) 1 (Ont. S.C.J. [Commercial List]), LeSage, C.J.S.C. at para. 8; *Sammi Atlas Inc., Re* (1998), 3 C.B.R. (4th) 171 (Ont. Gen. Div. [Commercial List]), at 173-4.

CCAA to facilitate restructuring should include consideration of interests beyond those of senior creditors.[35]

The *CCAA* was enacted in 1933, but was really only rediscovered as a valuable restructuring tool in the past 25 years. The *CCAA* has the simultaneous objectives of maximizing creditor recovery, preservation of going concern value where possible, preservation of jobs and communities affected by the firm's financial distress, rehabilitation of honest but unfortunate debtors, and enhancing the credit system generally.[36] These objectives can be measured by whether production has been maximized; whether there is a resultant generation of consumer surplus and overall welfare of the enterprise; whether the corporation has provided opportunities for workers to remain productive; whether a greater flow of profits to investors has been generated than would occur if they invested elsewhere; and whether the flow of benefits and size of return to suppliers and other creditors is such that this is optimal use of their capital and supplies, rather than directing their resources elsewhere.[37] A workout can be effective where these complex relationships interact in a cost effective, productive, and innovative manner.

One measure of a successful *CCAA* workout is the financial health of the corporation some years later. However, the nature of restructuring proceedings is shifting, such that the longer term financial health and wealth generating activity of the debtor may no longer be the only measure of a successful *CCAA* application. Although the public policy objectives of the statute remain the same, there are new actors entering the market and new efforts at controlling the process and outcome of a *CCAA* proceeding, such that these public policy goals may be at some risk. This is most evident in the discussion of DIP financing in chapter 4, but is highlighted throughout this text.

Notwithstanding the success of the *CCAA* in meeting its legislative objective of facilitating plans of arrangement and compromise with creditors, the statute is not without its critics. The skeletal nature of the statute means that the supervising judge is required to make numerous procedural and substantive decisions during the *CCAA* proceedings. There has been some criticism that this leaves judges with too much discretion and parties with too much uncertainty.[38] U.S. lenders, who often supply capital for a restructuring, are accustomed to a highly rules-based lending environment during insolvency and frequently are concerned about the lack of codification under the *CCAA*.

However, as will be discussed in chapter 3 on the role of the courts, examination of the caselaw reveals that the role of judges is twofold: supervising the proceedings

---

[35] *Fracmaster Ltd., Re* (1999), 11 C.B.R. (4th) 204 (Alta. Q.B.), Paperny, J., affirmed *Royal Bank* v. *Fracmaster Ltd.* (1999), 11 C.B.R. (4th) 230, 1999 ABCA 178 (Alta. C.A.) at paras. 18-23.

[36] For a discussion, see Janis P. Sarra, *Creditor Rights and the Public Interest, Restructuring Insolvent Corporations* (Toronto: University of Toronto Press, 2003).

[37] Margaret Blair, *Ownership and Control: Rethinking Corporate Governance for the Twenty-First Century* (Washington, DC: Brookings Institute, 1995) at 240.

[38] Andrew Kent, "Comment on Professor Yamauchi's Paper" (2004) 40 Canadian Business L.J. 295.

and weighing the prejudice to parties of particular decisions, and tempering the activities of the most aggressive and powerful parties in the restructuring process. The *CCAA* is a statute that facilitates bargaining. However, that bargaining occurs in light of radically different economic stakes in the financially distressed company, unequal bargaining power, and frequently, information asymmetries. While it is not realistic to expect a level playing field in a *CCAA* workout, the court's role in balancing interests and prejudice has become an extremely significant one.

As will be seen throughout this text, Parliament has addressed the uncertainty question in its proposed amendments to the *CCAA* in Chapter 47. A number of current practices of the court will be codified for the first time, enhancing the transparency of particular rights and remedies in such proceedings, and arguably creating greater certainty in some cases. At the same time, Parliament has chosen to leave a fair degree of discretion with the court in its exercise of jurisdiction under the *CCAA*.

3. Policy Instruments

The primary instrument under the *CCAA* is to grant a stay of proceedings against the debtor corporation so that it has breathing room to develop a going forward business and financial plan with its creditors. The *CCAA* maintains the *status quo* in terms of the debtor's financial relationships for the period of the stay, while the debtor corporation negotiates with creditors and seeks approval for a plan that will allow it to continue operating.[39] It provides a structured environment in which the debtor corporation can carry on business and retain control over assets during the negotiations.[40] The courts have also held that a public policy objective is to permit a broad balancing of stakeholder interests in the insolvent corporation.[41]

One of the objectives of an efficient insolvency system is that it discourages both premature liquidation and deferred liquidation. Premature liquidation arises because over-caution by directors and officers in respect of their own liability risk leads to filing of bankruptcy prematurely, or creditors move to enforce their claims on all or substantially all of the assets without a prior determination of whether there is going concern value in the enterprise. The *CCAA* provides debtors with a tool to act prior to this point as it provides a stay of proceedings without having to become bankrupt and the temporary stay allows for negotiations with creditors who might otherwise enforce their claims and prematurely insist that assets be liquidated.[42] Deferred liquidation is where directors and officers have not acted in a timely manner to deal with the firm's financial distress, specifically, to file under the *CCAA* or under the

---

[39] *Quintette Coal Ltd.* v. *Nippon Steel Corp.* (1990), 80 C.B.R. (N.S.) 98 (B.C. S.C.).

[40] *Blue Range Resource Corp., Re* (2000), 192 D.L.R. (4th) 281, 20 C.B.R. (4th) 187 (Alta. C.A.).

[41] *Nova Metal Products Inc.* v. *Comiskey (Trustee of)* (1990), 1 C.B.R. (3d) 101, (sub nom. *Elan Corp.* v. *Comiskey*) 1 O.R. (3d) 289 (Ont. C.A.); *Air Canada, Re* (2004), 47 C.B.R. (4th) 189 (Ont. S.C.J. [Commercial List]). For a discussion, see Janis P. Sarra, *Creditor Rights and the Public Interest, Restructuring Insolvent Corporations* (Toronto: University of Toronto Press, 2003).

[42] A restructuring by the debtor or a going concern sale by a creditor may provide economic efficiency.

proposal or bankruptcy provisions of the *BIA* in a timely manner; hence, there has been unnecessary further depletion of assets that has harmed creditors' claims. Chapter 2 deals at length with the stay provisions and how they serve as a policy instrument in achieving the goals of the statute.

The second principal instrument of the statute is that it provides a framework in which negotiations can take place for a plan of compromise or arrangement. After the court grants the stay, the debtor corporation can then identify the various stakeholders with a claim or interest in the company and identify the scope of that interest. The debtor corporation then initiates communication and negotiations, in some cases having to deal with immediate relationship issues that arise from the debtor having filed under the *CCAA*. The framework then facilitates negotiations for a viable business plan that deals with the myriad of different kinds of claims, interests and concerns about the future of the debtor.

Another policy instrument is the scope of judicial powers in terms of the court's supervision of the proceedings. In the period between the initial stay order and the court's final approval of a plan, there are a myriad of questions that parties bring to the court in terms of determining rights, carriage of the proceedings, the need for interim financing to continue operating, seeking the assistance of the court in mediation or adjudication of particular disputes, and advice sought by the monitor as the court-appointed officer. For example, in *Canadian Airlines*, the Court dealt with key issues such as set off, missed claims dates, valuing of particular assets and ancillary proceedings under the U.S. *Bankruptcy Code*.[43] The supervisory function of the courts as a principal policy instrument for advancing the objectives of the statute is explored in chapter 3 on the role of the courts.

4. Challenges for Learning about *CCAA* Proceedings

One of the challenges for understanding the *CCAA* is that there is little codification in the statute. Hence, most information as to the scope and parameters of the *CCAA* can be found in the proceedings themselves, and in judgments rendered by the courts. Even more of a challenge is that in a number of instances, where there is no disagreement by parties as to particular procedures or decisions, there is only a handwritten endorsement by the court, which is not reported in the caselaw, or there may be no judgment at all. Hence there can often be only a limited public record of what occurs in a workout. The statute creates a framework for negotiation, and most of what occurs in cases does not occur in the court room. This reflects an important public policy objective; specifically, that the best plans of arrangement and compro-

---

[43] *Canadian Airlines Corp., Re*, [2001] A.J. No. 226, 2001 CarswellAlta 240 (Alta. Q.B.); *Ontario* v. *Canadian Airlines Corp.* (2000), 2000 CarswellAlta 1336, [2000] A.J. No. 1321 (Alta. Q.B.); Norm McPhedran, "Canadian Airlines - The Last Tango in Calgary: Key Issues Faced by the Monitor", (Insolvency Institute of Canada, Toronto: 2000) and Geoffrey Morawetz, "Controversial Legal Rulings, Canadian Airlines – The Last Tango in Calgary", (Insolvency Institute of Canada, Toronto: 2000) (http://www.westlawecarswell.com).

mise are those that are built on consensus, where there is broad support from multiple classes of creditors. In a number of instances, the debtor will have a going forward relationship with creditors and thus arriving at a plan that is suitable to creditors is an essential building block to a going forward business plan.

There is also a lack of a systematic database on *CCAA* proceedings. While access to information has recently improved because of monitors or their legal counsel posting court orders, claims process information and other information on websites, there continues to be a lack of systematic information about the nature of cases and their outcomes. Moreover, once the debtor corporation emerges from *CCAA* proceedings, that information is usually removed from websites and hence is no longer in the public domain. This lack of public information is likely to change if currently proposed amendments to the *CCAA* in Chapter 47 are proclaimed in force, as the Office of the Superintendent of Bankruptcy will then be given a legislative mandate to collect information.

Finally, there are some interesting challenges for thinking about the mix of common law and civil law as the *CCAA*, as a federal insolvency statute, is interpreted in different jurisdictions. There has been considerable convergence of judicial approach to the *CCAA* in recent years, but there continues to be some difference, particularly when the *CCAA* proceeding must implicate provincial corporations law, securities law or preferences statutes.

5. Learning Objectives and Methodology of the Text

This text presents a framework for understanding and applying the *CCAA*. It examines the design of the Canadian insolvency system, including the court's jurisdiction and how the administration of insolvency proceedings works. It provides the reader with an understanding of how the *CCAA* and the caselaw generated under it have shaped the process, from interim relief to exit from protection of the stay provisions. The text sets out the history and current practice under the *CCAA*. It discusses general principles and illustrates them through examples of cases and excerpts from judgments. It is aimed at providing readers with a comprehensive introduction to the statutory provisions and how they are interpreted by the courts or generally applied by parties. For those using this text to study the *CCAA*, there are both questions for review of materials and policy questions throughout the text to assist in understanding the statute.

The learning objectives of this text are to allow readers to acquire a basic understanding of:

- the legal, financial and management issues underlying *CCAA* proceedings;
- the regulatory environment in which insolvent corporations must devise a workout plan;
- the requirements to commence a proceeding under the *CCAA;*
- financing operations during and after a restructuring;

- the role of the courts and their officers in insolvency proceedings;
- how interests align or diverge during a workout;
- the governance of the financially distressed company; and
- the financing and control issues raised by cross-border proceedings.

For purposes of this text, debtor, debtor corporation and debtor company are used interchangeably.

II. OVERVIEW OF THE CANADIAN RESTRUCTURING SYSTEM

1. The *CCAA* Process – Historical Development

The enactment of the *CCAA* in 1933 must be situated in the context of existing bankruptcy legislation at the time, as well as the then prevailing economic conditions of the depression.[44] Early bankruptcy legislation in Canada dates back to 1869, but it was repealed in 1880 because of the amount of fraud and abuse by debtors. After that, numerous provincial statutes were enacted to meet debt collection needs, although there was a serious lack of uniformity in these statutes.[45] National bankruptcy legislation was enacted in 1919 after creditor groups lobbied for national consistency in the administration of bankrupt estates.[46] The 1919 bankruptcy legislation applied to both companies and individuals for the first time, and allowed debtors to make compromise proposals prior to bankruptcy, subject to creditor approval and court sanction. This legislation was driven by creditors who wanted to ensure that where they worked out arrangements with debtor companies, they had the ability to bind minority and dissenting creditors through court orders.[47] However, the effectiveness of this early legislation was undermined, as it did not bind secured creditors who could defeat a proposal by moving to enforce their claims.[48] The rehabilitation provisions of the legislation received little scrutiny at the time, the focus of the *Bankruptcy Act* being on the efficient administration and liquidation of estates.[49]

Amendments to the *Bankruptcy Act* were enacted in 1923 as the result of abuses of debtors and unqualified trustees; these amendments disallowed proposals for restructuring or compromise before bankruptcy.[50] Given the difficulty in reviving a com-

---

[44] *An Act to Facilitate Compromises and Arrangements between Companies and Their Creditors*, S.C. 1933, c. 36, 23-24 George V., Royal Assent May 23, 1933.

[45] Richard McLaren, *Canadian Commercial Reorganization, Preventing Bankruptcy* (Toronto: Canada Law Book, 1999) at 1-4, 1-6.

[46] *Bankruptcy Act*, S.C. 1919, c. 3.

[47] T. Telfer, "Reconstructing Bankruptcy Law" (1995) 24 C. B. L. J. 357 at 358-9, 361.

[48] J. Ziegel, "The Modernization of Canada's Bankruptcy Law in a Comparative Context" (1998) 33 Texas International Law Journal 1.

[49] T. Telfer, "Reconstructing Bankruptcy Law" (1995) 24 C. B. L. J. 357 at 393, 401.

[50] Richard McLaren, *Canadian Commercial Reorganization, Preventing Bankruptcy* (Toronto: Canada Law Book, 1999) at 1-6. L. Duncan and W. Reilley, *Bankruptcy in Canada*, 2nd ed. (Toronto, Canadian Legal Authorities Ltd., 1933) at 168.

pany once it is bankrupt, these amendments resulted in defeat of almost all efforts to restructure financially distressed companies, leading in turn to a number of premature liquidations. Thus by 1933, existing legislation such as the *Bankruptcy Act* and the *Winding-up Act* essentially provided only for liquidation of a company.[51] Yet growing capitalization and concentration of wealth in existing enterprises meant that when a firm experienced financial difficulty, firm failure affected not only the owners of the company, but large numbers of creditors and employees as well. Thus, the *CCAA* was introduced to facilitate compromises and arrangements between companies and their creditors.

In introducing the *CCAA* in 1933, the government observed that the limited mechanisms under existing statutes inevitably resulted in the entire disruption of the corporation, loss of goodwill, and sale of assets on a discounted basis.[52] The *CCAA* was based on the British *Companies Act of 1929*, which provided for compromises with creditors.[53] The impetus for reform came largely from the rise of credit industry organizations that aggressively lobbied for an enhanced debt collection structure. There had been no means by which creditors could reach an amicable settlement in such a way as to permit the company to continue in business through reorganization.

The court was empowered to hear applications proceeding conjointly under the *CCAA* and provincial corporations law, in order to facilitate compromises and arrangements and allow for a change in the capital structure. One of the express purposes was to provide a mechanism to bind both secured and unsecured creditors, unlike proposals under pre-existing bankruptcy legislation.[54]

Legislators recognized the harm caused by loss of investments, including employment and credit losses in the firm. The Honourable Arthur Meighen, in presenting the Government's bill, said:

> the depression has brought almost innumerable companies to the point where some arrangement is necessary in the interest of the company; in the interests of employees, because the bankruptcy of the company would throw the employees on the street, and in the interest of security holders, who may decide that it is much better to make some sacrifice than run the risk of losing all in the general debacle of bankruptcy.[55]

The original *CCAA* was initially viewed by unsecured trade creditors as inadequate to protect their interests because of the amount of control debtor corporations were

---

[51] *Winding-up Act*, R.S.C. 1906, c. 144, now the *Winding-up and Restructuring Act*, R.S.C. 1985, c. W-11.

[52] Secretary of State Honourable C. H. Cahan, Remarks on the Introduction of Bill 77 (20 April 1933), Dominion of Canada, Official Report of the Debates, House of Commons, 4th session, 17th Parliament 23-24 George V, Volume IV (Ottawa: King's Printer, 1933) at 4090.

[53] *Ibid.* The 1933 legislation required a majority of creditors by class and three-quarters in value of those voting to approve the plan before the court would sanction it. *Companies Act, 1929*, 1929, c. 23 (U.K.).

[54] Secretary of State Cahan, Committee as a Whole Debates on *CCAA* (9 May 1933) (Ottawa, King's Printer, 1933) at 23. Second reading (24 April 1933), third reading (9 May 1933).

[55] Honourable Arthur Meighen, (10 May 1933), Debates of the Senate of the Dominion of Canada, 1933 Official Report, 4th session, 17th Parliament, 23-24 George V (Ottawa: King's Printer, 1933) at 474.

able to exercise in the restructuring process. As a result, a bill introduced in 1938 sought to repeal the legislation.[56] However, the *CCAA* was not repealed, and debate continued sporadically with respect to the amount of control exercised by debtor companies. In 1953, the *CCAA* was amended to limit its application to companies that had issued bonds or debentures under a trust deed as a means to limit access to its use to larger publicly held companies. The rationale was that there was less opportunity for debtor corporations to act entirely self-interestedly in the *CCAA* process when they were publicly held.[57] During this period, use of the *CCAA* focused on reorganization of companies with complicated public debt structures, where there was an indenture trustee to monitor or control the corporation.[58]

Thus, the *CCAA* was originally enacted with a policy objective of providing a mechanism by which insolvent companies could avoid bankruptcy through "workable and equitable" restructuring plans.[59] The underlying notion was that if the creditors receive only the liquidation value of the corporation, they would receive considerably less than the value might be as a going concern. An effective reorganization scheme would assist in preserving going concern value of insolvent companies that have a good chance of survival, would prevent the loss of jobs, and would help ensure that investors and creditors were not deprived of their claims or the opportunity to share in the value of future activities of the company.

There were few *CCAA* applications for many years.[60] In 1947, the Québec Court of Appeal held that the purpose of the legislation was remedial and rehabilitative, and that the court's discretionary power was aimed at helping to effect a successful restoration of the business enterprise if the requisite creditor approvals of a plan of arrangement had been accomplished.[61] Stanley Edwards, in the only article written about the *CCAA* for a period of almost 40 years, discussed the statute's public policy objectives:

> Reorganization may give to those who have a financial stake in the company an opportunity to salvage its intangible assets. To accomplish this they must ordinarily give up some of their nominal rights, in order to keep the enterprise going until business is better or defects in management can be remedied. . .it is in the interests of the public to continue the enterprise. . .especially if it employs large numbers of workers who would be thrown out of work by its liquidation, . . .and this (public

[56] J. Honsberger, *Debt Restructuring: Principles and Practice* (Aurora: Canada Law Book, 1993) at 9.04.

[57] Prior to 1997, courts recognized the creation of instant trust deeds to by-pass this requirement. In 1997 the requirement was eliminated from the statute.

[58] Janis P. Sarra, *Creditor Rights and the Public Interest, Restructuring Insolvent Corporations* (Toronto: University of Toronto Press, 2003).

[59] Stanley Edwards, "Reorganizations under the *Companies' Creditors Arrangement Act*" (1947) 25 Canadian Bar Review 587 at 589-90.

[60] See for example, *Dairy Corp. of Canada, Re*, [1934] O.R. 436 (Ont. C.A.), the first judgment setting out the tests for determining whether the plan is fair and reasonable.

[61] *Feifer* v. *Frame Manufacturing Corp.* (1947), 28 C.B.R. 124 (Que. C.A.).

> interest) is undoubtedly a factor which the court would wish to consider in deciding whether to sanction a plan under the *CCAA*.[62]

The *CCAA* fell, for the most part, into disuse for half a century. Notwithstanding its existence, Canada's insolvency system historically favoured liquidation. It was not until the *CCAA* was rediscovered as a helpful restructuring tool in the past 25 years that there has been a shift towards a regime that encourages restructuring. The renewed interest in the *CCAA* was driven by a need to find alternatives to premature liquidation, given the size and impact of firm failure with the growth in debt financing, failures from leveraged buyouts and fluctuating products markets, and competition for capital in an increasingly global market.

When the *Bankruptcy and Insolvency Act (BIA)* was amended in 1992 to facilitate restructuring of insolvent enterprises through the proposal provisions, there was some debate regarding the necessity of having two restructuring statutes. The *CCAA* was left intact as a buffer in case the changes to the *BIA* were subsequently found to be flawed or ineffective to restructure enterprises. It was then thought that the *BIA* would become the tool of choice to restructure enterprises, and that the *CCAA* could be repealed at a later date. The experience in the first 5 years of implementation of the new provisions of the *BIA* demonstrated that while there was an increased use of the restructuring provisions under the *BIA*, there was still considerable restructuring activity being channelled through the *CCAA*, which pointed to a need to preserve the availability of this statute for the more complex situations. As a consequence, the 1997 amendments to bankruptcy and insolvency legislation did not include repeal of the *CCAA*, rather, the *CCAA* was amended to make it more accessible, to restrict its use to larger companies, and to provide some harmonization with provisions of the *BIA*. During the latest round of legislative amendments under Chapter 47, there was almost no call for repealing the *CCAA*.

Mr. Justice James Farley made the following observation in *Stelco Inc.*, regarding the evolution of the statute:

> ¶ 19 I would also note that the jurisprudence and practical application of the bankruptcy and insolvency regime in place in Canada has been constantly evolving. The early jails of what became Canada were populated to the extent of almost half their capacity by bankrupts. Rehabilitation and a fresh start for the honest but unfortunate debtor came afterwards. Most recently, the *Bankruptcy Act* was revised to the *BIA* in 1992 to better facilitate the rehabilitative aspect of making a proposal to creditors. At the same time, the *CCAA* was amended to eliminate the threshold criterion of there having to be debentures issued under a trust deed. . .. The size restriction was continued as there was now a threshold criterion of at least $5 million of claims against the applicant. While this restriction may appear discriminatory, it does have the practical advantage of taking into account that the costs (administrative costs including professional fees to the applicant, and indeed to the other parties who retain professionals) is a significant amount, even when viewed from the perspective of $5

[62] Stanley Edwards, "Reorganizations under the *Companies' Creditors Arrangement Act*" (1947) 25 Canadian Bar Review 587 at 592-3.

> million. These costs would be prohibitive in a smaller situation. Parliament was mindful of the time horizons involved in proposals under *BIA* where the maximum length of a proceeding including a stay is six months (including all possible extensions) whereas under *CCAA,* the length is in the discretion of the court, judicially exercised in accordance with the facts and the circumstances of the case. Certainly sooner is better than later. However, it is fair to observe that virtually all *CCAA* cases which proceed go on for over six months and those with complexity frequently exceed a year.[63]

With proposed amendments under Chapter 47, Parliament has codified some of the jurisprudence under the *CCAA,* but has clearly determined that it is a useful statute to have for the restructuring of insolvent corporations.

2. Commencing a *CCAA* Proceeding

A *CCAA* proceeding is commenced by a notice of application or originating summons, called the initial application.[64] Either the debtor corporation or a creditor can make the initial application for a stay or propose a plan of compromise or arrangement, although in the vast majority of cases, it is the debtor corporation that seeks protection of the *CCAA*.[65]

Hearing the initial application under the *CCAA*, the court can make an order commencing the proceeding and granting an initial stay order, with or without the debtor corporation having given notice to creditors.[66] As will be discussed in the section on notice below, the granting of *ex parte* orders under the *CCAA* has been somewhat contested. Courts have held that the stakeholders should be given as broad notice as possible. Hence, in recent years, there has been a shift away from granting stays on an *ex parte* basis. However, where *ex parte* stays are found to be necessary, the court will grant them for very limited periods until appropriate notice can be given.[67]

A stay of proceedings is almost always requested in an initial application under the *CCAA,* and such a request must be accompanied by a statement indicating the cash flow of the company and copies of all financial statements, audited or unaudited, prepared during the year preceding the application, and if there are no financial

---

[63] *Stelco Inc., Re* (2004), 48 C.B.R. (4th) 299 (Ont. S.C.J. [Commercial List]), leave to appeal refused (2004), 2004 CarswellOnt 2936 (Ont. C.A.), leave to appeal refused (2004), 2004 CarswellOnt 5200 (S.C.C.).

[64] Section 10, *CCAA*.

[65] See, for example, the *SLMSoft* (Court File No. 03-CL-005013) (Ont.) and *Cadillac Fairview* (Court File No. B348/94) (Ont.) cases. In *Cadillac Fairview*, it was Whitehall Street Real Estate Ltd. Partnership, a U.S. "vulture" fund that made the *CCAA* application on December 19, 1994. The corporation did not hear about the application until after the initial order was made.

[66] Section 11(1), *CCAA*.

[67] *Blue Range Resource Corp., Re* (2000), 192 D.L.R. (4th) 281, 20 C.B.R. (4th) 187 (Alta. C.A.) at para. 7. See the discussion below regarding "come-back orders" as a mechanism to address deficiencies in granting *ex parte* orders.

statements in that period, then a copy of the most recent statement.[68] The court has the discretion, on an initial application for a stay order, to make an order on such terms as it wishes to impose, for a period not to exceed 30 days.[69] The court can order a stay on all proceedings taken, or that might be taken, in respect of the debtor under the *BIA* or *WURA*; restrain further proceedings in any other action, suit, or proceeding of the company; and prohibit, until otherwise ordered by the court, the commencement of, or proceeding with, any other action, suit or proceeding against the debtor company.[70] The parties can seek an extension of this initial stay for longer periods, as the court deems necessary in the circumstances.[71]

The *CCAA* specifies that the court is not to make an initial order or another order unless the applicant satisfies the court that the applicant has acted and is acting in good faith and with due diligence.[72] The stay does not restrain rights under eligible financial contracts, discussed at length in chapter 6.[73]

The courts have held that the purpose of the statutory regime set out in the *CCAA* is to facilitate compromises and arrangements between companies and their creditors in order to allow the corporation to continue to operate for the benefit of all stakeholders.[74] The British Columbia Court of Appeal in *Hongkong Bank of Canada* v. *Chef Ready Foods* observed that there are devastating social and economic effects of bankruptcy and liquidation because shareholder investments are destroyed, unemployment creates hardships on workers, and creditors recover little of their claims.[75]

The definition of creditor under the *CCAA* is reasonably broad and mirrors somewhat the language of the *BIA*. Secured creditor is defined in the *CCAA* as a holder of a mortgage, hypothec, pledge, charge, lien or privilege, assignment, transfer of property of a debtor company as security for indebtedness, or a holder of a bond secured by any of these, and any trustee under any trust deed or instrument securing any such bonds.[76] Unsecured creditor is defined as any creditor of the company that is not a secured creditor, and a trustee for the holders of any unsecured bonds issued under a trust deed or other such instrument.[77] Thus, the statutory definitions of

---

[68] Section 11(2), *CCAA*.

[69] Section 11(3), *CCAA*.

[70] Section 11(3), *CCAA*.

[71] Section 11(4), *CCAA*.

[72] Section 11(6), *CCAA*.

[73] Section 11.1(2), *CCAA*.

[74] *Lehndorff General Partner Ltd., Re* (1993), 17 C.B.R. (3d) 24 (Ont. Gen. Div. [Commercial List]) at 31; *Reference re Companies' Creditors Arrangement Act (Canada)*, [1934] S.C.R. 659 (S.C.C.) at 661; *Quintette Coal Ltd.* v. *Nippon Steel Corp.* (1990), 2 C.B.R. (3d) 303 (B.C. C.A.), affirming (1990), 2 C.B.R. (3d) 291 (B.C. S.C.), leave to appeal refused (1991), 7 C.B.R. (3d) 164 (note) (S.C.C.).

[75] *Hongkong Bank of Canada* v. *Chef Ready Foods Ltd.*, [1991] 2 W.W.R. 136, 51 B.C.L.R. (2d) 84 (B.C. C.A.) at 88.

[76] Section 2, *CCAA*.

[77] Section 2, *CCAA*. Similarly, the trustee is an unsecured creditor for purposes of the Act except that the trustee does not have the right to vote at a creditors' meeting in respect of the bonds.

creditor are very expansive, and have been interpreted to include tort claimants as contingent creditors.[78]

The purpose of a *CCAA* stay order is to maintain the *status quo* for a specified limited period of time so that a proposed plan can be developed and presented to creditors for their consideration.[79] The statute allows the insolvent corporation to carry on business in a manner that allows time to undertake discussions with creditors and regulatory authorities, and to attract outside investment. The stay enables the debtor to prepare, file and seek approval from creditors, and ultimately the court, of a proposed plan.

Mr. Justice Donald Brenner of the British Columbia Supreme Court in *Pacific National Lease Holding Corp.*, summed up the principles to consider in applications under the *CCAA*:

> (1) The purpose of the *CCAA* is to allow an insolvent company a reasonable period of time to reorganize its affairs and prepare and file a plan for its continued operation subject to the requisite approval of the creditors and the Court.
>
> (2) The *CCAA* is intended to serve not only the company's creditors but also a broad constituency, which includes the shareholders and the employees.
>
> (3) During the stay period the *Act* is intended to prevent manoeuvres for positioning amongst the creditors of the company.
>
> (4) The function of the Court during the stay period is to play a supervisory role to preserve the *status quo* and to move the process along to the point where a compromise or arrangement is approved or it is evident that the attempt is doomed to failure.
>
> (5) The *status quo* does not mean preservation of the relative pre-debt status of each creditor. Since the companies under *CCAA* orders continue to operate, and having regard to the broad constituency of interests the *Act* is intended to serve, preservation of the *status quo* is not intended to create a rigid freeze of relative pre-stay positions.
>
> (6) The Court has a broad discretion to apply these principles to the facts of a particular case.[80]

---

[78] For a discussion of tort claimants, see chapter 6. Section 12 of the *CCAA*, which defines "claim" as any indebtedness, liability or obligation of any kind that, if unsecured, would be a claim provable in bankruptcy within the meaning of the *Bankruptcy and Insolvency Act*. By virtue of sections 121(2) and 135(1.1) of the *BIA*, a contingent or unliquidated claim is not a claim provable unless and until it has been determined to be a claim by the trustee, and has been valued by the trustee; however, the *CCAA* does not have a similar provision.

[79] *Northland Properties Ltd., Re* (1988), 73 C.B.R. (N.S.) 146 (B.C. S.C.); *Sairex GmbH* v. *Prudential Steel Ltd.* (1991), 8 C.B.R. (3d) 62 (Ont. Gen. Div.).

[80] *Pacific National Lease Holding Corp., Re* (August 17, 1992), Doc. A922870 (B.C. S.C.) at 10; see also *Alberta-Pacific Terminals Ltd., Re* (1991), 1991 CarswellBC 494, [1991] B.C.J. No. 1065 (B.C. S.C.).

The initial stay under the *CCAA* is for a maximum of 30 days, but can be extended by the court for any length of time that the court, in its discretion, finds appropriate. The court has held that the granting of any additional stay of proceedings after the initial stay will be based on the court's assessment of whether the debtor company has worked diligently and in good faith towards the development of a plan.[81] Where parties are negotiating in good faith and making meaningful progress towards a plan, the court has been flexible in granting extensions of the stay period to meet the goals of the statute.

If a stay of proceedings is ordered, a monitor is appointed under the *CCAA* proceeding and unless otherwise ordered by the court, the monitor must send a copy of the order within ten days after the order is made to every known creditor that has a claim against the debtor of more than $250.[82] The monitor may or may not perform a role similar to that of a trustee under the proposal provisions of the *BIA*, depending on the scope of the court's order. The monitor is almost always an insolvency professional with accounting or turnaround expertise, represented also by legal counsel in the *CCAA* proceedings. The court has discretion to direct the monitor to perform duties such as acting as liaison with the creditors and giving an opinion on the debtor corporation's ability to meet the requirements of a revised business plan.

Although appointment of a monitor had become accepted practice in *CCAA* applications, it became mandatory with the 1997 statutory amendments.[83] The role of the monitor is now defined under the *CCAA* and includes having access to the company's records and property to the extent necessary to assess the company's financial affairs. The monitor must also file a report with the court at least seven days prior to any creditors' meeting or at such times as the court directs. This report sets out the state of the corporation's business and financial affairs and any material adverse change in projected cash flow or financial circumstances. The monitor advises creditors of the filing of the report and carries out any additional functions that the court may direct. These duties often include assisting the corporation in developing a plan of arrangement or facilitating negotiations with creditors. Monitors are discussed in greater detail in chapter 8, particularly the evolution of their role in recent years and proposals for legislative reform.

In the majority of *CCAA* cases, the directors and officers of the corporation remain responsible for its assets and operations, and try to craft a plan that is acceptable to creditors. The monitor, as an officer of the court, ensures that the corporate officers do nothing that would unnecessarily deplete the resources available to satisfy creditors' claims. Decision-making by corporate directors and officers is also subject to closer scrutiny by creditors once the corporation files a *CCAA* application. The plan developed can also compromise claims against the directors that arose before the *CCAA* proceeding where the claims relate to their duties as directors.[84] This is to

[81] *Doaktown Lumber Ltd., Re* (1996), 39 C.B.R. (3d) 41 (N.B. C.A.).

[82] Section 11(5), *CCAA*.

[83] Section 11.7(3), *CCAA*.

[84] Section 5.1 *CCAA*. This is discussed at length in Chapter 5.

encourage directors to remain during the workout process so that their knowledge and expertise can assist in devising a viable plan.

The court's role is a supervisory one, discussed at considerable length in the next chapter. This role is very different from the court's role in applications or actions where parties are asking for a remedy based on particular previous conduct and the court has the benefit of hindsight and full evidence on both the events and the statutory or contractual framework that allocates the rights sought to be enforced. Under the *CCAA*, many questions decided by the court are not rights based determinations.[85] Rather, in addition to its supervisory role on an ongoing basis during the *CCAA* proceeding, the court's role is to be satisfied that the statutory requirements have been met in terms of creditor approval, and that the proposal is "fair and reasonable" in all the circumstances. Courts have reinforced the notion that the *CCAA* provides a structured environment for the negotiation of compromises and arrangements between a debtor corporation and its creditors for the benefit of both.[86] The underlying premise is that it is better for the company, its shareholders, employees and creditors to have the company operating in such a manner that it can meet its credit obligations, rather than creditors being able to receive only discounted payment at liquidation or sale value, and have shareholders and employees lose their investments. While the *CCAA* does not have an express purpose clause, the courts have been consistent in their findings regarding both the debt collection and rehabilitative nature of the statute.[87]

The *CCAA* supports creditors' rights by requiring a minimum threshold of creditor support by a majority in number and 2/3 majority in value of those voting in a class before the court will sanction the plan.[88] It balances creditors' rights to enforce with an entitlement by shareholders and their agents to devise acceptable viable business plans. Thus, the stay provisions facilitate the arrangement of refinancing, the consideration of diverse creditor interests, the time to discern and negotiate with creditors who have both converging and diverging interests, and thus the ability to achieve broad support for the proposed plan of arrangement or compromise.[89] The lack of codified requirements under the *CCAA* gives the parties, under the supervision of the court, the flexibility to craft constructive and timely workout plans to preserve the business. In some cases, this may include liquidation under the *CCAA* where it allows the parties high asset value realization or where a going concern sale could not be achieved through another process such as a receivership.[90]

---

[85] The court is required to make some rights determinations in the context of facilitating the negotiations, as discussed in Chapter 3.

[86] *Nova Metal Products Inc.* v. *Comiskey (Trustee of)* (1990), 1 C.B.R. (3d) 101, (sub nom. *Elan Corp.* v. *Comiskey*) 1 O.R. (3d) 289 (Ont. C.A.).

[87] *Hongkong Bank of Canada* v. *Chef Ready Foods Ltd.* (1990), 4 C.B.R. (3d) 311 (B.C. C.A.).

[88] It is important to note that it is 2/3 of those voting in terms of the value of their claims and not 2/3 of the capitalization of the corporation. The issue of who was in a particular class of creditors was the subject of considerable litigation in the 1980s and 1990s. For a discussion, see chapter 7.

[89] Janis P. Sarra, *Creditor Rights and the Public Interest, Restructuring Insolvent Corporations* (Toronto: University of Toronto Press, 2003).

[90] *Royal Bank* v. *Fracmaster Ltd.* (1999), 11 C.B.R. (4th) 230, 1999 ABCA 178 (Alta. C.A.).

3. Advantages and Disadvantages of Using the *CCAA* as compared with the *BIA* Proposal Process

The *BIA* and *CCAA* provide alternate but complementary regimes for companies to make proposals or plans of arrangement or compromise with their creditors with a view to becoming economically viable. Some corporations can choose which regime they will utilize, but, as noted above, the *CCAA* applies only where there are claims against the debtor corporation or affiliated debtor companies in an amount exceeding five million dollars.[91] The restructuring provisions of the *BIA* are generally aimed at small to medium sized enterprises. However, the *BIA* is a remedy available to larger debtors that seek the stability and specificity of its proposal scheme. While the *BIA* and *CCAA* are distinct statutes, in some instances, the language of the two statutes has been aligned.[92]

The *CCAA* is aimed solely at providing a scheme for restructuring of insolvent corporations, although, as discussed throughout this text, it has been now recognized as a tool to effect a liquidation. As with the *BIA*, restructuring can include amending terms of existing debt, such as rescheduling principal repayment, extending maturity dates, altering interest rates or forgoing a portion of the interest or principal owed by the debtor corporation. It also allows the corporation to restructure in such a manner as to allow parties to participate, based on a proportional basis, in the value generated by the company as a result of the reorganization and going concern value generated from it. Prior to 1992, the court could not bind secured creditors under the *BIA*. However, under the *CCAA,* the debtor corporation could receive a court-ordered stay of secured creditors' claims, making this an attractive forum in which to seek restructuring.

Under the *BIA,* the debtor, either a sole proprietor or a company, can file either a proposal, or more commonly, a notice of intention to make a proposal, either of which gives rise to an automatic stay.[93] If a secured creditor has already taken possession of secured assets prior to the filing of the notice of intention, it is not stayed. Similarly, if the secured creditor gave a section 244 notice of intention to enforce security more than 10 days prior to the filing of the notice of intention to file a proposal or the filing of a proposal, or if the debtor waived the requirement for the 10 day notice, it is not stayed.

One advantage of the *BIA* proposal provisions is that the automatic stay means that the debtor corporation does not incur the cost of seeking a court-imposed stay. However, the scope of the stay is specified in the *BIA* and there is little room to alter

[91] Section 3(1), *CCAA*. There is a separate regime aimed at allowing consumer debtors to restructure their debts, not addressed in this book; see Division II, Consumer Proposals, *BIA*.

[92] For example, defining debtor company, or most of the cross-border insolvency provisions. In *Parisian Cleaners & Laundry Ltd.* v. *Blondin* (1938), 20 C.B.R. 452 (Qué. C.A.), the Court held that the *CCAA* and *BIA* are distinct statutes and one is not auxillary to the other. See also *Québec (Sous-ministre du Revenu)* v. *Wynden Canada Inc.* (1982), 47 C.B.R. (N.S.) 76 (Que. S.C.).

[93] Sections 50, 50.4(1), 69.31, *BIA*.

its scope, making these provisions less costly and more certain, but less flexible in terms of tailoring the stay to particular circumstances of the debtor.[94] For smaller debtors with less complex debt and equity issues facing them, there is considerable appeal to this level of codification.

Under the *CCAA,* the stay is not automatic and the court must determine whether it is appropriate in the circumstances to grant a stay. The stay is the point of access to *CCAA* negotiations and hence is usually granted, but the court may limit the scope or timing of the stay. Similarly, claims against directors are automatically stayed under the *BIA* but not the *CCAA*. However, the *CCAA* allows the court to make such an order and this protection is routinely set out in the initial order.

Unlike the *BIA*, under the *CCAA*, extensions on the initial stay are not limited to fixed periods or a fixed maximum, although the courts have made it clear that they expect an expeditious process.

Both a *BIA* proposal and a *CCAA* plan of arrangement and compromise require the support of creditors for the plan in the amount of majority of creditors representing two-thirds of the value of voting creditors' or class of voting creditors' claims, as well as the sanction of the court in respect of the fairness and reasonableness of the plan. As noted in the introduction, any reorganization of the equity of the corporation requires concurrent proceedings under the federal, provincial or territorial corporations statutes, as bankruptcy and insolvency are areas of federal jurisdiction, while property and civil rights are areas of provincial jurisdiction under the Canadian *Constitution*.[95]

Often parties need to utilize more than one piece of legislation in a workout. If there are amendments to share structure, these must be effected under arrangement proceedings of the applicable corporations' legislation, as there are no such provisions under either the *BIA* or the *CCAA*.[96] In some cases, where there are public shareholders, the court has sanctioned mechanisms such as special committees of independent directors, hired specialized expertise and court ordered meetings of public shareholders to assist in determining the fairness of a proposed arrangement.[97] However, shareholders routinely do not receive a vote where plans are relying on the arrangement provisions of corporations statutes, particularly where their equity interests have no value as the claims by creditors are to all assets of the debtor corporation.

The objective of corporate restructuring under both the *BIA* and the *CCAA* is to preserve the corporation as a going concern notwithstanding the fact that it is

---

[94] Janis P. Sarra, *Creditor Rights and the Public Interest, Restructuring Insolvent Corporations* (Toronto: University of Toronto Press, 2003).

[95] The *Constitution Act, 1867*, as amended. Sections 91 and 92 of the *Constitution Act, 1867* provide for the areas of exclusive jurisdiction of the federal Parliament and provincial legislatures.

[96] *Dylex Ltd., Re* (January 23, 1995), Doc. B-4/95 (Ont. Gen. Div. [Commercial List]), Houlden J.A.

[97] *Olympia & York Developments Ltd., Re* (1993), (sub nom. *Olympia & York Developments Ltd.* v. *Royal Trust Co.*) 18 C.B.R. (3d) 176 (Ont. Gen. Div.).

financially distressed, if there is a prospect that it can become viable. By placing a stay on the ability of creditors to enforce their claims for a limited period, creditors cannot force the corporation into bankruptcy. The *quid pro quo* of the stay is that any proposal, plan of arrangement or compromise must have the requisite level of support in order to receive the sanction of the court. Amendments to the *BIA* and *CCAA* since 1992 have in part been aimed at enhancing the fairness and efficiency of the system. In introducing the 1992 amendments, the Government expressly stated that the objectives were to better protect all marketplace participants, consumers, workers and companies by better balancing debtor and creditor rights; by making rehabilitation rather than liquidation the focus of the legislation; by helping viable businesses better survive short-term downturns; by preserving jobs; and by giving greater protection to unpaid suppliers and wage earners.[98]

The *BIA* proposal proceedings are used for all sizes of business, from sole proprietorships to larger corporations. In particular, the *BIA* affords smaller companies without complex ownership or debt arrangements a mechanism to develop proposals to restructure or compromise debts in order to avoid bankruptcy. The *BIA* proposal provisions have increased in use, particularly since the 1992 amendments that allowed for proposals to bind secured creditors. This has led to fewer bankruptcies overall. In 1994, there were 743 commercial restructuring proposals under the *BIA*, compared with 11,810 business bankruptcies.[99] In 2004, there were 1,728 proposals under the *BIA*, compared with 8,128 business bankruptcies. Of those total of 9,856 business insolvencies in 2004, 7,075 were sole proprietorships.[100]

The federal Office of the Superintendent of Bankruptcy (OSB) exercises broad oversight over the *BIA*. However, in respect of *BIA* proposals, it is the licensed trustee, as the court-appointed officer, and the court itself that exercise the oversight of the debtor's proposal process. The proposal provisions under the *BIA* are highly rule driven, with most of the standards and process for developing a proposal specified by the statute. For the financially troubled small business or corporation, the certainty of the statutory proposal provisions can reduce the cost of negotiations with creditors and of numerous court appearances. Thus both statutory schemes play an important role in the restructuring of insolvent businesses.

During the stay period under the *BIA* provisions, the debtor has an obligation to work in good faith and with due diligence to formulate a proposal.[101] These obligations are equivalent to those under the *CCAA*. Under the *BIA*, creditors cannot make proposals or force the company to apply for proposal proceedings, a negative

---

[98] Honourable Pierre Blais, Minister of Consumer and Corporate Affairs, Remarks (Canadian Insolvency Institute Conference, Ottawa, 1991) at 1, 4.

[99] Jacob Ziegel, Benjamin Geva and R.C.C. Cuming, *Secured Transactions in Personal Property, Suretyships and Insolvency, Volume III, Commercial and Consumer Transactions, Cases, Text and Materials*, 3rd ed. (Toronto: Emond Montgomery Publications Ltd., 1995) at 761.

[100] OSB, *Insolvencies in Canada 2004*, http://strategis.ic.gc.ca/epic/internet/inbsf-osb.nsf/en/br01476e.html. The OSB reports that sole proprietorship includes all non-incorporated businesses.

[101] Sections 50(12) and 50.4(9), *BIA*.

feature of the scheme.[102] In contrast, the *CCAA* allows creditors to develop and propose plans of arrangement or compromise, thus facilitating collaboration of stakeholders in devising a viable workout plan.[103] While it is usually the debtor that proposes the plan, senior lenders and the lender that provides funding to the debtor during the *CCAA* proceeding often have considerable control in the workout strategy, as discussed in chapter 4.

Before filing a proposal or notice of intention to file a proposal with the Official Receiver (the government official), the *BIA* requires that the debtor have the written consent of a licensed trustee who has agreed to act in the proposal. The trustee files the proposal and a cash-flow statement with the Official Receiver, prepared and signed by both the debtor corporation or sole proprietor and the trustee. The trustee is obligated to review and report on the reasonableness of the cash-flow statement, and must generally make this statement available to creditors on request.[104] The trustee is responsible for convening a meeting of creditors within 21 days of filing the proposal.[105] Once a notice of intention is given, the trustee must file the cash-flow statement and assessment of reasonableness within ten days. Failure to do so results in the debtor company being deemed to have made an assignment in bankruptcy.[106] The trustee advises the debtor in the preparation of the proposal, monitors its activities and reports to the court and creditors periodically. While the trustee has a statutorily prescribed duty to assist the debtor in developing a proposal, it must also be careful to have regard for the interests of both the debtor and the general body of creditors. The court has held that in the context of a proposal under the *BIA*, the trustee is not an agent of the debtor corporation, but rather, is an officer of the court and must impartially represent and protect the interests of creditors.[107]

---

[102] Conceivably, a creditor could indirectly compel a debtor to file a proposal. Section 50 of the *BIA* provides for a list of persons who may file a proposal in respect of a debtor. One of the persons listed is a receiver within the meaning of section 243 of the *BIA*, who could be a mandatary or agent of a secured creditor. As well in *J.S. McMillan Fisheries Ltd., Re* (1998), 1998 CarswellBC 405 (B.C. S.C.), the Court allowed an interim receiver appointed under section 47.1 of the *BIA* to file a proposal, notwithstanding the fact that the interim receiver is not one of the persons named in section 50 of the *BIA*.

A word of caution should be made here regarding the pitfalls of creditor sponsored plans. Since a proposal or a plan of arrangement is essentially a contract between the debtor company and the creditors, a plan imposed by creditors will have little chance of success unless the debtor subscribes to it completely, or the participation of the debtor becomes unnecessary (either through a dilution of the capital and change in management, or if the plan contemplates the cessation of the business activities). As such, a creditor sponsored plan may seem like a good idea, but may be impractical, if the plan has to be implemented by the debtor.

[103] *Algoma Steel Corp., Re* (1992), Ontario Court File No. B62191-A (Ont. Gen. Div.).

[104] Sections 50(2), 50(6), 50(7) and 50(8), *BIA*.

[105] Section 51, *BIA*.

[106] Sections 50.4(2) and 50.4(8)(a), *BIA*.

[107] *Canadian Glacier Beverage Corp.* v. *Barnes & Kissack Inc.* (1999), 6 C.B.R. (4th) 212 (B.C. S.C.) at para. 35; *Mutual Trust Co.* v. *Scott, Pichelli & Graci Ltd.* (1999), 11 C.B.R. (4th) 54 (Ont. Bktcy.), additional reasons at (1999), 11 C.B.R. (4th) 62 (Ont. Bktcy.).

If the proposal does not attract the required level of creditor support, a vote defeating it results in automatic bankruptcy.[108] Hence this differs from the *CCAA* in that a failed vote on a *CCAA* plan does not automatically give rise to a bankruptcy. Practically speaking, however, if a *CCAA* plan does not receive the requisite creditor support and the stay period expires or is terminated by the court, a receiver, trustee or liquidator can be appointed to realize on assets, sell the business or liquidate it. In practice, under the *BIA* proposal process, where a meeting of creditors is held and there is interest in finding an acceptable proposal, a "straw vote" is taken of the classes of creditors and if the requisite support does not exist, the parties attempt some renegotiation of the proposal. This is so that a failed "official vote" does not automatically result in an assignment in bankruptcy. If a class or classes of secured creditors reject the proposal, there is no deemed bankruptcy; rather, the secured creditors of that class are free to exercise their rights under their security without further regard to the proposal proceeding. Hence both statutes allow for a period of negotiation, but failing the debtor receiving sufficient support after a specified period, creditors are able to pursue their remedies that were stayed under the *BIA* or *CCAA* proceedings.[109]

Although a *BIA* proposal does not require the approval of secured creditors, given that they hold first rights to the property of the corporation, realistically, in almost all cases, their approval is necessary because enforcement of security by significant secured creditors will render a proposal unworkable. As a result, proposal approval is often expressly conditional on acceptance of the proposal by all classes of secured creditors. The same considerations exist for a proposed *CCAA* plan, in terms of garnering the support of the secured creditors in order to ensure that a plan is viable.

A debtor may make a proposal to creditors either before or after bankruptcy. In respect of a bankrupt company that negotiates a proposal with creditors prior to the trustee liquidating its assets, the inspectors must approve a proposal because the court's approval operates to annul the bankruptcy and to revest the bankrupt property in the debtor or any other party the court directs.[110] A *BIA* proposal proceeding can be continued under the *CCAA* if a proposal has not been filed under the *BIA*.[111]

While the initial stay is automatic, the court does have an important supervisory role throughout the *BIA* proposal proceedings. A trustee can bring a motion for directions on numerous matters. The debtor corporation can seek extension of the initial stay period from the court in up to 45-day increments to a maximum of six months in total. The court, in exercising its discretion to grant an extension, must be satisfied that the insolvent corporation has acted in good faith and with due diligence; that it would likely be able to make a proposal if an extension is granted; and that no

---

[108] Section 57, *BIA*.

[109] There are only very limited circumstances in which a debtor can convert from a proceeding under the *BIA* to a *CCAA* proceeding, or vice versa. See discussion in Chapter 7 regarding conversion of proceedings.

[110] Sections 50(7), 61(1), *BIA*.

[111] Section 11.6, *CCAA*.

creditor would be materially prejudiced by the granting of an extension.[112] The court does not have the discretion that it has under the *CCAA* to grant longer or more flexible stay periods. The tight time frame and maximum amount of stay period means that the debtor must act expeditiously to devise a proposal that is acceptable to creditors. A disadvantage is that the rigid time frame under the *BIA* can result in negotiations with only the largest creditors, in order to satisfy the minimum statutory requirement for creditor support.

Once creditors have accepted a proposal, the trustee must apply to the court for approval within a specified time, following notice and reporting requirements.[113] This mirrors the *CCAA* process. There is a series of highly codified requirements as to the content of the *BIA* proposal. The court must be satisfied that the proposal meets the statutory requirements, as well as consider whether the proposal is in the interests of the general body of creditors and the public interest in preserving the bankruptcy process.[114] The approved proposal effectively becomes a contract between the company and its creditors, breach of which might give rise to bankruptcy.[115] The effect of court approval is to make the proposal binding on all parties that the proposal is aimed at, including those unsecured creditors that voted against it and secured creditors that voted against the proposal but that were in a class that voted in favour in the requisite amounts. The *CCAA* does not have the same level of codification as a prerequisite to court approval, although in terms of meeting the threshold of creditor support as a prerequisite to approving a plan, the *CCAA* has the same double majority as required by the *BIA*.[116]

Given that a *BIA* proposal alters the rights of creditors, the court has held that it will ensure the provisions of the *BIA* have been strictly complied with.[117] For example, the *BIA* specifies that the court shall not approve the proposal where the assets of the corporation are not of a value equal to fifty cents on the dollar of the debtor's unsecured liabilities, although the court may provide for a lower percentage where it is satisfied that the debtor did not cause the deficiency.[118] The court must also be satisfied that the proposal provides for payment of preferred claims under section 136 of the *BIA* in priority to classes of ordinary creditors, and for payment of all fees and expenses of the trustee in respect of the proposal proceedings.[119] The proposal must also provide for payment of certain claims under the *Income Tax Act*,

---

[112] Section 50.4(9), *BIA*; *Baldwin Valley Investors Inc., Re* (1994), 23 C.B.R. (3d) 219 (Ont. Gen. Div. [Commercial List]).

[113] Section 58, *BIA*.

[114] *Eagle Mining Ltd., Re* (1999), 42 O.R. (3d) 571 (Ont. Bktcy.); *Aquatex Corp., Re* (1998), 8 C.B.R. (4th) 177 (Alta. Q.B.); *Sumner Co. (1984), Re* (1987), 64 C.B.R. (N.S.) 218 (N.B. Q.B.); *Stone, Re* (1976), 22 C.B.R. (N.S.) 152 (Ont. S.C.). Sections 59(2), 198, 199, 200, *BIA*.

[115] *Bruce* v. *Neiff Joseph Land Surveyors Ltd.* (1977), 23 C.B.R. (N.S.) 258 (N.S. C.A.). Section 63, *BIA*.

[116] There have been some attempts under *CCAA* proceedings to affect the future rights of creditors in a sanctioning order, see the discussion of *Doman Forest Products* in Chapter 7.

[117] *Mutual Trust Co.* v. *Scott, Pichelli & Graci Ltd.* (1999), 11 C.B.R. (4th) 54 (Ont. Bktcy.), additional reasons at (1999), 11 C.B.R. (4th) 62 (Ont. Bktcy.) at para. 18. *Re Davis* (1924), 5 C.B.R. 182 (S.C.).

[118] Section 59, *BIA*; *Eagle Mining Ltd., Re* (1999), 42 O.R. (3d) 571 (Ont. Bktcy.).

[119] Sections 60(1), (1.3), 136, *BIA*.

the *Canada Pension Plan* and the *Employment Insurance Act*, and similar provincial legislation, unless the Crown has otherwise consented.[120]

Even where the court has approved a proposal, it can have a continuing supervisory role in some instances. If there is a default in meeting the requirements of the proposal, or there is a subsequent discovery of a fraud on the court in the original approval process, or the proposal cannot continue without injustice or undue delay, the court may annul a proposal.[121]

The *CCAA* does not include the same level of codification of statutory requirements and there is no minimum threshold of dollar amount of claims that must be paid out under a plan. The *CCAA* also does not specify parties whose claims must be paid prior to creditors receiving payment, although proposed amendments under Chapter 47 will alter this and create new provisions giving a preference claim and align the *CCAA* and the *BIA* in this respect.[122]

While the proposal provisions under the *BIA* are a mechanism that affords an opportunity for expeditious development and approval of a viable business plan for the insolvent business, its rule driven features reduce flexibility in the workout process. This can be a disadvantage where there are diverse types of claims or a complex debt structure. However, the proposal provisions are generally viewed as less costly, because of the need for fewer court appearances and the certainty in regard to numerous features required of any proposal. This makes the *BIA* scheme more attractive for sole proprietorships, small to medium-sized businesses, or for large corporations where the claims are relatively uncomplicated. It is also a route that creditors sometimes prefer that the debtor corporation pursue because of the tight time frames and the certainty that there will either be a proposal or a bankruptcy within six months. Some regions, such as Québec and the Maritimes, have used proposals more frequently than plans of arrangement under the *CCAA*.

As with the *CCAA,* the definition of creditor under the *BIA* is broad enough to encompass numerous interests, including the claims of contingent creditors.[123] Contingent claimants have been recognized as unsecured creditors under both statutes. A creditor with a contingent claim has the onus of demonstrating that the claim is neither speculative nor remote; and while the claimant does not need to establish the probability success of the claim, it must lead some evidence of its claim and probable success.[124] Judicial oversight is key to ensuring that creditors' rights are impaired as little as possible during the period that their ability to realize on their claims is suspended. Given its rule driven features, the *BIA* does not pose the same kinds of challenges as the *CCAA*.

---

[120] Section 60(1.1), *BIA*; s. 224 (1.2), *Income Tax Act*.

[121] Section 63(1), *BIA*; *544553 B.C. Ltd.* v. *Sunshine Coast Mechanical Contractors Inc.* (2000), 2000 CarswellBC 1270, [2000] B.C.J. No. 1217 (B.C. C.A.).

[122] See discussion in chapter 6 regarding these proposed changes to treatment of claims.

[123] A contingent creditor is one that has a claim that has not yet been fully determined or proven.

[124] *Air Canada, Re* (2004), 2004 CarswellOnt 3320, 2 C.B.R. (5th) 23 (Ont. S.C.J. [Commercial List]) (CUPE Contingent Claim Appeal).

Another difference is that for years it was felt that the court could not grant interim financing, colloquially referred to as debtor in possession (DIP) financing, on a primed basis under the *BIA*, as the court did not have express authority to grant such relief. DIP financing, as discussed at length in chapter 4, allows the debtor corporation to borrow funds to keep operating during the *CCAA* proceeding. However, the courts have now authorized DIP financing in proposal proceedings under the *BIA* and proposed amendments under Chapter 47 will codify such jurisdiction.[125]

4. Québec Bijuralism and Harmonization

Civil law has an impact on the application of federal insolvency law in Québec, although in practice, there is considerable convergence in how the *CCAA* is interpreted and applied in Québec. Parliament enacted statutes in 2001 and 2004, aimed at harmonizing federal law with Québec civil law.[126] Consequent amendments were made to the *BIA* and the *Interpretation Act,* aimed at harmonization.[127]

The *Interpretation Act* specifies that both the common law and the civil law are equally authoritative and recognized sources of law of property and civil rights in Canada.[128] Unless otherwise provided by law, if it is necessary to refer to a province's rules, principles or concepts forming part of the law of property and civil rights, reference must be made to the rules, principles or concepts in force in the province at the time the enactment is being applied.[129] The statute also specifies that where an enactment contains both civil law and common law terminology or where the terminology has a different meaning in common law and civil law, the civil law terminology or meaning is to be adopted in Québec.[130]

Martin Desrosiers and David Tardif-Latourelle have observed that these harmonization efforts have resulted in the adoption of a Model Initial Order for applications under the *CCAA*.[131] Reference is made in this text where civil law has a particular impact on proceedings under the *CCAA*.

---

[125] *In the matter of a Bankruptcy Proposal of Bearcat Explorations Ltd. and Stampede Oils Inc.*, Doc. BK 01-84659, BK 01- 084660 (Alta. Q.B.). See also *Charon Systems Inc. / Charon Systemes inc., Re* (2001), [2001] O.J. No. 5129, 2001 CarswellOnt 4556 (Ont. S.C.J.), where the court ordered DIP financing for a *BIA* proposal proceeding, finding that the same principles underlie the proposal provisions of the *BIA* as underlie the *CCAA*.

[126] *Federal Law – Civil Harmonization Act, No. 1,* S.C. 2001, c. 4 and *Federal Law – Civil Harmonization Act, No. 2,* S.C. 2004, c. 25.

[127] *Interpretation Act,* R.S.C. 1985., c. I-21, as amended.

[128] *Ibid.* at section 8.1.

[129] *Ibid.* at section 8.1.

[130] *Ibid.* at section 8.2.

[131] For a discussion of the issue of harmonization, see Martin Desrosiers and David Tardif-Latourelle, "Insolvency and Restructuring in Québec: A Common Law Practitioner's Guide", in *Annual Review of Insolvency Law, 2005* (Toronto: Carswell, 2006), at 319-355. The Québec Model Order is Appendix 6 of this text.

5. Considerations for Choice of Proceeding under which to Conduct a Workout

Choice of legal framework for a workout strategy for the debtor and/or creditors will depend in large measure on the capital structure of the debtor company, the location and type of assets, the complexity of debt, the issue of what kinds of stakeholders and kinds of claims are made on the debtor's assets, the jurisdiction in which assets are situated, where the head office or centre of main interest is located, the corporate structure, and whether that structure is primarily domestic or crosses borders.

There are many parent-subsidiary relationships among Canadian corporations, often with highly integrated operational and capital structures. Many insolvencies involve corporate groups, including divisions, subsidiaries, affiliates, and co-venture arrangements, many of these involving entities in other countries, most frequently in the United States. One or more of the parent or subsidiaries may be insolvent, but other members of the corporate group may be financially healthy.

In addition to the factors that a single entity considers, there are multiple other considerations regarding the most appropriate forum when a corporate group is involved. The parent and/or some affiliated companies may be insolvent and others are not. The capital structures may be highly integrated across jurisdictions within Canada and across borders; for example, where the parent company and its subsidiaries are all parties to the same borrowing facility. In cross-border situations, where management or financial control is centralized, the corporate group may need to file concurrently in multiple jurisdictions in order to continue operating, because a stay in one jurisdiction is not sufficient to allow such a centralized structure to continue during the workout negotiation process. The specific objectives of the workout may influence filing choices. Chapter 9 discusses the challenges of cross-border proceedings under the *CCAA*, but these issues are equally relevant under the *BIA* proposal provisions.

The choice of insolvency proceeding will also depend on the choice of workout strategy itself. Factors involved in consideration of workout strategy include: what markets the debtor will serve in the future; what the optimal going-forward capital structure should be; how the debtor intends to attract new customers, clients and key employees; and the overall viability of the business plan. The legal framework for a workout, be it receivership, proceedings under the *CCAA* or *BIA,* or proceedings under provincial statutes, provides the debtor and its advisers with different tools to drive the end objective of the particular workout strategy chosen.

Questions for review of materials:

1. What are the principal policy instruments under the *CCAA*?

2. What are the principal differences between the *BIA* and the *CCAA* as a rescue mechanism?

3. When is a private workout appropriate for a financially distressed firm?

4. What is the requisite level of creditor support for a *CCAA* plan, and what does the court's sanction of a plan mean for creditors that voted against the plan? Is the same level of support required under a *BIA* proposal?

Questions for discussion:

1. What are the advantages and disadvantages of a *CCAA* proceeding as compared with a *BIA* proposal proceeding?

2. Should creditors be able to commence proposal proceedings, or is there some reason to distinguish such rights between the *CCAA* and the *BIA*?

3. Should the *BIA* and the *CCAA* continue to co-exist as insolvency restructuring statutes?

CHAPTER 2

ACCESS TO THE *CCAA* PROCESS

I. THE INITIAL ORDER

An initial order and an initial stay order under the *CCAA* are often one and the same, and the terms are used interchangeably. While it is not an essential component of the *CCAA* proceeding that there be a stay of proceedings, practically, it is usually necessary to allow the debtor respite from litigation and enforcement of various contractual and other obligations during the proceeding.[1] However, the court has the discretion whether or not to order a stay of proceedings, as well as discretion with respect to the scope of that stay.

The initial order under the *CCAA* is an order of the court finding that the debtor corporation is a company to which the *CCAA* applies; in effect, a finding that the debtor is a company as defined in the *CCAA*, has debts of five million dollars or more and is bankrupt or insolvent. If a plan of compromise or arrangement is proposed at the time of the initial application, called a pre-packaged plan, the initial order would also order that a meeting of the creditors be convened to vote on the plan.[2]

A key characteristic of an efficient restructuring tool is the ability to suspend actions against the debtor while the discussions towards a plan are continuing, to avoid a race of the swiftest creditors that would deplete the debtor's assets, and to re-balance the negotiating power between the debtor and the creditors. As such, an initial order without its accompanying stay order would be of little use, and the stay is customarily granted at the same time as the order is granted to commence the *CCAA* proceeding.[3] Given its importance in the context of a restructuring under the *CCAA*, this text will

---

[1] The restructuring would be jeopardized absent an order staying the proceedings, save for exceptional circumstances, such as where the plan is ready for implementation right from the outset and the creditors' meeting can be convened quickly, creditors have not already started legal proceedings, there is strong support for the proposed plan from the creditors, etc. The occurrence of all of these circumstances at the same time is highly unlikely.

[2] In some circumstances, a meeting of shareholders would also be called, as discussed in chapter 7.

[3] The first application made for a stay order under the *CCAA* is referred to in section 11 of the *CCAA*, as the "initial application", and thus the order made in respect of this application is usually referred to as the initial order.

refer to the initial order as the practice knows it, namely a hybrid of the initial order and the stay order.

II. THE INITIAL STAY ORDER

1. Objective of the Stay Order

The stay order is a principal policy instrument of the *CCAA*, because it provides a period for the debtor company to negotiate with its creditors, without having to direct all of its time and resources to initiating, conducting or defending legal proceedings. The court has held that its task under the *CCAA* is to facilitate an effective process aimed at compromises and arrangements, thus it is essential that the debtor be afforded a respite from litigation during the period that it is attempting to carry on as a going concern and to negotiate a plan acceptable to creditors.[4] The stay affords the company a limited period in which to develop a plan and negotiate with creditors to seek their support. It enhances the ability of the debtor corporation to concentrate its efforts on negotiating a plan of compromise or arrangement.[5] Hence, Canadian courts have liberally interpreted the stay provisions in order to facilitate the negotiation process and meet the objective of the statute.[6]

2. Granting the Initial Stay Order

On application for the initial stay order, the debtor proposes a draft order. An example of an initial order, in the *Air Canada* case, is included as Appendix 2 to this book. Initially, the courts applied different versions of a similar test in determining whether to grant an initial stay under the *CCAA*. The British Columbia courts utilized a lower threshold, whereby the court would grant a stay unless the process was "doomed to failure", and Ontario courts a higher threshold, where the debtor was required to

---

[4] *Campeau* v. *Olympia & York Developments Ltd.* (1992), 14 C.B.R. (3d) 303 (Ont. Gen. Div.) at para. 17 *First Treasury Financial Inc.* v. *Cango Petroleums Inc.* (1991), 3 C.B.R. (3d) 232 (Ont. Gen. Div.); *Ursel Investments Ltd., Re* (1991), 2 C.B.R. (3d) 260 (Sask. Q.B.), reversed (1992), 10 C.B.R. (3d) 61 (Sask. C.A.).

[5] *Campeau* v. *Olympia & York Developments Ltd.* (1992), 14 C.B.R. (3d) 303 (Ont. Gen. Div.); *Air Canada, Re* (2004), 47 C.B.R. (4th) 177 (Ont. S.C.J. [Commerical List]) (Always Travel Inc. – Leave to Proceed Motion).

[6] One of the main objectives of the stay order is to maintain the *status quo* while the negotiations are continuing with creditors. In view of the finality and validity of deeming and termination provisions in civil law, the practice that evolved in Québec is to provide in the initial order that it applies retroactively. The standard order developed between the Québec Bar and the judiciary provides that the initial order applies as and from one minute past midnight on the day before the order is rendered. This ensures that no creditor can terminate a contract (including, for instance, invoking the insolvency to terminate an insurance policy) while the debtor is presenting its application or while the court is deciding whether the relief should be granted, which might render the relief moot.

demonstrate that there is a "reasonable prospect of a viable workout".[7] However, the tests essentially converged after several years, particularly as the courts moved to recognize the rehabilitation goals of the statute. Given the objectives of the *CCAA*, the court will generally grant the initial stay unless it finds that the *CCAA* application is merely an effort by the debtor to avoid its obligations to creditors or that creditors have lost all confidence in management of the corporation.[8]

While it is much easier now for the debtor to receive the initial stay order than it was two decades ago, the court must be satisfied that an order is appropriate in the circumstances before it will exercise its discretion to make the order. Madam Justice Barbara Romaine of the Alberta Court of Queen's Bench in *Matco Capital Ltd.* v. *Interex Oilfield Services Ltd.* declined to grant an initial *CCAA* order on the basis that there was no evidence to suggest that there was any possibility of the debtor restructuring its affairs.[9] The Court observed that while the burden is placed on an applicant for an initial *CCAA* order to show that it has a reasonable possibility of restructuring, the burden is not an onerous one.[10] The Court held:

> ¶8 As Matco points out, Interex is in the same position it was when it solicited bridge financing from Matco in May of this year, and there is no evidence that any of its efforts from that time have resulted in a refinancing source stepping forward. Added to this is the surfacing of substantial builders' liens and the corporate governance problems that Interex now faces. The prospect of any successful refinancing looks dire. If what is really more likely is a liquidating *CCAA*, the consideration becomes whether such a resolution is better advanced through existing management in a *CCAA* proceeding, or through a receivership. Given that there is now evidence that Interex is essentially rudderless, with a CEO who will likely be terminated today and a board of directors that is under threat of replacement from a major shareholder, the balance of efficient resolution tips in favour of a receivership.

In making an application under the *CCAA*, the debtor corporation does not have to demonstrate at the initial stay application stage that it has a feasible plan, although the courts have held that the debtor corporation is wise to have consulted with major creditors in advance of the application, in order to ascertain their willingness to co-operate in the negotiation of a workout. The Québec Superior Court has held that the debtor does not need to have first made an arrangement with secured creditors, as then the approval or rejection of the plan would be in the control of secured creditors, not the entire group of creditors and the court.[11]

---

[7] *Philip's Manufacturing Ltd., Re* (1992), 9 C.B.R. (3d) 25 (B.C. C.A.), leave to appeal refused (1992), 15 C.B.R. (3d) 57 (note) (S.C.C.), at 28. See also *Sharp-Rite Technologies Ltd., Re* (2000), 2000 CarswellBC 128, [2000] B.C.J. No. 135 (B.C. S.C.); *Bargain Harold's Discount Ltd.* v. *Paribas Bank of Canada* (1992), 10 C.B.R. (3d) 23 (Ont. Gen. Div.).

[8] *Ibid.*

[9] *Matco Capital Ltd.* v. *Interex Oilfield Services Ltd.* (August 1, 2006), Docket No. 060108395 (Alta. Q.B.) Oral Reasons for Judgment, Romaine J.

[10] *Ibid.* at para. 6.

[11] *Taché Construction ltée* c. *Banque Lloyds du Canada* (1990), 5 C.B.R. (3d) 151 (Qué. S.C.).

The Québec Superior Court, however, has found in several instances that an initial order should not be made, or that the relief granted should be very limited, unless a plan of compromise and arrangement is in existence at the time the application is filed.[12] That position is premised on a decision of the Québec Court of Appeal in *Groupe Bovac Ltée*, which held that at the time of the application, the plan must be in existence, although the plan could be modified or varied after that time.[13] With respect, these decisions of the Québec Superior Court do not seem to take into consideration the fact that the *CCAA* was modified in 1997, after the judgment of the Court of Appeal was rendered in *Groupe Bovac Ltée*, introducing a limit on the length of the stay granted on an initial application for a stay order. It seems evident that the reason for a time-limited stay is that Parliament recognized that the debtor might need a period to prepare a plan. As a consequence, a requirement that a plan or a draft of a plan exist before an initial order is made is overly onerous on the debtor.[14] It appears that the judgment of the Court of Appeal in *Groupe Bovac Ltée* is now dated as a result of the changes to the *CCAA* in 1997.

The *CCAA* stay provision is a protective device, not only for the benefit of the debtor corporation, but also for a broad constituency of stakeholders.[15] The statutory scheme contemplates that the rights and remedies of various stakeholders might be temporarily sacrificed through imposition of the stay. The most common period for the initial stay is the statutory maximum of 30 days. However, where the court grants an initial stay in face of opposition from key creditors, the stay period imposed can be shorter, with a fixed date to come back before the court. Prior to the amendments limiting the length of the stay, the court frequently required the debtor corporation to establish to the court's satisfaction that it had a reasonable chance of successfully negotiating with creditors, prior to the court granting the stay.[16]

If a *CCAA* proceeding is not commenced, senior secured creditors have a number of self-help remedies available to immediately realize on their claims. Where the liquidation value fully satisfies their claims, they may be resistant to the time and cost of a process that may maximize enterprise value, but not necessarily enhance the realizable value of their claims. The purpose of the stay is to grant a limited period in which to determine whether a viable plan can be developed and to allow dissemination of information to creditors to allow them to assess their options. The stay order prevents one creditor from gaining an advantage over other creditors

---

[12] See, as an example, *Boutiques San Francisco Incorporées, Les Ailes de la Mode Incorporées, et Les Éditions San Francisco Incorporée* v. *Richter & Associés Inc, Monitor* (December 17, 2003), Doc. 500-11-022070-037 (Qué. S.C.), Clément J. (unreported).

[13] *Banque Laurentienne du Canada* c. *Groupe Bovac Ltée* (1991), 1991 CarswellQue 39 (Qué. C.A.).

[14] In practice, some of the applications contain general statements as to the company's restructuring intentions, (such as an intention to rationalize its business, reduce costs, terminate leases, decrease staff complement, etc.), the usefulness of which is doubtful in determining what exactly will be the form and content of the restructuring plan, but which seems to satisfy the court that a draft of a plan is in place.

[15] *Hongkong Bank of Canada* v. *Chef Ready Foods Ltd.* (1990), 4 C.B.R. (3d) 311 (B.C. C.A.).

[16] *Inducon Development Corp., Re* (January 3, 1992), Ontario Crt File No. B364/92 (Ont. Gen. Div.).

while the company is attempting to devise a workout plan, preventing a race to the assets.[17]

The Alberta Court of Queen's Bench in *Hunter Trailer* held that "*status quo*" during the stay period is not merely preservation of pre-stay debt status, but rather, is preservation of the *status quo* in the sense of preventing manoeuvres by creditors that would impair the ability of the corporation to operate while it and its creditors determine whether there is a viable workout.[18] The stay is temporal, for a specified period, and does not permanently take away a creditor's cause of action.[19]

Even where some secured creditors are initially opposed to a stay pursuant to the *CCAA*, the court has held that "all affected constituencies must be considered, including secured and unsecured creditors, preferred creditors, employees, landlords, shareholders and the public generally".[20] Although the stay is a temporary loss of control by senior creditors, the courts are giving effect to the legislation. The balance of convenience must weigh in favour of granting the stay, given that the court will not lightly interfere with creditors and other claimants seeking to enforce their rights.[21]

3. Terms and Conditions of the Initial Stay Order

Section 11 of the *CCAA* provides a broad jurisdiction to impose terms and conditions on the granting of the stay and section 11(4) includes the power to vary the stay and allow the company to enter into agreements to facilitate the restructuring, provided that the creditors have the final decision under section 6 whether or not to approve the plan. The Ontario Court of Appeal has held that the point of the *CCAA* process is not simply to preserve the *status quo* but to facilitate restructuring so that the company can successfully emerge from the process.[22] The Court of Appeal held that it is important to take into account the dynamics of the debtor's particular situation.

The stay order can prohibit the company from issuing further debt, disposing of assets or applying cash flow other than in the ordinary course of business.[23] Where an action has commenced against the debtor corporation and a third party prior to the debtor seeking protection of the *CCAA*, the court can order a stay of proceedings

---

[17] *Woodward's Ltd., Re* (1993), 17 C.B.R. (3d) 236 (B.C. S.C.); *Northland Properties Ltd., Re* (1988), 73 C.B.R. (N.S.) 141 (B.C. S.C. [In Chambers]); *Sairex GmbH* v. *Prudential Steel Ltd.* (1991), 8 C.B.R. (3d) 62 (Ont. Gen. Div.).

[18] *Hunters Trailer & Marine Ltd., Re* (2001), 2001 CarswellAlta 964, [2001] A.J. No. 857 (Alta. Q.B.); *Alberta-Pacific Terminals Ltd., Re* (1991), 8 C.B.R. (3d) 99 (B.C. S.C.) at 105.

[19] *Quinsam Coal Corp., Re* (2000), 20 C.B.R. (4th) 145 (B.C. C.A. [In Chambers]).

[20] *Hunters Trailer & Marine Ltd., Re* (2001), 2001 CarswellAlta 964, [2001] A.J. No. 857 (Alta. Q.B.) at para. 16; *Smoky River Coal Ltd., Re* (2001), 28 C.B.R. (4th) 127 (Alta. C.A.); *Bargain Harold's Discount Ltd.* v. *Paribas Bank of Canada* (1992), 7 O.R. (3d) 362 (Ont. Gen. Div.) at 370-71.

[21] *Campeau* v. *Olympia & York Developments Ltd.* (1992), 14 C.B.R. (3d) 303 (Ont. Gen. Div.).

[22] *Stelco Inc., Re* (2005), 2005 CarswellOnt 6283 (C.A.), affirming (2005), 2005 CarswellOnt 5023 (Ont. S.C.J. [Commercial List]).

[23] *Northland Properties Ltd., Re* (1988), 69 C.B.R. (N.S.) 266 (B.C. S.C.).

not only against the debtor, but against the third party under the general power possessed by the court in civil matters.[24] The court can also stay the commencement or continuation of actions against directors that arose before the commencement of the *CCAA* proceeding. This stay relates to obligations of the company where the directors are liable in their capacity as directors.[25]

The section 11 stay does not, however, have the effect of prohibiting a person from requiring immediate payment for goods, services, use of leased or licensed property or other valuable consideration provided after the order is made; or requiring the further advance of money or credit.[26] Earlier concern that the exercise of judicial discretion preserving the *status quo* during the stay period would require the lenders of operating capital to continue lending, was ameliorated when the *CCAA* was amended in 1997 to clarify that the effect of a stay order does not require the further advance of money or credit.[27] If a person supplies goods and services to the debtor corporation or if the debtor continues to occupy or use leased or licensed property, no stay order can be made in respect of payment for the use of the goods, services, lease or licensed property after the order was made.[28] The court can also create a post-filing charge in favour of such creditors, as discussed in chapter 4.

The court has limitations in imposing a stay. These include the effect of a stay on eligible financial contracts;[29] restraining certain officials with respect to their duties under specific legislation;[30] restraining a proceeding by a beneficiary against a person, other than the debtor, who is obligated under a letter of credit or letter of guarantee;[31] imposing a stay on the Crown in a situation where a secured creditor has a right to enforce its security against the accounts receivable of the debtor company or where the debtor has defaulted on an obligation to make a remittance after the initial order;[32] and imposing a stay in respect of a creditor who holds security on aircraft objects.[33] In such cases, the court may not impose a stay, or the stay will have a limited application or be limited in time.

---

[24] *Campeau* v. *Olympia & York Developments Ltd.* (1992), 14 C.B.R. (3d) 303 (Ont. Gen. Div.).

[25] Section 11.5, *CCAA*.

[26] Section 11.3, *CCAA*.

[27] Section 11.3, *CCAA*.

[28] Section 11.3, *CCAA*.

[29] Section 11.1, *CCAA*.

[30] Section 11.11, *CCAA*.

[31] Section 11.2, *CCAA*.

[32] Section 11.4(2), *CCAA*.

[33] Section 11.31, *CCAA*. This last exception to the court's discretion in granting a stay relates to the obligations of Canada under international treaties. The article was added by S.C. 2005, chapter 3, *An Act to implement the Convention on International Interests in Mobile Equipment and the Protocol to the Convention on International Interests in Mobile Equipment on Matters Specific to Aircraft Equipment.*

If a creditor has knowledge of and fails to comply with a *CCAA* stay order, the creditor is in contempt of court, and the court has refused to hear the creditor until it has purged the contempt.[34]

4. Come-back Provisions

Interested persons who wish to have an initial *CCAA* order granting a stay of proceedings in respect of a debtor set aside or varied, can bring the matter before the court. The courts now commonly add a "come-back" provision in the initial *CCAA* order, which specifies that parties can come before the court in an application to vary or amend the order. The Model Initial Order in Ontario provides an example of a come-back clause in an initial *CCAA* order:

> 44. THIS COURT ORDERS that any interested party (including the Applicant and the Monitor) may apply to this Court to vary or amend this Order on not less than seven (7) days' notice to any other party or parties likely to be affected by the order sought or upon such other notice, if any, as this Court may order.[35]

The Ontario Superior Court has held that such persons should not feel constrained about relying on the come-back clause in the *CCAA* order to seek a variance of the initial stay order. Mr. Justice Farley in *Muscletech Research & Development Inc., Re* particularly stressed the parties' ability under the come-back provisions:

> ¶ 5 As this order today is being requested without notice to persons who may be affected, I would stress that these persons are completely at liberty and encouraged to use the comeback clause found at paragraph 59 of the Initial Order. In that respect, notwithstanding any order having previously been given, the onus rests with the applicants (and the applicants alone) to justify *ab initio* the relief requested and previously granted. Comeback relief, however, cannot prejudicially affect the position of parties who have relied bona fide on the previous order in question. This endorsement is to be provided to the creditors and others receiving notice.[36]

Hence, the Court has held that the *CCAA* debtor or other applicant for the initial *CCAA* order has the onus on a come-back motion to satisfy the court that the existing terms of the *CCAA* order should be upheld.[37]

---

[34] *Philip's Manufacturing Ltd., Re* (1991), 9 C.B.R. (3d) 17 (B.C. S.C.), reversed on other grounds (1992), 9 C.B.R. (3d) 25 (B.C. C.A.), leave to appeal refused (1992), 15 C.B.R. (3d) 57 (note) (S.C.C.).

[35] Ontario Model Order, at para. 44. See Appendices 3 to 7 for full text of Model Orders.

[36] *Muscletech Research & Development Inc., Re* (2006), 2006 CarswellOnt 264, [2006] O.J. No. 167 (Ont. S.C.J. [Commercial List]).

[37] *Warehouse Drug Store Ltd., Re* (2005), 2005 CarswellOnt 1724 (Ont. S.C.J. [Commercial List]).

5. Limits on the Scope of the Stay

Mr. Justice David Tysoe of the British Columbia Supreme Court in *Doman Industries Ltd.*, gave a helpful summary of the scope of the stay under a *CCAA* proceeding:

> ¶ 15 The law is clear that the court has the jurisdiction under the *CCAA* to impose a stay during the restructuring period to prevent a creditor relying on an event of default to accelerate the payment of indebtedness owed by the debtor company or to prevent a non-creditor relying on a breach of a contract with the debtor company to terminate the contract. It is also my view that the court has similar jurisdiction to grant a permanent stay surviving the restructuring of the debtor company in respect of events of default or breaches occurring prior to the restructuring. In this regard, I agree with the following reasoning of Spence J. at para. 32 of the supplementary reasons in *Playdium*:
>
>> In interpreting s. 11(4), including the "such terms" clause, the remedial nature of the *CCAA* must be taken into account. If no permanent order could be made under s. 11(4) it would not be possible to order, for example, that the insolvency defaults which occasioned the *CCAA* order could not be asserted by the Famous Players after the stay period. If such an order could not be made, the *CCAA* regime would prospectively be of little or no value because even though a compromise of creditor claims might be worked out in the stay period, Famous Players (or for that matter, any similar third party) could then assert the insolvency default and terminate, so that the stay would not provide any protection for the continuing prospects of the business. In view of the remedial nature of the *CCAA*, the Court should not take such a restrictive view of the s. 11(4) jurisdiction.
>
> ¶ 16 Spence J. made the above comments in the context of a third party, which had a contract with the debtor company. In my opinion, the reasoning applies equally to a creditor of the debtor company in circumstances where the debtor company has chosen not to compromise the indebtedness owed to it. The decision in *Luscar Ltd.* v. *Smoky River Coal Ltd.*, [1999] A.J. No. 676, is an example of a permanent stay being granted in respect of a creditor of the restructuring company.
>
> ¶ 17 Accordingly, it is my view that the court does have the jurisdiction to grant a permanent stay preventing the Senior Secured Noteholders and the Trustee under the Trust Indenture from relying on events of default existing prior to or during the restructuring period to accelerate the repayment of the indebtedness owing under the Notes. It may be that the court would decline to exercise its jurisdiction in respect of monetary defaults but this point is academic in the present case because the Doman Group does intend to pay the overdue interest on the Notes upon implementation of the Reorganization Plan.
>
> . . .
>
> ¶ 20 The third issue is whether the court has the jurisdiction to effectively stay the operation of Section 4.16 of the Trust Indenture. Although I understand that there is an issue as to whether the giving of 85% of the equity in the Doman Group to the

Unsecured Noteholders as part of the reorganization would constitute a change of control for the purposes of the current version of the provincial forestry legislation, counsel for the Doman Group conceded that it would constitute a Change of Control within the meaning of Section 4.16.

¶ 21 The language of s. 11(4) of the *CCAA*, on a literal interpretation, is very broad and the case authorities have held that it should receive a liberal interpretation in view of the remedial nature of the *CCAA*. However, in my opinion, a liberal interpretation of s. 11(4) does not permit the court to excuse the debtor company from fulfilling its contractual obligations arising after the implementation of a plan of compromise or arrangement.

¶ 22 In my view, there are numerous purposes of stays under s. 11 of the *CCAA*. One of the purposes is to maintain the *status quo* among creditors while a debtor company endeavours to reorganize or restructure its financial affairs. Another purpose is to prevent creditors and other parties from acting on the insolvency of the debtor company or other contractual breaches caused by the insolvency to terminate contracts or accelerate the repayment of the indebtedness owing by the debtor company when it would interfere with the ability of the debtor company to reorganize or restructure its financial affairs. An additional purpose is to relieve the debtor company of the burden of dealing with litigation against it so that it may focus on restructuring its financial affairs. As I have observed above, a further purpose is to prevent the frustration of a reorganization or restructuring plan after its implementation on the basis of events of default or breaches which existed prior to or during the restructuring period. All of these purposes are to facilitate a debtor company in restructuring its financial affairs. On the other hand, it is my opinion that Parliament did not intend s. 11(4) to authorize courts to stay proceedings in respect of defaults or breaches which occur after the implementation of the reorganization or restructuring plan, even if they arise as a result of the implementation of the plan.[38]

Hence while the stay accomplishes numerous public policy purposes and the courts have adopted a very liberal approach to assist in meeting the objectives of the statute, Mr. Justice Tysoe declined to order a stay in respect of future defaults or breaches that occur after the implementation of the *CCAA* plan.

The court has authority to make stay orders against third parties. The court has held that it can make stay orders against parties who are not creditors of the debtor, where the actions of the third party could potentially prejudice the success of a proposed plan.[39]

The court has also found jurisdiction to extend the stay over non-corporate entities. In *Calpine Canada Energy Ltd.*, there were partnerships related to the debtor and a dispute arose as to whether the partnerships should be stayed. The Alberta

[38] *Doman Industries Ltd., Re* (2003), 2003 CarswellBC 538, [2003] B.C.J. No. 562 (B.C. S.C. [In Chambers]).

[39] *Lehndorff General Partner Ltd., Re* (1993), 17 C.B.R. (3d) 24 (Ont. Gen. Div. [Commercial List]); *Norcen Energy Resources Ltd.* v. *Oakwood Petroleums Ltd.* (1988), 72 C.B.R. (N.S.) 1 (Alta. Q.B.); *Cansugar Inc., Re* (2005), 2005 CarswellNB 308, [2005] N.B.J. No. 277 (N.B. Q.B.); *Muscletech Research & Development Inc., Re* (2006), 2006 CarswellOnt 6230 (Ont. S.C.J.).

Court of Queen's Bench held that while the *CCAA* does not grant the court express power to stay proceedings against non-corporate entities, the court has inherent jurisdiction to grant a stay of proceedings where it is just and convenient to do so. The court concluded that given the complex corporate and debt structure of the Calpine group, the cross-border nature of the proceedings, and the evidence before it that irreparable harm could accrue to the Calpine group if the stay was not granted, it was just and reasonable to stay the proceedings against the partnerships.[40]

6. Extension of the Stay

After the initial 30 day period, which is the maximum period that the initial stay is available under an initial order, an applicant can seek to extend the stay for longer limited periods. The court's granting or denial of an extension of the stay order will depend in part on the amount of confidence creditors and the court have in the progress being made by the debtor in its negotiations for a viable workout plan.[41] In applications for extension of the initial thirty-day stay period, the court applies tests of good faith, due diligence and balancing of prejudice to creditors in determining whether to extend the stay period.[42] The applicant must establish that circumstances exist that make the order appropriate; and that the applicant has acted and continues to act in good faith and with due diligence.[43]

The British Columbia Supreme Court has held that the debtor corporation has an obligation to demonstrate measurable and substantive progress towards a plan if an extension is to be granted, and the court will also consider the economic impact on stakeholders and members of the surrounding community.[44] Thus, even where the exercise of discretion is not as constrained by express requirements as it is in the sanctioning of the plan, there is a substantial degree of certainty in the tests applied to the exercise of that discretion. As with the initial stay order, the extension of a stay is only a temporary suspension of creditors' rights.

Generally, the court wants assurance that corporate officers understand the reason for the firm's insolvency, so that they have a realistic sense of whether there is a potentially viable plan that can be devised. On granting an extension, the court can order the monitor to report cash flow projections on a regular basis to senior creditors

---

[40] *Calpine Canada Energy Ltd., Re* (2006), 19 C.B.R. (5th) 187 (Alta. Q.B.) Romaine J.; *Lehndorff General Partner Ltd., Re* (1993), 17 C.B.R. (3d) 24 (Ont. Gen. Div. [Commercial List]).

[41] Janis Sarra, "Judicial Exercise of Inherent Jurisdiction under the *CCAA*", (2004) 40 Canadian Business Law Journal 280.

[42] Section 11(4), *CCAA*; *Royal Oak Mines Inc., Re* (1999), 1999 CarswellOnt 625, [1999] O.J. No. 709 (Ont. Gen. Div. [Commercial List]), Blair J.; *Playdium Entertainment Corp., Re* (2001), 2001 CarswellOnt 3893, [2001] O.J. No. 4252 (Ont. S.C.J. [Commercial List]), additional reasons at (2001), 31 C.B.R. (4th) 309 (Ont. S.C.J. [Commercial List]); *Simpson's Island Salmon Ltd., Re* (2005), 2005 CarswellNB 781, [2005] N.B.J. No. 570 (N.B. Q.B.).

[43] Section 11(4), *CCAA*.

[44] *Skeena Cellulose Inc., Re* (2001), 2001 CarswellBC 2226, [2001] B.C.J. No. 2226 (B.C. S.C.).

so that they have timely notice of any further deterioration in the financial position of the debtor corporation.[45]

The courts have held that approval of the creditors is not a prerequisite for extension of a stay; rather, the extension is for the benefit of all the company's stakeholders, not just the creditors.[46] All affected constituencies must be considered, including secured, preferred and unsecured creditors, employees, landlords, shareholders and the public generally. The Ontario Court of Appeal in *Stelco Inc.*, held that it must be a matter of judgment for the supervising judge to determine whether a proposed plan is doomed to fail, and that where a plan is supported by the other stakeholders and the independent monitor, and is a product of the business judgment of the board, it is open to the supervising judge to conclude that the plan was not doomed to fail and that the process should continue.[47]

In *Rio Nevada Energy Inc.*, considering whether to extend a stay under the *CCAA*, the Alberta Court of Queen's Bench held that:

> ¶ 32 As to whether circumstances exist that make the continuation of the stay appropriate, there are a number of factors that must be taken into account. The continuation of the stay in this case is supported by the basic purpose of the *CCAA*, to allow an insolvent company a reasonable period of time to reorganize and propose a plan of arrangement to its creditors and the court and to prevent manoeuvres for positioning among creditors in the interim; *Re Pacific National Lease Holding Corp.; Meridian Developments Inc.* v. *Toronto Dominion Bank.* Westcoast has not satisfied the Court that an attempt at an acceptable compromise or arrangement is doomed to failure at this point in time. Negotiations for restructuring a sale or refinancing are ongoing, and there has been a strengthening of the management team. Rio Nevada continues in business, and plans are underway to remediate its two major wells, which will significantly increase the company's rate of production. A Monitor is in place, which provides comfort to the creditors that assets are not being dissipated and current operations are being supervised. The extension sought is not unduly long, and is supported by the secured creditors other than Westcoast. The costs of the *CCAA* proceedings are likely no less onerous than the costs of a receivership in these circumstances, and the relief sought under the *CCAA* less drastic to all constituencies than the order that would likely have to be made in a receivership.[48]

Where a company sought and received a stay under the *CCAA* as a means of achieving a global resolution of numerous product liability actions, and a complainant alleged bad faith as to activities of the debtor pre-filing of the *CCAA* application, the Ontario Superior Court held that the good faith test in considering an extension of the stay relates only to the debtor's conduct during the *CCAA* proceeding, not to

---

[45] *Starcom International Optics Corp., Re* (1998), 3 C.B.R. (4th) 177 (B.C. S.C.).

[46] *Taché Construction ltée* c. *Banque Lloyds du Canada* (1990), 5 C.B.R. (3d) 151 (Qué. S.C.).

[47] *Stelco Inc., Re* (2005), 2005 CarswellOnt 6283 (Ont. C.A.), at para. 24, affirming (2005), 2005 CarswellOnt 5023 (Ont. S.C.J. [Commercial List]).

[48] *Rio Nevada Energy Inc., Re* (2000), 2000 CarswellAlta 1584, [2000] A.J. No. 1596 (Alta. Q.B.).

prior conduct; and the Court was satisfied that the debtor was proceeding with due diligence and good faith and extended the stay.[49]

The Court also held that where product liability actions pertained only to products formerly sold by a debtor, the liability of the third parties was derivative of, and inextricably linked to, the liability of the debtor and as a result, the stay of proceedings was extended in the initial *CCAA* order to the third parties with respect to the product liability actions. The Court held that it was premature to challenge the settlement and release of claims against third parties as part of a restructuring plan prior to the sanction hearing when the restructuring plan will be considered for approval by the court. The Court further held that where creditors have sufficient information with which to consider and vote in respect of a restructuring plan, it is inappropriate and unnecessary to permit such creditors to require further investigation or additional information in respect of pre-*CCAA* transactions involving the *CCAA* debtors, and the court will not approve the appointment of an investigator to that end.[50]

In *Hunters Trailer & Marine Ltd.*, an application for extension of the stay and increase in DIP financing was dismissed by the Court, which held that the debtor had failed to lead evidence that the benefits of extending the stay and granting further DIP financing clearly outweighed the potential prejudice to creditors; and held that there was insufficient evidence of a reasonable prospect of successfully restructuring and a lack of confidence in governance of the debtor.[51] The Court thus allowed the debtor to remain in the *CCAA* process for just under two months, and then terminated the proceeding when it found a lack of evidence of a potential successful restructuring.

Hence, the courts will exercise their discretion not to extend the stay where they find no evidence of progress being made in the development of a plan acceptable to creditors, or where they conclude that there is concern that DIP financing is being used as a means to delay inevitable liquidation, or where there is a lack of confidence in the governance of the debtor corporation.

---

[49] *Muscletech Research & Development Inc., Re* (2006), 2006 CarswellOnt 264 (Ont. S.C.J. [Commercial List]).

[50] *Muscletech Research & Development Inc., Re* (2006), 2006 CarswellOnt 6230 (Ont. S.C.J.).

[51] *Hunters Trailer & Marine Ltd., Re* (2002), [2002] A.J. No. 603, 2002 CarswellAlta 611 (Alta. Q.B.) at paras. 10, 14. Subsequently, during the *Hunters Trailer & Marine Ltd.* bankruptcy proceedings, an issue arose as to the costs incurred during the *CCAA* part of the process. The issue arose in the context of whether or not the trustee had acquired any priority in interests under an insurance policy by giving notice to the insurers. While the Alberta Court found that the interest of the trustee in bankruptcy in the insurance policy was subject to the rights of the assignees of the policies, it held that the trustee should not have to bear the costs of the *CCAA* process, the interim receivership or the bankruptcy. The Court held that notice was only relevant to determining priority among assignees, at para. 90. The Court thus directed the trustee to calculate the cost burden over all security. The only exception was insurance proceeds, if any, payable to one assignee, to the extent that Court had found these potential proceeds exempt from execution.

7. The Problem of Overreach

The stay order has sometimes been contested. There has been an issue in respect of whether the orders overreach in terms of the scope of the order. The applicant under the *CCAA* drafts the order, which can be 20-40 pages or more, and the court is asked to endorse the order with few parties having received notice or the opportunity to make submissions to the court. The court was frequently faced with extensive orders, sought on a very short notice basis such that the court did not have the appropriate time or submissions from parties to assist it in fully considering the extent or impact of the order.

In *Royal Oak Mines*, the Court expressed concern about the growing complexity of initial orders being sought under the *CCAA* stay provisions.[52] The Court acknowledged the efficiency of bringing pre-packaged draft orders in which the debtor corporation has first sought the input and approval of senior creditors. However, the Court expressed concern about the growing tendency to attempt to incorporate provisions to meet all eventualities that may arise during the *CCAA* proceedings. The Court held that given that stay applications are made on short or no notice, the extensive relief being sought at the initial order stage is beyond what could appropriately be accommodated within the bounds of procedural fairness. The Court held that it must balance the need to move quickly with the requirement that parties be given an opportunity to digest the information and advance their interests. The Court acknowledged the need for a certain degree of complexity in initial orders, but urged more readily understandable language in initial orders, suggesting that "they should not read like trust indentures".

This reasoning was subsequently endorsed by other courts, although it did little to curb the overreach. In *Big Sky Living Inc.*, in an order appointing an interim receiver, the Alberta Court of Queen's Bench struck out a number of provisions as not necessary for the protection of the estate, observing that the order sought to limit the rights of parties that had not received notice of the application.[53]

The Supreme Court of Canada in *GMAC Commercial Credit Corporation - Canada* v. *TCT Logistics Inc.* also discussed the issue of orders that overreach what is appropriate, in the context of a receivership order.[54] The Court held:

> ¶50 Trustees, receivers and the specialized courts by which they are supervised, are entitled to a measure of deference consistent with their undisputed expertise in the effective management of a bankruptcy. Flexibility is required to cure the problems in any particular bankruptcy. But guarding that flexibility with boiler plate immunizations that inoculate against the assertion of rights is beyond the therapeutic reach of the *Bankruptcy and Insolvency Act.*

---

[52] *Royal Oak Mines Inc., Re* (1999), 1999 CarswellOnt 625, [1999] O.J. No. 709 (Ont. Gen. Div. [Commercial List]), at paras. 8, 9, 15, 17.

[53] *Big Sky Living Inc., Re* (2002), 37 C.B.R. (4th) 42 (Alta. Q.B.).

[54] *GMAC Commercial Credit Corp. - Canada* v. *TCT Logistics Inc.*, 2006 SCC 35 (S.C.C.). For a discussion of this case, see chapter 6.

While trade suppliers, workers and other unsecured creditors can take advantage of the "come-back" clause, as discussed above, in reality, most of them do not have the sophistication to appreciate remedies that they may have because of failure of the debtor corporation to give notice of extensive stay orders. As the Court observed in *Royal Oak Mines Inc.*, the come-back clauses in initial orders do not provide an answer to "overreaching" initial orders because while there is no formal onus on a party applying to vary the initial order, the momentum established in the process creates an inherent disadvantage to the party seeking to alter its provisions.[55]

8. Model Orders – Creating Consistency in the System

A number of bar associations and insolvency practitioners across Canada have now developed model initial *CCAA* orders, working with the courts in their jurisdictions. The model orders are aimed at expediting the commencement of proceedings. They are also aimed at dealing with the issue of overreach of orders.

Model Initial Orders have now been developed in Ontario and Québec and are being drafted in British Columbia and Alberta. These orders are included as Appendices to this text.[56] In developing these orders, members of the profession and the court have worked to ensure that the orders reflect commercial realities.

Model orders can still be tailored to meet the needs of the particular debtor. However, parties are to provide the court with a black-lined copy that identifies all the wording of the order sought where it varies from the model order. In this way, the court and other parties to the proceeding can easily identify where the applicant seeking to commence proceedings under the *CCAA* has determined that it needs relief that differs from the model order. Hence, the practice in most jurisdictions is that the party seeking the order must advise the court where the order departs from the model order, thus increasing both understanding of the scope of the order and expediting the process.

9. Lifting or Setting Aside the Stay

The court has the discretion to lift or set aside the stay, and in determining whether to grant a request by a party to lift or set aside the stay, the court will balance the interests of all parties. The court must be satisfied that there is prejudice to a particular creditor if the creditor is not allowed to proceed with its claim, but this alone is not enough. The court is generally reluctant to lift the stay because the purpose of the stay period is to allow the insolvent corporation reprieve from litigation so that it

---

[55] *Royal Oak Mines Inc., Re* (1999), 1999 CarswellOnt 625, [1999] O.J. No. 709 (Ont. Gen. Div. [Commercial List]), at paragraphs 27, 28.

[56] Appendices 3 to 7 of this text.

can direct its resources to negotiating a viable plan with creditors.[57] The court is often concerned that lifting the stay for one creditor will lead to similar requests from other creditors, and that these requests could destabilize the restructuring. Where the negotiations for a plan appear to be progressing and there is no evidence of material prejudice to creditors, the court has refused to lift the stay.[58]

In *Stelco Inc.*, the Ontario Superior Court held that the stay of proceedings in respect of a debtor under the *CCAA* should not be lifted to permit litigation in respect of a conspiracy claim to proceed against the debtor where a claims process for determining the conspiracy claim had been previously established by a claims officer.[59] The Court held that the claims officer should be permitted to render its decision in respect of the conspiracy claim pursuant to the claims process; and if necessary, the claimant could then appeal the claims officer's decision.

In *Air Canada,* where proposed class action litigation was complex and would have had an adverse impact on restructuring efforts, the court refused to lift the stay to permit the action to proceed.[60] In *Ivaco*, an insurer sought to lift a stay so that it could enforce its security by terminating insurance policies; the Court refused, stating that to allow the creditor to enforce its security by terminating insurance policies financed under contracts with the insolvent company would amount to an indirect but devastating attack on the stay.[61] To lift the stay would give the insurer an inappropriate advantage over other unsecured creditors, as well as over secured creditors with priority.[62]

The court has lifted the stay in order to protect the interests of particularly vulnerable claimants where the public interest weighs in favour of lifting the *CCAA* stay, as it did for some tort claims in the *Red Cross* contaminated blood case. During negotiation of a *CCAA* plan, the Court in *Red Cross* lifted the stay to allow fifteen transfusion-related lawsuits to proceed, on the basis that there were compelling reasons that these proceedings be allowed to proceed, given the reduced life expectancy of the claimants.[63] In the same case, the Court dismissed a motion by former management employees seeking a lift of the stay to determine a related-employer issue; the Court held that the purpose of the stay was to give the debtor respite from

---

[57] *Toronto Stock Exchange Inc.* v. *United Keno Hill Mines Ltd.* (2000), 48 O.R. (3d) 746 (Ont. S.C.J. [Commercial List]).

[58] *Canadian Airlines Corp., Re* (2000), 19 C.B.R. (4th) 1 (Alta. Q.B.).

[59] *Stelco Inc., Re* (2005), 2005 CarswellOnt 1732 (Ont. S.C.J. [Commercial List]).

[60] *Air Canada, Re* (2004), 47 C.B.R. (4th) 177, 2004 CarswellOnt 481 (Ont. S.C.J. [Commercial List]) (Always Travel Inc. – Leave to Proceed Motion).

[61] *Ivaco Inc., Re* (2003), 2003 CarswellOnt 6097, 1 C.B.R. (5th) 204, 6 P.P.S.A.C. (3d) 261 (Ont. S.C.J. [Commercial List]).

[62] See also *Stelco Inc., Re* (2004), [2004] O.J. No. 1915, 49 C.B.R. (4th) 283, 12 C.C.L.I. (4th) 26, 6 P.P.S.A.C. (3d) 268 (Ont. S.C.J. [Commercial List]), leave to appeal allowed (2004), 4 C.B.R. (5th) 115 (Ont. C.A.), reversed (2005), 9 C.B.R. (5th) 307 (Ont. C.A.) (CAFO unearned insurance premium motion).

[63] This was because the costs of defence proceedings were to be borne by the insurer and thus would not come from the assets.

litigation and here, there was nothing to take these particular claimants out of the *CCAA* claims process.[64]

Where creditors are concerned about a preference payment or fraudulent conveyance that allegedly occurred prior to the *CCAA* filing, they can seek a temporary lifting of the *CCAA* stay to allow the filing of a petition in bankruptcy. This petition is then stayed until the outcome of the *CCAA* process is known. If the debtor subsequently becomes bankrupt, this fixes the date from which a trustee can look backward and challenge payments either as fraudulent preferences or as fraudulent conveyances. If there is a *CCAA* plan sanctioned by the court, the preference or other reviewable transaction claims are usually settled within the plan, and the filing under the *BIA* is discontinued.

In *Toronto Stock Exchange Inc.* v. *United Keno Hill Mines*, the Court refused to lift a stay to allow the Toronto Stock Exchange to pursue proceedings on whether to suspend trading on the corporation's securities.[65] The Court held that the *CCAA*, the *Toronto Stock Exchange Act* and the Ontario *Securities Act* were all instruments of public policy and that the serious risk to those involved in survival of the firm and the public interest in restructuring outweighed the largely speculative allegation of prejudice to the Toronto Stock Exchange in the execution of its public interest mandate. The Court held that where there are two streams of public interest implicated, the interests of affected parties must be weighed.

The Court's reasoning in *Toronto Stock Exchange Inc.* v. *United Keno Hill Mines* is consistent with its approach to *CCAA* stays, with refusal by the courts to lift the stay for human rights enforcement and employment standards claims during the stay period, on the basis that enforcement rights under remedial legislation must be temporarily suspended in the larger public interest of giving the debtor corporation time to devise a business plan acceptable to creditors. As with securities legislation, these claims involve remedial statutes and public interest considerations. However, the judgment raised an interesting public policy question regarding the public interest in allowing trading in worthless equity.

Chapter 47, when proclaimed in force, will change this situation, allowing regulators under provincial, territorial and federal legislation to pursue investigation and enforcement proceedings that do not involve orders for financial payments.

In contrast to the Toronto Stock Exchange case, in *Milner Greenhouses Ltd.* v. *Saskatchewan*, the Court observed that the *CCAA* stay is directed to commercial as opposed to penal activities. Accordingly, the Court held that the prosecution of offences under the *Occupational Health and Safety Act* were not stayed by section 11, although the stay would apply to the enforcement of any fines imposed following

---

[64] *Canadian Red Cross, Endorsement* (April 26, 1999), Ontario Court File No. 98-CL-002970, Blair J. (Ont. Gen. Div. [Commercial List]), at 6.

[65] *Toronto Stock Exchange Inc.* v. *United Keno Hill Mines Ltd.* (2000), 48 O.R. (3d) 746 (Ont. S.C.J. [Commercial List]).

a successful prosecution.[66] There were similar carve outs in the Stelco *CCAA* proceedings regarding environmental and health and safety applications.

In *PSINet Ltd.*, the Court distinguished between what it properly considers its role and that more appropriately left to the legislative process.[67] The issue was whether to lift the *CCAA* stay to allow re-registration of a formerly perfected security interest under the *Personal Property Security Act (PPSA)*. Prior to the discovery of the lapse during the *CCAA* proceeding, the parent corporation was considered an unsecured creditor. The Court observed that while legislative intervention may be required to close a gap in the statutory language, there was nothing in that language to prevent re-registration, and the court exercised its discretion to allow this. The court observed that this substantially reduced the realization value for unsecured creditors, and ordered both costs of the proceeding and some adjustment to the terms of the *CCAA* plan to account for the expenditure of time and money by unsecured creditors who had previously had an expectation of greater recovery.[68]

The court will often lift the stay so that a lien may be filed, in order to protect creditors from prejudice from time limits on the filing of lien claims. The court will also lift the stay to allow a lien claim to be perfected, where the creditor risks losing the claim.[69] The court does not need to rule on the validity of the claim or its status as a lien in order to exercise its discretion to lift the stay.[70] The Court found it was appropriate to lift the stay of proceedings in a debtor company's *CCAA* and receivership proceedings for the limited purpose of validating a secured creditor's amended *PPSA* registration, as such registration did not affect the debtor company's reorganization efforts and there was not any prejudice to the debtor company or its creditors.[71]

Where a plan of arrangement had been approved three years prior and was close to completion, the Court held that it was appropriate to lift the *CCAA* stay to allow certain creditors to access insurance proceeds, as it did not impair the principles underlying the *CCAA*.[72]

In *Air Canada,* where a disputed human rights claim had been determined within the *CCAA* proceeding under a claims review process, the court would not grant leave

---

[66] *Milner Greenhouses Ltd.* v. *Saskatchewan* (2004), 2004 CarswellSask 280, [2004] 9 W.W.R. 310, 50 C.B.R. (4th) 214, 2004 SKQB 160 (Sask. Q.B.); *Occupational Health and Safety Act*, S.S. 1993, c. O-1.1.

[67] *PSINet Ltd., Re* (2002), [2002] O.J. No. 271 (Ont. S.C.J. [Commercial List]), affirmed (2002), 32 C.B.R. (4th) 102 (Ont. C.A.).

[68] *Ibid.*

[69] *Smoky River Coal Ltd., Re* (1999), 12 C.B.R. (4th) 116 (Alta. Q.B.); *Cansugar Inc., Re* (2003), 48 C.B.R. (4th) 225 (N.B. Q.B.).

[70] *Anvil Range Mining Corp., Re* (1998), 3 C.B.R. (4th) 93 (Ont. Gen. Div. [Commercial List]).

[71] *Brookside Capital Partners Inc.* v. *Kodiak Energy Services Ltd. (Receiver-Manager of)*, 2006 CarswellAlta 1036 (Alta. Q.B.).

[72] *United Properties Ltd., Re* (2005), 22 C.B.R. (5th) 274 (B.C. S.C. [In Chambers]).

to lift the stay of proceedings in a judicial review application because the underlying substance of the claims had been conclusively dealt with.[73]

10. Appeal of the Stay Order

Parties dissatisfied with a stay order can seek an appeal. In considering applications for leave to appeal the stay order, Canadian appellate courts have held that they will be cautious to intervene in the *CCAA* process, especially at an early stage, given that the supervising judge engages in a delicate balancing of interests that an appellate proceeding may upset or frustrate.[74]

Appellate courts have held that leave to appeal should not be granted where it would prejudice the prospects of restructuring the business for the benefit of stakeholders as a whole, and thus setting aside a stay order would be contrary to the spirit and objectives of the *CCAA*.[75] Appellate court judgments indicate that in *CCAA* cases, leave to appeal should be granted sparingly.[76] In *Northland Properties Ltd.* v. *Guardian Trust Co.,* the Court held that given the discretionary nature of a stay under the *CCAA*, the appellate courts will be reluctant to grant leave to appeal a stay order unless the judge committed an error in principle or overlooked material evidence.[77]

The Ontario Court of Appeal in *Stelco Inc.,* held that the appellate courts, in the context of a *CCAA* proceeding, will only grant leave to appeal where there are "serious and arguable grounds that are of real and significant interest to the parties."[78] This criterion is determined in accordance with a four-pronged test, namely, whether the point on appeal is of significance to the practice; whether the point is of significance to the action; whether the appeal is *prima facie* meritorious or frivolous; and whether the appeal will unduly hinder the progress of the restructuring process.[79] On the facts, the Court of Appeal held that the first three tests had been met and

---

[73] *Bird* v. *Air Canada* (2005), 2005 CarswellNat 249 (F.C.) (Grievance Procedure).

[74] *Algoma Steel Inc., Re* (2001), 2001 CarswellOnt 1742, [2001] O.J. No. 1943 (Ont. C.A.) at para. 8; *Pacific National Lease Holding Corp., Re* (1992), 15 C.B.R. (3d) 265 (B.C. C.A.).

[75] *Consumers Packaging Inc., Re* (2001), 27 C.B.R. (4th) 197 (Ont. C.A.).

[76] *Country Style Food Services Inc., Re* (2002), [2002] O.J. No. 1377, 2002 CarswellOnt 1038 (Ont. C.A. [In Chambers]); *Pacific National Lease Holding Corp., Re* (1992), 15 C.B.R. (3d) 265 (B.C. C.A. [In Chambers]); *Consumers Packaging Inc., Re* (2001), [2001] O.J. No. 3908, 27 C.B.R. (4th) 197 (Ont. C.A.), at 199 [C.B.R. (4th)].

[77] *Northland Properties Ltd.* v. *Guardian Trust Co.* (1988), 73 C.B.R. (N.S.) 163 (B.C. C.A. [In Chambers]).

[78] *Stelco Inc., Re* (2005), 9 C.B.R. (5th) 135, 75 O.R. (3d) 5 (Ont. C.A.) at para. 24, citing *Country Style Food Services Inc., Re* (2002), 2002 CarswellOnt 1038, 158 O.A.C. 30 (Ont. C.A. [In Chambers]), at para. 15. In Stelco's *CCAA* proceeding, however, because of the "real time" dynamic of the restructuring, Mr. Justice Laskin of the Ontario Court of Appeal granted an order expediting a motion for leave to appeal, directing that it be heard orally and, if leave granted, directing that the appeal be heard at the same time. The leave motion and the appeal were argued together, by order of the panel.

[79] *Country Style Food Services Inc., Re* (2002), 2002 CarswellOnt 1038, 158 O.A.C. 30 (Ont. C.A. [In Chambers]), at para. 15.

granted leave, observing that "the issue of the court's jurisdiction to intervene in corporate governance issues during a *CCAA* restructuring, and the scope of its discretion in doing so, are questions of considerable importance to the practice and on which there is little appellate jurisprudence."[80] As discussed in chapter 5, the appellate court overturned the lower court judgment.

III. THE DEFINITION OF INSOLVENCY

Unlike the *BIA*, the *CCAA* does not define "insolvent" or "insolvency." Although it is common practice to refer to the definition of "insolvent person" in the *BIA* in referring to insolvency in the context of the *CCAA*, the Ontario court has held that the test for insolvency under the *CCAA* differs from that under the *BIA* in order to meet the special circumstances and objectives of the *CCAA*. In *Stelco Inc.*, Mr. Justice Farley held that "insolvent" should be given an expanded meaning under the *CCAA* in order to give effect to the rehabilitative goal of the statute.[81] The Court concluded that it would defeat the purpose of the *CCAA* to limit or prevent an application until the financial difficulties of the applicant are so advanced that the applicant would not have sufficient financial resources to successfully complete its restructuring. Under this approach, a court should determine whether there is a reasonably foreseeable expectation at the time of filing that there is a looming liquidity condition or crisis that will result in the applicant running out of money to pay its debts as they generally become due in the future without the benefit of the stay and ancillary protection. How far forward the court should look will vary according to the complexity of and time required to complete a restructuring.

In the *Stelco Inc.* proceeding, the union sought to set aside the initial stay order under the *CCAA* on the basis that the debtor corporation was not insolvent. The Court's ruling was an application of the tests under the *BIA*, but with a view to the objectives of the *CCAA*, such that establishing insolvency was slightly less onerous than under the *BIA*.[82]

The Court in *Stelco Inc.*, held:

> ¶ 3 For the purpose of determining whether Stelco is insolvent and therefore could be considered to be a debtor company, it matters not what the cause or who caused the financial difficulty that Stelco is in as admitted by Locker on behalf of the Union. The management of a corporation could be completely incompetent, inadvertently or advertently; the corporation could be in the grip of ruthless, hard hearted and hard

[80] *Stelco Inc., Re* (2005), 9 C.B.R. (5th) 135, 75 O.R. (3d) 5 (Ont. C.A.).

[81] *Stelco Inc., Re* (2004), 2004 CarswellOnt 1211, 48 C.B.R. (4th) 299 (Ont. S.C.J. [Commercial List]), leave to appeal refused (2004), 2004 CarswellOnt 2936 (Ont. C.A.), leave to appeal refused (2004), 2004 CarswellOnt 5200 (S.C.C.). For a discussion of *Stelco*, see Vern W. DaRe, "Is 'Insolvency' Still a Prerequisite to Restructuring?", (2004) 49 C.B.R. (4th) 163.

[82] Stelco subsequently experienced a profitable fiscal quarter, raising a question for further consideration as to what happens when future forecasting is inaccurate and the debtor regains solvency during the *CCAA* stay period.

nosed outside financiers; the corporation could be the innocent victim of uncaring policy of a level of government; the employees (unionized or non-unionized) could be completely incompetent, inadvertently or advertently; the relationship of labour and management could be absolutely poisonous; the corporation could be the victim of unforeseen events affecting its viability such as a fire destroying an essential area of its plant and equipment or of rampaging dumping. One or more or all of these factors (without being exhaustive), whether or not of varying degree and whether or not in combination of some may well have been the cause of a corporation's difficulty. The point here is that Stelco's difficulty exists; the only question is whether Stelco is insolvent within the meaning of that in the "debtor company" definition of the *CCAA*. However, I would point out, as I did in closing, that no matter how this motion turns out, Stelco does have a problem which has to be addressed - addressed within the *CCAA* process if Stelco is insolvent or addressed outside that process if Stelco is determined not to be insolvent. The status quo will lead to ruination of Stelco (and its Sub Applicants) and as a result will very badly affect its stakeholder, including pensioners, employees (unionized and non-unionized), management, creditors, suppliers, customers, local and other governments and the local communities. In such situations, time is a precious commodity; it cannot be wasted; no matter how much some would like to take time outs, the clock cannot be stopped. The watchwords of the Commercial List are equally applicable in such circumstances. They are communication, cooperation and common sense. I appreciate that these cases frequently invoke emotions running high and wild; that is understandable on a human basis but it is the considered, rational approach which will solve the problem.

. . .

¶ 11 The Union, supported by the International United Steel Workers of America ("International"), indicated that if certain of the obligations of Stelco were taken into account in the determination of insolvency, then a very good number of large Canadian corporations would be able to make an application under the *CCAA*. I am of the view that this concern can be addressed as follows. The test of insolvency is to be determined on its own merits, not on the basis that an otherwise technically insolvent corporation should not be allowed to apply. However, if a technically insolvent corporation were to apply and there was no material advantage to the corporation and its stakeholders (in other words, a pressing need to restructure), then one would expect that the court's discretion would be judicially exercised against granting *CCAA* protection and ancillary relief. In the case of Stelco, it is recognized, as discussed above, that it is in crisis and in need of restructuring - which restructuring, if it is insolvent, would be best accomplished within a *CCAA* proceeding. Further, I am of the view that the track record of *CCAA* proceedings in this country demonstrates a healthy respect for the fundamental concerns of interested parties and stakeholders. I have consistently observed that much more can be achieved by negotiations outside the courtroom where there is a reasonable exchange of information, views and the exploration of possible solutions and negotiations held on a without prejudice basis than likely can be achieved by resorting to the legal combative atmosphere of the courtroom. A mutual problem requires a mutual solution. The basic interest of the *CCAA* is to rehabilitate insolvent corporations for the benefit of all stakeholders. To do this, the cause(s) of the insolvency must be fixed on a long term viable basis so that the corporation may be turned around. It is not achieved by positional bargaining in a tug of war between two parties, each trying for a larger slice of a defined size pie; it may be achieved by taking steps involving shorter term equitable sacrifices and implementing sensible approaches to improve productivity to ensure that the pie grows sufficiently for the long term to accommodate the reasonable needs of the parties.

. . .

¶ 24 . . . It seems to me that there is merit in considering that the test for insolvency under the *CCAA* may differ somewhat from that under the *BIA*, so as to meet the special circumstances of the *CCAA* and those corporations which would apply under it. In that respect, I am mindful of the above discussion regarding the time that is usually and necessarily (in the circumstances) taken in a *CCAA* reorganization restructuring which is engaged in coming up with a plan of compromise and arrangement. The *BIA* definition would appear to have been historically focused on the question of bankruptcy - and not reorganization of a corporation under a proposal since before 1992, secured creditors could not be forced to compromise their claims, so that in practice there were no reorganizations under the former *Bankruptcy Act* unless all secured creditors voluntarily agreed to have their secured claims compromised. The *BIA* definition then was essentially useful for being a pre-condition to the "end" situation of a bankruptcy petition or voluntary receiving order where the upshot would be a realization on the bankrupt's assets (not likely involving the business carried on - and certainly not by the bankrupt). Insolvency under the *BIA* is also important as to the Paulian action events (e.g., fraudulent preferences, settlements) as to the conduct of the debtor prior to the bankruptcy; similarly as to the question of provincial preference legislation. Reorganization under a plan or proposal, on the contrary, is with a general objective of the applicant continuing to exist, albeit that the *CCAA* may also be used to have an orderly disposition of the assets and undertaking in whole or in part.

. . .

¶ 25 It seems to me that given the time and steps involved in a reorganization, and the condition of insolvency perforce requires an expanded meaning under the *CCAA*. Query whether the definition under the *BIA* is now sufficient in that light for the allowance of sufficient time to carry through with a realistically viable proposal within the maximum of six months allowed under the *BIA*? I think it sufficient to note that there would not be much sense in providing for a rehabilitation program of restructuring/reorganization under either statute if the entry test was that the applicant could not apply until a rather late stage of its financial difficulties with the rather automatic result that in situations of complexity of any material degree, the applicant would not have the financial resources sufficient to carry through to hopefully a successful end. This would indeed be contrary to the renewed emphasis of Parliament on "rescues" as exhibited by the 1992 and 1997 amendments to the *CCAA* and the *BIA*.

. . .

¶ 40 . . . . However, I am of the view that that [*BIA* definition of insolvency] would be unduly restrictive and a proper contextual and purposive interpretation to be given when it is being used for a restructuring purpose even under *BIA* would be to see whether there is a reasonably foreseeable (at the time of filing) expectation that there is a looming liquidity condition or crisis which will result in the applicant running

> out of "cash" to pay its debts as they generally become due in the future without the benefit of the stay and ancillary protection and procedure by court authorization pursuant to an order. I think this is the more appropriate interpretation of *BIA* (a) test in the context of a reorganization or "rescue" as opposed to a threshold to bankruptcy consideration or a fraudulent preferences proceeding. On that basis, I would find Stelco insolvent from the date of filing. Even if one were not to give the latter interpretation to the *BIA* (a) test, clearly for the above reasons and analysis, if one looks at the meaning of "insolvent" within the context of a *CCAA* reorganization or rescue solely, then of necessity, the time horizon must be such that the liquidity crisis would occur in the sense of running out of "cash" but for the grant of the *CCAA* order. On that basis Stelco is certainly insolvent given its limited cash resources unused, its need for a cushion, its rate of cash burn recently experienced and anticipated.
>
> . . .
>
> ¶ 69 In the end result, I have concluded on the balance of probabilities that Stelco is insolvent and therefore it is a "debtor company" as at the date of filing and entitled to apply for the *CCAA* initial order. My conclusion is that (i) *BIA* test (c) strongly shows Stelco is insolvent; (ii) *BIA* test (a) demonstrates, to a less certain but sufficient basis, an insolvency and (iii) the "new" *CCAA* test again strongly supports the conclusion of insolvency. I am further of the opinion that I properly exercised my discretion in granting Stelco and the Sub Applicants the initial order on January 29, 2004 and I would confirm that as of the present date with effect on the date of filing. The Union's motion is therefore dismissed.[83]

The above excerpt illustrates that there are two elements to the decision, with the court determining the issue of insolvency not only on the cash flow test, but also on the basis that Stelco was insolvent based on a balance sheet basis. On balance, the Court found that Stelco was insolvent and that it had properly exercised its discretion in granting Stelco an initial stay order under the *CCAA*.[84] The Court considered the union's submission that under the court's definition, many companies in Canada would be technically insolvent, and observed that the court always has the discretion not to grant *CCAA* relief or to terminate that relief on a come-back application. It also observed that if a company were to cease paying its debts in order to come within the definition of insolvency, the court could view this as ill-advised game playing and refuse to exercise its discretion to grant the benefit of the *CCAA* stay if the debtor's actions were capriciously undertaken and there was not reasonable need.[85] The Court also observed that if a corporation did so capriciously, then one might well expect a creditor-initiated application so as to take control of the process and oust management and directors who authorized such unnecessary stoppage, and that in such a case, it is likely that a creditor application would find favour of judicial discretion.[86]

---

[83] *Stelco Inc., Re* (2004), 2004 CarswellOnt 1211, 48 C.B.R. (4th) 299 (Ont. S.C.J. [Commercial List]), leave to appeal refused (2004), 2004 CarswellOnt 2936 (Ont. C.A.), leave to appeal refused (2004), 2004 CarswellOnt 5200 (S.C.C.).

[84] *Ibid.* at para. 69.

[85] *Ibid.* at para. 8.

[86] *Ibid.*

IV. THE ISSUE OF NOTICE

1. Who is Entitled to Notice?

An application for a stay under the *CCAA* can be made without notice, although increasingly, the courts expect the applicant to have given notice. The reason for an *ex parte* order is because the debtor is trying to prevent creditors from moving to realize on their claims, essentially a "stampede to the assets" once creditors learn of the debtor's financial distress. If the *CCAA* application is made *ex parte*, the court has held that there must be full and frank disclosure of all relevant facts, although the material filed does not need to set out all the details of the company's financial position.[87]

In *Hester Creek Estate Winery Ltd.*, the Court held that it had been misled and that full and fair disclosure of relevant information had not been made; hence an *ex parte* order was not extended.[88]

As noted above, where a stay or other order is made without notice to parties, the courts frequently add a "come-back" clause, whereby parties can return to court at a later date to seek to set aside some or all of the order. The come-back order is viewed by the courts as the counterbalance to any prejudice suffered by creditors as a result of failing to receive notice.

2. Transparency and Potential Prejudice in Current Practice

Often employees, and where there are trade unions representing them, the trade unions, do not receive notice of the application for an initial stay order. For example, in each of the cases of *Anvil Range, Red Cross* and *Royal Oak Mines Inc.*, the workers and their unions were not given any notice of the proceedings until some discrete issue of pension liability, other fixed claims, or stays on grievance arbitration proceedings arose.

The reason often given for not providing workers or their unions with notice of the filing application is that there is a fear that employees will occupy the plant or engage in other misconduct in the hours before the stay is granted, although there have been no cases reported of such conduct. Often at the initial order stage, important decisions have already been made, including the court's sanction of initial orders that stay the rights of employees and limit the liability of court-appointed officers in terms of employment and labour law. This creates prejudice to employees, particularly those that are not unionized and do not have the resources to have their interests represented in the proceedings.

---

[87] *Philip's Manufacturing Ltd., Re* (1991), 9 C.B.R. (3d) 1 (B.C. S.C.); *229531 B.C. Ltd., Re* (1989), 72 C.B.R. (N.S.) 310 (B.C. S.C.).

[88] *Hester Creek Estate Winery Ltd., Re* (2004), 50 C.B.R. (4th) 73, 2004 CarswellBC 542, 2004 BCSC 345 (B.C. S.C. [In Chambers]).

However, advance notice and disclosure can be a complex issue. Unions, as the exclusive bargaining agent of workers, must report to their members, so confidentiality can be a problem. Premature disclosure can also be a problem for publicly held companies, and even in some instances private companies, where there is a risk of self-help actions by creditors and contract counter-parties.

The courts could require fuller disclosure at the outset of the process. Use of electronic communication has enhanced the possibility for cost effective and widely disseminated early disclosure. Early notice and disclosure to all creditors can facilitate the early identification of their interests and allow them to seek to enforce what participation and decision rights they can establish. Such disclosure in turn would reduce costs for workers, small trade creditors and other stakeholders seeking to participate. The direction by the courts to give additional notice and time to allow parties to consider their interests should act to enhance access to the process by those who traditionally have not been involved.

3. Legislative Reform

Chapter 47 does improve notice to creditors on DIP financing applications, as discussed in chapter 4. This will alleviate some of the problems associated with *ex parte* granting of operating financing on initial stay applications, without notice to creditors. However, it does not address the failure of parties to give notice to employees and unions.

Chapter 47 will not require notice as of right on initial filing of *CCAA* applications to stakeholders that are identifiable. The granting of *ex parte* initial stays should be restricted to urgent situations as they are now, with limited periods for parties to come back on notice, but a condition of granting the stay should be that the debtor be required to give notice to employees, their unions, local suppliers, governments and any known tort claimants.

Questions for review of materials:

1. What is the definition of insolvency under the *CCAA*, and does it differ from that under the *BIA*?

2. What is the purpose of a stay under an initial *CCAA* order?

3. What test does the court use for lifting a stay of proceedings?

4. What considerations does an appellate court take into account in granting leave to appeal an order made under the *CCAA*?

Questions for discussion:

1. This chapter discusses the issue of overreach of initial stay orders. Does the initial stay order in *Air Canada*, included as Appendix 2 of this text, provide the necessary stay or does it appear to be overreach?

2. Do you think that the test for insolvency in *Stelco Inc.*, is an appropriate definition? Why or why not?

3. In *Stelco Inc.*, why did the court conclude that the debtor was insolvent?

CHAPTER 3

THE ROLE OF THE COURTS IN *CCAA* PROCEEDINGS

I. THE JURISDICTION OF THE COURTS

The *CCAA* gives public policy recognition to the value of restructuring processes. The crux of the success of the *CCAA* as a restructuring tool has been the willingness of the courts to interpret the statute in a purposive manner. As the Québec Superior Court observed in *PCI Chemicals Canada Inc.*, the courts have consistently held that the *CCAA* should be interpreted in a fair, large and liberal manner, with the court considering the equities in each case.[1] Mr. Justice Tysoe of the British Columbia Supreme Court has observed that the successful reorganization of *Quintette Coal* was as a result of the flexibility of the *CCAA* and the court in allowing the parties time to craft a viable plan.[2]

As noted in the introduction, the *CCAA* is broad remedial legislation designed to facilitate a restructuring of debtor corporations in the interests of the company, its creditors and the public.[3] Unlike much litigation in which the court is assessing liability, harm or other conduct *ex post*, proceedings under the *CCAA* primarily engage the court's supervisory powers. The court's role is to approve the framework for negotiation, determining matters that will facilitate the process. It also has overall responsibility to ensure that the statutory requirements are met. The court is not

---

[1] *PCI Chemicals Canada Inc., Re* (2002), 2002 CarswellQue 831, [2002] J.Q. no. 433 (Que. S.C.). See also *Nova Metal Products Inc.* v. *Comiskey (Trustee of)* (1990), (sub nom. *Elan Corp.* v. *Comiskey*) 1 O.R. (3d) 289 (Ont. C.A.), *ibid.*; *Algoma Steel Corp.* v. *Royal Bank* (1992), 1992 CarswellOnt 2843, [1992] O.J. No. 795 (Ont. Gen. Div.).

[2] Mr. Justice Tysoe, "Quintette Coal – The Story of its Reorganization" in J. Ziegel and D. Baird, eds., *Case Studies in Recent Canadian Insolvency Reorganizations, In Honour of the Honourable Lloyd W. Houlden* (Toronto: Carswell, 1997) 377 at 396. *Quintette Coal Ltd., Re* (1991), 10 C.B.R. (3d) 197, 62 B.C.L.R. (2d) 218 (B.C. S.C.) at 240.

[3] *Playdium Entertainment Corp., Re* (2001), 2001 CarswellOnt 3893, [2001] O.J. No. 4252 (Ont. S.C.J. [Commercial List]), additional reasons at (2001), 31 C.B.R. (4th) 309 (Ont. S.C.J. [Commercial List]), at para. 27; *Armbro Enterprises Inc., Re* (1993), 22 C.B.R. (3d) 80 (Ont. Bktcy.); *Icor Oil & Gas Co.* v. *Canadian Imperial Bank of Commerce* (1989), 102 A. R. 161 (Alta. Q.B.) at 165; *Quintette Coal Ltd.* v. *Nippon Steel Corp.* (1990), 2 C.B.R. (3d) 303 (B.C. C.A.), leave to appeal refused (1991), 7 C.B.R. (3d) 164 (note) (S.C.C.); *Consumers Packaging Inc., Re* (2001), [2001] O.J. No. 3908, 27 C.B.R. (4th) 197 (Ont. C.A.).

usually required to adjudicate liability for prior decisions or actions of the debtor corporation.

The *CCAA* has evolved through judicial interpretation and the courts have held that its design and efficacy is that it is a flexible instrument for the restructuring of insolvent companies.[4] The court's role is one of judicial oversight of the process, a role that creates particular challenges in discerning and balancing the rights of creditors and other stakeholders.

While the court will defer to the business judgment of creditors in their approval of a final plan of arrangement or compromise, the primary function of the courts is to supervise the proceedings and to make rulings that keep the process moving when parties hit a particular impasse or there is a lack of clarity about their rights and responsibilities in the particular circumstance. In this respect, the skeletal framework of the statute and its resultant flexibility facilitate the supervisory role of the court.

There has been some critique that the courts have used their supervisory authority in favour of restructuring, and as a result, have implicitly favoured the interests of particular stakeholders.[5] This criticism ignores the legislative purpose of the statute and the nature of the judiciary's role. The courts have observed that the *CCAA* was designed to serve a "broad constituency of investors, creditors and employees", and thus the court will consider the individuals and organizations directly affected by the plan, as well as the wider public interest.[6] Those interests are generally, but not always, served by permitting a company to attempt a restructuring.[7] Judges adjudicate multiple disputes under a restructuring proceeding, interpreting the *CCAA* and its companion corporations, securities, personal property security, bank and bankruptcy statutes in the specific disputes before them. Hence its exercise of jurisdiction under a skeletal statute such as the *CCAA* must be undertaken within the context of a highly codified statutory regime. While the *CCAA* is primarily a procedural statute, the court is called on to make both substantive and procedural determinations.

---

[4] *Dylex Ltd., Re* (January 23, 1995), Doc. B-4/95 (Ont. Gen. Div. [Commercial List]), at 111; *Canadian Red Cross Society / Société Canadienne de la Croix-Rouge, Re* (1998), 5 C.B.R. (4th) 299, 72 O.T.C. 99 (Ont. Gen. Div. [Commercial List]), additional reasons at (1998), 5 C.B.R. (4th) 319 (Ont. Gen. Div. [Commercial List]), further additional reasons at (1998), 5 C.B.R. (4th) 321 (Ont. Gen. Div. [Commercial List]), leave to appeal refused (1998), 1998 CarswellOnt 5967, 32 C.B.R. (4th) 21 (Ont. C.A.), at para. 45.

[5] M. Barrack, "Is Judicial Activism in the Restructuring Field Skewing the Negotiating Process?" in *Corporate Restructurings and Insolvencies, Issues and Perspectives* (Toronto: Carswell, 1995) at 485, 491, 494.

[6] *Hongkong Bank of Canada* v. *Chef Ready Foods Ltd.* (1990), 4 C.B.R. (3d) 311 (B.C. C.A.); *Sklar-Peppler Furniture Corp. v. Bank of Nova Scotia* (1991), 8 C.B.R. (3d) 312 (Ont. Gen. Div.) at 314; *Skydome Corp., Re* (1998), 16 C.B.R. (4th) 118 (Ont. Gen. Div. [Commercial List]).

[7] *Hongkong Bank, ibid.*

1. Inherent Jurisdiction versus the Exercise of Judicial Discretion

The courts use both statutory interpretation and the use of inherent jurisdiction in their decision making in respect of the *CCAA*. Given that the statute is relatively short in nature, and given that the restructuring proceedings that are undertaken under the statute are very complex, the court has used both its statutory discretion and its inherent jurisdiction to make both procedural and substantive decisions that assist the parties in completing the negotiation process and that meet the overall objectives of the legislation. Debtor in possession (DIP) financing, whereby the court allows the debtor company to obtain financing from a lender during the *CCAA* proceeding to allow it to continue operating while it goes through the restructuring process, is one example of the exercise of this power, discussed at length in part 5 of this chapter. While statutory discretion and inherent jurisdiction have sometimes been conflated in judgments in *CCAA* proceedings, more recently the courts have tried to articulate the differences between the use of the two powers.[8]

The court is granted a broad discretion under section 11 of the *CCAA* to make any order it considers appropriate within its general power to grant a stay under the *CCAA* and this statutory discretion has been interpreted broadly. Section 11 specifies:

> 11(1) Notwithstanding anything in the *Bankruptcy and Insolvency Act* or the *Winding-up and Restructuring Act*, where an application is made under this Act in respect of a company, the court, on the application of any person interested in the matter, may, subject to this Act, on notice to any other person or without notice as it may see fit, make an order under this section.

The exercise of the court's inherent jurisdiction is a more sparingly used tool. Inherent jurisdiction is the exercising of the general powers of the court as the superior court of the province or territory. It has been used more generally by the court to control its process, or to fill in the gaps where legislation has not specified what is to occur in particular circumstances. In the context of its supervisory role under the *CCAA*, the court has defined inherent jurisdiction as a "residual source of powers, which the court may draw upon as necessary whenever it is just and equitable to do so, in particular, to ensure the observance of the due process of law, to prevent improper vexation or oppression, to do justice between the parties and to secure a fair trial between them".[9] Inherent jurisdiction cannot be exercised in a manner that conflicts with a statute and, because it is an extraordinary power, should be exercised

[8] *Skeena Cellulose Inc., Re* (2003), 43 C.B.R. (4th) 187 (B.C. C.A.); *Stelco Inc., Re* (2005), 2005 CarswellOnt 1188, [2005] O.J. No. 1171 (Ont. C.A.).

[9] Mr. Justice Farley, citing Halsbury's Volume 37, 4th Edition, at paragraph 14, in *Royal Oak Mines Inc., Re* (1999), [1999] O.J. No. 864, 1999 CarswellOnt 792 (Ont. Gen. Div. [Commercial List]) at paragraph 22. See also *80 Wellesley St East Ltd.* v. *Fundy Bay Builders Ltd.*, [1972] 2 O.R. 280 (Ont. C.A.).

only sparingly and in a clear case where there is cogent evidence that the benefits to all clearly outweighs the potential prejudice to a particular creditor.[10]

The British Columbia Court of Appeal in *Skeena Cellulose Inc.* held that decisions under the *CCAA* are, for the most part, made under the court's broad discretion, rather than inherent jurisdiction:

> ¶ 45 It is true that in "filling in the gaps" or "putting flesh on the bones" of the *CCAA* – for example, by approving arrangements which contemplate the termination of binding contracts or leases – courts have often purported to rely on their "inherent jurisdiction". Farley J. did so in *Dylex*, for example, at para. 8, and in *Royal Oak, supra*, at para. 4, the latter in connection with the granting of a "superpriority"; and Macdonald J. did so in *Westar, supra,* at 8 and 13. The court's use of the term "inherent jurisdiction" is certainly understandable in connection with a statute that confers broad jurisdiction with few specific limitations. But if one examines the strict meaning of "inherent jurisdiction", it appears that in many of the cases discussed above, the courts have been exercising a discretion given by the *CCAA* rather than their inherent jurisdiction. In his seminal article, "The Inherent Jurisdiction of the Court", (1970) 23 Current Legal Problems, Sir J.H. Jacob, Q.C., writes that the inherent jurisdiction of a superior court of law is "that which enables it to fulfill itself as a court of law." The author explains:
>
>> On what basis did the superior courts exercise their powers to punish for contempt and to prevent abuse of process by summary proceedings instead of by the ordinary course of trial and verdict? The answer is, that the jurisdiction to exercise these powers was derived, not from any statute or rule of law, but from the very nature of the court as a superior court of law, and for this reason such jurisdiction has been called "inherent." This description has been criticized as being "metaphysical," but I think nevertheless it is apt to describe the quality of this jurisdiction. For the essential character of a superior court of law necessarily involves that it should be invested with the power to maintain its authority and to prevent its process being obstructed and abused. Such a power is intrinsic in a superior court; it is its very life-blood, its very essence, its immanent attribute. Without such a power, the court would have form but would lack substance. . . . The juridical basis of this jurisdiction is therefore the authority of the judiciary to uphold, to protect and to fulfill the judicial function of administering justice according to law in a regular, orderly and effective manner. [at 27-28]

---

[10] *Sharp-Rite Technologies Ltd., Re* (2000), [2000] B.C.J. No. 135, 2000 CarswellBC 128 (B.C. S.C.) at paras. 43, 46. *Manderley Corp., Re* (2005), 2005 CarswellOnt 1082 (Ont. S.C.J.). This is subject to a much larger debate, as cases such as *Skeena-Cellulose* and *Ottawa Senators* consider the issue of the interplay between inherent jurisdiction and the specific provisions of statutes. For a discussion, see Mary Buttery, "Jurisdiction of the Court in *CCAA* Proceedings: An Examination of *Skeena Cellulose Inc.* v. *Clear Creek Contracting Ltd.*," in J. Sarra, ed., *Annual Review of Insolvency Law, 2003*, (Toronto: Carswell, 2004) at 275. *Baxter Student Housing Ltd.* v. *College Housing Co-operative Ltd.*, [1976] 2 S.C.R. 475 (S.C.C.) at 480. *Westar Mining Ltd., Re* (1992), 14 C.B.R. (3d) 88 (B.C. S.C.); *Hongkong Bank of Canada* v. *Chef Ready Foods Ltd.* (1990), 4 C.B.R. (3d) 307 (B.C. S.C.), affirmed [1991] 2 W.W.R. 136 (B.C. C.A.); *Canadian Asbestos Services Ltd.* v. *Bank of Montreal* (1992), 11 O.R. (3d) 353 (Ont. Gen. Div.), additional reasons at (1993), 13 O.R. (3d) 291 (Ont. Gen. Div.).

> The author also notes that unlike inherent jurisdiction, the source of statutory jurisdiction "is of course the statute itself, which will define the limits within which such jurisdiction is to be exercised, whereas the source of inherent jurisdiction of the court is derived from its nature as a court of law, so that the limits of such jurisdiction are not easy to define, and indeed appear to elude definition." (at 24.)
>
> ¶ 46 Applying this distinction to the issue at hand, I think the preferable view is that when a court approves a plan of arrangement under the *CCAA* which contemplates that one or more binding contracts will be terminated by the debtor corporation, the court is not exercising a power that arises from its nature as a superior court of law, but is exercising the discretion given to it by the *CCAA*. (As to the meaning of "discretion" in this context, see S. Waddams, "Judicial Discretion", (2001) 1 Cmnwth. L.J. 59.) This is the discretion, given by s. 11, to stay proceedings against the debtor corporation and the discretion, given by s. 6, to approve a plan which appears to be reasonable and fair, to be in accord with the requirements and objects of the statute, and to make possible the continuation of the corporation as a viable entity. It is these considerations the courts have been concerned with in the cases discussed above, rather than the integrity of their own process.[11]

The exercise of the court's discretion on either basis depends on the nature of the judicial function under the particular proceeding; the statutory framework and specific requirements that are implicated in a particular dispute; and a consideration what is just and reasonable in the circumstances, including a balancing of the interests of, and prejudice to, the stakeholders with an interest in the financially distressed firm. The Supreme Court of Canada has held that inherent jurisdiction has both substantive and procedural aspects and the courts have authority to exercise both.[12]

Inherent jurisdiction has its origins in the separation of legislative and judicial power, where the courts have taken jurisdiction to deal with matters not otherwise codified by parliaments and legislatures. The notion of equity in the exercise of that jurisdiction dates back to the 12th and 13th centuries, arising from a notion of conscience, protection of the vulnerable from the more powerful, and enforcement of relations of trust and confidence.[13] In the context of both common law and statutory interpretation, balancing equities and prejudice was part of the move toward purposive legal reasoning that has become today's hallmark of statutory interpretation.[14] The practice of reconciling conflicting doctrines, interests and statutes also dates back to this period.[15]

The Ontario Court of Appeal, in overturning a lower court judgment in *Stelco Inc.*, made the following observations regarding inherent jurisdiction under the *CCAA*:

---

[11] *Skeena Cellulose Inc., Re* (2003), 2003 CarswellBC 1399, [2003] B.C.J. No. 1335 (B.C. C.A.).

[12] *Assn. of Parents for Fairness in Education, Grand Falls District 50 Branch* v. *Société des Acadiens du Nouveau-Brunswick Inc.*, [1986] 1 S.C.R. 549 (S.C.C.) at paras. 123-5.

[13] J.C. Smith and D.N. Weisstub, *The Western Idea of Law,* (Toronto: Butterworths, 1983) at 330, 350.

[14] *Ibid.* at 620.

[15] *Ibid.* at 320-1.

[34] Inherent jurisdiction is a power derived "from the very nature of the court as a superior court of law", permitting the court "to maintain its authority and to prevent its process being obstructed and abused". It embodies the authority of the judiciary to control its own process and the lawyers and other officials connected with the court and its process, in order "to uphold, to protect and to fulfill the judicial function of administering justice according to law in a regular, orderly and effective manner". See I.H. Jacob, "The Inherent Jurisdiction of the Court" (1970) 23 Current Legal Problems 27-28. In Halsbury's Laws of England, 4th ed. (London: LexisNexis UK, 1973 —), vol. 37, at para. 14, the concept is described as follows:

> In sum, it may be said that the inherent jurisdiction of the court is a virile and viable doctrine, and has been defined as being the reserve or fund of powers, a residual source of powers, which the court may draw upon as necessary whenever it is just or equitable to do so, in particular, to ensure the observation of the due process of law, to prevent improper vexation or oppression, to do justice between the parties and to secure a fair trial between them.

[35] In spite of the expansive nature of this power, inherent jurisdiction does not operate where Parliament or the legislature has acted. As Farley J. noted in *Royal Oak Mines, supra,* inherent jurisdiction is "not limitless; if the legislative body has not left a functional gap or vacuum, then inherent jurisdiction should not be brought into play" (para. 4). See also, *Baxter Student Housing Ltd.* v. *College Housing Co-operative Ltd.,* [1976] 2 S.C.R. 475, 57 D.L.R. (3d) 1, at p. 480 S.C.R.; Richtree Inc. (Re) (2005), 74 O.R. (3d) 174, [2005] O.J. No. 251 (S.C.J.).

[36] In the *CCAA* context, Parliament has provided a statutory framework to extend protection to a company while it holds its creditors at bay and attempts to negotiate a compromised plan of arrangement that will enable it to emerge and continue as a viable economic entity, thus benefiting society and the company in the long run, along with the company's creditors, shareholders, employees and other stakeholders. The s. 11 discretion is the engine that drives this broad and flexible statutory scheme, and that for the most part supplants the need to resort to inherent jurisdiction. In that regard, I agree with the comment of Newbury J.A. in *Clear Creek Contracting Ltd.* v. *Skeena Cellulose Inc.,* [2003] B.C.J. No. 1335, 43 C.B.R. (4th) 187 (C.A.), at para. 46, that:

> . . . the court is not exercising a power that arises from its nature as a superior court of law, but is exercising the discretion given to it by the *CCAA*. . . . This is the discretion, given by s. 11, to stay proceedings against the debtor corporation and the discretion, given by s. 6, to approve a plan which appears to be reasonable and fair, to be in accord with the requirements and objects of the statute, and to make possible the continuation of the corporation as a viable entity. It is these considerations the courts have been concerned with in the cases discussed above, rather than the integrity of their own process.

[37] As Jacob observes, in his article "The Inherent Jurisdiction of the Court", supra, at p. 25:

> The inherent jurisdiction of the court is a concept which must be distinguished from the exercise of judicial discretion. These two concepts resemble each other, particularly in their operation, and they often appear to overlap, and are

therefore sometimes confused the one with the other. There is nevertheless a vital juridical distinction between jurisdiction and discretion, which must always be observed.

[38] I do not mean to suggest that inherent jurisdiction can never apply in a *CCAA* context. The court retains the ability to control its own process, should the need arise. There is a distinction, however – difficult as it may be to draw – between the court's process with respect to the restructuring, on the one hand, and the course of action involving the negotiations and corporate actions accompanying them, which are the company's process, on the other hand. The court simply supervises the latter process through its ability to stay, restrain or prohibit proceedings against the company during the plan negotiation period "on such terms as it may impose". Hence the better view is that a judge is generally exercising the court's statutory discretion under s. 11 of the Act when supervising a *CCAA* proceeding. The order in this case could not be founded on inherent jurisdiction because it is designed to supervise the company's process, not the court's process.[16]

Hence, the appellate courts in British Columbia and Ontario have tried to clarify the distinction between the exercise of discretion under the *CCAA* and the exercise of the court's inherent jurisdiction, locating most of the court's authority in *CCAA* proceedings under the broad discretion granted by the statute.

The Québec Superior Court in *MEI Computer Technology Group Inc.* held that it is now settled law that the *CCAA* is a remedial statute that is to be given a liberal interpretation to facilitate its objectives so as to facilitate a restructuring and continue the debtor as a going concern in the interim.[17] The Court held that the Québec courts share the same vision as to the liberal interpretation of the *CCAA*, and that in facilitating the achievement of the *CCAA's* objectives, courts have relied on their inherent jurisdiction or alternatively, on their broad discretion under s. 11 of the *CCAA,* as the source of judicial power to "fill the gaps" or "put flesh on the bones" of the statute.[18] Hence, the court in *MEI Computer Technology Group Inc.* fully embraced the use of inherent jurisdiction as a gap filling power, but then declined to use it to grant the remedy in the circumstances, based on indicia that the court found furthered the objectives and scheme of the *CCAA*.[19] The Court held that a lack of opposition to a particular motion is not good enough reason for the court to be lenient in a situation where the criteria recognized by the court in its jurisprudence are not otherwise met.[20]

Richard Jones has explored the scope and limits of judicial discretion, observing that the trend by the courts under the *CCAA* to assume increasing discretionary

---

[16] *Stelco Inc., Re* (2005), 2005 CarswellOnt 1188, [2005] O.J. No. 1171 (Ont. C.A.).

[17] *MEI Computer Technology Group Inc., Re* (2005), 2005 CarswellQue 3675, [2005] Q.J. No. 5744 (Que. S.C.) at para. 18, citing the Court of Appeal in *Stelco Inc., Re* at para. 32 and *United Used Auto & Truck Parts Ltd., Re* (2000), 2000 CarswellBC 414, [2000] B.C.J. No. 409 (B.C. C.A.) at para.12.

[18] *Ibid.* at paras. 19-20.

[19] *Ibid.* The case involved determining whether to grant a priority charge for a key employee retention program. For a discussion of the tests used by the courts, see the discussion in Chapter 5, Part IV.

[20] *Ibid.* at para. 21.

authority may have the courts determining rights that are not justiciable, in part because debtors and creditors are bringing disputes before the court that may more properly belong at the negotiation table.[21]

The court's role under the *CCAA* is primarily supervisory and it is the parties that have carriage of the negotiations. The court makes particular determinations during the process where the parties are unable to agree. These decisions facilitate the negotiation process, whether it results in a going concern solution or not. Moreover, the court must be periodically satisfied that the parties are making progress in the workout negotiations. Thus the role is both procedural and substantive in making rights determinations within the context of an ongoing negotiation process. The court has held that because of the remedial nature of the legislation, the judiciary will exercise its jurisdiction to give effect to the public policy objectives of the statute where the express language is incomplete, including endorsement of a survival program of the debtor corporation.[22]

While negotiations between creditors and other stakeholders are largely conducted in private and the court may encourage various forms of dispute resolution, the court has consistently declined to deal with matters of rights determination *in camera*, finding that these matters are more appropriately for public hearing. Private negotiation between the parties is a key policy instrument for a *CCAA* proceeding, accompanied by judicial determination to resolve disputes based on information and evidence led by the parties.[23] Rulings have a substantive component in that they define the framework, determine information or participation rights where parties cannot agree, determine allegations of prejudice, and keep the process moving towards an expeditious resolution. They are, for the most part, based on the broad discretion conferred by the *CCAA*. The objective of the statute is to facilitate compromises and arrangements, thus there is a legislative presumption in favour of allowing the debtor to try to negotiate a plan. The courts give effect to this objective.

Scholar Karen Gross observes that "messiness" is an inevitable part of the insolvency law social system and judges are called on to deal with the inherent complexities and problems of financial distress and the people implicated, while still respecting the statutory hierarchy and requirements of insolvency legislation.[24] Rather than seeking to achieve an impossible standard of objectivity, judges engaged in decision-making processes should interpret and apply legislation, while trying to be cognizant

---

[21] Richard B. Jones, "The Evolution of Canadian Restructuring: Challenges for the Rule of Law", in J. Sarra, ed., *Annual Review of Insolvency Law, 2005* (Toronto: Carswell, 2006) at 522.

[22] *Dylex Ltd., Re* (1995), 31 C.B.R. (3d) 106 (Ont. Gen. Div. [Commercial List]) at 110; *Olympia & York Developments Ltd. (Trustee of)* v. *Olympia & York Realty Corp.* (2001), [2001] O.J. No. 3394, 2001 CarswellOnt 2954 (Ont. S.C.J. [Commercial List]), additional reasons at (2001), 2001 CarswellOnt 4739 (Ont. S.C.J. [Commercial List]), affirmed (2003), 2003 CarswellOnt 5210 (Ont. C.A.); *NsC Diesel Power Inc., Re* (1990), 79 C.B.R. (N.S.) 1 (N.S. T.D.); *Westar Mining Ltd., Re* (1992), 14 C.B.R. (3d) 88 (B.C. S.C.); *Interpretation Act*, R.S.C. 1985, c. I-21, s. 12.

[23] Janis Sarra, "Judicial Exercise of Inherent Jurisdiction under the *CCAA*" (2004) 40 Canadian Business Law Journal 280.

[24] Karen Gross, "On the Merits: A Response to Professors Girth and White" (1999) American Bankruptcy Law Journal 485 at 488.

of their biases due to their race, gender and socio-economic class. It is also important that groups, who are not characteristically represented on the judiciary, be able to place their views before the court in order that those interests are considered. This is particularly important in insolvency, as the whole regime is structured on the basis that there is not enough current value in the corporation to satisfy all claims, and thus, any outcome must balance the risks at stake. Without these views being presented to the court, the balance will be struck in the absence of potentially vital information.

Where judges have publicly commented on their role in *CCAA* proceedings, it is evident that they are aware of the limits of their supervisory role. Mr. Justice Forsyth explained:

> It is my view that the courts should never be placed in a position or expected to assume a legislative function as contrasted to assuming a procedural function in the absence of specific statutory enactments . . . it does not flow from that, however, that simply because one constituent is opposed to a particular reorganization scheme, that the scheme should fail. I perceive the position of the court in such situations to be ensuring that the proposed arrangement is properly considered by all constituents affected, before final approval or rejection is sought.[25]

Mr. Justice Blair made this observation:

> In exercising their traditional adjudicative role judges must remember that they are judges. Their mandate is not to make political decisions, but to make judicial decisions. On the other hand, judges do not live in a vacuum. They are not impervious to the social and economic implications of matters that come before them. In dealing with causes which have a public dimension to them, such as business reorganizations, underlying consequences pertaining to the social and economic impact of the reorganization on the community form the setting in which the court exercises its supervisory jurisdiction over the process . . . while the social and economic consequences for the community of the closure or restructuring of a business are not of direct concern to the judge in making her or his judicial decisions, they may well affect the court's response to the processing of the reorganization and its approach to the resolution options.[26]

One issue that Canadian courts have yet to deal with in their supervisory capacity in a *CCAA* proceeding is credit derivatives and the potential to skew workout negotiations. Credit derivatives refer to a number of financial products that are in the market that allow parties to minimize or spread their risk in respect of investments. There are numerous kinds of credit derivatives, such as eligible financial contracts, collateralized debt obligations, credit-linked notes and credit default swaps.[27] In terms of determining the outcome of a restructuring proceeding, the

---

[25] Mr. Justice Forsyth, Alberta Court of Queen's Bench, "Judicial Discretion under the *CCAA*" in *Corporate Restructurings and Insolvencies* (Carswell: Scarborough, 1995) at 85-88.

[26] Mr. Justice Blair, in "The Judges Speak", in J. Ziegel, ed., *Current Developments in International and Comparative Corporate Insolvency Law* (Oxford University Press, 1994) at 768-9.

[27] ISDA Credit Derivatives Definitions, www.isda.org.

nature and complexity of these risk management tools creates new and complex challenges for insolvency law and the courts that have oversight of workout proceedings. The global market for credit derivatives is estimated to be 17.3 trillion in U.S. dollars in 2005.[28] Credit default swaps are the most prevalent credit derivative product. Essentially, credit default swaps allow a financial institution to hedge its risk of investment in a firm. For example, in a basic single-name credit default swap, one party, called the protection buyer, buys from the other party, the protection seller, protection against the credit risk associated with a principal amount (called the notional amount) of a debt obligation of a debtor, called the reference entity.[29] The protection buyer pays a premium, usually a fixed per annum rate, to the protection seller in exchange for credit protection under the contract.[30] Every credit default swap contract contains specified credit events relating to the reference entity (the debtor), which usually includes *CCAA* proceedings. If one of the credit events occurs, the protection seller pays the amount of protection either through a cash settlement or a physical settlement. If there is a cash settlement, the protection buyer is paid out the value of the swap, but retains its full claim in the *CCAA* proceeding. The significance is that debtor corporation and other stakeholders will likely not be aware that the creditor is fully hedged and hence may have little interest in a going forward strategy for the debtor company. To date, there has been no requirement to disclose this fully hedged position. While this topic is beyond the scope of this text, it is important to note that credit derivatives can affect the position that senior lenders take during negotiations for a *CCAA* plan and it is likely that in the near future, the courts will be called on to determine issues of transparency and disclosure of such hedging in the context of workout negotiations.[31]

2. Jurisdiction of Filing

The court has jurisdiction to hear an application under the *CCAA* if the debtor company has its head office or chief place of business in its province or territory, or if the debtor has no place of business in Canada, in any province in Canada within which any assets of the company are situated.[32] If the head office is in one province or territory and its chief operations are located in another, an application can be made in either jurisdiction.

---

[28] *Year-end 2005 Market Survey*, International Swaps and Derivatives Association Inc. (ISDA), 2006.

[29] *Credit Derivatives in Restructurings, Guidance Booklet*, (London: INSOL, 2006).

[30] Credit default swap contracts are often modeled on the ISDA standard form agreement, with any modifications contained in a schedule. (ISDA Standard Form Agreement), www.isda.org.

[31] For a full discussion of these issues, see E. Murphy, J. Sarra and M. Creber, "Credit Derivatives in Canadian Insolvency Proceedings, 'The Devil will be in the Details'", in *Annual Review of Insolvency Law, 2006*, (Toronto: Carswell, 2007).

[32] Section 9, *CCAA*.

While this definition appears clear, there have been numerous cases in which applications have been brought in jurisdictions other than where the debtor's head office or place of chief operations is located, most notably Ontario. This can create a problem of access to participation in proceedings for less senior creditors, including employees, when the proceedings are located far from the company's head office or centre of main operations. However, in one case where the head office was located in Manitoba and most of its assets were located in that province, the court in Saskatchewan declined to hear a *CCAA* application, finding that it should have been brought in Manitoba.[33]

There have been approximately 254 *CCAA* proceedings.[34] Chart 1 illustrates province of filing a *CCAA* proceeding.[35] It confirms that Ontario has had the largest number of filings, although British Columbia and Alberta have had surprisingly more proceedings than one would have predicted. Québec has had only a little over one quarter of the number of proceedings in Ontario. Two of Canada's territories, the Yukon and Nunavut, have had no filings, and the Northwest Territories has had two cases.

[33] *Oblats de Marie Immaculée du Manitoba, Re* (2002), 34 C.B.R. (4th) 76 (Sask. Q.B.).

[34] This figure comes from an empirical study currently being conducted by the author under a grant by SSHRC. As noted in Chapter 1, there is not currently a central repository of information regarding *CCAA* cases that allows for certainty in the total numbers.

[35] This table is part of an ongoing study, to be completed in 2007.

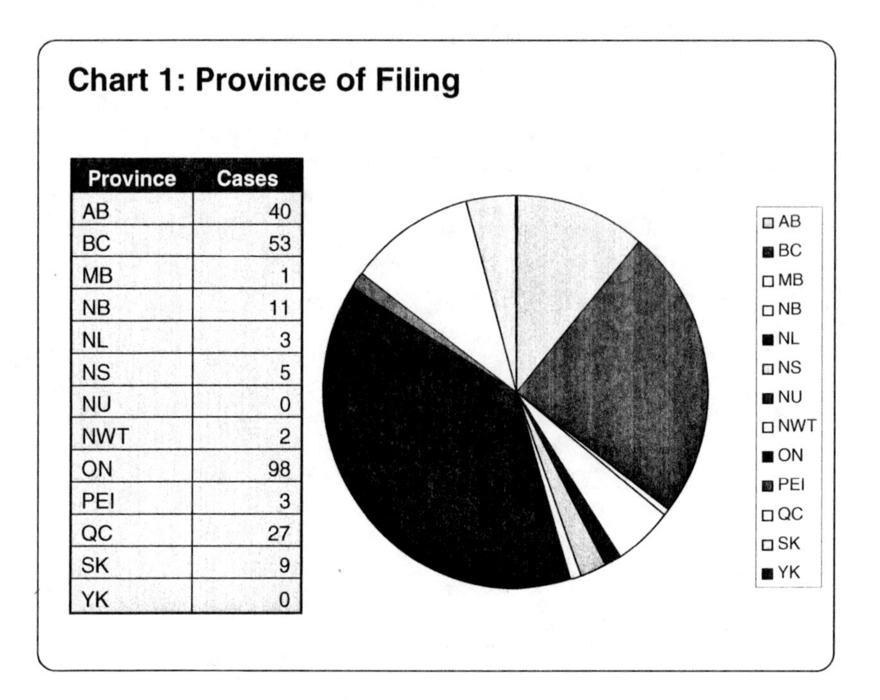

Province	Cases
AB	40
BC	53
MB	1
NB	11
NL	3
NS	5
NU	0
NWT	2
ON	98
PEI	3
QC	27
SK	9
YK	0

The Ontario numbers are not surprising, given the number of businesses registered in Ontario. The Québec numbers are low, given its relative economic importance. For a number of years, Québec headquartered companies more commonly filed proposals under the *BIA*, rather than *CCAA* proceedings. In a few cases, Québec headquartered companies filed *CCAA* proceedings in Ontario because of a higher degree of certainty offered by the procedures of the Ontario Superior Court Commercial List and the experience of judges in handling complex restructurings. The major operating lenders of many debtors were also located in Toronto and the creditors wanted proceedings in Ontario where they were assured of a timely process. There had also been a prior policy of the Québec Superior Court to handle all petitions individually and hence not have a single judge seized with carriage of the proceedings, which lengthened the time for access to the court and the decision-making process. This changed with the introduction of a commercial list in the Québec Superior Court two years ago; and Québec has seen a rise in the number of *CCAA* filings.[36]

3. The Court in its Supervisory Capacity

The courts have held that the *CCAA* is aimed at avoiding, where possible, the devastating social and economic consequences of the cessation of business opera-

[36] A commercial list has been introduced in the Montréal district, but is not yet available in other districts, although the possibility is under consideration. While a commercial list is not yet available, the court in other regions has been willing to seize itself of proceedings in complex or sensitive cases.

tions, and at allowing the corporation to carry on business in a manner that causes the least possible harm to employees and the communities in which it operates.[37]

a. The Fairness and Reasonableness Test

The fairness and reasonableness test is the one applied by the court in approving a *CCAA* plan of arrangement and compromise, although fairness is considered by the court at various stages of the process.[38] The fairness inquiry in sanctioning a proposed plan is an example of the court's exercise of discretion. The *CCAA* contemplates that the court will approve a plan of compromise or arrangement, and in exercising its discretion to order a vote, the court must consider whether the proposed plan has a reasonable chance of success.[39] Once the vote is held and the proposed plan receives the requisite creditor support, the court holds a sanctioning hearing in which it examines whether there has been strict compliance with the statutory requirements; whether all materials filed and procedures carried out were authorized by the *CCAA* and in compliance with previous court orders; and whether the plan is fair and reasonable.[40]

The Ontario Superior Court has held that:

> 'fairness' is the quintessential expression of the court's equitable jurisdiction – although the jurisdiction is statutory, the broad discretionary powers given to the judiciary by the legislation makes its exercise an exercise in equity – and 'reasonableness' is what lends objectivity to the process.[41]

Fairness is assessed by whether the plan is feasible, whether it fairly balances the interests of all the creditors, the company and its shareholders. The court has held that it must weigh the equities or balance the relative degrees of prejudice that might flow from granting or refusing the relief sought under the *CCAA*.[42] One measure of whether a plan is fair and reasonable is the parties' degree of approval of the plan.

---

[37] *Sklar-Peppler Furniture Corp.* v. *Bank of Nova Scotia* (1991), 8 C.B.R. (3d) 312 (Ont. Gen. Div.).

[38] *Philip Services Corp.* (1999), 1999 CarswellOnt 4673, [1999] O.J. No. 4232 (Ont. S.C.J. [Commercial List]).

[39] *Royal Bank* v. *Fracmaster Ltd.* (1999), 11 C.B.R. (4th) 230 (Alta. C.A.).

[40] *Canadian Airlines Corp.* (2000), 2000 CarswellAlta 662, [2000] A.J. No. 771 (Alta. Q.B.) at para. 95, leave to appeal refused (2000), 2000 CarswellAlta 919, [2000] A.J. No. 1028 (Alta. C.A. [In Chambers]), affirmed (2000), 2000 CarswellAlta 1556 (Alta. C.A.), leave to appeal refused (2001), 2001 CarswellAlta 888 (S.C.C.). See also *Quintette Coal Ltd., Re* (1992), 13 C.B.R. (3d) 146 (B.C. S.C.); *Dairy Corp. of Canada*, [1934] O.R. 436 (Ont. C.A.); *Olympia & York Developments Ltd.* v. *Royal Trust Co.* (1993), 17 C.B.R. (3d) 1 (Ont. Gen. Div. [Commercial List]), at 1; *Northland Properties Ltd., Re* (1988), 73 C.B.R. (N.S.) 175 (B.C. S.C.) at 182, affirmed (1989), 73 C.B.R. (N.S.) 195, 34 B.C.L.R. (2d) 122 (B.C. C.A.).

[41] *Olympia & York, ibid.* at 1.

[42] *Algoma Steel Corp.* v. *Royal Bank* (1992), 11 C.B.R. (3d) 1 (Ont. Gen. Div.); *Northland Properties Ltd., Re* (1988), 73 C.B.R. (N.S.) 175 (B.C. S.C.) at 182, affirmed (1989), 73 C.B.R. (N.S.) 195 (B.C. C.A.) at 201; *Quintette Coal Ltd.* v. *Nippon Steel Corp.* (1990), 51 B.C.L.R. (2d) 105 (B.C. C.A.) at 116, leave to appeal refused (1991), 55 B.C.L.R. (2d) xxxiii (note) (S.C.C.).

The court has held that parties generally know what is in their best interests, and in engaging in the fairness inquiry, the court will be reluctant to refuse to sanction a plan where creditors have strongly supported the plan. Its function is not to examine the details of the business plan in all its minutiae, nor will it second guess or substitute its own judgment for the business judgment of creditors involved in negotiating the plan in their own best interests.[43] Part of the assessment of fairness is to examine the sophistication of the creditors and whether they received experienced legal advice. At the point of the sanctioning hearing, the creditors have already expressed their support for the plan in the requisite statutory amounts and thus are representing to the court that in their business judgment the plan should be approved.

However, where parties disagree as to whether sufficient business judgment has been exercised, or believe that there has been unreasonableness or unfairness in the process followed to develop the content of the proposed plan, the court will consider the evidence and submissions of the parties and engage in a balancing of prejudices.[44] In *Canadian Airlines*, the Alberta Court of Queen's Bench held that the court's role in the sanctioning hearing is to consider whether the plan fairly balances the interests of all stakeholders. Accordingly, its role is to look forward and determine whether the plan represents a fair and reasonable compromise that will permit a viable commercial entity to emerge.[45] Thus it is important to situate the discussion about the court's exercise of discretion in the context of the statutory language that requires it be exercised to achieve express goals.

4. Judicial Discretion and the Scope of the Stay

As noted earlier, in *Royal Oak Mines*, the Court expressed concern about the growing complexity of initial orders being sought under the *CCAA* stay provisions.[46] The model orders being developed across Canada provide greater initial certainty and should avoid the worst cases of overreach. They are the result of the insolvency bar's agreement in terms of what is appropriate in an initial order.

The complexity and overreach of initial orders creates a particular dynamic. While parties can seek to set aside particular provisions, it is time consuming and costly to

[43] *Olympia & York Developments Ltd.* v. *Royal Trust Co.* (1993), 17 C.B.R. (3d) 1 (Ont. Gen. Div.); *Northland Properties, ibid.* at 205. Mr. Justice G.R. Forsyth, "Judicial Discretion under the *CCAA*" in *Corporate Restructurings and Insolvencies*, Queen's Annual Business Law Symposium, 1995 (Toronto: Carswell, 1995) at 88.

[44] Janis Sarra, "Judicial Exercise of Inherent Jurisdiction under the *CCAA*." (2004) 40 Canadian Business Law Journal 280.

[45] *Canadian Airlines Corp.* (2000), 2000 CarswellAlta 662, [2000] A.J. No. 771 (Alta. Q.B.) at para. 95, leave to appeal refused (2000), 2000 CarswellAlta 919, [2000] A.J. No. 1028 (Alta. C.A. [In Chambers]), affirmed (2000), 2000 CarswellAlta 1556 (Alta. C.A.), leave to appeal refused (2001), 2001 CarswellAlta 888 (S.C.C.).

[46] *Royal Oak Mines Inc., Re* (1999), 1999 CarswellOnt 625, [1999] O.J. No. 709 (Ont. Gen. Div. [Commercial List]), at paras. 8, 9, 15, 17.

appear before the court.[47] Arguably, there is also a hurdle in asking a court to set aside its own order and parties who are not regular players in the insolvency system may be reluctant to challenge what they perceive as the court's directive.[48] Since the rights suspended often affect vulnerable parties such as workers, pension beneficiaries and small trade suppliers, the overreach of these orders can prejudice particular interests in the workout process. Thus, although the stay may be temporary, care must be taken that the courts' discretion in granting the stay does not result in permanent, rather than merely temporary prejudice to these interests.[49]

The court's discretion under section 11 of the *CCAA* does not give authority to remove the directors and the Ontario Court of Appeal has held that any such authority could only be exercised under corporations law where the court finds oppression.[50]

One critique of the court's exercise of jurisdiction has been that the court applies the same considerations to creditors whose value is at greater risk as to those who are most likely to gain upside value through an eventual restructuring. This is really an argument for preferred treatment of secured creditors, who enjoy a higher priority if the debtor is liquidated.[51] Yet a restructuring proceeding is a step prior to liquidation, expressly aimed at suspending that priority of rights for a limited period in order to see if a negotiated outcome is possible. To accord secured creditors a different standard of deference on a stay application would defeat that legislative objective.[52] The Alberta Court of Queen's Bench in *Hunters Trailer* observed that "*status quo*" during the stay period is not merely preservation of pre-stay debt status, but rather, is preservation of the *status quo* in the sense of preventing manoeuvres by creditors that would impair the ability of the corporation to operate while it and its creditors determine whether there is a viable workout.[53]

The court's observation is particularly important in light of the rapid growth of distressed debt trading, in which the claim holders are increasingly not the parties who originally entered into the business relationship with the debtor corporation. Claims are now bought up across classes at a discounted value in order to try and influence the workout process. Thus, those seeking the preferred treatment in the decision regarding the stay may not be those who are attempting to protect the capital they put at risk in granting the corporation credit, but rather those who merely seek

---

[47] Janis P. Sarra, *Creditor Rights and the Public Interest, Restructuring Insolvent Corporations* (Toronto: University of Toronto Press, 2003).

[48] *Ibid.*

[49] *Ibid.*

[50] *Stelco Inc., Re* (2005), 2005 CarswellOnt 1188, 2 B.L.R. (4th) 238, 9 C.B.R. (5th) 135 (Ont. C.A.), discussed further in chapter 5.

[51] Janis P. Sarra, *Creditor Rights and the Public Interest, Restructuring Insolvent Corporations* (Toronto: University of Toronto Press, 2003). See also, Andrew Keay, "Insolvency Law: A Matter of Public Interest?" (2000) 51 Northern Ireland Legal Quarterly 509 at 533.

[52] *Ibid.*

[53] *Hunters Trailer & Marine Ltd., Re* (2001), 2001 CarswellAlta 964, [2001] A.J. No. 857 (Alta. Q.B.); *Alberta-Pacific Terminals Ltd., Re* (1991), 8 C.B.R. (3d) 99 (B.C. S.C.) at 105.

to maximize the profit on their discounted debt purchase.[54] To the extent that there is a moral claim in this argument based on the risk to creditors' capital, it loses much of its force in the absence of similar risk in a distressed debt transaction.[55] The court faces new challenges in balancing interests and in trying to mediate differences where there is a growing imbalance in bargaining power during the workout.

Where the court has become involved in mediating resolution of a plan, as in the *Air Canada* or *Algoma Steel* restructurings, the judge involved in the dispute resolution process is not the judge that ultimately conducts the plan sanctioning hearing.

5. Jurisdiction to Order DIP Financing

DIP financing is discussed at some length in chapter 4, but it is important to note here that the granting of such financing initially raised the question of the limits of both the court's discretion and its inherent jurisdiction, as well as the problems posed by the granting of DIP facilities on an *ex parte* basis.[56] There was considerable litigation on the court's authority to authorize DIP financing on a priority basis. The courts have found authority for granting super-priority financing under both the *CCAA* and their inherent jurisdiction.[57]

In finding that the court had jurisdiction to authorize DIP financing, the British Columbia Court of Appeal held that the effective achievement of the legislation's objectives requires a broad and flexible exercise of jurisdiction to facilitate a restructuring, and the court's equitable jurisdiction permits orders granting super-priority in some circumstances.[58] The court will engage in a balancing of prejudices between the parties, and secured creditors may be required to make some sacrifice because of the reasonably anticipated benefits for all stakeholders including employees, trade suppliers and other creditors.[59]

---

[54] Janis P. Sarra, *Creditor Rights and the Public Interest, Restructuring Insolvent Corporations* (Toronto: University of Toronto Press, 2003).

[55] *Ibid.*

[56] *Royal Oak Mines Inc., Re* (1999), 1999 CarswellOnt 625, [1999] O.J. No. 709 (Ont. Gen. Div. [Commercial List]) at para. 22. *United Used Auto & Truck Parts Ltd., Re* (1999), 12 C.B.R. (4th) 144 (B.C. S.C. [In Chambers]), affirmed (2000), 16 C.B.R. (4th) 141 (B.C. C.A.), leave to appeal allowed but appeal discontinued (2000), [2000] S.C.C.A. No. 142, 2000 CarswellBC 2132 (S.C.C.); *Dylex Ltd., Re* (January 23, 1995), Doc. B-4/95 (Ont. Gen. Div. [Commercial List]), Houlden J.A.; *T. Eaton Co., Re* (1997), 1997 CarswellOnt 5954, [1997] O.J. No. 6388 (Ont. Gen. Div.), Houlden J.A.

[57] Super-priority is discussed further in chapter 4, but refers to the court authorizing the debtor corporation to borrow funds for financing, giving the DIP lender a priority in its security over pre-existing secured lenders. Generally, the rule in secured financing recognizes secured lenders in order of their registration of secured claims and only allows a change in those priorities where a more senior lender agrees to subordinate its interest on a particular asset or type of claim.

[58] *United Used Auto & Truck Parts Ltd., Re* (1999), 12 C.B.R. (4th) 144 (B.C. S.C. [In Chambers]), affirmed (2000), 16 C.B.R. (4th) 141 (B.C. C.A.), leave to appeal allowed but appeal discontinued (2000), [2000] S.C.C.A. No. 142, 2000 CarswellBC 2132 (S.C.C.) at paras. 2, 9, 12.

[59] Janis P. Sarra, *Creditor Rights and the Public Interest, Restructuring Insolvent Corporations* (Toronto: University of Toronto Press, 2003).

However, the courts have cautioned that in balancing these interests, there should be cogent evidence that the benefit of DIP financing clearly outweighs the potential prejudice to the lenders whose security is being subordinated, and the court should make such orders only where there is a reasonable prospect of successfully restructuring.[60] Although the practice of *ex parte* approval of DIP financing on a primed basis is declining, it continues to be problematic.[61] Even on an urgent basis, notice should be given to creditors prior to subordinating their interests in order to avoid their having to incur the additional costs and onus of seeking to set aside an initial order approving DIP financing. While the courts have been fairly consistent in respecting the statutory hierarchy of creditors' claims, they have engaged in a balancing of multiple interests during the process, having regard to the express aims of the statute.

As will be seen in chapter 4 on financing a workout, the caselaw is now settled on the court's authority to order DIP financing and legislative reform will codify much of current practice. As will also be discussed, the notion of incremental approval of DIP financing during the *CCAA* proceeding, known colloquially as "drip DIPs", should be considered as a standard means of enhancing accountability of the debtor and the DIP lender during the process.

6. Judicial Discretion and the Public Interest

The courts have recognized the public interest involved in *CCAA* restructuring proceedings.[62] Madam Justice Paperny, then of the Alberta Court of Queen's Bench, held in *Canadian Airlines*:

> The court is assisted in the exercise of its discretion by the purpose of the *CCAA*: to facilitate the reorganization of a debtor company for the benefit of the company, its creditors, shareholders, employees and in many instances, a broader constituency of affected persons. Parliament has recognized that reorganization, if commercially feasible, is in most cases preferable, economically and socially, to liquidation.[63]

---

[60] *United Used Auto & Truck Parts Ltd., Re* (1999), 12 C.B.R. (4th) 144 (B.C. S.C. [In Chambers]), affirmed (2000), 16 C.B.R. (4th) 141 (B.C. C.A.), leave to appeal allowed but appeal discontinued (2000), [2000] S.C.C.A. No. 142, 2000 CarswellBC 2132 (S.C.C.); *Royal Oak Mines Inc., Re* (1999), 1999 CarswellOnt 625, [1999] O.J. No. 709 (Ont. Gen. Div. [Commercial List]) at para. 22.

[61] *Algoma Steel Inc., Re* (2001), 2001 CarswellOnt 1999, [2001] O.J. No. 1994 (Ont. S.C.J. [Commercial List]), leave to appeal refused (2001), 2001 CarswellOnt 1742, [2001] O.J. No. 1943 (Ont. C.A.). For a full discussion of DIP financing see, Janis Sarra, "Debtor in Possession Financing: The Jurisdiction of Canadian Courts to Grant Superpriority Financing in *CCAA* Applications" (2000) 23 Dalhousie Law Journal 337.

[62] This has been the subject of an entire book by the author, see Janis P. Sarra, *Creditor Rights and the Public Interest, Restructuring Insolvent Corporations* (Toronto: University of Toronto Press, 2003).

[63] *Canadian Airlines Corp.* (2000), 2000 CarswellAlta 662, [2000] A.J. No. 771 (Alta. Q.B.) at para. 95, leave to appeal refused (2000), 2000 CarswellAlta 919, [2000] A.J. No. 1028 (Alta. C.A. [In Chambers]), affirmed (2000), 2000 CarswellAlta 1556 (Alta. C.A.), leave to appeal refused (2001), 2001 CarswellAlta 888 (S.C.C.).

The Court in *Canadian Airlines* held that it could not limit its assessment of fairness to those directly affected by the plan. Canadian Airlines was concerned about loss of employees during the critical plan implementation period. The timing of the plan was crucial, as Canadian Airlines faced an imminent threat of closure because of financial distress due to market competition from the U.S.; lower than expected operating revenues; and higher airport terminal fees.[64] In order to minimize the risk of loss of public confidence in the airline, Canadian sought to negotiate with creditors and tried to garner the support of creditors prior to filing a plan.[65] At the point that Canadian filed under the *CCAA,* it had what is referred to as a "pre-packaged plan", whereby the majority of creditors had already negotiated with the debtor corporation prior to it filing for a *CCAA* order.

The restricted number of affected creditors in *Canadian Airlines* meant there was some risk that particular creditors could extract premiums in the workout.[66] The vast majority of creditors affected by the restructuring, the employees and trade creditors, were the "high value" creditors with the greatest interest in a viable workout plan and the greatest potential losses in a liquidation. However, while these parties were keenly interested in the *CCAA* proceedings and the success of the restructuring, their legal claims were not compromised and thus they did not have a vote in the *CCAA* proceedings. The Court expressly recognized these broader interests, including the risk to the public of "chaos to the Canadian transportation system". The Court held that companies are more than just assets and liabilities, even in insolvency, and that the fate of the corporation is tied to those who depend on it in various ways. The Court also acknowledged that while the 16,000 employees did not have claims affected by the plan, the job dignity and job security protections negotiated for the benefit of workers should not be jeopardized by liquidation. The Court held that in sanctioning a plan, that weight should be accorded to strong creditor support, but that a number of additional factors had to be considered, including the public interest. Madam Justice Paperny held that the objective of the *CCAA* "widens the lens" to balance a broader range of interests that includes creditors, shareholders, the company, employees and the public, and that an assessment of fairness must include reference of the plan's impact on all of these constituents.[67]

The Court in *Canadian Airlines* also took note of the ripple effects in the economy if the corporation was to cease operations, including airport authority losses, consumer losses, and loss of accessible air transportation to smaller Canadian commu-

---

[64] *Ibid.* at para. 36.

[65] *Ibid.* at para. 42.

[66] Sean Dunphy has observed that the pre-packaged plan in *Canadian Airlines* offered an expeditious and less costly workout, but also made the debtor corporation and the takeover bidder vulnerable to hold-out minorities, which became evident in disputes over class, share structure and terms of the plan. Sean Dunphy, "Canadian Airlines – The Last Tango in Calgary, Air Canada's Perspective" (Toronto: The Insolvency Institute of Canada, 2000) at 14 (http://www.westlawecarswell.com).

[67] *Canadian Airlines Corp.* (2000), 2000 CarswellAlta 662, [2000] A.J. No. 771 (Alta. Q.B.) at para. 144, leave to appeal refused (2000), 2000 CarswellAlta 919, [2000] A.J. No. 1028 (Alta. C.A. [In Chambers]), affirmed (2000), 2000 CarswellAlta 1556 (Alta. C.A.), leave to appeal refused (2001), 2001 CarswellAlta 888 (S.C.C.).

nities. The Court held that the plan represented a solid chance for continued existence, preserving the business, maintaining jobs, keeping trade creditors and suppliers whole, protecting consumers and preserving the integrity of the national transportation system. The Court held that fairness and reasonableness are not abstract terms, but they must be measured against the available commercial alternatives.

There had been some critical comment that judicial notice of the public interest has had the effect of increasing access to initial stays; and the court's consideration of diverse interests frequently justifies allowing the debtor a period to negotiate restructuring, over the objection of a group of creditors who have the ability to ultimately veto any plan.[68] Yet the courts have stressed that the stay provisions are time-limited remedies and that any suspension of creditor rights to enforce is temporary, absent agreement on a plan. The fact that there may initially be many stakeholders in favour of a workout and a few opposed, is not evidence of judicial bias. Rather, the few opposed are precisely so because, absent a *CCAA* proceeding, they can immediately realize on their claims and thus have little incentive to support the workout process. The liquidation value fully satisfies their claims, so naturally, they are resistant to the time and cost of a process that may maximize enterprise value, but not necessarily enhance the realizable value of their claims. Preventing a race to the assets is in part what the legislation is aimed at remedying.[69]

It is also important to observe that secured creditors' views of *CCAA* proceedings continue to evolve and there is no longer a typical institutional secured creditor reaction. Many institutional lenders now have considerable experience with *CCAA* proceedings, including the court's recognition of the broader public interest. If there are objections at the outset of a *CCAA* proceeding now, it is usually because of concerns that a secured position would erode and become unsecured, or that the amount of DIP financing would place a secured creditor's interests under water.[70]

Another criticism of the exercise of the court's discretion has been that there is an assumption that the public interest is served through restructuring as opposed to liquidation, when a restructuring process imposes significant costs on the operating lender and secured creditors, while benefiting other stakeholders. This critique is valid insofar as it suggests that the court should not always accept as a given that restructuring is more efficient at capturing enterprise value. It is important for parties to place some evidence before the court as to the potential upside value if a *CCAA* process is allowed to proceed.

---

[68] Peter Hamilton and George Wade, "Restructuring under the *CCAA*: An Examination of Principles and Solutions in Light of the Experience in the U.S.", in *Corporate Restructurings and Insolvencies, Issues and Perspectives* (Toronto: Carswell, 1995) at 10-13.

[69] Janis Sarra, "Judicial Exercise of Inherent Jurisdiction under the *CCAA*." (2004) 40 Canadian Business L.J. 280.

[70] "Under water" in this context being that there will not be sufficient value in remaining assets to meet the secured creditor's claim.

The principal concern underlying such criticisms is that there may be some redistribution of value in the restructuring process. Yet insolvency by definition means that there are not sufficient assets to meet debt obligations, and thus restructuring is about adjusting claims, trading debt for equity and other arrangements where parties are satisfied that there is potential long-term gain over liquidation.[71] Secured creditors are exposed to some risk of their collateral depreciating during the workout period, although the risks to unsecured creditors are frequently far greater. To an extent, senior creditors already adjust for the cost of firm financial distress in their credit decisions, including costs associated with court-supervised workouts. They also have the bargaining power during the *CCAA* process to win price adjustments in the cost of future financing that account for recognition of stakeholder interest or compromise of their claims.[72] Moreover, there are more general price adjustments in the market where there is a risk of firm failure and secured creditors have the economic bargaining power to make price adjustments to spread risk. However, there are also cases where secured creditors are not able to make price adjustments, and where their support of a plan is contingent on the plan reducing their going-forward exposure.

While the secured creditors may bear a portion of the *CCAA* process costs, they will have first call on any upside benefits to be extracted from a successful workout. Consideration of the public interest is one aspect of the court's assessment of the viability and fairness of the proposed plan within the existing statutory scheme of priorities. The court has held that there is a broader public dimension that must be considered and weighed in the balance, as well as the interests of those most directly affected.[73]

The *Red Cross CCAA* proceeding illustrates that what is in the public interest in *CCAA* proceedings is not always apparent. In considering a motion to adjourn a proceeding to approve a proposed asset sale that divested Red Cross of the national blood program where tight timing was critical, the Court, in deciding the issue, was required to balance multiple interests, those of the creditors, federal, provincial and territorial governments. It was clearly in the public interest to "ensure the seamless continuation of the delivery of safe blood products across Canada" and the preser-

---

[71] Janis Sarra, "Judicial Exercise of Inherent Jurisdiction under the *CCAA*" (2004) 40 Canadian Business L.J. 280.

[72] *Ibid.*

[73] *Skydome Corp., Re* (1998), 16 C.B.R. (4th) 118 (Ont. Gen. Div. [Commercial List]). Elsewhere, I have analyzed the "public interest" as a "short form" for the complex balancing of diverse interests in which the court engages in determining disputes that arise during a *CCAA* proceeding. If investments are properly valued, the "redistributive outcome" is really one of according value to human capital and other investments that should have been accorded a value much earlier in the process. Then any redistributive outcomes from recognizing those interests are really a tempering of the redistributive effects of the current regime, where value flows to capital claimants to the detriment of other kinds of investors. Janis P. Sarra, *Creditor Rights and the Public Interest, Restructuring Insolvent Corporations* (Toronto: University of Toronto Press, 2003).

vation of the human capital involved in that delivery.[74] However, the Court also took account of the public and private interest in allowing the Transfusion Claimants as creditors to be meaningfully involved in the process. The Court noted that the continued viability and safety of the blood system was absolutely essential and the failure to proceed created a serious risk of firm failure and loss of the service of key employees. On the other hand, to deny the adjournment would result in three classes of Transfusion Claimants being deprived of a reasonable opportunity to assess whether the asset sale would provide a maximization of returns on Red Cross' blood related assets.

The Court in *Red Cross* held that the *CCAA* process and approval of the sale of assets must be seen to be fair and reasonable to the Transfusion Claimants, whose interests lie at the heart of the process. The interests of the Transfusion Claimants, although a contingent interest in the sense of the type and quantum of claims, were nevertheless recognized as valid. Here, the Court noted that the people whose claims from blood contamination injuries resulted in the *CCAA* application, and for whose benefit the result of the sale process is aimed, were left out of the process until after the *CCAA* proceedings were commenced.[75] As a consequence, the Court granted an adjournment of two weeks to allow representative counsel a reasonable opportunity to assess the proposed asset sale. The Court's decision represented not only a balancing of the interests and prejudices at that stage of the proceeding, but also sent a message to Red Cross that the process must necessarily involve adequate notice and timely disclosure in order to make the participation of the contingent creditors and other stakeholders meaningful.

The court's view of public interest and diverse interests was recognized in *Curragh Inc.*, which was the first time that a Canadian court granted substantive rights to stakeholders beyond the value of their fixed capital claims.[76] The Court granted participation rights and substantive remedies to reflect the interests of a First Nation Council, and to the Territorial Government in a representative capacity on behalf of Yukon miners. The Court in *Curragh* also recognized the Ross River Denat Nation as a party, the first time that a First Nation had been recognized as a party in a commercial restructuring proceeding. The Ross River Dena Nation had three kinds of interests. It had relatively minor fixed capital claims owed to its economic development corporation, the Ross River Development Corporation (RRDC). The Ross River Dena Nation was also seeking to enforce First Nation land claims against the corporation, where it was asserting title to Curragh's lands. Finally, as part of the community affected by the social and economic losses from the firm's distress, it had a broader interest in the outcome of the proceedings. While the Court declined

---

[74] *Canadian Red Cross Society / Société Canadienne de la Croix-Rouge, Re* (1998), 5 C.B.R. (4th) 299, 72 O.T.C. 99 (Ont. Gen. Div. [Commercial List]), Blair J. at para. 7, additional reasons at (1998), 5 C.B.R. (4th) 319 (Ont. Gen. Div. [Commercial List]), further additional reasons at (1998), 5 C.B.R. (4th) 321 (Ont. Gen. Div. [Commercial List]), leave to appeal refused (1998), 1998 CarswellOnt 5967, 32 C.B.R. (4th) 21 (Ont. C.A.).

[75] *Ibid.*

[76] Frederick Myers and Edward Sellers, "Recognition of Social Stakeholders in Canadian Insolvency Proceedings" (1999) 11 Commercial Insolvency Reporter 6 at 68.

to hear the Nation's argument regarding land claims, treaty rights and the right to mine, it held that it would hear from the Nation as a party affected by the restructuring.[77] It found that the Nation "had an undoubted interest in the outcome of the proceedings, both because of the need for ongoing environmental maintenance of the mine site and because the future economic prospects of the RRDC remained contingent on ongoing operation of the Faro Mine".[78]

In 1998, the successor to Curragh, Anvil Range, also filed under the *CCAA*. In deciding a motion in the *Anvil Range* case, the Court expressly recognized the interests of "social stakeholders". This was a case in which the court permitted a concurrent *CCAA* proceeding and appointment of an interim receiver to ensure that the assets were preserved during the period of negotiations for a workout plan. In 1998, this concurrent process was a novel means of ensuring asset preservation pending a *CCAA* workout. Such concurrent proceedings are now relatively common. In *Anvil Range,* the interim receiver had filed a report with the Court, suggesting that it was unlikely that Faro Mine would re-open in the following two to five years, recommending to the court the sale of additional assets that it referred to as the "residual equipment". This equipment, including mine shovels and drills, were assets without which the mine could not become operational again.[79] The interim receiver and the majority of creditors argued that the court should endorse the recommendation, according considerable weight to the views of the court's appointed officer and the 90% of secured creditors that supported the asset sale. The court was asked to balance the likelihood of the mine reopening with the need to satisfy creditors' claims, the daily deterioration of equipment and the costs of the receiver to secure the equipment.[80] The union and the territorial government asked for an adjournment on the basis that it was not appropriate to require a sale where there was no marketing plan for the enterprise before the court and the sale would seal the fate of the mine prematurely by forfeiting the ability of the mine to reopen.[81]

The Court refused to allow the sale of further assets of Anvil Range. The Court found that the Union and the Yukon territorial government were "social stakeholders" representing workers and the Yukon public, based on a concern about jobs and the general public interest.[82] The Court found that it was difficult to be optimistic about the mine's future prospects and acknowledged that the "social stakeholders" had conceded that the chances of the mine reopening in the near future were slim. The Court held that it must always consider with great deference and weight the

---

[77] *R.* v. *Curragh Inc.* (May 7, 1994), (Ont. Gen. Div. [Commercial List]). The Court held that the RRDC was an "affected person" under the *CCAA* proceeding to the extent that Ross River Dena Nation members were residents in the immediate vicinity of the Faro Mine.

[78] Frederick Myers and Edward Sellers, "Recognition of Social Stakeholders in Canadian Insolvency Proceedings", (1999) 11 Commercial Insolvency Reporter 6 at 68.

[79] *Anvil Range Mining Corp., Re* (1998), 7 C.B.R. (4th) 51 (Ont. Gen. Div. [Commercial List]) (Endorsement) Blair J., at para. 1.

[80] *Ibid.*

[81] *Ibid.* Oral Submissions to the Court, Fred Myers, Counsel for Yukon Territorial Government, August 1998; *Interim Receiver's Report*, (14 August 1998).

[82] *Ibid.* at 2.

recommendations of its appointed officer, the receiver. Creditors are entitled to pursue their remedies; yet that entitlement is not entirely unrestricted, particularly where the secured creditor has sought a court-appointed receiver. Mr. Justice Robert Blair held that:

> The court in its supervisory capacity has a broader mandate. In a receivership such as this one, which works well into the social and economic fabric of a territory, that mandate must encompass having an eye for the social consequences of the receivership too. These interests cannot override the lawful interests of secured creditors ultimately, but they can and must be weighed in the balance as the process works its way through.[83]

The Court balanced the needs of the creditors with those of the social stakeholders. It found that the cash likely to be generated by the sale was not a large portion of the debt, particularly when the evidence suggested that there was not likely to be a material change in the value of the equipment if it was not sold that season. The Court further held that the interest saving over one year was not "too great a price to pay to preserve the social and political spirit of those who wish to see the mine re-open if at all possible".[84] Consequently, the Court adjourned the sale motion for several months, allowing the territorial government to undertake its analysis.

The courts have subsequently acknowledged the importance of considering the interests of social stakeholders in several *CCAA* cases. In *Skydome Corp.*, the Court cited the *Anvil Range* judgment, and in particular, the passage that recognized the court's mandate to consider the interests of social as well as economic stakeholders.[85] In *Enterprise Capital Management*, the Court adopted the *Anvil Range* reasoning in respect of considering the social and economic consequences and broader public dimension.[86] The Alberta Court of Appeal in *Fracmaster* held that the spirit of the *CCAA* contemplates an attempt at restructuring for the general benefit of all stakeholders.[87] There the Court of Appeal endorsed the lower court decision refusing to sanction a proposed plan because it was not aimed for the general benefit of stakeholders. In *Starcom,* the British Columbia Supreme Court endorsed the importance of social stakeholder concerns in the *CCAA* process. The Court held that the community protected under *CCAA* orders is greater than shareholders and creditors and encompasses suppliers, employees, municipalities and the broader community affected by the well being of the company.[88]

---

[83] *Anvil Range Mining Corp., Re* (1998), 7 C.B.R. (4th) 51 (Ont. Gen. Div. [Commercial List]) (Endorsement) Blair J., at para. 9.

[84] *Ibid.* at 5.

[85] *Skydome Corp., Re* (1998), 16 C.B.R. (4th) 118 (Ont. Gen. Div. [Commercial List]), Blair J.

[86] *Enterprise Capital Management Inc.* v. *Semi-Tech Corp.* (1999), 10 C.B.R. (4th) 133 (Ont. S.C.J. [Commercial List]), Ground J. at paras. 21, 22.

[87] *Royal Bank* v. *Fracmaster Ltd.* (1999), 11 C.B.R. (4th) 230 (Alta. C.A.) at paras. 36, 40.

[88] *Starcom, Re* (November 17, 1998), Saunders J. (B.C. S.C.).

7. Judicial Discretion and Liquidating *CCAAs*

One policy issue that has not to date been fully explored is whether the *CCAA* should be used to effect an organized liquidation that should properly occur under the *BIA* or receivership proceedings. Increasingly, there are liquidating *CCAA* proceedings, whereby the debtor corporation is for all intents and purposes liquidated, but not under the supervision of a trustee in bankruptcy or in compliance with all of the requirements of the *BIA*. While creditors still must vote in support of such plans in the requisite amounts, there may be some public policy concerns regarding the use of a restructuring statute, under the broad scope of judicial discretion, to effect liquidation. This usually happens when a receiver or trustee will not take an appointment due to possible liability concerns, given the language of section 14.02 of the *BIA*.

While the courts have endorsed liquidating *CCAA*s, there has not yet been a judgment that carefully considers both the benefits and prejudice to expanding the scope of the *CCAA* to allow for this. However, the cases regarding sale of assets, discussed in the next chapter, do set out the factors considered by the court in approving the sale itself.

In *1078385 Ontario Ltd.*, the plan of arrangement proposed by the secured creditors provided for the sale of the debtor's assets and a distribution to the secured creditors only.[89] Under the plan, no amount would be available to the unsecured creditors. The Court of Appeal endorsed the lower court finding that the fact that there is no recovery for the unsecured creditors does not necessarily mean that the plan is not fair and reasonable. The Court observed that "although the question of whether a plan of arrangement under which the assets of the debtor company will be disposed of and the debtor company will not continue as a going concern is contrary to the purposes of the *CCAA* may not have been resolved by this court,. . . this is not the first time a secured-creditor-led plan, which operates exclusively for the benefit of secured creditors and under which the assets of the debtor company will be disposed of and the debtor company will not continue as a going concern, has received court approval.[90] The Court appeared to recognize that even if the debtor company itself does not survive, if the liquidation results in an enhanced result for the creditors whose claims still had value, as compared to bankruptcy, the plan could be considered fair and reasonable.

---

[89] *1078385 Ontario Ltd., Re* (2004), 2004 CarswellOnt 8034 (Ont. C.A.). See also *Entreprises Microtec Inc., Re* (March 15, 2005), Doc. C.S. Montréal 500-11-024389-047 (Que. S.C.); *Papiers Gaspésia inc., Re* (2004), 2004 CarswellQue 10014, [2004] J.Q. no. 13392 (Que. C.A.).

[90] *Ibid.* at para. 30, referring to *Anvil Range Mining Corp., Re* (2001), 25 C.B.R. (4th) 1 (Ont. S.C.J. [Commercial List]), affirmed on other grounds (2002), 2002 CarswellOnt 2254, [2002] O.J. No. 2606 (Ont. C.A). The Court found that the applicant had not established any reasonable possibility that he had an economic interest in the debtor's assets.

In *Royal Bank of Canada* v. *Fracmaster Ltd.*, the Alberta Court of Appeal dismissed the appeal of a judgment that ordered a sale of assets under a receivership rather than under a *CCAA* proceeding.[91] The Court held:

> ¶ 16 Although there are infrequent situations in which a liquidation of a company's assets has been concluded under the *CCAA*, the proposed transaction must be in the best interest of the creditors generally: *Re Lehndorff General Partner Ltd.* (1993), 17 CBR (3d) 24 at 31 (Ont. Gen. Div.). There must be an ongoing business entity that will survive the asset sale. See, for example, *Re Canadian Red Cross Society*, [1998] O.J. No. 3306 (Ont. Gen. Div.), online: QL (OJ); *Re Solv-Ex Corporation and Solv-Ex Canada Limited*, (19 November, 1997), (Calgary), 9701-10022 (Alta. Q.B.). A sale of all or substantially all the assets of a company to an entirely different entity, with no continued involvement by former creditors and shareholders, does not meet this requirement. While we do not intend to limit the flexibility of the *CCAA*, we are concerned about its use to liquidate assets of insolvent companies which are not part of a plan or compromise among creditors and shareholders, resulting in some continuation of a company as a going concern. Generally, such liquidations are inconsistent with the intent of the *CCAA* and should not be carried out under its protective umbrella. The chambers judge did not err in concluding that the sale of assets to UTI would be an inappropriate use of the *CCAA*. We grant leave to appeal to UTI, but dismiss its appeal.

8. Legislative Reform

There has been an ongoing process of legislative reform in the past three years, culminating in Statutes of Canada Chapter 47, which has been enacted, but is not yet in force.[92] Chapter 47 amends the *BIA*, the *CCAA*, and creates a new wage earner protection program for insolvent firms. Further amendments are anticipated in 2007, prior to Chapter 47 coming into force.

Part of the reform process has been a consideration of the scope of the court's jurisdiction under the *CCAA*. Prior to introduction of the legislation, there were extensive public hearings conducted by the Senate Committee on Banking Trade and Commerce. In November 2003, the Senate Committee released a report reviewing the *BIA* and the *CCAA*.[93] In respect of the court's exercise of jurisdiction under the *CCAA*, the Senate Committee concluded that fundamentally, the current system is working well, endorsing the current flexibility of the statute:

---

[91] *Royal Bank of Canada* v. *Fracmaster Ltd.* (1999), 1999 CarswellAlta 539, [1999] A.J. No. 675 (Alta C.A.).

[92] *An Act to Establish the Wage Earner Protection Program Act, to amend the Bankruptcy and Insolvency Act and the Companies' Creditors Arrangement Act and to make consequential amendments to other Acts*, S.C. 2005, Chapter 47, Royal Assent November 25, 2005, not yet proclaimed in force as of December 30, 2006.

[93] Report of the Standing Senate Committee on Banking, Trade and Commerce, *Debtors and Creditors Sharing the Burden: A Review of the Bankruptcy and Insolvency Act and the Companies' Creditors Arrangement Act*, (Ottawa: November 2003), www.senate-senat.ca/bancom.asp.

> In particular, we know that the flexibility that is inherent in the *CCAA* is probably inconsistent with consistency and predictability, and may not result in fairness. Nevertheless, tradeoffs must be made and an appropriate balance must be struck. We believe that the need for flexibility is paramount with the *CCAA*, but urge relevant parties to respect the principles of predictability, consistency and fairness – to the extent that they can – when involved in proceedings under the *Act*.[94]

The Senate Committee recommended some codification in areas that have been particularly litigious. It recommended giving express jurisdiction to approve DIP financing on a primed basis, but on notice to affected secured creditors. It also recommended that the courts be required to consider seven factors in approving DIP financing, including: what arrangements have been made for governance of the debtor during the stay period, the length of time to determine whether or not there is a going concern solution; whether any creditors will be materially prejudiced; and whether the debtor has tabled a detailed cash flow statement for the following 120 days.[95] These factors had been proposed by The Insolvency Institute of Canada and the Canadian Association of Insolvency and Restructuring Professionals in their joint submission to the Senate Committee, and are largely adopted in the proposed amendments to the *CCAA*, as discussed in chapter 4.

The proposed amendments to the *CCAA* under Chapter 47 codify current practice in terms of filing documents and codify, for the first time, the authority of the court to permit DIP financing on a primed basis. Section 10 of the *CCAA* is amended by adding that an initial application must be accompanied by a statement indicating, on a weekly basis, the projected cash flow of the debtor company; a report containing the prescribed representations of the debtor company regarding the preparation of the cash flow statement, including the assumptions used in preparing the statement; and copies of all financial statements, audited or unaudited, prepared during the year before the application or, if no such statements were prepared in that year, a copy of the most recent such statement. These recommendations are also a codification of current practice, and are based on recommendations by The Insolvency Institute of Canada and the Canadian Association of Insolvency and Restructuring Professionals that the authority to allow DIP financing be codified and that some guidance be given to the court in the exercise of its discretion.

As the *CCAA* is currently framed, the requirement for the supply of a cash flow statement as well as audited and unaudited financial information exists, but is included as part of section 11(1) of the *CCAA*. In effect, the relocation of the documentary requirement from section 11 to section 10 when Chapter 47 is proclaimed means that a cash flow statement will be required in all cases, and not only where a stay of proceedings is requested. That is not a significant change, given that a stay of proceedings is almost always sought.

---

[94] *Ibid.* at 173-4.

[95] *Ibid.* at 100-105.

II. CASE MANAGEMENT OF *CCAA* PROCEEDINGS AND TIMELINESS OF THE PROCESS

In Canada, insolvency legislation is administered by the superior courts in each province. The existence of the Commercial List of the Ontario Superior Court and Québec Superior Court has facilitated a "hands-on" approach of the court in *CCAA* matters. Mr. Justice James Farley has been often quoted regarding the need for expeditious treatment of cases, specifically that: "co-operation, communication and common sense are the three commercial court canons driving Ontario's case-managed process".[96] In many Canadian jurisdictions, *CCAA* cases are case managed and assigned to justices with commercial expertise.

The Ontario Superior Court of Justice, Commercial List was the prototype for effective judicial oversight of restructuring proceedings. The expertise of the court and efficacy of its case-managed system highlights why the court has been effective in complex restructuring cases and why so many of *CCAA* applications were brought to this court in the 1990s. The key elements of the case-management system include facilitating negotiation, access to the case-managing judge, and the issuing of interim orders to keep the process both expeditious and accountable.

An effective restructuring system is premised on access to the court during the process. While restructuring should focus on commercial viability, the ability of parties to seek direction or have disputes resolved expeditiously ensures that the process of negotiations continues on a timely basis.

This commitment to timely and effective processes has been subsequently adopted by other Canadian courts. Effective 2003, the Québec Superior Court adopted a commercial list and case managed system, which has considerably enhanced the timeliness and efficiency of *CCAA* and other insolvency proceedings. In December 2004, the Alberta Court of Queen's Bench established a Commercial Practice Committee made up of justices of the court who have a particular interest and experience in dealing with commercial matters, an extension of long-standing informal practice of the Court.[97] *CCAA* proceedings are scheduled before members of the Commercial Practice Committee on a regular basis, with a procedure for expediting motions before the court. The British Columbia Supreme Court commenced a Commercial Chambers Mini-Pilot Project in December 2005, including moving *CCAA* proceedings within the ambit of the Commercial Chambers.[98] Other provinces have moved to case managing of *CCAA* files.

The Court of Queen's Bench of Manitoba in *Oblats de Marie Immaculée du Manitoba*, in a postscript to its judgment on a *CCAA* application, observed that the

---

[96] Mr. Justice Farley, Ontario Superior Court of Justice, 2001.

[97] Chief Justice Allan Wachowich, Notice to the Profession regarding the Commercial Practice Committee, (14 December 2004).

[98] Chief Justice Donald Brenner, Notice to the Profession regarding Commercial Chambers Mini-Pilot Project, (12 December 2005).

Manitoba Court of Queen's Bench has not accepted the principle of judicial specialization in insolvency and other commercial proceedings, and wrote the following:[99]

> ¶ 76 I would strongly encourage my colleagues to review their position and encourage the recognition of the Senate's Committee's conclusions of the need for such a specialization. That specialization has developed in Ontario with the establishment of a commercial list in Toronto.
>
> ¶ 77 The commercial list is administered and heard by a small group of judges who hear all the applications of this nature. They have become national experts through experience.
>
> ¶ 78 The benefit is not for the judges nor to the Court but rather for the public which results in an improved service and presumably one of a higher quality. The development of a specialized bar more able to serve the public is also a consequence.

The principal merit of a case-managed system is that matters can be dealt with fairly, expeditiously and efficiently. The Commercial List judges have experience, interest and expertise in corporate and commercial matters, and many issues arising under *CCAA* applications are dealt with in hours or days. The Commercial List hears cases in considerably less time than the court's regular trial list because parties adhere to its practice direction setting out fairly rigorous requirements.[100] The operating premise is that parties will have considerable input into the process and time frame of a restructuring application, but that once the process is in place, the court will expect parties to adhere to the schedule set. Given the exigencies of expeditious decision-making at the point of insolvency in order to prevent the further depletion of value for creditors, these practice directions assist parties with timely resolution of disputes.

The courts in British Columbia, Québec, Alberta and Ontario have also created practitioner advisory committees to assist in improving accessibility and efficiency in insolvency and other commercial cases.

In *CCAA* cases in Ontario, the court has created very liberal access to "9:30 appointments", which are ten-minute meetings with the case managing judge in chambers, commencing at 9:30 am, to resolve matters of scheduling, minor disputes on disclosure, consent matters, and simple directions. The court may endorse an order or just give informal but clear directions to the parties to ensure the process keeps moving forward, reducing the need to bring formal motions and thus controlling transaction costs. Although the supervising judge will deal with *ex parte* motions on an urgent basis, the court will not decide matters where adequate notice has not been given to

---

[99] *Oblats de Marie Immaculée du Manitoba, Re* (2004), [2004] M.J. No. 112, 2004 CarswellMan 104, 182 Man. R. (2d) 201, 2004 MBQB 71 (Man. Q.B.).

[100] The first practice direction was published in 1995, revised several times, with the most recent revisions in 2002, *Practice Direction Covering the Commercial List,* February, 2002, http://www.ontariocourts.on.ca/superior_court_justice/notices/commercial.htm.

interested parties, or where the matter should be properly decided in a public hearing in conformity with the principles of natural justice.

1. Dispute Resolution Tools

Dispute resolution is multifaceted. Key to *CCAA* proceedings is direct negotiations between parties with an interest in the insolvent corporation. Dispute resolution can be effective in redressing power imbalances in a *CCAA* workout. The court will facilitate negotiations to ensure that they take place on a principled basis, finding it has jurisdiction to order procedures that create access to justice, including disclosure, claims resolution processes and confidentiality regimes.[101]

In the 1992 *Algoma Steel* case, the Court, in an effort to facilitate the outstanding financing issues, ordered the parties to mediation. In that case, the parties had already agreed that the business plan was viable.[102] While the banks initially took the position that the court did not have the jurisdiction to issue the mediation order, they agreed to participate when the process appeared to be workable. The Court ordered the parties to meet with the Honourable George Adams in a process that Mr. Justice Farley described as "akin to court annexed alternative dispute resolution" because of the "special circumstances of the vital importance of Algoma to the essential viability of Sault Ste. Marie as a major Northern Ontario Community".[103] Success of the process was in measure due to the skills that Mr. Justice Adams brought to the mediation, assisting the banks and the union to craft an outcome acceptable to all stakeholders. The multi-faceted negotiation/mediation process also included the intervention of the Ontario Premier in an effort to assist parties to reach a compromise. The result of two intensive weeks of mediation was an agreed plan of arrangement that had high buy-in by the parties. Subsequent meetings of shareholders and creditors resulted in votes of greater than 95% support for the plan.[104]

The successful mediation in the 1991-92 *Algoma Steel CCAA* case was the genesis for the current Ontario civil law mandatory mediation regime. Mr. Justice Farley has written that a significant aspect of the Court's involvement in Algoma was its ability 'to encourage' the parties to negotiate and to exert every effort to reach a compromise, using court-involved mediation to assist with dismantling traditional walls between parties such as bankers and union represntatives.[105]

---

[101] *Skydome Corp., Re* (1998), 1998 CarswellOnt 5922, 16 C.B.R. (4th) 118 (Ont. Gen. Div. [Commercial List]).

[102] *Ibid.* at 763.

[103] James McCartney, "Algoma Steel Inc.: A Successful Restructuring" in J. Ziegel and D. Baird, eds., *Case Studies in Recent Canadian Insolvency Reorganizations* (Toronto: Carswell, 1997) at 234-5.

[104] *Algoma Steel Corp.* v. *Royal Bank* (1992), [1992] O.J. No. 795, 1992 CarswellOnt 2843 (Ont. Gen. Div.).

[105] Mr. Justice Farley, "The Judges Speak", in J. Ziegel, ed., *Current Developments in International and Comparative Corporate Insolvency Law* (Oxford University Press, 1994) at 764.

In *Air Canada,* Mr. Justice Warren Winkler acted as mediator in resolving a series of collective agreement disputes that assisted in parties being able to support the restructuring of the national airline.

In the *Red Cross CCAA* proceeding, a mediation process was conducted in respect of the pension claims with the Honourable Lloyd Houlden, a retired justice of the Ontario Court of Appeal.[106] The procedure was aimed at full and final resolution of the pension issues, in lieu of any civil action or process before any statutory pension regulatory agency, with any mediated or arbitrated resolution subject to approval of the Court.[107]

The parties in *Red Cross* also used dispute resolution techniques as alternatives to litigation in other parts of the *CCAA* proceeding. There was a $47 million pay equity claim by the Service Employees International Union, representing a sizable portion of the unsecured claims in the proceedings.[108] The use of negotiations as an alternative to litigation was key in resolving the claims amount and in allowing Red Cross to move the *CCAA* proceedings forward.[109] The settlement of the claims could allow the workers to receive pay equity adjustments, while ensuring that Red Cross met its statutory obligations.

III. THE ROLE OF THE APPELLATE COURT IN A *CCAA* RESTRUCTURING

Appeal of an order or reasons for judgment of the *CCAA* supervising judge lies with the courts of appeal. Often the time constraints involved in a *CCAA* proceeding means that no appeal is taken, as business and financial exigencies require an extremely timely workout.

---

[106] The sale and transfer of assets closed in September 1998 and $32 million of the proceeds went into escrow; the parties subsequently negotiated and then received Court approval for a procedure to resolve the pension liability issues. There were two additional escrow funds: $36 million for real property adjustments and $10 million to deal with residual transfer issues. *Canadian Red Cross Society / Société Canadienne de la Croix-Rouge, Re* (November 6, 1998), Court File No. 98-CL-00297 (Ont. S.C.J.), Blair J. (Order, Notice of Motion, Procedure of Potential Pension Claims), at paragraph 3.

[107] Parties were to resolve whether the Red Cross was entitled to pay administrative expenses from the pension fund; whether liability for pensions had transferred to the new blood agencies in plan obligations; and the amount of money to be used from the escrow fund to satisfy pension claims. Failing successful mediation, the parties agreed to litigate the matter before an arbitrator who would interpret the relevant collective agreements and legislation across Canada.

[108] Ontario *Pay Equity Act,* S.O. 1988, c. P.16, as amended. *Red Cross, ibid., Motion Record, Service Employees International Union,* (28 July 1999).

[109] *Canadian Red Cross Society / Société Canadienne de la Croix-Rouge, Re* (1999), 1999 CarswellOnt 3123, [1999] O.J. No. 3657 (S.C.J.). The Red Cross had been required to negotiate a pay equity plan pursuant to pay equity legislation, and had previously set aside $15 million in trust transferred from the provincial government to satisfy pay equity claims. However, during the *CCAA* proceedings, Red Cross took the position that it owed considerably less than $47 million in pay equity adjustments. During the workout proceedings, the Red Cross and the SEIU negotiated a settlement of the claims in the amount of $10.2 million in lump sum payment to workers covered by the pay equity plan.

There have been a number of judicial pronouncements on the role of the appellate courts during a *CCAA* proceeding. The British Columbia Court of Appeal in *Doman Industries Ltd.* held that where an order is made by the judge who is supervising the *CCAA* proceedings of the insolvent company from the beginning, the court will be very reluctant to grant leave to appeal the order.[110] The appellate court will exercise its power sparingly when asked to intervene with respect to decisions made during the course of a *CCAA* proceeding, as the *CCAA* judge is undertaking a careful and delicate balancing of numerous interests; and appellate proceedings may upset that balance and frustrate the process.[111] The appellate courts have held that they will be cautious about intervening in *CCAA* proceedings at an early stage, particularly where the order contains a come-back clause that allows parties to bring their concerns regarding a decision to the judge supervising the *CCAA* proceeding.[112]

Appellate courts will accord a high degree of deference when asked to interfere with the exercise of discretion of a *CCAA* court.[113] At the same time, discretionary decisions are not immune from review if the appellate court reaches the clear conclusion that there has been a wrongful exercise of discretion or there is a fundamental question of the lower court's jurisdiction.[114] Leave will be refused by the appellate court the appeal is of no general significance to the practice and where granting leave would disrupt the proposed plan that has been approved by the creditors.[115]

In *Stelco Inc.*, the Ontario Court of Appeal granted leave to hear an appeal of a judgment of the supervising judge under a *CCAA* proceeding.[116] It set out the tests for granting leave to appeal:

> [23] Because of the "real time" dynamic of this restructuring project, Laskin J.A. granted an order on March 4, 2005, expediting the appellants' motion for leave to appeal, directing that it be heard orally and, if leave be granted, directing that the appeal be heard at the same time. The leave motion and the appeal were argued together, by order of the panel, on March 18, 2005.
>
> [24] This court has said that it will only sparingly grant leave to appeal in the context of a *CCAA* proceeding and will only do so where there are "serious and arguable grounds that are of real and significant interest to the parties": *Country Style*

[110] *Doman Industries Ltd., Re* (2004), [2004] B.C.J. No. 1402, 2004 CarswellBC 1545, 2 C.B.R. (5th) 141 (B.C. C.A. [In Chambers]).

[111] *Pacific National Lease Holding Corp., Re* (1992), 15 C.B.R. (3d) 265 (B.C. C.A.); *Gauntlet Energy Corp., Re* (2004), 49 C.B.R. (4th) 225 (Alta. C.A.).

[112] *Algoma Steel Inc., Re* (2001), 25 C.B.R. (4th) 194 (Ont. C.A.).

[113] *New Skeena Forest Products Inc., Re* (2005), 2005 CarswellBC 705, 9 C.B.R. (5th) 278 (B.C. C.A.); *Pacific National Lease Holding Corp. Re* (1992), 1992 CarswellBC 524, 15 C.B.R. (3d) 265 (B.C. C.A. [In Chambers]); *Smoky River Coal Ltd., Re* (1999), 1999 CarswellAlta 491, 12 C.B.R. (4th) 94 (Alta. C.A.).

[114] *New Skeena Forest Products Inc., Re* (2005), 2005 CarswellBC 705, 9 C.B.R. (5th) 278 (B.C. C.A.).

[115] *Doman Industries Ltd., Re* (2004), 2004 CarswellBC 963, 50 C.B.R. (4th) 194, 2004 BCCA 253 (B.C. C.A. [In Chambers]).

[116] *Stelco Inc., Re* (2005), 2005 CarswellOnt 1188, [2005] O.J. No. 1171 (Ont. C.A.). For a discussion of the merits, see the discussion earlier in this chapter on inherent jurisdiction under the *CCAA*.

> *Food Services Inc. (Re),* [2002] O.J. No. 1377, 158 O.A.C. 30 (C.A.), at para. 15. This criterion is determined in accordance with a four-pronged test, namely,
>
> (a) whether the point on appeal is of significance to the practice;
>
> (b) whether the point is of significance to the action;
>
> (c) whether the appeal is prima facie meritorious or frivolous;
>
> (d) whether the appeal will unduly hinder the progress of the action.
>
> [25] Counsel agree that (d) above is not relevant to this proceeding, given the expedited nature of the hearing. In my view, the tests set out in (a) - (c) are met in the circumstances, and as such, leave should be granted. The issue of the court's jurisdiction to intervene in corporate governance issues during a *CCAA* restructuring, and the scope of its discretion in doing so, are questions of considerable importance to the practice and on which there is little appellate jurisprudence.[117]

In another appellate judgment in *Stelco Inc.*, the Ontario Court of Appeal considered an appeal by noteholders from an order that they claimed imposed "an expedited, summary '*CCAA*-style' claims process" for the determination of certain inter-creditor claims in the Stelco restructuring, alleging it was made without jurisdiction under the *CCAA* or through the court's inherent jurisdiction.[118] The Court, in dismissing the appeal, distinguished the types of cases in which appeal is appropriate:

> ¶ 1 THE COURT (oral endorsement):— The appellants are the holders of certain Convertible Notes of Stelco. They seek to set aside the order of Farley J. dated March 7, 2006, which they describe as imposing "an expedited, summary '*CCAA*-style' claims process" for the determination of certain inter-creditor claims in the Stelco restructuring. They assert that the order was made without jurisdiction either under the *CCAA* or through the exercise of the court's inherent jurisdiction, and that the order deprives them of their rights to require those who wish to assert Subordination Claims as against other Stelco creditors to prove those claims in a ordinary civil lawsuit with all the bells and whistles that go with such a proceeding.
>
> . . .
>
> ¶ 7 The appellants are creditors of Stelco and at least some of them participated in the negotiation of the Plan. In any event they voted on approval and the Plan was approved and is binding on them.
>
> ¶ 8 In short, the parties negotiated as part of the Plan, and agreed to – and the Court sanctioned – a mechanism for resolving "entitlements to the Turnover Proceeds". That is what this dispute is about. The evidence before Farley J. indicated that a significant portion of the Turnover Proceeds consists of potentially volatile marketable securities that could not be traded until this dispute is resolved. The procedure

---

[117] See also *Ketch Resources Ltd.* v. *Gauntlet Energy Corp. (Monitor of)* (2005), 2005 CarswellAlta 1527, [2005] A.J. No. 1400 (Alta C.A.); *Canadian Airlines Corp., Re* (2000), 261 A.R. 120 (Alta C.A.).

[118] *Stelco Inc., Re* (2006), 2006 CarswellOnt 3050, [2006] O.J. No. 1996 (Ont. C.A.).

created by Farley J. reflects this dynamic of the Stelco process and responds to the particular exigencies of this restructuring.

¶ 9 Mr. Macdonald argues that the appellants should be entitled to their full rights of process under the Rules of Civil Procedure and to put the respondents to compliance with the *Class Proceedings Act*. We do not agree. That is not what the Plan calls for, nor is it what we would expect in the context of a complicated and time-driven *CCAA* proceeding such as the Stelco restructuring. The Plan contemplates *directions* with respect to a *process to determine* entitlements to the Turnover Proceeds *on a timely basis*. If the parties and the Court had intended the subordination claims issue to be resolved by way of a regular lawsuit, they would simply have said so or left the Convertible Noteholders and the Senior Bondholders to their normal remedies. They did not.

¶ 10 This is not a pure inter-creditor dispute that is unconnected to the debtor, Stelco. It is a dispute that invokes – at least insofar as the subordination claims that have to be resolved for purposes of distribution of the Turnover Proceeds are concerned – the provisions of the Plan and the court's control of its own process in relation to matters pertaining to the roll out of the Plan.

¶ 11 Thus, the circumstances differ from those involved in either of the two prior Stelco cases to which we were referred. In *Re Stelco* (2005), 75 O.R. (3d) 5 (C.A.) – the directors case – the court was dealing with a matter relating to the company's role in the restructuring process as opposed to the court's role in the restructuring process. The present case pertains to the court's control over the restructuring process. In *Re Stelco*, [2005] O.J. No. 4883 (C.A.) – the classification case – the court observed that it is not a proper use of a *CCAA* proceeding to determine disputes between parties other than the debtor company. As pointed out above, however, the present case is not simply an inter-creditor dispute that does not involve the debtor company; it is a dispute that is inextricably connected to the restructuring process.

¶ 12 The Monitor duly applied to the Court, as required, and Farley J., exercising his jurisdiction as the supervising judge of the Stelco restructuring put a timely process in place – in *CCAA* Commercial List fashion – to resolve the entitlements to the Turnover Proceeds. His jurisdiction over the process of the *CCAA* restructuring extends at least to continued process-related matters concerning the rollout of the Plan in accordance with its provisions.

¶ 13 Farley J. is entitled to considerable deference in respect of this type of discretionary decision, which, as the respondent submits, is in the nature of an interlocutory, scheduling order. We see no basis for interfering with his order.

¶ 14 Accordingly, the appeal is dismissed.

In *Stelco Inc.*, the Ontario Court of Appeal in considering section 15(3) of the *CCAA*, which states that no appeal to the Supreme Court of Canada shall operate as a stay of proceedings unless and to the extent ordered by that court, held that it nevertheless had the jurisdiction to grant a stay of the order since section 15(3) of the *CCAA* only addresses stays actually on appeal, not applications for leave to appeal, as was the case at hand. The Court held that when leave to appeal to the Supreme Court of

Canada is sought, applications for a stay of the decision being appealed are to be brought at first instance to the court appealed from, rather than to the Supreme Court of Canada. The test to be applied when considering whether to stay an order of a court granted in the context of a company's *CCAA* proceedings pending a leave to appeal application relating to such order is: whether there is a serious question to be tried; whether the applicant would suffer irreparable harm if the stay is not granted; and the balance of convenience. Having regard to the interests of justice, the Ontario Court of Appeal held that no stay should be granted where to do so would effectively implement the decision of the supervising judge at a critical stage of the restructuring proceedings when the Court of Appeal had already held that the supervising judge had no jurisdiction to make such an order.[119]

Questions for review of materials:

1. What is the difference between statutory discretion and the court's exercise of inherent jurisdiction?

2. What is the scope of a stay under the *CCAA* and why is it important?

3. What is meant by fairness in the context of a *CCAA* proceeding?

Questions for discussion:

1. Do you agree with the specialization of a commercial list when, generally in Canada, we do not have a specialized judiciary?

2. What, in your view, is the appropriate balance between recognizing the public interest and protecting the rights of secured and unsecured creditors in a *CCAA* proceeding?

---

[119] *Stelco Inc., Re* (2005), 2005 CarswellOnt 1336 (Ont. C.A. [In Chambers]).

CHAPTER 4

FINANCING OPERATIONS DURING AND AFTER RESTRUCTURING

I. THE NEED FOR IMMEDIATE OPERATIONAL CAPITAL

Insolvent companies need operating capital to continue carrying on business during the period of the *CCAA* proceeding. Yet pre-filing creditors are often reluctant to advance further credit when their pre-existing claims may already be underwater. The company will often seek new financing to continue operations, as well as try to persuade trade suppliers to continue to advance credit during the period of negotiations for a workout.

II. DEBTOR IN POSSESSION FINANCING

Interim financing, colloquially referred to as debtor-in-possession (DIP) financing refers primarily to the working capital that the debtor corporation requires in order to keep operating during restructuring proceedings.[1] The premise underlying DIP financing is that it is a benefit to all stakeholders, as it allows the debtor to protect going-concern value while it attempts to devise a plan of arrangement acceptable to creditors. Although a number of practitioners refer to the bundle of types of priority financing and charges as debtor-in-possession financing, a distinction can be made between financing that allows the debtor corporation to continue operating during a brief period of workout negotiations (DIP financing) and a variety of other court ordered charges that are given priority in order to cover the expenses of the restructuring proceedings or protect particular vulnerable creditors (priming liens). Notwithstanding that there is no express language in the *CCAA* providing for DIP

[1] The term DIP financing is borrowed from the terminology used in restructuring proceedings under Chapter 11 of the U.S. *Bankruptcy Code*. (*US Code*, Title 11). Paragraphs §1107, §1108 and §364 of the U.S. *Bankruptcy Code*, read together, provide that a debtor in possession may obtain credit, and set out the rules applicable to this credit. While the terminology used in Canada is similar, the rules applicable to the interim financing are very different and should not be confused, as the U.S. rules are highly codified.

financing, Canadian courts have found that they have the jurisdiction to order DIP financing.[2]

Similarly, the courts have consistently affirmed their ability to order priming liens or priority charges in favour of insolvency officers during a *CCAA* proceeding. This allows the debtor corporation access to the professional services of the monitor, chief restructuring officer, other workout experts, and lawyers that can assist with a successful workout. Such financing orders have been approved by the courts to cover administrative charges in a *CCAA* proceeding;[3] to reduce director and officer liability exposure;[4] to cover expenses;[5] and for general operating purposes, including post-petition trade creditor charges.[6] DIP financing has also been approved in cross-border cases where there is a *CCAA* proceeding and an ancillary proceeding recognized by a U.S. court pursuant to former s. 304 (now chapter 15) of the U.S. *Bankruptcy Code* or a main proceeding in the U.S. with ancillary proceedings in Canada.[7] According super-priority financing has also been aimed at protecting or ensuring compliance with environmental obligations.[8]

Mr. Justice Clément Gascon of the Québec Superior Court has held that there are five principles currently operating in the court's consideration of applications for DIP financing and priority charges or priming liens: adequate notice of DIP financing and priming requests, so that creditors can fully assess the impact of DIP financing

---

[2] *United Used Auto & Truck Parts Ltd., Re* (1999), 12 C.B.R. (4th) 144 (B.C. S.C. [In Chambers]), affirmed (2000), 16 C.B.R. (4th) 141 (B.C. C.A.), leave to appeal allowed but appeal discontinued (2000), [2000] S.C.C.A. No. 142, 2000 CarswellBC 2132 (S.C.C.). *Dylex Ltd., Re* (January 23, 1995), Doc. B-4/95 (Ont. Gen. Div. [Commercial List]); *T. Eaton Co., Re* (1997), 1997 CarswellOnt 5954, [1997] O.J. No. 6388 (Ont. Gen. Div.). See articles J. Gollob, "Distressed Debt Lenders and their Impact on Restructurings and Workouts in Canada", *Annual Review of Insolvency Law, 2004* (Toronto: Carswell, 2005) 173-186 and Janis Sarra, "Governance and Control: The Role of Debtor-in-Possession Financing under the *CCAA*", *Annual Review of Insolvency Law, 2004* (Toronto: Carswell, 2005) 119-172.

[3] *Air Canada, Re* (2003), 2003 CarswellOnt 2465 (Ont. S.C.J. [Commercial List]); *United Used Auto & Truck Parts Ltd., Re* (1999), 12 C.B.R. (4th) 144 (B.C. S.C. [In Chambers]), affirmed (2000), 16 C.B.R. (4th) 141 (B.C. C.A.), leave to appeal allowed but appeal discontinued (2000), [2000] S.C.C.A. No. 142, 2000 CarswellBC 2132 (S.C.C.); *Simpson's Island Salmon Ltd., Re*, 2006 CarswellNB 420 (N.B. Q.B.).

[4] *Stelco Inc., Re* (2004), 2004 CarswellOnt 483, [2004] O.J. No. 549 (Ont. S.C.J. [Commercial List]); *Air Canada, Re* (2003), 2003 CarswellOnt 1220 (Ont. S.C.J. [Commercial List]); *Canada 3000 Inc., Re* (2001), Doc. Toronto 01-CL-4314 (Ont. S.C.J.); *Philip Services Corp., Re*, Doc. 99-CL-3442, 4166CP/98.

[5] *General Publishing Co., Re* (2003), [2003] O.J. No. 2358, 2003 CarswellOnt 2094 (Ont. S.C.J.); *Dylex Ltd., Re* (2002), [2002] O.J. No. 1505, 2002 CarswellOnt 1183 (Ont. S.C.J.), discussing this charge under the *CCAA* and the *BIA*. *Canadian Red Cross Society / Société Canadienne de la Croix-Rouge, Re*, Court File No. 98-CL-002970 (Ont. S.C.J.).

[6] *Smoky River Coal Ltd., Re* (2001), [2001] A.J. No. 1006, 2001 CarswellAlta 1035 (Alta. C.A.); *Westar Mining Ltd., Re* (1992), 14 C.B.R. (3d) 88 (B.C. S.C.); *T. Eaton Co., Re* (1997), 46 C.B.R. (3d) 293 (Ont. Gen. Div.).

[7] One example is *Consumers Packaging Inc., Re* (May 23, 2001) Doc. 01-CL-4147 (Ont. S.C.J. [Commercial List]); *Consumers Packaging Inc., Re* (May 30, 2001), Doc. 01-1865 (U.S. Bkty Crt. D. Del., 2001) and (June 12, 2001), Doc. 01-1865 (U.S. Bkty Crt. D. Del., 2001). However, there have been numerous other cases.

[8] *Royal Oak Mines Inc., Re* (2000), 2000 CarswellOnt 3686 (Ont. S.C.J. [Commercial List]).

decisions; sufficient disclosure; timeliness of the request; balancing the prejudice to creditors and other stakeholders; and the principle of granting priority financing as an extraordinary remedy.[9] Canadian courts apply these principles in an effort to find the optimal balancing of prejudices in the exercise of their jurisdiction to grant DIP financing or other priority charges. The court must weigh the likely risks against the likely gains of authorizing such financing. This is with a view to creating certainty in credit transactions while meeting the objectives of the *CCAA*.

1. Development of the Court's Exercise of Power

The origins of DIP financing were from the practice of a receiver securing capital on a super-priority basis to cover administration and operating expenses during a receivership, where the receiver believed that the debtor was worth more as a going concern. There had been considerable debate in the late 1990s regarding the use of DIP financing to provide capital during reorganization under the *CCAA*, much of it focused on the jurisdiction of the courts to grant such financing on a priority basis over pre-existing secured claims. This issue has largely been resolved through judicial direction on the scope and limits of DIP financing.

As discussed briefly in chapter 3, the courts have found authority for granting super-priority charges or DIP financing under both the *CCAA* and their inherent jurisdiction. The British Columbia Court of Appeal in *United Used Auto* held that the effective achievement of the *CCAA*'s objectives requires a broad and flexible exercise of jurisdiction to facilitate a restructuring, and the court's equitable jurisdiction permits orders granting super-priority in some circumstances.[10] Secured creditors may be required to make some sacrifice because of the reasonably anticipated benefits for all stakeholders. The Court of Appeal held that the objective of the *CCAA* extends beyond protecting assets for eventual realization by creditors.[11]

At the same time, the British Columbia Court of Appeal cautioned that granting DIP financing on a priority basis can erode the security of creditors and, thus, the court should make such orders only where there is a reasonable prospect of successfully restructuring.[12] This speaks to the necessity of the court balancing the prejudice to creditors, and the challenge of doing so where the upside potential of the DIP financing is not always clear.

---

[9] *Boutiques San Francisco Incorporées, Re* (2003), 2003 CarswellQue 13882, [2003] Q.J. No. 18940 (Que. S.C.), citing Janis Sarra, "Debtor in Possession Financing: The Jurisdiction of Canadian Courts to Grant Superpriority Financing in *CCAA* Applications" (2000) 23 Dalhousie Law Journal 337.

[10] *United Used Auto & Truck Parts Ltd., Re* (1999), 12 C.B.R. (4th) 144 (B.C. S.C. [In Chambers]), affirmed (2000), 16 C.B.R. (4th) 141 (B.C. C.A.), leave to appeal allowed but appeal discontinued (2000), [2000] S.C.C.A. No. 142, 2000 CarswellBC 2132 (S.C.C.) at paras. 2, 9, 12.

[11] *Ibid.* at paras. 25, 28, 30.

[12] *Ibid.* at para. 30. Instead, the Court granted an order funding the debtor's restructuring legal expenses, included as part of the administration charge as a limited substitute for DIP financing. See also *Simpson's Island Salmon Ltd., Re* (2005), 2005 CarswellNB 781, [2005] N.B.J. No. 570 (N.B. Q.B.) at paras. 16, 19.

The Alberta Court of Queen's Bench in *Hunters Trailer & Marine Ltd.* held that the *CCAA* is designed to serve a broad constituency of investors, creditors, and employees and that its effectiveness in achieving its objectives is dependent on a broad and flexible exercise of jurisdiction to facilitate a restructuring and continue the debtor as a going concern in the future.[13] While its jurisdiction is invoked when an initial application is made under the *CCAA*, the court is not limited to granting priority only for those costs that arise after the date of the application or initial order. The Court found that so long as the monies were reasonably advanced to maintain the *status quo* pending a *CCAA* application or the costs were incurred in preparation for the *CCAA* proceedings, "justice dictates and practicality demands that they fall under the super-priority granted by the court".[14]

The courts have cautioned that in balancing interests there should be cogent evidence that the benefit of DIP financing clearly outweighs the potential prejudice to the lenders whose position is being subordinated.[15] DIP financing requests in initial orders should be confined to what is reasonably necessary for the continued operation of the debtor corporation during a "brief but realistic period on an urgent basis".[16] DIP financing should be enough to "keep the lights on" and enable the debtor to keep up with the appropriate preventive maintenance measures.[17] In *Royal Oak Mines*, Mr. Justice Blair held that DIP financing orders involve "what may be a significant reordering of priorities from those in place before the application is made, not in the sense of altering the existing priorities as between the various secured creditors but in the sense of placing encumbrances ahead of those presently in existence".[18]

The granting of DIP financing may allow a corporation to keep operating in order to retain value while trying to negotiate a workout with creditors. For stakeholders, such as workers, trade creditors, or local governments, it may also result in preservation of their investments, at least for the period that a restructuring plan is being formulated.[19] According super-priority financing has also been aimed at ensuring compliance with environmental obligations, in the public interest.[20] The court, in

---

[13] *Hunters Trailer & Marine Ltd., Re* (2001), 2001 CarswellAlta 964, [2001] A.J. No. 857 (Alta. Q.B.) at paras. 32-34.

[14] *Ibid.* at para. 18, 51.

[15] *Skydome Corp., Re* (1998), 1998 CarswellOnt 5922, 16 C.B.R. (4th) 118 (Ont. Gen. Div. [Commercial List]) at 5; *Royal Oak Mines Inc., Re* (1999), 1999 CarswellOnt 792 (Ont. Gen. Div. [Commercial List]) at para. 22; *United Used Auto & Truck Parts Ltd., Re* (1999), 12 C.B.R. (4th) 144 (B.C. S.C. [In Chambers]), affirmed (2000), 16 C.B.R. (4th) 141 (B.C. C.A.), leave to appeal allowed but appeal discontinued (2000), [2000] S.C.C.A. No. 142, 2000 CarswellBC 2132 (S.C.C.); *Hunters Trailer & Marine Ltd., Re* (2000), [2000] A.J. 1550, 2000 CarswellAlta 1776 (Alta. Q.B.) at paras. 9, 10; *Hunters Trailer & Marine Ltd., Re* (2001), 2001 CarswellAlta 964, [2001] A.J. No. 857 (Alta. Q.B.); *Hunters Trailer &Marine Ltd., Re* (2002), [2002] A.J. No. 1638, 2001 CarswellAlta 1636 (Alta. Q.B.).

[16] *Royal Oak Mines Inc., Re* (1999), 6 C.B.R. (4th) 314 (Ont. Gen. Div. [Commercial List]).

[17] *Ibid.* at para. 24.

[18] *Ibid.*

[19] Janis Sarra, "Governance and Control: The Role of Debtor-in-Possession Financing under the *CCAA*", *Annual Review of Insolvency Law, 2004* (Toronto: Carswell, 2005) 119-172.

[20] *Royal Oak Mines Inc., Re* (2000), 2000 CarswellOnt 3686 (Ont. S.C.J. [Commercial List]).

balancing prejudices, will weigh the possibility of a going-concern solution that potentially creates long-term upside value for numerous stakeholders, with the risk of further depletion of value that may be able to satisfy claims on a short-term basis. This balancing of interest and prejudice is at the heart of most financing judgments. Notwithstanding these potential benefits to all stakeholders, absent careful scrutiny of the terms of the DIP financing agreement, granting access to short-term capital can increase the risk of harm to stakeholders if the terms approved by the court lead to a *CCAA* plan that prejudices their interests more than a liquidation outcome.[21]

In *Stelco Inc.*, the Court found that the debtor could not realistically expect any increase in its credit lines or access further outside funding, and that the DIP financing of $75 million was only available under *CCAA* protection.[22]

The court has distinguished between the existence of its jurisdiction and the exercise of the court's discretion under that jurisdiction. Banks, as senior lenders, often lay claim to all otherwise-unencumbered assets through general security agreements. This differs from lending practice in the United States, which is frequently asset-specific secured debt, not blanket security. In Canada, for the debtor seeking financing for a *CCAA* workout, there may be few, if any, unencumbered assets. Since a DIP lender is unwilling to lend at this stage of a company's financial health absent security, the priming of the DIP facility is a key aspect of the debtor's ability to attempt a workout. While the courts have determined that they have jurisdiction, there is a further step as to whether they will exercise their discretion under that jurisdiction to order DIP financing.[23]

The Québec courts were initially reluctant to grant DIP financing, in part because this involved applying common law principles; however, their comfort level in approving DIP financing orders has grown.[24] The Québec Superior Court approved DIP financing with a priming lien in an *ex parte* initial order in *Alis Technologies*

---

[21] Janis Sarra, "Governance and Control: The Role of Debtor-in-Possession Financing under the *CCAA*", *Annual Review of Insolvency Law, 2004* (Toronto: Carswell, 2005) 119-172.

[22] *Stelco Inc., Re* (2004), 2004 CarswellOnt 1211, [2004] O.J. No. 1257 (Ont. S.C.J.) at paras. 32-33, leave to appeal refused (2004), 2004 CarswellOnt 2936 (Ont. C.A.), leave to appeal refused (2004), 2004 CarswellOnt 5200 (S.C.C.).

[23] In a *BIA* proposal case heard by Madam Justice Romaine of the Alberta Court of Queen's Bench, a secured creditor objected to the granting of DIP financing on a priority basis. The Court approved the DIP facility, but subordinated it to the security of the objecting secured creditors with the terms of the DIP loan to be agreed on by creditors; *In the matter of a Bankruptcy Proposal of Bearcat Explorations Ltd. and Stampede Oils Inc.*, Doc. BK 01-84659, BK 01- 084660 (Alta. Q.B.).

[24] *Alis Technologies Inc., Re* (July 16, 2003), Doc. 500-11-021079-039 (Que. S.C.). DIP financing orders have also been made in *Mines Jeffrey Inc., Re* (October 7, 2002), Doc. 450-05-005118-027 (Que. S.C.), *Mines Jeffrey Inc., Re* (November 29, 2002), Doc. 450-05-005118-027 (Que. S.C.); *Papiers Gaspésia Inc., Re* (February 3, 2004), Doc. 500-11-022333-047 (Que. S.C.); *Concert Industries Ltd., Re* (August 5, 2003), Doc. 500-11-021197-039 (Que. S.C.); *Eaux Vives Harricana Inc., Re* (March 19, 2004), Doc. 500-11-022700-047 (Que. S.C.), *Eaux Vives Harricana Inc., Re* (April 15, 2004), Doc. 500-11-022700-047 (Que. S.C.); in Robert Tessier, "Le Financement du débiteur en possession et les charges prioritaires dans les réorganisations suivant la Loi sur les arrangements avec les créanciers des compagnies", September 2004, on file with author.

Inc.[25] The Québec courts have also granted priority charges to cover the monitor's fees and for the indemnification of directors and officers in a number of *CCAA* proceedings.[26] Robert Tessier has suggested that the Québec Superior Court will make a DIP financing order with a priming lien but will want to hear from existing creditors beforehand, except where the debtor can demonstrate an urgent need.[27] Hence the caselaw in Québec has aligned with that in other parts of Canada.

The Ontario Superior Court of Justice has also ordered a priming DIP facility for Québec based corporations over the objection of pre-filing secured lenders, where the *CCAA* proceeding was being managed out of Toronto.[28]

In *General Electric Capital Canada Inc.* v. *Euro United Corp.*, the Ontario Superior Court confirmed the inherent jurisdiction of the court to order DIP financing but refused to approve the DIP financing request.[29] The Court was not satisfied that super-priority financing of a DIP facility could be granted without prejudicing the interests of secured creditors in a manner that was not justified in the circumstances of the case. Instead, it granted a competing application by the lenders to appoint an interim receiver and approved a type of DIP financing in which the receiver borrowed funds from existing secured lenders to recommence operations and pursue restructuring and sales alternatives.[30]

DIP financing is not always needed by the debtor corporation. The debtor may be able to finance itself from cash flow from inventory and accounts receivable without new borrowing, and the ability to do this is protected by the *CCAA* stay.

Industry Canada reports that of data that it compiled on 79 *CCAA* cases, 30 *CCAA* proceedings had DIP financing approved by the court.[31] The average value of the DIP facility was $33.52 million. The DIP facility received a priority charge in 17 of 25 cases in which Industry Canada was able to find accurate data. Twenty-two of the studied *CCAA* proceedings were concluded as of December 2003, and of those files, 12 or just over half, were successful in restructuring under a *CCAA* plan of arrangement. In contrast, 16 of the 49 proceedings that did not receive DIP financing emerged from the *CCAA* proceeding with a restructuring plan approved by creditors and the court.[32]

---

[25] *Alis, ibid.*

[26] See for example, *Alis, ibid.*; *Boutiques San Francisco Incorporées, Re* (2003), 2003 CarswellQue 13882, [2003] Q.J. No. 18940 (Que. S.C.).

[27] Robert Tessier, "Le Financement du débiteur en possession et les charges prioritaires dans les réorganisations suivant la Loi sur les arrangements avec les créanciers des compagnies", September 2004, on file with author.

[28] *Ivaco Inc., Re* (2003) Court File No. 03-CL-5145 (Ont. S.C.J.).

[29] *General Electric Capital Canada Inc.* v. *Euro United Corp.* (1999), 1999 CarswellOnt 4908 (Ont. S.C.J. [Commercial List]).

[30] *Ibid.* This was accomplished through receiver's certificate.

[31] Gilles Gauthier, "DIP Financing in Insolvency Law Reform" December 2003. Of the 141 cases, 50 per cent were filed in Ontario, 35 per cent in Western Canada, 12 per cent in Québec and 3 per cent in Atlantic Canada.

[32] *Ibid.*

2. *Ex Parte* DIP Orders

DIP financing orders have been made *ex parte* in a number of cases, although the courts have made clear their concern about this practice. In *Royal Oak Mines*, the Court held that the reordering of priorities that DIP financing orders involve "should not be imported lightly, if at all, into the creditors' mix"; and that affected parties are entitled to a reasonable opportunity to think about their potential impact and to consider whether a *CCAA* proceeding is the appropriate approach to the insolvency in the circumstances.[33]

In *Algoma Steel Inc.,* the Ontario Superior Court of Justice granted a $50 million DIP financing order in the initial stay order, without notice given to the first secured creditors.[34] The operating lenders with an existing first charge on the debtor's current assets were the lenders of the DIP facility, secured by a first charge over the fixed assets and a second charge over current assets. In balancing the interests, the Court attempted to limit the priming effect on the noteholders' security by limiting draws on the DIP facility to $20 million in the first 30 days, with further subsequent restrictions made by the court.[35] It is evident that the Court had some concern in making the order on an *ex parte* basis, but was persuaded by the urgency of the request. The Court's endorsement emphasized that creditors who had not received notice should use the come-back clause and that "any interested party may apply to this court to vary or rescind this order". The first mortgage noteholders, who had claims of more than a half-billion dollars, then sought leave to appeal the decision.

The Ontario Court of Appeal dismissed the motion for leave to appeal the lower court's judgment in *Algoma Steel Inc.*[36] It held that the granting of an initial order on an *ex parte* basis is specifically authorized by s. 11(1) of the *CCAA*, noting that *CCAA* proceedings are often urgent, complex, and dynamic, and such was the case at Algoma.[37] The Court held that the granting of the DIP financing was on an urgent and interim basis because of a serious negative cash flow crisis, and that without short-term assistance, Algoma, one of the largest companies in the province, was at risk of ceasing operations.[38] It held that the motion for leave to appeal was premature, that the lower court had invited dissatisfied parties to bring motions back to the court on a timely basis, and that the appellate court would not lightly intervene in the early stage of a *CCAA* proceeding.

Similarly, in *Hunters Trailer & Marine Ltd.*, the Court observed that it is preferable that priority for administrative costs and DIP financing be dealt with on notice to

---

[33] *Royal Oak Mines Inc., Re* (1999), 6 C.B.R. (4th) 314 (Ont. Gen. Div. [Commercial List]) at para. 24.

[34] *Algoma Steel Inc., Re* (2001), [2001] O.J. No. 1994, 2001 CarswellOnt 1999 (Ont. S.C.J. [Commercial List]), leave to appeal refused (2001), [2001] O.J. No. 1943, 2001 CarswellOnt 1742 (Ont. C.A.).

[35] Janis P. Sarra, *Creditor Rights and the Public Interest, Restructuring Insolvent Corporations* (Toronto: University of Toronto Press, 2003).

[36] *Algoma Steel Inc., Re* (2001), [2001] O.J. No. 1943, 2001 CarswellOnt 1742 (Ont. C.A.).

[37] *Ibid.* at para. 7.

[38] *Ibid.* at para. 2.

all interested parties.[39] However, where circumstances warrant, priority may be granted on a limited basis, until the matter is considered on notice to those affected by the order. The Court found that the debtor corporation had brought the application *ex parte* because it was insolvent and there was a threat of seizure by some creditors.[40] The Court wrote an express provision in the order, permitting any motion to vary the order or to seek other relief on two days' notice, a provision that was not acted on immediately by the creditors. The Court held that if super-priority cannot be granted without the consent of secured creditors, the protection of the *CCAA* would effectively be denied the debtor corporation. The stay in *Hunters Trailer* was subsequently amended, and the amounts under the DIP facility and the administrative charge were reduced. As noted in chapter 2, the court subsequently terminated the proceeding.

There were a number of cases in the late 1990s in which debtors sought approval for new lenders or prefiling subordinated lenders to supply the DIP financing, often on an *ex parte* basis, notifying few, if any, creditors. Such *ex parte* applications are now less common, giving the court's direction that notice should be given on applications for DIP financing. Where such applications are sought *ex parte,* the approval of the DIP financing agreement *ex parte* means that pre-filing creditors are often not given the opportunity to scrutinize the terms of the facility and have meaningful input into those terms prior to the debtor signing the agreement. Even where there is "notice", it often involves pre-filing creditors getting a 40-page financing agreement the night before the motion, with an inability to fully consider the favourable treatment being given to the DIP lender, sometimes to the prejudice of pre-filing creditors.[41]

While there is a "come-back" clause in initial *CCAA* orders that allows parties that did not receive notice or received inadequate notice of motions regarding DIP financing to come before the court and object to the terms, this has not, to date, frequently been used. In part, this may be due to confusion as to the appropriate onus on come-back clauses. Arguably, the onus should continue to rest with the debtor, as applicant of the initial stay, particularly where the order has been granted *ex parte*.[42]

---

[39] *Hunters Trailer & Marine Ltd., Re* (2000), [2000] A.J. No. 1550, 2000 CarswellAlta 1776 (Alta. Q.B.); *Hunters Trailer & Marine Ltd., Re* (2001), [2001] A.J. No. 857, 2001 CarswellAlta 964 (Alta. Q.B.) at para. 34.

[40] *Ibid.* at para. 32.

[41] For example, *In the matter of the Companies' Creditors Arrangement Act and Teleglobe Inc.* (May 15, 2002), Doc. 02-CL-4528 (Ont. S.C.J. [Commercial List]).

[42] For a full discussion, see Janis Sarra, "Governance and Control: The Role of Debtor-in-Possession Financing under the *CCAA*", *Annual Review of Insolvency Law, 2004* (Toronto: Carswell, 2005) 119-172.

3. Benefits of Oversight Controls

A lender offering DIP financing during a *CCAA* workout expects a bundle of rights to accompany the financing, in terms of credit arrangements and fees, protection against being primed by new post-filing lenders, and in respect of oversight controls during the period that the debtor continues to operate while it is negotiating a plan of arrangement and compromise.

One issue is whether creditors in Canada have been very active, where truly necessary, to affect governance matters when debtor corporations are insolvent. Historically, there was a sense that insolvency was caused by reasonably unforeseen outside circumstances, and thus that existing directors and officers should be retained; or that resignation of directors, or requests for their resignation, would signal internal dispute or create a vacuum that would concern customers and suppliers. However, there are a number of cases in which governance is deficient and creditors need to provide some oversight of the debtor during this period where there are governance deficiencies that must be corrected if the debtor's business is to become viable.

Most DIP facilities are provided by existing lenders, usually to protect their pre-filing position, so that no other lender has priority over their claim. Canadian institutional investors can be reluctant to prime each other, giving that they have ongoing relationships in a relatively small market, and are likely to face the converse situation in the next *CCAA* proceeding.

Often pre-existing lenders realistically consider prior loans as a sunk cost, which has little value unless the debtor is able to devise a viable workout strategy.

DIP financing may provide another oversight mechanism for managerial activity during negotiations for a viable plan of arrangement. Where the DIP lender is a pre-filing creditor, it may have a strong interest in the success of the business going-forward, both in terms of satisfying its existing claims and the expected value from a continuing lending relationship with the debtor.[43] In such a case, there is likely to be a convergence of interest with less-protected creditors that have a stake in the firm as a going concern. Unsecured and undersecured creditors may also benefit from the provision of continued working capital and from any governance improvements negotiated by the DIP lender in the DIP financing agreement. DIP lenders also have considerable access to information in undertaking their due diligence prior to negotiating a DIP financing agreement. This means that the DIP lender may be the party best positioned at the commencement of *CCAA* proceedings to determine that there is a potential upside value to be generated by having the debtor corporation restructured through a *CCAA* proceeding.[44]

The DIP lender that has an ongoing relationship with the debtor corporation or seeks an ongoing credit or equity relationship, while naturally self-interested in its nego-

---

[43] *Ibid.*

[44] *Ibid.*

tiations, is less likely to push the debtor prematurely into liquidation. New DIP lenders may or may not have the same timelines as pre-filing lenders. They may be interested in a going-forward relationship or only in a rapid turnaround of their capital. Their specific interest will direct the control terms they secure.

In many cases, oversight exercised by creditors can enhance governance, in the sense of providing another check on the activities of corporate directors and officers. However, there may also be situations that call for a governance change, but DIP lenders and other secured creditors are not prepared to intervene, as there is a risk that their ability to sell claims would be hampered because they would fall within the definition of insider trading under securities legislation.[45]

In *Laidlaw,* the Ontario Superior Court rejected an application for a shareholders' oversight committee to participate in the *CCAA* proceedings, including negotiation for a plan and mediation efforts with a senior creditor.[46] The court held that there was no reasonable prospect for shareholders to salvage any equity and therefore there was no economic interest to protect. Thus, it was inappropriate to appoint a shareholder oversight committee with a first charge on the assets, as the costs would be inappropriately borne by creditors who already faced a severe discounting of their claims.

4. Use of DIP Financing Agreements to Control Governance

Governance of the debtor corporation plays a significant role in the potential success and, hence, upside value that may be generated by a successful workout, and DIP financing is being utilized as a tool in both Canada and the United States to influence governance.[47] The ability to attract financing on a competitive basis is key to the restructuring effort. While this has historically come from pre-filing operating or other senior secured lenders, today's workouts involve a mix of pre-filing and new creditors. The growth of distressed debt investors in insolvency workouts has created

---

[45] Too much control exerted over the debtor corporation draws creditors into the definition of insider within the meaning of securities laws. Where creditors anticipate trading or selling their claims during the *CCAA* proceeding, they do not wish to hamper this ability by becoming subject to insider trading rules under Canadian securities law. As a result, there may be situations in which assertion of control rights to improve governance would be appropriate, but lenders do not act. Hence, there are two possible outcomes that could be prejudicial. The first is that the DIP lender exercises excessive control rights, such that other lenders are reluctant to intervene, leading to a skewed process. Arguably, in this case, the DIP lender may be acquiring fiduciary obligations if it is acting more as a shadow director. The second potential outcome is that if no creditor acts to correct governance deficiencies, leaving directors and officers with control where there are governance concerns, there could be a lack of accountability in regard to their actions; *ibid.*

[46] *Laidlaw Inc., Re* (2002), 2002 CarswellOnt 790, [2002] O.J. No. 947 (Ont. S.C.J. [Commercial List]); see also *Canadian Airlines Corp.* (2000), 20 C.B.R. (4th) 1 (Alta. Q.B.), leave to appeal refused (2000), 2000 CarswellAlta 919 (Alta. C.A. [In Chambers]), affirmed (2000), 2000 CarswellAlta 1556 (Alta. C.A.), leave to appeal refused (2001), 2001 CarswellAlta 888 (S.C.C.).

[47] Janis Sarra, "Governance and Control: The Role of Debtor-in-Possession Financing under the *CCAA*", *Annual Review of Insolvency Law, 2004* (Toronto: Carswell, 2005) 119-172.

new pressure for timely turnaround and workout plans that generate short-term returns on their investments.[48]

DIP financing offers working capital that provides the breathing space to the debtor corporation during the *CCAA* proceeding, to allow it to identify and remedy the source of financial distress. While there has long been an active market for secured credit in Canada, a new market has arisen for DIP financing. DIP lenders are able to secure generous initial fees, higher interest rates and super-priority for the capital that they make available to the financially distressed firm. While this is arguably a risk premium, the super-priority granted to draws on the DIP facility actually make the transactions lower risk than pre-filing secured claims.[49]

The limited pool of DIP lenders provides them with considerable bargaining power in negotiations for a DIP financing agreement. Traditionally, the pre-filing operating lender or other senior secured creditor provided DIP financing for *CCAA* debtor corporations. Where they were not pre-filing lenders, however, the banks have not traditionally offered DIP financing. U.S. lenders have entered the Canadian market with considerable experience from U.S. workouts, and given the thinness of the market, DIP lenders are able to secure both extremely favourable financing terms, as well as extensive control rights in the provisions of the DIP financing agreement. An example was the Teleglobe DIP financing agreement, in which the DIP lender was expressly given the right to approve any form of order coming before the court.[50]

Canadian courts have endorsed these DIP financing agreements because they have been persuaded that the agreement is the only realistic means for the debtor corporation to keep operating while it attempts to negotiate a viable restructuring plan with its creditors. The DIP lender is presented as the "only game in town", and the court is advised that all the jobs will be lost if the DIP agreement is not approved. Control terms in a DIP agreement can create serious risk of prejudice to stakeholders. For example, the DIP lender can threaten to declare default on the agreement if particular motions are brought before the court or if the debtor takes particular positions where creditors bring motions. Other provisions can specify default of the DIP financing agreement if the court makes particular orders. The courts have not yet had the opportunity to consider whether such provisions are harmful to the integrity of the *CCAA* process.

If the debtor is able to secure capital from existing senior operating lenders, the governance structure may not change, except that the lender imposes more stringent monitoring and, in some cases, control rights on the use of the DIP financing. Where creditors have confidence in the oversight and management of the debtor corporation and they determine that a going-concern outcome to the *CCAA* proceeding maxi-

---

[48] *Ibid.*

[49] *Ibid.*

[50] *In the matter of the Companies' Creditors Arrangement Act and Teleglobe Inc.* (May 15, 2002), Doc. 02-CL-4528 (Ont. S.C.J. [Commercial List]). This is a normal practice of the DIP lender to protect its interest but can also serve to prevent the debtor from considering strategies or bringing motions that better serve the interests of multiple stakeholders.

mizes value for them, they are likely to provide the DIP facility. Existing creditors can often make a decision on DIP financing quickly, given that they have already acquired knowledge of the debtor's financial position and may have sector-specific information that has informed previous credit decisions.[51] Hence, they may have lower transaction costs in conducting the due diligence required in DIP financing decisions. Even where their claims are already covered because of their security, pre-filing secured creditors may agree to provide DIP financing where they want to ensure that their position is not compromised during the workout process, that the debtor restructures in a manner that maximizes protection of their interests, or to maintain some control over the debtor during the proceedings.

Where the lender is a pre-existing subordinated secured lender, such as a specific asset secured creditor, the creditor's claim is often unaffected by a reorganization proceeding, and the creditor is less likely to support DIP financing, as it means delay in realizing on its claim. On the other hand, Dowdall and Seigel have suggested that subordinated pre-filing lenders may benefit from the provision of DIP financing that is aimed at satisfying senior secured claims at the outset or early in the process, in that by paying out senior creditors, subordinated lenders could arguably enhance their recovery from the reduced professional fees and through their ability to assert some control over the process.[52]

One trend is that certain equity sponsors organize their strategy to shift control early in the process towards their interests. They buy up the debt across classes at a discounted value and provide the DIP financing under stringent controls. Alternatively, they can buy most of the debt from a single class, but purchase that debt through several entities, and thus control the vote of the class through the "head count" numbers as well as the total value of claims. This strong creditor position then allows them to put in the equity bid and to be assured that it is accepted across the classes of creditors. While parties are entitled to conduct their affairs to maximize value, this creates new challenges for the court in exercising its supervisory powers in terms of its ability to balance stakeholder interests.

The DIP facility is often negotiated prior to the initial filing of the *CCAA* application, and usually contains a declaration in the court order approving the DIP financing agreement that the DIP lender will be an unaffected creditor in any plan of compromise or arrangement. This is a device to ensure that the DIP lender is fully secured without any risk that its claims will be compromised. A series of covenants and conditions for granting the DIP facility give the DIP lender considerable control over the restructuring proceeding.

---

[51] Janis Sarra, "Governance and Control: The Role of Debtor-in-Possession Financing under the *CCAA*", *Annual Review of Insolvency Law, 2004* (Toronto: Carswell, 2005) 119-172.

[52] S.E. Seigel and D.R. Dowdall, "The Latest Word on *CCAA* Interim Financing: DIP Financing and Alternative Financing Arrangements" Paper, December 2003 at 8, on file with author. It is unclear how often this currently occurs in a *CCAA* proceeding.

A new DIP lender may have little concern about the outcome of the *CCAA* proceeding, since its claims are fully protected and it has no pre-filing debt that may be underwater. Given the controls that it extracts in the DIP financing agreement, the DIP lender may unduly pressure the debtor corporation to consider its interests above those of other creditors. It may also pressure the debtor company to engage in particular bargaining or litigious conduct that unnecessarily prejudices pre-filing creditors and dictates the outcome of bargaining, confident that the size of the DIP facility and the conditions under which it was granted will prevail.

Where the DIP lender is not a pre-filing creditor, it may have different timelines in terms of satisfying its claims. As a consequence, the DIP creditor may encourage the debtor corporation to consider liquidation prematurely, when there is still value in the debtor that could accrue to junior secured and unsecured creditors. Similarly, it may press for a going concern sale to third parties when a sale to existing creditors would satisfy a greater percentage of claims or produce less prejudice to claims overall. Since an objective of *CCAA* proceedings is to facilitate a process whereby the debtor is given the opportunity to devise a viable plan of arrangement, the courts should consider the potential prejudice to these objectives where DIP lenders have imposed control rights that prevent directors and officers from decision-making in the interests of the firm and all its stakeholders.[53]

The debtor corporation remains in control during the workout process, as the legislative scheme envisions, but not necessarily the directors and officers, who might be replaced or encouraged to resign. The DIP facility changes this dynamic. The ability of directors and officers to bargain the terms of the DIP facility may allow them more room to negotiate overall with other stakeholders in finding the most appropriate plan of arrangement or compromise. However, it may also allow them to entrench their roles and their practices. If creditors have confidence in the oversight and management of the business, there may not be concern. Whether the DIP facility is for administration costs or operational capital during a brief but reasonable period, there is the potential for greater upside value if a viable plan can be developed that receives the requisite creditor support.[54]

The difficulty is where there is a lack of confidence in governance by the vast majority of creditors, but the DIP facility has the effect of entrenching the directors and officers. In some cases, corporate officers negotiate a specific provision that the debtor cannot change management and that such a change would be considered a default of the DIP agreement. Creditors are not given full access to the terms of the agreement and, thus, do not know of the existence of such terms at the point that the court endorses the DIP agreement.[55]

---

[53] Janis Sarra, "Governance and Control: The Role of Debtor-in-Possession Financing under the *CCAA*", *Annual Review of Insolvency Law, 2004* (Toronto: Carswell, 2005) 119-172.

[54] *Ibid.*

[55] *Ibid.*

In *Stelco Inc.*, an unexplored issue was what may have been the pressure on the debtor under the DIP financing agreement to extract wage and pension concessions in order to meet the terms of the DIP financing agreement.

The control issue in respect of DIP lenders arises because the market for such lenders continues to be thin. Canadian based DIP lenders are still not that common, except where the lender is a pre-filing creditor. More traditional operating lenders in Canada have not moved aggressively into the DIP lending market, notwithstanding the super-priority charge granted in most cases. U.S. lenders can be cautious about entry into the market because they are accustomed to a rule-based U.S. insolvency framework. More recently, traditional pre-filing lenders are selling their debt, rather than seeking remedies under insolvency law. Another factor may be that there continues to be a stigma in Canada associated with firm failure or bankruptcy. The lack of a healthy market for DIP lending could be due to a combination of these factors.

The nature of workout financing in Canada is increasingly similar to capital movements in the United States. Karen Gross has observed that the U.S. lending market has shifted in recent years, and that there has been an enormous development in the bond market, particularly in unsecured high yield debt, as well as a robust secondary market for distressed debt.[56] These lenders have a much more active role in Chapter 11 proceedings, and, hence, debtors today must deal with an array of new entities and new financial products, and while some vulture funds may favour speed and liquidity, other creditors may support longer term strategies.[57] Gross suggests that the new players in a Chapter 11 proceeding are those entities that are increasingly interested in acquiring the assets of the debtor in order to combine them with the assets of healthier companies or put them to other higher uses, observing that: "these asset-purchasers exercise real power in Chapter 11 cases as the prices they are willing to pay and the conditions upon what they purchase affect the outcome of the Chapter 11 case and define the surviving entity, if there is one that survives". Hence, it is often the asset purchasers, rather than the secured creditors, that exercise control in the Chapter 11 workout.

a. Overreach

A recent pattern is that Canadian courts grant the DIP financing order and then reduce it under the come-back clause, causing, in some cases, needless and costly court appearances. The cost may not be so great when measured against what is at stake. However, there has been some unwillingness by courts to change orders under the come-back clause, and this can result in prejudice to parties. Parties must be prepared to use the come-back clause, and the courts must be more willing to consider it, particularly where little information was available during the initial hearing to

---

[56] Karen Gross, "A Response to J.J. White's Death and Resurrection of Secured Credit: Finding Some Trees but Missing the Forest" (2004) 12 Am. Bankr. Inst. L. Rev. 203 at 207-210.

[57] *Ibid.* at 209-210.

grant the order.[58] A distinction needs to be made between the need for an immediate stay order and any urgent need for DIP financing. There should be careful scrutiny as to what is needed until creditors can reasonably be given notice, and what is needed in the short term "to keep the lights on", but not required until creditors have had the opportunity to consider their position and make their submissions to the court.[59]

There is a growing practice in Canada of arranging DIP financing in an amount far in excess of what the debtor corporation anticipates needing, ostensibly to increase market confidence and provide creditors with some assurance that their post-filing claims will be met. However, the size of the DIP facility also allows for increased up-front fees, higher costs associated with heightened reporting requirements to the DIP lender, and, arguably, more control elicited as a function of providing the DIP financing.[60] As the market for DIP financing increases, the competition means that the margin on a DIP facility itself is not that great, but the DIP lender makes its real profit on the up-front fees. Creditors should be afforded the opportunity to assess the amount of the DIP facility, the fee structure and the control elicited in the DIP financing agreement as a condition of financing. The key question is how to maintain the flexibility of the current regime while ensuring the integrity of the decision-making process in respect of DIP financing and other priority charges.

Ultimately, the key question is whether there is a viable financing alternative. Most DIP lenders will want similar protections in exchange for advancing capital to the debtor corporation. However, if there is competition to provide the financing, it is less likely that there will be over-reaching. In *Air Canada,* there was great concern about the preference issue, but no financing alternative emerged and the court was never asked to rule on the appropriateness of the provisions.

5. Cross-collateralization

Cross-collateralization refers to using a DIP priority charge to secure pre-filing claims. The *Air Canada CCAA* proceeding marked yet another stage of development in DIP financing in Canada in that the court approved cross-collateralization. The DIP lender General Electric Capital Canada Inc. (GE) was able to bootstrap subordinated claims through the granting of the DIP facility for US$700 million, the largest DIP facility in Canadian history.[61] This was particularly significant in an industry with relatively few hard assets and a potentially soft customer base. Under the DIP financing arrangement, GE secured performance of pre-filing obligations owed under aircraft leases to its affiliated company GE Capital Aviation Services

---

[58] *Ibid.*

[59] *Royal Oak Mines Inc., Re* (1999) , 1999 CarswellOnt 1067, [1999] O.J. No. 1364 (Ont. Gen. Div. [Commercial List]).

[60] Janis Sarra, "Governance and Control: The Role of Debtor-in-Possession Financing under the *CCAA*", *Annual Review of Insolvency Law, 2004* (Toronto: Carswell, 2005) 119-172.

[61] *Air Canada, Re* (2003), 2003 CarswellOnt 1220 (Ont. S.C.J. [Commercial List]).

Inc., in addition to the security on the DIP facility itself. This cross-collateralization thus enhanced the position of a subordinated lender in terms of the priorities of claims. The leases would not have been fully covered under a liquidation and, hence, the affiliated company was at risk of losing part of its claims, as the deficiency would rank *pari passu* with other unsecured creditors. By cross-collateralizing 22 of the 100 aircraft leased, these claims now ranked in priority to unsecured creditors with the endorsement of the court.

The Court in *Air Canada* also insulated GE and GE Capital Aviation from any preference claim in the event that Air Canada became bankrupt. There were no objecting parties before the court because they recognized the reality of the need for a vote of confidence in the debtor and because there was a lack of co-ordination between the junior creditors. This worked to the debtor and DIP lender's advantage and, hence, the preference issues were not fully considered. The GE order was somewhat controversial among unsecured creditors, just as similar attempts to cross-collateralize have been controversial in the United States. In part, this is because such a transaction could be considered a preference under the *BIA*, absent a court order and in the event of a failure of the restructuring effort.[62]

The *Air Canada* DIP facility has created new impetus for DIP lenders to seek to expand their security and their control rights. It will be interesting to observe whether or not the court grants such rights in other circumstances. If cross-collateralization becomes a practice in Canada, it will create new incentives for creditors lower in the hierarchy of claims to consider offering DIP financing as a means to better secure their claims, which, in turn, could reduce the risk of premature liquidation and enhance the possibility of a going-concern plan. Equally, however, it may allow preferences that would not otherwise be allowed, negating the public-policy purposes underlying preference protections.[63] It is also likely to create new incentives for existing senior lenders to offer DIP financing as a means of preventing such shifting of priorities. Hence, cross-collateralization may be a double-edged development, and further cases are required to understand their impact on *CCAA* proceedings. At minimum, the courts should rigorously scrutinize the implications of any cross-collateralization in terms of the overall objectives of the *CCAA*, particularly in the absence of specific statutory language addressing this issue.[64]

---

[62] In *Air Canada*, the court may well have assessed the preference nature of the cross-collateralization, but no creditor brought a motion before it seeking to set aside that aspect of the DIP financing arrangement.

[63] Janis Sarra, "Governance and Control: The Role of Debtor-in-Possession Financing under the *CCAA*", *Annual Review of Insolvency Law, 2004* (Toronto: Carswell, 2005) 119-172.

[64] Air Canada also secured a DIP facility of $350 million from the Canadian Imperial Bank of Commerce (CIBC). CIBC had contracted with Air Canada for a lengthy period for the purchase of Aeroplan frequent flyer points for distribution to holders of one of its credit cards (Aerogold). This contract was repudiated by Air Canada and the claims for damages were unsecured claims against the debtor corporation. During the *CCAA* proceeding, Air Canada and CIBC negotiated a revised contract in which Air Canada received larger payments for each frequent flyer point and a $350 million DIP facility. Air Canada could repay amounts owing under the DIP facility by issuing Aeroplan points, and by May 2004 the entire amount of the DIP facility had been repaid by the supply of points. In considering whether to sanction this arrangement, which normally would be an unsecured claim, the

In *Air Canada*, no draws were made on the DIP facility in the first six months, and only US$243 million of the total US$700 million approved by the court was drawn after the first year in *CCAA* proceedings.[65] There may be incentive effects associated with granting such a large DIP facility when the debtor corporation is unlikely to need the full amount. The size of the DIP facility can enhance marketplace confidence, but huge standby fees can be prejudicial to creditors, and, hence, a point of inquiry is precisely how much DIP financing is required to secure that confidence.

Where there is a non-arm's length DIP lender, there is a risk that it will use the terms of the DIP financing agreement to extend liability protection for its directors well beyond what should reasonably be expected. Arguably, this is what occurred in the *Teleglobe* case.[66] BCE was a DIP lender that was non-arm's length, in the sense that it was a pre-filing lender and had BCE directors as nominees on the Teleglobe board. BCE's refusal to provide further financing as a pre-existing lender was a contributing factor in causing the firm's failure. In providing the DIP financing, BCE sought to insulate the directors that were cross-listed between BCE and Teleglobe by insisting on extremely broad releases to cover any of the directors' actions. Combined with the fact that it sought priority for the DIP facility, the conflicts of interest are apparent.[67]

6. Access to Information Regarding the Terms

One difficulty in recent DIP facilities is that the debtor has signed confidentiality agreements with respect to the terms of the DIP financing arrangement. Creditors are often prohibited from viewing these terms, even though, as suggested above, the DIP lender may be extracting control terms that are contrary to the public policy objectives of the *CCAA*.

In other instances, creditors are given access, but are required to sign overly broad confidentiality statements. For democratic organizations, such as trade unions, the

court ordered a market solicitation process and, when satisfied, issued an order endorsing the arrangement, providing protection that the new Aerogold agreement could not be repudiated by Air Canada, and granting CIBC a charge over the new agreement: *Air Canada, Re* (May 14, 2003), Doc. 03-CL-4932, [2003] O.J. No. 2267 (Ont. S.C.J. [Commercial List]); see also *Air Canada, Re* (2003), [2003] O.J. No. 1617, 2003 CarswellOnt 1662 (Ont. S.C.J. [Commercial List]). As Huff and Rogers have observed, this order provided CIBC some assurances in respect of the DIP facility and provided Air Canada with working capital during the *CCAA* proceeding without impairing its future liquidity by having to commit to future onerous payments; P. Huff and L. Rogers, "Fortune Favours the Bold: Lending in a *CCAA* Proceeding and Priority Charges to Facilitate Restructurings" (2004) 16 Comm. Insol, R. 57, 2004 C.C.I.R. Lexis 10 at 5.

[65] The substantive purpose was to create market stability, given that, at the time, Air Canada had just survived the SARS crisis, and the war in Iraq had commenced.

[66] *In the matter of the Companies' Creditors Arrangement Act and Teleglobe Inc.* (May 15, 2002), Doc. 02-CL-4528 (Ont. S.C.J. [Commercial List]).

[67] For a discussion of the differences between Canadian and U.S. DIP financing, see Janis Sarra, "Governance and Control: The Role of Debtor-in-Possession Financing under the *CCAA*", *Annual Review of Insolvency Law, 2004* (Toronto: Carswell, 2005) 119-172.

inability to disclose information to their members in order to be accountable to them for positions that they are taking in negotiations, creates unnecessary conflicts in the workout process. To date, the courts have not yet issued a judgment dealing with this recognition of the commercial reality of different stakeholders and their varied accountability structures.

7. Drip DIPs and Accountability

More recently, Canadian courts have granted "Drip DIPs" that require the debtor to come before the court on notice to creditors each time it seeks to draw down another tranche of funds. The only exposure of the DIP lender is the amount already advanced, and creditors have more input, and hopefully more information, on which to assess their positions as the process unfolds. Gradual release of funds in the first 30 days or few months could generate a higher degree of accountability.

Drip DIPs frequently are structured so that the debtor can draw down according to an anticipated schedule; hence it is not necessary to come back before the court if there is no deviation from the schedule that would have adverse consequences for other creditors.

Andrew Kent, Alex MacFarlane, and Adam Maerov have observed that the introduction of "Drip DIPs" may address the problem of excessively large DIP facilities. Kent *et al* point to the Drip DIP facilities in the *Ivaco* and *Royal Oak* cases as examples of where the debtor corporation is permitted to draw down only on a portion of an unused DIP facility that is required for its continued operations during the restructuring process.[68] In order to access another tranche of the DIP facility, the debtor must apply to the court on notice to all affected stakeholders. They suggest that this may offer one means of ensuring that stakeholders are provided with timely information of the financing requirements of the debtor and the opportunity to provide their views to the court on the necessity of the draw down, as well as acting as a temper on any managerial slack that has arisen from a generous DIP facility.[69]

8. Post-petition Trade Credit and Other Post-Filing Charges

The court can order a range of post-filing charges, often on specific assets, as a means to protect trade suppliers and other creditors that continue to supply goods and services and are essential to the successful workout of the debtor company.

While the court cannot compel a supplier to continue to extend credit to the debtor during a *CCAA* proceeding, the court can protect trade suppliers that choose to supply goods or credit during the stay period by granting them a charge on the assets

[68] Andrew Kent, Alex MacFarlane and Adam Maerow, "Who is in Control? A Commentary on Canadian DIP Lending Practices", May 2004.

[69] *Ibid.*

of the debtor that will rank ahead of other claims.[70] While section 11.3 of the *CCAA* states that no stay of proceedings can have the effect of prohibiting a person from requiring immediate payment for goods, services or the use of leased or licensed property, or requiring the further advance of money or credit, trade suppliers were often continuing credit only to find that they had lost further assets during the workout period because of their priority in the hierarchy of claims. Hence the practice of post-petition trade credit priority charges developed, first recognized in Alberta.

The court has held that if such a post-petition charge is made, the terms and scope of the charge should be clearly defined, including whether the costs of repairing and maintaining leased equipment are covered by the priority charge in addition to the lease payments.[71] A post-filing charge created by a court must be done clearly and with specificity. A charge directing the vendors of a debtor company to complete the sale transaction in accordance with the terms of an agreement of purchase and sale will not suffice to create a charge in favour of the purchaser of a debtor company in priority to secured creditors where, after adjustments, it transpired that the purchaser had made an over-payment with respect to the purchase price.[72]

In *Air Canada*, the Court held that the stay did not prohibit a lessor from requiring payment for the ongoing use of a leased airplane; however, in keeping with commercial reasonableness and to prevent one lessor from obtaining an ongoing priority that would be unwarranted *vis à vis* other lessor creditors, a reconciliation obligation was split between the pre-filing and post-filing obligations of the debtor.[73]

The court can also lift the *CCAA* stay to allow a creditor to be paid where the creditor can show that without payment of its account, it would have to terminate a service that was essential for carrying out the debtor's business.[74]

In *Air Canada*, the Court held that in exceptional circumstances, the court may permit payments to unsecured creditors during a *CCAA* process if they are critical to the debtor being able to continue its business.[75]

9. Allocating the Costs of DIP Financing

The court has provided direction on how the costs of a *CCAA* proceeding should be allocated. The Alberta Court of Queen's Bench in *Hunters Trailer & Marine Ltd.*

---

[70] *Westar Mining Ltd., Re* (1992), 14 C.B.R. (3d) 88 (B.C. S.C.); *Smoky River Coal Ltd., Re* (2000), 19 C.B.R. (4th) 281 (Alta. Q.B.), reversed (2001), 28 C.B.R. (4th) 127 (Alta. C.A.).

[71] *Smoky River Coal Ltd., Re* (2001), 28 C.B.R. (4th) 127 (Alta. C.A.); see also *Mosaic Group Inc., Re* (2004), 3 C.B.R. (5th) 40 (Ont. S.C.J.).

[72] *Mosaic Group Inc., Re* (2004), [2004] O.J. No. 2323, 2004 CarswellOnt 2254, 3 C.B.R. (5th) 40 (Ont. S.C.J.).

[73] *Air Canada, Re* (2004), 47 C.B.R. (4th) 182 (Ont. S.C.J. [Commercial List]) [TA lessor's motion for rental payments].

[74] *Quintette Coal Ltd.* v. *Nippon Steel Corp.* (1990), 80 C.B.R. (N.S.) 98 (B.C. S.C.).

[75] *Air Canada, Re* (2003), 45 C.B.R. (4th) 163 (Ont. C.A.).

held that all of the major secured creditors should be liable for a portion of the *CCAA* costs.[76] The Court held that while some creditors who are less than fully secured stand to benefit the most from a successful reorganization, equity informs the decision to be made by the court. Each case must be judged on its facts, and the court found that it was equitable in the instant case that creditors share the risk. However, the Court held that equity did not call for an equal allocation of costs; rather, equitable as opposed to equal treatment is the objective of *CCAA* proceedings. The Court observed that all creditors can point to costs that cannot be attributed to assets over which they hold security; however, the DIP financing is to meet the urgent needs of the company during the sorting-out period, and it was for the benefit or potential benefit of all creditors. The court's recognition of the need for an equitable allocation is aimed at a mid-ground between one creditor bearing all the costs and all creditors sharing equally. The notion that financing is a potential benefit to all creditors is critical to the equitable allocation of costs.

In allocating *CCAA* costs, including the monitor's professional fees and amounts advanced by DIP lenders, the British Columbia Court of Appeal held that an order issued in a *CCAA* proceeding contravenes section 11.3(b) of the *CCAA*, which states that no order shall have the effect of requiring the further advance of money or credit, if such order provides that a secured creditor seeking to recover the asset against which it holds security must, as a condition of such recovery, pay to the receiver the amount of certain costs incurred in the *CCAA* proceedings allocated to such asset by the receiver where such payment will result in the creditor paying funds in excess of the value of its security interest.[77]

With respect to sharing the cost of primed charges, the British Columbia Supreme Court in *Western Express Air Lines Inc.*, dismissed an application by a creditor for a declaration that an aircraft lessor was required to share in certain charges created during the course of *CCAA* proceedings as the aircraft leases were true leases not sales financing.[78] The Court found that the charges under the *CCAA* order could not attach to the aircraft lessors as the lessors were not creditors of the debtor and there was no basis for them to bear a portion of the existing charges.[79] Hence the characterization of the lease will be a factor on which the court determines cost sharing in a *CCAA* proceeding.

Jean-Daniel Breton has observed that in the *Western Express Air Lines* judgment, the result appears to depend on whether a lease is a true lease or a security instrument, as this will be a determining factor in assessing whether the lessor will be required

---

[76] *Hunters Trailer & Marine Ltd., Re* (2001), [2001] A.J. No. 1638, 2001 CarswellAlta 1636 (Alta. Q.B.) at para. 15.

[77] *New Skeena Forest Products Inc., Re* (2005), 2005 CarswellBC 705, 9 C.B.R. (5th) 278 (B.C. C.A.).

[78] *Western Express Air Lines Inc., Re* (2005), 2005 CarswellBC 72 (B.C. S.C.). The leases did fall under section 3(c) of the *PPSA* (British Columbia), which deems a lease for a term of more than one year to be a security agreement for limited purposes; however, the Court held that this deemed security interest does not mean that a secured creditor that takes a security interest in the leased goods can claim priority over the lessor. The security interest attaches only to the interest of the lessee.

[79] *Ibid.*

to share in certain charges created during the course of *CCAA* proceedings, i.e. whether the lessor is liable to see the leased assets used as collateral for the DIP financing and thereby see its position primed by the DIP lender.[80] He argues that the result may be different depending on the manner in which a lease is characterized in the personal property legislation of each province. Thus, if the debtor has a place of business in several provinces, it seems possible that a lessor could see its leased assets primed in one province but not in another, in respect of leases that otherwise have identical language. Breton suggests that the problem is compounded in Québec, since it would seem that as a result of a recent decision of the Supreme Court of Canada, a lease would never be assimilated to a financing arrangement.[81]

III. LEGISLATIVE REFORM

In 2002, the Joint Task Force on Business and Insolvency Law Reform suggested that the *CCAA* provide that 1) unsecured claims for goods and services provided post-filing have priority over pre-filing unsecured claims, 2) after filing for *CCAA* protection, the debtor should not obtain additional credit from any person without first giving appropriate notice of the proceeding, 3) the court shall not permit a *CCAA* case to continue if it is not satisfied that adequate arrangements are in place for payment of post-filing goods and services, and 4) the court has jurisdiction to order any existing critical suppliers of goods and services to supply the debtor during the reorganization proceeding on normal pricing terms so long as effective arrangements assure payment.[82]

The proposed amendments to the *CCAA* in Chapter 47 codify DIP financing provisions and allow other post-filing charges, essentially codifying existing practice, but directing the court's exercise of discretion more clearly. If Chapter 47 is proclaimed in force, section 11.2 of the *CCAA* will specify:

> *Interim financing*
>
> 11.2 (1) A court may, on application by a debtor company, make an order, on any conditions that the court considers appropriate, declaring that the property of the company is subject to a security or charge in favour of any person specified in the order who agrees to lend to the company an amount that is approved by the court as being required by the company, having regard to its cash-flow statement,
>
> (a) for the period of 30 days following the initial application in respect of the

---

[80] Jean-Daniel Breton, Comment, June 2006, on file with author.

[81] *Ibid.*, citing *Lefebvre, Re* (2004), 2004 CarswellQue 2831 (S.C.C.). Breton observes that the same difficulty may exist as relates to conditional sale agreements, or instalment sales under the *Québec Civil Code*, in view of the findings of the Supreme Court of Canada in *Ouellet, Re* (2004), 2004 CarswellQue 2833 (S.C.C.).

[82] Joint Task Force on Business Insolvency Law Reform Report (March 15, 2002) at 18, online: The Insolvency Institute of Canada website http://www.insolvency.ca/dhtml/en/page/papers.q/indexType$Topic/indexID$10/a$index.html at 9-11 (Recommendations 12-14, 17).

company if the order is made on the initial application in respect of the company; or

(b) for any period specified in the order if the order is made on any application in respect of a company other than the initial application and notice has been given to the secured creditors likely to be affected by the security or charge.

Restriction

(2) An order may be made under subsection (1) in respect of any period after the period of 30 days following the initial application in respect of the company only if the monitor has reported to the court under paragraph 23(1)(b) that the company's cash-flow statement is reasonable.

Rank

(3) The court may specify in the order that the security or charge ranks in priority over the claim of any secured creditor of the company.

Other orders

(4) The court may specify in the order that the security or charge ranks in priority over any security or charge arising from a previous order made under subsection (1) only with the consent of the person in whose favour the previous order was made.

Factors to be considered

(5) In deciding whether to make an order referred to in subsection (1), the court must consider, among other things,

(a) the period during which the company is expected to be subject to proceedings under this Act;
(b) how the company is to be governed during the proceedings;
(c) whether the company's management has the confidence of its major creditors;
(d) whether the loan will enhance the prospects of a viable compromise or arrangement being made in respect of the company;
(e) the nature and value of the company's assets; and
(f) whether any creditor will be materially prejudiced as a result of the company's continued operations.[83]

---

[83] The Government has announced its intention to further clarify the notice provisions, specifically, that it will table amendments in 2007 whereby an application for interim financing must be made "on notice to the secured creditors who are likely to be affected by the security or charge" under s. 11.2; and changing the language of s. 11(5)(b) to read: "how the company's business and financial affairs are to be managed during the proceeding" and other proposed changes; *Notice of Ways and Means Motion to introduce an Act to amend the Bankruptcy and Insolvency Act, the Companies' Creditors Arrangement Act, the Wage Earners Protection Act and Chapter 47 of the Statutes of Canada, 2005*, (December 8, 2006, Library of Parliament).

Hence the amendments provide some direction to the court in the exercise of its discretion. They also codify the ability to prime the financing over pre-existing lenders, again codifying current practice but enshrining the provisions in the legislation to address any residual concerns about the court's jurisdiction to make such orders. It allows the court to approve a financing charge for up to 30 days where there has not been notice, or a longer period, where notice has been provided and the monitor has reported to the court on the finances of the debtor. The language codifies the court's ability to prime the charges and it codifies factors to be taken into consideration, without fettering the court's discretion to take into account other factors.

IV. ASSET SALES DURING THE *CCAA* PROCESS

Asset sales can be used to finance a restructuring through a sale of some of the assets to facilitate a going forward solution for the rest of the debtor company or they can be the final outcome of a *CCAA* proceeding.

In *Red Cross*, the Court approved the sale of assets of the national blood program pending development of a proposed plan.[84] The proposed sale arose out of governmental and public pressure to ensure the safe delivery of blood and blood products across Canada.[85] The Court held that it had jurisdiction to make the order, both in its power to impose terms and conditions in the granting of a stay under the *CCAA* and based on its inherent jurisdiction to fill gaps in legislation to give effect to the objectives of the *CCAA*.[86] In undertaking the balancing of interests and prejudices on the sale motion, the Court examined expert evidence, the assumptions underlying the proposals, the positions of key stakeholders such as the federal, provincial and territorial governments, employees, health care providers and the tort (transfusion) claimants. The Court held that the appropriate criteria for determining whether to approve a sale of assets included:

- whether the debtor has made a sufficient effort to obtain the best price and has not acted improvidently;
- consideration of the interests of parties;
- the efficacy and integrity of the process by which offers had been obtained; and
- whether there has been any unfairness in the working out of the process.

---

[84] *Canadian Red Cross Society / Société Canadienne de la Croix-Rouge, Re* (1998), 5 C.B.R. (4th) 299 (Ont. Gen. Div. [Commercial List]).

[85] A Commission of Inquiry had previously examined the blood system in Canada. Mr. Justice Horace Krever in the Final Report of the Commission recommended the immediate development of a new blood system in order to protect public safety and the creation of a no-fault scheme for compensation of blood related injury. Mr. Justice Krever, *Commission of Inquiry on the Blood System in Canada, Final Report* (Ottawa: Government of Canada), Part IV at 1030, 1044.

[86] *In the Matter of the Companies' Creditors Arrangement Act, Canadian Red Cross/La scoieté canadienne de la croix-rouge* (August 19, 1999), Court File No. 98-CL-002970 (Ont. S.C.J.) Blair J. (Endorsement), at para. 21.

These tests were adopted from the tests that the court applies in a receivership to a sale of assets, as set out in *Royal Bank* v. *Soundair Corp.*[87] The Court in *Red Cross* concluded that the value that would be recovered with the sale, 169 million dollars, was as close to the maximum likely to be obtained. After the debt to the bank was paid and claims of other creditors defrayed, there would still be 70-100 million dollars in a trust fund to satisfy transfusion claims. The Court considered whether the sale was fair and reasonable in all the circumstances and engaged in a balancing of the interests at risk and considered the prejudice to all stakeholders affected by the decision.

The Ontario Superior Court of Justice held that it was appropriate to re-open a sales process for a very short time frame to consider further offers for a debtor company's assets under the *CCAA* where there was the potential that a new offer would lead to a much-improved return for the unsecured creditors than an existing firm offer. The Court distinguished the decision in *Royal Bank* v. *Soundair Corp.* in the circumstances, given there was the potential for a much-improved return for unsecured creditors. The Court also found that although there was a risk to the estate of further costs and time in connection with the re-opening of the sales process, such risks were warranted in the circumstances since the unsecured creditors, as the stakeholders who would bear such risks, were prepared to assume the risks.[88]

In *Boutiques San Francisco Inc.*, the Québec Superior Court considered the following factors in determining whether to approve a sale of assets: the bank syndicate supported the sale; the monitor had advised the court that the offer was adequate and acceptable; the debtor had received no other offer; the offer was greater than the liquidation value of the company; the sale would result in continued employment for most employees; and it represented the best price possible after having conducted a sale process.[89] In the same *CCAA* proceeding, considering a request to authorize alienation of certain assets, the Court observed that one of the goals of the *CCAA* is to encourage an orderly and fair process. The Court held that the debtor and monitor had put in place a reasonable process for the selection of offers aimed at an efficient, equitable, transparent and rapid search for the best result to the ultimate benefit of all creditors. While a competitive bid offered a better price with more conditions, the Court held that price is not the only guide, and on balance, the Court approved the application and authorized the debtor to conclude an agreement of lease and sale of fixed assets.[90]

In a third judgment in *Boutiques San Francisco Inc.*, the Court held that a sale process was reasonable, sufficient and equitable in that the market was canvassed, the received offers were analyzed and those with insufficient price or unacceptable financial conditions were rejected, and an offer was selected subject to certain conditions being met. Overall, the Court was satisfied that the offer accepted was

---

[87] *Royal Bank* v. *Soundair Corp.* (1991), 7 C.B.R. (3d) 1 (Ont. C.A.).

[88] *1587930 Ontario Ltd., Re* (2006), 2006 CarswellOnt 6419 (Ont. S.C.J. [Commercial List]).

[89] *Boutiques San Francisco Inc., Re* (2004), 2004 CarswellQue 10918 (Que. S.C.).

[90] *Boutiques San Francisco Inc., Re* (2004), 2004 CarswellQue 753, 5 C.B.R. (5th) 197 (Que. S.C.).

the highest price and most advantageous conditions, observing that major creditors supported the sale; almost all of the employees would remain employed under the successor company; and the debtor could continue to operate without the sizeable weekly losses that it was incurring.[91]

In *Skydome Corp.*, when an offer was made for purchase during the *CCAA* proceeding, the Court ordered the monitor to conduct an auction bidding process, to determine whether this or another offer was the most appropriate for sale of the debtor company.[92]

The British Columbia Supreme Court held that it is appropriate to exercise its inherent jurisdiction and sanction a delay of the calling of a creditors' meeting to approve a debtor company's plan of arrangement where it is necessary to ensure that there is enough time to allow for the sale and replacement of the key operating assets of the debtor company in accordance with the plan. The Court found that the purpose of the *CCAA* was to preserve the debtor as a viable operation and that the preservation and reorganization could only take place if the creditors' meeting was delayed and that the "status quo" could only be maintained by ensuring that the debtor had equipment to operate its business.[93]

The court has exercised its discretion to refuse to impose conditions on a court-approved sale process and has allowed a monitor to proceed with an offer, even where a new offer arising following the bid deadline could have preserved jobs.[94] The Court held that to rule otherwise would amount to unfairness in the working out of the sale process to the detriment of the current purchaser and the secured creditors; interfere with the efficacy and integrity of the sale process; and prefer the interests of one party over others. In determining the appropriateness of the sale process, the Court considered whether the monitor made a sufficient effort to get the best price and did not act improvidently; the interests of all parties; and whether there was any unfairness in the process.

There can be *CCAA* plans that are essentially a sale of assets or sale of the business as a whole. These can be conducted by a court-appointed officer, such as an interim receiver, or they can also be conducted by the debtor itself in a *CCAA* proceeding. Debtor corporations can also seek approval under the *CCAA* of a pre-packaged plan, which means that the debtor has already conducted a canvass of the market and has negotiated a purchase plan or other plan of compromise and arrangement that already has the support of the majority of creditors at the time that the debtor files for *CCAA* protection. Pre-packaged plans can be helpful where the debtor is trying to preserve customer goodwill or other market value and time is of the essence in working out its financial distress. However, equally, a pre-packaged sale of assets plan is not

[91] *Boutiques San Francisco Inc., Re* (27 février 2004), no C.S. Montréal 500-11-022070-037, EYB 2004-55240 (Que. S.C.).

[92] *Skydome Corp., Re* (1998), 16 C.B.R. (4th) 125 (Ont. Gen. Div. [Commercial List]).

[93] *Hawkair Aviation Services Ltd., Re*, 2006 CarswellBC 1637 (B.C. S.C. [In Chambers]).

[94] *Tiger Brand Knitting Co., Re* (2005), 2005 CarswellOnt 1240 (Ont. S.C.J.), leave to appeal refused (2005), 2005 CarswellOnt 8387 (Ont. C.A.).

necessarily subject to the same scrutiny of process that a public asset sale process is, and hence the court must be satisfied that the sale plan is maximizing value for creditors.

In general, a court will accept a proposed sale process under the *CCAA* when it has been recommended by a monitor and is supported by the major creditors. The Court in *Ivaco* held that its discretion to vary the process should be exercised only in exceptional circumstances.[95] The Ontario Superior Court of Justice has held that there is no need to appoint an interim receiver to carry out a sale of substantially all the assets during a *CCAA* proceeding; and prior to a plan being filed, the court can, after a proper call for tenders, approve a sale by the debtor directly to the purchaser where a sale is the only viable alternative for the debtor.[96]

This approach can be contrasted with *Royal Bank of Canada* v. *Fracmaster Ltd.*, which was discussed in chapter 3, where, during *CCAA* proceedings, the Court declined to order a meeting of creditors to vote on a debtor's plan that called for a sale of assets under a sale process that had been conducted by the debtor. Instead, the Court appointed a receiver/manager to conduct the sale. The Court expressed concern about the use of the *CCAA* to liquidate assets of insolvent companies that are not part of a plan that results in some continuation of a company as a going concern.[97]

Hence, control by the debtor of a sale of assets process is not completely uncontested, given that, unlike a court-appointed officer who has an obligation to ensure the process is fair and maximizing value, the debtor can have conflicting interests in the sale process.

1. Stalking Horse Bids

Stalking horse processes under the *CCAA* are a relatively new phenomenon. The term "stalking horse" comes originally from using a horse or a painted screen of a horse to serve as a screen to camouflage hunters as they stalked their prey.[98] In the insolvency context, it is used to signify a situation where the debtor makes an agreement with a potential bidder for a sale of the debtor's assets or business, and that agreement forms part of a process whereby an auction or tendering process is conducted to see if there is a better and higher bidder that will result in greater returns to creditors. The premise is that the stalking horse has undertaken considerable due diligence in determining the value of the debtor corporation, and other

[95] *Ivaco Inc., Re* (2004), 2004 CarswellOnt 2397, 3 C.B.R. (5th) 33 (Ont. S.C.J. [Commercial List]).

[96] *Consumers Packaging Inc., Re* (2001), 27 C.B.R. (4th) 194 (Ont. S.C.J. [Commercial List]), leave to appeal refused (2001), 27 C.B.R. (4th) 197 (Ont. C.A.).

[97] *Royal Bank of Canada* v. *Fracmaster Ltd.* (1999), 1999 CarswellAlta 539, [1999] A.J. No. 675 (Alta. C.A.).

[98] D.F. Cohen & D.S. Kolesar, "Canadian Perspective on the Chapter 11 Stalking Horse Bid Process", (2004) 21 Nat. Insol. Review 25.

potential bidders can rely, to an extent, on the value attached by that bidder based on that due diligence.

"Stalking horse auction" processes have been used in the U.S. in many asset sales under the U.S. *Bankruptcy Code.* Canadian courts have endorsed such processes in cross-border proceedings. In an auction, the preliminary bid by the stalking horse bidder is disclosed to the market and becomes the base amount that parties can then outbid, driving up the price and hence the value to meet creditors' claims.

The stalking horse bidder in a *CCAA* proceeding enters the process knowing that it may not be the eventual purchaser. Hence it negotiates a price for its participation and the cost of its due diligence activities, usually in the form of a "break fee", which it will receive if it is not ultimately successful in its bid for the debtor company. In this sense, it is similar to a white knight in a takeover transaction, in that the size of the break fee must be large enough to be auction generating and small enough not to be auction inhibiting.

The U.S. courts have determined that a break fee of 1-2% is reasonable.[99] Although the caselaw in the U.S. on approval of fees is uneven, the court has held that it will take the following factors into account in determining whether to approve a break fee: whether the fee correlated with a maximization of value to the estate; whether the request is arm's length; the degree of stakeholder support; whether the proposed fee is a fair and reasonable percentage of the proposed purchase price; any potential chilling effect on the market; the existence of safeguards; and whether there is an adverse impact on any opposing unsecured creditors.[100]

As noted above, in a Canadian proceeding, the court uses the tests in *Royal Bank* v. *Soundair Corp.* as factors in the consideration of a sale in the context of insolvency proceedings, including a stalking horse proceeding. A stalking horse process can be approved where there is an urgent need to create stability and preserve market confidence in order to conduct a sale in a short time frame.[101]

In Canada, the few stalking horse proceedings that have occurred are more akin to a tendering process. However, as several commentators have pointed out, the lines have become more blurred in respect of the processes.[102] In some cases, there are concurrent processes, where a sale process is being conducted at the same time as the debtor is trying to devise a plan to attract new equity investors as part of a *CCAA*

---

[99] Daniel R. Dowdall and Jane O. Dietrich, "Do Stalking Horses Have a Place in Intra-Canadian Insolvencies?", in Janis Sarra, ed., *Annual Review of Insolvency Law, 2005* (Toronto: Carswell, 2006) at 1-14.

[100] *Hupp Industries, Re,* 140 B.R. 191 (Bankr. N.D. Ohio, 1992). Dowdall and Dietrich report that there are also topping fees, overbid increment protections and in some cases, rights of first refusal; however, the courts in some cases have been reluctant to grant these economic incentives, *ibid.* at 7-8.

[101] Daniel R. Dowdall and Jane O. Dietrich, "Do Stalking Horses Have a Place in Intra-Canadian Insolvencies?", in Janis Sarra, ed., *Annual Review of Insolvency Law, 2005* (Toronto: Carswell, 2006) at 2.

[102] *Ibid.*

workout.[103] In addition to approving break fees, the courts can also approve a stay fee, which serves as an incentive for the stalking horse bidder to leave its bid open for a certain period of time.[104]

Daniel Dowdall and Jane Dietrich have observed that the increasing number of stalking horse proceedings that are conducted by the debtor and not a neutral court-appointed officer raise new concerns about the process.[105] First, the stalking horse can exert considerable control over timelines, making them very tight such that other bidders do not have a meaningful opportunity to undertake their due diligence. Second, stalking horse bidders may insist on restrictive terms in respect of who may be treated as a qualified bidder. Third, management has a conflict of interest where they are negotiating key employee retention packages, bonuses or other perquisites; and while these are ostensibly subject to some control in terms of the court's sanctioning process, the tight timeliness may create pressure to approve such plans, even where the court might otherwise have concerns.[106]

There are two recent cases that illustrate some of the issues that arise in a stalking horse type of proceeding, *A&B Sound* and *Stelco Inc.*, both of which are discussed briefly below.[107]

The *A&B Sound CCAA* restructuring was what debtor counsel described as an unintended evolution of a stalking horse sale process, recognizing stalking horse processes for the first time in British Columbia.[108] A&B Sound had a retail business with 800 employees, selling pre-recorded music and high-end consumer electronics products. In 2005, its liabilities exceeded $55 million, and it was experiencing severe financial distress due to stiff market competition and a variety of other factors.[109] What began as an out of court sale process aimed at divestiture, became a *CCAA* process when a large unsecured supplier creditor filed a petition for a receiving order against the debtor. A&B then filed for protection under the *CCAA* in order to be able to complete the sale process. The debtor had quietly canvassed the market for a purchaser, hoping to retain its customer goodwill. Once it filed under the *CCAA*, it hoped to successfully conclude a pre-packaged *CCAA* plan with a bidder, Sun Capital Partners Group. Sun Capital had previously worried about a competitive bidding process and hence had negotiated an exclusive right to negotiate with the debtor for a sale of the business, plus a $500,000 break fee in the event that A&B's

---

[103] An example was the *Stelco* case.

[104] See for example, *Tiger Brand Knitting Co., Re* (2005), 9 C.B.R. (5th) 315 (Ont. S.C.J.), leave to appeal refused (2005), 19 C.B.R. (5th) 53 (Ont. C.A.).

[105] Daniel R. Dowdall and Jane O. Dietrich, "Do Stalking Horses Have a Place in Intra-Canadian Insolvencies?", in Janis Sarra, ed., *Annual Review of Insolvency Law, 2005* (Toronto: Carswell, 2006) at 8.

[106] *Ibid.*

[107] For a full discussion, see Dowdall and Dietrich, *ibid.*, and Michael Fitch and Kibben Jackson, "Face the Music: The *A.&B. Sound CCAA* Proceeding- A Stalking Horse of a Different Colour", in Janis Sarra, ed., *Annual Review of Insolvency Law, 2005* (Toronto: Carswell, 2006) at 15.

[108] Michael Fitch and Kibben Jackson, *ibid.* at 15.

[109] For a full discussion of the facts, see *ibid.*

business was sold to another party or the debtor voluntarily undertook a liquidation of assets.[110]

A&B received the initial *CCAA* stay order, and the debtor developed a somewhat complex but timely strategy to deal with the claims process and bring the matter to creditors for a vote. Essentially, the *CCAA* plan proposed that A&B's business be sold, the secured debt paid in full, and the unsecured creditors were to receive their *pro rata* share of remaining proceeds of sale.[111]

However, when the debtor sought an order from the British Columbia Supreme Court to convene a meeting of creditors to consider and vote on the plan, two potential other bidders sought an extended public sale process. One of the bidders, Best Buy/Future Shop, had declined to participate in the debtor's earlier canvass of the market. The other, Seanix, had negotiated with the debtor during the early market canvass, but discussions had fallen through on the question of financial disclosures of the potential bidder. Seanix and Best Buy/Future Shop both brought motions seeking access to all records and other information concerning A&B's business to which Sun Capital had access during its due diligence process.

The supervising judge granted the order sought by A&B to convene the creditors' meeting, but also granted Seanix the disclosure order, finding that Seanix had previously participated in the market canvass; did not require regulatory approval that would delay the *CCAA* process; and that if Seanix were to subsequently make an offer to purchase the debtor's business, the court could deal with the efficacy of the process on a subsequent application.[112] The judge dismissed the disclosure motion of Best Buy/Future Shop on the basis that it had declined to participate in the early market canvass; and that the required regulatory approvals from the Investment Canada and Competition Bureau would be time consuming and make any offer too conditional for creditors to properly assess.

Seanix did put in an offer on the same terms as Sun Capital, except it increased the purchase price to 70% of book value, 8% higher than Sun Capital, plus a payment of $2.5 million, compared with Sun Capital's $1 million.[113] Hence creditors could compare both offers relatively easily. Essentially, Sun Capital had become the stalking horse, even in a process where it had specifically contracted not to do so

[110] *Ibid.* at 21, 24.

[111] *Ibid.* at 26. The British Columbia Supreme Court was very cooperative in facilitating the process, notwithstanding that it had some novel features, such as a reverse claims process in which creditors were given notice of the amount of their claim and were to file notices only where they disputed the claims; and an *ex parte* order permitting the debtor to bring an application for an order approving the plan for dissemination to creditors prior to receiving an order confirming the debtor's entitlement to protection from creditors. There was a complex process for converting to a *BIA* process and realizing on the sale. *Ibid.* at 21, 22.

[112] *Ibid.* at 25.

[113] *Ibid.* at 28-29.

through the exclusivity provisions. In the end result, the Seanix plan was the one accepted by creditors and at the sanctioning hearing, was effectively uncontested.[114]

Michael Fitch and Kibben Jackson have subsequently observed that with the full benefit of hindsight, Sun Capital may have made a strategic blunder in requiring the break fee at the same time as seeking to maintain exclusive bargaining rights, because the court likely saw the existence of the break fee as its protection in the event its bid was not successful.[115] Another view, however, is that if other parties had come forward, there is some question as to whether Sun Capital's exclusivity would have persuaded the court not to let them bid. Fitch and Jackson observe that in future cases, it would be fairer to all parties if a stalking horse process is explicitly approved at the outset of the *CCAA* proceeding with the cooperation of one potential purchaser and clear directions as to process.

The *Stelco Inc.* case differed in that the parties consciously entered into a stalking horse type of proceeding. Dowdall and Dietrich have observed that the stalking horse process in Stelco was purported to meet an urgent need to create stability within a timeframe that was shorter than normally required for a full sale process, and that in such cases, break fees and other economic incentives are the price for creating stability.[116] In *Stelco Inc.*, the Court approved a bid from Deutsche Bank as a stalking horse bid.[117] Deutsche Bank was a significant bondholder of Stelco. The bid had been generated as a means to assure one of Stelco's largest customers that there was certainty in the debtor emerging as a viable company. While this initial reason was resolved prior to the court's approval of the bid, the court nevertheless approved the bid as a stalking horse process.

Dowdall and Dietrich have observed that the bid in *Stelco Inc.*, contained conditions that stakeholders and one competing bidder had argued could never be fulfilled, specifically, that Stelco and its union enter into a binding collective agreement at one of the facilities where the agreement had expired and that Stelco would continue to enjoy the pension holiday that the government had previously approved and that it not be required to pay down its pension deficiency over time.[118] Ultimately, the stalking horse bid failed because the conditions could not be met.[119]

There are still a number of unresolved policy issues in respect of stalking horse proceedings. In the A&B case, Best Buy/Future Shop was a direct and aggressive competitor of the debtor, and there were serious concerns regarding confidentiality

---

[114] For a detailed description of all the procedural "jockeying", see *ibid.* at 15-36.

[115] *Ibid.* at 35.

[116] Daniel R. Dowdall and Jane O. Dietrich, "Do Stalking Horses Have a Place in Intra-Canadian Insolvencies?", in Janis Sarra, ed., *Annual Review of Insolvency Law, 2005* (Toronto: Carswell, 2006) at 2.

[117] *Stelco Inc., Re* (2004), 2004 CarswellOnt 5076 (Ont. S.C.J. [Commercial List]).

[118] Daniel R. Dowdall and Jane O. Dietrich, "Do Stalking Horses Have a Place in Intra-Canadian Insolvencies?", in Janis Sarra, ed., *Annual Review of Insolvency Law, 2005* (Toronto: Carswell, 2006) at 11.

[119] Stelco eventually emerged from *CCAA* proceedings intact as an operating entity.

that would have become an issue had the court granted the disclosure order. There is also the question of the appropriate level of break fees, and the level that is accepted in the context of Canadian takeover cases would appear too high for situations where the firm is financially distressed. Hence some guidance by the courts would be helpful. There are also control issues in respect of the debtor and the stalking horse bidder, particularly where there is no court-appointed officer, such as a receiver trustee or monitor, conducting the sale process. The potential for exploitation or inappropriate handling of the process needs further consideration. Finally, if the stalking horse bidder can negotiate terms that are impossible to achieve, then the deal will not happen. As has been suggested occurred in *Stelco Inc.*, there is a risk of shifting assets to that bidder in the form of break fees and other incentives without a concomitant financial risk for the bidder.

One suggestion is that the court should, if concerns exist about the completeness or fairness of a stalking horse process, approve the bid only as a stalking horse bid and not as a final agreement, hence creating incentive on the parties to ensure a complete and fair process in order for any bid to be viewed as a final bid.[120]

It is also important to note that corporate officers may have a conflict of interest in such negotiations, particularly where there are salary or retention issues or other incentives being negotiated as part of the mix in the negotiations.

One policy option would be for the court to seek a meaningful opinion from a court-appointed officer as to the fairness and efficacy of the stalking horse process, even where the debtor has carriage of the process. This might inject a level of neutrality or at least an impartial second set of eyes on the process, in order to reduce the inherent conflicts faced by officers of the debtor. This is a common approach in *CCAA* sales. In a *CCAA* proceeding, the court normally relies on reports of the monitor. If the monitor is actively involved in the sale process, it performs a role very similar to a bankruptcy receivership.

V. EXIT FINANCING

Exit financing refers to a loan made to the debtor corporation or other capital raised at the time of implementation of the *CCAA* plan of arrangement and/or compromise. The exit financing is used to repay the DIP lender and provide operating capital post-closing.

Stalking horse proceedings, new injections of equity and a restructured debt configuration are all forms of financing the debtor's exit from *CCAA* proceedings, although they can have very different results in terms of whether a viable entity goes forward. This additional capital must be used in conjunction with pre-filing lenders agreeing to compromise the amount or payment schedules of pre-existing loans.

---

[120] *Ibid.* at 12.

The objective is to ensure that the debtor corporation has sufficient capital post the *CCAA* proceeding to effectively implement its new business plan, governance structure and/or operational changes.

The court can approve a request by the debtor corporation to seek a party that will make an equity investment, and where the parties have agreed on a process to solicit such an investment, the court may hold the parties to the process and refuse an adjournment to consider another potential offer.[121]

The increasing involvement of distressed debt purchasers is significant for the potential to find exit financing. Such financiers can be categorized into three broad types. The first are distressed trading funds. They are looking for a trading event and their objective is a rapid turnaround of their capital investment, with no interest in the outcome of the insolvency proceeding (hence the nickname vulture funds). Any outcome that increases the value of their claims within a short time frame is likely to draw the support of these creditors. Distressed trading funds may also trade a distressed debt numerous times as the value of the security fluctuates in value during a restructuring proceeding. In such instances, there is uncertainty in terms of who are the claimants in a restructuring proceeding at any given moment in time, which may affect the ability to attract exit financing.

The second type of distressed debt purchaser is the hedge fund, in which credit risk is allocated over numerous investments in distressed businesses. While not as focused on instant turnaround of the value of the claim, hedge funds do have monthly or quarterly profit and payment obligations that create particular pressure to push the debtor to complete the insolvency proceeding and payout the value of the claim. Here again, depending on the nature and type of claim, there can be considerable pressure to move to rapid liquidation of the firm's assets in order to ensure timely payment of claims. Hedge funds, by their nature, structure their purchase of debt so that if there is a call on the capital of the fund, they have the liquidity to meet the call.

The third, private equity funds, are increasingly involved in exit financing. Private equity funds frequently have a longer time horizon for their investments than other distressed debt purchasers, often 5-7 years, and are interested in obtaining the maximum value of the enterprise, whether through a going concern restructuring or liquidation. Such lenders frequently assess the operational and managerial inefficiencies in determining whether there is a viable business plan that allows the firm to continue operating. They may have purchased claims prior to or during the insolvency proceeding, or they may be offering the exit financing for the firm that is seeking to restructure. Often, private equity funds bargain a governance role going forward, whether it is on the board of directors or through control provisions in respect of their choice of CEO or other key personnel during and immediately after the restructuring period.

---

[121] *Air Canada, Re* (2003), 47 C.B.R. (4th) 163 (Ont. S.C.J. [Commercial List]).

In terms of exit financing, industry investors are at a competitive advantage because they know the industry and have established lenders that also know the commercial potential of purchase of a competitor's business. U.S. vulture funds, while more general, can afford some losses because of the large amount, variety of investments and ability to spread risk; thus they are able to act quickly in restructuring processes to offer funding and secure priority.[122]

The nature of exit financing is changing rapidly, and the distressed debt financing entities are increasingly the party with the liquidity and capital to finance exit of the corporation. If they take an equity stake as the price of that capital, the interest is frequently short term, but the distressed debt lenders are in control of the capital and governance decisions on exit. While beyond the scope of this text, it deserves much further consideration of how they may affect *CCAA* workouts in the future.

Questions for review of materials:

1. What is the purpose of debtor in possession financing and where does it rank in comparison to other secured debt?
2. What is cross-collateralization?
3. What is post-petition trade credit and how have the courts dealt with it?
4. What tests does the court use for asset sales during a *CCAA* proceeding?

Questions for discussion:

1. What governance and control issues does DIP financing raise and what would be the appropriate public policy mechanism to remedy any problems?
2. When a debtor has already negotiated a plan with a potential purchaser, should the courts allow a stalking horse process over the objection of the debtor? What would be the policy rationale of such a decision?
3. Is there a problem with creditors trying to assess competing offers, particularly where they contain terms that are complex and not easily compared? How would you remedy or reduce this problem?

---

[122] Janis P. Sarra, *Creditor Rights and the Public Interest, Restructuring Insolvent Corporations* (Toronto: University of Toronto Press, 2003).

CHAPTER 5

GOVERNANCE OF THE INSOLVENT CORPORATION DURING THE *CCAA* PROCEEDING

I. CHALLENGES FOR GOVERNANCE OF THE FINANCIALLY DISTRESSED FIRM

In most *CCAA* proceedings, the directors and officers retain their oversight and management of the debtor corporation during the period of negotiations for a plan. Hence, corporate governance is key because skills that are required for oversight of a financially healthy company can be quite different than those required for turnaround of an insolvent firm. For example, if a financial downturn is expected to be short-lived, the existing board and management must have the appropriate skills and experience to ameliorate the financial difficulties by seeking new financing before a crisis creates a spiral into bankruptcy.

Corporate governance is the legal and practical system for the exercise of power and control in the business and includes the relationship between the corporation and its directors, officers, shareholders, creditors, and other stakeholders. Governance is a function of the statutory regime that imposes duties on directors and officers; the common law fiduciary duties that constrain actions; mandatory disclosure and proxy requirements of securities law; the corporation's internal governance procedures; and capital structure.[1] Governance decisions are aimed at strategic planning, ensuring good management, risk assessment, efficient use of assets, sustainability, accountability to residual claimants, and containing transaction costs. Unless governance problems are addressed in the restructuring decisions, going-concern value will not be enhanced, the firm will ultimately fail, and costs of that failure will be borne largely by creditors.[2]

---

[1] J. Gordon, "The Shaping Force of Corporate Law in the New Economic Order" (1997) 31 U. Richmond Law Review, 1473 at 1474.

[2] Lynn LoPucki and George Triantis, "A Systems Approach to Comparing U.S. and Canadian Reorganization of Financially Distressed Companies" in Jacob Ziegel, ed., *Current Developments in International and Comparative Corporate Insolvency Law* (Oxford: Clarendon Press, 1994) at 102, 104.

For a financially healthy company, the directors and officers have oversight and control of the corporation, engaging in the full range of decisions regarding strategic planning, capital raising and utilization, risk assessment, and operations. Generally, creditors have limited or no control over governance, other than covenants that senior secured creditors bargain as a condition of extending credit. These dynamics shift when the firm is in financial distress. Creditors can now lay claim to most, if not all, of the assets of the corporation, and shareholders' claims have little, if any, value. While directors' duties remain foremost to the corporation, they may not fully appreciate that the residual claimants to the assets of the corporation are now the creditors, not the shareholders. While creditors ultimately have control rights in the sense that they can vote against the plan of arrangement or compromise, the officers of the debtor corporation have carriage of the process.

Most directors and officers act in the best interests of the corporation, even when dealing with the firm's insolvency. At the point of a firm's financial distress, however, there is a risk that directors and officers will unnecessarily further deplete assets that are available to satisfy creditors' claims because they are unlikely to be in the same role post-restructuring and have little more to lose than reputational capital. There are also risks to their workout strategy where their own exit from the firm in the form of a golden parachute is being negotiated at the same time as a workout plan, DIP financing and new capital and operational structure. Where directors and officers are unable or unwilling to address the governance issues, they should be replaced during the process. Similar issues exist when directors are conducting a "stalking horse" sale, as discussed in chapter 4. Since these negotiations are not subject to the courts' or creditors' scrutiny until they are already settled, this can create the wrong incentive effects in the negotiation of workout financing.

1. Who Should Govern the Financially Distressed Firm?

Generally in corporations, directors are responsible for oversight and strategic direction and managers are responsible for the overall operations. In a number of *CCAA* cases, directors and officers continue during the stay period in these roles. However, where there is a loss of confidence in the directors and/or managers, creditors will seek to have an interim receiver or other insolvency officer appointed to take over governance of the corporation. Turnaround experts are employed in many cases, either as advisors or to take over management and control of the debtor company. As is discussed below, these professionals have particular turnaround skills that existing directors and officers may not have. New people brought into the insolvent firm may not always be receivers or turnaround professionals. If creditors have lost confidence in existing management, they may insist that one or more new managers be brought in as the *quid pro quo* for supporting the proposed reorganization. This approach is not just limited to DIP lenders. Even where directors and officers are able to continue managing during the *CCAA* process, a condition of finalizing the plan is often the replacement of existing management and directors.

Governance is always important, but becomes even more so during insolvency because the forms of monitoring and default control by creditors that temper director conduct are temporarily stayed under the *CCAA* proceeding. When a firm is not under *CCAA* protection, a secured creditor has power to act in the event that the debtor corporation engages in particular kinds of conduct or fails to perform as agreed to in the financing document. Secured creditors are generally able to negotiate default control rights and self-help remedies, even for financially healthy firms. However, the default and attendant control rights are usually only activated at the point that the firm is in financial distress. The *CCAA* stays a number of these pre-existing control rights for the duration of the *CCAA* proceeding, unless the court expressly lifts the stay. At the same time, the debtor is seeking working capital during this period, and frequently the terms negotiated by the DIP lender are expressly exempted from the stay. Hence, at insolvency, the debtor corporation is cash-strapped and vulnerable to control terms being imposed.[3]

More generally, the shift in corporate finance to complex and highly dynamic global capital markets has also seriously influenced governance of the insolvent corporation during the period of decision-making regarding its future. The breadth and range of financial instruments that debtor corporations can utilize means that they face multiple and often divergent interests of creditors, which must be addressed during negotiations for a plan of arrangement under the *CCAA*. Trading in claims or physical settlement of credit default swaps means that there is often turnover in who the debtor has to deal with during the course of a *CCAA* proceeding.

Governance is also important at the time the debtor is preparing to complete its restructuring. Once the protection of the restructuring statute is lifted, markets, as well as how successful the reorganization has been at curing the operational and financial ills, will be a major determinant of the firm's survival. Hence, corporate governance, including how decisions are made in respect of going forward capital structure and business plan, are key elements to a *CCAA* workout.

II. ROLE OF THE CORPORATE BOARD

The role of the corporate board as a whole continues during insolvency. Its role is to provide independent advice on the strategic decisions of the corporation. The challenge is that the board may not have anticipated the firm's financial distress, and may not have a strategic plan for dealing with it. Moreover, many of the indicia of good board behaviour do not really apply in the insolvency context in the same way. For example, meetings are likely to be held frequently and on an urgent basis, with little time for reflective consideration of the decisions made. Fear of liability may drive the decision making. Succession planning takes on a whole new meaning, in that the board may be called on to decide about a chief restructuring officer or other replacement of its management team immediately or on exit from the *CCAA*.

---

[3] Janis Sarra, "Governance and Control: The Role of Debtor-in-Possession Financing under the *CCAA*", *Annual Review of Insolvency Law, 2004* (Toronto: Carswell, 2005) 119-172.

The board is likely to face pressures from both investors and creditors, as there are no longer sufficient assets to satisfy the corporation's outstanding claims.

1. Conflicts and Contributions

The directors are frequently shareholders themselves, both because of the closely held nature of many Canadian firms and because good governance practice today generally encourages directors to be remunerated largely in equity ownership. This may create some conflicts of interest in how the directors approach their oversight of the restructuring negotiations. The board may also require a different type of oversight of their managers, as they are also in a conflict of interest position as they work through the process. This may necessitate more aggressive oversight, creating new tensions between inside and outside directors.

At the same time, a diverse board with healthy connections to the sector in which the debtor company operates, may have considerable advice to offer in the workout period. The board has the continuity to appreciate what has worked and what has not worked in the past. The diversity of views may offer insights into possible new injections of equity into the company or the structuring of debt financing, or ideas about restructuring the operational side of the business. Independent directors can be particularly helpful to a chief restructuring officer who takes over management of the corporation. The courts generally do not interfere with the corporate board of an insolvent corporation under *CCAA* proceedings.

In *Stelco Inc.*, the Ontario Court of Appeal held that the court is not entitled to usurp the role of the directors and management in conducting what are in substance the company's restructuring efforts. The corporate activities that take place in the course of the workout are governed by the legislation and legal principles that normally apply to such activities. The court is not catapulted into the shoes of the board of directors or into the seat of the chair of the board when acting in its supervisory role in the restructuring. The Court of Appeal held that what the court does under section 11 of the *CCAA* is establish the boundaries of the playing field and act as a referee in the process. The Court held that the company's role in the restructuring, and that of its stakeholders, is to work out a plan or compromise that a sufficient percentage of creditors will accept and the court will approve and sanction. In the course of acting as referee, the court has authority to effectively maintain the *status quo* in respect of an insolvent company while it attempts to gain the approval of its creditors for the proposed compromise or arrangement that will be to the benefit of both the company and its creditors. The Court in *Stelco Inc.* observed that the fact that section 11 did not itself provide the authority for a *CCAA* judge to order the removal of directors, however, did not mean that the supervising judge was powerless to make such an order. The Court held that section 20 of the *CCAA* offers a gateway to the oppression remedy and other provisions of the *Canada Business Corporations Act (CBCA)* and similar provincial statutes.[4]

[4] *Canada Business Corporations Act*, R.S.C. 1985, c. C-44.

Chapter 47, when proclaimed in force, will amend the *CCAA* to grant the court power to remove directors, specifying that the court may, on application of any person interested in the matter, make an order removing from office any director if the court is satisfied that the director is unreasonably impairing or is likely to unreasonably impair the possibility of a viable plan or is acting or likely to act inappropriately as a director in the circumstances.[5]

2. Fiduciary Obligations during Insolvency

The scope of directors' duties when the firm is financially distressed was recently decided by the Supreme Court of Canada in *Peoples Department Stores*.[6] Prior to the Supreme Court of Canada judgment in *Peoples Department Stores*, discussed below, Canadian courts had begun to recognize a shift in fiduciary obligation at the point of insolvency, finding that the directors' duty to a corporation as a whole extends to not prejudicing the interests of creditors in an insolvency context.[7] The Supreme Court of Canada in *Peoples Department Stores* ruled that the duty of directors and officers under the *CBCA* does not change when the corporation is approaching or is in financial distress, and that directors and officers owe their fiduciary duties solely to the corporation at all times.[8] It held that directors owe a duty of care to creditors, but that duty does not rise to a fiduciary obligation. However, in acting in the best interests of the corporation, the Court held that it may be legitimate for directors to consider the interests of shareholders, employees, suppliers, creditors, consumers, and the environment.

Courts in the U.K., Australia and the United States have long recognized that directors must consider the interests of creditors when the corporation is insolvent, although there are differences in opinion as to when that obligation arises.[9]

---

[5] Section 11.5(1), Chapter 47 (proposed amendment to the *CCAA*).

[6] *Peoples Department Stores Ltd. (1992) Inc., Re* (2003), [2003] Q.J. No. 505, 2003 CarswellQue 145 (Que. C.A.), leave to appeal allowed (2003), [2003] S.C.C.A. No. 133, 2003 CarswellQue 3487, 2003 Carswell Que 3488 (S.C.C.), affirmed (2004), [2004] S.C.J. No. 64, 2004 CarswellQue 2862, 2004 Carswell Que 2863 (S.C.C.).

[7] *Peoples Department Stores Ltd. (1992) Inc., Re* (1998), 1998 CarswellQue 3442, [1998] Q.J. No. 3571 (Qué. S.C.) (Bankruptcy and Insolvency Division) (Greenberg J.), reversed (2003), 2003 CarswellQue 145 (Que. C.A.), leave to appeal allowed (2003), 2003 CarswellQue 3487 (S.C.C.), affirmed (2004), 2004 CarswellQue 2862 (S.C.C.). *Canbook Distribution Corp.* v. *Borins* (1999), 45 O.R. (3d) 565 (Ont. S.C.J.) at para. 16; *Sidaplex-Plastic Suppliers Inc.* v. *Elta Group* (1998), 40 O.R. (3d) 563 (Ont. C.A.). See also J. Ziegel "Creditors as Corporate Stakeholders: The Quiet Revolution-an Anglo-Canadian Perspective" (1993) 43 U. T. L. J. 511.

[8] *Ibid.*

[9] See for example: *Winkworth* v. *Edward Baron Development Co.*, [1987] 1 All E.R. 114 (U.K. H.L.); *Walker* v. *Wimborne* (1976), 50 A.L.J.R. 446 (Australia H.C.). See also Andrew Keay, "The Director's Duty to Take into Account the Interests of Company Creditors: When is it Triggered?" (2001) 25 Melbourne University Law Review 315; Janis Sarra, "Taking the Corporate Ship Past the Plimsoll Line, Director and Officer Liability when the Corporation Founders" (2001) 10 International Insolvency Review 229.

Prior to the judgment in *Peoples Department Stores*, the caselaw was mixed as to whether the obligation to act in the corporation's best interest was an obligation to maximize shareholder value or some broader obligation.[10] By expressly declining to equate shareholder interest with the corporation's interest, the Supreme Court of Canada in *Peoples Department Stores* recognizes that creditors' interests and other interests must be considered. Directors always face competing interests in the exercise of their duties; however, the Supreme Court did not clarify how these duties are to be reconciled either in or outside of insolvency. The Court held that the directors must strive for a "better" corporation, observing that best interest of the corporation means maximization of the value of the corporation. This is a helpful measure of best interests. Arguably, where directors and officers are acting to maximize this value, they will have met their fiduciary obligations. The Court's reasoning provides a mechanism for stakeholders to hold directors and officers accountable where their duties are not carried out in a manner that maximizes value for the corporation. How the courts balance the various interests implicated in the firm's financial distress will be the key to whether this recognition is effective.

3. Statutory Duty of Care to Creditors

The Supreme Court of Canada in *Peoples Department Stores* held that directors do owe a duty of care to creditors pursuant to section 122(1)(b) of the *CBCA*; specifically, they must exercise the care, diligence and skill that a reasonably prudent person would exercise in comparable circumstances. Since the corporation was not expressly mentioned in section 122(1)(b), the Court held that it "appeared obvious" that the duty was owed to creditors in addition to shareholders.[11] The Court held that the standard of care is an objective one, expressly declining to adopt the standard that had been applied in Canada for the past decade, whereby conduct has been assessed on a subjective and objective basis.

The Supreme Court held that in order for a plaintiff to succeed in challenging a business decision, he or she must establish that the directors acted in breach of the duty of care and in a way that caused injury to the plaintiff.[12] Directors and officers will not be in breach of the duty of care under section 122(1)(b) of the *CBCA* if they act prudently and on a reasonably informed basis. The decisions they make must be reasonable business decisions in light of all the circumstances about which the directors or officers knew or ought to have known. In determining whether directors have acted in a manner that breached the duty of care, perfection is not demanded. The Court held that courts are ill-suited and should be reluctant to second-guess the application of business expertise to the considerations that are involved in corporate

[10] See for example, *820099 Ontario Inc.* v. *Harold E. Ballard Ltd.* (1991), 1991 CarswellOnt 142, [1991] O.J. No. 266 (Ont. Gen. Div.), affirmed (1991), 1991 CarswellOnt 141, [1991] O.J. No. 1082 (Ont. Div. Ct.); *Westfair Foods Ltd.* v. *Watt* (1991), 115 A.R. 34 (C.A.), leave to appeal refused, [1991] 3 S.C.R. viii (note) (S.C.C.).

[11] *Peoples Department Stores Ltd. (1992) Inc., Re*, 2004 SCC 68, [2004] 3 S.C.R. 461 (S.C.C.) at para. 57.

[12] *Ibid.* at para. 66.

decision making, but they are capable, on the facts of any case, of determining whether an appropriate degree of prudence and diligence was brought to bear in reaching what is claimed to be a reasonable business decision at the time it was made.[13]

While the *Peoples Department Stores* case was brought under the *CBCA* and *BIA*, both federal statutes, the case took place in Québec, which differs from the rest of Canada in that it is a civil law regime. The Supreme Court held that the civil law in Québec serves as a supplementary source of law to federal legislation and since there is no express entitlement of creditors to sue directors directly for their breach of duties, it is appropriate to have recourse to the *Québec Civil Code (CCQ)* to determine how rights grounded in a federal statute should be addressed in Québec and how section 122(1) *CBCA* provisions can be harmonized with the principles of civil liability.[14] The Supreme Court considered the duty of care where there are not contractual obligations such as a guarantee of debt. To determine the applicability of extra-contractual liability, the Court observed that it is necessary to refer to art. 1457 of the *CCQ*, with three elements relevant to the integration of the director's duty of care into the principles of extra-contractual liability: who has the duty ("every person"), to whom is the duty owed ("another") and what breach will trigger liability ("rules of conduct").[15] The Court held that directors and officers come within the expression "every person" and that the word "another" can include creditors. The Court held that art. 1457 is broad and has been given an open and inclusive meaning.[16] It held that this interpretation can be harmoniously integrated with the duty of care in section 122(1)(b) of the *CBCA*, which does not specifically refer to an identifiable party as the beneficiary of the duty and requires that "[e]very director and officer of a corporation in exercising their powers and discharging their duties shall ... exercise the care, diligence and skill that a reasonably prudent person would exercise in comparable circumstances." Thus, the Court held that the identity of the beneficiary of the duty of care is much more open-ended and includes creditors.[17]

This new recognition of a statutory duty that is owed to creditors as well as shareholders and other stakeholders has not yet been tested post the *Peoples Department Stores* judgment.

[13] *Ibid.* at para. 67.

[14] *Ibid.* at para. 29.

[15] Art. 1457 *CCQ* specifies that every person has a duty to abide by the rules of conduct which lie upon him or her, according to the circumstances, usage or law, so as not to cause injury to another and where the person fails in this duty, he or she is responsible for any injury he or she causes to another person by such fault and is liable to reparation for the injury, whether it be bodily, moral or material in nature. The person is also liable, in certain cases, to reparation for injury caused to another by the act or fault of another person or by the act of things in his or her custody.

[16] *Ibid.* at para. 56.

[17] *Ibid.* at para. 57.

4. Oppression Remedies

Oppression remedy provisions specify a "statutory lifting of the corporate veil" for the conduct of directors that is oppressive, unfairly prejudicial to, or unfairly disregards the interests of particular stakeholders.[18] The courts have recognized that creditors and trustees in bankruptcy can be proper persons to bring oppression claims.[19] The remedy is available only in limited circumstances, and the court has made it clear that it will not allow debt actions to be routinely turned into oppression actions. Unfair prejudice encompasses the protection of the underlying expectation of the creditor in its arrangement with the corporation, the detriment to the interests of the creditor, and the extent to which the acts complained of were unforeseeable or the creditor could reasonably have protected itself from such acts.

The Supreme Court of Canada in *Peoples Department Stores* characterized the oppression remedies under section 241(2) of the *CBCA* and similar provincial corporate statutes as granting the broadest rights to creditors of any common law jurisdiction.[20] An oppression remedy is a remedy granted by the court where it is satisfied that the corporation's directors have exercised their powers or conducted the company's affairs in a manner that is oppressive, unfairly prejudicial to or unfairly disregard the interests of any security holder, creditor, director or officer.[21] The availability of this remedy was a key part of the Court's reasoning and conclusion that there was no need to extend the directors' statutory fiduciary duty to require that creditors' interests be considered when the corporation was in the vicinity of insolvency.[22] The Court held that the oppression remedy provides a mechanism for creditors to protect their interests from the prejudicial conduct of directors and that the availability of such a broad oppression remedy undermines any perceived need to extend the fiduciary duty imposed on directors by section 122(1)(a) of the *CBCA* to include creditors.[23] This reasoning suggests that the Court believes the oppression remedy provides ample protection to those interests while they are at the greatest risk.

This broad statutory protection against unfairness is accompanied by an equally robust remedial jurisdiction. The court's general power to rectify oppressive and unfair consequences by any order it thinks fit is bolstered by a lengthy list of specific

---

[18] See for example, ss. 245, 248, Ontario *Business Corporations Act*, R.S.O. 1990, c. B.16. *Adecco Canada Inc.* v. *J. Ward Broome Ltd.* (2001), 2001 CarswellOnt 1173, [2001] O.J. No. 454 (Ont. S.C.J. [Commercial List]) (Swinton, J.), additional reasons at (2001), 2001 CarswellOnt 1173 (Ont. S.C.J. [Commercial List]).

[19] *Sammi Atlas Inc., Re* (1998), 49 C.B.R. (3d) 165 (Ont. Gen. Div. [Commercial List]).

[20] *Peoples Department Stores Ltd. (1992) Inc., Re*, 2004 SCC 68, [2004] 3 S.C.R. 461 (S.C.C.); *Canada Business Corporations Act*, R.S.C. 1985, c. C-44, as amended (*CBCA*) at para. 48. For a full discussion of these issues, see Janis Sarra, "The Oppression remedy, the *Peoples'* Choice", in *Annual Review of Insolvency Law, 2005* (Toronto: Carswell, 2006).

[21] *CBCA* s. 241(2) sets out the conditions that can form the basis for an oppression remedy application.

[22] *Peoples Department Stores Ltd. (1992) Inc., Re*, 2004 SCC 68, [2004] 3 S.C.R. 461 (S.C.C.) at para. 51.

[23] *Ibid.* at para. 51.

remedial powers the court can exercise, from enjoining the corporation to ordering its dissolution and liquidation.

The Supreme Court in *Peoples Department Stores* also discussed the relationship between directors' duties and the interests of other corporate stakeholders:

> We accept as an accurate statement of law that in determining whether they are acting with a view to the best interests of the corporation it may be legitimate, given all the circumstances of a given case, for the board of directors to consider, *inter alia*, the interests of shareholders, employees, suppliers, creditors, consumers, governments and the environment.[24]

Although the Court referred to the fact that the interests of creditors became more relevant in the vicinity of insolvency for the purposes of obtaining standing as a complainant under the *CBCA*, the Court gave no indication as to whether or under what circumstances the interests of employees, suppliers, consumers, government and environmental claimants would be sufficiently relevant to obtain standing as a complainant.

Although the oppression remedy is broad, the availability and scope of the remedy varies from statute to statute in Canada, and the Québec *Companies Act* and Prince Edward Island *Companies Act* do not contain an oppression remedy.[25] Most Canadian corporate law statutes include a definition of complainant that does not specifically mention creditors. In Alberta, creditors are expressly listed in the oppression provision; however, a creditor's right to bring the application is still subject to the exercise of the court's discretion that the creditor is a proper person to bring the application.[26] In New Brunswick, creditors are included in the definition of complainant for both the oppression remedy and derivative action provisions, making it the only corporate law statute in Canada where creditors have the ability to bring an oppression remedy application as of right.[27]

The definition of security holder includes both debt and equity securities. Hence if a creditor owns debt that is a security, such as bonds or debentures, then the creditor has status as of right to bring an oppression remedy application. All other creditors, however, are not granted status as of right except in New Brunswick.[28]

---

[24] *Ibid.* at para. 42.

[25] For a discussion of the lack of an oppression remedy under the Québec *Companies Act*, see Stéphane Rousseau, "The Liability of Directors towards Creditors in Civil Law: A Note on *Peoples Department Stores Inc.* v. *Wise*", in *Annual Review of Insolvency Law, 2003* (Toronto: Carswell, 2004). PEI *Companies Act*, R.S.P.E.I., 1998, c. C-14.

[26] Alberta *Business Corporations Act*, RSA 2000, c. B-9 (*ABCA*), section 239. Under s. 239, creditors can seek to bring a derivative action as of right, but leave of the court is required to bring an oppression claim. See also *Bull HN Information Systems Ltd.* v. *L.I. Business Solutions Inc.* (1994), 23 Alta L.R. (3d) 186 (Alta. Q.B.) at paras. 2 and 26.

[27] New Brunswick *Business Corporations Act*, S.N.B. 1981, c. B-9.1 (*NBBCA*), s. 163(c). Other than security holders, who do have the right to bring a complaint.

[28] New Brunswick *Business Corporations Act*, S.N.B. 1981, c. B-9.1 (*NBBCA*), at section 163(c).

The conditions under which the court will grant an oppression remedy under the *OBCA* are the most expansive of all the Canadian corporate statutes, as they include actions that have not yet occurred. The *OBCA* remedy includes any actions threatened to effect a result or powers of the directors that are threatened to be exercised in a manner that is oppressive, unfairly prejudicial to or unfairly disregards the interests of the complainant.[29] Hence the Ontario remedy covers past, current and future threatened conduct.

The British Columbia *Business Corporations Act* remedy specifies different conditions of oppressive conduct and unfair prejudice to different parts of the test, but covering proposed conduct in some circumstances. It specifies that the court can grant a remedy where:

> the affairs of the company are being or have been conducted, or that the powers of the directors are being or have been exercised, in a manner oppressive to one or more of the shareholders, including the applicant, or that some act of the company has been done or is threatened, or that some resolution of the shareholders or of the shareholders holding shares of a class or series of shares has been passed or is proposed, that is unfairly prejudicial to one or more of the shareholders, including the applicant.[30]

The statute makes no mention of unfair disregard of the interests protected.

Hence there is inconsistency in access across Canada, both in terms of who is a complainant as of right and the timeline of the impugned action. In all jurisdictions where the remedy exists, however, the court can make any interim or final order it considers appropriate.[31]

Generally, the credit bargain is that creditors will be paid for their goods, services or capital according to the terms of the arrangement with the debtor company. Creditors are not concerned about their claims when the company is financially healthy. Hence, the analysis that shareholders are the residual claimants and have a great interest in aligning the interests of the corporation with their interests makes sense when viewed from a capitalization perspective.[32] However, as the financial condition of the corporation worsens, the risk of trade creditors or capital lenders not being paid on a timely basis increases. If the corporation becomes insolvent, the creditors become the residual interest holders, and shareholder interests are minimal or have been wiped out. This residual interest is a critical aspect of oppression claims at the point of insolvency or as the firm slides toward insolvency.

---

[29] Ontario *Business Corporations Act*, R.S.O. 1990, c. B.16 (*OBCA*), section 248(2).

[30] British Columbia *Business Corporations Act*, S.B.C. 2002, c. 57, section 227(2).

[31] *OBCA*, s. 248(3); *BCBCA*, s. 227(3); *ABCA*, s. 242(3); *SBCA*, s. 234(3), *MCA*, s. 234(3); *NBBCA*, s. 166(3); *NSCA*, Sched. 3, 1999, s. 5(3); *NFLDCA*, s. 371(3); *NWTBCA*, s. 243(3); *NBCA*, s. 243(3).

[32] Janis Sarra, "The Oppression Remedy: The *Peoples'* Choice", *Annual Review of Insolvency Law, 2005* (Toronto: Carswell, 2006) at 111-156.

The Ontario Court of Appeal in *Stelco Inc.*, held that the powers of a judge under section 11 of the *CCAA* may be applied together with the provisions of the *CBCA*, including the oppression remedy provisions of that statute. However, the Court of Appeal held that court removal of directors is an exceptional remedy and one that is rarely exercised in corporate law. In determining whether directors have fallen foul of their obligations, more than some risk of anticipated misconduct is required before the court can impose the extraordinary remedy of removing a director from his or her duly elected or appointed office. The Court of Appeal held that the evidence was far from reaching the standard for removal, and the record did not support a finding that there was a sufficient risk of misconduct to warrant a conclusion of oppression, even if such a remedy had been sought.

a. The Definition of Complainant under Oppression Provisions

The oppression remedy is available to a "complainant" as that term is defined in the *CBCA* and most other Canadian corporations statutes.[33] The present statutory language creates two classes of potential claimants: a defined class where the individual falls within one of the relationships with the corporation defined in the statute, and an undefined class of potential claimants who are, in the court's opinion, "a proper person". Creditors that are not security holders may apply for an oppression remedy by asking a court to exercise its discretion and grant them status as a "proper person" to make an application.[34] Although the criteria for standing to bring an oppression remedy application do not specify any limits on who may commence the application, the criteria for those who may obtain a remedy for unfair prejudice or unfair disregard of their interests is apparently restricted to members of a defined class of complainants.[35]

The term security is not defined in the Nova Scotia *Companies Act*, although it is defined in the *CBCA* and other statutes. Where an issue recently arose in *Harbert Distressed Investment Master Fund, Ltd.* v. *Calpine Canada Energy Finance* as to whether bond holders were complainants within the meaning of the Nova Scotia statute, the Court held that the term "security" can include a bond, relying on the definition in *Black's Law Dictionary*.[36] The Court found that the applicants were

---

[33] Under the *CBCA*, a complainant for purposes of the oppression remedy includes: a current or former registered holder or beneficial owner of a security of a corporation or any of its affiliates, a current or former director or officer of a corporation or any of its affiliates, the Director, or any other person who, in the discretion of a court, is a proper person to make an application. Section 238, *CBCA*.

[34] *Peoples Department Stores Ltd. (1992) Inc., Re*, 2004 SCC 68, [2004] 3 S.C.R. 461 (S.C.C.) at para. 50.

[35] Janis Sarra, "The Oppression Remedy: The *Peoples'* Choice", *Annual Review of Insolvency Law, 2005* (Toronto: Carswell, 2006) at 111-156.

[36] *Harbert Distressed Investment Master Fund Ltd.* v. *Calpine Canada Energy Finance II ULC* (2005), 2005 CarswellNS 342, [2005] N.S.J. No. 317 (N.S. S.C.) at paras. 116-117; *Black's Law Dictionary*, 7th ed. (St. Paul, Minn.: West Group, 1999).

registered holders or beneficial owners of securities of the respondents and thus came within the definition of complainant under the statute.[37]

The caselaw regarding who is a "proper person" appears to be primarily in respect of creditors other than those holding security.[38] The criteria set out in *First Edmonton Place Ltd.* have been adopted by a number of courts across Canada.[39] The creditor must be in a position that is analogous to that of a minority shareholder in that it has a particular legitimate interest in how the corporation is being managed or has a direct financial interest in the way in which directors are conducting the business of the corporation.[40] The act complained of must constitute a breach of the underlying reasonable expectation of the applicant.[41] Reasonable expectations are a question of fact, with the courts finding that they are not just a wish list but expectations that could be said to have been considered as part of the arrangement between the complainant and the corporation.[42] This reasoning is much narrower than the more recent direction of the Supreme Court of Canada in *Peoples Department Stores.*

The court will decline to grant creditors status where the interest is too remote, where the creditor is not proceeding in good faith, where the complainant was not a creditor at the time of the impugned action, or where the acts complained of have nothing to do with the debt.[43] Although some courts have declined to grant status where the claim is contingent, others have held that the contingent nature of the

---

[37] *Harbert Distressed Investment Master Fund, ibid.* at para. 118. The Court in *Harbert Distressed Investment Master Fund* also found that the definition of "affiliate" for purpose of bringing an oppression application must be given a broad interpretation, again drawing on the statutory language and *Black's Law Dictionary, ibid.* at paras. 125-128.

[38] For a discussion, see Janis Sarra and Ronald B. Davis, *Director and Officer Liability in Corporate Insolvency*, (Toronto: Butterworths Canada Ltd., 2002) at 34-43.

[39] *First Edmonton Place Ltd.* v. *315888 Alberta Ltd.* (1988), 40 B.L.R. 28 (Alta Q.B.), appeal adjourned (1989), 45 B.L.R. 110 (Alta C.A.); followed in: *Mackenzie* v. *Craig* (1999), 171 D.L.R. (4th) 268 (Alta. C.A.) at para. 17; *Precision Feeds Ltd.* v. *Rock Lake Colony Ltd.* (1993), 1993 CarswellMan 338, [1993] M.J. No. 561, 93 Man. R. (2d) 1 (Man. Q.B.), motion for stay of proceedings pending appeal dismissed as applicants failed to establish that there was an arguable point for appeal (1994), 1994 CarswellMan 242, 93 Man. R. (2d) 13, [1994] M.J. No. 115 (Man. Q.B.); *Downtown Eatery (1993) Ltd.* v. *Ontario* (2001), 200 D.L.R. (4th) 289 (Ont. C.A.), leave to appeal refused (2002), 2002 CarswellOnt 246, [2001] S.C.C.A. No. 397 (S.C.C.).

[40] *First Edmonton Place, ibid.*; Janis Sarra and Ronald B. Davis, *Director and Officer Liability in Corporate Insolvency*, (Toronto: Butterworths Canada Ltd., 2002) at 34-43; *Royal Trust Corp. of Canada* v. *Hordo* (1993), 10 B.L.R. (2d) 86 (Ont. Gen. Div. [Commercial List]); *Levy-Russell Ltd.* v. *Shieldings Inc.* (1998), 41 O.R. (3d) 54 (Ont. Gen. Div.), additional reasons at (1998), 1998 CarswellOnt 5916 (Ont. Gen. Div.), leave to appeal refused (1998), 1998 CarswellOnt 4778 (Ont. Gen. Div. [Commercial List]). This reasoning comes from the fact that the remedy was originally enacted as a shareholder remedy in the 1970s.

[41] *LeBlanc* v. *Corp. Eighty-Six Ltd.* (1997), 37 B.L.R. (2d) 129 (N.B. C.A.).

[42] *820099 Ontario Inc.* v. *Harold E. Ballard Ltd.* (1991), 1991 CarswellOnt 142, [1991] O.J. No. 266 (Ont. Gen. Div.), affirmed (1991), 1991 CarswellOnt 141, [1991] O.J. No. 1082 (Ont. Div. Ct.); *Naneff* v. *Con-Crete Holdings* (1995), 23 O.R. (3d) 481, 23 B.L.R. (2d) 286 (Ont. C.A.).

[43] Janis Sarra and Ronald B. Davis, *Director and Officer Liability in Corporate Insolvency*, (Toronto: Butterworths Canada Ltd., 2002) at 34-43; *Jacobs Farms Ltd.* v. *Jacobs* (1992), 1992 CarswellOnt 3215, [1992] O.J. No. 813 (Ont. Gen. Div.); *Royal Trust Corp. of Canada* v. *Hordo* (1993), 10 B.L.R. (2d) 86 (Ont. Gen. Div. [Commercial List]) at para. 12.

claim is not a bar to the court exercising its discretion to grant status as a complainant where the claim is not uncertain or speculative.[44]

The Supreme Court in *Peoples Department Stores* held that:

> the fact that creditors' interests increase in relevancy as a corporation's finances deteriorate is apt to be relevant to, *inter alia*, the exercise of discretion by a court in granting standing to a party as a 'complainant' under section 238(d) of the *CBCA* as a 'proper person' to bring a derivative action in the name of the corporation under ss. 239 and 240 of the *CBCA*, or to bring an oppression remedy claim under section 241 of the *CBCA*.[45]

b. Limits of the Oppression Remedy

There is discrepancy between the definition of complainant and the interests that are offered protection by the oppression remedy. While a complainant may include anyone the court considers a proper person, the statute only provides a remedy when corporate actions are oppressive towards, unfairly prejudicial to, or unfairly disregard the interests of any security holder, creditor, director or officer.[46] Some courts have held that this means only interests in relation to a claimant's position as a shareholder, creditor, director or officer of a corporation are protected by the oppression remedy.[47] The court has held that the question of being able to qualify as a complainant by meeting the requirements of s. 238 of the *CBCA* is a separate and distinct matter from that of having sustainable grounds of oppression within the meaning of s. 241, which "requires a connection between the aggrieved share-

---

[44] Sarra and Davis, *ibid.* at 36; *A E Realizations (1985) Ltd.* v. *Time Air Inc.* (1994), 127 Sask. R. 105 (Q.B.) at para. 23, affirmed (1995), 131 Sask. R. 249 (Sask. C.A.); *Downtown Eatery (1993) Ltd.* v. *Ontario* (2001), 200 D.L.R. (4th) 289 (Ont. C.A.), leave to appeal refused (2002), 2002 CarswellOnt 246, [2001] S.C.C.A. No. 397 (S.C.C.); *Gestion Trans-Tek Inc.* v. *Shipment Systems Strategies Ltd.* (2001), 2001 CarswellOnt 4270, [2001] O.J. No. 4710 (Ont. S.C.J.).

[45] *Peoples Department Stores Ltd. (1992) Inc., Re*, 2004 SCC 68, [2004] 3 S.C.R. 461 (S.C.C.) at para. 49. The caselaw in the U.S. is converging somewhat in this respect, see: *Production Resources Group, L.L.C.* v. *NCT Group, Inc.*, 863 A.2d 772, 790 (Del. Ch., 2004). The legal framework differs, however, in that there is not an oppression remedy under Delaware corporate law, and the duty of care is a common law duty, as opposed to codified in the statute. See also Ronald B. Davis, "The Bonding Effects of Directors' Statutory Wage Liability: An Interactive Corporate Governance Explanation", (2002) 24 *Law and Policy* 405 at 417.

[46] *Catalyst Fund General Partner I Inc.* v. *Hollinger Inc.* (2004), 2004 CarswellOnt 4772, [2004] O.J. No. 4722 (Ont. S.C.J.) at para. 94, affirmed (2006), 2006 CarswellOnt 1416 (Ont. C.A.).

[47] *Clitheroe* v. *Hydro One Inc.* (2002), 2002 CarswellOnt 3919, [2002] O.J. No. 4383 (Ont. S.C.J.) at para. 26, dealing with the wrongful dismissal claim of the corporation's CEO outside of the insolvency context. Other courts have held that a claim for wrongful dismissal by an employee can only be included in an oppression remedy claim where the employment is closely connected with their rights as a shareholder, officer and director and the dismissal is part of a pattern of oppressive conduct, also outside of the insolvency context: *Naneff* v. *Con-Crete Holdings* (1995), 23 O.R. (3d) 481, 23 B.L.R. (2d) 286 (Ont. C.A.). See also *Benedetti* v. *North Park Electronics (1980) Ltd.* (1997), 1997 CarswellOnt 559, [1997] O.J. No. 597 (Ont. Gen. Div.), affirmed (1997), 1997 CarswellOnt 5079, [1997] O.J. No. 5244 (Ont. Div. Ct.).

holder(s) and the actions/inactions that are oppressive or unfairly prejudicial to or that unfairly disregard the interests of that shareholder."[48]

The Ontario Court of Appeal observed in *UPM-Kymmene Corp.* v. *UPM Kymmene Miramichi Inc.* that the oppression remedy provisions in corporate statutes allow a "statutory lifting of the corporate veil" to hold directors accountable for their conduct or the power they have exercised in a manner that is oppressive or unfairly prejudicial to the interests of the complainant as a security holder, creditor, director or officer.[49]

The oppression remedy originated in the United Kingdom in an attempt to provide a less drastic remedy than Winding-up or dissolving the company when its majority shareholders or the directors they elected acted in a way that would otherwise justify a court ordering the wind-up of the company on just and equitable grounds.[50] When an oppression remedy was inserted in most Canadian corporations statutes, the grounds for court intervention were expanded from oppressive action to include unfair prejudice and unfair disregard of the protected interests.

Directors have a defence under oppression remedy provisions in that they can establish that the exercise of their power was not oppressive, unfairly prejudicial to or unfairly disregarding of interests.

c. The Conditions under which an Oppression Remedy may be Granted

In most provinces, there are three types of conduct that can be remedied through the oppression provisions: oppressive conduct, unfairly prejudicial conduct and unfairly disregarding conduct. In *Piller Sausages & Delicatessens Ltd.*,[51] the Ontario Supe-

---

[48] *Ford Motor Co. of Canada, Ltd.* v. *Ontario (Municipal Employees Retirement Board)* (2004), 2004 CarswellOnt 208, [2004] O.J. No. 191 (Ont. S.C.J.) at para. 238, additional reasons at (2005), 2005 CarswellOnt 1412 (Ont. S.C.J. [Commercial List]), reversed (2006), 2006 CarswellOnt 13 (Ont. C.A.), leave to appeal refused (2006), 2006 CarswellOnt 5134, 2006 CarswellOnt 5135 (S.C.C.).

[49] *UPM-Kymmene Corp.* v. *UPM-Kymmene Miramichi Inc.* (2002), 214 D.L.R. (4th) 496 (Ont. S.C.J.) at para. 3, additional reasons at (2002), 2002 CarswellOnt 3579 (Ont. S.C.J. [Commercial List]), affirmed (2004), 2004 CarswellOnt 691, [2004] O.J. No. 636 (Ont. C.A.).

[50] The U.K now has a statutory remedy of "unfair prejudice" to a specific member (shareholder) or members generally, which mirrors Canadian oppression provisions but allows claims of both a personal and derivative nature. In 1989, the U.K. *Companies Act* was amended to read:

> s. 459(1) A member of a company may apply to the court by petition for an order under this Part on the ground that the company's affairs are being or have been conducted in a manner which is unfairly prejudicial to the interests of its members generally or of some part of its members (including at least himself) or that any actual or proposed act or omission of the company (including an act or omission on its behalf) is or would be so prejudicial.

The broad scope of remedies is set out in section 461. For a discussion see Janis Sarra, *Review of the Derivative Action Provisions of the Canada Business Corporations Act, Policy Implications and Options*, Research Report to Corporations Canada, April 30, 2005.

[51] *Piller Sausages & Delicatessens Ltd.* v. *Cobb International Corp.* (2003), 35 B.L.R. (3d) 193 (Ont. S.C.J.), affirmed (2003), 40 B.L.R. (3d) 88 (Ont. C.A.). See also *Olympia & York Developments Ltd. (Trustee of)* v. *Olympia & York Realty Corp.* (2001), [2001] O.J. No. 3394, 2001 CarswellOnt 2954 (Ont. S.C.J. [Commercial List]) at paras. 30-31, additional reasons at (2001), 2001 CarswellOnt 4739 (Ont. S.C.J. [Commercial List]), affirmed (2003), 68 O.R. (3d) 544 (Ont. C.A.).

rior Court of Justice, affirmed by the Ontario Court of Appeal, described the different standards:

> ¶ 17 "Oppressive" has been interpreted as meaning burdensome, harsh or wrongful: *Scottish Cooperative Wholesale Society Ltd.* v. *Meyer,* [1959] A.C. 324; *Burnett* v. *Tsang* (1985), 29 B.L.R. 196.
>
> ¶ 18 "Unfairly prejudicial" has been held to mean "acts that are unjustly or inequitably detrimental": *Diligenti* v. *R.W.M.D. Operations Kelowna* (1996), 1 B.C.L.R. 36.
>
> ¶ 19 "Unfairly disregards" has been held to mean "unjustly or without cause, pay no attention to, ignore or treat as of no importance the interests of security holders, creditors, directors or officers": *Stech* v. *Davies* (1987), 53 Alta. L.R. (2d) 373.
>
> ¶ 20 It appears that the progression from "oppressive" to "unfairly prejudicial" to "unfairly disregards" involves decreasingly stringent requirements: *Journet* v. *Superchef Food Industries Ltd.,* (1984), 29 B.L.R. 206.
>
> ¶ 21 An applicant need not show *mala fides* on the part of the respondents, as it is the effect of their actions, rather than their intent, which is material: *Brant Investments Ltd.* v. *Keeprite Inc.* (1991), 3 O.R. (3d) 289; *Palmer* v. *Carling-O'Keefe Breweries of Canada Ltd.* (1989), 67 O.R. (2d) 161.
>
> ¶ 22 Jurisprudence shows that these provisions of the CBCA are remedial and should be interpreted broadly in considering a complainant's interest. Each such application is fact specific. The reasonable expectations of the parties, the nature of the acts complained of and the methods by which they were carried out must be all considered.
>
> ¶ 23 Amongst the factors to be considered is included the reasonable expectation of a creditor that debtors will not engage in conduct after becoming a creditor, and during and after a trial, that will hinder satisfaction of a judgment: *Levy-Russell Ltd.* v. *Shieldings Inc.* (1998), 41 O.R. (3d) 54, leave to appeal refused (1998), 42 O.R. (3d) 215.
>
> ¶ 24 Also included in the factors to be considered are the history and nature of the corporation, the nature of the relationship between the parties, general commercial practice, and detriment to the creditor's interests where those who control a closely held corporation transfer assets and pay shareholder loans with the result that the creditor remains unpaid with no likelihood of recovery: *Gigna, Sutts* v. *Harris* (1997), 36 B.L.R. (2d) 210.[52]

[52] The reasoning in *Piller Sausages & Delicatessens Ltd.* was recently endorsed in *Harbert Distressed Investment Master Fund Ltd.* v. *Calpine Canada Energy Finance II ULC* (2005), 2005 CarswellNS 342, [2005] N.S.J. No. 317 (N.S. S.C.).

Oppressive conduct has been defined as that which is "burdensome, harsh and wrongful" and has been held to have two aspects.[53] If there is no legal right to commit the adverse act, it is considered oppressive without a requirement for bad faith; but if the act is legally authorized, it may still be oppressive if done in bad faith.[54] In this branch of the oppression remedy, the focus is on the character and motivation of the action taken. However, under the unfair prejudice and unfair disregard branches of the oppression remedy, the focus is on the effect on the injured complainant of the conduct.[55] This has been interpreted as conduct that unfairly disregards the complainant's interests, conduct that unjustly or without cause fails to pay attention to, or ignores or treats as of no importance the interests of security holders, creditors, directors or officers.[56] In this aspect of the oppression remedy, there need not be any bad faith or an intention to harm the complainant.[57] The remedy is available to protect a complainant's legal rights, as well as reasonable expectations arising out of the course of dealing between the parties or corporate law itself.[58]

d. Reasonable Expectations and Creditors

The notion of reasonable expectations arises from early cases, where the court made clear that the remedy was not available solely to protect strict legal rights, but rather, to protect the reasonable expectations of the complainant.[59] Outside the insolvency

---

[53] *Scottish Co-op. Wholesale Soc. Ltd.* v. *Meyer*, [1958] 3 All E.R. 66 (U.K. H.L.); *Mahoney* v. *Taylor* (1996), 1996 CarswellBC 1441, [1996] B.C.J. No. 1479 (B.C. S.C.) at para. 24.

[54] *Mahoney, ibid.*

[55] *Nystad* v. *Harcrest Apartments Ltd.* (1986), 1986 CarswellBC 123, [1986] B.C.J. No. 3145 (B.C. S.C.) at para. 24; *Piller Sausages & Delicatessens Ltd.* v. *Cobb International Corp.* (2003), 35 B.L.R. (3d) 193 (Ont. S.C.J.), affirmed (2003), 40 B.L.R. (3d) 88 (Ont. C.A.).

[56] *Piller Sausages & Delicatessens Ltd., ibid.*; *Harbert Distressed Investment Master Fund, Ltd.* v. *Calpine Canada Energy Finance II ULC* (2005), 2005 CarswellNS 342, [2005] N.S.J. No. 317 (N.S. S.C.); *Nystad* v. *Harcrest Apartments Ltd, ibid.*; *Olympia & York Developments Ltd. (Trustee of)* v. *Olympia & York Realty Corp.* (2001), [2001] O.J. No. 3394, 2001 CarswellOnt 2954 (Ont. S.C.J. [Commercial List]) at paras. 30-31, additional reasons at (2001), 2001 CarswellOnt 4739 (Ont. S.C.J. [Commercial List]), affirmed (2003), 68 O.R. (3d) 544 (Ont. C.A.).

[57] *Downtown Eatery (1993) Ltd.* v. *Ontario* (2001), 200 D.L.R. (4th) 289 (Ont. C.A.), leave to appeal refused (2002), 2002 CarswellOnt 246, [2001] S.C.C.A. No. 397 (S.C.C.). See also Janis P. Sarra and Ronald B. Davis, *Director and Officer Liability in Corporate Insolvency*, (Toronto: Butterworths Canada Ltd., 2002) at 37; *Ferguson* v. *Imax Systems Corp.* (1983), 150 D.L.R. (3d) 718 (Ont. C.A.) at 727, leave to appeal refused (1983), 2 O.A.C. 158 (note), 52 N.R. 317 (note) (S.C.C.); *Brant Investments Ltd.* v. *KeepRite Inc.* (1991), 3 O.R. (3d) 289 (Ont. C.A.).

[58] *UPM-Kymmene Corp.* v. *UPM-Kymmene Miramichi Inc.* (2002), 214 D.L.R. (4th) 496 (Ont. S.C.J.), additional reasons at (2002), 2002 CarswellOnt 3579 (Ont. S.C.J. [Commercial List]), affirmed (2004), 2004 CarswellOnt 691, [2004] O.J. No. 636 (Ont. C.A.).

[59] *Westfair Foods Ltd.* v. *Watt* (1991), 115 A.R. 34 (C.A.), leave to appeal refused, [1991] 3 S.C.R. viii (note) (S.C.C.). In *820099 Ontario Inc.* v. *Harold E. Ballard Ltd.*, the Court held that shareholder interests would appear to be intertwined with shareholder expectations and that they must be expectations that could be said to have been or ought to have been considered as part of the compact of the shareholders, *820099 Ontario Inc.* v. *Harold E. Ballard Ltd.* (1991), 1991 CarswellOnt 142, [1991] O.J. No. 266 (Ont. Gen. Div.), affirmed (1991), 1991 CarswellOnt 141, [1991] O.J. No. 1082 (Ont. Div. Ct.); see also *Naneff* v. *Con-Crete Holdings* (1995), 25 O.R. (3d) 481, 23 B.L.R. (2d) 286 (Ont. C.A.); *Themadel Foundation* v. *Third Canadian Investment Trust Ltd.* (1998), 38 O.R. (3d) 749 (Ont. C.A.) at 753-4.

context, the reasonable expectations test arises from the fact that minority shareholders may not have the means to hold corporate officers accountable for their actions through the mechanism of board elections and annual general meetings. Creditors may be similarly situated in that they cannot elect directors and officers and yet in insolvency, the directors may act in a manner that is oppressive or unfairly disregards or unfairly prejudices the interests of creditors.

Most successful oppression remedy proceedings brought by creditors have involved closely held corporations, where the directors caused assets to be transferred out of the reach of creditors, often to their own financial gain. The remedy has not generally been granted where directors have mismanaged the corporation, resulting in unfair prejudice to creditors in respect of their claims.

The courts have held that unfair prejudice encompasses the protection of the underlying expectation of the creditor in its arrangement with the corporation.[60] The courts have tended to interpret "reasonable expectations" narrowly, particularly for creditors whose expectations are often defined by a credit arrangement and the extent to which acts complained of were foreseeable such that the creditor could have protected itself in the bargain through security or covenants or refusing to extend credit.[61] Where creditors have sufficient bargaining power to obtain these protections in the credit arrangement, there may be no problem with this reasoning; however, many creditors cannot bargain for governance protections in their credit arrangements due to information asymmetries and lack of bargaining power.

Creditors expect to be paid in the ordinary course, and they generally are, except where directors and officers engage in preferences, settlements or the siphoning off of corporate assets. Creditors arguably have a reasonable expectation that directors will manage or engage in oversight that does not unnecessarily deplete corporate assets that may be available to meet their claims. Yet when directors are insulated from claims due to a narrow definition of what reasonable expectations may entail, incentives may be created to act contrary to those expectations.

In *First Edmonton Place*, the Court held that the elements of determining unfairness in deciding whether or not to order a remedy, specifically, the protection of the underlying expectation of a creditor in its arrangement with the corporation, the extent to which the acts complained of were unforeseeable and the detriment to the creditor's interests, are a list of considerations that are not exhaustive.[62]

The New Brunswick Court of Appeal in *ADI Ltd.* found oppressive conduct and unfair disregard of creditors' interests where the corporation embarked on a series

[60] *Downtown Eatery (1993) Ltd.* v. *Ontario* (2001), 200 D.L.R. (4th) 289 (Ont. C.A.), leave to appeal refused (2002), 2002 CarswellOnt 246, [2001] S.C.C.A. No. 397 (S.C.C.); *Sidaplex-Plastic Suppliers Inc.* v. *Elta Group Inc.* (1995), 131 D.L.R. (4th) 399 (Ont. Gen. Div. [Commercial List]) at para. 16, reversed (1998), 162 D.L.R. (4th) 367 (Ont. C.A.); *First Edmonton Place Ltd.* v. *315888 Alberta Ltd.* (1988), 40 B.L.R. 28 (Alta Q.B.), appeal adjourned (1989), 45 B.L.R. 110 (Alta C.A.).

[61] *First Edmonton Place Ltd., ibid.*

[62] *Ibid.* at 57.

of otherwise legal transactions with no substantial business purpose other than to defeat the claims of a creditor, finding a director personally liable.[63]

The current reasonable expectation test used by the courts in determining whether a remedy should be granted may serve an important gate-keeping function in terms of the type of actions that give rise to a remedy, hence protecting the duly diligent director from frivolous claims. The significance of the caselaw that emphasizes that the reasonable expectation test is an objective standard is critically important. In respect of creditors, however, the courts need a clearer articulation of how that objective test is to be applied. For example, the court may need to develop principles for application to unsecured and involuntary creditors, recognizing their inability to bargain for protection against oppressive, unfairly prejudicial or unfairly disregarding conduct. They may also need to provide guidance on what principles operate in granting a remedy to unliquidated and contingent claims in particular circumstances.

e. Trustees and Oppression Remedies

While not directly relevant to the *CCAA*, it is important to note that in bankruptcy, trustees may be able to bring an oppression application, and the availability of this mechanism is a factor for parties to consider during *CCAA* proceedings, particularly where they face collective action problems.

It has only become clear in recent years that trustees can bring an oppression claim in some circumstances. In 1991, the Court in *Canada (Attorney General)* v. *Standard Trust Co.* held that a trustee takes the property of the bankrupt as it finds it and has no higher rights than the corporation itself; hence the trustee was not a proper person to seek oppression remedy relief.[64] It was another decade before the Court in *Olympia & York Developments Ltd. (Trustee of)* found that a trustee could bring an oppression application in its role as representative of creditors.[65] The court reasoned that since creditors can bring applications, the trustee in the course of its duties to seek remedies for creditors should be able to bring an oppression claim. The court held that bankruptcy legislation generally encourages collective action on the part of the trustee as the effective and efficient way of proceeding.[66] Essentially, the trustee operates in several capacities, including having obligations to creditors generally; and exercises its discretion to pursue remedies under sections 91-101 of the *BIA* as representative of creditors. Hence when the court considers the trustee's status, it

---

[63] *ADI Ltd.* v. *052987 N.B. Inc.* (2000), [2000] N.B.J. No. 467, 22 C.B.R. (4th) 1 (N.B. C.A.) at paras. 65, 66 and 72, leave to appeal refused (2001), 2001 CarswellNB 253, [2001] S.C.C.A. No. 48 (S.C.C.).

[64] *Canada (Attorney General)* v. *Standard Trust Co.* (1991), 5 O.R. (3d) 660 (Ont. Gen. Div.).

[65] *Olympia & York Developments Ltd. (Trustee of)* v. *Olympia & York Realty Corp.* (2001), [2001] O.J. No. 3394, 2001 CarswellOnt 2954 (Ont. S.C.J. [Commercial List]), additional reasons at (2001), 2001 CarswellOnt 4739 (Ont. S.C.J. [Commercial List]), affirmed (2003), 68 O.R. (3d) 544 (Ont. C.A.).

[66] *Ibid.* at para. 30.

should be the creditor representation part that is foremost in the court's consideration of granting the complainant status under the oppression remedy provisions.[67]

Trustees in bankruptcy have now been found on several occasions to be appropriate parties to bring oppression claims, in effect on behalf of creditors, in order to protect creditors where the alleged conduct was oppressive, unfairly prejudicial to or unfairly disregarded the interests of creditors.[68]

f. Examples of Oppression Cases Involving Creditors

In *Sidaplex-Plastics Suppliers Inc.* v. *Elta Group Inc.*, the Ontario Court of Appeal held that the conduct of the corporation and its sole director/officer/shareholder was unfairly prejudicial to or unfairly disregarded the interests of a judgment creditor that had sought an oppression remedy.[69] The respondent corporation had failed to renew a letter of credit, which was to be security for a judgment debt owing to the plaintiff. All other creditors' claims had been met and the sole director had benefited from the lapse because he had used the corporation's assets to relieve his exposure under a personal guarantee. The Court held that this action had unfairly prejudiced or unfairly disregarded the plaintiff creditor's interests within the oppression provisions of the *OBCA* and found the director personally liable. Since the corporation no longer had assets, the court held that it was appropriate to rectify the matter by requiring the director to personally compensate the creditor for the loss.[70]

In *369413 Alberta Ltd.* v. *Pocklington*, the Alberta Court of Appeal held that where a director and shareholder had acquired a valuable asset for nominal consideration at the expense of the insolvent corporation's creditors and had promoted the interests of one shareholder at the expense of creditors, the director was not acting in the best interests of the corporation and thus was held personally liable.[71]

In *Adecco Canada Inc.* v. *J. Ward Broome Ltd.*, the Court held a director personally liable for foreclosure transactions that caused unfair prejudice and had unfairly disregarded the interests of unsecured creditors.[72] As directing mind of two companies, the Court held that the director stood to benefit if Newco foreclosed on the assets of Oldco because the surplus generated after accounting for the old company's

---

[67] Janis Sarra, "The Oppression Remedy: The *Peoples'* Choice", in *Annual Review of Insolvency Law, 2005* (Toronto: Carswell, 2006) at 111-156.

[68] *Ibid.*; *Dylex Ltd. (Trustee of)* v. *Anderson* (2003), 2003 CarswellOnt 819, 63 O.R. (3d) 659 (Ont. S.C.J.).

[69] *Sidaplex-Plastic Suppliers Inc.* v. *Elta Group Inc.* (1995), 131 D.L.R. (4th) 399 (Ont. Gen. Div. [Commercial List]) at para. 5, reversed (1998), 162 D.L.R. (4th) 367 (Ont. C.A.).

[70] *Ibid.* at para. 24.

[71] *369413 Alberta Ltd.* v. *Pocklington* (2000), 2000 CarswellAlta 1295, [2000] A.J. No. 1350 (Alta. C.A.) at paras. 60, 67, 69, 88.

[72] *Adecco Canada Inc.* v. *J. Ward Broome Ltd.* (2001), 2001 CarswellOnt 1173, 21 C.B.R. (4th) 181 (Ont. S.C.J. (Commercial List)), additional reasons at (2001), 2001 CarswellOnt 1173 (Ont. S.C.J. [Commercial List]). For a discussion, see, Janis P. Sarra and Ronald B. Davis, *Director and Officer Liability in Corporate Insolvency*, (Toronto: Butterworths Canada Ltd., 2002) at 40.

secured debt would accrue to the benefit of Newco instead of the unsecured creditors, allowing the latter to continue in business without the burden of old debts.[73] On the facts, the Court held that an unsecured creditor would reasonably expect that the secured creditor would have proceeded to collect the accounts receivable rather than foreclose, and that even if it had chosen to foreclose, the creditor could have reasonably expected the debtor to object to the foreclosure during the notice period.[74] The Court held that the respondents failed to demonstrate that the foreclosure was a reasonable business decision, rather than a form of self-dealing.[75] It held that the director had caused unfair prejudice to and had unfairly disregarded the interests of the unsecured creditor; the director was held personally liable and was ordered jointly and severally liable with Newco to pay the sum of the value of assets in excess of the amount owing on the bank loan.[76]

In *Fiber Connections,* a debtor sought a motion to approve an amended proposal under the *BIA* and terminate a unanimous shareholders' agreement (the "USA") and terms of a prior proposal.[77] The Ontario Superior Court of Justice held that a corporation can qualify as a proper person to make an oppression application under section 248 of the Ontario *Business Corporations Act* against the corporation where: (a) a shareholder is attempting to oppose the corporation's proposal under the *BIA* by relying on a USA that requires the shareholder's consent to amend the share structure; (b) the corporation is a party to the USA; (c) the contemplated restructuring cannot be carried out without a change to the share structure, which requires actions on the part of the corporation; (d) all of the other shareholders and creditors of the corporation consent to the remedy sought in the name of the corporation; and (e) the corporation is a necessary party to the remedy. The Court further held that it is oppressive to a corporation and its stakeholders to permit a shareholder to exercise its veto right under a USA and end the corporation's prospect for a restructuring when virtually all of the shareholders, directors, creditors and employees believe that the corporation has a future.

The Court in *Fiber Connections* held that it cannot be the reasonable expectation of all shareholders of a corporation, whose shares have no economic value, that one shareholder can deprive them of the possibility of achieving some value through a restructuring by employing a veto, the effect of which would put the corporation into bankruptcy. In the event it was found in error in respect of the ability to find a corporation a complainant oppressed under the *OBCA*, the Court held that it has the

---

[73] *Ibid.*, citing s. 245(c), *OBCA*.

[74] *Ibid.* at para. 24; the notice period was under s. 65 of the *Personal Property Security Act*, R.S.O. 1990, c. P.10, and would have required a disposition of the collateral and an accounting for the surplus.

[75] *Ibid.* at para. 25.

[76] *Ibid.* at paras. 28-30. Given that there were other unsecured creditors as well as the applicant Adecco, the court ordered that the sums to be paid by the director and Newco should be made available to satisfy the claims of all creditors, not just the applicant.

[77] *Fiber Connections Inc.* v. *SVCM Capital Ltd.* (2005), 2005 CarswellOnt 1963 (Ont. S.C.J.), leave to appeal granted (2005), 2005 CarswellOnt 1834, 10 C.B.R. (5th) 201 (Ont. C.A. [In Chambers]). A unanimous shareholder agreement is allowed under Canadian corporations statutes to allow shareholders to remove some powers from the directors and vest those decision making powers, duties and liabilities in the shareholders themselves. See for example, section 146 of the *CBCA*.

jurisdiction under the *BIA* to set aside the USA and approve the proposal in order to prevent one shareholder, with no economic interest, from blocking a restructuring that is in the best interests of the stakeholders. Since shareholders under a USA assume directors' duties to the extent that the USA allows them to exercise the powers of directors, the Court was, in effect, ruling on whether or not the exercise of the veto was in the best interests of the corporation.

Canadian courts, to date, appear not to have granted an oppression remedy to employees, or, where they have, it has been in their capacity as a shareholder or officer of the corporation.[78] Generally, in Canadian law, employee complaints of whatever kind are limited to the human rights, employment and labour statutory schemes, given that employment standards, labour relations, workers' compensation, human rights, pension law, etc., are viewed as comprehensive regimes that cover the full scope of employee complaints regarding the conduct of directors and officers. While in the normal course of business dealings this may make some sense, the issue is whether employees should also have access to the oppression remedy in some circumstances.

g. Business Judgment Rule

On finding that directors owe a duty of care to creditors, the Supreme Court in *Peoples Department Stores* also made the strongest statement to date regarding deference by the courts to directors' and officers' business judgments, explicitly enshrining a "business judgment rule". Prior to this decision, the judgments of Canadian courts were mixed as to whether Canada has a business judgment rule, although many courts have held that the court should defer to some extent to the business judgments of directors and officers in their duly diligent activities. The Supreme Court held:

> ¶ 64 The contextual approach dictated by s.122(1)(b) of the *CBCA* not only emphasizes the primary facts but also permits prevailing socio-economic conditions to be taken into consideration. The emergence of stricter standards puts pressure on corporations to improve the quality of board decisions. The establishment of good corporate governance rules should be a shield that protects directors from allegations that they have breached their duty of care. However, even with good corporate governance rules, directors' decisions can still be open to criticism from outsiders. Canadian courts, like their counterparts in the United States, the United Kingdom, Australia and New Zealand, have tended to take an approach with respect to the enforcement of the duty of care that respects the fact that directors and officers often have business expertise that courts do not. Many decisions made in the course of business, although ultimately unsuccessful, are reasonable and defensible at the time

[78] See for example, *Joncas* v. *Spruce Falls Power and Paper Co. Ltd.* (2000), 48 O.R. (3d) 179 (Ont. S.C.J.), affirmed (2001), 15 B.L.R. (3d) 1 (Ont. C.A.); *Clitheroe* v. *Hydro One Inc.* (2002), 2002 CarswellOnt 3919, [2002] O.J. No. 4383 (Ont. S.C.J.); *Vlasbom* v. *NetPCS Networks Inc.* (2003), 2003 CarswellOnt 538, [2003] O.J. No. 535, 31 B.L.R. (3d) 255 (Ont. S.C.J.), additional reasons at (2003), 2003 CarswellOnt 2093 (Ont. S.C.J.).

> they are made. Business decisions must sometimes be made, with high stakes and under considerable time pressure, in circumstances in which detailed information is not available. It might be tempting for some to see unsuccessful business decisions as unreasonable or imprudent in light of information that becomes available *ex post facto*. Because of this risk of hindsight bias, Canadian courts have developed a rule of deference to business decisions called the "business judgment rule", adopting the American name for the rule.

On the facts of the case, the Court found that the implementation of a new inventory purchase policy was a reasonable business decision that was made with a view to rectifying a serious and urgent business problem and found that the directors were not liable for a breach of their duty of care in respect of the creditors of *Peoples Department Stores*.[79] The Supreme Court did not really specify how the business judgment rule is to be applied in Canada, having formally recognized its existence. The U.S. formulation of the standard has been that directors must have acted free of any conflicting interests, in which case a high degree of deference is accorded. Where there are conflicting interests, the burden shifts to directors to demonstrate the entire fairness of the impugned transaction.[80]

One further issue in the *Peoples Department Stores* case was that directors were on both sides of the impugned transaction in the sense that the directors were the same people for both corporations. This raises the question of how deference to business judgment should operate when the directors are directors of the two corporations involved in the same transaction and hence arguably have a conflict of interest where granting credit or other decision benefits one corporation to the detriment of another. In *Peoples Department Stores,* the Supreme Court failed to fully consider that the directors were on both sides of the transaction where they extended credit from the Peoples Department Stores to the affiliated but separate Wise Stores. In such a case of conflicting interests, there should be a heightened scrutiny of directors' conduct.[81]

In *UPM-Kymmene Corp.*, the Ontario Court of Appeal endorsed the lower court finding that the business judgment rule "recognizes the autonomy and integrity of a corporation and the expertise of its directors" since they are "in the advantageous position of investigating and considering first-hand the circumstances that come before it and are in a far better position than a court to understand the affairs of the corporation and to guide its operation".[82] There, the Ontario Court of Appeal held

---

[79] *Ibid.* at paras. 68-70.

[80] *Pente Investment Management Ltd.* v. *Schneider Corp.* (1998), 40 B.L.R. (2d) 244 (Ont. Gen. Div. [Commercial List]), affirmed (1998), (sub nom. *Maple Leaf Foods Inc.* v. *Schneider Corp.*) 42 O.R. (3d) 177 (Ont. C.A.). The *CBCA* ss. 120(7) requires any transaction in which a director has an interest be reasonable and fair to the corporation at the time when it is approved by those directors who do not have an interest, following full disclosure of the interest by the interested director.

[81] Janis Sarra, "The Oppression Remedy: The *Peoples'* Choice", in *Annual Review of Insolvency Law, 2005* (Toronto: Carswell, 2006) at 111-156.

[82] *UPM-Kymmene Corp.* v. *UPM-Kymmene Miramichi Inc.* (2002), 214 D.L.R. (4th) 496 (Ont. S.C.J.) at para. 6, additional reasons at (2002), 2002 CarswellOnt 3579 (Ont. S.C.J. [Commercial List]), affirmed (2004), 2004 CarswellOnt 691, [2004] O.J. No. 636 (Ont. C.A.).

that the director's deliberations fell far short of the exercise of prudent judgment.[83] The Ontario Superior Court in *UPM-Kymmene* held the following in respect of how the business judgment rule is to be applied:

> ¶ 153 However, directors are only protected to the extent that their actions actually evidence their business judgment. The principle of deference presupposes that directors are scrupulous in their deliberations and demonstrate diligence in arriving at decisions. Courts are entitled to consider the content of their decision and the extent of the information on which it was based and to measure this against the facts as they existed at the time the impugned decision was made. Although Board decisions are not subject to microscopic examination with the perfect vision of hindsight, they are subject to examination.

The Court in *Air Canada* held that directors' duties and obligations are to the corporation, no matter who nominates the director.[84] Where creditors have not challenged the governance of the debtor corporation, the court will defer to the business judgment of directors and officers. In assessing a governance decision during a *CCAA* proceeding, the court must be satisfied that creditors as a whole are receiving fair and equitable treatment and that there has been a balancing of interests, with parties sharing the pain of compromise on an equitable basis, as well as the potential for "gain" in a viable going forward plan.[85]

h. Scope of Remedies

The remedies offered under oppression provisions of corporations statutes are broad, granting the court the discretion to make any interim or final order it thinks fit, including orders restraining conduct complained of; an order appointing a receiver-manager; an order to regulate the corporation's affairs by amending articles or creating or amending a unanimous shareholder agreement; an order directing the issue or exchange of securities; an order appointing directors in place of or in addition to existing directors; an order directing the corporation or any other person to pay a security holder any part of the money paid by the security holder for securities; an order varying or setting aside a transaction or contract to which the corporation is a party and compensating the corporation or any other party to the transaction or contract; an order requiring a corporation, within the time specified, to produce to the court or an interested person financial statements or an accounting in such other form as the court may determine; an order compensating an aggrieved person; an order directing rectification of the register or other records of the corporation; and/

---

[83] *Ibid.* at para. 7.

[84] *Air Canada, Re* (2003), 2003 CarswellOnt 5243 (Ont. S.C.J. [Commercial List]) at para. 5. See also *820099 Ontario Inc.* v. *Harold E. Ballard Ltd.* (1991), [1991] O.J. No. 266, 1991 CarswellOnt 142 (Ont. Gen. Div.), additional reasons at (May 7, 1991), Doc. RE 1305/90 (Ont. Gen. Div.), affirmed (1991), 1991 CarswellOnt 141 (Ont. Div. Ct.).

[85] *Air Canada, ibid.* at para. 9.

or a winding-up order; an order directing an investigation; and an order requiring a trial of any issue.[86]

The courts have a wide discretion to fashion a remedy appropriate to the circumstances; however, the remedy fashioned should be limited to rectifying the conduct complained of. Numerous courts have cited Mr. Justice Farley in *820099 Ontario Inc.* v. *Harold E. Ballard Ltd.*, that the remedy to correct an oppressive act "should be done with a scalpel, and not a battle axe" and that the task of the court is to even the balance, not tip it in favour of the injured party.[87]

In *Canadian Airlines,* a motion was brought to lift the *CCAA* stay to pursue oppression claims against the officers of Canadian Airlines and Air Canada, alleging that the officers had stripped Canadian Airlines of valuable assets such as flight routes, lease arrangements and goodwill in a manner that was oppressive, that the nature of the takeover transaction had contained material misrepresentations in terms of returning Canadian Airlines to a viable operation, and that their actions made a post-takeover stand-alone corporation impossible. The applicants also alleged that the use of the Alberta *Business Corporations Act* was oppressive in the manner in which it allowed conversion and retraction of all common shares at a value of $1, thus eliminating minority shareholder interest in the restructured corporation, and was oppressive in allowing the preferred shares held by 853350 Alberta to be converted to common shares. Instead of granting the motion to lift the stay, the Alberta Court of Queen's Bench ordered the oppression allegations to be heard in the context of the fairness inquiry at the plan sanctioning hearing.

Madam Justice Marina Paperny in *Canadian Airlines* held that "oppression is the antithesis of fairness" and thus it was appropriate to consider the issue in the context of the proposed plan, specifically, whether the corporation's actions were "unauthorized matters" or unfair. The Court held that the rights and expectations of creditors and shareholders in respect of oppression remedies must be viewed through the lens of insolvency. Equity and fairness are measured or considered in the context of the rights, interests or reasonable expectations of the complainants. Here, eliminated rights were in the context of an insolvency workout, not because of oppressive conduct. The Court held that the breach of the debenture terms did not impact differently on the applicant creditor than other defaults under the moratorium. The Court also held that pre-filing negotiations were to be encouraged as facilitating the objectives of the *CCAA* and as such were not oppressive. The negotiations and

---

[86] Section 241(3) *CBCA*. See also *OBCA*, s. 248 (3); *BCBCA*, s. 227(3); *ABCA*, s. 242(3); *SBCA*, s. 234(3), *MCA*, s. 234(3); *NBBCA*, s. 166(3); *NSCA*, 2nd Sch., 1999, s. 5(3); *NFLDCA*, s. 371(3); *NWTBCA*, s. 243(3); *NBCA*, s. 243(3).

[87] *820099 Ontario Inc.* v. *Harold E. Ballard Ltd.* (1991), [1991] O.J. No. 266, 1991 CarswellOnt 142 (Ont. Gen. Div.), at para. 140, additional reasons at (May 7, 1991), Doc. RE 1305/90 (Ont. Gen. Div.), affirmed (1991), 1991 CarswellOnt 141 (Ont. Div. Ct.).

arrangements pre-*CCAA* filing had prevented bankruptcy and created the stability to facilitate the workout.[88]

In respect of the oppression claims under the proposed share reorganization, the Court in *Canadian Airlines* held that the Alberta *Business Corporations Act* allows corporate articles, including share structure and rights, to be amended in the context of a *CCAA* plan.[89] It held that the conduct of Air Canada could only be oppressive if there was either a going concern alternative under which there was shareholder and creditor value in excess of that anticipated by the proposed plan, or if a liquidation would have allowed recovery for unsecured creditors and shareholders. The Court considered a liquidation analysis prepared by the monitor, which estimated that liquidation would result in a shortfall to secured creditors; realization of 1-3 cents on the dollar for unsecured creditors; and no recovery by shareholders. There were no known alternative going-concern purchasers after more than a year of the corporation searching. Thus the Court rejected the oppression claims and approved the capital reorganization. The Court held that the plan did not harm shareholders because their economic interest in the corporation had vanished before the *CCAA* proceedings.[90]

In the context of approving a stalking horse proceeding in *Stelco Inc.*, Mr. Justice Farley held that any difficulties in the process would be met by the duty owing by directors of the corporation to maximize its value and by the threat of action pursuant to the oppression remedy under the *CBCA*.[91] Citing the *Peoples Department Stores* judgment, the Court held that the oppression remedy provisions are powerful weapons that directors and officers should be cognizant of in exercising their duty to the corporation, noting that the remedy does not require that wrongdoing be involved.

In the context of granting a leave to commence a derivative action under the British Columbia *Business Corporations Act* and an oppression action against the same defendants, the British Columbia Supreme Court relied on *Peoples Department Stores* to make the following observation:[92]

---

[88] *Canadian Airlines Corp.* (2000), 2000 CarswellAlta 662, [2000] A.J. No. 771 (Alta. Q.B.) at paras. 95, 140, leave to appeal refused (2000), 2000 CarswellAlta 919, [2000] A.J. No. 1028 (Alta. C.A. [In Chambers]), affirmed (2000), 2000 CarswellAlta 1556 (Alta. C.A.), leave to appeal refused (2001), 2001 CarswellAlta 888 (S.C.C.).

[89] Sections 167, 185, Alberta *Business Corporations Act*, S.A. 1981, c. B-15, as amended. Resurgence appealed the order sanctioning the Plan of Arrangement and Compromise. The Alberta Court of Appeal dismissed the application, finding that the Court's jurisdiction was limited to either upholding the Plan or setting it aside. The Court of Appeal held that the role of the supervising judge in ensuring a timely and orderly resolution of workout issues, as well as the effect on the interests of all parties were factors to be considered in *CCAA* proceedings. It endorsed the lower court's reasoning that oppression must be assessed in the context of the insolvency and reasonable expectations of creditors.

[90] *Canadian Airlines Corp., Re* (2000), 2000 CarswellAlta 919, [2000] A.J. No. 1028 (Alta. C.A.).

[91] *Stelco Inc., Re* (2004), 2004 CarswellOnt 5076, [2004] O.J. No. 4899 (Ont. S.C.J. [Commercial List]) at para. 3.

[92] *Carr* v. *Cheng*, (2005), 2005 CarswellBC 695, [2005] B.C.J. No. 664 (B.C. S.C.) at para. 25.

> The Supreme Court of Canada said at paras. 42-44 that best interests of the company did not simply mean best interests of the shareholders and that from an economic perspective, best interests means the maximization of the value of the corporation. Depending on the circumstances, best interests can include consideration of the interests of shareholders, employees and others. The main goal is the maximization of the value of the corporation. It is best for a corporation to be profitable, well capitalized and with strong prospects. The deterioration of the corporation's financial stability is to be avoided. It appears to this court to be in the best interest of the company to proceed with a derivative action in the circumstances here when the core financial stability of the company appears to be threatened.[93]

These observations appear to indicate that the courts are taking direction from the Supreme Court of Canada in terms of the broad nature of the remedy. However, in another judgment in *Stelco*, the Ontario Court of Appeal, at least on the governance issues, appears to have a less generous view on the scope of the remedy.[94] Although oppression had not been argued, the Court held that it would be a high standard to meet before actual conduct has risen to the level of misconduct required to trigger oppression remedy relief.[95]

The Ontario Superior Court in *Catalyst Fund General Partner I Inc.* v. *Hollinger Inc.*, granted an oppression application removing directors that were motivated to place their own interests ahead of those of the company and public shareholders, finding that director removal is an extraordinary remedy, but that it is appropriate where the continuing presence of the incumbent directors is harmful to both the company and the interests of corporate stakeholders and where the appointment of new director(s) would remedy the oppressive conduct.[96]

In *Harbert Distressed Investment Master Fund*, the Nova Scotia Supreme Court, after dealing with preliminary issues such as jurisdiction and standing, determined an oppression application under the Nova Scotia *Companies Act (NSCA)*.[97] Harbert is an investment fund specializing in distressed and high yield debt securities, registered in the Cayman Islands with business carried on largely from New York.[98]

---

[93] *Ibid.* at paras. 25-26.

[94] *Stelco Inc., Re* (2005), 2 B.L.R. (4th) 238, 9 C.B.R. (5th) 135 (Ont. C.A.) at paras. 48-49.

[95] *Ibid.* at para. 47. The Court of Appeal cited those provisions of the Supreme Court judgment that discussed best interests of the corporation and the legitimacy in some circumstances of considering the interests of shareholders, employees, suppliers, creditors, consumers, governments and the environment, with a view to creating a better corporation and without favouring the interests of any one group of stakeholders, *ibid.* at para. 60.

[96] *Catalyst Fund General Partner I Inc.* v. *Hollinger Inc.* (2004), 2004 CarswellOnt 4772, [2004] O.J. No. 4722 (Ont. S.C.J.), affirmed (2006), 2006 CarswellOnt 1416 (Ont. C.A.) at paras. 68, 72, citing D. Peterson, *Shareholder Remedies in Canada* (Markham: LexisNexis Butterworths, 1989).

[97] *Harbert Distressed Investment Master Fund, Ltd.* v. *Calpine Canada Energy Finance II ULC* (2005), 2005 CarswellNS 342, [2005] N.S.J. No. 317 (N.S. S.C.). See the Court's reasoning on issues of jurisdiction and standing at paras. 60-94. Nova Scotia *Companies Act*, s. 5, Third Schedule.

[98] *Ibid.* at para. 2. The other applicant, Wilmington Trust Company, is a Delaware banking corporation and trustee in relation to the bonds. Two of the respondent companies, Calpine Canada Energy Finance II ULC and Calpine Canada Resources Company are unlimited liability companies pursuant to the *NSCA*. Two other respondent affiliated companies are corporations organized under the laws

It bought a series of senior notes or bonds.[99] Citing *Peoples Department Stores*, the Nova Scotia Supreme Court held that while the court has the ability in the appropriate circumstances to grant relief from oppressive, unfairly prejudicial or unfairly disregarding conduct, the court must be careful not to inappropriately intrude into the legitimate conduct of a company's business.[100]

On the facts in *Harbert Distressed Investment Master Fund*, the Court held that the respondent companies had unfairly disregarded the interests of the bondholders, in that one of the affiliated companies had taken its interest in a valuable asset (proceeds it received from a transaction) and substituted an asset of more dubious value (unsecured promissory notes) and that it acquiesced in the upstreaming of funds from a transaction out of its control, despite the fact that the result would be that it would lose control of its most meaningful asset with no direct benefit to it.[101] The Court found that these actions were contrary to both a clause of a term debenture (that the bondholder oppression applicants were not party to) and to the bondholder applicant's interests, in that the affiliated respondent companies, by failing to enforce their rights to preserve and protect their assets, unfairly disregarded the interests of the bondholders.[102] The court held that it was entitled to consider all of the surrounding circumstances, including the debenture, even where the applicants were not party to it and thus could not sue directly on the debenture.

The Court in *Harbert Distressed Investment Master Fund* also found that the parent corporation had unfairly disregarded the interests of the affiliate's bondholders; the closely held nature of the companies and interrelated directors meant that the company could not now ignore the very corporate structure that it elected.[103] However, with respect to the remedy, the court held that a sophisticated investor that decides to become a security holder knowing that the impugned conduct is occurring cannot be said to have had reasonable expectations to the contrary or maintain that it has been oppressed. Hence, Harbert's application for a remedy (and that of another company it purchased for) was not granted.[104] However, for the bondholders that purchased prior to the impugned conduct, the Court held that it could grant a remedy, finding that it was appropriate that different security holders be treated differently,

---

of Jersey in the Channel Islands and the parent, Calpine Corporation, is registered under Delaware company law, trading on the NYSE.

[99] *Ibid.* at paras. 7, 8.

[100] *Ibid.* at paras. 106, 107. It endorsed the above-cited reasoning in *Piller Sausages & Delicatessens Ltd.* in respect of the differences in each condition or standard under the remedy and held that oppression cases are fact driven.

[101] *Ibid.* at paras. 129, 135 and 136.

[102] *Ibid.* at para. 138.

[103] *Ibid.* at para. 141.

[104] *Ibid.* at paras. 169-181, 188. The Court distinguished this finding from a situation where the complainant purchased a security in order to bring a derivative application, based primarily on the "reasonable expectations" part of the test for an oppression remedy.

as their reasonable expectations in respect of the directors' conduct may differ for good reason, beyond a subjective view of the matter.[105]

5. Indemnification of Directors during the Workout Process

When a firm is financially distressed, director and officer liability insurance is often difficult or expensive to obtain. This is because often few or no assets are available to indemnify the officers, and insurance companies do not like the risks. As a result, the courts in the initial stay orders frequently order indemnification of directors and officers, so that those who may be key to the workout process will stay during the restructuring period.[106]

The stay of claims against directors during the *CCAA* proceeding allows the parties to consider whether a compromise or arrangement can be made in respect of these claims, as discussed in the next part of this chapter, while encouraging directors, where they are required to assist in devising a workout strategy for the debtor company, to carry on in their oversight capacity. The stay of proceedings against directors does not stay actions against directors on a guarantee given by the director relating to the company's obligations or an action seeking injunctive relief against a director in relation to a company.[107] Any person who manages or supervises the business and affairs of the company where all the directors have resigned or been removed by shareholders without replacement, is deemed to be a director for purposes of the stay provisions.[108]

In addition to negotiating golden parachutes, there is an increasing tendency for directors to seek large and extensive director and officer (D&O) liability protection. Directors can legitimately ask for protection going forward, as this encourages them to stay during the workout process. However, some directors attempt to get liability

---

[105] *Ibid.* at para. 190-192. The Court ordered the trustee to provide to the respondents and the court a list of all Finance II bondholders that fulfilled the criteria of having purchased the bonds prior to September 1, 2004 and continuing to hold them as of the date of the judgment. An order would then issue requiring Calpine to maintain in the control of the affiliate sufficient proceeds from the sale transaction to cover the face value of the bonds, and where there were not sufficient funds, the Court ordered the parent company to place in the affiliate's control an additional amount to cover the value. The order was to further provide that the affiliate would conduct its business in a proper and efficient manner so as to preserve and protect its business and assets.

[106] To the extent that an insurance policy exists to cover directors and officers (D&O) liability, the initial order usually specifically provides that these policies cannot be terminated by the insurer, in addition to ordering a D&O liability indemnification charge. In view of the finality and validity of deeming and termination provisions in civil law, the practice that evolved in Québec is to provide in the initial order that it applies retroactively. The standard order developed between the Québec Bar and the judiciary provides that the initial order applies as and from one minute past midnight on the day before the order is rendered. This ensures that no creditor can terminate a contract (including, for instance, invoking the insolvency to terminate an insurance policy) while the debtor is presenting its application or while the court is deciding whether the relief should be granted, which might render the relief moot.

[107] Section 11.5(2), *CCAA*.

[108] Section 11.5(3), *CCAA*.

protection for prior conduct. This could become problematic. In one instance, the DIP lender used the DIP negotiations to seek as broad a release as possible for those of its directors that were involved on the debtor corporation's board.[109]

In the Air Canada restructuring, there was a directors' insurance policy, a directors' trust and a directors' charge. The Court held that there should be some exposure to liability and ordered that affected directors and officers would be required to make a contribution of 5% of the amount of the directors' charge utilized for the protection or indemnification, that amount to go into the general fund for the benefit of creditors.[110] The Court also viewed the directors' trust favourably in terms of its application to pre-filing obligations, but was of the view that it was inappropriate for the insurance to be applied to the pre-filing obligations.

Currently, many *CCAA* orders include indemnification for directors with a first charge on the assets, as a means to limit their liability exposure and encourage them to stay during the workout period. Unlike a universal safe harbour that would then give rise to *ex ante* incentives to neglect their duty to consider the interests of creditors, the protection here is granted by the court under the supervised *CCAA* proceeding where creditors have notice of the indemnification and can make representations. This ability of creditors to make representations to the court in those instances where such protection is not appropriate due to the failure to consider the creditors' interests provides the proper *ex ante* incentives to directors to discharge their duties diligently. Stakeholders such as employees, pensioners and community members affected by environmental harms also have an opportunity to challenge the first charge and have the court make a determination as to the scope of liability protection.

In *Afton Food Group Ltd.*, the Ontario Superior Court of Justice held that the indemnification provisions in a debtor company's initial *CCAA* order and continued in a receivership order in favour of directors will extend to liabilities for which the former directors of the debtor company may be personally liable and that existed before the date of the initial *CCAA* order if such liabilities otherwise fall within the scope of the indemnities included in the initial *CCAA* order. A directors' charge that secures the indemnification provisions in the orders is exclusive of legal fees and disbursements that have been paid by the debtor company to counsel for the former directors in accordance with the terms of the orders. The Court further held that a group of former directors of the debtor company are entitled to retain separate counsel and the indemnity regarding legal fees applies to the reasonable fees and disbursements of their counsel in connection with a claim that has been asserted against such group of former directors by another former director of the debtor company.[111]

---

[109] See the discussion of BCE and *Teleglobe*, Court File No. 02-CL-4528.

[110] *Air Canada, Re* (2003), 42 C.B.R. (4th) 173 (Ont. S.C.J.).

[111] *Afton Food Group Ltd., Re* (2006), 2006 CarswellOnt 3002 (Ont. S.C.J.).

III. COMPROMISE OF CLAIMS AGAINST DIRECTORS

The *CCAA* allows for a compromise of claims against directors as part of the terms of a plan of arrangement.[112] Hence, there is an incentive to retain control and oversight during the workout negotiations to ensure that the debtor corporation exits from *CCAA* protection with no claims personally against the directors. The positive aspect of this liability protection is that directors will stay with the debtor corporation and provide important informational capital and helpful oversight during this period.[113] This assumes, of course, that directors are actively involved and have been engaged in oversight prior to the firm's financial distress, a role for directors that is somewhat uneven across different companies. The financial distress of the firm also places new demands on directors' time, in that strategic decisions are being made, frequently even on a daily basis, during the *CCAA* stay period, given the pressure to find a going forward strategy.

Under section 5.1 of the *CCAA,* a plan of compromise or arrangement may include in its terms provision for the compromise of claims against directors of the company that arose before commencement of *CCAA* proceedings and that relate to the obligations of the company where the directors are in their capacity as directors liable for payment of such obligations.[114] The ability to compromise claims may encourage directors to enter proceedings earlier and thus may prevent value from being lost because the firm's financial distress is dealt with on a timely basis. The downside of the liability protection is the risk to the firm from director self-dealing or self-protecting to the detriment of the general body of creditors.[115]

There are exceptions to this safe harbour protection. Section 5.1 of the *CCAA* specifies that claims against directors cannot be compromised where they relate to contractual rights of one or more creditors arising from contracts with a director or directors; claims based on allegations of misrepresentations made by directors to creditors; or claims based on allegations of wrongful or oppressive conduct by the directors. This provision reduces the risk that directors will engage in misconduct because such claims cannot be compromised under the plan.

The court may declare that a claim against directors shall not be compromised if the court is satisfied that the compromise would not be fair and reasonable in the circumstances.[116] Where directors have been removed or have resigned without replacement, the *CCAA* specifies that any person who manages or supervises the management of the business and affairs of the debtor corporation is deemed to be a director for purposes of the section.[117]

---

[112] Section 5.1, *CCAA*.

[113] *General Publishing Co.* (2003), 2003 CarswellOnt 275 (Ont. S.C.J.) at para. 6, affirmed (2004), 1 C.B.R. (5th) 202 (Ont. C.A.).

[114] Section 5.1(1), *CCAA*.

[115] *SLMSoft Inc., Re* (2003), 2003 CarswellOnt 4402 (Ont. S.C.J.).

[116] Section 5.1(3), *CCAA*.

[117] Section 5.1(4), *CCAA*.

In *Canadian Airlines*, the clause of the *CCAA* plan that compromised claims against directors did not make clear that the compromise was only relating to claims that arose prior to commencement of the proceedings and failed to make clear that the compromise excluded claims excepted by section 5.1(3) of the *CCAA*. The Court, during the sanctioning process, amended the plan to add words that clarified both of these statutory requirements.[118] The plan in that case also released claims against third parties such as officers and employees, and the Court held that although the *CCAA* does not expressly authorize a release of such claims, it does not prohibit such releases; hence it approved the release of claims.

While section 5.1 of the *CCAA* is helpful, it is often not a central focus for directors, as they have much less control over the outcome of the process than creditors. Jean-Daniel Breton has questioned the usefulness of the provisions of the *CCAA* purportedly protecting directors, as the liabilities that are most often a cause of concern for directors are obligations towards employees or towards governments; and the conditions giving rise to liability under the statutes creating these directors' personal obligations are not present in the context of a restructuring under the *CCAA*. He suggests that typically, under employment standards legislation, tax laws or supplementary pension plan legislation, the conditions giving rise to liability on a joint and several basis with the corporation include that the corporation has been sued for the debt and the judgment was incapable of being satisfied, or the company has been the object of liquidation proceedings or has become bankrupt, and the claim filed could not be satisfied.[119]

IV. CORPORATE MANAGERS – INFORMATIONAL CAPITAL OR ENTRENCHMENT?

The role of pre-filing corporate managers in a *CCAA* restructuring depends in large measure on the reasons for the financial distress, the relationship of the managers with the board, whether there is a need for a chief restructuring officer, and sometimes, the views of the most senior lenders.

The CEO and other officers may be integrally involved in the workout, bringing important informational capital to the development of a plan of arrangement or compromise. They can contribute industry or sector expertise; have a firm-specific understanding of supplier arrangements, operations and collective agreements; and

---

[118] *Canadian Airlines Corp., Re* (2000), 20 C.B.R. (4th) 1 (Alta. Q.B.), leave to appeal refused (2000), 2000 CarswellAlta 919 (Alta. C.A. [In Chambers]), affirmed (2000), 2000 CarswellAlta 1556 (Alta. C.A.), leave to appeal refused (2001), 2001 CarswellAlta 888 (S.C.C.).

[119] See the text by Jean-Daniel Breton, "Reorganizations: Objectives Contemplated and Achieved by Legislative Changes since 1992", in J. Sarra, ed., *Annual Review of Insolvency Law, 2003* (Toronto: Carswell, 2004). Breton suggests that the specific condition that the corporation has commenced restructuring proceedings under the *BIA* or *CCAA* is not customarily mentioned as one of the triggering conditions. For example, see section 131(2) of the Ontario *Business Corporations' Act*, R.S.O. 1990, chapter B.16, section 323(2) of the *Excise Tax Act*, R.S.C 1985, c. E-15 as amended, and section 53 of the Québec *Supplemental Pension Plans Act*, R.S.Q., chapter R-15.1.

may have a healthy relationship with pre-filing operating lenders. They are frequently also members of the board of directors and stay in that capacity as well.

Equally, however, it may be that the senior officers have significantly contributed to the firm's financial distress and senior creditors, in particular, want some assurance that the assets will not be further unnecessarily depleted during the stay period. In such cases, the debtor corporation (its directors and/or officers) may agree to a chief restructuring officer (CRO) or other turnaround expert to take over operations and negotiations for a plan. Alternatively, the parties may agree that the officers stay in place for a period, but that the monitor will take a more active role in oversight of decisions. A further alternative is that the parties may seek to have an interim receiver appointed within the context of the *CCAA* proceeding. In such cases, whether or not officers remain will depend on those who retain or acquire decision making power during the period of the *CCAA* proceedings. There is always some degree of management change. Often industry experts are hired, rather than a chief restructuring officer.

The board of directors of the debtor corporation often wants managers to remain because of the contributions they can make or because they have longstanding relationships as directors. In cases where it is important to retain senior officers to facilitate the workout, the courts have approved key employee retention plans (KERPs). KERPs can offer managers significant compensation to remain at the company, a golden parachute that guarantees their financial security on exit, and other incentives that encourage these officers to remain with the debtor corporation pending completion of the workout, and sometimes afterwards. KERPs can prevent the untimely loss of skills at a time when the debtor company is trying to continue to operate.[120]

However, there are also a number of instances in which officers use their strategic position to appropriate benefits for themselves. One example, discussed in chapter 4, is where managers are negotiating the size of the DIP facility at the same time they are bargaining for their own KERP or exit strategy. In such cases, there is a conflict of interest, as the officers may negotiate an excessive amount of DIP financing to ensure that the debtor corporation has the financial capacity to meet their compensation demands. Arguably, the *Air Canada* case was an example of this conflict. In other instances, officers bargain terms of DIP financing agreements that prohibit the board from replacing them without the approval of the DIP lender, a strategy that can firmly entrench the officers and can create the wrong incentive effects in terms of how those officers interact with the DIP lender and other stakeholders. While there are few cases to date in Canada, this is an area that may give rise to some litigation.

The Québec Superior Court recently considered the question of inherent jurisdiction in the context of a request to authorize a priority charge for an employee retention

[120] Recent amendments to the U.S. *Bankruptcy Code* have placed new limitations on the use of KERPs under Chapter 11 reorganization proceedings.

program.[121] In *MEI Computer Technology Group Inc.*, Mr. Justice Clément Gascon considered a request for a priming charge for an employee retention program in a *CCAA* proceeding for four groups of employees, including the project managers, key analysts, management and the chief restructuring officer.[122] The debtor sought a priority charge that ranked behind all existing secured debt but ahead of all subsequent security and all unsecured creditors. The Court drew an analogy with the tests used to determine whether or not to grant priming charges in a DIP facility, finding them helpful to its consideration of the issue before the court. The Court held that it would not exercise its inherent jurisdiction to allow the creation of a charge in favour of the employee retention program for the following reasons:

- The charge was aimed at guaranteeing the payment of base amounts to the employees covered, regardless of the outcome of the *CCAA* proceeding, even if the *CCAA* process ended up in liquidation; and thus it was difficult to justify the creation of the charge as the caselaw suggests priming orders should be made only when there exists a reasonable prospect of restructuring.

- The charge would essentially entail the financing of a salary increase for remaining employees by its unsecured creditors, including trade creditors and employees; and that it was difficult to see how this was just and equitable, particularly when, as creditors in the same class, they would likely be paid less than 100% of their claims and many employees had lost their employment.

- The balance that must exist between interest and prejudice among creditors of the same class was not present here.

- The burden of the charge was not shared equitably between the debtor's creditors; if the charge was really key to the debtor's ability to restructure, it was difficult to understand why the charge was created without apportioning some of the cost to secured creditors who would benefit directly from a successful restructuring.

- The cash flow projections were such that there appeared to be other practical ways to structure payments of the base amounts of the employee retention program and to reassure employees so that they stayed, such as tranches to employees over a shorter period.

- Finally, the court was not persuaded that such a charge was necessary to "keep the lights on", and therefore it was not a clear case warranting the creation of an additional charge.[123]

---

[121] *MEI Computer Technology Group Inc., Re* (2005), 2005 CarswellQue 3675, [2005] Q.J. No. 5744 (Que. S.C.).

[122] *Ibid.*

[123] *Ibid.* at para. 26.

This reasoning helpfully used a set of underlying principles to determine whether the court should exercise its discretion in the circumstances to grant a priority charge.

The role of managers is often not visible to participants in the *CCAA* proceeding, because the "face" of the negotiator may not be the officer that is calling the shots. Yet corporate managers can be a pivotal force in either developing the workout plan or standing in the way of development of an effective plan.

V. THE ROLE OF THE CHIEF RESTRUCTURING OFFICER

In the past 15 years, there has been the growing use of chief restructuring officers (CROs) in *CCAA* workouts, frequently appointed in the initial stay order. This development is a governance response to creditor concerns that directors that may have skills appropriate to oversee financially healthy corporations may not have the skills or expertise to deal with a turnaround situation.

The CRO is vested with responsibility to steer the insolvent firm through the negotiation for a plan and the restructuring process. CROs tend to be "turnaround experts" that take over control of the corporation, replacing most of the functions of both the CEO and the directors. Algoma Steel, Loewen and Consumers Packaging Inc. are all recent examples of *CCAA* cases that utilized a CRO.[124] The appointment of a CRO can result in higher creditor confidence, particularly where creditors attribute the firm's financial distress to failures of governance. The CRO can also serve as a buffer between equity investors, directors, officers and creditors, undertaking the often tough negotiations required for an effective workout. As a new participant, the CRO has all the advantages of a fresh assessment of the financial distress and the potential for refinancing and a viable workout.

In *Ivaco,* the Court permitted the participation of a chief restructuring officer in the sale process of an insolvent company.[125] The CRO assessed the various bids and weighed each against the possibility of a stand alone restructuring, and ultimately made recommendations. The Court held that it would consider the following factors in examining the appropriate role of a CRO involved in the sale of an insolvent company: (1) that fairness to all creditors is a pre-requisite to a satisfactory sale process; (2) that a sale process should not result in one unsecured creditor receiving a secret benefit or advantage over other unsecured creditors; (3) that the sale process

---

[124] *Consumers Packaging Inc., Re* (2001) Toronto File No. 01-CL-4147 (Ont. S.C.); M. Forte, "The Recognition and Roles of the Chief Restructuring Officer in Canadian Insolvency Proceedings" (2001) 14 Comm. Insolvency Review 4.

[125] *Ivaco Inc., Re* (2004), 2004 CarswellOnt 2397, 3 C.B.R. (5th) 33 (Ont. S.C.J. [Commercial List]). For a general discussion, see Edward Sellers *et al.*, "Governance of the Financially Distressed Corporation: Selected Aspects of the Financing and Governance of Canadian Enterprises in Cross-Border Workouts" and Geoffrey Morawetz, "Under Pressure: Governance of the Financially Distressed Corporation", in Janis Sarra, *Corporate Governance in Global Capital Markets* (UBC Press, 2003).

must be seen to be fair and transparent; and (4) that the sale process ought to be determined by the court after considering the advice of the monitor, the position of the insolvent company and the positions of the creditors.[126]

A CRO was successfully utilized in the *Consumers Packaging Inc.* (CPI) proceeding, a company that supplied most of the domestic glass bottle market in Canada. It was publicly listed on the Toronto Stock Exchange, but 63.6% held by a shareholder who was also CEO and Chair of the board. CPI faced problems that included a pension deficit liability, aging capital assets, long-term fixed price contracts and enormous increases in input costs. When the corporation began to experience financial distress in 2001, the corporate board struck an Independent Restructuring Committee, recognizing the need for an independent assessment of the financial distress while preventing a control change and acceleration of financial obligations that would have been triggered by debt defaults or dilution of majority shareholder interest.[127] The committee hired a CRO who assumed operational control of the corporation, facilitated a complex debt arrangement and going concern sale process of CPI's principal operating assets under the supervision of the *CCAA* judge.

The workout in *Consumers Packaging Inc.* ultimately generated a value of $61 million greater than CPI's estimated liquidation value. The purchaser assumed the pension plan deficit of $35-45 million and other employee obligations.[128] Edward Sellers observes that the workout was facilitated by early recognition that an independent committee of directors and an independent CRO were needed to effectively assess and implement the corporation's options for a viable plan. The restructuring was accomplished by the going concern sale, driven by factors that included value maximization for almost all interested parties, preservation of supply relationships for ordinary trade creditors, preservation of more than 2,400 direct jobs, successor protection of the pension plan, and prevention of major disruption to the glass container and beverage market in Canada.[129]

1. Issues of CRO Accountability

Given that the CRO is a court-appointed officer, the supervision of the court can ensure a measure of accountability that is normally a function of the relationship between the corporate board and senior managers. If the CRO is court-appointed, arguably it has obligations to the court and must act neutrally with respect to stakeholders. If CROs have taken over the oversight or management of the affairs of the debtor corporation, arguably they also acquire a statutory duty of care to creditors and are required to consider the interests of all stakeholders with an interest

---

[126] *Ivaco, ibid.*

[127] Edward Sellers *et al.*, "Governance of the Financially Distressed Corporation: Selected Aspects of the Financing and Governance of Canadian Enterprises in Cross-Border Workouts", in Janis Sarra, *Corporate Governance in Global Capital Markets* (UBC Press, 2003) at 38.

[128] *Ibid.* at 44.

[129] *Ibid.* at 45.

in the process, as directed by the Supreme Court of Canada in *Peoples Department Stores.*[130] They also have reporting obligations to the court.

However, another view is that the CRO's objective is to maximize the value of fixed capital claims while managing the turnaround of the company. In which case, to whom does the CRO owe obligations? It may depend on the mandate of the CRO in terms of whether to restructure internally, seek a sale of the debtor corporation to third parties as a going concern, or facilitate a liquidation outcome. These issues have not yet been canvassed before Canadian courts, leaving the issue of fiduciary obligation of CROs an open question.

Most of the CRO's compensation is performance-incentive driven: performance measured by return to creditors. Hence there is some risk that the CRO will fail to recognize or take into account the interests of all stakeholders. Where the CRO is selected by the DIP lender, there may also be a risk of the CRO deferring to the interests of the DIP lender to the detriment of other creditors' interests.

CROs have also taken the benefit of D&O liability protection charges in DIP financing or stay orders. *CCAA* orders tend to protect the CRO from all of the usual liability that directors and officers face in respect of wage and other claims.[131] While the CRO frequently performs an important business function and can enhance the debtor's prospects of successfully restructuring in a *CCAA* proceeding, agency issues arise in terms of CRO decision making that can shift value to senior secured creditors to the disadvantage of longer term, but junior, secured or unsecured creditors. These risks are mitigated somewhat by the supervisory role of the court. However, just as the agency costs of management of the insolvent firm may be a key factor in firm success or failure, the potential agency costs of CROs needs further study.

VI. A GOVERNANCE ROLE FOR EMPLOYEES?

For the solvent corporation, creditors generally exercise a governance function by their pricing and terms of debt.[132] Operating lenders exercise a monitoring function because of re-evaluation processes for loan renewals, access to information about cash-flow and expenditures through provision of banking services and early warning signals on payment default.[133] Most employees, however, do not have the bargaining

---

[130] *Peoples Department Stores* was discussed at length earlier in this chapter; *Peoples Department Stores Ltd. (1992) Inc., Re*, 2004 SCC 68, [2004] 3 S.C.R. 461 (S.C.C.).

[131] There remains some concern about the validity of such orders granting blanket protection to court-appointed officers without notice to affected parties, in particular as regard to employment related claims. See for instance *Big Sky Living Inc., Re* (2002), 2002 CarswellAlta 875 (Alta. Q.B.), and *GMAC Commercial Credit Corp. - Canada* v. *TCT Logistics Inc.*, 2006 SCC 35 (S.C.C.).

[132] G. Triantis and R. Daniels, "The Role of Debt in Interactive Corporate Governance" (1985), 83 Cal. Law Review 1073; M. Jensen and W. Meckling, "Theory of the Firm: Managerial Behaviour, Agency Cost and Ownership Structure" (1976), 3 Journal of Fin. Econ. 305; B. Adler, "An Equity-Agency Solution to the Bankruptcy-Priority Puzzle" (1993) J. of Legal Studies 73.

[133] Triantis and Daniels, *ibid.* at 1083-4.

power to acquire a governance role in the corporation, even though their investment is almost exclusively with the company in terms of their labour inputs and the deferred compensation system, and hence their risk is highly undiversified.[134] Only when a firm is financially distressed is there a possibility that employees or their union in a representative capacity can acquire a governance role as part of the workout and compromise of their claims. That is what occurred in the first *Algoma Steel* restructuring; employees and their union acquired a governance role under a co-determination model that was enshrined in the corporate articles, a model that allowed employees to participate directly on the corporate board and allowed for joint decision-making on numerous operational and fundamental change issues. The co-determination structure carried the corporation through another decade of operations and wealth generating activity before Algoma was required to file under the *CCAA* once again because of market competition and less than ideal timing on accessing the debt market.

In the second *Algoma Steel* restructuring, secured creditors utilized the threat of exit to force governance change during negotiations for the workout, notwithstanding the fact that the insolvency was not attributed to the governance structure. Rather, Algoma's financial distress was primarily attributed to long-term debt load, and market and currency fluctuations. Nevertheless, the price of the compromise for Noteholders as the senior affected creditors was a majority of seats on the corporate board. Arguably, they were able to use their bargaining leverage to extract a premium in debt terms and percentage of equity ownership for their support of the plan because they would receive 85% realization on liquidation and because they were not "high value" creditors in the sense of a long-term interest in the corporation's viability. The union did not have much bargaining leverage during the 2001 negotiations, primarily because of its concern for the 8,000 pension beneficiaries whose interests were at risk, as well as the current job security of members. Moreover, the union recognized that in order for Algoma to survive and remain competitive in global markets, additional capital expenditures were needed, and capital necessarily raised through equity as opposed to debt. While the union retained some residual governance rights, such as three nominee directors and a role in material change to operations, its voting shares were eliminated and many governance rights associated with them.[135]

The *Algoma Steel* experience suggests that while there is a role for employees in the governance of the corporation, such a role is only possible when the equity of the corporation is available at such a severely discounted price that employees can afford to make a further investment in a firm where their investments are already at

[134] Canada is widely recognized as having a deferred compensation system, which means that employees work today for future promised benefits, such as pensions or health benefits. Hence, the compensation for current work performed is deferred until some later point in the employment relationship. It also refers to the fact that historically, many employees work hard in their earlier years, but continue to be paid a full wage in their pre-retirement years, because full compensation for the earlier labour was deferred until these years.

[135] Steve Boniferro, Vice-President Algoma Steel (21 December 2001). *Memorandum of Agreement*, Algoma 2001 Plan, on file with author.

risk. While employees and their trade unions often do not wish a governance role and prefer to retain the traditional relationship between labour and management, the Algoma experience suggests that there can be considerable benefits for employees and other stakeholders implicated in the debtor corporation's activities in terms of not only maximizing the firm's health, but also creating a healthier and sustained work environment for employees.[136]

The treatment of employee claims and collective agreements in *CCAA* proceedings are discussed in the next chapter.

Questions for review of materials:

1. How does corporate governance differ for the insolvent firm?

2. What is the fiduciary obligation of directors when a firm is insolvent?

3. What is the duty of care of directors when a corporation is insolvent?

4. How is the oppression remedy relevant to the insolvency context and what are the tests for a finding of oppression?

Questions for discussion:

1. Should the same level of deference apply where directors are acting in the "interests" of two or more corporations in a related party transaction, and should there be a heightened scrutiny as to whether they acted prudently and on a reasonably informed basis, given their potential conflict of interest?

2. How are courts likely to apply the statutory duty of care to creditors?

3. Is the Supreme Court of Canada's reasoning on fiduciary obligation in *Peoples Department Stores* persuasive?

4. To whom does a chief restructuring officer owe its obligations?

---

[136] For a full discussion of the Algoma Steel co-determination experience, see Janis P. Sarra, *Creditor Rights and the Public Interest, Restructuring Insolvent Corporations* (Toronto: University of Toronto Press, 2003).

CHAPTER 6

TREATMENT OF CLAIMS

I. INTRODUCTION

Ultimately, the fate of the company in a *CCAA* proceeding depends on whether the debtor corporation can secure sufficient creditor support for the proposed plan. The rights of creditors cannot be compromised unless the creditor has been given the right to vote in the appropriate class on the proposed plan. The creditors' vote must be in accordance with the procedure approved by the court; the classes in which creditors are appropriately placed has voted by a majority in number and two-thirds in value in support of the plan; and the court has approved the plan on the basis that it is fair and reasonable.[1]

Section 12(2) of the *CCAA* addresses only the determination of who is a creditor, and not the value of the claim.[2] The onus is on any claimant to prove its claim, although there are exceptions, as in the *A&B Sound* restructuring process, in which the court approved a reverse claims process.[3] Other cases using this type of process include *Canadian Airlines.* Where a contingent claimant seeks to prove its claim, it must show that the claim is not speculative or remote; however, the Ontario Superior Court in *Air Canada* held that contingent creditors need not establish that success is probable.[4]

The binding force of the plan of arrangement or compromise arises from the *CCAA* through the sanction of the court, not from the effect of terms mutually agreed upon.[5] However, an agreement between creditors in a *CCAA* plan, such as a valid subordination agreement, will be enforced by the court as a valid contract.[6] The Court in

---

[1] *Olympia & York Developments Ltd.* v. *Royal Trust Co.* (1993), 1993 CarswellOnt 182, (sub nom. *Olympia & York Developments Ltd., Re*) 12 O.R. (3d) 500 (Ont. Gen. Div.); *Menegon* v. *Philip Services Corp.* (1999), 11 C.B.R. (4th) 262 (Ont. S.C.J. [Commercial List]).

[2] *Air Canada, Re* (2004), [2004] O.J. No. 3048, 2004 CarswellOnt 2946, 2 C.B.R. (5th) 18 (Ont. S.C.J. [Commercial List]) (*Canada Labour Code* Claims).

[3] See discussion in chapter 4 under stalking horse proceedings.

[4] *Air Canada, Re* (2004), 2004 CarswellOnt 3320, 2 C.B.R. (5th) 23 (Ont. S.C.J. [Commercial List]) (CUPE contingent claim appeal).

[5] *Cable Satisfaction International Inc.* v. *Richter & Associés inc.* (2004), 2004 CarswellQue 810, 48 C.B.R. (4th) 205 (Que. S.C.).

[6] *Air Canada, Re* (2004), 2004 CarswellOnt 1842, 2 C.B.R. (5th) 4 (Ont. S.C.J. [Commercial List]).

Stelco Inc. held that the *CCAA* addresses compromises or arrangements between a company and its creditors and does not address a change of relationship among creditors *vis-à-vis* the creditors themselves and not directly involving the company.[7]

There is no hierarchy of debts set out in the *CCAA*, and the statute only identifies secured and unsecured creditors. However, if the debtor corporation in a *CCAA* proceeding fails to devise a viable plan acceptable to creditors, it will almost always be liquidated, either in bankruptcy proceedings or receivership; hence parties bargain in the shadow of the *BIA*. However, the parties in a *CCAA* proceeding are not strictly bound by that hierarchy of claims, allowing considerable flexibility in the negotiations for a workout plan. The court determines classification of creditors for purposes of voting on a *CCAA* plan, discussed in the next chapter.

The Saskatchewan Court of Queen's Bench in *Worldwide Pork Co.* v. *Agricultural Credit Corp. of Saskatchewan*, in determining the amount of a creditor's claim pursuant to section 12 of the *CCAA*, held that a claim will be given no value for voting purposes where it is plain and obvious that it has no foundation or is frivolous; the amount of a claim may be determined on the information filed with the court or after the trial of an issue; and the debtor company, after admitting the amount of a claim for voting purposes, retains its right to contest liability for other purposes.[8] The Court emphasized that although it is important for disputed claims to be resolved expeditiously, it is also important that the debtor company's focus not be diverted from completing a *CCAA* plan on which its economic survival depends.[9]

II. PROVABLE CLAIMS

Section 12 of the *CCAA* sets out the definition of claim, linking it to the *BIA* provisions:

> *Definition of "claim"*
>
> 12. (1) For the purposes of this Act, "claim" means any indebtedness, liability or obligation of any kind that, if unsecured, would be a debt provable in bankruptcy within the meaning of the Bankruptcy and Insolvency Act.
>
> *Determination of amount of claim*
>
> (2) For the purposes of this Act, the amount represented by a claim of any secured or unsecured creditor shall be determined as follows:

---

7 *Stelco Inc., Re*, 2005 CarswellOnt 6483 (S.C.J. [Commercial List]), affirmed (2005), 2005 CarswellOnt 6510 (Ont. C.A.), additional reasons at (2005), 2005 CarswellOnt 6818 (Ont. C.A.), further additional reasons at (2006), 2006 CarswellOnt 5194 (Ont. C.A.).

8 *Worldwide Pork Co.* v. *Agricultural Credit Corp. of Saskatchewan* (2006), [2006] S.J. No. 31, 2006 CarswellSask 82 (Sask. Q.B.).

9 *Ibid.*

(a) the amount of an unsecured claim shall be the amount

(i) in the case of a company in the course of being wound up under the Winding-up and Restructuring Act, proof of which has been made in accordance with that Act,

(ii) in the case of a company that has made an authorized assignment or against which a bankruptcy order has been made under the Bankruptcy and Insolvency Act, proof of which has been made in accordance with that Act, or

(iii) in the case of any other company, proof of which might be made under the Bankruptcy and Insolvency Act, but if the amount so provable is not admitted by the company, the amount shall be determined by the court on summary application by the company or by the creditor; and

(b) the amount of a secured claim shall be the amount, proof of which might be made in respect thereof under the Bankruptcy and Insolvency Act if the claim were unsecured, but the amount if not admitted by the company shall, in the case of a company subject to pending proceedings under the Winding-up and Restructuring Act or the Bankruptcy and Insolvency Act, be established by proof in the same manner as an unsecured claim under the Winding-up and Restructuring Act or the Bankruptcy and Insolvency Act, as the case may be, and in the case of any other company the amount shall be determined by the court on summary application by the company or the creditor.

Admission of claims

(3) Notwithstanding subsection (2), the company may admit the amount of a claim for voting purposes under reserve of the right to contest liability on the claim for other purposes, and nothing in this Act, the Winding-up and Restructuring Act or the Bankruptcy and Insolvency Act prevents a secured creditor from voting at a meeting of secured creditors or any class of them in respect of the total amount of a claim as admitted.

Chapter 47 will replace section 12 by the following:

Fixing of deadline for filing claims

12. The court may make an order fixing a deadline for creditors to file their claims against a company for the purpose of voting at a creditors' meeting held under section 4 or 5.[10]

The Court in *Stelco Inc.* discussed the notion of provable claims, in the context of determining whether the debtor corporation was insolvent:

---

[10] The Government announced its intention to amend further s. 12 to specify: "The court may fix deadlines for the purposes of voting and for the purposes of distributions under a compromise or arrangement". *Notice of Ways and Means Motion to introduce an Act to amend the Bankruptcy and Insolvency Act, the Companies' Creditors Arrangement Act, the Wage Earners Protection Act and Chapter 47 of the Statutes of Canada, 2005,* (December 8, 2006, Library of Parliament).

¶51 S. 121(1) and (2) of the *BIA,* which are incorporated by reference in s.12 of the *CCAA,* provide in respect to provable claims:

> S. 121(1) All debts and liabilities, present or future, to which the bankrupt is subject on the day on which the bankrupt becomes bankrupt or to which bankrupt may become subject before the bankrupt's discharge by reason of any obligation incurred before the day on which the bankrupt becomes bankrupt shall be deemed to be claims provable in proceedings under this Act.
>
> (2) The determination whether a contingent or unliquidated claim is a provable claim and the valuation of such claim shall be made in accordance with s. 135.

¶52 Houlden and Morawetz *2004 Annotated, supra* at p. 537 (G28(3)) indicates:

> The word "liability" is a very broad one. It includes all obligations to which the bankrupt is subject on the day on which he becomes bankrupt except for contingent and unliquidated claims which are dealt with in s. 121(2). However contingent and unliquidated claims would be encompassed by the term "obligations".

. . .

¶57 With the greatest of respect for my colleague, I disagree with the conclusion of Ground J. in *Enterprise Capital, supra* as to the approach to be taken to "due and accruing due" when he observed at pp. 139-140:

> In my view, the obligations, which are to be measured against the fair valuation of a company's property as being obligations due and accruing due, must be limited to obligations currently payable or properly chargeable to the accounting period during which the test is being applied as, for example, a sinking fund payment due within the current year. Black's Law Dictionary defines "accrued liability" as "an obligation or debt which is properly chargeable in a given accounting period, but which is not yet paid or payable". The principal amount of the Notes is neither due nor accruing due in this sense.

¶58 There appears to be some confusion in this analysis as to "debts" and "obligations", the latter being much broader than debts ... I pause to note that an insolvency test under general corporate litigation need not be and likely is not identical, or indeed similar to that under these insolvency statutes. As well, it is curious to note that the cut off date is the end of the current fiscal period which could have radically different results if there were a calendar fiscal year and the application was variously made in the first week of January, mid-summer or the last day of December. Lastly, see above and below as to my views concerning the proper interpretation of this question of "accruing due".

¶59 It seems to me that the phrase "accruing due" has been interpreted by the courts as broadly identifying obligations that will "become due". See *Viteway* below at pp. 163-4 - at least at some point in the future . . . every obligation of the corporation in the hypothetical or notional sale must be treated as "accruing due" to avoid orphan obligations. In that context, it matters not that a wind-up pension liability may be discharged over 15 years; in a test (c) situation, it is crystallized on the date of the test. See *Optical, supra* at pp. 756-7; *Re Viteway Natural Foods Ltd.* (1986), 63 C.B.R. (N.S.) 157 (B.C.S.C.) at pp. 164-63-4; *Re Consolidated Seed Exports Ltd.* (1986), 62 C.B.R. (N.S.) 156 (B.C.S.C.) at p. 163.

III. CLAIMS BAR ORDER AND EXTENSION OF TIME FOR FILING CLAIMS

The court may make a claims bar order, whereby creditors are required to file their claims by a fixed date, after which claims are barred.[11] A claims bar order provides a timely mechanism to allow creditors to assess and vote on a proposed plan and to facilitate the court ordering completion of the *CCAA* proceeding.[12] The court usually directs how to provide notice of the claims procedure, which can be a direct mailing to creditors, a publication notice in newspapers, or some other mechanism. The court also frequently appoints a claims officer, who is given authority to adjudicate any disputed claims. The party can appeal the claims officer's determination of the claim to the judge who is supervising the *CCAA* proceeding.

In limited circumstances, the court may grant an extension for the filing of claims. In *Blue Range Resources Corp.*, the Alberta Court of Appeal held that the court should apply the following considerations:

i. Was the delay caused by inadvertence and if so, was the creditor acting in good faith? Inadvertence can include carelessness, negligence and accident, but must be unintentional.

ii. What is the effect of extending the time for filing claims and any prejudice caused by the late filing? Prejudice includes consideration of whether the creditors who filed in time will lose, as a result of the late filing, a realistic opportunity to do anything that they might otherwise have done.

iii. If the late filing has caused relevant prejudice, can it be alleviated by attaching appropriate conditions to the order permitting the late filing?

---

[11] Unlike the *BIA*, which has a claims bar process incorporated as part of the statute in section 149, the *CCAA* does not expressly provide for any claims bar process. The concept of a claims bar process in a *CCAA* proceeding was "borrowed" from concepts that exist under Chapter 11 of the U.S. *Bankruptcy Code*. Given the importance of finality in the process, the courts drew on their jurisdiction to create claims bar processes. It should be noted that the claims bar process as provided in the U.S. *Bankruptcy Code* (see Rule 3003(c)(3) of the *Federal Rules of Bankruptcy Procedure*) is very different from the one that has been adopted in the *CCAA* proceedings to date, as there is more finality to a claim bar order made by the court in a case under Chapter 11. The process adopted by the courts in proceedings under the *CCAA* is similar to that provided for in section 149 of the *BIA*, whereby a creditor can ask the court for an extension of time to file, even after the deadline has expired, and the court may allow such an extension if it is satisfied with the merits of the application or the explanation of the delay in proving the claim. See *Blue Range Resource Corp., Re* (2000), 2000 CarswellAlta 1145 (Alta. C. A.), additional reasons at (2001), 2001 CarswellAlta 1059 (Alta. C.A.), leave to appeal refused [2001] S.C.R. viii (S.C.C.).

[12] *Blue Range Resource Corp., Re* (2000), 15 C.B.R. (4th) 192 (Alta. C.A. [In Chambers]).

iv. If relevant prejudice cannot be alleviated, are there any other considerations that could nonetheless warrant an order for late filing?[13]

Generally, the court is reluctant to exclude claims that could be dealt with in the *CCAA* claims process. The Saskatchewan Court of Queen's Bench in *Printwest Communications Ltd.* v. *Saskatchewan Cooperative Financial Services Ltd.* held that the claims of two unions for severance pay, arising from a collective bargaining agreement, should not be granted special status and dealt with outside of a debtor's *CCAA* plan of arrangement with the effect that the claims are paid in full, since claims for severance pay arising from a collective bargaining agreement did not, in the particular circumstances, fall into the category of essential services provided during the *CCAA* reorganization period in order to enable the debtor company to function.[14] The Court held that such a result would be unfair and unreasonable to other unsecured creditors, such as suppliers of goods and services, who would only recover a fraction of their claims.

IV. SET-OFF

The law of set-off applies notwithstanding the existence of *CCAA* proceedings. The objective of set-off is to avoid the perceived injustice to a creditor who has mutual dealings with an insolvent debtor of having to pay in full what it owes to the debtor while having to take a discounted value of the debt owing to it. Set-off requires a mutuality of debt.[15] Section 18.1 of the *CCAA* specifies:

> 18.1 The law of set-off applies to all claims made against a debtor company and to all actions instituted by it for the recovery of debts due to the company in the same manner and to the same extent as if the company were plaintiff or defendant, as the case may be.

Under section 18.1 of the *CCAA*, the principles of legal setoff permit pre-filing debts to be set off against post-filing debts; there is no change in mutuality as there would be in a bankruptcy situation.[16]

The court has held that it does not undermine the purposes of the *CCAA* to allow a creditor to raise a claim for set-off.[17] Set-off claims should be carefully scrutinized in *CCAA* proceedings because the effect may be to give preference to certain creditors. The British Columbia Court of Appeal in *Cam-Net Communications* v. *Van-*

---

[13] *Ibid.*

[14] *Printwest Communications Ltd.* v. *Saskatchewan Cooperative Financial Services Ltd.* (2005), 2005 CarswellSask 508 (Sask. Q.B.).

[15] L.W. Houlden, G. B. Morawetz and J. P. Sarra, *The 2006 Annotated Bankruptcy and Insolvency Act* (Toronto: Carswell, 2006) at 508.

[16] *Air Canada, Re* (2003), 2003 CarswellOnt 4016, 45 C.B.R. (4th) 13 (Ont. S.C.J. [Commercial List]).

[17] *Cam-Net Communications* v. *Vancouver Telephone Co.* (1999), 71 B.C.L.R. (3d) 226, 182 D.L.R. (4th) 436 (B.C. C.A.).

couver Telephone Co., in considering a claim for equitable set-off, described the public policy concern:

> Using, or rather misusing, the law of set-off is one example of how persons with a claim against the company in reorganization might attempt to escape the *CCAA* compromise. A party claiming set-off . . . realizes its claim on a dollar-for-dollar basis while other creditors, who participated in the *CCAA* proceedings, have their claims reduced substantially. For this reason, the legislative intent animating the *CCAA* reorganization regime requires that courts remain vigilant to claims of set-off in the reorganization context.[18]

The Ontario Court of Appeal in *Algoma Steel Inc.* v. *Union Gas Ltd.* held that the court must consider the issue of equitable, as well as legal set-off.[19] The Court of Appeal held that equitable set-off is available where there is a claim for a sum whether liquidated or unliquidated. The Court summed up the principles for its consideration of an equitable set-off claim as:

- The party relying on a set-off must show some equitable ground for being protected against the adversary's demands.
- The equitable ground must go to the very root of the plaintiff's claim.
- A cross-claim must be so clearly connected with the demand of the plaintiff that it would be manifestly unjust to allow the plaintiff to enforce payment without taking into consideration the cross-claim.
- The plaintiff's claim and the cross-claim need not arise out of the same contract.
- Unliquidated claims are on the same footing as liquidated claims.

The Court in *Skydome* declined to grant set-off where a party to the *CCAA* proceeding had failed to comply with its order.[20] The Court held:

> ¶ 20 CMC must comply with the terms of the *CCAA* Orders. The Orders have not been appealed, and CMC did not choose to move to vary them until after it was faced with this Motion by SkyDome to compel it to comply. Parties affected by a *CCAA* Order - as with any other Order - are not entitled to ignore that Order, much less to flout it, simply because they don't like its effect on them or because they wish to use the difficulties caused to the *CCAA* company by their non-compliance as a lever to enhance their bargaining position with the debtor company. It is patently clear that that is exactly what CMC and Mr. Black were intent on accomplishing here, and it cannot be sanctioned.

---

[18] *Ibid.* at 235.

[19] *Algoma Steel Inc.* v. *Union Gas Ltd.* (2003), 63 O.R. (3d) 78 (Ont. C.A.).

[20] *Skydome Corp., Re* (1999), [1999] O.J. No. 221, 1999 CarswellOnt 208 (Ont. Gen. Div. [Commercial List]).

¶ 21 CMC acknowledges, as I have indicated, that it has failed to comply with the Initial Order to the extent of $177,774.00 (see affidavit of G. Montegu Black, sworn January 20, 1999). In addition, it is admitted that a further $73,961.00 was payable under the CMC Agreement by January 15, 1999, a date which has now passed. For the reasons explained above, it is my view that CMC is obliged to account and to pay over all advertising revenues received by it in relation to the period pre-dating the termination of the Agreement. I therefore order that CMC pay to SkyDome immediately the sum of $251,645.00, being the sum of the foregoing two amounts. In addition, CMC is required to account to SkyDome forthwith as to the balance of the advertising revenues which have been received by it (less commissions) prior to Friday, December 18, 1998, and not remitted to SkyDome. After that accounting has been furnished, if the parties cannot agree, a motion may be made for the establishment of a court procedure to settle the accounting. The balance of the amounts found due on the accounting are to be paid to SkyDome forthwith thereafter.

¶ 22 Given its conduct, CMC does not come to court with clean hands. I am not prepared to permit an equitable remedy of set-off to be applied against the sums improperly held back following the granting of the Initial Order. CMC is entitled, of course, to assert its claims to set-off as claimant/creditor in the *CCAA* proceedings.

¶ 23 The cross-motion, however, is dismissed. I see nothing in the situation of CMC which puts it in a position different from other creditors of SkyDome who assert that they have claims of one sort or another against the Company. Those claims are stayed under the *CCAA* Orders, so that SkyDome will have the capacity to concentrate its time and resources and the energies of its personnel on attempting to gain the support of its creditors to a restructuring. If the stay were to be lifted to permit CMC to pursue its claims, it would be difficult to argue that others should not be accorded the same relief. The whole purpose of the proceeding would be nullified.

V. INTERACTION WITH PROVINCIAL PERSONAL PROPERTY SECURITY LEGISLATION

Secured creditors generally protect their priority ranking over personal property assets by registering financing statements to perfect their security agreements. The registries and priority rules that apply to these security agreements are primarily governed by provincial or territorial law, setting out a priority of claims based on date of perfection of the claim.[21] All Canadian provinces other than Québec have adopted personal property security legislation (PPSA) that regulates "the creation, perfection and enforcement of a security interest in a debtor's assets, and creates a system for determining the priority of competing interests in collateral."[22] The PPSA applies to "every transaction that in substance creates a security interest, without

[21] Perfection is a process of registering a security interest under provincial and territorial personal property security statutes, whereby meeting the specific requirements of the statute generally grants the creditor a priority over subsequently registered claims.

[22] McMillan Binch Mendelsohn LLP, *Secured Lending in Canada* (2005) at 3, online: <http://www.mcmillanbinch.com/Upload/Publication/MBM_ACLF_Secured%20Lending%20in%20Canada.pdf>.

regard to its form and without regard to the person who has title to the collateral."[23] The rules for hypothecs in Québec are similar.[24]

Personal property security legislation generally defines security interest as an interest in personal property that secures payment or performance of an obligation. PPSAs are intended as a notice system that identifies which creditors are asserting a secured claim against the debtor. This notice system serves to resolve priority disputes between creditors when there are multiple claims on the assets of the debtor.[25] The *BIA* recognizes such registration; however, a security interest must be perfected under the PPSA, or it is subordinate to the interest of a trustee in bankruptcy under the *BIA* and to other secured creditors. The *CCAA* is not codified in the same way; however, the courts have recognized this provincial legislation.[26]

There are instances in which the *CCAA* and provincial PPSAs do not neatly mesh and the courts are required to make determinations reconciling competing claims. Two examples are the treatment of intangible information and equipment lessors during the restructuring process.

The section 11 provisions of the *CCAA* stay operating lenders from enforcing their security without leave of the court.[27] As noted in chapter 2, such lenders can apply to the court to lift the stay for a limited time or purpose; however, it is incumbent on the party seeking to lift the stay to demonstrate prejudice before the court will consider granting the order. Recall, however, that the *CCAA* specifies that the stay does not have the effect of prohibiting a lessor from requiring immediate payment for goods, services, or use of leased or licensed property after the initial stay order is made. Section 11.3 specifies:

> 11.3 No order made under section 11 shall have the effect of
>
> (a) prohibiting a person from requiring immediate payment for goods, services, use of leased or licensed property or other valuable consideration provided after the order is made; or
>
> (b) requiring the further advance of money or credit.[28]

---

[23] See for example the B.C. *Personal Property Security Act,* R.S.B.C. 1996, c. 359, s. 2(1)(a).

[24] Martin Desrosiers and David Tardif-Latourelle, "Insolvency and Restructuring in Québec: A Common Law Practitioner's Guide", in *Annual Review of Insolvency Law, 2005* (Toronto: Carswell, 2006), at 319-355.

[25] S. Weisz *et al.,* "Striking an Imbalance: The Treatment of Equipment Lessors Under Section 11.3 of the *CCAA*" (2003) 20 Nat'l Insolv. Rev. 45, 2003 C.N.I.R. LEXIS 11 at 20.

[26] L.W. Houlden, G.B. Morawetz and J.P. Sarra, *Bankruptcy and Insolvency Law in Canada,* 3rd ed., vol.1, (Toronto: Carswell, 2006) at ND-73.

[27] Except in respect of aircraft objects, in which case the stay has an application that is limited in time and in scope, whether the aircraft object is subject to a security interest, is leased or has been acquired pursuant to a conditional sale agreement. See section 11.31 of the *CCAA*.

[28] Chapter 47 will amend s. 11.3 to specify:

> 11.3 (1) The court may, on the application of a debtor company, make an order assigning the rights and obligations of the company under any agreement to any person, to be specified by the court, who has agreed to the assignment.

In determining whether equipment lessors with financing leases should or should not fall within the ambit of section 11.3 of the *CCAA*, courts have adopted the distinction between a true lease and a financing lease under personal property security legislation. Courts dealing with leases in a *CCAA* proceeding have held that the benefit of section 11.3 only covers "true leases" and not financing arrangements.[29]

In *PSINet Ltd.*, the Ontario Superior Court held that the leases in question were financing arrangements, whose purpose was to secure a loan that was provided before the stay order was made; and the payments owed were repayments for that loan. PSINet had selected the equipment to meet its specifications, and had paid all taxes, levies and insurance costs. The bank had provided no warranties, and on default, was entitled to recover the present value of the entire remaining term of the lease. On any default, the debtor was entitled to a credit for any amounts realized by the bank on the sale or disposition of the equipment. The arrangement contemplated PSINet acquiring equity in the property. Therefore, the Court held that the leases in question were best characterized as equipment financing leases, rather than true leases within the scope of the *CCAA*. Any other determination would give the bank an unfair advantage over the other creditors of PSINet who were bound by the stay.[30]

In *Gauntlet Energy Corp.*, the Alberta Court of Queen's Bench held that intangible information, such as seismic data, was personal property under the Alberta *Personal Property Security Act* and the *CCAA*.[31] The Court applied *PPSA* priority rules in the case of three conditional sales agreements between the debtor company Gauntlet and the supplier of the data, Pulse. The Court rejected the supplier's argument that

---

Notice

(2) The applicant must give notice of the assignment in the prescribed manner to every party to the agreement.

Exceptions

(3) Subsection (1) does not apply in respect of rights and obligations

(a) iunder an eligible financial contract within the meaning of subsection 11.05(3);

(b) under a collective agreement; or

(c) that are not assignable by reason of their nature.

Factors to be considered

(4) In deciding whether to make an assignment, the court must consider, among other things,

(a) whether the person to whom the rights and obligations are to be assigned would be able to perform the obligations; and

(b) whether it would be appropriate to assign the rights and obligations to that person.

Restriction

(5) The court may not make an order assigning an agreement unless it is satisfied that all financial defaults in relation to the agreement will be remedied.

[29] Derrick C. Tay and Orestes Pasparakis, "Whose Law Is It Anyway? A Principled Approach to *PPSA* Conflict of Laws Rules" in Janis Sarra, ed., *Annual Review of Insolvency Law 2004* (Toronto: Thomson Carswell, 2004) at 493.

[30] *PSINet Ltd., Re* (2001), 26 C.B.R. (4th) 288 (Ont. S.C.J.).

[31] *Gauntlet Energy Corp., Re* (2003), 2003 CarswellAlta 1209, [2003] A.J. No. 1062 (Alta. Q.B.); R.S.A. 2000, c. P-7.

confidential information was not "property" at law and could not be subject to the *PPSA*.[32] It held that the debtor's secured lender, Alberta Treasury Branches (ATB), had a prior secured interest in the data because Pulse had not registered its security agreement and the residual priority provision of the Alberta *PPSA* applied.[33]

It should be noted that Québec law does not provide for the distinction between a "true lease" and a lease entered into as a financing arrangement. The Québec *Civil Code* contemplates that some lease agreements (in French, credit-bail) are structured in a way such that they are merely a financing transaction, in that the lessor orders the asset from a third party supplier on instructions and specifications received from the lessee, the third party supplier is directly responsible to the lessee for warranties, and the lessee assumes all of the risks associated with the leased asset.[34]

One issue is how the *CCAA* interfaces with the personal property security regime in terms of how preferences are treated in insolvency. In *General Chemical Canada Ltd.*, the Ontario Superior Court summarized how the Ontario *PPSA* interacts with insolvency:[35]

> The *PPSA* sets up a scheme for "perfection" of security interests in personal property. An unperfected security interest will be subordinated to a perfected security interest in the same collateral [*Personal Property Security Act,* section 20(1)(a)(i)]. While registration of a financing statement is the way to perfect general security agreements, such as those at issue in this case, this does not apply to certain statutory liens, which do not require registration [sections 4(1)(a) and (b)]. The PPSA, and thus its registration requirements, do not apply to either statutory liens, or deemed trusts arising out of a statute. Thus, the *PPSA* does not apply to the deemed trusts or statutory liens established by the *PBA* [*Pension Benefits Act*] in favour of the pension administrator. In situations where a debtor is bankrupt, however, the *PPSA* says that these statutory liens arise on the effective date of the bankruptcy [*PPSA,* section 20(2)(a)(i)].
>
> . . .
>
> [74] The question of priority is dependent on many things. As far as Harbert is concerned, their rights are easy to determine. There is no question that their security interest was perfected on March 31, 2004. The real question is whether the pension

---

[32] *Ibid.* at 4. As a result of the *Gauntlet* decision, seismic companies can use data as collateral.

[33] Douglas Nishimura, "Treatment of the Ownership of Intangible Information in a *CCAA* Context: Gauntlet", (2003) 16 Comm. Insol. R. 1, 2003 C.C.I.R. LEXIS 10 at 6.

[34] See in this respect articles 1842 to 1846 of the Québec *Civil Code*. Such an agreement (as well as a lease agreement that extends over one year) needs to be published in the Register of Personal and Movable Real Rights, the Québec equivalent to the PPSA registry, and if published, the property rights of the lessor are opposable to third parties. The property rights are opposable as and from the date of the leasing agreement if they are published within 15 days (Article 1847 of the Québec *Civil Code*). While this type of agreement is similar to a financing lease arrangement in a Common Law province, and requires publication to be opposable to third parties, this type of agreement may not be susceptible of being treated as a financing arrangement: *Lefebvre, Re* (2004), 2004 CarswellQue 2831 (S.C.C.).

[35] *General Chemical Canada Ltd., Re* (2006), 2006 CarswellOnt 4675, 22 C.B.R. (5th) 298 (Ont. S.C.J. [Commercial List]), judgment of Madam Justice Mesbur.

> plan administrator would have had lien rights prior to this date, and if so, in what amount.
>
> [75] The *BIA* sets out a scheme of distribution among secured, preferred and unsecured creditors. It does not, however, determine the priorities of secured creditors among themselves. In bankruptcy, priorities between competing secured creditors in the same collateral are determined according to the "first in time" rule, subject to the principles of equity. Therefore, where the equities between two competing secured creditors are equal, the creditor whose security arose first will have priority over the other.

On the facts, including timing of particular payments to the pension administrator, the Court held that the *PPSA* secured claim was to be met first.[36]

In *Stelco Inc.*, the Ontario Court of Appeal considered the issue of whether, when an insured has fully paid for a policy of insurance and assigns its right to receive a refund of any unearned premiums, this a security interest that is transferred; and whether it is necessary to file notice of the security interest under the *PPSA* or whether the security interest is exempt from registration by virtue of a combination of section 4(1)(c) of the *PPSA* and the Ontario *Insurance Act,* or at common law.[37] In allowing the appeal, the Court held that the right to any unearned premiums was created when the policy was funded, but the realization of that interest was contingent on the happening of a future event, namely, the non-payment of premiums and the cancellation of the policy. Nevertheless, the right was an interest. The wording of the exclusion in section 4(1)(c) of the *PPSA* was clear and was to be read as including the assignment of unearned premiums under a policy of insurance.[38] The values of certainty, uniformity, and ease of commerce were promoted if section 4(1) of the *PPSA* were construed so as to exempt a requirement to register its interest in any unearned premiums.[39]

One question is the monitor's status in respect of unperfected security interests under personal property security statutes. Current legislation specifies that an unperfected security interest is not effective against a receiver or trustee in bankruptcy.[40] Since the language of some personal property security statutes, such as the Ontario *PPSA,* specifies that an unperfected security interest is not effective against a person who represents creditors, the question is whether a monitor, acting on behalf of the debtor's estate as a whole and creditors as claimants, could be found to fall within that language.

---

[36] *Ibid.* at paras. 83, 84.

[37] *Stelco Inc., Re* (2005), 9 C.B.R. (5th) 307 (Ont. C.A.). *Personal Property Security Act*, R.S.O. 1990, c. P.10; *Insurance Act*, R.S.O. 1990, c. I.8.

[38] *Ibid.* at paras. 11, 13, 24.

[39] *Ibid.* at para 19. For a discussion of this issue generally, see Jacob Ziegel, "Unearned Insurance Premiums as Security Interests under The Canadian Personal Property Security Acts", (2004) 1 C.B.R. (5th) 173 at 179.

[40] See for example, section 20(1), Ontario *PPSA*, R.S.O. 1990, c. P.10.

In Québec, rather than a personal property security system, there is a system based on prior claims and hypothecs.[41] It imports a notion of common pledge to creditors, with the property of the debtor charged with the performance of its obligations.[42] The Québec *Civil Code* defines a prior claim as a claim to which the law attaches the right for a creditor to be preferred over other creditors, and prior claims rank according to the order specified in the statute, without regard to their date; they rank ahead of movable or immovable hypothecs.[43] Movables are analogous to personal property and immovables are analogous to real property.[44] A hypothec is a real right on a movable or immovable property made liable for the performance of an obligation and it confers a right on a creditor to follow the property into the hands of third parties, to take possession or payment or to dispose of the property.[45] Hypothecation can take place only according to specified conditions and formalities authorized by the law, and can be created in particular circumstances by delivery, also called a pledge. The hypothec can be conventional or legal, depending on whether it arises from agreement of the parties or operation of the law.[46]

Martin Desrosiers and David Tardif-Latourelle, in discussing the Québec system of hypothecs and common pledges, have observed that the harmonization amendments made to the *BIA* with respect to prior claims constituting a real right, were not extended to the definition of secured creditor under the *CCAA*. On analyzing the caselaw, they suggest that on the basis of principles established by the courts, there would need to be an irreconcilable conflict between provisions of the *CCAA* and the Québec *Civil Code* before it could be concluded that a prior claim that does not constitute a real right could be treated as unsecured pursuant to the *CCAA*.[47]

VI. EXECUTORY CONTRACTS - CURRENT TREATMENT

Executory contracts are frequently affected both under the stay provisions of the *CCAA* and in the final plan of arrangement or compromise. Executory contracts are generally contracts under which both parties still have obligations to perform, such that the failure to perform the contract is likely to cause a material breach that

---

[41] Article 2644, Québec *Civil Code*.

[42] For a helpful discussion, see Martin Desrosiers and David Tardif-Latourelle, "Insolvency and Restructuring in Québec: A Common Law Practitioner's Guide", in *Annual Review of Insolvency Law, 2005* (Toronto: Carswell, 2006), at 319-355.

[43] Articles 2651, 2657, Québec *Civil Code*.

[44] Martin Desrosiers and David Tardif-Latourelle, "Insolvency and Restructuring in Québec: A Common Law Practitioner's Guide", in *Annual Review of Insolvency Law, 2005* (Toronto: Carswell, 2006), at 322.

[45] Articles 2660, 2664, Québec *Civil Code*.

[46] Martin Desrosiers and David Tardif-Latourelle, "Insolvency and Restructuring in Québec: A Common Law Practitioner's Guide", in *Annual Review of Insolvency Law, 2005* (Toronto: Carswell, 2006), at 323. A conventional hypothec can be granted only by a person having the capacity to alienate the property hypothecated, whereas legal hypothecs arise from the law, specifically, Article 2724 of the Québec *Civil Code*. *Ibid.* at 323-324.

[47] *Ibid.* at 336.

excuses the performance of the other party.[48] Common examples of executory contracts include real estate leases, employment contracts, an uncompleted construction contract under which the customer agrees to pay the builder as the work progresses, or a contract for the continued supply of goods or services for which the supplier periodically bills the customer.[49]

The ability of the debtor corporation to carry on business during the *CCAA* stay period frequently depends on the continued performance of executory contracts. However, due to its financial distress, the debtor company is often in material breach of the contracts, and in the normal course of commercial dealing, the other party to the contract would have the right to terminate for the debtor's failure to perform.

While the *CCAA* does not expressly deal with executory contracts, Canadian courts have drawn on their discretionary powers to prevent a creditor from terminating an executory contract with the debtor, or to allow the debtor to terminate an executory contract notwithstanding provisions in the contract that would otherwise prevent its termination.[50] In *T. Eaton Co.,* the Ontario Superior Court held:

> It is clear that under *CCAA* proceedings debtor companies are permitted to unilaterally terminate in the sense of repudiate leases and contracts without regard to the terms of those leases and contracts including any restrictions conferred therein that might ordinarily (i.e. outside *CCAA* proceedings) prevent the debtor company from so repudiating the agreement. To generally restrict debtor companies would constitute an insurmountable obstacle for most debtor companies attempting to effect compromises and reorganizations under the *CCAA*. Such a restriction would be contrary to the purposive approach to *CCAA* proceedings followed by the courts to this date.[51]

Many initial stay orders under the *CCAA* specify that all executory contracts are to continue unless assigned or terminated by the debtor. Thus, the debtor is not usually required within a specified time to make a formal election to retain an executory contract, assign the contract, or to terminate it. From a practical perspective, however, any termination must occur in time to allow the resulting damage claim to be quantified and dealt with in the debtor's plan of arrangement and compromise.

An initial stay order under the *CCAA* will usually be quite specific in terms of the contracts to be preserved and often prohibits the termination of executory contracts. The Alberta Court of Appeal observed in *Blue Range Resource Corp.*;

---

[48] Joint Task Force on Business Insolvency Law Reform Report (March 15, 2002) at 18, online: Insolvency Institute of Canada website http://www.insolvency.ca/dhtml/en/page/papers.q/indexType$Topic/indexID$10/a$index.html at 18.

[49] *Ibid.* at 18.

[50] *Lehndorff General Partner Ltd., Re* (1993), 17 C.B.R. (3d) 24 (Ont. Gen. Div. [Commercial List]) at para. 11. See also *Gaz métropolitain Inc.* v. *Wynden Canada Inc.* (1982), 44 C.B.R. (N.S.) 285 (Que. S.C.) at 290-1, affirmed (1982), 45 C.B.R. (N.S.) 11 (Que. C.A.) and *Quintette Coal Ltd.* v. *Nippon Steel Corp.* (1990), 51 B.C.L.R. (2d) 105 (B.C. C.A.) at 111-12, leave to appeal refused (1991), 55 B.C.L.R. (2d) xxxiii (note) (S.C.C.).

[51] *T. Eaton Co., Re* (1999), 14 C.B.R. (4th) 288, 1999 CarswellOnt 3542, [1999] O.J. No. 4216 (Ont. S.C.J. [Commercial List]) at para. 7.

> The court's discretionary powers under section 11 have been interpreted to restrain any conduct "the effect of which is, or would be, seriously to impair the ability of the debtor company to continue in business during the compromise or arrangement negotiating period". . .. Accordingly, a court-ordered stay will usually prohibit creditors from terminating contracts with the debtor company.[52]

A plan of arrangement and compromise may repudiate leases or terminate contracts, regardless of restrictions placed on those contracts. Any claims arising from that repudiation are unsecured claims for damages.[53]

An excerpt from three paragraphs of the Initial Stay Order in *Air Canada*, the full order of which is contained in Appendix 2 of this text, is illustrative of stay provisions in an initial order in respect of executory contracts:

> 6. THIS COURT ORDERS that during the Stay Period, no person, firm, corporation, governmental authority, or other entity shall, without leave, discontinue, fail to renew, alter, interfere with or terminate any right, contract, arrangement, agreement, licence or permit in favour of an Applicant or the Applicants' Property or held by or on behalf of an Applicant, including as a result of any default or non-performance by an Applicant, the making or filing of these proceedings or any allegation contained in these proceedings.
>
> 7. THIS COURT ORDERS that, during the Stay Period, (a) all persons, firms, corporations, governmental authorities, airport or air navigation authorities or any other entity (including, without limitation, NAV Canada, Office of the Superintendent of Financial Institutions ("OSFI"), IBM Canada Limited and BCE Nexxia Inc.) having written or oral agreements with an Applicant (including, without limitation, leases, pooling or consignment agreements, multilateral interline traffic agreements, codeshare agreements, Tier III Commercial Agreements, gate access agreements, frequent flyer programs or statutory or regulatory mandates) for the supply of goods and/or services (including, without limitation, computer software and hardware, aircraft parts, aircraft maintenance services and related equipment, ground handling services and equipment, catering, office supplies and equipment, reservations, employee uniforms, crew accommodations, meals and commissary, communication and other data services, accounting and payroll servicing, insurance or indemnity, clearing, banking, cash management, credit cards or credit card processing, transportation, utility or other required services), by or to an Applicant or any of the Applicants' Property are hereby restrained until further order of this Court from discontinuing, failing to renew on terms no more onerous than those existing prior to these proceedings, altering, interfering with or terminating the supply of such goods or services so long as the normal prices or charges for such goods and services received after the date of this order are paid in accordance with present payment practices, or as may be hereafter negotiated from time to time, and (b) subject to section 11.1 of the *CCAA*, all persons being party to fuel consortia agreements, or agreements or arrangements for hedging the price of, or forward purchasing of fuel, are hereby

---

[52] *Blue Range Resource Corp., Re* (2000), 192 D.L.R. (4th) 281, 20 C.B.R. (4th) 187 (Alta. C.A.) at para. 7.

[53] Section 8, *CCAA*; *Citibank Canada* v. *Chase Manhattan Bank of Canada* (1991), 5 C.B.R. (3d) 165 (Ont. Gen. Div.).

> restrained from terminating, suspending, modifying, cancelling, or otherwise interfering with such hedging agreements or arrangements, notwithstanding any provisions in such agreements or arrangements to the contrary.
>
> . . . .
>
> 11. THIS COURT ORDERS that, without limiting the generality of paragraph 7 hereof, all credit card companies (including Visa, Mastercard, American Express and Diners Club International) and credit card processing companies (including, without limitation, Global Payments Inc. and Global Payments Direct, Inc.) are hereby restrained from stopping, withholding, redirecting or otherwise interfering with any payments to any of the Applicants or any amount in an Applicant's account(s) against any indebtedness owing to that credit card company by an Applicant or contingent claims not in accordance with past practice, or from discontinuing, failing to renew on terms no more onerous than those existing prior to these proceedings, altering, interfering with or terminating such credit card arrangements.

Canadian courts have allowed the debtor to terminate or assign executory contracts and then negotiate a compromise of claims for damages arising out of the termination or assignment.[54] In *Playdium Entertainment Corp.*, the Ontario Superior Court of Justice allowed a debtor to assign an executory contract without the consent of the counter-party, even though the contract contained a clause that restricted assignment.[55] The correctness of the judgment in *Playdium Entertainment Corp.*, has been somewhat contested, given that the court did not have the benefit of arguments from parties on both sides. Parties to whom a contract is likely to be assigned will usually require the debtor company to obtain an order confirming the assignment of the contract.

The British Columbia Court of Appeal in *Skeena Cellulose Inc.* upheld a lower court judgment terminating evergreen logging contracts. The Court of Appeal explained its reasoning as follows, making the distinction between the exercise of discretion and use of inherent jurisdiction:

> ¶ 37 In the exercise of their 'broad discretion' under the *CCAA*, it has now become common for courts to sanction the indefinite, or even permanent, affecting of contractual rights. Most notably, in *Re Dylex Ltd.* (1995) 31 C.B.R. (3d) 106 (Ont. Ct. (Gen. Div.)), Farley J. followed several other cases in holding that in "filling in the gaps" of the *CCAA*, a court may sanction a plan of arrangement that includes the termination of leases to which the debtor is a party. (See also the cases cited in Dylex, at para. 8; *Re T. Eaton Co.* (1999) 14 C.B.R. (4th) 288 (Ont. S.C.), at 293-4; *Smoky River Coal; supra,* and *Re Armbro Enterprises Inc.* (1993) 22 C.B.R. (3d) 80 (Ont. Ct. (Gen. Div.)), at para. 13.) In the latter case, R.A. Blair J. said he saw nothing in principle that precluded a court from "interfering with the rights of a landlord under a lease, in the *CCAA* context, any more than from interfering with the rights of a

---

[54] *Playdium Entertainment Corp., Re* (2001), 2001 CarswellOnt 3893, 31 C.B.R. (4th) 302 (Ont. S.C.J. [Commercial List]), additional reasons at (2001), 31 C.B.R. (4th) 309 (Ont. S.C.J. [Commercial List]); *T. Eaton Co., Re* (1999), 14 C.B.R. (4th) 288 (Ont. S.C.J. [Commercial List]).

[55] *Playdium Entertainment Corp., ibid.*

secured creditor under a security document. Both may be sanctioned when the exigencies of the particular reorganization justify such balancing of the prejudices." In its recent judgment in *Syndicat national de l'amiante d'Asbestos inc.* v. *Jeffrey Mines Ltd* [2003] Q.J. No. 264, the Québec Court of Appeal observed that "A review of the jurisprudence shows that the debtor's right to cancel contracts prejudicial to it can be provided for in an order to stay proceedings under s. 11." (para. 74.)

¶ 38 But in approving and implementing compromises and arrangements under the statute, courts are concerned with more than the efficacy of the plans before them and their acceptability to creditors. Courts also strive to ensure fairness as between the unsecured, secured and preferred creditors of the corporation and as between the debtor and its creditors generally. . . .

¶ 46 . . . . I think the preferable view is that when a court approves a plan of arrangement under the *CCAA* which contemplates that one or more binding contracts will be terminated by the debtor corporation, the court is not exercising a power that arises from its nature as a superior court of law, but is exercising the discretion given to it by the *CCAA*. (As to the meaning of "discretion" in this context, see S. Waddams, "Judicial Discretion", (2001) 1 Cmnwth. L.J. 59.) This is the discretion, given by s. 11, to stay proceedings against the debtor corporation and the discretion, given by s. 6, to approve a plan which appears to be reasonable and fair, to be in accord with the requirements and objects of the statute, and to make possible the continuation of the corporation as a viable entity. It is these considerations the courts have been concerned with in the cases discussed above, rather than the integrity of their own process.

. . .

¶ 50 It follows in my view that in approving an arrangement in which the debtor corporation terminates a replaceable logging contract, a *CCAA* court is not overriding "provincial legislation" as the intervenor contends. Nor is the court "overriding" the terms of the contract: it is merely exercising the discretion given to it by the statute to approve a plan of arrangement. The breach of contract is recognized as a matter of fact by the court, but is not "permitted" in the sense that the licence holder is somehow immunized from the usual consequences of its breach at law or in Equity. Finally, even if the Forest Act or Regulation did prohibit the termination of replaceable contracts, the federal government's powers with respect to bankruptcy and insolvency would become applicable once the *CCAA* was invoked and the doctrine of paramountcy would operate to resolve any direct conflict.[56]

The Court of Appeal observed that the debtor corporation Skeena had provided the Chambers judge below with an explanation as to why it chose to reduce the volume of timber allocated to Skeena's evergreen contractors, and why it chose to terminate the particular contracts of the appellants rather than to terminate all contracts. The Court found that there was a business case for its actions.[57] The Court held that the key to the fairness analysis lies in the very breadth of that constituency and wide range of interests that may be properly asserted by individuals, corporations, gov-

---

[56] *Skeena Cellulose Inc., Re* (2003), 2003 CarswellBC 1399, [2003] B.C.J. No. 1335 (B.C. C.A.).

[57] *Ibid.* at para. 57.

ernment entities and communities.[58] It held that in the absence of evidence that the debtor company was motivated by anything other than a desire to improve the debtor corporation's financial prospects for survival post-arrangement, the court could not conclude that the Chambers judge erred in ruling that the termination of the appellants' replaceable contracts was a valid part of the reorganization plan.[59]

The court does not always grant the relief sought. In *Doman Industries*, the British Columbia Supreme Court declined to terminate replaceable logging contracts as conditions precedent to the implementation of a restructuring plan.[60] The Court adopted the approach of the court in *Dylex* in weighing the competing interests and prejudices of the parties and in deciding what was fair and reasonable.[61] In the absence of sufficient evidence to support the conclusion that the proposed contract terminations were fair and reasonable, the Court declined to make the order. Evidence simply that the company would be more profitable if the terminations were effected was not sufficient reason to terminate the contracts. In distinguishing *Skeena Cellulose Inc.*, the Court in *Doman Industries*, concluded that the conditions relating to the terminations were not true conditions precedent, and that the restructuring would not be jeopardized if the conditions were not satisfied.[62]

Executory contracts can include intellectual property licenses under which the licensor has agreed to provide maintenance and update facilities and the licensee pays royalties. One area of concern is the licensee's ability to protect its rights when the licensor becomes insolvent and disclaims a license for intellectual property. While an insolvent debtor corporation wishes to terminate the license to avoid the ongoing provision of support services, the licensee may require the intellectual property for the continuation of its own business.[63] In *Eaton's*, the Court held that a debtor is entitled to unilaterally terminate contracts, including license arrangements, and provide for the liability and damages in its plan of restructuring.[64] The Court held that a license transfers no proprietary interest that would protect the licensee by way of specific performance or mandatory injunction, and that in determining requests

---

[58] *Ibid.* at para. 60.

[59] *Ibid.* at para. 61.

[60] *Doman Industries Ltd., Re* (2004), [2004] B.C.J. No. 1149, 2004 CarswellBC 1262, 1 C.B.R. (5th) 7 (B.C. S.C.), leave to appeal refused (2004), [2004] B.C.J. No. 1402, 2004 CarswellBC 1545, 2 C.B.R. (5th) 141 (B.C. C.A. [In Chambers]).

[61] *Dylex Ltd., Re* (1995), 1995 CarswellOnt 54, [1995] O.J. No. 595, 31 C.B.R. (3d) 106 (Ont. Gen. Div. [Commercial List]).

[62] *Doman Industries Ltd., Re* (2004), [2004] B.C.J. No. 1149, 2004 CarswellBC 1262, 1 C.B.R. (5th) 7 (B.C.S.C.), leave to appeal refused (2004), [2004] B.C.J. No. 1402, 2004 CarswellBC 1545, 2 C.B.R. (5th) 141 (B.C. C.A. [In Chambers]). For a discussion of *Doman,* see M. Fitch and K. Jackson, "Pulp Friction: The Protracted Restructuring of the Doman Forest Companies", Janis Sarra, ed., *Annual Review of Insolvency Law, 2004* (Carswell, 2005) at 1-28.

[63] Elyse Rosen, "The Fate of a Technology Licence When the Licensor Becomes Insolvent" (2003) 20 Nat'l Insolv. Rev. 32, 2003 C.N.I.R. LEXIS 6 at 2-3; Scott A. Bomhof, "An Update on the Proposed Reforms to the *BIA* and *CCAA*" (2003) 16 Comm. Insol. R. 10, 2003 C.C.I.R. LEXIS 12 at 4.

[64] *Eaton's,* at para. 7, cited in Mario J. Forte and Amanda C. Chester, "Licenses and the Effects of Bankruptcy and Insolvency Law on the Licensee" 13 Comm. Insol. R. 25 at 40.

for termination, the court would balance prejudice to all parties with an interest in the proceedings.[65]

The *CCAA* was amended in 2005 to deal with specific problems that arose out of the insolvency of several airline companies in respect of aircraft leases. The stay provisions now specify that a stay order under the *CCAA* cannot restrict a lessor or secured lender of aircraft objects (a defined term), from taking possession if the insolvent aircraft lessee does not maintain the aircraft or cure any defaults in payments within 60 days.[66]

1. Claims Relating to Real Property Leases

The courts have allowed termination of leases where necessary for the development of a plan. The Alberta Court of Appeal has held that where such a lease is terminated as part of a *CCAA* restructuring, a proper assessment of the landlord's damages must be made and the resulting claim dealt with in the *CCAA* restructuring.[67] The court has held that unless there is an admission of the amount owed, the valuation of a landlord's claim should be made by the court in the normal course in a *CCAA* proceeding.

Section 12 does not import all of the provisions of the *BIA* when determining the amount of a claim. In *Alternative Fuel Systems,* where a landlord sought to apply the *BIA* and Alberta provincial *Landlord's Rights on Bankruptcy Act*, the Alberta Court of Queen's Bench determined that the flexibility of the debtor to formulate a plan of arrangement would be hindered by the application of the more rigid rules set out in the *BIA* and the provincial legislation.[68]

The debtor corporation must provide proper notice of termination, or claims are not compromised under a *CCAA* plan. The Ontario Court of Appeal in *Ivorylane Corp.* v. *Country Style Realty Ltd.* held that a pre-*CCAA* claim for arrears of rent under a lease is not barred, and may be asserted in full against a reorganized *CCAA* company following its emergence from *CCAA* proceedings where: the lease in question was not repudiated as part of the *CCAA* proceedings; the claimant, whose claim should have been known to the debtor company and documented in the debtor company's books, never received formal notice of the *CCAA* proceedings or of a claims procedure order providing for a claims bar date; and the claimant did not see the claims bar notice published in the newspaper: The Court found that the plan itself made it clear that: a real property lease that has not been repudiated or terminated and in respect of which there has been no written agreement to allow a claim was an "unaffected obligation" under the plan; the debtor company was deemed to have ratified each unexpired lease to which it was a party, unless such lease was previously

---

[65] *Eaton's, ibid.* citing, *Heap* v. *Hartley* (1889), 42 Ch. D. 461 (Eng. C.A.) at 468-9.

[66] Section 11.31, *CCAA*.

[67] *Alternative Fuel Systems Inc, Re* (2004), 47 C.B.R. (4th) 1, 2004 CarswellAlta 64 (Alta. C.A.).

[68] *Alternative Fuel Systems Inc., Re* (2003), 46 C.B.R. (4th) 8, 2003 CarswellAlta 1262 (Alta. Q.B.), affirmed (2004), 47 C.B.R. (4th) 1, 2004 CarswellAlta 64 (Alta. C.A.).

repudiated or terminated or previously expired or terminated pursuant to its own terms; and any agreement to which the debtor company is a party as at the effective date of the plan was to remain in full force and effect unamended and the debtor company was obliged to perform such agreement and was prohibited from repudiating it by reason of the fact that the debtor company had sought and obtained *CCAA* relief or that a reorganization had been implemented.[69]

The Ontario Court of Appeal in *Veltri Metal Products Co.* held that in order for proceeds of sale of the debtor's interest in real property to constitute trust monies under sections 7 and 9 of the *Construction Lien Act* (the "*CLA*") in favour of construction lien claimants who made improvements to the real property interest sold, the proceeds of sale must, *inter alia*, be monies in the hands of the debtor or received by the debtor as owner. Here, the lien was registered against the title of the leased property, including the leasehold interest of the debtor. Where there is a sale of assets under the *CCAA,* including the leasehold interest and title vested in the purchaser free and clear, the proceeds are substituted for the debtor's assets and are subject to claims of the debtor's secured creditors, the sale proceeds cannot constitute trust funds in favour of construction lien claimants under the *CLA* since, in such circumstances, a debtor is not an owner of the assets sold to the extent that secured creditors have an interest therein.[70] The Court in that case held that the debtor had no interest in or right to any of the net sale proceeds ultimately paid to and held by the monitor appointed in the *CCAA* proceedings; and at best, the debtor simply acts as a conduit for the receipt by the monitor of the sale proceeds.[71]

2. Trade Suppliers

Another form of executory contract is supply agreements, such as the logging contracts referred to above. A stay order under the *CCAA* frequently contains provisions prohibiting creditors from terminating contracts with the debtor corporation. However, the debtor corporation can, subject to the court's supervision, terminate or breach a contract, and damage claims arising from the termination or breach become unsecured claims. The prohibition against terminating contracts does not apply to contracts that are "eligible financial contracts", as discussed below.[72]

While section 81.1 of the *BIA* allows unpaid suppliers who sold or delivered goods to make a demand to a bankrupt for return of the goods within 30 days of delivery under certain conditions, these rights do not exist under the *CCAA* and suppliers are

---

[69] *Ivorylane Corp.* v. *Country Style Realty Ltd.* (2005), 2005 CarswellOnt 2516, 11 C.B.R. (5th) 230 (Ont. C.A.).

[70] *Veltri Metal Products Co., Re* (2005), 2005 CarswellOnt 3326 (Ont. C.A.).

[71] *Ibid.*

[72] Section 11.1(1)(h), *CCAA; Blue Range Resource Corp., Re* (2000), 192 D.L.R. (4th) 281, 20 C.B.R. (4th) 187 (Alta. C.A.).

stayed from repossession of goods.[73] However, where the court is concerned about prejudice to the suppliers, it may make orders that attempt to fashion some remedy. For example, in *Woodward's*, the Court ordered that if the company in *CCAA* proceedings subsequently went into receivership or bankruptcy, the *CCAA* period would not be counted for purposes of the 30 day rule, and that suppliers would have access to funds of the receiver to the extent that they could identify the funds as proceeds of the sale of the goods.[74] This is now a standard clause in *CCAA* stay orders. However, in *Woodward's*, the Court would not set aside the funds in a trust during the period that the *CCAA* plan was being negotiated.[75]

Prior to the reform of the Québec *Civil Code* in 1994, a supplier of movable property in Québec had the right to resolve a sale and revendicate property within 30 days of delivery, in the case of bankruptcy, if the property remained in the possession of the purchaser.[76] However, the Court has held that the *CCAA* stay applies to suppliers with rights of revendication, and on the facts, the Court would not grant leave to lift the stay for such suppliers as the individual rights of creditors must yield to the collective rights of all creditors to advance the goals of the *CCAA*.[77]

In *Doman Industries Ltd.*, a creditor filed a lien claim after the insolvent company entered into *CCAA* protection, and the initial order provided that the company could continue to make payments only in respect of obligations incurred after the filing date. The British Columbia Supreme Court found that the prior practice of applying payments to the oldest debts was varied by the initial order. While the order did

---

[73] The initial *CCAA* order can contain a provision suspending any rights to repossess for the period during which the stay order is in effect. As an example, the standard form of order developed between the Québec Bar and the judiciary contains such a provision, see Appendix 6 of this text.

[74] *Woodward's Ltd., Re* (1993), 17 C.B.R. (3d) 253 (B.C. S.C.), leave to appeal refused (1993), 22 C.B.R. (3d) 25 (B.C. C.A.).

[75] Of note is that the initial order in the matter of the arrangement of *Woodward's Ltd.* was rendered relatively soon after the implementation of the new provisions of the *BIA* creating the right for suppliers to recover recently delivered merchandise. Given the lack of jurisprudence on the issue at the time, the portion of the judgment relating to a tracing of funds in the hands of the receiver may no longer be valid reasoning. Under the provisions of section 81.1 of the *BIA*, merchandise can only be recovered where (*inter alia*) the merchandise is in the possession of the debtor, the trustee or the receiver, is identifiable and in the same state as at the time of delivery, and has not been resold or is not subject to an agreement of sale at arm's length.

[76] Under the previously existing *Civil Code of Lower Canada* (*CCLC*), the right of resiliation of a contract was provided for in article 1543 of the *CCLC*. This right could be exercised by a seller of movable property at any time for reason of non-payment, although the right was restricted to a period of 30 days following delivery in case of bankruptcy. The Court in Québec had found that this right to retroactively annul the sale was not incompatible with the provisions of the *Bankruptcy Act* (as it was then known). See in this regard *Alcools de commerce Inc.* v. *Corp. de produits chimiques de Valleyfield* (1985), 57 C.B.R. (N.S.) 225 (Que. C.A.). Since the reform, the Québec *Civil Code* provides that when a contract is not being fulfilled, it may be resolved (deemed to have never existed) or resiliated (terminated for the future), without necessity of judicial proceedings (see articles 1605 and 1606 of the *Civil Code*). If the contract is a sale of movable property, the seller can ask that the sale be resolved and revendicate the merchandise, within 30 days of delivery, if the property is still entire and in the same condition. However this right cannot be invoked if the sale was with a term, which makes this right largely irrelevant in a context of bankruptcy or insolvency (Article 1741 of the *Civil Code*).

[77] *Steinberg Inc.* c. *Colgate-Palmolive Canada Inc.* (1992), 13 C.B.R. (3d) 139 (Que. S.C.).

provide for optional payment of pre-existing debts if, in the normal course of business, it was clear that the payments made particular reference to individual invoices that were submitted after the initial order. The cheques were cashed, and therefore the Court held that the lien for invoices submitted in the thirty days immediately prior to the filing of the lien was invalid.[78]

In the context of the court's treatment of tradepersons' claims, where a proceeding to determine the validity of a woodsmen's lien was exempted from the stay, two defendant banks claiming security pursuant to the *Bank Act* were permitted to participate in the hearing, not only with respect to the issue as to priority between the bank's security and the lien, but also with respect to the validity of the liens themselves and the writs of attachment. Once the banks were added as defendants, the Court held that the *Woodsmen's Liens Act* did not expressly or implicitly restrict their rights to challenge the validity of the liens.[79]

With respect to letters of credit, section 11.2 of the *CCAA* specifies:

> 11.2 No order may be made under section 11 staying or restraining any action, suit or proceeding against a person, other than a debtor company in respect of which an application has been made under this Act, who is obligated under a letter of credit or guarantee in relation to the company.

Letters of credit in place at the time of filing have usually been provided as a condition of supplying critical goods or services to the debtor; and since the counter-party to the agreement is, pursuant to section 11.3, entitled to withhold provision of goods and/or services during the *CCAA* process if it cannot obtain reasonable security for payment from the debtor, keeping letters of credit in place during a *CCAA* proceeding can be an important mechanism to allow the debtor corporation to continue operating.[80]

3. Public Utilities

Public utility companies are in a special position in a proceeding under the *CCAA*, whether or not the supply contracts are documented as long term agreements or a

---

[78] *Doman Industries Ltd., Re* (2004), 2004 CarswellBC 1741, 2 C.B.R. (5th) 149, 2004 BCSC 991 (B.C. S.C. [In Chambers]).

[79] *Glassville Logging Co.* v. *Juniper Lumber Co.* (2003), 2003 CarswellNB 441, 46 C.B.R. (4th) 275, 2003 NBQB 366 (N.B. Q.B.), leave to appeal allowed (2003), 2003 CarswellNB 474, 1 C.B.R. (5th) 51 (N.B. C.A.), reversed (2004), 2004 CarswellNB 104, 2004 CarswellNB 105, (sub nom. *Wicklow Logging Co.* v. *Juniper Lumber Co.)* 270 N.B.R. (2d) 346, 1 C.B.R. (5th) 53, 2004 NBCA 10 (N.B. C.A.), additional reasons at (2004), 2004 CarswellNB 294, 2004 CarswellNB 295, 1 C.B.R. (5th) 55, 2004 NBCA 10 (N.B. C.A.). There are numerous provincial statutes that protect tradeperson's labour by allowing the tradeperson (working in construction, woodwork, repairing, etc.) to place a lien on the assets of the debtor, in order to encourage timing payment for work performed.

[80] Evelyn H. Biery, Patrick T. McCarthy, Richard J. Wilson, Melissa M. Smith, and Patricia L. Barsalou, "Treatment of Forward Contracts in Insolvency Cases: A Comparison of U.S. and Canadian Law", in Janis Sarra, ed., *Annual Review of Insolvency Law, 2004* (Toronto: Carswell, 2005) at 59-118.

month to month arrangement. In a *CCAA* proceeding, the initial order will usually compel the public utility companies to continue providing the services on an on-going basis. Section 11.3 of the *CCAA* provides that the initial order cannot have the effect of prohibiting a person from requiring an immediate payment for goods supplied or services rendered after the order is made, or requiring the further advance of money or credit. In effect, section 11.3 of the *CCAA* is intended to provide a measure of protection to those people dealing with the insolvent debtor after the initial order, with a view to maintaining a *status quo*.

Public utility companies, by the nature of their services, cannot easily benefit from the protection afforded by section 11.3 of the *CCAA*, in that they cannot know with certainty in advance of a delivery what the delivery will be and therefore the price to be paid, and cannot practically monitor usage and prepare an invoice on a daily basis. The problem they face is one of ensuring that they receive payment for the supplies after the initial order.

To alleviate this difficulty, public utility companies have attempted to argue that their standard agreement with the insolvent debtor provides for an advance deposit, and that it is merely a temporary "favour" if the deposit requirement is waived in respect of a customer, prior to the insolvency. Public utility companies then suggest that reinstating the requirement for a deposit would not be a departure from the terms of the initial order, which usually requires that the services continue on the same terms, conditions and pricing as those in effect prior to the making of the initial order. This argument has had very limited success.[81]

More recently in *Meubles Dinec*, Hydro Québec, the supplier of electricity in Québec, was able to convince the court that in view of its billing practices and administrative delays in issuing invoices and receiving payments from the debtor, it would be appropriate for it to demand a deposit as a way to obtain the protection afforded to other suppliers by virtue of section 11.3 of the *CCAA*.[82] In the *Meubles Dinec* case, the Court of Appeal referred to an earlier case in which the court had rejected a request from a natural gas supplier for a one month deposit, inferring that the decision is fact specific.

4. Eligible Financial Contracts

Eligible financial contracts have, since 1997, enjoyed a special status under the *CCAA*, aimed at maintaining the integrity of Canadian capital markets. The stay provisions of the *CCAA* do not apply to eligible financial contracts.

In 1994, prior to the 1997 amendments, Confederation Treasury Services Ltd. (CTS), a wholly-owned subsidiary of Confederation Life Insurance, filed under the *CCAA*

---

[81] *Abattoir Coquelicot Inc., Re* (1993), 1993 CarswellQue 40 (Que. S.C.).

[82] *Meubles Dinec Inc., Re* (2006), 2006 CarswellQue 4986, [2006] J.Q. No. 5160 (Que. C.A.), File 200-09-005532-061.

when its parent experienced a liquidity crisis. At the time of the parent corporation's financial distress, CTS had both cash and "in the money" assets from a number of derivative contracts. The initial *CCAA* order stayed parties from accelerating, terminating or cancelling contracts, including derivative contracts.[83] CTS was granted the ability to terminate "out of the money" contracts, while preserving its position in "in the money" derivative contracts.[84] Subsequently, one party brought a motion asking the court to find that CTS had failed to properly terminate derivative contracts to which it was a party. The Court held that the stay continued, since the *CCAA* was not amended in 1992 at the time the *BIA* was amended to exempt a range of derivative and commodity contracts from the automatic stay of proceedings during a proposal proceeding.[85]

The *CCAA* was subsequently amended in 1997, exempting eligible financial contracts from the stay provisions and aligning the *CCAA* with the *BIA* provisions. The 1997 amendments added a definition of eligible financial contracts and clarified that the ability to exercise set-off rights is preserved.[86]

Section 11.1 of the *CCAA* specifies:

> "eligible financial contract" means
>
> (a) a currency or interest rate swap agreement,
>
> (b) a basis swap agreement,
>
> (c) a spot, future, forward or other foreign exchange agreement,
>
> (d) a cap, collar or floor transaction,
>
> (e) a commodity swap,
>
> (f) a forward rate agreement,
>
> (g) a repurchase or reverse repurchase agreement,
>
> (h) a spot, future, forward or other commodity contract,
>
> (i) an agreement to buy, sell, borrow or lend securities, to clear or settle securities transactions or to act as a depository for securities,
>
> (j) any derivative, combination or option in respect of, or agreement similar to, an agreement or contract referred to in paragraphs (a) to (i),

---

[83] *Confederation Treasury Services Ltd., Re* (1994), 1994 CarswellOnt 2224, [1994] O.J. No 1992 (Ont. Gen. Div. [Commercial List]).

[84] I. B. Nadler, "Treatment of Derivative Transactions in Insolvencies", (1995) 12 Nat'l Insol. Rev. 6 79-82 at 81.

[85] *Confederation Treasury Services Ltd. (Trustee of)* v. *Hees International Bancorp Inc.* (1997), 45 C.B.R. (3d) 204 (Ont. Gen. Div. [Commercial List]), affirmed (1998), 1998 CarswellOnt 4421 (Ont. C.A.); section 65.1, *BIA*. The court observed that the *BIA* provisions provided an example of how the competing public policy was to be balanced.

[86] *Blue Range Resource Corp., Re*, [2000] 11 W.W.R. 117, 2000 ABCA 200 (Alta C.A.), see also *Air Canada, Re* (2003), 45 C.B.R. (4th) 13 (Ont. S.C.J. [Commercial List]). The Court in *Blue Range* found that pre-filing claims could be set-off against post-filing claims.

(k) any master agreement in respect of any agreement or contract referred to in paragraphs (a) to (j),

(l) any master agreement in respect of a master agreement referred to in paragraph (k),

(m) a guarantee of the liabilities under an agreement or contract referred to in paragraphs (a) to (l), or

(n) any agreement of a kind prescribed;

"net termination value"

"net termination value" means the net amount obtained after setting off the mutual obligations between the parties to an eligible financial contract in accordance with its provisions.

No stay, etc., in certain cases

(2) No order may be made under this Act staying or restraining the exercise of any right to terminate, amend or claim any accelerated payment under an eligible financial contract or preventing a member of the Canadian Payments Association established by the Canadian Payments Act from ceasing to act as a clearing agent or group clearer for a company in accordance with that Act and the by-laws and rules of that Association.

Existing eligible financial contracts

(3) For greater certainty, where an eligible financial contract entered into before an order is made under section 11 is terminated on or after the date of the order, the setting off of obligations between the company and the other parties to the eligible financial contract, in accordance with its provisions, is permitted, and if net termination values determined in accordance with the eligible financial contract are owed by the company to another party to the eligible financial contract, that other party shall be deemed to be a creditor of the company with a claim against the company in respect of the net termination values.

The objective of eligible financial contracts is primarily to manage risk. Evelyn Biery, Patrick McCarthy *et al* have observed that many factors have contributed to the rise of eligible financial contracts, including deregulating electricity markets and continental natural gas and petroleum markets that have been forcibly reshaped by the collapse of many of the giant energy traders, these markets characterized by a volatile foreign currency exchange, interest rate and commodity price environment.[87] They suggest that derivative contracts aimed at risk management continue to experience incredible growth as a result.

[87] Evelyn H. Biery, Patrick T. McCarthy, Richard J. Wilson, Melissa M. Smith, and Patricia L. Barsalou, "Treatment of Forward Contracts in Insolvency Cases: A Comparison of U.S. and Canadian Law", in Janis Sarra, ed., *Annual Review of Insolvency Law, 2004* (Toronto: Carswell, 2005) at 59-118.

Biery *et al* observed that the 1997 provisions leave the debtor in the situation where it can only continue to preserve the value of "in the money" derivative or commodity contracts if it liquidates those positions prior to filing under the *CCAA,* or seeks consent of the counter-parties to those contracts to continue them after obtaining an initial order; and that it also leaves the counter-parties free to terminate, set-off and realize on security held for those contracts.[88]

Evelyn Biery and her co-authors describe derivatives in the following way:

> Derivatives are contracts under which liabilities arise as a result of changes in the value of a currency, fungible commodity, stock, index or some other financially significant variable to which the contract is tied. Derivatives have evolved to allow businesses to manage risk by buying what is essentially a form of insurance against a material adverse change in a financial component of their operations. . ..
>
> The first is the problem of finding a party whose payment amounts and the timing of whose payments precisely offset those of the counter-party, and at the same time one whose concerns regarding the direction the currency may move are exactly opposite to those of the counter-party. The second problem, which is at the core of the special rules which govern derivative and similar contracts in insolvencies in Canada is that both parties must be completely creditworthy – and remain so for the term of the transaction – because eliminating risk is the entire purpose of the arrangement. The prospect that one party may become unable to fulfill its obligations in the face of an adverse movement in the price of the underlying commodity, currency or other variable is antithetical to the purpose of the arrangement.
>
> For these reasons a sizeable business has grown up in providing hedges against risk to parties on a wide variety of financial variables, in a wide variety of industries. It will come as no surprise, given the volatility of the prices of commodities such as oil and natural gas, which the various players in the energy industry have for many years sought ways to protect themselves against the risks of commodity price fluctuations. . ..
>
> There are many sorts of such "financial" arrangements available, in which the party with whom the buyer, seller, or other party is contracting never intends to deal with the commodity itself, either by taking delivery of it or otherwise, but nonetheless undertakes to provide protection against pricing, delivery or other risk for the buyer or seller of the commodity. There are two small but important distinctions between these purely financial arrangements and true insurance. First, these arrangements do not require an actual loss to be suffered for payment to occur. Second, the party purchasing the arrangement need not have an insurable interest such as ownership in the underlying asset.[89]

There are generally two types of derivatives. Over the counter derivatives, often referred to as "swaps", are privately negotiated derivatives, customized to meet

[88] *Ibid.*

[89] *Ibid.*

parties' needs; and standardized exchange-traded derivatives are called futures.[90] While futures are guaranteed by the clearing organization that provides the credit worthiness assurances, swaps can also be offered by financial institutions (either as intermediary or seller), which provides counter-parties with comfort regarding performance.[91]

Over the counter derivative contracts usually set provisions for when parties are materially "out of the money", specifically, providing for cash deposits or letters of credit. To quote Biery *et al* again:

> . . . . contracts usually provide (at least in the energy industry) that security by way of cash deposits, or letters of credit may be demanded where one party is materially "out of the money" on its obligations under the contract - i.e., the price at which it had committed to buy, sell, or provide other pricing protection has become negative when compared to the then-current market price of the underlying commodity or financial variable involved. This process of comparing contract prices to market prices to determine whether the value of a contract was negative or positive from one party's point of view is known as "marking to market" and is done frequently over the term of such contracts to ensure that the "in the money" counter-party knows when to demand security to ensure that it will not be exposed to excessive financial risk if the "out of the money" counter-party cannot perform its obligations. Failure by the out of the money counter-party to provide security when required also lets an "in the money" party know that it is necessary to terminate the agreement and place its risk elsewhere before matters get worse.[92]

The first reported case under the 1997 section 11.1 provisions on eligible financial contracts was *Blue Range Resource Corp.*[93] Blue Range was an oil and gas exploration and production company that had committed to forward sales of natural gas in amounts that exceeded its production. Most of the forward sales were at prices below the then-current market prices for natural gas, meaning that Blue Range was required, in order to meet its obligations under its sale contracts, to purchase some gas at the higher "spot" market price, and deliver it under its contracts at a loss.[94] Blue Range's four largest contracts were with Enron Canada Limited.[95] Enron

---

[90] International Swaps and Derivatives Association, Inc. (www.isda.org). ISDA has developed standardized contracts that are widely used to document both "physical" and "financial" over the counter transactions.

[91] Evelyn H. Biery, Patrick T. McCarthy, Richard J. Wilson, Melissa M. Smith, and Patricia L. Barsalou, "Treatment of Forward Contracts in Insolvency Cases: A Comparison of U.S. and Canadian Law", in Janis Sarra, ed., *Annual Review of Insolvency Law, 2004* (Toronto: Carswell, 2005) at 59-118.

[92] *Ibid.* at 87-88.

[93] *Blue Range Resource Corp., Re* (1999), 245 A.R. 172, 12 C.B.R. (4th) 173 (Alta. Q.B.), leave to appeal allowed (1999), 1999 CarswellAlta 809 (Alta. C.A.), reversed (2000), 2000 CarswellAlta 1004 (Alta. C.A.).

[94] Evelyn H. Biery, Patrick T. McCarthy, Richard J. Wilson, Melissa M. Smith, and Patricia L. Barsalou, "Treatment of Forward Contracts in Insolvency Cases: A Comparison of U.S. and Canadian Law", in Janis Sarra, ed., *Annual Review of Insolvency Law, 2004* (Toronto: Carswell, 2005) at 59-118.

[95] Previously called Enron Capital & Trade Resources Canada Corp. In the early 1990s, the parent corporation Enron had introduced the idea of a "Gas Bank," in which it became the market maker for trading in natural gas in North America. *Ibid.*

Canada brought an application to court under the *CCAA* proceeding for a declaration that its gas contracts were eligible financial contracts. The lower court held that the key consideration in deciding whether a forward contract was afforded the protection of section 11.1 should be whether the contract was financial or physical in nature, finding that if the purpose of the contract is only financial in nature and is not intended to lead to the actual delivery of the commodity, then it should be found to be an eligible financial contract".[96]

On appeal, the Alberta Court of Appeal reversed the lower court's decision and found that Enron Canada's agreements were eligible financial contracts, rejecting the distinction between financial and physical contracts, as it found that distinction would render the inclusion of many of the contracts listed in section 11.1 of the *CCAA* meaningless as some eligible financial contracts can only be settled physically.[97] The Court observed, however, that by including physically settled contracts in the category of eligible financial contracts, it created a risk that a wider range of purchase and sale agreements could be afforded the protection of section 11.1 in *CCAA* proceedings, hence increasing a risk of defeating the express goals of the *CCAA*.[98] The Court of Appeal limited the definition of "commodities" to:

> . . . interchangeable, and readily identifiable as fungible commodities capable of being traded on a futures exchange or as the underlying asset of an over-the-counter derivative transaction. Commodities must trade in a volatile market, with a sufficient trading volume to ensure a competitive trading price, in order that the "forward commodity contract" may be "marked to market" and their value determined. This removes from the ambit of section 11.1(1)(h) contracts for commercial merchandise and manufactured goods which neither trade on a volatile market or are completely interchangeable for each other.[99]

The Court's tests were two-fold, specifically, that items identified as eligible financial contracts must be financial hedges and risk management tools and the classification must produce a fair result.[100] The Court of Appeal further held:

> If forward gas contracts are not exempt from the *CCAA* stay provisions and no offsetting deductions are permitted, available credit quickly will be gobbled up. As a result, risk management companies will limit the capital they can allocate to this market or ask cash-strapped gas producers to put up additional security to cover any

---

[96] *Blue Range Resource Corp., Re* (1999), 245 A.R. 172, 12 C.B.R. (4th) 173 (Alta Q.B.) at para. 30, leave to appeal allowed (1999), 1999 CarswellAlta 809 (Alta. C.A.), reversed (2000), 2000 CarswellAlta 1004 (Alta. C.A.). The judgment was criticized on the basis that derivatives often have both physical and financial components and that with respect to forward sales, the credit risk was the same, whether or not physical delivery at maturity was contemplated. M. R. Smith, "Basic Derivatives for the Oil and Gas Company" (2001) 39 Alta. L. Rev. 152 at 175.

[97] *Blue Range Resource Corp., Re* (2000), 192 D.L.R. (4th) 281, 20 C.B.R. (4th) 187 (Alta. C.A.) at para. 29. The court pointed out the undesirability of allowing debtors to "cherry pick" between contracts, as business would be encouraged to migrate to jurisdictions that protected physically settled transactions.

[98] *Ibid.* at para. 39. Thus, the intent to limit the application of section 11.1 appears to have some following.

[99] *Ibid.* at para. 45.

[100] *Ibid.* at paras. 44, 50.

> shortfalls. The unfortunate effect will be reduced availability of physical forward gas sales contracts to small producers who are most in need of hedges to manage price risks. It will also encourage business to migrate to the United States where physically settled transactions are protected under United States bankruptcy law, putting Canadian risk management companies at a competitive disadvantage. These results weaken the risk management structure within the derivative market and are contrary to the object of the eligible financial contract amendment.

Finding that Enron Canada's gas contracts were eligible financial contracts, the Court of Appeal held that this produced a fair result in that producers under *CCAA* protection that lose the benefit of their eligible financial contracts when they were terminated by the counter-parties could still sell their gas in the spot market or arrange new, possibly better, long term contracts; and counter-parties were able to net out their agreements with an insolvent party, crystallize their losses and deal with their risk exposure through new contracts.[101]

Two years later, with the collapse of its parent Enron in the United States, Enron Canada experienced a credit squeeze, which in turn opened a majority of Enron Canada's contracts to demands for security by "in the money" counter-parties while triggering termination provisions in others. Enron Canada wanted to find a way to preserve the value in its "in the money" over the counter contracts, and brought an application under section 192 of the *Canada Business Corporations Act* for an order staying the termination rights of its counter-parties and requiring them to continue to perform their obligations under their over the counter contracts with Enron Canada, until such time as Enron Canada could locate a new party or a different mechanism to provide credit support for its obligations under those contracts.[102] The Court dismissed the application, relying on the Court of Appeal judgment in *Blue Range* to find that there is equally good reason to honour the underlying public policy considerations for solvent and insolvent companies.[103]

Subsequently, the Ontario Court of Appeal considered whether long-term gas supply contracts were eligible financial contracts in *Androscoggin Energy LLC.*[104] A U.S. company, Androscoggin, had entered into long-term gas supply contracts with AltaGas Ltd. and Pengrowth Corporation in Alberta, who were to supply gas over a ten year period to Androscoggin's generation facility at a specified price. The contracts did not anticipate the rapid increase in the market price of natural gas. Androscoggin filed a Chapter 11 reorganization proceeding under the U.S. *Bankruptcy Code* and obtained section 18.6 *CCAA* recognition and stay in Ontario.[105] The Ontario Court of Appeal held that the gas supply contracts should not be considered eligible financial contracts, but even if they were, there was no right to

---

101 *Ibid.* at 52, 53. However, the Court held that not every purchase and sale agreement of natural gas was a forward commodity contract within the meaning of s. 11.1.

102 *Enron Canada Corp., Re* (2001), [2001] A.J. No. 1611, 2001 CarswellAlta 1675 (Alta. Q.B.).

103 *Ibid.*

104 *Androscoggin Energy LLC, Re* (2005), 75 O.R. (3d) 552 (Ont. C.A.).

105 See chapter 9 for a discussion of recognition orders.

terminate them.[106] The Court agreed with the reasoning in *Blue Range* in not drawing a distinction between physically settled and financially settled transactions as the basis for characterizing eligible financial contracts. The Ontario Court of Appeal further held that eligible financial contracts must serve a financial purpose unrelated to physical settlement of the contract, specifically, managing the risk of a commodity by providing the non-defaulting party the ability to terminate the agreement on the event of filing for protection, to offset or net its obligations and to re-hedge its position. In addition to these hallmarks, the court will have regard to the overall contract.[107] The Court of Appeal held:

> [15] The appellants submit that their contracts are EFCs within s. 11.1(1) of the CCAA as interpreted by Fruman J.A. in *Blue Range, supra.* I disagree. The contracts in issue before Fruman J.A. served a financial purpose unrelated to the physical settlement of the contracts. The reasons in Blue Range indicate that the contracts Fruman J.A. examined enabled the parties to manage the risk of a commodity that fluctuated in price by allowing the counterparty to terminate the agreement in the event of an assignment in bankruptcy or a *CCAA* proceeding, to offset or net its obligations under the contracts to determine the value of the amount of the commodity yet to be delivered in the future, and to re-hedge its position. Unlike the contracts found to be EFCs in *Blue Range, supra,* the contracts in issue here possess none of these hallmarks and cannot be characterized as EFCs. However, mere pro forma insertion of such terms into a contract will not result in its automatic characterization as an EFC. Regard must be had to the contract as a whole to determine its character.

Further, the Court of Appeal held that under the terms of the contracts before it, the Alberta companies were not entitled to terminate as long as payments were made under the contract and because the terms of the contract did not entitle the appellants to termination.[108]

More recently, in *Calpine*, Madam Justice Barbara Romaine of the Alberta Court of Queen's Bench, in dismissing an application for a declaration that a supply agreement was an "eligible financial contract" within the meaning of section 11.1 of the *CCAA*, held that the contract had none of the hallmarks of an eligible financial contract; specifically, the contract was not a stand-alone supply contract, the supply price was neither fixed nor predetermined, the term of the contract and the volumes to be produced were uncertain and not defined, and allowing the termination of the contract would not meet the fairness of result test.[109] The Court further held that the contract before it had no offsetting or netting provisions, and that both *Blue Range* and *Androscoggin* judgments had referred to the importance of such provisions to the concept of an eligible financial contract.[110] The Court found that:

---

[106] *Ibid.* at paras. 7, 8.

[107] *Ibid.* at para. 13-15.

[108] *Ibid.* at paras. 18, 21. For a comment on this case, see David Mann, "Eligible Financial Contracts Revisited: The Androscoggin Experience", in J. Sarra, ed. *Annual Review of Insolvency Law, 2005* (Toronto: Carswell, 2006) at 541.

[109] *Calpine Canada Energy Ltd., Re* (2006), 2006 CarswellAlta 446, [2006] A.J. No. 412 (Alta. Q.B.).

[110] *Ibid.* at para. 19.

> ¶ 19 The COP Agreement, due to its nature, cannot be "marked to market", which is contrary to the characteristic noted at paragraph 46 of *Blue Range* that "(f)orward gas contracts ... have a calculable cash equivalent". The COP Agreement, again due to its nature, has no offsetting or netting provisions. Both the *Blue Range* and *Androscoggin* decisions refer extensively to the importance of such netting-out provisions to the concept of eligible financial contracts: *Blue Range* at paras. 8, 9, 13, 20, 21, 27, 30 and 53; *Androscoggin* at para. 15. Without suggesting that such provisions are necessary in every case before a contract is found to be an eligible financial contract, or that every contract that includes such provisions must be a priori be an eligible financial contract, the importance of such provisions to the determination of whether the contract is truly a derivative or risk management instrument cannot be overemphasized.

While the enumeration in the *CCAA* of types of contracts excluded from the statutory stay can be helpful, it can create problems for new types of contracts developed in the market, where they resemble the types of contracts enumerated under the *CCAA*, but do not fall within the statutory language. This highlights one of the difficulties in enumerating a list as opposed to setting out the types of contracts that the legislation seeks to protect. Further clarity in the statutory language may have prevented problems posed in *Blue Range* and *Androscoggin*. This is an area that is in need of further legislative reform, in order to arrive at greater clarity.

Chapter 47 amends the eligible financial contract provisions to include that forfeiture of terms cannot be stayed.[111] It does not, however, address the challenge of new types of contracts being developed in the market.[112]

VII. CONCURRENT LABOUR RELATIONS AND INSOLVENCY LAW SYSTEMS

Just as with the personal property security regime, courts are called on to reconcile tensions between labour relations law, which is provincial, territorial and federal, and federal insolvency law. Generally, where the laws do not conflict, the courts are reluctant to interfere with rights and processes under employment and labour relations law. In the context of the *CCAA,* however, the question is how to reconcile the temporary stay received by the debtor with rights of employees, who are often some of the most vulnerable creditors in a restructuring proceeding.

Even observing employment and labour relations law, although staying some rights for a limited period, the practical reality is that the debtor corporation needs to have

---

[111] Proposed section 11.05(1).

[112] As this book goes to press, the Government has announced that it will introduce amendments to take the definition of eligible financial contract out of the statute and place it in a regulation, in order to give it the flexibility to amend the definition as new products become available; *Notice of Ways and Means Motion to introduce an Act to amend the Bankruptcy and Insolvency Act, the Companies' Creditors Arrangement Act, the Wage Earners Protection Act and Chapter 47 of the Statutes of Canada, 2005,* (December 8, 2006, Library of Parliament).

dealt with the claims of employees and their trade unions if it is to successfully exit the *CCAA*. While employees' wage claims are often paid during the course of the restructuring, there are instances in which debtors may have failed to meet several payrolls before filing under the *CCAA* or have met base payroll, but failed to pay vacation, overtime or similar compensation owing to employees.[113] There is also the question of the collective agreements, and here, there has been considerable litigation regarding the scope and limits of employees' continued protection.

1. Collective Agreements

The *CCAA* does not currently contain any express statutory language addressing the issue of treatment of collective agreements at the point of insolvency. This is because labour relations in Canada fall under section 92(13) as part of civil rights under the *Constitution Act, 1867*, and hence is, the legislative domain of the provincial and territorial governments, as well as the federal government in respect of employees covered under the *Canada Labour Code*.

Collective agreements and employment contracts reflect deferred compensation systems. At the point of insolvency, the debtor corporation has often already extracted its portion of the value from the collective agreement, leaving only the cost side commitment, i.e. protection of seniority rights, health and pension benefits. Hence, debtors may seek to disclaim such contracts as they have already derived the benefit of them without full payment.

There has been some question as to the most effective means of addressing collective agreements within the context of a *CCAA* proceeding. There have been a number of proceedings in which parties to collective agreements have been able to agree on a restructuring plan, and in some instances, amendments to the collective agreement. However, there have been several cases in which debtor corporations have contested the scope of the *CCAA* in terms of its impact on labour relations legislation. In some cases, debtors have sought to use insolvency as a means of inappropriately bypassing or reducing their obligations under existing labour relations legislation. There have also been situations in which the collective agreements are a barrier to a successful going forward strategy, and a mechanism is needed to address this situation, aimed at providing a balance in insolvency restructuring, having regard to the constitutional division of powers; the distinction between a temporary stay of rights or claims and a permanent one; and the integrity and efficacy of both the insolvency system and the labour relations system.

While there was some initial inconsistency in Canadian judgments regarding the effect of insolvency or bankruptcy on collective agreements, there has recently been convergence among appellate courts that insolvency and bankruptcy do not termi-

[113] In cases where a smaller debtor cannot meet payroll, it is unlikely to have enough cash to do a *CCAA* filing and will more likely access the *BIA* under either proposal or bankruptcy proceedings.

nate collective agreements for all purposes.[114] The Supreme Court of Canada in *GMAC Commercial Credit Corporation – Canada* v. *TCT Logistics Inc.*, discussed below, has now clarified that a collective agreement does not terminate on receivership or bankruptcy.[115]

The premise of labour relations legislation is that it facilitates labour peace. Collective agreements provide security for employees and certainty for debtor companies in the conduct of their business because they can plan operations around known labour costs and be assured of no strike activity or other economic sanction during the life of the collective agreement. When a collective agreement is in place, dispute over the alleged non-compliance of either party with its terms are referred to mandatory binding arbitration for final resolution. Equally, however, the system is premised on economic pressure, specifically, the provision of specified periods in which collective agreements are to be re-negotiated and a highly codified scheme for when parties to the collective bargaining relationship can resort to economic sanctions in the form of strike/lock-out or work to rule as part of the bargaining process. However, even during the period of negotiations leading up to the point where the use of economic sanctions is permitted, stability is provided through a statutory "freeze" on working conditions during the negotiations. These dynamics shift during insolvency because of the financial distress of the debtor company, the concurrent legislative scheme that facilitates restructuring, and the involvement of multiple interested stakeholders that have an interest in the debtor's financial distress and potential restructuring.[116]

With respect to the status of collective agreements on bankruptcy, the Ontario Superior Court in *Royal Crest Lifecare Group Inc.* held that a collective agreement is not terminated for all purposes in bankruptcy, and that labour relations legislation must be interpreted liberally to achieve its objectives.[117] The Court held that "the collective agreement is not terminated but rather it is put into suspended animation, to be revived if, as, and when a purchaser with a personal economic interest in the operation of the business acquires the business".[118] The Ontario Court of Appeal in *Royal Crest Lifecare Group Inc.* upheld the lower court judgment that in bankruptcy,

---

[114] *Royal Crest Lifecare Group Inc., Re* (2003), 2003 CarswellOnt 683, [2003] O.J. No. 756 (Ont. S.C.J.), affirmed (2004), 2004 CarswellOnt 190, [2004] O.J. No. 174 (Ont. C.A.), leave to appeal refused (2004), 2004 CarswellOnt 2984, [2004] S.C.C.A. No. 104 (S.C.C.). The Court held that the collective agreement is not terminated, but placed in "suspended animation", at para. 30. *Saan Stores Ltd.* v. *Nova Scotia (Labour Relations Board)* (1999), 172 D.L.R. (4th) 134 (N.S. C.A.), which held that bankruptcy does not terminate a collective agreement for all purposes.

[115] *GMAC Commercial Credit Corp. – Canada* v. *TCT Logistics Inc.*, 2006 SCC 35 (S.C.C.).

[116] For a full discussion of these issues, as well as the successor employer issues, see Janis Sarra, *Proposed Model of a Federal Insolvency Collective Bargaining Process,* Final Report to Industry Canada, March 5, 2005.

[117] *Royal Crest Lifecare Group Inc., Re* (2003), 2003 CarswellOnt 683, [2003] O.J. No. 756 (Ont. S.C.J.), affirmed (2004), 2004 CarswellOnt 190, [2004] O.J. No. 174 (Ont. C.A.), leave to appeal refused (2004), 2004 CarswellOnt 2984, [2004] S.C.C.A. No. 104 (S.C.C.) at para. 17, 23, noting with approval *Saan Stores Ltd.* v. *Nova Scotia (Labour Relations Board)* (1999), 172 D.L.R. (4th) 134 (N.S. C.A.) at 154.

[118] *Ibid.* at para. 30. The Court dismissed the application as premature.

collective agreements are not terminated, noting that the bankruptcy judge had expressly recognized the existence and importance of the collective agreements.[119]

In the context of *CCAA* proceedings, in *Mine Jeffrey inc.*, the Québec Court of Appeal held that the monitor in a *CCAA* proceeding does not have the authority to suspend provisions of the collective agreement and that it must bargain with the trade union for changes to the collective agreement.[120]

In *GMAC Commercial Credit Corp. – Canada* v. *TCT Logistics Inc.*, a bankruptcy case, the Supreme Court of Canada identified the issue as the extent to which the collective bargaining rights of employees as creditors in a bankruptcy must yield to the overall objective in a bankruptcy of maximizing the ability of creditors to minimize their losses; and in particular, whether employees should be entitled to the same access to a remedy as other stakeholders who attempt to impugn a trustee's conduct.[121] The Supreme Court held that the powers given to the bankruptcy court under section 47(2) of the *BIA* are powers to direct the interim receiver's conduct, and the bankruptcy court does not have jurisdiction to decide whether an interim receiver is a successor employer within the meaning of labour relations legislation. Powers granted to the bankruptcy court to direct an interim receiver's conduct do not explicitly or implicitly confer authority on the bankruptcy court to make unilateral declarations about the rights of third parties affected by other statutory schemes.[122] Section 72(1) of the *BIA* specifies that unless there is a conflict with the *BIA,* any legislation relating to property and civil rights is deemed to be supplemental to, and not abrogated by, the *BIA*. The effect of section 72(1) is that the *BIA* is not intended to extinguish legally protected labour relations rights that are not in conflict with the *BIA*.[123]

Trustees and receivers are entitled to a measure of deference consistent with their expertise in the effective management of a bankruptcy; however, the Supreme Court held that guarding the flexibility given to such officers with boilerplate immunizations that inoculate against the assertion of rights is beyond the therapeutic reach of the *BIA*.[124] The right to seek a successor employer declaration pursuant to provincial labour relations legislation does not conflict with the bankruptcy court's authority under section 47(2). The Court held that if the section 47 net were interpreted widely enough to permit interference with all rights that, though protected by law, represent an inconvenience to the bankruptcy process, it could be used to extinguish all rights;

---

[119] *Royal Crest Lifecare Group Inc., Re* (2003), 2003 CarswellOnt 683, [2003] O.J. No. 756 (Ont. S.C.J.), affirmed (2004), 2004 CarswellOnt 190, [2004] O.J. No. 174 (Ont. C.A.), leave to appeal refused (2004), 2004 CarswellOnt 2984, [2004] S.C.C.A. No. 104 (S.C.C.) at paras. 34, 35.

[120] *Mine Jeffrey inc., Re* (2003), 2003 CarswellQue 90, [2003] Q.J. No. 264 (Que. C.A.).

[121] *GMAC Commercial Credit Corp. - Canada* v. *T.C.T. Logistics Inc.*, 2006 SCC 35 (S.C.C.) at para. 2.

[122] *Ibid.* at para. 45.

[123] *Ibid.* at para. 47.

[124] *Ibid.* at para. 50.

explicit language would be required before such a sweeping power could be attached to section 47.[125]

Unions are not allowed to proceed before labour relations boards without the bankruptcy court's approval. In considering an application for leave to bring an application to the labour relations board, the Supreme Court held that the *Mancini* test under section 215 of the *BIA* is the appropriate test, specifically, if the evidence discloses a *prima facie* case, leave should be granted.[126] The principles in *Mancini* are: leave should not be granted if the action is frivolous, vexatious or manifestly unmeritorious; nor should leave be granted where the materials filed do not disclose a cause of action; and the court is not required to make a final assessment of the merits of the claim before granting leave.[127] The Supreme Court held that this test strikes the appropriate balance between the protection of trustees and receivers from frivolous tactical suits, while preserving, to the maximum extent possible, the rights of creditors and others as against the trustee or receiver.[128] The bankruptcy court should not convert the leave mechanism in section 215 into blanket insulation for court-appointed officers, and there is no reason to impose a higher threshold in a labour relations case, as it would read into the *BIA* a lower tolerance for the rights of employees represented by unions than for other creditors and there is nothing in the *BIA* that suggests this dichotomy. The Court held that the integrity and efficiency of the bankruptcy process are sufficiently advanced by directing bankruptcy courts to deny leave to frivolous and merely tactical suits.[129]

GMAC Commercial Credit Corp. – Canada v. *TCT Logistics Inc.* is a clear case of the court setting limits on the court's broad authority to make express orders where the object of the order is already subject to an extensive statutory regime. While not diminishing the authority of the bankruptcy court to direct the conduct of insolvency officers, the judgment does clearly indicate that courts should be careful to consider the statutory framework under federal insolvency legislation and under federal, provincial and territorial legislation. The general powers granted to the bankruptcy court to direct an interim receiver's conduct do not explicitly or implicitly confer authority on the bankruptcy court to make unilateral declarations about the rights of third parties affected by other statutory schemes. There was no gap filling role to be played by the court on the facts of *GMAC Commercial Credit Corp. – Canada* v. *TCT Logistics Inc.*

It is important to note that a successor employer declaration is a declaration of statutory responsibilities (and potential liability), not an application impugning action. Section 14.06 *BIA* immunity for insolvency professionals is already quite broad, as it should be, given the important function these officers perform. Section 14.06

---

[125] *Ibid.* at para. 51.

[126] *Ibid.* at para. 59. *Mancini (Trustee of)* v. *Falconi* (1993), (sub nom. *Mancini (Bankrupt)* v. *Falconi*) 61 O.A.C. 332 (Ont. C.A.).

[127] *GMAC Commercial Credit Corp. - Canada* v. *TCT Logistics Inc.*, 2006 SCC 35 (S.C.C.) at para. 57, citing *Mancini, ibid.* at para. 7.

[128] *Ibid.* at para. 61.

[129] *Ibid.* at para. 62.

specifies that notwithstanding anything in federal or provincial law, where the trustee carries on the business of the debtor or continues employment of the debtor's employees, the trustee is not personally liable in respect of any claim against the debtor that arose before or upon the trustee's appointment. Hence any liability can only arise from the professional's conduct after its appointment. The Supreme Court judgment clarifies that the receiver or trustee operating a business has an obligation to comply with the law for the limited period that it is vested with responsibility under insolvency proceedings.

In reconciling insolvency and labour relations law, the potential harm sought to be prevented is that potential purchasers not use the appointment of insolvency professionals to by-pass obligations that they have under labour relations legislation. Where collective agreements are in place, employers have exclusive management powers under labour relations legislation, including the unilateral right to shut down operations and terminate employment, but the scheme requires particular obligations to be met when such actions are taken. The problem in cases such as *GMAC* is that parties and their counsel may view their interests too narrowly, given their specialization in insolvency or in labour relations.

This problem was averted to by Mr. Justice Farley in *Stelco Inc.*[130] Insolvency proceedings involve an intricate complementary and sometimes discordant set of statutes that advance multiple public policy goals. The court's ability to consider the bankruptcy process as a whole is informed by the entire statutory framework, including banking legislation, provincial personal property security legislation, labour relations law and a host of other statutes.

In *CCAA* proceedings, there have been few judgments defining the relationship of insolvency and labour relations legislation, and hence parties frequently agree to a plan of arrangement where bargaining has occurred under the uncertainty of what courts would or would not require. However, it is clear from the Supreme Court of Canada judgment in *GMAC* that collective agreements continue to operate during insolvency and that courts will defer to the highly codified legislative system for labour relations where it does not conflict with the express language of the statute.

In *Stelco Inc.*, the union had argued that there were numerous production efficiencies that could be achieved without the massive wage concessions being sought, and the Court recognized this point but suggested that these discussions could be carried out under the protection of the *CCAA*. The Court appears to have recognized the problem of unions having to negotiate twice, once with the debtor and then potentially with new buyers or new creditors, as occurred in the *Air Canada* proceeding.

Prior to the release of the Supreme Court of Canada judgment in *GMAC Commercial Credit Corp. – Canada* v. *TCT Logistics Inc.*, the British Columbia Supreme Court in *Hawkair Aviation Services Ltd.* held that the broad scope of the *CCAA* stay postponed the exercise of rights of employees and the union to bring a certification

---

[130] *Stelco Inc., Re* (2004) O.J. No. 4092.

application pursuant to the Canada *Labour Code*.[131] A certification application is brought to the labour relations board and if approved, places the union in a collective bargaining relationship with a company. The Court held that the *status quo* was a non-unionized workplace and the Court declined to lift the stay to allow employees to proceed with the application on the basis that there was no evidence of injustice to the employees; the debtor company had insufficient resources to deal with the application at the time; there was no evidence that employees' rights would be lost by the passage of time; and allowing the application to proceed would impair the ability of the debtor to concentrate on devising the *CCAA* plan.[132] The findings in cases such as this are likely to change, given the reasoning of the Supreme Court of Canada regarding the standard to be applied to applications for leave.

2. Legislative Reform regarding Collective Bargaining

The treatment of collective agreements has become highly contested in the current legislative reform debate. Two factors are driving public policy debates regarding treatment of collective agreements on insolvency. Debtors and senior lenders are concerned that there is no codified process to deal with collective agreements and thus uncertainty in the insolvency proceeding where the trade union and the debtor do not agree on whether changes to the collective agreement are essential to the restructuring. Trade unions are concerned that debtors are seeking insolvency protection in order to shed collective agreements, in an attempt to bypass the existing labour relations system that has been carefully designed to balance the interests of employers and employees.[133]

The proposed amendments to the *CCAA* in Chapter 47 attempt to codify, for the first time, the relationship between collective agreements and *CCAA* proceedings. The provisions of Chapter 47 expressly state that collective agreements continue during insolvency.[134] The law clarifies that the debtor corporation cannot disclaim a collective agreement. It mandates a good faith bargaining process, having the

---

[131] *Hawkair Aviation Services Ltd., Re* (2006), 2006 CarswellBC 1007, [2006] B.C.J. No. 938 (B.C. S.C.).

[132] *Ibid.* at para. 35.

[133] See for example, submissions by the Canadian Autoworkers, the United Steelworkers and the Canadian Labour Congress to the Standing Senate Committee on Banking Trade and Commerce consideration of amendments to the *BIA* and *CCAA*, 2002. For a general discussion of labour relations issues during insolvency, see S. Wahl, "Bankruptcy and Insolvency: High Stakes Poker at the Collective Bargaining Table", in *Annual Review of Insolvency Law, 2004* (Carswell, 2005) 243-254; P. Bélanger, "Collective Agreements and Employment Contracts: What Obligations are Transmitted to the Purchaser of a Bankruptcy Business?", in *Annual Review of Insolvency Law, 2004* (Carswell, 2005) 255-282; and J. Morrison, "Labour Pains: A Review of Recent Ontario Court and Labour Board Decisions Regarding Successor Employer Liability for Receivers", *Annual Review of Insolvency Law, 2004* (Carswell, 2005) 311-330. See also L.W. Houlden, G.B. Morawetz and J.P. Sarra, *Bankruptcy and Insolvency Law of Canada,* 3rd ed. (Toronto: Carswell, 2006) N§ 16(5A) Terminating Contracts.

[134] Section 33(1), *CCAA*, as proposed by Chapter 47.

labour relations system largely govern that bargaining. Chapter 47 sets out a series of provisions in respect of collective agreements, specifically:

- Where a debtor company and the union representing its employees fail to reach a voluntary agreement to revise provisions of the collective agreement, the court has jurisdiction to grant an order authorizing the company to serve a "notice to bargain" on the bargaining agent.

- The application to the court must be made on five days notice.

- The court may issue the order only if it is satisfied that:

    - the insolvent debtor would not be able to make a viable plan of arrangement and compromise, taking into account the terms of the collective agreement;

    - the insolvent debtor has made good faith efforts to renegotiate the provisions of the collective agreement; and

    - the failure to issue the order is likely to result in irreparable damage to the insolvent person.[135]

- The vote of the creditors in respect of a plan of arrangement under the *CCAA* may not be delayed solely because the period provided in the laws of the jurisdiction governing collective bargaining between the debtor and the bargaining agent has not expired.[136]

- If the parties to the collective agreement agree to revise the collective agreement after proceedings have been commenced under the *CCAA*, the bargaining agent has a claim, as an unsecured creditor, for an amount equal to the value of concessions granted by the bargaining agent with respect to the remaining term of the collective agreement.[137]

- Once the court grants a notice to bargain, it may, subject to any terms and conditions it specifies, make an order requiring the debtor to make available to the bargaining agent any information specified by the court in the debtor's possession or control that relates to the debtor's business or financial affairs and that is relevant to the collective bargaining between the insolvent person and the bargaining agent.

The provision clarifying that the collective agreement remains in force absent any agreement to change it, is a provision that will provide greater certainty to all parties to the insolvency proceeding that the *status quo* continues during the stay period. This will prove an important starting point in the workout process and will clarify

---

[135] Section 33(3), Chapter 47. There are mirror provisions in the *BIA*.

[136] Section 33(4), Chapter 47.

[137] Sections 65.12(4), 33(5), Chapter 47.

for parties not familiar with the labour relations system in Canada that there is a continued public policy commitment to this system, as well as that of the *CCAA*. When proclaimed in force, Chapter 47 will avoid unnecessary litigation on the status of the collective agreement during insolvency and bankruptcy and will assist parties in deciding their positions on the restructuring process.

For the purpose of this section of Chapter 47, the parties to a collective agreement are the insolvent debtor and the bargaining agent who are bound by the collective agreement. This provision is helpful in clarifying that third parties cannot interfere directly with the collective agreement negotiations during a *CCAA* proceeding.[138]

While the "notice to bargain" provisions proposed for the *CCAA* constitute a positive first step in encouraging the parties to come to a negotiated compromise regarding provisions of the collective agreement, the provisions may be insufficient in that they fail to provide a timely process to arrive at a final solution to the collective bargaining issues, issues that are often critical to the successful outcome of the restructuring proceeding. There is no mechanism proposed in Chapter 47 or elsewhere that grants the court or an arbitrator the authority to bind the parties where there is no agreement. It will likely take some time, once Chapter 47 is proclaimed, for parties to fully appreciate that even with these limitations in the law, it is in their collective interest to bargain for a timely and positive outcome, given the time pressures created by the firm's financial distress and the risk of liquidation and permanent loss of jobs.

VIII. PROTECTION OF WAGES ON INSOLVENCY

Currently in Canada, on bankruptcy, employees have a preferred claim, ranking fourth in priority after secured creditors and specified administrative and other charges.[139] Section 136(1)(d) of the *BIA*, subject to the rights of secured creditors, gives employees a preferred claim in a bankruptcy of up to $2,000 for unpaid wages, salaries and like entitlements earned during the six months immediately preceding the bankruptcy and, in the case of a traveling salesperson, an additional $1,000 for expenses incurred during the preceding six months. Vacation pay is considered to be wages or a preferred claim to the extent that it accrues during the six months preceding the bankruptcy. Compensation owing that is greater than the statutory preferred claim is an unsecured claim. Severance and termination claims are treated as ordinary unsecured claims.[140]

---

[138] Although realistically, senior lenders or the DIP lender have a strong influence on the position taken by the debtor in such negotiations.

[139] Section 136(1), *BIA*, ranking after reasonable funeral and testamentary expenses, the costs of administration, and the Office of the Superintendent of Bankruptcy levy.

[140] See *Crabtree (Succession de)* c. *Barrette* (1993), 1993 CarswellQue 25 (S.C.C.); *Nolisair International Inc., Re* (1999), 1999 CarswellQue 1716 (Que. C.A.); *Rizzo & Rizzo Shoes Ltd., Re* (1998), 1998 CarswellOnt 1 (S.C.C.). The exclusion of severance or termination pay from the preferred claim portion of an employee may not necessarily be excluded in every instance; see the comments by Madam Justice Otis in *Nolisair*, dealing with the *BIA* and the Canada *Labour Code*, L.R.Q. 1985, c.

One study of 94 business bankruptcies in 1991 found that employees overall received an average of 7% of their total unsecured wage claims and only 31% of their fourth ranking preferred wage claims.[141] Hence, employees with unpaid wages have been left with little recovery in many Canadian bankruptcies.

There are carve-outs from the preferred claim status for related persons who were employees.[142] Wage claims of present or former spouses or common law partners are postponed until all claims of other creditors are satisfied.[143] Wage claims of other relatives and officers and directors are unsecured, as opposed to preferred claims.[144] There is currently no national wage earner protection fund, although, as discussed below, Chapter 47 will create such a program if it is proclaimed in force.

Employees who are owed wages at the time of bankruptcy must pursue collection of those wages on their own; and although provincial employment standards legislation facilitates the collection process, employees must discern their rights and file a complaint with the appropriate officials.[145] There is no obligation on the employer or the insolvency officer to advise employees of their rights.

The *CCAA* does not expressly address the treatment of wages, other than the references to the *BIA,* discussed earlier. However, parties bargain under the *CCAA* with the knowledge that the bankruptcy priorities will become effective if the *CCAA* process fails. While employees' wage claims are usually met if the debtor corporation continues to operate, it is the broader definition of compensation, including severance and termination pay, that is not generally covered in full under a *CCAA* plan. Employees do, however, benefit from *CCAA* plans where they can continue to work and are not receiving merely the liquidation value of their claims.

L-2. The requirement for a claim to receive a priority ranking under section 136(1)(d) of the *BIA* is that the claim must be for wages, salaries or remuneration relating to services rendered prior to the bankruptcy. It is conceivable that a collective agreement could provide for a form of compensation that accrues on a day by day basis, earned continuously by the employee, but only becomes payable on termination of employment, in a manner and amount similar to severance or termination. In this circumstance, it is still an open question as to whether this type of compensation could benefit from the preference referred to in section 136(1)(d) of the *BIA*.

[141] K. Davis and J. Ziegel, "Assessing the Economic Impacts of a New Priority Scheme for Unpaid Wage Earners and Suppliers of Goods and Services" (1998), http://strategis.ic.gc.ca/SSG/c100150e.html#BIA-consult at Appendix B, Table 3.

[142] Related persons is a defined term.

[143] Section 137(2), *BIA*.

[144] Sections 138, 140, *BIA*.

[145] Ronald B. Davis, "After the Fall: Trustees, Receivers and Employees of Insolvent Businesses under Bill C-55", in Janis Sarra, ed., *Annual Review of Insolvency Law, 2005* (Toronto: Carswell, 2006) at 258.

1. Proposed Creation of a National Wage Earner Protection Program

Chapter 47 will create both a national wage earner protection scheme and new priorities for employee claims, and will impose positive obligations to advise workers of their rights. It extends similar treatment to workers in respect of their unpaid wage and pension contribution claims, whether the debtor is under receivership or in bankruptcy proceedings.

Chapter 47, if proclaimed, will create for the first time, a program for making payments to individuals in respect of wages owed to them by employers who are bankrupt or subject to a receivership. The *Wage Earner Protection Program Act* ("*WEPP*") provides for payments to individuals who have been terminated and who have unpaid wages as at the date of bankruptcy or receivership, with certain restrictions on quantum and eligibility. Currently, in many commercial insolvencies where employees are terminated on bankruptcy or receivership, there are unpaid wages, leaving worker's vulnerable in the short term in their ability to meet their living expenses. The *WEPP* is aimed at relieving some of this hardship.

The features of the proposed *WEPP* are:

- The maximum amount that may be paid to an eligible individual in respect of a bankruptcy or receivership is the greater of $3,000 and an amount equal to four times the maximum weekly insurable earnings under the *Employment Insurance Act*, less any deductions applicable under a federal or provincial law.[146]

- Payments will be made out of the federal government Consolidated Revenue Fund.[147]

- Wages expressly include vacation pay and exclude severance or termination pay.[148]

- Wages must be earned during the six months immediately preceding the date of bankruptcy or the first day on which there was a receiver appointed.[149]

- The onus is on individual employees to apply for the wage payments to the Minister.

---

[146] Section 7(2) of the *Wage Earner Protection Program Act* ("*WEPP*"), as introduced by Chapter 47.

[147] Section 35, *WEPP*, as introduced by Chapter 47.

[148] Section 2(1), *WEPP*, as introduced by Chapter 47 specifies: 2(1) In this Act, "wages" includes salaries, commissions, compensation for services rendered, vacation pay and any other amounts prescribed by regulation but does not include severance or termination pay.

[149] Section 7(1), *WEPP*, as introduced by Chapter 47.

- Employees who were a director or officer of the employer or who had a controlling interest in the employer's business or who occupied a managerial position are not entitled to receive a *WEPP* payment.[150]

The Crown is subrogated to any rights of an individual for amounts paid under *WEPP* against the bankrupt or insolvent employer and the directors.[151] *WEPP* payments cannot be assigned or pledged as security.[152]

To receive a payment, an individual must apply to the Minister in the form and manner, and within the period, provided for in the regulations.[153] If the Minister determines that the applicant is eligible for a payment, the Minister must approve the making of the payment.[154] An individual can request a review of any determination, and the Minister can review and confirm, vary or rescind the determination.[155] The decision is final except for appeal to an adjudicator only on a question of law or a question of jurisdiction.[156]

The duties of the trustees and receivers under the proposed *WEPP* are much more proactive in respect of employees and are aimed at informing workers of both their right to apply under the *WEPP* and the amount that is owing to them. Trustees and receivers are to:

- identify each individual who is owed wages by a bankrupt or insolvent employer that were earned during the period of six months immediately before the date of the bankruptcy or the first day on which there was a receiver in relation to the employer;

- determine the amount of wages owing to each individual in respect of that six-month period;

- advise the former employees, who have unpaid wages, of the existence of the *WEPP* and conditions under which payments may be made;

- provide the Minister and each individual, in accordance with the regulations, with information in relation to the individual and the amount of wages owing to the individual in respect of the six-month period;

- inform the Minister when discharged if a trustee, or duties completed if a receiver.[157]

---

[150] Section 6(2), *WEPP*, as introduced by Chapter 47.
[151] Section 36, *WEPP*, as introduced by Chapter 47.
[152] Section 37, *WEPP*, as introduced by Chapter 47.
[153] Section 8, *WEPP*, as introduced by Chapter 47.
[154] Section 9, *WEPP*, as introduced by Chapter 47.
[155] Sections 11, 12, *WEPP*, as introduced by Chapter 47.
[156] Sections 13-16, *WEPP*, as introduced by Chapter 47.
[157] Sections 21-22, *WEPP*, as introduced by Chapter 47.

Currently, in operating situations, the receiver or trustee pays wages in the normal course. However, this occurs where companies continue to operate through a restructuring or sale process. *WEPP* provides for only one process to be followed if there are unpaid wages on the date of bankruptcy or receivership; there is no provision for a second option whereby the receiver or trustee would pay the wages owing at the date of receivership/bankruptcy. *WEPP* should provide for an option whereby unpaid wages can be paid by a receiver or trustee, in order to expedite money being placed in the hands of employees and to deal with tax forms and employee deduction issues.[158]

There are extensive anti-abuse measures included in *WEPP* for various offences, including sanctions for failure by a trustee and receiver to comply with their statutory responsibilities.

Section 38 the *WEPP* specifies that every person commits an offence who:

- makes a false or deceptive entry, or omits to enter a material particular, in any record or book of account that contains information that supports an application under the *Act*;

- in relation to an application under this *Act*, makes a representation that the person knows to be false or misleading;

- in relation to an application under this *Act*, makes a declaration that the person knows is false or misleading because of the non-disclosure of facts;

- being required under this *Act* to provide information, provides information or makes a representation that the person knows to be false or misleading;

- obtains a payment under this *Act* by false pretence;

- being the payee of any cheque issued as a payment under this *Act*, knowingly negotiates or attempts to negotiate it knowing that the person is not entitled to the payment or any part of the payment; or

- participates in, assents to or acquiesces in any of the above acts or omissions.

A prosecution for an offence may be commenced at any time within six years after the time when the subject-matter of the prosecution arose. It is also an offence to delay or obstruct a person in the exercise of his or her powers or the performance of his or her duties under the *WEPP*.[159] Persons guilty of an offence are liable on

---

[158] This is a recommendation of the Canadian Association of Insolvency and Restructuring Professionals and The Insolvency Institute of Canada in their joint Legislative Review Task Force Report, 2005.

[159] Section 39, *WEPP*, as introduced by Chapter 47. The Government has announced that it will add a due diligence defence when it proposes amendments to the WEPP in 2007; *Notice of Ways and Means Motion to introduce an Act to amend the Bankruptcy and Insolvency Act, the Companies' Creditors*

summary conviction to a fine of not more than $5,000 or to imprisonment for a term of not more than six months, or to both.[160]

2. Wage Priorities

There are a number of proposed new priorities under Chapter 47. The statute will add section 81.3 to the *BIA*, which will give unpaid employees security over all current assets of the bankrupt:

- The *BIA* will provide for a super-priority for wages in a bankruptcy to the extent of $2,000 and for expenses of a traveling salesperson to the extent of $1,000.[161]

- The priority is on all current assets of the bankrupt.

- This priority ranks above every other claim, right, charge or security against the debtor's current assets, regardless of when the claim or right arose, except for the priority for the 30 day goods rights of unpaid suppliers; priority rights granted to farmers, fishers and aquaculturists; and source deductions.[162]

- Section 81.4 provides for similar wage priority provisions as section 81.3 but in a receivership.

- If a trustee or receiver disposes of current assets covered by a secured claim, the trustee or receiver is liable for the claim to the extent of the amount realized on the disposition and is subrogated in and to all rights of the employee in respect of the amounts paid to that person by the trustee or receiver.[163]

- A court is not to sanction a plan of arrangement under the *CCAA* or a proposal under the *BIA* unless the plan provides for payment to the employees and former employees of the amount secured under these provisions.

- Section 136(1)(d) gives preferred status to the amount of wages, salaries, commissions, compensation or disbursements referred to in the super-priority provisions that was not paid.

The effect of the new priority is to give employees, but in reality, the federal government who acquires the rights of subrogation under the *WEPP*, a claim that

---

Arrangement Act, the Wage Earners Protection Act and Chapter 47 of the Statutes of Canada, 2005, (December 8, 2006, Library of Parliament).

160 Section 40, *WEPP*, as introduced by Chapter 47.

161 Section 81.3, *BIA*, as modified by Chapter 47.

162 Section 81.1-81.3, *BIA*, as modified by Chapter 47.

163 Sections 81.3(5), 81.4(5), *BIA*, as modified by Chapter 47.

must be satisfied ahead of secured creditors' claims. The wage provisions are also aimed at preventing a moral hazard for insolvent businesses and their secured creditors that would arise if the only legislative change was the introduction of the *WEPP*.[164] The proposed priority discourages debtor corporations from skipping payments to employees so that increased assets are available for payment of secured creditors' claims.

Most significant for purposes of a *CCAA* proceeding is that a court is not to sanction a plan of arrangement under the *CCAA* or a proposal under the *BIA*, unless the plan provides for the payment to the employees and former employees of the amount secured under these provisions.

IX. PENSION CLAIMS

Pension claims in *CCAA* proceedings are based on the requirements of pension legislation and the contract of employment between the debtor corporation and its employees. One source of claims that may arise is the (now increasingly rare) circumstance in which there is a surplus in the plan. Another source of claims is the debtor corporation's failure to make contributions as and when required by pension legislation.

1. Ownership of Pension Surplus Amounts

Pension plan surpluses arise when the value of the plan's assets exceeds the projected cost of its benefits. The calculation of the projected cost is made by an actuary. When a plan is ongoing, the surplus is only notional, since both asset values and projected costs can change with changes in the variables affecting them. It is only when a pension plan is terminated and assets are sold in order to pay all benefits earned in the plan that the actual amount of any surplus can be determined.[165]

Ownership of a surplus in a pension plan is an issue in *CCAA* proceedings because if the debtor corporation is able to claim ownership of all or a portion of the surplus in the plan, it could serve as a source of funding for a restructuring plan.

Surplus ownership turns on the original terms of the funding arrangements for the pension plan, and in particular, whether or not the contributions and investment income are held in a trust. Unless the debtor corporation has reserved an express power to revoke that trust in the document creating the trust, ownership of any surplus in the plan following its termination will vest in the plan members.[166] Other

---

[164] Ronald B. Davis, "Doomed to Repeat History? Retiree Benefits and the Reform of Canada's Insolvency Laws", in *Annual Review of Insolvency Law, 2004* (Toronto: Carswell, 2005) 199-242.

[165] *Schmidt* v. *Air Products of Canada Ltd.*, [1994] 2 S.C.R. 611 (S.C.C.) at para. 87 - 89.

[166] *Ibid.* at para. 58.

forms of funding arrangements may be more amenable to post-creation amendments granting the debtor corporation ownership of any surplus.[167]

Some pension legislation provides alternatives to litigating the issue of surplus ownership in the courts by allowing payment of surplus to debtor corporations through a surplus sharing agreement ratified by a prescribed percentage of pension plan members.[168] In some jurisdictions, there is also a mechanism for binding arbitration concerning pension surplus disputes.[169]

2. Failure to Remit Contributions

Where there is no surplus in a pension plan, then issues may arise concerning the failure to make contributions when required and the resolution of any deficiencies in the plan's funding. Ronald Davis sets out the provisions by which the regulatory regime for pension plan benefits under the Ontario *Pension Benefits Act (PBA)* tries to reduce the impact of insolvency on pension plan members:[170]

> In order to be eligible for registration, the pension plan must also "provide for funding sufficient to provide the pension benefits, ancillary benefits and other benefits under the pension plan in accordance with this Act and the regulations" and obligates the employer to make contributions in the manner and at the time prescribed to a pension fund or insurance company, as the case may be.[171] Thus, the sufficiency of the funding arrangements for the benefits is subject to a merit test by the regulator at the time of registration. The *PBA* Regulation adds more specificity to the employer's contribution obligation by requiring the pension plan document set out the employer's contribution to the annual "normal cost" of the plan's benefits as well as any unfunded liabilities of the plan, with the normal cost being determined by an actuarial calculation.[172]
>
> After a plan is registered, it must have actuarial reports concerning its funded status prepared and submitted to the regulator at least every three years or when changes are made that change the contributions required and/or the plan's liabilities.[173] If these reports disclose that additional liabilities have been created or existing liabilities have been increased, then the employer must make additional special contributions calculated by an actuary as sufficient to pay-off these liabilities over a five to fifteen year time frame.[174] These provisions provide a stream of contributions into the pension fund or insurance company that are required to be sufficient to fund the benefits provided. However, the accumulation of sufficient assets will not benefit the

[167] *Ibid.* at para. 48.

[168] *PBA* Reg., R.R.O. 1990, Reg. 909, (Ontario) s. 8.

[169] *Pension Benefits Standards Act* (British Columbia), R.S.B.C. 1996, c. 352, s. 62.

[170] Ronald B. Davis, "Restructuring Proceedings and Pension Fund Deficits: A Question of Risk and Reward", in J. Sarra, ed. *Annual Review of Insolvency Law* – 2003, (Toronto: Carswell, 2004) 29 – 65.

[171] *Ibid.* citing *Pension Benefits Act*, R.S.O., 1990, c. P.8, as amended (Ontario) (*PBA*), ss. 55(1) & (2).

[172] *Ibid.* citing *PBA* Reg., R.R.O. 1990, Reg. 909, ss. 4(1) & 13 [hereinafter Reg.].

[173] *Ibid.* citing Reg. (Ont.), ss. 14(1) & 3(1).

[174] *Ibid.* citing Reg. (Ont.), s. 5(1).

> employees in the case of insolvency unless they are not available to the employer to use to prop up the company if it enters financial difficulties nor available to other creditors as part of the employer's estate.
>
> The rules relating to pension plans registered with federal income tax regulators provide this aspect of protection from insolvency risk by requiring that pension benefits be funded by one of an insurance contract to provide annuities to eligible employees; a trust fund in the hands of a trust company or board of trustees of a duly constituted trust; a separate pension corporation, or an arrangement administered by the federal or provincial governments.[175] The *PBA* also makes provision for a separation from the employer by limiting those who can be administrators of the pension fund to a government, an insurance company, a trust whose trustees are a trust company, board of trustees, or a corporate pension society, and a body assigned the role by legislation (in distinction from those who can administer the "plan").[176] This requirement protects the contributions that have been remitted to the pension fund from insolvency risk by removing them from an insolvent employer's estate and from the ability of the employer to gain access to the funds for support during financial difficulties. The *PBA* also imposes a duty on the fund administrator not to allow the fund administrator's interests to conflict with their duties towards the fund's beneficiaries.[177]
>
> The only remaining solvency risk with respect to pre-funding is that the contributions due but not yet remitted, and/or the balance of any special payments required to liquidate unfunded liabilities will not be remitted prior to the employer's insolvency and the resulting shortfall will lead to a reduction in the plan's benefits. However, the *PBA* attempts to reduce the risk by deeming the amounts due but not yet remitted as trust funds in the hand of the employer, and by subjecting employers (and in the case of corporations, the responsible officers and directors) to personal liability for the contributions due. These provisions do not eliminate the risk because the deemed trust can always be attacked as ineffective against the scheme of distribution under paramount federal insolvency legislation or the relevant individuals may also be insolvent. However, they do generate somewhat compelling incentives for the responsible officials to ensure timely payment of the contributions.

Thus when the debtor corporation becomes insolvent, there are two possible sources of claims arising from its pension plan. First, it may not be current in the remittance of contributions required to pay both the normal cost of the benefits accruing in the plan and the special payments required to extinguish unfunded liabilities. Second, the outstanding balance of any unfunded liabilities may become due immediately, if the plan is terminated. Even if the plan is not terminated, if there is a sizeable unfunded liability, the payments required to extinguish it over the prescribed period may be a hurdle for any successful restructuring.

---

[175] *Ibid.* citing Canada Customs and Revenue Agency, 'Information Circular 72-13R8 - Employees' Pension Plans' (1988) (accessed 8 November 2003) <Forms and Publications, Canada Customs and Revenue Agency>, s. 6(e).

[176] *Ibid.* citing *PBA*, s. 22(6) & Reg. (Ont.), s. 54.

[177] *Ibid.* citing *PBA*, s. 22(4).

Negotiations for a plan are necessarily informed by the alternatives for recovery of various creditors outside of the *CCAA*, such as in a bankruptcy. Pension legislation tries to enhance this recovery for pension contributions by deeming that any unremitted contributions are held in trust by the debtor corporation. In addition, the Ontario *PBA* gives the pension fund administrator a statutory lien and charge over the unremitted contributions.[178] Courts have given effect to such claims against insolvent debtor corporations outside of bankruptcy proceedings.[179]

However, once a bankruptcy proceeding has been commenced, the scheme of distribution under the *BIA* cannot be changed by provincial legislation. Courts have held that provincial legislation creating deemed trusts over certain funds is ineffective in creating a trust over those funds for the purposes of the *BIA* unless the funds are also the subject of a trust at common law.[180] In circumstances such as pension contributions, courts often rely on the failure to hold the specific funds separate from other assets of the debtor corporation as having destroyed the certainty of subject matter necessary for a valid common law trust.

In *Ivaco Inc.*, the Ontario Superior Court considered a motion by the Superintendent of Financial Services (Ontario) for an order directing the monitor to distribute part of the proceeds of sale of the debtor, Ivaco's, businesses to four non-union pension plans to protect the pension beneficiaries.[181] The debtor had suspended making special payments to liquidate funding deficiencies into the pension plans, claiming that it would not have sufficient funds to continue operations until a sale of the debtor's businesses was completed. In the sale of the businesses, the purchaser assumed the unionized worker pension plans. The deficit in the non-union plans was estimated to be $23 million. Part of this deficiency was to be covered by the Ontario Pension Benefits Guarantee Fund. The Court dismissed the motion, finding that the Superintendent had overstated its claims that the pensioners were the only creditors to provide a source of financing. There were other creditors who contributed to the financial stability of the debtor's companies. Although there was a deemed trust in favour of the pension beneficiaries prior to bankruptcy, the priorities changed in a bankruptcy situation. There was no evidence that a trust was created for the purposes of a bankruptcy situation. None of the required funds was segregated or earmarked for the pension beneficiaries. Furthermore, the Superintendent did not make such a

---

[178] *PBA*, s. 57(5).

[179] *Toronto Dominion Bank* v. *Usarco Ltd.* (1991), 42 E.T.R. 235 (Ont. Gen. Div.) where the failure of an applicant to pursue a bankruptcy petition meant that pension administrator's claim for contributions due was to be determined under non-bankruptcy law, statutory deemed trust and lien and charge was effective; contributions to be paid from assets of debtor in priority to all other claimants.

[180] *I.B.L. Industries Ltd., Re* (1991), 2 O.R. (3d) 140 (Ont. Bktcy.); see also, *Edmonton Pipe Industry Pension Plan Trust Fund (Trustees of)* v. *350914 Alberta Ltd.* (2000), 2000 CarswellAlta 484, [2000] A.J. No. 583 (Alta. C.A.), leave to appeal refused (2001), 2001 CarswellAlta 57, [2000] S.C.C.A. No. 408 (S.C.C.) in which the Court held that it was not necessary that the funds be held separate from the employer's general bank account in order to find a common law trust, if the amounts were identifiable through calculations.

[181] *Ivaco Inc., Re* (2005), 2005 CarswellOnt 3445, [2005] O.J. No. 3337 (Ont. S.C.J. [Commercial List]), affirmed (2006), 2006 CarswellOnt 6292 (Ont. C.A.). See also *General Chemical Canada Ltd., Re* (2006), 2006 CarswellOnt 4675, 22 C.B.R. (5th) 298 (Ont. S.C.J. [Commercial List]), Mesbur, J.

request as a condition of the sale of the businesses. An administrative lien would also be ineffective in a bankruptcy. The Superintendent was unable to demonstrate why the court should refuse to order a bankruptcy. Furthermore, it was unable to demonstrate why the bankruptcy should not proceed in the ordinary course. The Court held that:

> The Ivaco Companies are still involved in the CCAA proceedings. It cannot be reasonably disputed that it is not reasonably possible for the Ivaco Companies to be restructured. In pith and substance what has happened is that there has been a liquidating *CCAA* proceeding.
>
> ¶ 10 The National Bank, the Bank of Nova Scotia, the Informal Committee of Noteholders, and a very major trade creditor, QIT - Fer et Titane Inc., wish to have the proceedings transformed into BIA proceedings. It would not appear to me that there has been any conduct alleged to have been taken by any of these BIA desirous parties which would be considered "inequitable" in the sense of *Bulut* v. *Brampton (City)* (2000), 48 O.R. (3d) 108 (C.A.); *Re Christian Brothers of Ireland* (2004), 69 O.R. (3d) 507 (S.C.J.). See also *Unisource Canada Inc. (cob Barber-Ellis Fine Papers)* v. *Hong Kong Bank of Canada* (1998), 43 B.L.R. (2d) 226 (Ont. Gen. Div.), affirmed [2000] O.J. No. 947, 15 P.P.S.A.C. (2d) 95 (Ont. C.A.); AEVO Co. v. D & A Macleod Co. (1991), 4 O.R. (3d) 368 (Gen. Div.).
>
> ¶ 11 While in a non-bankruptcy situation, the Ivaco Companies' assets are subject to a deemed trust on account of unpaid contributions and wind up liabilities in favour of the pension beneficiaries by s. 57(3) of the *Pension Benefits Act* (Ontario), in a bankruptcy situation, the priority of such a statutory deemed trust ceases unless there is in fact a "true trust" in which the three certainties of trust law are found to exist, namely (i) certainty of intent; (ii) certainty of subject matter; and (iii) certainty of object. For these three certainties to be met, the trust funds must be segregated from the debtor's general funds. See *British Columbia* v. *Henfrey Samson Belair Ltd.*, [1989] 2 S.C.R. 24, 59 D.L.R. (4th) 726 (S.C.C.); *British Columbia* v. *National Bank* (1994), 119 D.L.R. (4th) 669 (B.C.C.A.); *Bassano Growers Ltd.* v. *Price Waterhouse Inc.* (1998), 6 C.B.R. (4th) 199 (Alta. C.A.); *Re IBL Industries Ltd.* (1991), 2 O.R. (3d) 140 (Gen. Div.); *Continental Casualty Co.* v. *Macleod-Stedman Inc.* (1996), 141 D.L.R. (4th), 36 (Man. C.A.). There is no evidence that any of the "required" funds have been segregated or earmarked for the pension beneficiaries; nor did the Superintendent make such a request as a condition of the Heico deal being closed. Since there has been no such segregation, the deemed statutory trusts would not be effective as trusts upon the happening of a bankruptcy: see Henfrey at p. 141.
>
> ¶ 12 An administrator's lien pursuant to s. 57(5) of the *Pension Benefits Act* (Ontario) would also be ineffective in a bankruptcy. Section 2(1) of the *BIA* provides that a "secured creditor" includes a person who holds a lien (i.e. a "true lien") on a debt which is actually owing. Even though provincial legislation may deem something to be a lien, that deeming does not make it a s. 2(1) BIA "lien": see *New Brunswick* v. *Peat Marwick Thorne Inc.* (1995), 37 C.B.R. (3d) 268 (N.B.C.A.). While provincial legislation may validly affect priorities in a non-bankruptcy situation, once bankruptcy has occurred s. 136(1) of the *BIA* determines the status and priority of claims: see *Deloitte, Haskins & Sells Ltd.* v. *Alberta (Workers' Compensation Board)*, [1985] 1 S.C.R. 785, 19 D.L.R. (4th) 577 (S.C.C.); *Husky Oil Oper-*

ations Ltd. v. *Minister of National Revenue,* [1995] 3 S.C.R. 453, 128 D.L.R. (4th) 1 (S.C.C.).

In upholding the lower court judgment in *Ivaco Inc.,* the Ontario Court of Appeal held that the *CCAA* does not impose a legal obligation on a debtor company to pay unpaid contributions to a pension plan while it is under the protection of the *CCAA,* and that there is not a gap between the *CCAA* and *BIA* in which a deemed trust under sections 57(3) and 57(4) of the *Pension Benefits Act* (Ontario) for unpaid pension contributions and wind-up liabilities can be executed.[182]

Pension plan administrators could also try to include a claim for unremitted pension contributions in the fourth ranking preference claim for unpaid employee compensation under the *BIA*. However, a decision of the Ontario Court of Appeal expressed doubt that pension contributions could be included in the fourth ranking preference claim for employee compensation because of difficulties in making a connection between the amount of pension contribution with any particular employee's service rendered over the six months prior to bankruptcy.[183] Thus, claims for unremitted pension contributions are ordinary unsecured claims in bankruptcy.

In terms of continuing contributions during a *CCAA* proceeding, in one cross-border proceeding, the Court held that there was no evidence that the debtor did not have sufficient funds to make the Canadian pension funding payments or that its DIP arrangements were such that it could not make such payments or that an application was made to the DIP lenders for consent to make such payments.[184] Hence the Court ordered the debtor to continue to make contributions to its funded pension plans, and pay all outstanding arrears.

As for the unpaid balance of a funding deficiency, the pension legislation does not require immediate repayment unless the pension plan is terminated by the debtor corporation or by the pension regulator. Instead it provides for regular payments over a period of five years in amounts necessary to eliminate the deficiency over that period. However, even these payments can result in a significant claim on the debtor corporation's cash flow. In *Air Canada*, the *CCAA* monitor reported that the estimated shortfall in funding of the Air Canada pension plans was $1.8 billion dollars if the pension plan was terminated immediately.[185] According to the monitor's report, the annual contributions required to extinguish the funding shortfall over the

---

[182] *Ivaco Inc., Re*, 2006 CarswellOnt 6292 (Ont. C.A.).

[183] *Abraham* v. *Canadian Admiral Corp. (Receiver of)* (1993), 13 O.R. (3d) 649 (Ont. Gen. Div.), reversed (1998), 39 O.R. (3d) 176 (Ont. C.A.), leave to appeal refused (1998), 120 O.A.C. 196 (note) (S.C.C.). For a discussion, see Ronald B. Davis, "Doomed to Repeat History? Retiree Benefits and the Reform of Canada's Insolvency Laws", in *Annual Review of Insolvency Law, 2004* (Carswell, 2005) at 262-4.

[184] *United Air Lines Inc., Re* (2005), 2005 CarswellOnt 1078, 9 C.B.R. (5th) 159 (Ont. S.C.J. [Commercial List]).

[185] Eighth Report of Monitor, July 31, 2003, *Air Canada, Re*, No. 03-CL-4932 ((Ont. S.C.J. (Commercial List)) 2003), paragraphs 15 & 16, this was an increase of approximately $500 million over a previous estimate, an increase that was attributed to the decline in long-term interest rates by Air Canada's actuaries.

statutorily dictated maximum period of five years were estimated to be $539 million. In *Stelco*, the parties eventually agreed to a structured funding regime in which Stelco was obligated to make regularly scheduled payments. Stelco also had to make additional payments to the pension plans once its free cash-flow exceeded a certain fixed amount.[186]

As part of its *CCAA* restructuring in 2001, Algoma Steel's plan of arrangement contained replacement pension compromises whereby Algoma's pension plan liabilities were restructured, reducing the projected pension cash costs by $124 million. Each of the existing pension plans was divided into two separate plans, an "Active Plan" and a "Retiree Plan", with the Ontario Superintendent of Financial Services responsible for the administration of the plans until they were to be wound-up; with structured payments from the pension fund, the debtor corporation and provincial government loans.[187] Current pension benefit levels were protected, but future inflation increases were removed as part of the workout agreement. In *Algoma Steel,* the pension losses would have been devastating to a very vulnerable set of stakeholders and the workout provided a better outcome than liquidation.[188]

All of these examples illustrate that a solution to a funding deficiency in a pension plan may prove to be a crucial element in a restructuring in a *CCAA* proceeding. The cooperation of both pension plan members and the pension regulator will be vital to achieving success.

3. Legislative Reform

While the issue of pension deficits and failure of debtor corporations to remit pension contributions in a timely fashion is an issue that should be addressed (and enforced) much earlier in the firm's financial life cycle, Chapter 47 is aimed at addressing an acute aspect of the failure to remit contributions.

Under Chapter 47, employee contributions that were collected but not remitted to the pension fund; the employer contribution for the normal cost of a pension plan; or the sums due but not paid under a defined contribution plan will be a secured claim over all the assets of the insolvent debtor or bankrupt.[189] Normal cost is the cost of benefits excluding special payments that are to accrue during a plan year as determined on the basis of a going concern valuation. Hence normal cost liabilities exclude special payment obligations that are generally required to be made by an

---

[186] McCarthy Tétrault LLP, CCAA Restructuring Proceedings, Stelco Inc: "Pension Agreement dated March 31, 2006 between Stelco Inc. and Superintendent of Financial Services, *et al*" in CCAA Plan Documents - Pension Agreement at http://www.mccarthy.ca/en/ccaa/ccaa_detailed.asp?company_id=1 (last visited August 29, 2006).

[187] For a discussion, see Janis P. Sarra, *Creditor Rights and the Public Interest, Restructuring Insolvent Corporations* (Toronto: University of Toronto Press, 2003).

[188] The Court ordered independent legal advice, paid for as a priority administration charge, in order to provide pensioners with advice prior to voting on the plan.

[189] Section 81.5, *BIA*, as modified by Chapter 47.

employer-sponsor of a defined benefit plan to fund, over a period of time, unfunded plan liabilities or solvency deficiencies.[190] Hence, the super-priority does not extend to any unfunded solvency deficiency in a defined benefit pension plan.

Chapter 47 creates a security interest, ranking above every other claim, right, charge or security, regardless of when that charge arose on all the person's assets in both bankruptcy and receivership situations.[191] This pension contribution security will have a lower priority than the payment of unpaid wage claims, and rank below the deemed trust for employee source deductions; however, the class of assets over which the security is granted is broader than that enjoyed by the wage claims discussed above, and pension contributions will still have to be paid prior to any payment being made to secured creditors.

Some have argued that such statutory super-priorities will have the effect of potentially reducing available credit to companies from operating lenders, particularly for mature debtor companies with significant defined benefit plans, and will add further uncertainty generally for operating and term lenders in valuing their collateral; and have suggested that any super-priority for pension obligations should be against current assets of the business only.[192] However, others have suggested that the priority will create the appropriate incentive effects in terms of ensuring that debtors remit contributions in a timely fashion prior to the insolvency, as their creditors will be seeking such assurances in their continued advancement of credit.

Also under Chapter 47, no plan of arrangement and compromise under the *CCAA* is to be approved by the court unless it provides for payment of outstanding pension plan contributions.[193] Currently, proposals under the *BIA* must provide for payment of employee preferred claims, but there are no such provisions for pension contributions. The *CCAA* is currently silent on this issue. Chapter 47 will require parties to take into account wage and pension secured claims in devising a plan of arrangement and compromise under the *CCAA*, or they will not receive the sanction of the court for the workout plan.

Under the new legislation, the court may approve a proposal or plan that does not allow for the payment of the amount if it is satisfied that the relevant parties have entered into an agreement, approved by the relevant pension regulator, respecting the payment of those amounts.[194]

---

[190] The amount of pension plan contributions secured should be an amount equal to the sum of all amounts that were deducted from the employees, plus accrued "normal cost" as defined in subsection 2(1) in the *Pension Benefits Standards Regulations, 1985*.

[191] Sections 81.5(2) and 81.6(2), *BIA*, as modified by Chapter 47.

[192] The Canadian Association of Insolvency and Restructuring Professionals and The Insolvency Institute of Canada in their joint Legislative Review Task Force Report, 2005.

[193] Sections 6(5), *CCAA* and 60(1.5), *BIA*, as amended by Chapter 47.

[194] Sections 60(1.6), *BIA* , 6(6), *CCAA*, as amended by Chapter 47.

X. CROWN CLAIMS AND DEEMED TRUSTS

1. Stay of Crown Claims

Section 21 of the *CCAA* provides that "this Act is binding on Her Majesty in right of Canada or a province". Consequently, a stay of proceedings under section 11 of the *CCAA* is binding on the Crown. In *CCI Industries Ltd.*, the Alberta Court of Queen's Bench also held that under section 21, a plan of arrangement is binding on the Crown.[195]

Among the Crown claims that can be stayed under the *CCAA* are claims for deductions under federal or provincial legislation from employees' wages. However, if a plan is approved by the court, such claims must be paid within six months, unless the Crown consents otherwise.[196] The stay order can address the Crown's recourse under section 224(1.2) of the *Income Tax Act* (*ITA*);[197] or any provision of the *Canada Pension Plan* (*CPP*) or of the *Employment Insurance Act* (*EIA*) that refers to this provision of the *ITA* and provides for the collection of a contribution under the *CPP*, or an employee's or employer's premium under the *EIA*, and of any related interest, penalties or other amounts if the company is a tax debtor under that subsection or provision. The stay is for such period as the court considers appropriate, but ending not later than: the expiration of the order; the refusal of a plan by the creditors or the court; six months following the court sanction of a plan; the default by the company on any term of a plan; or the performance of a compromise or arrangement in respect of the company.[198] There are similar provisions for provincial legislation that have a similar purpose.

When the stay is in effect, the debtor must continue payments to the Crown. However, the stay ceases to be of effect if the debtor defaults on payment of any amount that becomes due under these provisions or any creditor is or becomes entitled to

[195] *CCI Industries Ltd., Re*, 2005 ABQB 675, 2005 CarswellAlta 1261 (Alta. Q.B.) at para. 26.

[196] Sections 11.4(1), 18.2(1), *CCAA*.

[197] The *ITA* provides one of the Crown's administration and enforcement recourses, for a sort of garnishment in certain circumstances. This "garnishment" right is provided for in section 224(1.2) of the *ITA*, and can be used by the Crown to recover from a debtor an amount that would be due to the Crown, through the issuance by the Minister of National Revenue of a demand letter. The amounts that can be recovered through this provision would be amounts that can be assessed by virtue of section 227(10.1) of the *ITA*. In substance, those amounts would include any amount that is required to be withheld at source, together with interest and penalties. The *CPP* and *EIA* create similar rights, by incorporating the *ITA* provisions by reference, to recover the amounts due in respect of employer and employee contributions, interest and penalties. One issue that is yet undetermined is the quantification of the Crown's rights, as relates to section 224(1.2) of the *ITA*. The *CCAA* is worded to cover all amounts that are of a kind that could be subject to a demand under section 224(1.2) of the *ITA*. Jean Daniel Breton has argued that it would appear that the only amounts that could be subject to such a demand would be limited to the collectible value of the debtor's accounts receivable. Thus, the question remains, if the debtor does not have any accounts receivable (as might be the case for a retailer), or if they have little or no value, whether the amount of the Crown's rights under section 18.2 of the *CCAA* should be reduced commensurately; Jean-Daniel Breton, Comment, June 2006, on file with author.

[198] Section 11.4, *CCAA*.

realize a security on any property that could be claimed by the Crown in exercising these rights.[199] The stay ceases at the time of the default, not when the Crown issues a requirement to pay, and the court has jurisdiction to determine whether a stay order has ceased to be in effect pursuant to the *CCAA*.[200]

A *CCAA* stay also prevents the Crown from taking garnishment proceedings under section 317(3) of the *Excise Tax Act.* The Court has held that the fact that section 317(3) states that it applies notwithstanding any other enactment of Canada other than the *BIA,* but does not refer to the *CCAA,* does not deprive the court of the power to stay garnishment proceedings pursuant to that provision, as the court is merely suspending, not taking away the rights.[201] If the proposed plan is rejected by creditors or the court and the stay ends, the Crown can proceed with garnishment.

2. Priority of Crown Claims

As per sections 18.3(1) and 18.4(1) of the *CCAA*, the deemed trust claim of Canada Revenue Agency for unpaid G.S.T. was not applicable in *CCAA* restructurings, and thus the Crown's claims for G.S.T. could only be unsecured claims.[202] In implementing budget provisions in 2000, the federal government made changes to a number of provisions in various fiscal laws, to improve the administration and enforcement provisions in certain areas, and to provide greater harmonization between the various similar provisions in fiscal laws. One of the changes made was to the deemed trust provisions contained in section 222 of the *ETA*.[203] While the changes consisted largely of wording modifications, they had the effect of causing a change to the provisions of section 222 of the *ETA,* which was subsequent in time to the implementation of sections 18.3 and 18.4 of the *CCAA*. The changes made to section 222 of the *ETA* did not take into consideration the provisions of sections 18.3 and 18.4 of the *CCAA*, implemented in 1997. This caused an inconsistency between the clear provisions of section 222 of the *ETA*, and the equally clear provisions of sections 18.3 and 18.4 of the *CCAA*.

---

[199] Section 11.4(2), *CCAA.*

[200] *United Used Auto & Truck Parts Ltd., Re* (2000), 20 C.B.R. (4th) 289 (B.C. S.C. [In Chambers]).

[201] *Minister of National Revenue* v. *Points North Freight Forwarding Inc.* (2000), 24 C.B.R. (4th) 184 (Sask. Q.B.).

[202] *BlueStar Battery Systems International Corp., Re* (2000), 2000 CarswellOnt 4837, 25 C.B.R. (4th) 216, 10 B.L.R. (3d) 221 (Ont. S.C.J. [Commercial List]), cited in L.W. Houlden, G.B. Morawetz and J.P. Sarra, *Bankruptcy and Insolvency Law in Canada,* 3rd ed., vol. 4 (Toronto: Carswell, 2006) at 10A-68.10.

[203] It should be noted that the amount due in respect of the G.S.T. and the amount of the deemed trust created by virtue of section 222 of the *ETA* could be different amounts, and the difference could be significant. This results from the different basis of calculation for the two amounts. With regard to the G.S.T. liability, the amount is established in relation to the G.S.T. charged to customers (whether or not it has been collected), less input tax credits, remittances and other miscellaneous tax adjustments such as the tax relief for bad debts. With respect to the deemed trust, the amount is established based on the G.S.T. actually collected from customers, less input tax credits and remittances.

After the amendment was in force, the Alberta Court of Queen's Bench found in *Solid Resources Ltd.* that section 18.3 of the *CCAA* and section 222 of the *ETA* were in conflict and could not stand together.[204] The Court held that the *ETA*, being the more recent statute, should prevail.[205] The reasoning in *Solid Resources* was applied in *Gauntlet Energy Corp.,* in which the Court held that through the use of the notwithstanding provision and the express exclusion of the *BIA* but not the *CCAA* in the subsequent *ETA* statute, Parliament had signalled its intention that the latter general legislation should prevail over the earlier specific legislation. The Court concluded that section 222(3) of the *ETA* effectively repealed section 18.3(1) of the *CCAA* with respect to G.S.T. and therefore, the G.S.T. obligation could not be compromised by a plan of arrangement under the *CCAA*.[206]

In *Ottawa Senators Hockey Club Corp.,* the Ottawa Senators Hockey Club Corporation and several related companies filed under the *CCAA*.[207] The Crown claimed priority for unremitted G.S.T. and for interest and penalties under the Excise Tax Act (*ETA*). The Crown's claims to priority were disputed by two creditors, the Canadian Imperial Bank of Commerce and Fleet National Bank. The Ontario Court of Appeal held that the issue was a conflict between section 18.3(1) of the *CCAA*, which the Court found was a specialized statute, and section 222 of the *ETA*, which was a statute of general application. The Court held that section 18.3 of the *CCAA* was enacted prior to sections 222(1) and (3) of the *ETA*. The effect of section 18.3(1) of the *CCAA* was that G.S.T. amounts that are deemed to be a trust under the *ETA* would only be considered as trust property if they constituted a trust at common law or in equity, which the Crown conceded was not the case. However, section 222(3) of the *ETA* stated the opposite. It provided that if an amount is deemed under section 222(1) to be held in trust for the Crown and is not remitted according to the *ETA*, property of the debtor in an amount of equal value is deemed to be held in trust for the Crown and does not form a part of the property of the debtor. The conflict could not be resolved by the trumping words that are often found in statutes because both statutes contain specific words: "notwithstanding any provision in federal or provisional legislation" in section 18.3(1) of the *CCAA*, and "Despite . . . any other enactment of Canada (except the *BIA*)" in section 222(3) of the *ETA*.

The Court of Appeal in *Ottawa Senators Hockey Club Corp.*, held that the overarching rule of statutory interpretation is that statutory provisions should be interpreted to give effect to the intention of the legislature in enacting the law. This primary rule takes precedence over all maxims, canons or aids relating to statutory interpretation, including the maxim that the specific prevails over the general. The Court held that the *BIA* and the *CCAA* are closely related federal statutes and it was not conceivable that Parliament would specifically identify the *BIA* as an exception,

---

[204] *Solid Resources Ltd., Re* (2002), 2002 CarswellAlta 1699, [2002] A.J. No. 1651, 40 C.B.R. (4th) 219 (Alta. Q.B.).

[205] *Ibid.* at para. 84. See also *Gauntlet Energy Corp.,* 2003 ABQB 894, 2003 CarswellAlta 1735, [2003] A.J. No. 1504 (Alta. Q.B.).

[206] *Gauntlet Energy Corp.,* 2003 ABQB 894, 2003 CarswellAlta 1735, [2003] A.J. No. 1504 (Alta. Q.B.).

[207] *Ottawa Senators Hockey Club Corp., Re* (2005), 73 O.R. (3d) 737 (Ont. C.A.).

but accidentally fail to consider the *CCAA* as a possible second exception. The Court of Appeal held that the omission of the *CCAA* from section 222(3) of the *ETA* was almost certainly a considered omission. Ordinary rules of interpretation hold that general statutes are set aside by subsequent general legislation, even without a "notwithstanding clause". Therefore, the only possible interpretation of "notwithstanding any inconsistent provision" is that it applies to prior special legislation, which would otherwise have precedence. By virtue of the rule of effectivity, such a clause must be construed as applying to prior special legislation. Hence, the deemed trust provisions of the *ETA* apply in *CCAA* proceedings.[208]

The *CCAA* stay order also does not stay or restrain the exercise by the Minister of Finance or the Superintendent of Financial Institutions of any power, duty or function assigned to them by the *Bank Act*, *the Cooperative Credit Associations Act*, the *Insurance Companies Act or the Trust and Loan Companies Act*; the exercise by the Governor in Council, the Minister of Finance or the Canada Deposit Insurance Corporation of any power, duty or function assigned to them by the *Canada Deposit Insurance Corporation Act*; or the exercise by the Attorney General of Canada of any power assigned by the *WURA*.[209]

3. Governmental Involvement in *CCAA* Proceedings

In addition to the usual Crown claims relating to source deductions and G.S.T., various levels of government are sometimes involved in *CCAA* proceedings. Governments frequently quietly assist in restructuring, for example, forgiving various kinds of debt as part of the restructuring strategy.

While all creditors must make compromises in the restructuring process, governments must compromise more so in the sense that they have competing public policy objectives of debt collection and encouraging the survival of businesses. On the one hand, they wish to collect monies owing through tax instruments, contributions to CPP and workers' compensation, as well as industrial start-up or recapitalization loans. On the other hand, closure of operations can have devastating effects for local communities in terms of decreased local tax bases, lost tax revenues from financial difficulties faced by spin-off economic activities, and increased costs of social supports in terms of employment insurance and welfare assistance.[210]

Thus governments will often assist the restructuring through debt forgiveness, loan guarantees or other adjustment measures. In the 1991-2 Algoma workout, the Ontario Government used the incentive of more than a hundred million dollars in loan guarantees to help bring parties to the bargaining table. As part of the negotiated restructuring, it relieved lenders and preferred shareholders from environmental

---

[208] *Ibid.* at paras. 43-46.

[209] Section 11.11, *CCAA*.

[210] Janis P. Sarra, *Creditor Rights and the Public Interest, Restructuring Insolvent Corporations* (Toronto: University of Toronto Press, 2003).

liability in the event of default and realization of the security, and these environmental waivers facilitated negotiations.[211]

XI. PREFERENCES AND REVIEWABLE TRANSACTIONS

Preferences occur when an insolvent debtor makes a payment to one creditor or undertakes a transaction in the period leading up to bankruptcy that involves a conveyance or transfer of property to the benefit of one or more creditors at the expense of others.[212] Reviewable transactions are generally transfers for undervalue between non-arm's length parties, i.e. when a party sells assets for less than they are worth.[213] These transactions may in some cases be fraudulent. Provisions to avoid preferential payments and other reviewable transactions exist both in the *BIA* and in provincial legislation.[214] Reviewable transactions under the *BIA* include settlements, which are gifts, transfers and similar transactions to dispose of assets that would otherwise be available to satisfy creditors' claims.[215]

The *CCAA* does not create a direct mechanism to permit creditors to challenge settlements, reviewable transactions and unfair preferences, as these rights exist under other statutes. Instead, creditors may seek a temporary lift of the *CCAA* stay to file a petition in bankruptcy, which is then stayed during the *CCAA* proceedings, but preserves time frames for challenging reviewable transactions and preferences. In such a case, these claims are then usually dealt with in the course of the negotiations for a *CCAA* plan, but are preserved and able to be realized on if the *CCAA* proceeding fails and the debtor corporation becomes bankrupt.

The existing *BIA* provisions have been criticized for not being sufficiently comprehensive, leading to a fragmented approach for regulating preferences and transfers at undervalue in bankruptcies and insolvencies.[216] Parallel provisions under provincial assignments, preferences and conveyances legislation overlap with federal bankruptcy legislation, with different standards across provincial jurisdictions. Provincial legislation is used more frequently, as many creditors find the federal legislation to

---

[211] The Ontario Government offered some protection for the operating lender as consideration for it extending a further bridge loan of $60 million; default would have granted possession rights without attracting any environmental liability. The federal and provincial governments provided funding for employee training and older workers' adjustments. The Ontario Government adopted a special securities regulation that gave protection to directors and officers against personal liability arising out of future operations, and that gave Algoma and Algoma Finance the status of reporting issuers. G. Marantz, "Facilitating Arrangements – A Dynamic Process", in *Corporate Restructurings and Insolvencies, Issues and Perspectives* (Toronto: Carswell, 1995) at 507.

[212] L.W. Houlden, G.B. Morawetz and J.P. Sarra, *Bankruptcy and Insolvency Law in Canada,* 3rd ed., vol. 1, (Toronto: Carswell, 2006) at ND-43.

[213] *Ibid.*

[214] Sections 95-100, *BIA*. See also, for example, the *Assignments and Preferences Act* (Ontario) R.S.O. 1990, c. A.33.

[215] Section 91, *BIA*.

[216] L.W. Houlden, G.B. Morawetz and J.P. Sarra, *Bankruptcy and Insolvency Law in Canada,* 3rd ed., vol. 1, (Toronto: Carswell, 2006) at ND-43.

be insufficiently concrete and inefficient.[217] Some practitioners have suggested that the provisions of the provincial legislation should be included in the federal insolvency legislation to create a single comprehensive piece of legislation for bankruptcy situations.[218] The existing legislation's reliance on the concepts of fraud and intent to determine whether these kinds of transactions occurred is also problematic, as fraud and intent are "difficult to prove and can require costly and lengthy litigation".[219]

The Chapter 47 amendments reform the preferences, settlements and reviewable transactions provisions substantially, including proposing transfers at undervalue in order to bring consistency to the treatment of these claims. One question is whether the reviewable transaction remedies under the *BIA* should be available during the course of a *CCAA* proceeding.

XII. ENVIRONMENTAL CLAIMS

A key governance issue has been environmental liability at the point of insolvency. This liability poses some important challenges for the restructuring regime. Where restructuring efforts fail, environmental protection and clean up costs are frequently borne by environmental authorities and ultimately taxpayers. Often at the point of a *CCAA* proceeding, all of the outstanding environmental issues that the corporation has been deferring for years come to the fore, and in many cases, particularly in the resource extraction and manufacturing sector, there are millions of dollars in remediation liabilities.[220] Liability for environmental remediation generally runs with the land, and creditors, managers and other stakeholders must necessarily consider the risks of environmental liability in considering whether or not to restructure and in considering the potential value of a sale of the business.

Environmental protection legislation imposes personal and corporate liability for environmental harm. However, environmental liability or tort claims arising out of environmental harm may be such that they impair the ability of the debtor corporation to pay its debts, thus precipitating insolvency. Uncertainties about the extent of liability may hinder the corporation's ability to obtain further financing for restruc-

---

[217] *Ibid.*

[218] *Ibid.*

[219] *Ibid.* at ND-44. The issue of preferences is another area where the Canadian bankruptcy and insolvency system is significantly different from the U.S. model. Under the U.S. model, all transfers are voidable, if they occurred while the debtor was insolvent and within the suspect period, and had the effect of providing a greater return to the creditor than it would receive in a case under Chapter 7 of the U.S. *Bankruptcy Code*. The intent of the debtor is not a factor in determining whether the transaction is voidable. Under the Canadian system, the party seeking to void a preference will have to demonstrate an intent to prefer on the part of the debtor, although in this endeavour will benefit from a rebuttable presumption if the creditor was, in fact, preferred. The provisions in the U.S. *Bankruptcy Code* addressing preferences are found in Chapter 5.

[220] Janis P. Sarra, *Creditor Rights and the Public Interest, Restructuring Insolvent Corporations* (Toronto: University of Toronto Press, 2003).

turing, given that the value of the security is uncertain.[221] Given the scope of potential liability, decisions about converting debt to equity in a restructuring or exercising enhanced oversight are shaped by the environmental liability that creditors may be acquiring, particularly if there is some element of being a "person responsible" for the source of the contaminant. Environmental liability is also an important consideration in determining whether to approve a plan. Since these costs are often unknown at the point at which a debtor corporation is in *CCAA* proceedings, this can pose a barrier to successful resolution of the insolvency.

In order to reduce the distributive effects of environmental liability, both capital costs of remediation and long-term costs to quality of land, water, air and human health must be appropriately valued in decision-making about the future of the corporation.

Workouts facilitate availability of financing for environmental maintenance or remediation by clarifying that creditors can conduct investigations or offer financing, and not be concerned that they are acquiring the prior liability of the corporation. The availability of lender liability agreements with environmental authorities and "brownfields legislation" aimed at apportioning the risk and liability of revitalization of abandoned or contaminated lands during a workout, recognized the benefits of restructuring to environmental protection.[222] These agreements are no longer as common with the amendments to the *CCAA* that now expressly set out a mechanism for dealing with environmental remediation issues, as discussed below.

Environmental costs are not considered administration costs, and the costs of environmental remediation do not rank ahead of other claims in priority to any distribution to other parties of payouts of other assets, except as provided in section 11.3 of the *CCAA*, creating incentives for the Crown to negotiate going concern solutions to environmental liability problems with creditors.[223] There is a strong public interest in ensuring that someone is taking responsibility for environmental protection at a time when a debtor corporation is trying to devise a workout plan under the *CCAA*.

In 1997, the *CCAA* was amended to give priority to Crown claims for environmental clean-up costs over all other charges on the real property affected,[224] and the ability of insolvency officers to abandon or release their interest in property.[225] These amendments were aimed at encouraging creditors, through their officers, to consider

[221] Derrick Tay, "The Impact of Potential Environmental Law Liability on Creditors' Rights" (Canadian Bar Association Conference, Toronto, 1991) at 5-8.

[222] Ontario *Brownfields Statute Law Amendment Act, 2001*, S.O. 2001, c. 17, amending ss. 168.18, 168.19 of the Ontario *Environmental Protection Act*. The Brownfields Act makes similar amendments to the Ontario *Water Resources Act*, S.O. 1992, as amended, and to the Ontario *Pesticides Act*, S.O. 1993, c. 27, as amended. It includes directors, officers and agents of secured creditors.

[223] As discussed earlier, section 11.3 specifies that the *CCAA* order shall not have the effect of prohibiting a person from requiring immediate payment for goods, services or use of leased or licensed property after the order is made or requiring the further advance of money or credit.

[224] Section 11.8(8), *CCAA*.

[225] *Ibid.* See ss. 19, 148.1, 168.20 of the Ontario *Environmental Protection Act*; s. 89.11 of the Ontario *Water Resources Act*; and s. 31.5 of the Ontario *Pesticides Act*.

taking steps to remedy the environmental problems instead of abandoning the property.[226]

Section 11.8 of the *CCAA* specifies:

> *Liability in respect of environmental matters*
>
> (3) Notwithstanding anything in any federal or provincial law, a monitor is not personally liable in that position for any environmental condition that arose or environmental damage that occurred
>
> (a) before the monitor's appointment; or
>
> (b) after the monitor's appointment unless it is established that the condition arose or the damage occurred as a result of the monitor's gross negligence or wilful misconduct.
>
> *Reports, etc., still required*
>
> (4) Nothing in subsection (3) exempts a monitor from any duty to report or make disclosure imposed by a law referred to in that subsection.
>
> *Non-liability re certain orders*
>
> (5) Notwithstanding anything in any federal or provincial law but subject to subsection (3), where an order is made which has the effect of requiring a monitor to remedy any environmental condition or environmental damage affecting property involved in a proceeding under this Act, the monitor is not personally liable for failure to comply with the order, and is not personally liable for any costs that are or would be incurred by any person in carrying out the terms of the order,
>
> (a) if, within such time as is specified in the order, within ten days after the order is made if no time is so specified, within ten days after the appointment of the monitor, if the order is in effect when the monitor is appointed or during the period of the stay referred to in paragraph (b), the monitor
>
> (i) complies with the order, or
>
> (ii) on notice to the person who issued the order, abandons, disposes of or otherwise releases any interest in any real property affected by the condition or damage;

---

[226] The provisions of section 11.8 of the *CCAA* were written to mirror similar provisions contained in section 14.06 of the *BIA*, when the provisions of the *BIA* were expanded to extend the protection that was available to bankruptcy trustees to other types of mandates in which an insolvency professional might be involved. The provisions in the *CCAA* are geared towards providing protection of a monitor where it has assumed a governance role. The role of the monitor is addressed in greater detail in chapter 8 of this text.

(b) during the period of a stay of the order granted, on application made within the time specified in the order referred to in paragraph (a) or within ten days after the order is made or within ten days after the appointment of the monitor, if the order is in effect when the monitor is appointed, by

(i) court or body having jurisdiction under the law pursuant to which the order was made to enable the monitor to contest the order, or

(ii) the court having jurisdiction under this Act for the purposes of assessing the economic viability of complying with the order; or

(c) if the monitor had, before the order was made, abandoned or renounced any interest in any real property affected by the condition or damage.

Stay may be granted

(6) The court may grant a stay of the order referred to in subsection (5) on such notice and for such period as the court deems necessary for the purpose of enabling the monitor to assess the economic viability of complying with the order.

Costs for remedying not costs of administration

(7) Where the monitor has abandoned or renounced any interest in real property affected by the environmental condition or environmental damage, claims for costs of remedying the condition or damage shall not rank as costs of administration.

Priority of claims

(8) Any claim by Her Majesty in right of Canada or a province against a debtor company in respect of which proceedings have been commenced under this Act for costs of remedying any environmental condition or environmental damage affecting real property of the company is secured by a charge on the real property and on any other real property of the company that is contiguous thereto and that is related to the activity that caused the environmental condition or environmental damage, and the charge

(a) is enforceable in accordance with the law of the jurisdiction in which the real property is located, in the same way as a mortgage, hypothec or other security on real property; and

(b) ranks above any other claim, right or charge against the property, notwithstanding any other provision of this Act or anything in any other federal or provincial law.

Claim for clean-up costs

(9) A claim against a debtor company for costs of remedying any environmental condition or environmental damage affecting real property of the company shall

> be a claim under this Act, whether the condition arose or the damage occurred before or after the date on which proceedings under this Act were commenced.

According to Industry Canada, the policy objectives of these reforms to the *CCAA* and mirror provisions in the *BIA* were to "advance sustainable development objectives by promoting the clean-up of environmentally contaminated properties of bankrupt debtors or debtors reorganizing under the *BIA* or *CCAA* . . . avoid "orphan site" problems, alert environment ministries quickly to environmental problems and provide available funds from the estate to help finance the clean-up".[227]

The Ontario Superior Court in *General Chemical Canada Ltd.*, recently discussed how the similar *BIA* provisions work:[228]

> As to environmental issues, the Crown's claim "for costs of remedying any environmental condition or environmental damage affecting real property" is given priority under section 14.06(7) of the *Bankruptcy and Insolvency Act*, and is a statutory exception to the general scheme under the *BIA*. Any claim by either the federal or provincial Crown for the costs of remedying any environmental condition or damage affecting real property is "secured by a charge on the real property and on any other real property of the debtor that is contiguous" to the real property, and "is related to the activity that caused the environmental damage or charge." Subsection 14.06(7)(a) makes the Crown's charge enforceable in the same way as a mortgage or charge on real property, and subsection (b) makes this Crown charge against the realty rank above any other claim, right or charge against the property.
>
> The *EPA* (*Environmental Protection Act)* permits the MOE to issue orders to a polluter to clean up polluted property. This right extends, in some limited circumstances, to issuing these kinds of orders to interim receivers or trustees in bankruptcy, but only in exceptional circumstances, namely, where there is danger to the health or safety of any person, there is an impairment or serious risk of impairment of the quality of the natural environment, or there is injury or damage or serious risk of injury or damage to any property or to any plant or animal life [*EPA*, s. 168.20(1)]. Unless these exceptional circumstances exist, the MOE is prohibited from issuing orders to receivers or trustees unless the order arises from the gross negligence or wilful misconduct of the receiver or trustee [*EPA*, s. 168.19(1)].

This system has worked well under both the *CCAA* and the *BIA*. Lenders can conduct their due diligence on environmental issues, which are often less serious than they might have feared without investigation, knowing that if there is a very serious problem, they do not face open-ended liability. The result has been fewer abandoned properties.

---

[227] Industry Canada, "Sustainable Development Strategies: 1997-2000", online: Industry Canada website <http://strategis.ic.gc.ca/epic/internet/insd-dd.nsf/en/sd00052e.html>.

[228] *General Chemical Canada Ltd., Re* (2006), 2006 CarswellOnt 4675, 22 C.B.R. (5th) 298 (Ont. S.C.J. [Commercial List], Mesbur J.

XIII. TORT CLAIMS

The term "creditor" includes tort claimants as contingent creditors within the meaning of insolvency legislation, if the contingent creditors can establish a provable claim.

The *Red Cross* case was the first in Canada to have tort claimants involved as key creditors in the *CCAA* process. For tort claimants, the liability of the corporation arises from its past actions. Given the serious nature of the harm incurred, it is likely that such claimants are not supportive of having the corporation survive. Thus, absent some incentive to vote in favour of a plan of arrangement, such as recovery greater than the liquidation value of their claims, it is unlikely that tort claimants will support a plan.[229] Generally, contingent creditors are likely to support a plan if some compromise of their claims today provides greater realization on their claims in the future. However, for health related claims, time may be of the essence. Where there is the possibility of third party payment of the claims, as in *Red Cross*, the *CCAA* process can be used as bargaining leverage for extracting a better settlement. While this is vitally important for the contingent creditors, it can place at risk the negotiations for a viable restructuring plan for the debtor corporation.[230]

In the United States, trust funds have been created as a mechanism to satisfy mass tort claims. However, where health effects have not yet manifested themselves, due to long latency periods, there may be a problem with *ex ante* determination of the amount of trust funds required to be set aside for the future satisfaction of claims, when no one really knows the full extent of harms that may arise.[231] There may be a further question as to the constitutionality of the courts being able to bind future tort claimants who have been exposed to the past actions of the corporation, but the harms have not yet manifested themselves.[232] Essentially, binding future tort claimants, without either due process or relative certainty in the amount of money that needs to be vested in the trust to cover these claims, can work to disenfranchise future tort claimants.[233] On the other hand, if future claimants cannot be bound, the only alternative for the debtor may be liquidation, in which case future claimants would have no remedy at all.

In order for corporations to seek the protection of the *CCAA*, they must be insolvent; hence, by definition, there are not sufficient assets remaining in the corporation to satisfy all the tort claims. The *Red Cross* insolvency was precipitated by more than $8 billion in tort claims by thousands of Canadians ill or dying from contaminated

---

[229] Janis P. Sarra, *Creditor Rights and the Public Interest, Restructuring Insolvent Corporations* (Toronto: University of Toronto Press, 2003).

[230] *Ibid.*

[231] *Ibid.*

[232] G.M. Cole, "A Calculus Without Consent: Mass Tort Bankruptcies, Future Claimants and the Problem of Third Party Non-Debtor Discharge", (1999) 84 Iowa Law Review 753.

[233] Janis P. Sarra, *Creditor Rights and the Public Interest, Restructuring Insolvent Corporations* (Toronto: University of Toronto Press, 2003).

blood products.[234] More than 230 actions and 10 class actions involved claimants suffering from Hepatitis C (HCV), HIV, Creutzfeld Jakob disease, or some combination of these illnesses as the result of inadequate testing and screening. Hence in *Red Cross,* many of the health harms had already manifested themselves. As a not-for-profit corporation, the Red Cross had operated a blood donor operation since 1940, and had operated Canada's National Blood System with funding from federal and provincial governments since 1977. Services of the Red Cross included supply of blood and blood products, disaster relief, homemaker services, and international relief and crisis intervention. The Red Cross employed almost ten thousand people at the time of the *CCAA* filing. The quantum of remedies claimed and the cost of defending hundreds of actions would have resulted in the bankruptcy of Red Cross and as a consequence, Red Cross sought and obtained insolvency protection pursuant to the *CCAA*.[235]

In a report arising out of a national inquiry into Canada's blood system, Mr. Justice Krever had noted that no amount of money would make up for the pain, suffering and premature death caused by the blood related injuries.[236] Thus while the claims were of a contingent nature in the *CCAA* proceeding and the individual claims had yet to be determined, the interests of the Transfusion Claimants had already been established before the Red Cross filed under the *CCAA*.[237] A workout plan was subsequently successfully negotiated.[238] There have also been tort claims in the context of other harms caused by the debtor.[239]

The Muscletech *CCAA* proceeding in 2006 was precipitated by numerous product liability claims in the U.S. from the chemical ephedra and from prohormones used in dietary supplements that the debtor manufactured and sold. With respect to the tort claims, the Ontario Superior Court of Justice considered the question of whether plaintiffs in an uncertified class action could file claims in the *CCAA* proceeding on behalf of themselves and all other similarly situated plaintiffs.[240] The products liability actions had been stayed under both the *CCAA* and U.S. Chapter 15 proceedings.[241] There was a claims process set up, which involved a first assessment of

---

[234] *In the Matter of the Companies' Creditors Arrangement Act, Canadian Red Cross/La societé canadienne de la croix-rouge* (August 19, 1999), Court File No. 98-CL-002970 (Ont. S.C.J.) Blair J. (Endorsement).

[235] There were also cross-claims and third party claims from hospitals and governments.

[236] Mr. Justice Horace Krever, *Commission of Inquiry on the Blood System in Canada, Final Report,* (Ottawa: Government of Canada), Part IV at 1030.

[237] *Canadian Red Cross Society, Re* (July 20, 1998), Court File No. 98-CL-002970 (Ont. S.C.J.), Blair J. (Initial order) at 2.

[238] For a full discussion of this case, see Janis P. Sarra, *Creditor Rights and the Public Interest, Restructuring Insolvent Corporations* (Toronto: University of Toronto Press, 2003).

[239] *Oblats de Marie Immaculée du Manitoba, Re* (2004), [2004] M.J. No. 112, 2004 CarswellMan 104, 182 Man. R. (2d) 201, 2004 MBQB 71 (Man. Q.B.).

[240] *Muscletech Research & Development Inc., Re* (2006), 2006 CarswellOnt 4929 (Ont. S.C.J. [Commercial List]) Mesbur J. There are ongoing *CCAA* and U.S. Chapter 15 ancillary proceedings, as discussed in chapter 9.

[241] *Ibid.* at para. 10, the Court noted that such an order under U.S. proceedings is a Temporary Restraining Order and Preliminary Injunction, referred to as an Adversary Proceeding.

claims by the monitor; a process for resolving disputed claims; and a claims bar date.

In considering the issue of representative claims, the Court observed that the *CCAA* neither expressly permits nor forbids representative claims, and that "claim" under section 12(1) of the statute makes reference to the *BIA*. In turn, the *BIA* has a mechanism to determine whether a contingent or unliquidated claim is a provable claim.[242] The Court held that while it is possible to have a representation order in *CCAA* proceedings, to date, there has not been a judgment that extended such orders to permit a "representative proof of claim" to be filed. The Court held that while a representative claim may be possible, the question was whether the case before it was a proper one to permit this kind of representative claim, without the necessity of the individual members of the class filing claims.[243]

The Court in *MuscleTech Research and Development Inc.* held that the *CCAA* process adequately protected the interests of the potential claimants, had they availed themselves of the process. The Court noted that other individuals had filed claims within the prescribed period and that if members of the representative plaintiff's proposed class had wished to file claims, they had as much notice and opportunity as other parties. The Court held that the process adequately protected the interests of the potential claimants and they chose not to utilize the process. The Court declined to exercise its discretion to allow the representative claims or lift the stay to permit certification motions to proceed in the U.S.[244] The Court held that changing and increasing the landscape of claimants after the claims bar date and after the settlement of thirty of the ephedra claims could cause prejudice to the eventual success of the *CCAA* process. The Court held that all the arguments by the representative plaintiffs should have been made when the Call for Claims Order was made. The process gave adequate opportunity for anyone with a claim to file a proof of claim; the forms were accessible and in plain language, and the products liability claimants all managed to make individual claims even where they were involved in class actions. Hence the Court concluded that to allow representative or class claims at this date would be prejudicial to the entire claims process and would impair the integrity of the *CCAA* process. Hence the Court declined to exercise its discretion.

With the introduction in 2006 of new secondary market civil liability regimes under Ontario securities legislation and in January 2007 under Alberta and Manitoba securities legislations, there is also likely to be an increased number of securities laws claims that are filed prior to or during insolvency proceedings.

In one cross-border proceeding, the Court certified a class action relating to allegations of misrepresentation in a public offering. However, it declined to approve the settlement of both U.S. and Canadian class actions as premature within the *CCAA* process, because to do so would have given one group of unsecured claimants an

---

[242] *Ibid.* at para. 29, citing section 135(1.1), *BIA*.

[243] *Ibid.* at para. 37.

[244] *Ibid.* at paras. 41-44.

unwarranted advantage over another, would have impaired the ability of some claimants to engage in full and complete negotiations, and prematurely placed the restructuring at risk.[245] Thus the Court adjourned the question of approval of the settlement to a date contemporaneous with the sanctioning hearing, with notice to be sent to all members of the class. The settlement was subsequently approved at the sanction hearing.

XIV. RELATED PARTY CLAIMS

The treatment of related party claims is codified in the *BIA*. However, the courts have held that the *BIA* treatment of related party claims cannot be applied automatically to *CCAA* proceedings.[246] Resolution of related party claims has been a key issue in a number of *CCAA* restructurings, including *Mirant Canada Energy Marketing Ltd., PSINet Ltd., AT&T Canada Inc.*, and *Uniforêt Inc.*[247] Natasha MacParland observes that in each of these cases, resolution of the related party claims, because of their size and nature, was key to arriving at a successful restructuring plan.[248] For example, in the *AT&T Canada Inc.* proceeding, the inter-company claims were restructured to provide a tax benefit for the post-*CCAA* corporation and in *Uniforêt Inc.*, while initially controversial, the related party claims were treated the same as certain other arm's length creditors.[249] MacParland suggests that the courts use a variety of tools such as the classification of creditors, the determination of the fairness and reasonableness of the proposed plan, and substantive consolidation to overcome issues raised by the treatment of related party claims, with a view to facilitating a workout between the debtor corporation and its creditors.[250]

---

[245] *Menegon* v. *Philip Services Corp.* (1999), 1999 CarswellOnt 3240, [1999] O.J. No. 4080 (Ont. S.C.J. (Commercial List)).

[246] *Olympia & York Developments Ltd., Re* (March 14, 1994), Doc. B125/92, [1994] O.J. No. 1335 (Ont. Gen. Div. [Commercial List]); *Campeau Corp., Re* (1992), 10 C.B.R. (3d) 100, 86 D.L.R. (4th) 570 (Ont. Gen. Div.), leave to appeal refused (1992), 86 D.L.R. (4th) 570n (Ont. C.A.), leave to appeal refused (1992), 86 D.L.R. (4th) 570n (S.C.C.). Related parties are defined under s. 2 of the *BIA* as: individuals connected by blood relationship, marriage, common-law partnership or adoption; a corporation and a person who controls the corporation, if it is controlled by one person, a person who is a member of a related group that controls the corporation, or any person connected in the manner set out in paragraph (a) to a person described in subparagraph (i) or (ii); or; and two corporations related in a number of specified ways under the *BIA* (a list of six types of relationships).

[247] *Mirant Canada Energy Marketing Ltd., Re* (2003) Doc. Calgary 0301-11094 (Alta. Q.B.); *PSINet Ltd., Re* (2001), Doc. Toronto, 01-CL-4155 (Ont. S.C.J.); *AT&T Canada Inc., Re* (2002), Doc. Toronto 02-CL-004715 (Ont. S.C.J.); and *Uniforêt Inc., Re* (2002), Doc. S.C. Montréal 500-05-064436-015 (Qué. S.C.).

[248] Natasha MacParland, "How Close is Too Close? The Treatment of Related Party Claims in Canadian Restructurings", in *Annual Review of Insolvency Law, 2004* (Carswell, 2005) 355-398.

[249] *Ibid.*

[250] *Ibid.*

XV. PUBLIC INTEREST GENERALLY

A *CCAA* court-supervised proceeding involves cost, control and public interest. The court has held that the *CCAA* is broad remedial legislation designed to facilitate a restructuring of debtor corporations in the interests of the company, its creditors and the public.[251] In that context, the *CCAA* contemplates that the rights and remedies of various stakeholders might be temporarily sacrificed. In *Quintette Coal,* the British Columbia Court of Appeal observed that an important consideration in sanctioning a plan was the public interest in having the company survive, given the significance of coal to the British Columbia economy.[252]

Courts have observed that the *CCAA* was designed to serve a "broad constituency of investors, creditors and employees" and thus the court will consider the individuals and organizations directly affected by the plan, as well as the wider public interest, an interest that is generally, but not always, served by permitting a company to attempt a restructuring.[253] The *CCAA* is aimed at avoiding, where possible, the devastating social and economic consequences of loss of business operations, and is aimed at allowing the corporation to carry on business in a manner that causes the least possible harm to employees and the communities in which it operates.[254]

Hence the treatment of claims in a *CCAA* proceeding is undertaken with the public interest in mind. Public interest under the current regime is not a substantive objective, but rather, is a "short form" for the complex balancing of diverse interests that the court engages in determining claims and disputes that arise during a *CCAA* proceeding and in approving a plan.[255] Consideration of the public interest is one aspect of the court's assessment of the viability and fairness of the proposed plan within the existing statutory scheme of priorities. The Court has held that there is a broader public dimension that must be considered and weighed in the balance, as well as the interests of those most directly affected.[256] One scholar has suggested that the public interest in insolvency law involves taking into account interests that society has regard for, and that are wider than the interests of those parties directly involved in a particular case, the debtor and creditors.[257]

---

[251] *Playdium Entertainment Corp., Re* (2001), 2001 CarswellOnt 3893, [2001] O.J. No. 4252 (Ont. S.C.J. [Commercial List]), additional reasons at (2001), 31 C.B.R. (4th) 309 (Ont. S.C.J. [Commercial List]), at para. 27; *Armbro Enterprises Inc., Re* (1993), 22 C.B.R. (3d) 80 (Ont. Bktcy.); *Icor Oil & Gas Co.* v. *Canadian Imperial Bank of Commerce* (1989), 102 A. R. 161 (Alta. Q.B.) at 165.

[252] *Quintette Coal Ltd.* v. *Nippon Steel Corp.* (1990), 2 C.B.R. (3d) 303 (B.C. C.A.), leave to appeal refused (1991), 7 C.B.R. (3d) 164 (note) (S.C.C.).

[253] *Hongkong Bank of Canada* v. *Chef Ready Foods Ltd.* (1990), 4 C.B.R. (3d) 311 (B.C. C.A.); *Sklar-Peppler Furniture Corp.* v. *Bank of Nova Scotia* (1991), 8 C.B.R. (3d) 312 (Ont. Gen. Div.) at 314.

[254] *Sklar-Peppler, ibid.*

[255] Janis P. Sarra, *Creditor Rights and the Public Interest, Restructuring Insolvent Corporations* (Toronto: University of Toronto Press, 2003).

[256] *Skydome Corp., Re* (1998), 1998 CarswellOnt 5922, 16 C.B.R. (4th) 118 (Ont. Gen. Div. [Commercial List]) (Endorsement).

[257] Andrew Keay, "Insolvency Law: A Matter of Public Interest?" (2000) 51 Northern Ireland Legal Quarterly 509 at 533.

Although extremely rare, communities have participated in a workout in an organized fashion, even though they have no fixed capital claims, representing one form of the public interest. An example was the 1991-92 *Algoma Steel CCAA* proceeding. Given the enormous impact that the closure would have had on Sault Ste. Marie, the community created a non-profit organization called Algoma Community Action Team (CAT). Within a short time period, more than 22,000 community residents had taken out memberships, donating $165,000 to help CAT lobby and assist with the restructuring negotiations. CAT's contribution to the process was that it secured information from Algoma on the source of the financial distress and disseminated it to the public, independent of the corporation and the union. It also mobilized the community to pressure various levels of government to support the restructuring, including delegations to politicians and documentation of the economic and social harms caused by the failure of U.S. steel plants.

Questions for review of materials:

1. What is an eligible financial contract and how does its treatment differ from other executory contracts under the *CCAA*?

2. What is a provable claim within the meaning of the *CCAA*?

3. What tests does the court use in determining whether to grant an extension for the filing of claims?

4. What changes will the Wage Earner Protection Program implement?

Questions for discussion:

1. Does the Supreme Court of Canada in *GMAC Commercial Credit Corp.* find the appropriate balance between insolvency legislation and labour relations legislation?

2. Do changes to environmental liability provisions in the *BIA* and *CCAA* create the appropriate balance between environmental cleanup and protecting the monitor when a firm is in *CCAA* proceedings?

3. What is the appropriate role of the courts in being concerned about the public interest when the *CCAA* is largely a commercial statute?

CHAPTER 7

APPROVING PLANS OF ARRRANGEMENT AND COMPROMISE

I. INTRODUCTION

In most cases, the debtor corporation proposes a plan of arrangement and compromise, however, creditors also have the ability to propose a plan. The courts have held that creditors seeking to file a plan must submit an outline of a plan in making an application under the *CCAA*, and in the absence of a plan that permits the debtor to continue operating, the court will dismiss the application.[1] The court has refused to allow a class of secured creditors to file a plan for its class alone, as it would have the effect of giving that class of creditors a veto over the restructuring of the debtor corporation.[2]

Where an insolvent corporation is essentially sold to creditors in compromise of their claims, they acquire a heightened interest in governance post-plan implementation that is not satisfied through the pricing mechanism of debt. Hence they may have a strong interest in the governance measures that comprise part of the plan sought to be approved.

II. CLASSIFICATION OF CREDITORS

The definition of classes of creditors for voting purposes is often crucial to a successful restructuring.[3] Section 6 of the *CCAA* specifies that where a majority in number, representing two-thirds in value of each creditor or class of creditors, present and voting in person or by proxy at the meeting, agree to any compromise or arrangement as proposed or as altered or modified at the meeting, the compromise or arrangement may be sanctioned by the court. A debtor may offer a plan of a

---

1 *Enterprise Capital Management Inc.* v. *Semi-Tech Corp.* (1999), 10 C.B.R. (4th) 133 (Ont. S.C.J. [Commercial List]).

2 *Doman Industries Ltd., Re* (2003), 41 C.B.R. (4th) 29, 14 B.C.L.R. (4th) 153 (B.C. S.C. [In Chambers]).

3 *Campeau Corp., Re* (1991), 10 C.B.R. (3d) 100, 86 D.L.R. (4th) 570; *Oakwood Petroleum Products* (1988), 72 C.B.R. (N.S.) 1 (Alta. Q.B.); *Northland Properties Ltd., Re* (1988), 73 C.B.R. (N.S.) 171 (B.C. S.C. [In Chambers]).

compromise or arrangement to secured creditors only, in those circumstances where the assets of the debtor corporation will not be sufficient to generate recovery for any unsecured creditors.[4]

The debtor company usually proposes the definition of classes, and where there is a dispute, the court will determine classes for purposes of voting on the *CCAA* plan. The courts generally interpret class in a manner that promotes the statutory objective of facilitating restructuring.[5]

Given that a precondition to approval of a proposed plan of arrangement or compromise is the requisite creditor support in each class of creditors, the determination of "class" becomes a key issue in *CCAA* proceedings. Numbers are key, as creditors placed in classes in which the other creditors are very supportive of the debtor corporation have much less chance of vetoing a proposed plan. As a consequence, both creditors and the debtor corporation typically try to frame the classes in such a way as to maximize their voice and control rights in the restructuring process. Since Canadian insolvency law does not have formal "cram-down" provisions, where a plan can be approved even if some classes reject it, as exists in U.S. legislation, the definition of class becomes a point of negotiation for creditors and the debtor.

There has been considerable litigation on the issue of what comprises a "class of creditors" for purposes of the *CCAA*. Early *CCAA* cases adopted an anti-fragmentation approach, grouping creditors with a sufficient community of interest and rights so as not to fragment the voting process unneccessarily and thus allow one creditor to influence negotiations unduly or defeat the proposed plan.[6] Creditors often seek to be placed in separate classes based on the type of security or its legal or commercial attributes so that they can exercise effective veto and have enhanced bargaining power in the workout. The courts have been careful to approve classes in a manner that ensures similar interests and priorities are grouped, thus minimizing the potential for any one creditor to unfairly manipulate the process.

The debtor corporation's employees are often included in a single class with other unsecured creditors in the plan. In *Woodward's Ltd.*, the British Columbia Supreme Court refused to classify terminated employees as a separate class, including them with other unsecured creditors who were more supportive of the plan.[7] The definition of class can thus be used as a form of "cram down" of the plan on dissenting creditors

---

[4] *Anvil Range Mining Corp., Re* (2001), 25 C.B.R. (4th) 1 (Ont. S.C.J. [Commercial List]), affirmed (2002), 34 C.B.R. (4th) 157 (Ont. C.A.), additional reasons at (2002), 38 C.B.R. (4th) 5 (Ont. C.A.), leave to appeal refused (2003), 2003 CarswellOnt 730 (S.C.C.); *Philip Services Corp.* (1999), 1999 CarswellOnt 4673, [1999] O.J. No. 4232 (Ont. S.C.J. [Commercial List]).

[5] The *CCAA* segregates the creditors in two categories, namely secured and unsecured. It is clear from sections 4 and 5 of the *CCAA* that there could be more than one class in each of these categories.

[6] *Woodwards Ltd., Re* (1993), 84 B.C.L.R. (2d) 206 (B.C.S.C.); *Armbro Enterprises Inc., Re* (1993), 22 C.B.R. (3d) 80 (Ont. Bktcy.).

[7] *Woodwards Ltd., Re, ibid.*. Michael Fitch, "Store Wars: The Saga of Woodwards' Reorganization" in J. Ziegel and D. Baird, eds., *Case Studies in Recent Canadian Insolvency Reorganizations, In Honour of the Honourable Lloyd W. Houlden* (Toronto: Carswell, 1997) at 535.

within a class.[8] The fact that classes can be creatively constructed and that their designation requires court approval, results in a situation where the courts have endorsed plans that use the definition of classes of creditors to facilitate acceptance of a plan.

The courts generally have applied a "commonality of interest" test. If the court finds that a different state of facts exists among creditors, which may differently affect their minds and judgment, they are to be divided into different classes. A class should be made up of creditors whose rights are "not so dissimilar as to make it impossible for them to consult together with a view to their common interest".[9] In *Canadian Airlines*, the Alberta Court of Queen's Bench held that classes should be determined having regard for "legal interests", and that commonalty of interest is to be viewed purposively, bearing in mind the objective of the *CCAA* to facilitate restructuring plans.[10]

In addition to commonality of interest concerns, the Ontario Court of Appeal recently held that a court dealing with a classification of creditors issue needs to be alert to concerns about the confiscation of legal rights and about avoiding what the parties have referred to as "a tyranny of the minority". The classification of creditors is determined by their legal rights in relation to the debtor company, as opposed to their rights as creditors in relation to each other. The Court of Appeal expressly held that to the extent that other authorities at the trial level in other jurisdictions may suggest the contrary, the court disagreed. The Court held that to hold the classification and voting process hostage to the vagaries of a potentially infinite variety of disputes as between already disgruntled creditors who have been caught in the maelstrom of a *CCAA* restructuring, runs the risk of hobbling that process unduly. It could lead to the very type of fragmentation and multiplicity of discrete classes or sub-classes of classes that might well defeat the purpose of the *CCAA*. The Court of Appeal held that it is important to remember that classification of creditors, like most other things pertaining to the *CCAA*, must be crafted with the underlying purpose of the *CCAA* in mind, namely facilitation of the reorganization of an insolvent company through the negotiation and approval of a plan of compromise or arrangement between the debtor company and its creditors, so that the debtor company can continue to carry on its business to the benefit of all concerned.[11]

---

[8] Cram-down in this sense refers to creditors being placed in classes such that during the vote for the plan, the majority of the creditors in any given class is in favour of the plan, thus "forcing" the plan on the minority.

[9] *Norcen Energy Resources Ltd.* v. *Oakwood Petroleums Ltd.* (1988), 72 C.B.R. (N.S.) 20 (Alta. Q.B.); *NsC Diesel Power Inc., Re* (1990), 79 C.B.R. (N.S.) 1 (N.S. T.D.).

[10] *Canadian Airlines Corp., Re* (2000), 19 C.B.R. (4th) 12 (Alta. Q.B.), leave to appeal refused (2000), 19 C.B.R. (4th) 33 (Alta. C.A. [In Chambers]).

[11] *Stelco Inc., Re* (2005), 2005 CarswellOnt 6818 (Ont. C.A.), further additional reasons at (2006), 2006 CarswellOnt 5194 (Ont. C.A.).

1. Examples of Specific Classification Disputes

The debtor usually structures classes of creditors to enhance the possibility of successful endorsement of the plan. In *Canadian Airlines*, Air Canada purchased the claims of a number of unsecured creditors. Air Canada's claims were placed in a class with other unsecured creditors, thus enhancing prospects for that class to vote in favour of the plan in the required amounts specified by the statute. Unsecured noteholders and four minority shareholders opposed the decision to allow Air Canada to vote its assigned claims in the class with all unsecured creditors. The Court allowed Air Canada to vote the claims in advance of determination of the issue in order to expedite the process and ordered segregation of the votes until the classification issue was determined.

The Court in *Canadian Airlines* then decided the classification issue at the plan sanctioning hearing. The Court held that the determination of class was a fact driven one, and that it would apply the following principles: commonality of interest should be viewed on the basis of preventing excessive fragmentation and interests within a class need not be identical; interests are to be determined by the legal rights of the creditor in relation to the debtor, before and under the plan and in the event of liquidation; and commonality of interest should be given a purposive interpretation having regard to the restructuring objectives of the *CCAA*. Specifically, the court should resist classification approaches that potentially jeopardize viable plans. The Court concluded that Air Canada's votes could be counted in the unsecured class.[12] The case also illustrates the importance of approval of the plan by both number (head count) of creditors and the value of claims. Air Canada was only one creditor for the purpose of the head-count part of the statutory test, but the value of its claims was substantial.

In a case where the Federal Crown was a creditor in a proposed *CCAA* plan and also a co-defendant in a class action commenced by former residents of a First Nations residential school; and the plan provided that the plaintiffs in the class action and the Federal Crown be grouped in the same class, the Court held that there was no commonality of interest and that this attempt at classification was "a blatant effort to compromise" the Crown's claim as the single largest creditor without allowing the Crown an appropriate say in the vote.[13]

In *Minds Eye Entertainment Ltd.* v. *Royal Bank*, a creditor that claimed a common lien over tapes prepared with respect to the production of a television series was not entitled to be classified with the senior secured creditor banks on the basis that the

[12] *Canadian Airlines Corp., Re* (2000), 2000 CarswellAlta 662, [2000] A.J. No. 771 (Alta. Q.B.) at paras. 95, 103, leave to appeal refused (2000), 2000 CarswellAlta 919, [2000] A.J. No. 1028 (Alta. C.A. [In Chambers]), affirmed (2000), 2000 CarswellAlta 1556 (Alta. C.A.), leave to appeal refused (2001), 2001 CarswellAlta 888 (S.C.C.). The Court of Appeal in this case held that the judge had not erred in deferring the class issues to the fairness hearing. This outcome makes sense in the circumstances of Canadian Airlines and given the deference of appellate courts in *CCAA* proceedings.

[13] *Oblats de Marie Immaculée du Manitoba, Re* (2004), [2004] M.J. No. 112, 2004 CarswellMan 104, 182 Man. R. (2d) 201, 2004 MBQB 71 (Man. Q.B.).

property on which the lien was asserted was not that valuable, and it was not unfair or unreasonable to exclude the creditor from the senior secured creditor category.[14] In that case, members of a class of creditors that had provided essential labour services to the debtor were classified in one class as they belonged to the Writers Guild of Canada and the Court concluded that a creditor, by becoming a member of the Guild, had no independent status to object to a settlement negotiated by the Guild in the proceeding; the Guild bound all its members.

In *Steinberg Inc.*, the *CCAA* plan classified unsecured creditors into six sub-classes and one of those, comprising creditors with claims less than $1,000, was to be paid in full.[15] The Court held that sub-classification was not unreasonable or inequitable and that there was nothing improper in this arrangement. The Court held that it was unnecessary to obtain a majority vote of each sub-class, and that a majority vote of the entire class was sufficient.

In *Fairview Industries Ltd.*, the Court granted a separate class of preferred creditors for classified holders of statutory liens, which ranked lower than secured creditors but ahead of unsecured creditors.[16]

In *Uniforêt Inc.*, one class of creditors was composed of holders of U.S. notes, secured by a charge on the assets of the debtor.[17] The Court found that the plan, which proposed to pay each noteholder for the first US$25,000, the lesser of US$25,000 or the face amount of the notes held by the note holder, with the remaining balance, if any, to be exchanged for new notes, was acceptable. Hence, the claims were treated differently based on their monetary value, even if they were in the same class.

The court will also consider the timing of objections to definition of class. In *Armbro Enterprises*, when a landlord sought separate class status, the Court held that there was sufficient community of interest between the landlord and other unsecured creditors, and that a separate class would cause unnecessary fragmentation.[18] The Court also found that the landlord had adequate notice and had failed to raise the matter early in the process. To wait until the sanctioning hearing to object to the definition of class was too late, unless there was some sort of substantial injustice. Here the Court did not find such injustice existed. Thus where stakeholders are seeking decision rights through the definition of class, they will have to establish those interests early in the process.

---

[14] *Minds Eye Entertainment Ltd.* v. *Royal Bank* (2003), 2003 CarswellSask 921, 2003 SKQB 565, 1 C.B.R. (5th) 85, 246 Sask. R. 314 (Sask. Q.B.).

[15] *Steinberg Inc., Re* (1993), 23 C.B.R. (3d) 243 (Qué. S.C.).

[16] *Fairview Industries Ltd.* (1991), 11 C.B.R. (3d) 71 (N.S. T.D.).

[17] *Uniforêt Inc., Re* (2002), 40 C.B.R. (4th) 251 (Qué. S.C.), leave to appeal refused, (2002), 40 C.B.R. (4th) 281 (Qué. C.A.). The terms bond and debenture are often used interchangeably. They are a formal obligation of the company for money loaned or advanced to it.

[18] *Armbro Enterprises Inc., Re* (1993), 22 C.B.R. (3d) 80 (Ont. Bktcy.).

Landlords have been treated differently in terms of classification depending on the particular facts in a case. In contrast to *Armbro Enterprises,* in *Grafton-Fraser Inc.* v. *Canadian Imperial Bank of Commerce*, the Court held that it was proper to separate the landlords and the unsecured creditors into two classes because if the landlords were grouped with unsecured creditors, there would be greater difficulty in ascertaining the amounts of their claims, and because under the plan, the landlords were enjoined from exercising the contractual and statutory remedies that they would ordinarily enjoy when a tenant becomes insolvent.[19]

Grafton-Fraser Inc. v. *Canadian Imperial Bank of Commerce* was distinguished in *San Francisco Gifts Ltd.*, where San Francisco had obtained protection under the *CCAA*, had abandoned its leases with the landlords and took assets from the premises.[20] The landlords argued that they should be placed in a separate class because they had distinct legal rights, their claims were difficult to value and they were preferred over other creditors in the class. The Alberta Court of Queen's Bench held that the landlords' right to pursue distraint against the companies was unique but this was not sufficient to warrant a separate class. The landlords' claims were not difficult to value. The plan was amended to preserve any cause of action the landlords would have against any party who aided San Francisco in removing assets from their premises. Madam Justice Topolniski made the following observation regarding classification of landlords in separate classes:

> ¶ 11 The commonality of interest test has evolved over time and now involves application of the following guidelines that were neatly summarized by Paperny J. (as she then was) in *Resurgence Asset Management LLS* v. *Canadian Airlines Corp.* ("Canadian Airlines"):
>
> 1. Commonality of interest should be viewed based on the non-fragmentation test, not on an identity of interest test.
> 2. The interests to be considered are the legal interests that a creditor holds *qua* creditor in relationship to the debtor prior to and under the Plan as well as on liquidation.
> 3. The commonality of interests should be viewed purposively, bearing in mind the object of the *CCAA*, namely to facilitate reorganizations if possible.
> 4. In placing a broad and purposive interpretation on the *CCAA*, the Court should be careful to resist classification approaches that would potentially jeopardize viable Plans.
> 5. Absent bad faith, the motivations of creditors to approve or disapprove [of the Plan] are irrelevant.
> 6. The requirement of creditors being able to consult together means being able to assess their legal entitlement as creditors before or after the Plan in a similar manner.
>
> ¶ 12 To this pithy list, I would add the following considerations:

---

[19] *Grafton Fraser Inc.* v. *Canadian Imperial Bank of Commerce* (1992), 1992 CarswellOnt 164, [1992] O.J. No. 812 (Ont. Gen. Div.).

[20] *San Francisco Gifts Ltd., Re* (2004), 2004 CarswellAlta 1241, [2004] A.J. No. 1062 (Alta. Q.B.), leave to appeal refused (2004), 5 C.B.R. (5th) 300 (Alta. C.A.).

(i) Since the *CCAA* is to be given a liberal and flexible interpretation, classification hearings should be dealt with on a fact specific basis and the court should avoid rigid rules of general application.

In determining commonality of interests, the court should also consider factors like the plan's treatment of creditors, the business situation of the creditors, and the practical effect on them of a failure of the plan (notes omitted).

. . .

¶ 28 I find that the Plan does not adequately address the objecting landlords' unique legal entitlement to claim damages against persons who aided their tenant in clandestinely removing goods from the premises. In making this finding, I considered the following to be significant factors:

1. Unlike the ability to follow and seize goods, which has been rendered academic, this right of action is potentially meaningful.
2. The Plan does not offer compensation for deprivation of this right of action, resulting in a "confiscation" of the objecting landlords' right as described in Sovereign Life.
3. Unlike claims that would be extinguished on a bankruptcy of the companies, this right of action would survive since it is against third parties.

. . .

¶ 50 However, I find that the Plan does not adequately address their right to claim damages against persons who aided a tenant in clandestinely removing goods from the premises. Rather than create a separate voting class for the objecting landlords, I direct that the Plan be amended to preserve any cause of action the objecting landlords and others in their position might have against any party who aided San Francisco in clandestinely removing its assets from their premises.

III. ORDERING A VOTE AND CREDITOR APPROVAL

The process for creditors to vote on the proposed plan must be approved by the court. The court has the discretion not to order a meeting of creditors to consider a plan.

In exercising its discretion to order a vote, the court must consider whether the proposed plan of arrangement has a reasonable chance of success.[21] This threshold prevents unnecessary costs being expended in calling and conducting a vote where it is evident at the outset that there is not yet sufficient support by creditors to vote in favour of the plan.

---

[21] *Royal Bank of Canada* v. *Fracmaster Ltd.* (1999), 1999 CarswellAlta 539, [1999] A.J. No. 675 (Alta. C.A.).

Once the court orders a vote on a proposed plan, creditors are to vote by class in their consideration of whether to accept the plan. As noted earlier, a majority in number representing two thirds in value of claims in each class, present or represented at the meeting, must support the plan before the court will consider sanctioning the plan of compromise or arrangement.

Creditors cannot be bound by the *CCAA* plan if they were not given an opportunity to vote on it.[22] The court will also not consider a plan where it has not been considered and voted on by creditors.[23] Even if a creditor does not attend the meeting to vote on the plan, if the creditor received notice and the opportunity to vote, the creditor will be bound to the plan and will receive any benefits accruing to the class of creditors under which it was classified if the requisite approvals and court sanction occur.[24]

In considering whether to stay an order of the court pending an appeal, the Ontario Court of Appeal in *Stelco Inc.* held that the supervising judge has the ultimate power to approve or reject a *CCAA* restructuring plan, and that certain irreparable harm perceived by an applicant was potentially reparable within the restructuring process.[25]

IV. THE STATUS OF SHAREHOLDERS IN A *CCAA* PLAN

Technically, the issue of shareholders and their status is dealt with by the relevant corporations statute, not the *CCAA*; however, the status of shareholders can become an issue during the course of a *CCAA* proceeding. Often there is no equity remaining in the debtor corporation and hence shareholders have no claim on the assets. In such cases, a vote by shareholders is not required to approve a *CCAA* plan. During the stay period, the court can make a standstill order against the debtor company prohibiting the issuance of further shares.[26]

In *Boutiques San Francisco*, the Québec Superior Court held that creditors were the only parties with claims on the assets. Relying on the judgment in *Loewen Group Inc.*, which found that the shareholders do not have an economic interest remaining in an insolvent company and hence did not have the right to veto a proposed plan to sell all or substantially all of the assets, the Court in *San Francisco* held that a proposed sale did not require approval of shareholders, given their lack of interest

[22] *Menegon* v. *Philip Services Corp.* (1999), 11 C.B.R. (4th) 262 (Ont. S.C.J. [Commercial List]); *Doman Industries Ltd., Re* (2003), 41 C.B.R. (4th) 29, 14 B.C.L.R. (4th) 153 (B.C. S.C. [In Chambers]).

[23] *Cable Satisfaction International Inc.* v. *Richter & Associés inc.* (2004), 48 C.B.R. (4th) 205 (Qué. S.C.).

[24] *Lindsay* v. *Transtec Canada Ltd.* (1994), 28 C.B.R. (3d) 110 (B.C. S.C.), leave to appeal refused (1995), 31 C.B.R. (3d) 157 (B.C. C.A.).

[25] *Stelco Inc., Re* (2005), 2005 CarswellOnt 1336 (Ont. C.A. [In Chambers]).

[26] *Northland Properties Ltd., Re* (1988), 69 C.B.R. (N.S.) 266 (B.C. S.C.).

remaining in the corporation.[27] The Court authorized the purge of rights under the *Code de procédure civile du Québec*.[28]

In *Stelco Inc.*, the debtor corporation negotiated a plan and the arrangement acknowledged that the reorganization would in essence eliminate the existing shareholders based on the shares having no value.[29] The Court dismissed a motion of a group seeking adjournment of the plan sanctioning hearing for 60 days on the basis that the group had not presented credible evidence that existing equity had any value independent of the proposed arrangement, and that despite a comprehensive capital raising and asset sale process in a well canvassed market, no interested party had come forward to conclude a different deal.[30]

Where shareholders neither contribute funds required by the plan, nor participate in the arrangement or the reorganization, they have no standing to contest a proposal. In *Cable Satisfaction International Inc.* v. *Richter & Associés inc.*, the Québec Superior Court held that an amendment to the plan was made by the creditors and voted on at the creditors meeting pursuant to which the 2% participation of the shareholders contemplated in the original plan was eliminated. The Court concluded that the elimination of the shareholders' participation was not unfair as they were contributing nothing to the attempt to re-organize the company.[31]

In some cases, there is value in the tax losses of the debtor corporation such that shareholders can bargain some realization in the *CCAA* plan. This is possible only in some provinces, such as British Columbia and Québec. Under the *CBCA, OBCA* and corporations statutes of some other provinces, a "plan of reorganization" can restructure equity without a shareholder vote if the equity investment has no value.

A key component of the Canadian restructuring scheme is the integration of federal tax law facilitating restructuring. A workout can, under the *CCAA,* involve conversion of debt to equity through mechanisms such as issuing of distressed preferred shares, which qualify for special treatment for five years under the *Income Tax Act*.[32] Dividends received on the shares are tax deductible in computing taxable income, thus providing a lower cost means of financing a restructuring. It allows insolvent

---

[27] *Boutiques San Francisco Inc., Re* (2004), 2004 CarswellQue 10918, 7 C.B.R. (5th) 189 (Que. S.C.). See also *Loewen Group Inc. Loewen Group Inc., Re* (2002), 32 C.B.R. (4th) 54 (Ont. S.C.J. [Commercial List]); *Cable Satisfaction International Inc.* v. *Richter & Associés inc.* (2004), 48 C.B.R. (4th) 205 (Qué. S.C.).

[28] *Boutiques San Francisco Inc., ibid.*

[29] *Stelco Inc., Re* (2006), 17 C.B.R. (5th) 78 (Ont. S.C.J. [Commercial List]) (Sanction Hearing). As noted below, the Court held that creditors voted on and approved the arrangement in excess of the statutory two-thirds requirements and there was no creditor opposition to the proposed plan. The Court sanctioned the plan as fair, reasonable and equitable, finding that the debtor corporation had met all the requirements of the *CCAA*.

[30] *Ibid.*

[31] *Cable Satisfaction International Inc.* v. *Richter & Associés inc.* (2004), 2004 CarswellQue 810, 48 C.B.R. (4th) 205 (Que. S.C.).

[32] Sections 80, 112, 248, *Income Tax Act,* R.S.C. 1985, c. 1, as amended. D. M. Sherman, ed., *The Practitioners Income Tax Act*, 5th supplement (Toronto: Carswell, 2000).

firms to offer incentives to investors, including existing creditors, who might not otherwise be willing to provide additional financing. The court has held that the issuance of such shares facilitates restructuring of the debtor corporation by exchanging debt for equity and reducing financing costs.[33]

Another example of shareholder involvement is where the debtor undertakes a debt/equity restructuring without using DIP financing. Often a debt/equity restructuring is done when market conditions are poor. Creditors hope that they will recover losses if the equity value rises post-restructuring.

V. CONSOLIDATION OF PROCEEDINGS

The court will allow a consolidated plan of arrangement or compromise to be filed for two or more related companies in appropriate circumstances. For example, in *PSINet Ltd.,* the Court allowed consolidation of proceedings for four companies that were intertwined and essentially operated as one business.[34] The Court found that the filing of a consolidated plan avoided complex issues regarding the allocation of the proceeds realized from the sale of the assets, and that although consolidation by its nature would benefit some creditors and prejudice others, the prejudice had been ameliorated by concessions made by the parent corporation, which was also the major creditor.[35] Other cases of consolidated proceedings, such as *Philip Services, Canadian Airlines, Air Canada* and *Stelco*, all proceeded without issues in respect of consolidation.

Generally, the courts will determine whether to consolidate proceedings by assessing whether the benefits will outweigh the prejudice to particular creditors if the proceedings are consolidated. In particular, the court will examine whether the assets and liabilities are so intertwined that it is difficult to separate them for purposes of dealing with different entities. The court will also consider whether consolidation is fair and reasonable in the circumstances of the case.

VI. INCOME TRUSTS AND INSOLVENCY

The rapid growth of income trusts in Canada has raised the question of how such trusts are to be dealt with in insolvency.[36] There are a myriad number of ways to structure a business income trust, but in its most simple form, a trust fund sells trust

---

[33] *Pioneer Distributions Ltd.* v. *Bank of Montreal*, [1995] 1 W.W.R. 48 (B.C. S.C.) at paras. 17-20.

[34] *PSINet Ltd., Re* (2002), 33 C.B.R. (4th) 284 (Ont. S.C.J. [Commercial List]). The Court observed that the record keeping of the companies was deficient.

[35] See M. Rotsztain and N. De Cicco, "Substantive Consolidation in *CCAA* Restructurings: A Critical Analysis", in *Annual Review of Insolvency Law, 2004* (Toronto: Carswell, 2005) at 331-354.

[36] For a discussion of these issues, see Susan M. Grundy and Linc A. Rogers, "When the Cash Doesn't Flow: Dealing with Income Trusts in Financial Difficulty", in *Annual Review of Insolvency Law, 2004* (Toronto: Carswell, 2005) at 29-58.

units to the public and the funds raised are invested in an entity that carries on the business operations. This underlying operating entity is usually a corporation or a limited partnership. The unitholders are the beneficiaries of the trust and the trustees hold the equity interests in the operating entity. Business income trusts are used to flow cash from an operating business into the hands of investors through this structure.[37] To date, however, there has been little experience with business income trusts and insolvency, including how they interact with their operating entities.

The proposed amendments to the *CCAA* under Chapter 47 would expressly include income trusts under the definition of company for the purposes of the *CCAA*, codifying the ability of income trusts to utilize the *CCAA* to restructure.[38] Under the proposed language, income trust: "means a trust (a) that has assets in Canada, and (b) the units of which are traded on a prescribed stock exchange".[39] For purposes of stays or compromises of claims against directors, the definition of director under the *CCAA* will be amended to include the trustees of an income trust.[40]

VII. COURT APPROVAL OF THE PLAN

1. Statutory Requirements

The court has discretion to approve a plan of compromise or arrangement once creditors have voted in favour of the plan in the requisite amounts. The court holds a sanctioning hearing at which it will examine three criteria: whether there has been strict compliance with all the statutory requirements; whether all materials filed and procedures carried out were authorized by the *CCAA*; and whether the plan is fair and reasonable.[41]

---

[37] Common uses for a business trust include real estate investment funds and oil and gas funds. There are considerable tax savings to the use of this structure. Business income trusts had become so popular in Canada that in 2002, 86 per cent of initial public offerings were income trusts, although recent announcements regarding potential changes to the way they are taxed has considerably slowed down their growth. Michele Robitaille & Mike Hoehn, "Business Income Trusts Evolving into a Core Asset Class", National Bank Financial: Equity Research (March 6, 2003) at 1.

[38] Section 2, *CCAA*, as modified by Chapter 47.

[39] *Ibid.* The Government has announced that it will amend further the definition of income trust to clarify that it includes trusts that are listed (not just traded) on a prescribed stock exchange or where "the majority of its units are held by a trust whose units are listed on a prescribed stock exchange on the day on which proceedings commence"; *Notice of Ways and Means Motion to introduce an Act to amend the Bankruptcy and Insolvency Act, the Companies' Creditors Arrangement Act, the Wage Earners Protection Act and Chapter 47 of the Statutes of Canada, 2005*, (December 8, 2006, Library of Parliament).

[40] *Ibid.*

[41] *Quintette Coal Ltd., Re* (1992), 13 C.B.R. (3d) 146 (B.C. S.C.); *Dairy Corp. of Canada*, [1934] O.R. 436 (Ont. C.A.); *Olympia & York Developments Ltd.* v. *Royal Trust Co.* (1993), 17 C.B.R. (3d) 1 (Ont. Gen. Div.); *Northland Properties Ltd., Re* (1988), 73 C.B.R. (N.S.) 175 (B.C. S.C.) at 182, affirmed (1989), 73 C.B.R. (N.S.) 195 (B.C. C.A.); *BlueStar Battery Systems International Corp., Re* (2000), 2000 CarswellOnt 4837, 25 C.B.R. (4th) 216 (Ont. S.C.J. [Commercial List]).

In terms of the statutory requirements, the debtor corporation must have proven that it is insolvent within the meaning of the legislation. The court will also assess the appropriateness of the classes; and confirm that the meetings were held and votes conducted in compliance with the statutory scheme and that the plan was approved by the requisite double majority.[42]

Although it is usually the debtor corporation that seeks approval of the plan before the court, creditors can seek approval.[43] Where an interim receiver has been appointed in the context of a *CCAA* proceeding, the interim receiver can also apply for an order sanctioning the plan.[44] Once the court sanctions a plan, it becomes binding on the debtor company and on its creditors.

The court has the discretion to adjourn an application to sanction a plan, but will not do so to allow for further negotiation where the creditor seeking the adjournment did not propose any amendments at the creditors' meeting to vote on the proposed plan, the creditor was not affected by the plan and the adjournment request was made only shortly before the sanctioning hearing.[45]

2. The Fairness Inquiry

The court will review the plan to determine whether it is fair, reasonable and equitable.[46] In assessing the fairness and reasonableness of a plan, the court has held that "'fairness' is the quintessential expression of the court's equitable jurisdiction – although the jurisdiction is statutory, the broad discretionary powers given to the judiciary by the legislation makes its exercise an exercise in equity – and 'reasonableness' is what lends objectivity to the process".[47] Fairness is assessed by whether the plan is feasible, whether it fairly balances the interests of all the creditors, the company and its stakeholders. The court has held that it must weigh the equities or balance the relative degrees of prejudice that might flow from granting or refusing the relief sought under the *CCAA*.[48]

---

[42] *Canadian Airlines Corp., Re* (2000), 20 C.B.R. (4th) 1 (Alta. Q.B.), leave to appeal refused (2000), 2000 CarswellAlta 919 (Alta. C.A. [In Chambers]), affirmed (2000), 2000 CarswellAlta 1556 (Alta. C.A.), leave to appeal refused (2001), 2001 CarswellAlta 888 (S.C.C.).

[43] For an example of where creditors brought the application for approval and the court sanctioned the plan, see *Paris Fur Co.* v. *Nu-West Fur Corp.* (1950), 30 C.B.R. 193 (Qué. S.C.), leave to appeal refused (1950), 30 C.B.R. 197 (Qué. C.A.), where a plan was guaranteed in part by an officer of the debtor and accepted by the requisite number of creditors. When the debtor subsequently declined to bring the plan to the court for sanctioning, creditors made an application to sanction the plan so that the guarantees were not lost and received approval of the court for the plan.

[44] *Anvil Range Mining Corp., Re* (2001), 21 C.B.R. (4th) 194 (Ont. S.C.J. [Commercial List]).

[45] *GT Group Telecom Inc., Re* (2002), 38 C.B.R. (4th) 203 (Ont. S.C.J. [Commercial List]).

[46] *Air Canada, Re* (2004), 2004 CarswellOnt 1842, 2 C.B.R. (5th) 4 (Ont. S.C.J. [Commercial List]).

[47] *Olympia & York Developments Ltd.* v. *Royal Trust Co.* (1993), 17 C.B.R. (3d) 1 (Ont. Gen. Div.) at 1.

[48] *Algoma Steel Corp.* v. *Royal Bank* (1992), 11 C.B.R. (3d) 1 (Ont. Gen. Div.); *Northland Properties Ltd., Re* (1988), 73 C.B.R. (N.S.) 175 (B.C. S.C.) at 201, affirmed (1989), 73 C.B.R. (N.S.) 195 (B.C. C.A.); *Campeau Corp., Re* (1992), 10 C.B.R. (3d) 104 (Ont. Gen. Div.); *Quintette Coal Ltd.* v. *Nippon*

In *Canadian Airlines*, the Alberta Court of Queen's Bench held that its role in the sanctioning hearing is to consider whether the plan fairly balances the interests of all stakeholders; to look forward and determine whether the plan represents a fair and reasonable compromise that will permit a viable commercial entity to emerge.[49] The court will also consider factors such as whether the proposed plan brings more value to creditors than a bankruptcy or liquidation alternative, whether there has been any oppressive conduct towards creditors, whether there is retention of jobs and support by the debtor's unions, and the public interest in a successful workout strategy.[50] One measure of whether a plan is fair and reasonable is the parties' degree of approval of the plan. The court has held that parties generally know what is in their best interests, and in engaging in the fairness inquiry, the court will be reluctant to refuse to sanction a plan where creditors have strongly supported the plan.

Thus, fairness and reasonableness are assessed in the context of a proposed plan's impact on creditors, having regard to the purpose of the statutory scheme. Courts will look at all categories of interest holders in assessing if compromises are fair and reasonable in the circumstances.[51] The plan must be inherently fair, reasonable and equitable and in exercising its discretion to approve an agreement, the court will consider the relationship between the debtor corporation and stakeholders.[52] The courts have held that reference should be made to the substance, not the form, of a plan and that there is nothing in the *CCAA* that prohibits a creditor from agreeing to subordinate its claim to another creditor; hence the Court in *Air Canada* approved a plan that included an agreement among some of the insolvent company's creditors to subordinate their debts to the debts of other creditors.[53]

A plan that preserves the business but under new ownership may also meet the objectives of the *CCAA*.[54] In the concurrent Canada-U.S. court approval of *PSINet* asset sale, the Court held that the sale generated the highest enterprise value, was in the best interests of creditors, preserved 200 jobs and prevented service disruption to corporate accounts.[55]

In *Stelco Inc.*, the Court held that all creditors had voted on and approved the arrangement in excess of the statutory two-thirds requirements and there was no

---

Steel Corp. (1990), 51 B.C.L.R. (2d) 105 (B.C. C.A.) at 116, leave to appeal refused (1991), 55 B.C.L.R. (2d) xxxiii (note) (S.C.C.).

[49] *Canadian Airlines Corp., Re* (2000), 20 C.B.R. (4th) 1 (Alta. Q.B.), leave to appeal refused (2000), 2000 CarswellAlta 919, [2000] A.J. No. 1028 (Alta. C.A. [In Chambers]), affirmed (2000), 2000 CarswellAlta 1556 (Alta. C.A.), leave to appeal refused (2001), 2001 CarswellAlta 888 (S.C.C.).

[50] *Canadian Airlines Corp., Re* (2000), 20 C.B.R. (4th) 1 (Alta. Q.B.), leave to appeal refused (2000), 2000 CarswellAlta 919 (Alta. C.A. [In Chambers]), affirmed (2000), 2000 CarswellAlta 1556 (Alta. C.A.), leave to appeal refused (2001), 2001 CarswellAlta 888 (S.C.C.).

[51] *Campeau Corp., Re* (1992), 10 C.B.R. (3d) 104 (Ont. Gen. Div.); *Algoma Steel Corp.* v. *Royal Bank* (1992), [1992] O.J. No. 795, 1992 CarswellOnt 2843 (Ont. Gen. Div.).

[52] *Air Canada, Re* (2003), 2003 CarswellOnt 5296, 47 C.B.R. (4th) 163 (Ont. S.C.J. [Commercial List]) (Canada-Germany Co-operation Agreement).

[53] *Air Canada, Re* (2004), 2004 CarswellOnt 1842, 2 C.B.R. (5th) 4 (Ont. S.C.J. [Commercial List]).

[54] *Consumers Packaging Inc., Re* (2001), 27 C.B.R. (4th) 197 (Ont. C.A.).

[55] *PSINet Ltd., Re* (2002), 33 C.B.R. (4th) 284 (Ont. S.C.J. [Commercial List]).

creditor opposition to the proposed plan; the Court sanctioned the plan as fair, reasonable and equitable, finding that the debtor corporation had met all the requirements of the *CCAA*.[56]

3. Objections to the Proposed Plan

A plan must be approved by each class of creditors that will be affected by the plan. However, a *CCAA* plan can be tailored so that it only applies to some classes of creditors. In *Olympia & York Developments*, the Court held that approval of a plan by all classes of creditors is not always necessary, where the plan is found to be fair and reasonable and the plan specifies that the claims of creditors who rejected the plan were not bound by its provisions and hence none of their rights taken away.[57] Only 27 of 35 classes of creditors had voted in favour of the plan; however, the Court approved the plan because it met the statutory requirements, was fair and reasonable and did not bind the classes that had voted against the plan.

Timing of opposition to a plan can be significant in the court's consideration. Where a creditor objected to a plan on the basis that it was neither fair nor reasonable, the Court considered that the same creditor had taken no objection to the application by the debtor companies to submit a consolidated plan to creditors, observing that at the time the debtors sought the consolidation, the creditor was aware that the consolidated plan would deprive it of the right to seek to recover on its guarantees, and neither objected to nor appealed the consolidation. As a result, the Court sanctioned the plan.[58]

Where a plan has been accepted by creditors, the party seeking to have the court refuse the proposed plan must establish that it is unethical or that there are "serious grounds" for refusing to sanction it.[59]

Where objections to a plan were based on corporate governance concerns, the Court observed that the directors of the insolvent corporation owe duties to the corporation, and not to the nominator of the director, and concluded there was no evidence that the directors failed to exercise their fiduciary duties.[60]

---

[56] *Stelco Inc., Re* (2006), 17 C.B.R. (5th) 78 (Ont. S.C.J. [Commercial List]) (Sanction Hearing).

[57] *Olympia & York Developments Ltd.* v. *Royal Trust Co.* (1993), 17 C.B.R. (3d) 1 (Ont. Gen. Div.) at 1, 11; see also *Multidev Immobilia Inc.* v. *S.A. Just Invest,* (1988), 70 C.B.R. (N.S.) 91, [1988] R.J.Q. 1928 (Que. S.C.). In *Philip Services*, the Court held that the debtor could amend its plan to only apply to secured creditors when there was no value in the business for unsecured creditors and the alternative was rejection of the plan; *Philip Services Corp.* (1999), 1999 CarswellOnt 4673, [1999] O.J. No. 4232 (Ont. S.C.J. [Commercial List]).

[58] *Global Light Telecommunications Inc., Re* (2004), 2004 CarswellBC 1249, 2 C.B.R. (5th) 210, 2004 BCSC 745 (B.C. S.C.).

[59] *École Internationale de Haute Esthétique Edith Serei Inc. (Receiver of)* c. *Edith Serei Internationale (1987) Inc.* (1989), 78 C.B.R. (N.S.) 36 (Que. S.C.) at 38.

[60] *Air Canada, Re* (2004), 47 C.B.R. (4th) 169, 2004 CarswellOnt 469 (Ont. S.C.J. [Commercial List]) (Approval of Global Restructuring Agreement).

Where a proposed plan under the *CCAA* was not, in the opinion of the court, workable or practical and secured creditors were not prepared to accept it, the Court refused to permit the plan to be filed and lifted the stay in order to permit the secured creditors to appoint a receiver to realize on the assets.[61] Similarly, the courts have found that where it is obvious that a *CCAA* plan cannot succeed, the court may rescind the stay so that a petition in bankruptcy can be filed and a trustee in bankruptcy administer the estate.[62]

In considering objections to the plan in *Red Cross*, the Ontario Superior Court observed that many of the transfusion claimants had died and thousands were suffering, and that nothing the court could do would remedy these harms. Measured against this background, the Court noted that the *CCAA* regime must seem inadequate to many, but the process provided a mechanism "whereby some order, some closure and some measure of compensatory relief" was given, while at the same time offering to Red Cross the possibility of continuing to supply humanitarian services.[63] In approving the plan, the Court held that it was fair to all affected by it, and reasonable in the circumstances. The Court should approve a plan if it is "inherently fair, inherently reasonable and inherently equitable" and here, the plan "balanced the various competing interests in an equitable fashion".[64] The Court considered three letters opposing the plan in the context of the thousands of claimants voting in favour. While it had read the poignant letters carefully, the Court found that the huge majority of transfusion claimants had supported the plan as the best possible outcome for them in the circumstances. Although the transfusion claimants were not the type of business creditors normally affected by a *CCAA* plan, the Court held that they were the ones most touched by the events leading up to the proceedings, and that their voting support of the plan should be accorded equal if not more deference as that normally granted to creditors by the court. The high level of support, the fact that they were advised by representative counsel, and the changes made as a result of negotiations among all interested parties were all factors for the court. The Court acknowledged that the bitterness of the claimants was understandable given the harms they had experienced, but that in the balancing, the continuation of Red Cross' non-blood related activities was important.[65]

The *Red Cross CCAA* plan was dependent on approval of the settlement by the courts seized with the tort class actions that were proceeding against Red Cross, the federal and provincial governments and others in Ontario, Québec and British Columbia, because it resolved those claims against Red Cross and other defendants. The Ontario Court initially denied the motion to approve the settlement. It held that there was insufficient evidence of the contribution of pharmaceutical companies,

---

[61] *Fracmaster Ltd., Re* (1999), 11 C.B.R. (4th) 204 (Alta. Q.B.), affirmed *Royal Bank* v. *Fracmaster Ltd.* (1999), 11 C.B.R. (4th) 230, 1999 ABCA 178 (Alta. C.A.).

[62] *United Maritime Fishermen Co-op., Re* (1988), 68 C.B.R. (N.S.) 170, reversed on other grounds (1988), 69 C.B.R. (N.S.) 161 (C.A.).

[63] *Canadian Red Cross Society / Société Canadienne de la Croix Rouge, Re* (2000), 2000 CarswellOnt 3269, [2000] O.J. No. 3421 (Ont. S.C.J.) at para. 6.

[64] *Ibid.* at para. 20.

[65] *Ibid.* at para. 28.

doctors, hospitals and insurers named as defendants, in order for the court to assess whether releases should be granted. The Court held that this information was also necessary so that class members could determine whether or not to exercise their right to opt out of the class proceedings. The Court also concluded that the proposal paid nothing to the "derivative claimants", the family members and relatives of infected persons, and was aimed at extinguishing their rights if they failed to opt out.[66] The Ontario Court subsequently approved the settlement when the requisite evidence was led and the settlement was adjusted to allow for compensation for the derivative claimants, as did the British Columbia and Québec courts.[67]

4. Deference to Business Judgment at the Plan Sanctioning Hearing

The court has held that its function is not to examine the details of the business plan in all its minutiae, nor will it second guess or substitute its own judgment for the business judgments of creditors involved in negotiating the plan in their own best interests.[68] Rather, the court's role is to satisfy itself that the plan is feasible and that it fairly balances the interests of the company, its creditors and its shareholders. Part of that assessment is to examine the sophistication of the creditors and whether they received experienced legal advice. At the point of the sanctioning hearing, the creditors have already expressed their support for the plan in the requisite statutory amounts and thus are representing to the court that in their business judgment the plan should be approved. However, where parties disagree as to what that business judgment is, or believe that there has been unreasonableness or unfairness in the process, the court will consider the evidence and submissions of the parties and engage in a balancing of prejudices.[69]

---

[66] *McCarthy* v. *Canadian Red Cross Society* (2001), 2001 CarswellOnt 509, [2001] O.J. No. 567 (Ont. S.C.J.), additional reasons at (2001), 2001 CarswellOnt 2255 (Ont. S.C.J.).

[67] *Killough* v. *Canadian Red Cross Society* (2001), 2001 CarswellBC 1527, [2001] B.C.J. No. 1481 (B.C. S.C.) at para. 20; *McCarthy* v. *Canadian Red Cross Society* (2001), 2001 CarswellOnt 509, [2001] O.J. No. 567 (Ont. S.C.J.) at paras. 15-17, additional reasons at (2001), 2001 CarswellOnt 2255 (Ont. S.C.J.). The Court held that the reasonableness inquiry under a *CCAA* plan differs from that under a class proceeding settlement. The former requires a balancing of interests with a view to carrying on business with the least harm to creditors, employees and the community. For class proceedings, the court must be satisfied that the proposed settlement is fair, reasonable and in the best interests of those affected by it, and in that exercise, the court must be concerned with the interests of the class as a whole rather than individual members. The court will consider the risks and costs of trial, the likelihood of recovery in the action, the amount of discovery evidence, the terms of the settlement, the experience and recommendation of counsel, any independent assessment of the settlement, the cost and likely duration of trial, and the presence of good faith and absence of collusion. The Court determined that the settlement was fair, reasonable and in the best interests of the class as a whole. See also *Surprenant* c. *Société canadienne de la Croix-Rouge* (10 juillet 2001), no C.S. Montréal 500-06-000120-002, EYB 2001-26790, [2001] J. Q. No. 3717 (Que. S.C.).

[68] *Olympia & York Developments Ltd.* v. *Royal Trust Co.* (1993), 17 C.B.R. (3d) 1 (Ont. Gen. Div.), at 1; *Northland Properties Ltd., Re* (1988), 73 C.B.R. (N.S.) 175 (B.C. S.C.) at 205, affirmed (1989), 73 C.B.R. (N.S.) 195 (B.C. C.A.).

[69] *Ibid.*

Mr. Justice Forsyth of the Alberta Court has observed that the true test of judicial discretion is that it is exercised to ensure a level playing field for discussion and allowing all constituents an equal opportunity to put forward their position, while recognizing at all times that ultimately the success or failure should be based on a business judgment, rather than a judicial decision under the guise of judicial discretion.[70]

5. Modification or Interpretation of an Approved Plan

Section 6 of the *CCAA* allows creditors to alter or modify the plan of compromise or arrangement at the meeting of creditors to vote on a proposed plan. Such alterations can be made anytime up to the voting on a plan.[71] If a plan is altered at the meeting of creditors, there is no obligation by the debtor to distribute the amended plan to creditors.[72]

Where an alteration or modification of the plan is proposed after the court has directed the meeting, the court has the discretion to adjourn the meeting or convene a further meeting.[73] Where the proposed change is made after a meeting at which creditors have voted on a plan, the court also has the discretion not to direct a further meeting of any class of creditors or shareholders that in the opinion of the court is not adversely affected by the alteration or modification and the court can proceed to sanction the plan.[74] However, the courts have held that any changes to the plan when making a sanctioning order should be limited to technical as opposed to substantive changes.[75]

If substantive changes are required, creditors should be allowed to vote on the altered or modified plan. In one case, this alteration was the specific dates that payments were to be made, which the debtor was unable to meet because of an appeal.[76] In *Ball Machinery Sales Ltd.*, the Court held that amendments could be made to a plan after it has received creditor approval if the court has determined that the changes would not be materially prejudicial to the interests of creditors.[77] In that case, the Court amended provisions of the plan dealing with the release of claims against directors, officers and employees.

In *Telesystem International Wireless Inc.,* where proposed amendments to a *CCAA* plan were of a technical nature and did not alter the substance of stakeholder rights,

---

[70] Mr. Justice G.R. Forsyth, "Judicial Discretion under the *CCAA*" in *Corporate Restructurings and Insolvencies*, Queen's Annual Business Law Symposium, 1995 (Scarborough: Carswell, 1995) at 88.

[71] *Keddy Motor Inns Ltd., Re* (1992), 13 C.B.R. (3d) 245, 110 N.S.R. (2d) 246 (N.S. C.A.).

[72] *Cardlink Worldwide Inc., Re* (2001), 31 C.B.R. (4th) 206 (B.C. S.C. [In Chambers]).

[73] Section 7, *CCAA*.

[74] Section 7, *CCAA*. See *Quintette Coal Ltd., Re* (1991), 10 C.B.R. (3d) 197, 62 B.C.L.R. (2d) 218 (B.C. S.C.).

[75] *Wandlyn Inns Ltd., Re* (1992), 15 C.B.R. (3d) 316 (N.B. Q.B.).

[76] *Keddy Motor Inns Ltd., Re* (1992), 13 C.B.R. (3d) 262, 113 N.S.R. (2d) 431 (N.S. T.D. [In Chambers]).

[77] *Ball Machinery Sales Ltd., Re* (2002), 37 C.B.R. (4th) 39 (Ont. S.C.J.).

the claims process under the plan had been completed, and where the granting of further powers and duties to the monitor was in accordance with the plan, the Court ordered that all powers of directors and shareholders were to vest in the monitor and that the monitor was to take any and all appropriate measures in order to continue the liquidation of debtor and ultimately proceed with its dissolution, in accordance with the amended plan.[78]

The court will not amend a plan after the sanction hearing unless there are exceptional circumstances.[79] The court will be reluctant to imply terms into a plan of arrangement that would alter contractual relations.

The Alberta Court of Queen's Bench held that a plan of compromise or arrangement would not be interpreted to include an implied term that allowed a claimant to apply to a court to extend a drop dead date that applied under the plan to an action that had been commenced by the claimant against the debtor company, in order to permit the continued prosecution of such action, where there were no persuasive reasons or exceptional circumstances to imply such a term. The agreements in question were negotiated by sophisticated parties and the claimant voted in favour of the plan.[80] The fact that another party had been expressly given the right to apply for an extension suggested that the parties turned their minds to the issue of whether to include a broader extension provision and rejected such an approach. In such circumstances, the court will decline to exercise its inherent jurisdiction or its statutory jurisdiction under the *CCAA* to amend the plan.[81]

6. Sealing Orders and Public Policy

Generally, court records are open to the public as a means of ensuring confidence in the justice system. However, in the context of a *CCAA* proceeding, the courts have been asked to seal particular financial information or commercial agreements that may be sensitive, so that competitors of the debtor as prospective bidders for its assets cannot gain unfair advantage. These sealing orders can be temporary or permanent.

Outside of the insolvency context, the Supreme Court of Canada has given direction on when a sealing order is appropriate in court proceedings. In *Sierra Club of Canada*, the Supreme Court held that the discretion to grant a confidentiality order must be exercised in accordance with *Charter* principles because a confidentiality order will have a negative effect on the section 2(b) right to freedom of expression and openness of the court process.[82] A confidentiality (sealing) order should only

---

[78] *Telesystem International Wireless Inc., Re* (2005), 2005 CarswellQue 10684 (Que. S.C.).

[79] *Algoma Steel Corp.* v. *Royal Bank* (1992), 11 C.B.R. (3d) 11, 8 O.R. (3d) 449, 55 O.A.C. 303 (Ont. C.A.), leave to appeal refused (1992), 10 O.R. (3d) xv (note) (S.C.C.).

[80] *Teragol Investments Ltd.* v. *Hurricane Hydrocarbons Ltd.* (2005), 2005 CarswellAlta 587 (Alta. Q.B.).

[81] *Ibid.*

[82] *Sierra Club of Canada* v. *Canada (Minister of Finance)* (2002), 2002 CarswellNat 822, [2002] S.C.J. No. 42 (S.C.C.) at paras. 36-52.

be granted when (1) such an order is necessary to prevent a serious risk to an important interest, including a commercial interest, in the context of litigation because reasonably alternative measures will not prevent the risk; and (2) the salutary effects of the confidentiality order, including the effects on the right of civil litigants to a fair trial, outweigh its deleterious effects, including the effects on the right to free expression, which includes the public interest in open and accessible court proceedings. Three important elements are subsumed under the first branch of the test. First, the risk must be real and substantial, well grounded in evidence, posing a serious threat to the commercial interest in question. Second, the important commercial interest must be one that can be expressed in terms of a public interest in confidentiality, where there is a general principle at stake. Finally, the judge must consider not only whether reasonable alternatives are available to such an order, but also to restrict the order as much as is reasonably possible while preserving the commercial interest in question.[83] Hence, the courts are generally reluctant to make sealing orders, except in limited circumstances.

In the context of a *CCAA* proceeding, the debtor corporation in *Stelco Inc.*, brought a motion for a permanent sealing order regarding confidential information, and the order was granted, subject to any interested party asking for review, on notice to the debtor. The Ontario Superior Court of Justice held that there had been minimal redaction of the financial material; that there was minimal negative effect to the concept of an open court; that reasonable alternative measures would not have prevented the risk to the debtor corporation; and that the salutary effects of a confidentiality order as to the elements redacted outweighed any deleterious effects.[84]

In another request for a sealing order in *Stelco Inc.*, the Court dismissed a motion for a sealing order on the affidavit of a financial analyst sworn on behalf of certain equity holders.[85] The Court held that sealing orders cannot be granted merely because parties involved agree to have the material sealed or withdrawn, and that the applicant had presented no evidence that having the blacked-out material available to the public would cause any harm to it or to anyone privy to it. While the court would consider exclusion where the material is truly irrelevant, in making such a determination, the court should take an expansive view of relevance in order to safeguard the principle of ensuring that the interests of justice and public awareness and scrutiny be maintained by having an open court system.[86]

---

[83] *Ibid.*

[84] *Stelco Inc., Re* (2006), 17 C.B.R. (5th) 76 (Ont. S.C.J.) (Sealing Order for Confidential Information).

[85] *Stelco Inc., Re* (2006), 17 C.B.R. (5th) 95 (Ont. S.C.J.) (Sealing Order – re Taylor affidavit).

[86] *Ibid.*

7. Appeal of Plan Sanctioning Orders

In reviewing *CCAA* sanctioning orders, the appellate courts have held that leave will be granted sparingly, that the court must be satisfied that there are serious and arguable grounds that are of real and significant interest to the parties.[87]

In *Country Style Food Services,* where retail franchisees became aware of differential treatment after a plan was approved, the Ontario Court of Appeal declined to grant leave because the information was disclosed on the website and in proxy circulars to creditors.[88] While the franchisees were not on the notice list, the monitor had sent notice of the website to the franchisees and they could have discovered this information with due diligence. The Court observed that where a franchisor seeks *CCAA* protection, even though the statute contemplates notice only to creditors, it may be appropriate to give franchisees notice and the opportunity to request participation rights.

8. Powers of the Court after Sanctioning a Plan

While for the most part, the role of the court is completed on sanctioning of a plan of arrangement, there can be issues arising out of implementation of the plan that require direction or advice of the court. If parties encounter problems with interpreting the requirements of the plan, they can seek direction of the court that approved the plan.[89]

The court has interpreted the plan after it has been sanctioned, where a provision of the plan is unclear. For example, in *Red Cross*, an issue arose after the plan was sanctioned in respect of the appropriate law governing limitation periods. The Court held that in making such a determination, the court should apply fairness and reasonableness considerations with the aim of minimizing prejudice to creditors; however, since the sanctioned plan is also in the nature of a contract, the principles governing the interpretation of contracts must also apply.[90] The court may decline to determine a question where it does not involve the interpretation or administration of the sanctioned plan.[91]

In *Algoma Steel*, the Court allowed a creditor with a potential claim against the debtor corporation's insurers to bring proceedings against the debtor, notwithstanding a provision in the *CCAA* plan that specified that all claims of creditors were to

[87] *Blue Range Resource Corp., Re* (1999), 12 C.B.R. (4th) 186 (Alta. C.A.); *Cineplex Odeon Corp.* (2001), 24 C.B.R. (4th) 201 (Ont. C.A.); *Consumers Packaging Inc., Re* (2001), 27 C.B.R. (4th) 197 (Ont. C.A.).

[88] *Country Style Food Services Inc., Re* (2002), [2002] O.J. No. 1377, 2002 CarswellOnt 1038 (Ont. C.A. [In Chambers]).

[89] *Horizon Village Corp., Canada, Re* (1991), 8 C.B.R. (3d) 25 (Alta. Q.B.).

[90] *Canadian Red Cross Society / Société Canadienne de la Croix-Rouge, Re* (2002), 35 C.B.R. (4th) 43 (Ont. S.C.J.).

[91] *United Properties Ltd.* v. *642433 B.C. Ltd.* (2003), 43 C.B.R. (4th) 144 (B.C. C.A.).

be discharged and cancelled.[92] The Court held that the claim against the debtor was to be limited to the amount of proceeds of the insurance.

If a *CCAA* plan is sanctioned by the court and the debtor subsequently does not comply with the terms of the plan, the existence of the plan does not serve as a bar to creditors filing a petition in bankruptcy or the making of a receivership order.[93]

9. Example of a *CCAA* Ratification Order

Appendix 8 of this text is an example of a judgment sanctioning a *CCAA* plan, which also includes the entire plan of arrangement and compromise in the judgment.[94] The Québec Superior Court in *Uniforêt* dealt with objections to the plan, its contents and whether it met the statutory tests for approval of a proposed plan.

VIII. CONVERSION TO AND FROM *BIA* PROPOSAL PROCEEDINGS

The *CCAA* and *BIA* allow a proceeding to be converted from one statute to the other under certain conditions.

Section 11.6 of the *CCAA* specifies:

> 11.6 Notwithstanding the *Bankruptcy and Insolvency Act,*
>
> (a) proceedings commenced under Part III of the *Bankruptcy and Insolvency Act* may be taken up and continued under this Act only if a proposal within the meaning of the Bankruptcy and Insolvency Act has not been filed under that Part; and
>
> (b) an application under this Act by a bankrupt may only be made with the consent of inspectors referred to in section 116 of the Bankruptcy and Insolvency Act but no application may be made under this Act by a bankrupt whose bankruptcy has resulted from
>
> (i) the operation of subsection 50.4(8) of the *Bankruptcy and Insolvency Act,* or
>
> (ii) the refusal or deemed refusal by the creditors or the court, or the
>
> (iii) annulment, of a proposal under the Bankruptcy and Insolvency Act.

Conversely, section 66(2) of the *BIA* specifies:

---

[92] *Algoma Steel Corp.* v. *Royal Bank* (1992), 11 C.B.R. (3d) 11 (Ont. C.A.), leave to appeal refused (1992), 10 O.R. (3d) xv (note) (S.C.C.).

[93] *D.W. MacIntosh Ltd., Re* (1939), 21 C.B.R. 206 (Ont. Bktcy.).

[94] *Uniforêt inc., Re* (2003), 2003 CarswellQue 3404, [2003] Q.J. No. 9328 (Qué. S.C.), affirmed (2003), 2003 CarswellQue 1843, 44 C.B.R. (4th) 158 (Que. C.A.), leave to appeal refused (2004), 2004 CarswellQue 237 (S.C.C.).

66(2) Notwithstanding the *Companies' Creditors Arrangement Act*,

(a) proceedings commenced under that Act shall not be dealt with or continued under this Act; and

(b) proceedings shall not be commenced under Part III of this Act in respect of a company if a compromise or arrangement has been proposed in respect of the company under the *Companies' Creditors Arrangement Act* and the compromise or arrangement has not been agreed to by the creditors or sanctioned by the court under that Act.

In reading the above sections together, it is apparent that Parliament sought to limit "forum shopping" that would have allowed a debtor whose restructuring proceeding was unsuccessful under one statute to recommence the process under the other legislation. Reading the provisions of the *CCAA* and *BIA* together, it would appear that restructuring proceedings under the *CCAA* and *BIA* should not co-exist. There are two exceptions to the general principle that the debtor should complete the process under one statute or the other, but not both. First, is the situation where a debtor chose to commence proceedings by filing a notice of intention under the *BIA* and realises partway through the restructuring process, prior to filing a proposal, that additional time is required, in which case the debtor could apply to convert the proceedings to a *CCAA* restructuring plan, through the operation of section 11.6(a) of the *CCAA*. Second is the situation where the debtor, the creditors and the court agree that the restructuring would better be conducted as a proposal proceeding under the *BIA*, and the plan proposed under the *CCAA* has not already been refused by creditors; in which case the conversion can be made pursuant to section 66.2(b) of the *BIA*. The courts have allowed a debtor to file a proceeding under the *BIA* even though a proceeding under the *CCAA* had been initiated, provided that a plan had not yet been rejected by creditors or sanctioned by the court.[95]

Questions for review of materials:

1. What tests does the court use for determining classes of creditors entitled to vote on a proposed *CCAA* plan?

2. What tests does the court apply in sanctioning a plan of arrangement and compromise under the *CCAA*?

3. What issues does the judgment in *Uniforêt Inc.* (in Appendix 8) raise in terms of whether the court should sanction the *CCAA* plan?

---

[95] *SAAN Stores Ltd./Magasins SAAN Ltée, Re* (2005), 2005 CarswellOnt 1482, 12 C.B.R. (5th) 35 (Ont. S.C.J. [Commercial List]) Farley J. (Transition and Stay Extension Order); *Manderley Corp., Re* (2005), 2005 CarswellOnt 1082 (Ont. S.C.J.).

Questions for discussion:

1. Should the courts defer to the business judgment of creditors, or do they have a broader mandate under the *CCAA*?

2. Should shareholders have a voice in the *CCAA* proceeding?

3. Is there a problem with confidential financial information about the debtor corporation being in the public domain during *CCAA* proceedings such that its competitors can gain access to information? Have the courts found the appropriate balance in determining requests for sealing orders?

CHAPTER 8

THE ROLE OF THE COURT'S OFFICERS

I. INTRODUCTION

Reference has been made throughout this text to the role of the court's officers in *CCAA* proceedings. These officers include the monitor and in some cases, interim receivers. The CRO, discussed in chapter 5 on governance of the insolvent corporation, is also sometimes a court-appointed officer, although the courts have had little occasion to determine the scope and contours of that role. The role of the court's officers is constantly evolving under *CCAA* proceedings, and the evolution has raised some questions regarding how such officers are to balance the multiple interests implicated in a restructuring.

This chapter tracks the evolution of the role of monitor and examines its vital contribution to *CCAA* restructuring proceedings. It examines the issue of auditors serving as monitors, and monitors serving in a more robust role. It also explores the use of interim receivers in *CCAA* restructuring proceedings and discusses the challenges for all of these court appointed officers in their role of assisting the parties and the court.

II. THE ROLE OF THE MONITOR

1. Evolution of the Role

Prior to 1997, there was no express statutory language regarding monitors in the *CCAA*. However, Canadian courts had exercised their inherent jurisdiction to appoint monitors in *CCAA* proceedings, to monitor the business and financial affairs of the debtor corporation, provide independent information to the court on the progress of the proceedings, and assist in administrative matters, such as notifying creditors, and organizing and managing the meeting of creditors.

In 1997, the legislation was amended to make the appointment of monitors mandatory where a stay order is granted, codifying much of the then existing practice.[1]

---

[1] Sections 11.5, 11.7, *CCAA*.

The monitoring role does not divest the debtor of its governance structure, and the directors and officers continue to have oversight and control of the corporation unless the court orders otherwise under the oppression remedy of corporations' statutes.[2] The monitor has an obligation to act independently and to consider the interests of the debtor corporation and all creditors.[3] The monitor is an officer of the court.[4]

Prior to codification, the role of monitor arose as a means of enhancing creditors' access to information and a mechanism to provide assistance to the court in its oversight of the *CCAA* proceeding. Monitors were appointed to monitor the affairs of the corporation during the workout process.[5] The appointment of a monitor was initially driven by creditors seeking enhanced disclosure from debtor corporations during *CCAA* proceedings, as a means of reducing transaction costs associated with court appearances in disputes regarding the scope and timing of financial disclosure, and to provide some measure of control over the operations during the restructuring period.

The introduction of the monitor in *CCAA* proceedings was also, in part, a Canadian response to the U.S. practice of having creditors' committees in Chapter 11 workouts, with the debtor company paying for counsel and financial advisors of the creditors, a practice that was viewed as often highly confrontational and expensive. Under Canadian proceedings, the monitor, as an officer of the court, provides independent observation and oversight of the debtor's activities during the *CCAA* process, providing an accountability check for creditors without the time and expense of a creditors' committee. Given the independent role envisioned, in a number of instances, the company's outside auditor acted as monitor.

The 1997 codification of the monitor's role reflected the growing practice of appointing monitors and was based on recommendations of the Task Force studying the *CCAA*, which had suggested that mandatory appointment of a monitor would give creditors in *CCAA* applications the protection of a professional and impartial "watchdog", similar to the protection provided by the proposal trustee under a *BIA* proposal proceeding.[6]

Although initially, creditors sought the appointment of a monitor to protect their interests, the practice evolved that the debtor corporation selected and proposed a

---

[2] *Stelco Inc., Re* (2005), 2005 CarswellOnt 1188, [2005] O.J. No. 1171 (Ont. C.A.). The directors and officers could also, arguably, all resign and the monitor could be appointed to step into their role.

[3] *United Used Auto & Truck Parts Ltd., Re* (1999), 12 C.B.R. (4th) 144 (B.C. S.C. [In Chambers]), affirmed (2000), 16 C.B.R. (4th) 141 (B.C. C.A.), leave to appeal allowed but appeal discontinued (2000), [2000] S.C.C.A. No. 142, 2000 CarswellBC 2132 (S.C.C.).

[4] *Mines Jeffrey inc., Re*, (sub nom. *Syndicat national de l'amiante d'Asbestos c. Mine Jeffrey inc.*) [2003] R.J.Q. 420 (Que. C.A.); *Boutiques San Francisco Inc.* (2005), 5 C.B.R. (5th) 197 (Que. S.C.).

[5] *Northland Properties Ltd., Re* (1988), 73 C.B.R. (N.S.) 175 (B.C. S.C.), affirmed (1989), 73 C.B.R. (N.S.) 195 (B.C. C.A.); *United Co-Operatives of Ontario* (August 1984), unreported. Monitors were considered advisors, whereas interim receivers had management responsibilities.

[6] *Report of the Task Force on the CCAA to the Bankruptcy and Insolvency Advisory Committee Working Group on Commercial Reorganizations, Bankruptcies and Receiverships*, 1994 at 3.

monitor in its initial application to the court to commence a *CCAA* proceeding. Debtors and their advisors rapidly came to the conclusion that it was more productive for the debtor to ask for the appointment of the monitor right at the inception of the proceeding, as this provided more transparency and credibility to the process, thereby enhancing the chance of a successful workout.

2. Scope of the Monitor's Role

The *CCAA* sets out the duties of the monitor, including, that it shall monitor the company's business and affairs; have access to and examine the company's property; file reports with the court on both a periodic and specified basis on the state of the business' financial affairs; report on any material adverse change in the company's projected cash flow or financial circumstances; and advise creditors of reports filed with the court. The provisions also direct debtor corporations to provide the assistance necessary for the monitor to carry out its functions. The court can also exercise its discretion to direct the monitor to perform certain functions as it considers appropriate in the circumstances.

The duties of the monitor are set out in section 11.7 of the *CCAA:*

> 11.7(3) Functions of the monitor – The monitor shall
>
> (a) for the purposes of monitoring the company's business and financial affairs, have access to and examine the company's property, including the premises, books, records, data, including data in electronic form, and other financial documents of the company to the extent necessary to adequately assess the company's business and financial affairs;
>
> (b) file a report with the court on the state of the company's business and financial affairs, containing the prescribed information,
>
> > (i) forthwith after ascertaining any material adverse change in the company's projected cash-flow or financial circumstances,
> >
> > (ii) at least seven days before any meeting of creditors under section 4 or 5, or
> >
> > (iii) at such other times as the court may order;
>
> (c) advise the creditors of the filing of the report referred to in paragraph (b) in any notice of a meeting of creditors referred to in section 4 or 5; and
>
> (d) carry out such other functions in relation to the company as the court may direct.

If there is a material adverse change in the debtor's projected cash flow or financial circumstances, the *CCAA* specifies that the monitor must file a report on the state of the debtor's business and financial affairs forthwith.[7] The monitor must also file reports at least seven days before creditors' meetings and at such times as the court

---

[7] Section 11.7(3)(b), *CCAA*.

may order, and advise creditors of the filing of the report.[8] In many cases, monitors' reports are now posted on their websites or that of the legal counsel acting for the monitor in a *CCAA* proceeding or the debtor corporation's webpage, and hence are more accessible than previously.

As noted in chapter 3, the court's role in a *CCAA* proceeding is largely supervisory, undertaking both procedural and substantive rulings where the parties need direction or clarification regarding rights during the process of workout negotiations. The monitor, as a court-appointed officer, is to represent all stakeholders in monitoring the debtor's affairs during the proceeding and providing opinions to the court. The monitor's fees are paid for out of the assets of the debtor corporation on a priority basis, and the courts have justified the exercise of their discretion to order this security of payment because the monitor is an officer of the court.[9] The priority granted for the administration charge securing the monitor's compensation ensures that the monitor's reasonable fees and disbursements are paid.[10]

As originally conceived, the monitor had a relatively narrow monitoring and reporting function to the court and creditors. When the role of monitor was codified in 1997, the language of the statute reflected this role. The monitor is precisely as its name suggests; it is appointed to monitor the debtor during the proceeding, to ensure that the debtor does not engage in any conduct that will prejudice the interests of the creditors and other stakeholders. The monitor also assists the debtor in remaining compliant with the terms of the initial court order, as there can be confusion at the operational level regarding the scope of permitted activity once the stay protection is granted. However, the role of the monitor has been continually evolving, and while the statutory language envisions more of a monitoring role, the courts have liberally interpreted section 11.7(3)(d), which allows the court to direct the monitor to carry out such other functions in relation to the debtor company as the court may direct. This expanded role has been very effective in many *CCAA* proceedings.

The monitor can serve as a stabilizing force in the sense of reassuring creditors because it is monitoring the debtor's business and affairs, projected cash flow and appropriate use of assets and is monitoring managerial conduct in the operation of the business during the stay period. Given the limited size of the Canadian market of insolvency professionals and the less litigious legal culture in Canada than in the

---

[8] Section 11.7(3), *CCAA*.

[9] *Starcom International Optics Corp., Re* (1998), 3 C.B.R. (4th) 177 (B.C. S.C.); *Fairview Industries Ltd., Re* (1991), 11 C.B.R. (3d) 43, 109 N.S.R. (2d) 12 (N.S. T.D.); *Canadian Asbestos Services Ltd.* v. *Bank of Montreal* (1992), 16 C.B.R. (3d) 114, 11 O.R. (3d) 353 (Ont. Gen. Div.), additional reasons at (1993), 13 O.R. (3d) 291 (Ont. Gen. Div.).

[10] The courts will assess the reasonableness of a monitor's or receiver's account on the basis of numerous facts, such as the nature, extent and value of assets over which there is responsibility; the complications encountered; the degree of assistance provided by the debtor; time spent; the monitor or receiver's knowledge, experience and skills; the result of efforts; and costs of comparable services: *Agristar Inc., Re* (2005), 2005 CarswellAlta 841, [2005] A.J. No. 727 (Alta. Q.B.); *Belyea* v. *Federal Business Development Bank* (1983), 1983 CarswellNB 27, [1983] N.B.J. No. 41 (N.B. C.A.).

United States, there has also developed a level of confidence and trust between professionals that serve as monitors and the creditors that are repeat players in insolvency proceedings. This confidence and trust can facilitate proceedings and enhance the effectiveness of the monitor. Equally, however, the monitor must be cognisant of the fact that for stakeholders that are new to the process, the trust and co-operation among repeat players can create a perception of bias. The monitor must be scrupulous in fulfilling its obligation to consider and balance the interests of all stakeholders.

Monitors increasingly navigate the debtor through the complexity of the *CCAA* process, providing business judgment, negotiation skills and financial advice. The monitor can act as mediator or facilitator, bringing the parties together in an effort to build consensus on a viable going forward business plan. In some cases, the monitor has had significant input in developing the plan of arrangement. The monitor makes judgment calls on levels of disclosure to creditors and timing of that disclosure and increasingly takes positions on disputes before the court during the *CCAA* proceeding. These multiple roles may be needed, yet one issue is whether they create a real or perceived conflict with the obligation of the monitor to monitor the debtor on behalf of all stakeholders.

While there was a period after codification of the role of monitor where creditors were concerned that monitors proposed by the debtor corporation were acting as advocates of the debtor, the court quickly dispensed with any misconceptions monitors might have in respect of their duties. Canadian courts have consistently held that the monitor is an officer of the court and has an obligation to act independently.[11] The courts have held that the duty of the monitor is to act in the best interests of all stakeholders with an interest in the proceeding.[12]

This need for impartiality was reinforced in the endorsement of Mr. Justice Farley of the Ontario Superior Court of Justice in the *JTI-MacDonald Corp.* proceeding, in dismissing a motion to terminate the *CCAA* proceeding and in granting an extension of the stay. [13] The Court reminded the monitor and parties to the proceeding:

> ¶2 I expect that the monitor which has reconfirmed its obligation and responsibility to be fair and objective as amongst the applicant and all the stakeholders to make certain that these discussions commence forthwith and continue in a reasonable fashion — and that status reports (without impinging on privilege and confidentiality)

---

[11] *Hickman Equipment (1985) Ltd., Re* (2002), 34 C.B.R. (4th) 203, 214 Nfld. & P.E.I.R. 126 (Nfld. T.D.) at para. 33; *Siscoe & Savoie* v. *Royal Bank* (1994), 29 C.B.R. (3d) 1 (N.B. C.A.), at para. 28, leave to appeal refused (1995), 32 C.B.R. (3d) 179n (S.C.C.); *United Used Auto & Truck Parts Ltd., Re* (1999), 12 C.B.R. (4th) 144 (B.C. S.C. [In Chambers]), at para. 20, affirmed (2000), 16 C.B.R. (4th) 141 (B.C. C.A.), leave to appeal allowed but appeal discontinued (2000), 2000 CarswellBC 2132 (S.C.C.).

[12] *Royal Oak Mines Inc., Re* (1999), 11 C.B.R. (4th) 122 (Ont. Gen. Div. [Commercial List]) at para. 6; *PSINet Ltd., Re* (2002), 30 C.B.R. (4th) 226 (Ont. S.C.J. [Commercial List]), at para. 12, affirmed (2002), 32 C.B.R. (4th) 102 (Ont. C.A.).

[13] *In the Matter of the Companies' Creditors Arrangement Act and JTI-MacDonald Corp.* (September 14, 2004), Doc. 04-CL-5530 (Ont. S.C.J. [Commercial List]).

> be given in the monitor's regular reports which are to be made available to all interested persons in the ordinary course.

The role of the monitor as impartial officer has allowed the court flexibility in the orders it makes directing the activities of the monitor.

In *Skydome Corp.*, an insolvency involving Toronto's baseball and football sports complex, the monitor was directed to co-ordinate a sale process: to ask for expressions of interest in an auction, arrange for confidentiality agreements in the bid process, set up an advisory committee of stakeholders, assess the offers, and bring a recommendation to the court.[14] These functions were undertaken in the context of *CCAA* proceedings, but were akin to the role of a receiver in disposing of assets. In approving the monitor's recommendations as fair and reasonable, the Court applied the tests used in that analogous situation, specifically, whether the monitor had made a sufficient effort to obtain the best price and had not acted improvidently; had considered the interests of all parties affected; the integrity and efficiency of the process by which offers were obtained; and whether there had been any unfairness in the workout process.

Where a monitor carries out the business of the debtor corporation, the monitor does not become personally liable to pay for liabilities that arose before or upon the monitor's appointment.[15] The monitor is also protected from liability for environmental damage.[16]

There can also be an expansion in the role of a monitor if the debtor breached the initial order. This was done in the Royal Oak Mines *CCAA* proceeding. First, the monitor's supervisory and reporting mandate was expanded, and eventually, the monitor was appointed as interim receiver to replace management.

The courts accord a high level of deference to decisions of the monitor. For example, in *Tiger Brand Knitting Co.*, the Ontario Superior Court of Justice held that a monitor should not be enjoined from proceeding with an offer submitted as part of a court-approved sale process, even where a new offer arising following the bid deadline may preserve jobs, since this would amount to an unfairness in the working out of the sale process to the detriment of the current purchaser and the secured creditors; interfere with the efficacy and integrity of the sale process; and prefer the interests of one party, the new prospective purchaser or the union representing the employees, over others.[17]

---

[14] *Skydome Corp., Re* (February 19, 1999), Blair J. (Ont. Gen. Div. [Commercial List]) (Endorsement), citing *Royal Bank* v. *Soundair Corp.* (1991), 7 C.B.R. (3d) 1 (Ont. C.A.) and *Crown Trust Co.* v. *Rosenberg* (1986), 60 O.R. (2d) 87 (Ont. H.C.).

[15] Section 11.8, *CCAA*.

[16] Sections 11.8(3) - 11.8(8), *CCAA*.

[17] *Tiger Brand Knitting Co., Re* (2005), 2005 CarswellOnt 1240 (Ont. S.C.J.).

3. DIP Financing and Monitors

The monitor provides opinions to the court as to the need for, and scope of, DIP financing and an opinion as to the terms being extracted as part of the financing agreement.[18] How the monitor balances interests is crucially important, given the high level of deference by the court to its recommendations.

In most cases, the monitor's fees do not depend on the size of the DIP financing, and as discussed in chapter 4, the size of the DIP facility is often to reassure suppliers. Monitors can be very helpful to the debtor corporation in bringing competition to DIP financing proposals, which may lead to better terms for the debtor.

Another view, however, is that DIP lenders can take advantage of the fact that they are negotiating the terms of the financing agreement at the same time that the monitor is sorting out its fees pre-filing. Given that the monitor is not yet appointed by the court prior to filing, it may not be able to serve as an appropriate accountability check on the scope and terms of the DIP financing agreement.

4. The Auditor as Monitor

Another key issue is whether the auditor of a debtor corporation should serve as monitor. While in both theory and in law, the financial statements of the company are the work product of the company and its officers, with the auditor providing only an opinion on the financial statements, a company's auditor, while formally having an arm's length role in auditing the financial records of the company, in reality, frequently works closely with corporate officers. The auditor's views can heavily influence the work of the company in financial reporting. In other cases, a controlling or managing shareholder may push the auditor to see the statements its way, resulting in "auditor capture". Close relationships can develop between external auditors and corporate officers, particularly where the audit partner is not rotated every few years.

Industry Canada has estimated that approximately 33% of *CCAA* proceedings have involved a monitor that had been the auditor of the debtor corporation, primarily occurring in smaller and mid-market workouts.[19] Unlike the *BIA,* which excludes the auditor or accountant of a debtor from acting as its trustee in bankruptcy in a liquidation proceeding, except in particular circumstances, there is no similar statutory provision under the *CCAA*. Section 13.3(1) of the *BIA* specifies:

[18] *Starcom International Optics Corp., Re* (1998), 3 C.B.R. (4th) 177 (B.C. S.C.); *Fairview Industries Ltd., Re* (1991), 11 C.B.R. (3d) 43, 109 N.S.R. (2d) 12 (N.S. T.D.); *Canadian Asbestos Services Ltd.* v. *Bank of Montreal*, 16 C.B.R. (3d) 114, [1992] G.S.T.C. 15, 11 O.R. (3d) 353 (Ont. Gen. Div.), additional reasons at (1993), 1993 CarswellOnt 816 (Ont. Gen. Div.). The monitor's fees are paid for out of the assets of the debtor corporation on a priority basis, and the courts have justified the exercise of their discretion to order this security of payment because the monitor is an officer of the court.

[19] Industry Canada Statistics, on file with author.

> 13.3(1) Where trustee is not qualified to act – Except with the permission of the court and on such conditions as the court may impose, no trustee shall act as trustee in relation to the estate of a debtor
>
> (a) where the trustee is, or at any time during the preceding two years was,. . . . . .
>
> (iv) the auditor, accountant or solicitor, or a partner or employee of the auditor, accountant or solicitor, of the debtor;. . . .

Section 13.3(1) was aimed at preventing conflicts of interest, responding to a series of judgments in which the court held that it is improper for affiliated parties to become the trustee.[20]

In fact, the language of the *CCAA* is quite the opposite. Section 11.7 of the *CCAA* specifies that the monitor is appointed to monitor the business and affairs of the debtor, and expressly notes that the auditor may be appointed as monitor:

> 11.7 (1) *Court to appoint monitor* – When an order is made in respect of a company by the court under section 11, the court shall at the same time appoint a person, in this section and in section 11.8 referred to as "the monitor", to monitor the business and financial affairs of the company while the order remains in effect.
>
> (2) *Auditor may be monitor* – Except as may be otherwise directed by the court, the auditor of the company may be appointed as the monitor.

The courts have held that it is not improper for the auditor of a debtor corporation to become the monitor in a *CCAA* proceeding as the monitor is viewed as more akin to an independent auditor.[21]

In small and mid-market workouts under the *CCAA*, the auditor is more likely to act as monitor because there are not sufficient assets remaining to pay for the costs of two insolvency professionals. Hence the practical realities of the debtor's financial situation drive the decision about the dual use of the professional, as less time and expense is incurred in coming up to speed on the debtor's financial situation. In this, the interest of the debtor corporation may converge with that of creditors, since payment of the professional comes out of the debtor's assets as a first charge and creditors will weigh the double costs against concerns about conflicts of interest or impartiality of the monitor.[22] Yet the auditor as monitor can create a problem of perception of conflict of interest and in some instances, an actual conflict in the insolvency proceedings. One issue is whether the efficiencies generated by the dual role, in terms of more timely proceedings, reduction of information asymmetries

---

[20] *Walter W. Shaw Co., Re* (1922), 16 Sask. L.R. 275, 68 D.L.R. 616, 3 C.B.R 198, [1922] 3 W.W.R. 119 (Sask. K.B.); *Erie Gas Co., Re* (1938), 20 C.B.R. 14, 1938 CarswellOnt 86, [1938] O.J. No. 227 (Ont. S.C.); and *Tannis Trading Inc.* v. *Camco Food Services Ltd. (Trustee of)* (1988), 67 C.B.R (N.S.) 1, 63 O.R. (2d) 775, 49 D.L.R. (4th) 128 (Ont. S.C.).

[21] *Hickman Equipment (1985) Ltd., Re* (2002), 34 C.B.R. (4th) 203 (Nfld. T.D.).

[22] Janis Sarra, "Ethics and Conflicts, The Role of Insolvency Professionals in the Integrity of the Canadian Bankruptcy and Insolvency System" (2004) 13 *International Insolvency Review* 167-212.

and confidence of officers, are sufficient to overcome any perception of bias. In Canada, there have been very few cases where creditors have objected to the auditor serving as monitor and hence there is little caselaw as guidance. In the rare case where senior creditors have objected, the monitor/auditor has resigned and been replaced by an independent firm.

Allowing auditors to act as monitors has arguably assisted in reducing both premature and deferred liquidations by encouraging the debtor's directors and officers to file in a timely manner and determine whether there is a viable business plan that may be acceptable to creditors on a going forward basis. In *Hickman Equipment*, the Court found that this was a reason for allowing the auditor to act as monitor.[23]

In discussing whether the auditor should be allowed to act as the monitor appointed in *CCAA* proceedings, the debate has focused primarily on the issue of a conflict of interest, real or perceived, of the monitor, in its dealings with the creditors and the debtor.

In considering the reasons why a conflict might be thought to exist when the auditor serves as monitor, the issue is whether the auditor may be tempted to favour the debtor in dealing with other stakeholders, either because of a long standing friendly relationship with the debtor, or because the monitor may be tempted to make heroic unwarranted efforts at restructuring a failed business in order to maintain an income stream from audit fees, in effect looking after its own interest instead of that of others. Jean-Daniel Breton has argued that the case for a conflict of interest on the part of the auditor acting as monitor is at best weak, in view of the safeguards that exist through rules of ethics, market forces and court supervision.[24] He suggests that the auditor should in fact be precluded from acting as monitor, but not for reasons of conflict of interest; rather, for professional reasons arising from the auditor's responsibilities towards its client, and restrictions placed on the auditor's allowable activities by the auditors' professional rules of ethics or statutory restrictions. Examples of these restrictions are found, for instance, in the *Sarbanes-Oxley Act of 2002*;[25] which apply to any Canadian debtor corporation with securities trading in the U.S. Rules promulgated under *Sarbanes-Oxley* forbid certain activities by an auditor, such as "appraisal or valuation services, fairness opinions, or contribution-in-kind reports" or "management functions or human resources".[26] Other examples are rules of ethics prohibiting the auditor from managing assets of his client;[27] or rules of ethics forbidding the disclosure of confidential information concerning the audit client.[28] These examples represent functions that a monitor could conceivably

---

[23] *Hickman Equipment (1985) Ltd., Re* (2002), 34 C.B.R. (4th) 203 (Nfld. T.D.) at paras. 8, 23 and 49.

[24] Jean-Daniel Breton, "Senate Committee Recommendation no. 35 – A Career Limiting Move?", in *Annual Review of Insolvency Law, 2004* (Toronto: Carswell, 2005).

[25] One Hundred Seventh Congress of the United States of America, Second Session. The text can be found at http://news.findlaw.com/hdocs/docs/gwbush/sarbanesoxley 072302.pdf.

[26] *Sarbanes-Oxley Act of 2002*, Title II, section 201.

[27] Rules of Professional Conduct of the Canadian Institute of Chartered Accountants, Rule 204.4(22).

[28] Code of Ethics of Chartered Accountants of the Province of Québec, section 48. The Code of Ethics can be found at http://www.ocaq.qc.ca/pdf/ang/2_protection/ code_of_ethics.pdf.

be required to fulfill. The issue of confidentiality is thorny, as the monitor, as an officer of the court, could have an obligation to disclose information it knows, while the monitor has a concurrent obligation to keep information confidential. Breton suggests that in view of the fact that situations change in the course of the restructuring proceedings, the auditor could face problems arising from its position as auditor, and not from its position as monitor, if it assumes the role of monitor in a *CCAA* proceeding.[29]

Chapter 47, when proclaimed in force, will restrict the ability of an auditor to act as monitor, except in particular circumstances, as discussed later in this chapter.

5. Officer of the Court

Canadian courts have held that the monitor is an officer of the court and has an obligation to act independently and to consider the interests of the debtor and its creditors.[30] The courts have also held that the duty of the monitor is to act in the interests of all stakeholders with an interest in the proceeding.[31] This broader notion of the monitor's duties recognizes that multiple stakeholders may be interested in the proceedings. The Ontario Superior Court of Justice in *Royal Oak Mines* held that the monitor's role is to be neutral and to act in the best interests of all concerned.[32] In *PSINet Ltd.*, Mr. Justice Farley of the Ontario Superior Court held that there was no jurisprudence to support an argument that a monitor represents the interests of creditors in the same way as a trustee in bankruptcy, receiver or liquidator, given that the monitor does not act as an asset collector for purposes of distribution to creditors.[33]

The need for the monitor's impartiality goes to the perception of parties, particularly those that are not repeat players in the system, so that the integrity of the insolvency system is maintained. As an officer of the court, the monitor's obligation is to review the parties' positions and then give an opinion based on its expertise. The expertise that the monitor brings to the proceeding is financial expertise, not legal expertise. Even where the monitor has retained legal expertise, its role is not to become the advocate of the debtor corporation or any other party. This kind of legal advocacy can lead to failed confidence in the integrity of the system.

---

[29] Jean-Daniel Breton, "Senate Committee Recommendation no. 35 – A Career Limiting Move?", in *Annual Review of Insolvency Law, 2004* (Toronto: Carswell, 2005).

[30] *Fairview Industries Ltd., Re* (1991), 11 C.B.R. (3d) 43, 109 N.S.R. (2d) 12 (N.S. T.D.) at para. 75; *Siscoe & Savoie* v. *Royal Bank* (1994), 29 C.B.R. (3d) 1 (N.B. C.A.) , leave to appeal refused (1995), 32 C.B.R. (3d) 179n (S.C.C.); *United Used Auto & Truck Parts Ltd., Re* (1999), 12 C.B.R. (4th) 144 (B.C. S.C. [In Chambers]), at para. 20, affirmed (2000), 16 C.B.R. (4th) 141 (B.C. C.A.), leave to appeal allowed but appeal discontinued (2000), 2000 CarswellBC 2132 (S.C.C.); *Hickman Equipment (1985) Ltd., Re* (2002), 34 C.B.R. (4th) 203 (Nfld. T.D.) at para. 33.

[31] *Royal Oak Mines Inc., Re* (1999), 11 C.B.R. (4th) 122 (Ont. Gen. Div. [Commercial List]) at para. 6.

[32] *Ibid.*

[33] *PSINet Ltd., Re* (2002), 30 C.B.R. (4th) 226 (Ont. S.C.J. [Commercial List]), at para. 12, affirmed (2002), 32 C.B.R. (4th) 102 (Ont. C.A.), discussed in the context of being a representative of creditors for purposes of the *PPSA*.

The court has held that the monitor is to provide an independent assessment of the debtor's financial status and actions during the proceeding.[34] The court's recognition of impartiality has resulted in a very high level of deference by the court to the monitor's opinion. Where the opinion is contested by multiple stakeholders, the court may exercise slightly less deference, although it is still difficult for stakeholders to succeed where their objections do not align with the monitor's opinion. Even where the court has very serious reservations regarding the opinion of the monitor, it will recognize the monitor's experience, expertise and objectivity, but may caution the monitor about the necessity of remaining impartial, either at the court hearing or in any reasons for judgment issued.[35] However, the deference to the monitor will depend on how independent and objective the monitor is; and the court's assessment of that independence and objectivity may be influenced by past experience with the particular monitor, by the particular subject matter, and by how controversial the opinion offered is.

Hence, the need for the monitor to be accountable to the court and to all stakeholders and to be objective in performance of its obligations is key to the court's continued recognition of and deference to the monitor's opinion. It is also key to ethical practice that the monitor is fulfilling its fiduciary obligations and reducing the scope of potential conflicts of interest in the proceeding.

How the insolvency officer undertakes the balancing of interests is crucially important, given the high level of deference by the court to its recommendations. Where the monitor understands its role to be one of ensuring that all interests are considered, the process tends to be more successful, transaction costs lower, and there is greater buy-in by all parties, whatever the final outcome of the proceeding. The Court in *Laidlaw* explains the dynamic; the Court held that the monitor as a court-appointed officer must "objectively look out for" and be concerned with protection of the "reasonable interests of all stakeholders", including the shareholders.[36] However, where shareholders' interests are so far underwater that they have no reasonable expectation of having a positive economic interest, there is no economic interest to protect.

Where such officers consider primarily the interests of secured creditors or accord little value to the interests of unsecured creditors or other stakeholders, they may not have adequately performed their role. The outcome of the proceedings, whether a restructuring or a sale, can suffer because value may not have been maximized or transaction costs may have increased from litigation by those parties that believe their interests were not considered. In *T. Eaton Co.*, the Court reminded the monitor of the necessity of remaining neutral and objective in the *CCAA* proceedings.[37]

---

[34] *Canadian Imperial Bank of Commerce* v. *Quintette Coal Ltd.* (1991), 1 C.B.R. (3d) 253, 53 B.C.L.R. (2d) 34 (B.C. S.C.).

[35] See for example, the discussion regarding the CIBC Aerogold Agreement in *Air Canada, Re* (May 14, 2003), Doc. 03-CL-4932, [2003] O.J. No. 2267 (Ont. S.C.J. [Commercial List]).

[36] *Laidlaw Inc., Re* (2002), 2002 CarswellOnt 790, [2002] O.J. No. 947 (Ont. S.C.J. [Commercial List]) at paras. 2-9.

[37] *T. Eaton Co., Re* (1999), 1999 CarswellOnt 4112, 14 C.B.R. (4th) 298 (Ont. S.C.J. [Commercial List]).

6. Further Development of the Monitor's Role

Andrew Kent and Wael Rostom have suggested that the role and functions of a monitor were conceived of as being different from those of a trustee, and that the issue is more one of perception about the appearance of fairness and integrity in the restructuring process rather than an issue of substance.[38] They observe that increasingly, the monitor is taking on the role of "super-monitor", performing a whole new range of functions. For example, the monitor frequently advises management on how to adjust to the restructuring process and deal with the various stakeholder groups at the same time that the monitor is monitoring compliance by the debtor with the various restrictions contained in the initial order. The monitor also increasingly acts as the debtor's financial advisor, particularly in respect of small or mid-sized companies, in order to realize substantial cost savings. The monitor can also facilitate constructive negotiations between the debtor and creditors with respect to the terms of the restructuring, particularly where creditors do not have full confidence in existing managers.

The caselaw reflects these further developments in that the monitor's role, as ordered by the court, is often shaped to meet the exigencies of the particular proceeding. In some cases, where there is a loss of confidence in management, the monitor has effectively replaced the board and senior management and has assumed control of the reorganization process. An example is the *Royal Oak* case.[39]

In *Calpine Canada Energy Ltd.,* the Alberta Court of Queen's Bench ordered an expanded role for a monitor, finding that a supervisory role for the monitor was a method of alleviating the stresses that had occurred between the debtor and an income fund managed by the debtor.[40]

The expanded role is sometimes contested, and the courts consider the professionalism and impartiality of the officer in deciding specific issues where the monitor's views are contested. In *Mirant Canada Energy Marketing*, a court order under the *CCAA* provided that severance amounts could be paid at the discretion of the monitor, and the monitor refused to pay the full amount of a severance claim having regard to the effect the payment would have on other employees.[41] The Court found that the monitor had properly exercised its discretion in the circumstances. In *Jackpine*

---

[38] Andrew Kent and Wael Rostom, "The Auditor as Monitor in *CCAA* proceedings: What is the Debate?", in *Annual Review of Insolvency Law, 2003* (Toronto: Carswell, 2004) at 197-210, citing Canada, Parliament, "Proceedings of the Standing Senate Committee on Banking, Trade and Commerce" Issue No. 17, February 11, 1997.

[39] *Royal Oak Mines Inc., Re* (1999), 11 C.B.R. (4th) 122 (Ont. Gen. Div. [Commercial List]. Kent and Rostom observe that industry groups have recommended that the power to appoint a manager be expressly incorporated into the *CCAA,* citing The Insolvency Institute of Canada and the Canadian Association of Insolvency and Restructuring Professionals, Joint Task Force on Business Insolvency Law Reform Report (March 15, 2002) at 18, online: Insolvency Institute of Canada website http://www.insolvency.ca/dhtml/ en/page/papers.q/indexType$Topic/indexID$10/a$index.html at 50.

[40] *Calpine Canada Energy Ltd., Re* (2006), 2006 CarswellAlta 277 (Alta. Q.B.).

[41] *Mirant Canada Energy Marketing Ltd., Re* (2004), 2004 CarswellAlta 352, 1 C.B.R. (5th) 252 (Alta. Q.B.), additional reasons at (2004), 2004 CarswellAlta 561, 1 C.B.R. (5th) 261 (Alta. Q.B.).

Forest Products Ltd., where the monitor participated in an application by a secured creditor to replace it, which was defended by other secured creditors, the monitor was not awarded costs; the British Columbia Supreme Court held that a monitor as an impartial officer of the court ought not to pursue its own interest in defending the appointment.[42]

There are also cases, such as *Air Canada*, where the monitor had a higher level of credibility with stakeholders than the management of the debtor corporation. In such cases, the courts have allowed the monitor greater authority in trying to facilitate a positive outcome to the negotiations for a plan. Arguably, in the case of *Air Canada*, a successful workout may not have been possible but for the efforts and credibility of the monitor. While courts should not rubber stamp the actions or opinions of the monitor, where it plays a highly facilitative role and garners the respect of stakeholders, its expanded role advances the public policy objectives of the legislation.

7. Monitor's Reports and the Issue of Compellability

As an officer of the court, the monitor has been found not to be compellable to give evidence in a proceeding, although the monitor reports to the court on a regular basis. The monitor's reports have been found to be "not evidence" and hence not generally subject to cross-examination; rather, as an officer of the court, the monitor is to act "lawfully, fairly and honourably".[43] In Ontario, the court has held that insolvency officers will not generally be subject to cross-examination of their reports, while acknowledging that these court-appointed officers do occasionally make themselves available for examination in the spirit of co-operation and common sense.[44]

The Ontario Superior Court of Justice in *Bell Canada International Inc.* held that although the situation did not warrant it in the instant case, an officer of the court may be cross-examined on a report in exceptional or unusual circumstances.[45] Such circumstances could include situations where the monitor refused to co-operate in clarifying a part of its report or in not expanding on any element in the report as may be reasonably requested. The Court held that the reasonability of a request must take into account the objectivity and neutrality of the officer of the court; specifying that: "woe betide any officer of the court who did not observe his duty to be neutral and objective".[46] This judgment indicates that one of the monitor's duties is to clarify

---

[42] *Jackpine Forest Products Ltd., Re* (2004), 2004 CarswellBC 87, 2004 BCSC 20, 27 B.C.L.R. (4th) 332, 47 C.P.C. (5th) 313, 49 C.B.R. (4th) 110 (B.C. S.C.).

[43] *In the Matter of Bell Canada International Inc.* (October 29, 2003), Court File 02-CL-4553 (Ont. S.C.J.) (Endorsement) at para. 6.

[44] *Mortgage Insurance Co. of Canada* v. *Innisfill Landfill Corp.* (1995), 30 C.B.R. (3d) 100 (Ont. Gen. Div. [Commercial List]) at 101-102; see also *Anvil Range Mining Corp., Re* (2001), 21 C.B.R. (4th) 194 (Ont. S.C.J. [Commercial List]); *Canadian Airlines Corp.* (2000), 20 C.B.R. (4th) 1 (Alta. Q.B.), leave to appeal refused (2000), 2000 CarswellAlta 919 (Alta. C.A. [In Chambers]), affirmed (2000), 2000 CarswellAlta 1556 (Alta. C.A.), leave to appeal refused (2001), 2001 CarswellAlta 888 (S.C.C.).

[45] *In the Matter of Bell Canada International Inc.* (October 29, 2003), Court File 02-CL-4553 (Ont. S.C.J.) (Endorsement) at para 8.

[46] *Ibid.*; *Confederation Treasury Services Ltd., Re* (1995), 37 C.B.R. (3d) 237 (Ont. Bktcy.).

information to stakeholders based on a reasonableness test. Failing this, the court may in exceptional circumstances compel the monitor to be examined. It also indicates that the court's deference will depend on the monitor complying with its duty to be impartial, objective and fulsome in its reporting.

The monitor's report offers an opinion to the court as to the accuracy of the information or the wisdom of particular proposed actions. This is not problematic if the monitor is not acting as an advocate for the debtor corporation. However, where it is, it is unclear that the courts have yet generally recognized that this may be problematic for creditors and other stakeholders seeking to challenge the monitor's conclusions. This has implications for interim decisions during the course of *CCAA* proceedings, such as a sale of assets during the proceeding and the court's reliance on the monitor for its business judgment.[47] Rarely has the court preferred the evidence of creditors or disregarded the opinion of the monitor.

In the *Canadian Airlines* proceeding, the noteholders sought to cross-examine the monitor on its liquidation analysis. It was the first time that such an issue had come before the court. Madam Justice Paperny of the Alberta Court of Queen's Bench concluded that cross-examination might not be necessary if the monitor provided further information. It directed the noteholders and dissenting shareholders to send written questions to the monitor, finding that if the need arose, the court would put questions to the monitor in the courtroom. The monitor subsequently answered almost 70 questions in two Special Reports and the issue became moot.

The Court's approach in *Canadian Airlines* reflected the public interest in full disclosure of the monitor's reasoning while protecting the monitor as an officer of the court.[48] Monitors would generally be far less effective if they were at risk of being compelled to be cross-examined on each of their reports or opinions to the court.

However, the courts have cautioned that monitors' reports should not include information that really should be led as evidence by the debtor corporation in a *CCAA* proceeding. The use of the monitor's report to insulate the debtor from cross-examination may have implications for the dispute resolution process under the *CCAA* as the debtor may have a tactical advantage in the bargaining process where the monitor acts as advocate.

The Ontario Superior Court of Justice in *Bell Canada International* commented on this risk of the debtor shirking its disclosure obligations through the use of the

---

[47] *Consumers Packaging Inc., Re* (2001), 27 C.B.R. (4th) 194 (Ont. S.C.J. [Commercial List]), leave to appeal refused (2001), 27 C.B.R. (4th) 197 (Ont. C.A.).

[48] In *Innisfil Landfill Corp.*, the Ontario Court declined to allow cross-examination of a receiver on the basis that no need was established and that the receiver, as a court officer, did not make reports in an affidavit form. *Mortgage Insurance Co. of Canada* v. *Innisfill Landfill Corp.* (1995), 30 C.B.R. (3d) 100 (Ont. Gen. Div. [Commercial List]).

monitor's report.[49] It observed that there have been problems with motions supported by nothing other that the monitor's report. The Court held that if a matter is reasonably expected to be contentious or turns contentious, it is important to have an affidavit from the moving party and time to allow cross-examination.[50] This represents recognition by the court that the monitor may risk its impartiality or the perception of impartiality if its reporting role is used inappropriately to insulate parties from cross-examination.

8. Mediators in a *CCAA* Proceeding

As discussed in chapter 3, there have been several cases where the court has used mediation to resolve particular disputes within a *CCAA* proceeding. The Ontario Superior Court of Justice in *Stelco Inc.* noted that an experienced mediator under a *CCAA* proceeding should be given the highest degree of flexibility in his or her approach to and handling of a mediation between all stakeholders of an insolvent corporation. The Court noted that if the monitor feels it appropriate, it may recommend a third party's proposal for the stakeholders' consideration, in addition to the monitor's proposal. The Court held that if any stakeholder does not voluntarily participate in the mediation, then the monitor, at the mediator's request, may move for an order that such participation be directed and ordered by the court.[51]

Hence the monitor and mediator perform distinct roles, but the monitor continues to fulfill its monitoring and facilitative functions, supporting the mediation process where appropriate.

9. Legislative Reform

There has been considerable debate about the scope of the role of monitors, often cast as the "skinny versus robust role" debate. The "skinny" monitor is one that performs the traditionally more narrow monitoring functions. The "robust" monitor is where the monitor is engaged in the full range of roles, including facilitating workout negotiations, advising the debtor on a draft plan, negotiating terms of DIP and exit financing or conducting a sale process. The issue is whether the robust monitor becomes more of an advocate of the debtor corporation than an impartial court-appointed officer. There are legitimate concerns on either side of this debate. Layered into the debate is the issue of auditors as monitors, as described above.

The Standing Senate Committee on Banking, Trade and Commerce in its 2003 report on reform of the *BIA* and the *CCAA* made a series of recommendations

[49] *In the Matter of Bell Canada International Inc.* (October 29, 2003), Court File 02-CL-4553 (Ont. S.C.J.) (Endorsement) at para 9.

[50] *Ibid.*

[51] *Stelco Inc., Re* (2005), 2005 CarswellOnt 2010, 11 C.B.R. (5th) 163 (Ont. S.C.J. [Commercial List]).

regarding the role of monitors, trustees and other insolvency professionals.[52] It observed:

> The Committee is firmly of the opinion that roles and responsibilities that would create conflicts of interest- whether real or perceived – for trustees, monitors or other insolvency practitioners must be avoided. If other stakeholders perceive these individuals to be in a position of conflict, then their faith in the integrity of our insolvency system and their sense of fairness in the process are reduced. While this occurrence has negative implications for Canadian stakeholders, the effects extend to foreign investors and thereby to the Canadian economy. The insolvency system in Canada must be – and must be seen to be- fair and transparent.[53]

In respect of the role of insolvency professionals, the Senate Committee recommended that:

> 48. The *Bankruptcy and Insolvency Act* and the *Companies' Creditors Arrangement Act* be reviewed in order to identify and eliminate any opportunities for the roles and responsibilities of insolvency practitioners to place them in a real or perceived conflict of interest. Moreover, in order to ensure that all practitioners fulfil their duties with a high level of integrity, the federal government should adopt guidelines for insolvency practitioners regarding professional conduct and conflicts of interest, expanding upon Rules 34 to 53 of the *Bankruptcy and Insolvency Act* where appropriate.[54] . . .

The Senate Committee's reasoning was that all officers of the court involved in proceedings under the *BIA* or the *CCAA* should act in a manner characterized by good faith, competent execution of their duties and freedom from real or perceived conflicts of interest.[55] It called for disclosure of any circumstances that could be construed as a conflict of interest. The Senate Committee also suggested that behaviour consistent with these standards would generate fairness, predictability and transparency, and would increase the confidence of both domestic and international stakeholders in the integrity of the bankruptcy system.[56] It further recommended limits on permitting the auditor to serve as monitor.[57]

David Baird has written about the need for the "skinny monitor" model and has proposed that the duties of the monitor should be divided up, creating an "administrator" appointed by the debtor and a monitor appointed by the creditors' com-

---

[52] *Debtors and Creditors Sharing the Burden: A Review of the Bankruptcy and Insolvency Act and Companies' Creditors Arrangement Act*, Report of the Standing Senate Committee on Banking, Trade and Commerce (November 2003).

[53] *Ibid.* at 186.

[54] *Ibid.* at 185. Rule 34 of the Code of Ethics specifies that every trustee shall maintain the high standards of ethics that are central to the maintenance of public trust and confidence in the administration of the Act. Rule 35 specifies that for the purposes of sections 39 to 52, "professional engagement" means any bankruptcy or insolvency matter in respect of which a trustee is appointed or designated to act in that capacity pursuant to the Act.

[55] *Ibid.* at 150-151.

[56] *Ibid.* at 151.

[57] *Ibid.* at recommendation 35.

mittee.[58] He suggests that the administrator would be responsible for all the administrative procedures required for processing and implementing a plan of arrangement, similar to a proposal trustee under the *BIA*, including the accuracy of the cash flow statements, receiving proofs of claim and calling meetings of creditors. Under Baird's proposed model, the administrator would be able to assume the role of financial advisor, strategist and advocate for the company if the debtor corporation wished, and that in such a defined role, the auditor could act as administrator. Baird then argues for a narrower role for the monitor, dealing with matters where independence from the debtor corporation is required, commenting on the reasonableness of the cash flow statements, acting as whistle blower if there is a material change of circumstances, and commenting on the merits and fairness of the plan.[59]

Chapter 47, when proclaimed in force, will further codify the role of monitor. It will also place restrictions on who can be a monitor. Proposed section 11.7 specifies:

> *Court to appoint monitor*
>
> 11.7 (1) When an order is made on the initial application in respect of a debtor company, the court shall at the same time appoint a person to monitor the business and financial affairs of the company. The person so appointed must be a trustee, within the meaning of subsection 2(1) of the *Bankruptcy and Insolvency Act*.
>
> *Restrictions on who may be monitor*
>
> (2) Except with the permission of the court and on any conditions that the court may impose, no trustee may be appointed as monitor in relation to a company
>
> (a) if the trustee is or, at any time during the two preceding years, was
>
> (i) a director, an officer or an employee of the company,
>
> (ii) related to the company or to any director or officer of the company, or
>
> (iii) the auditor, accountant or legal counsel, or a partner or an employee of the auditor, accountant or legal counsel, of the company; or
>
> (b) if the trustee is
>
> (i) the trustee under a trust indenture issued by the company or any person related to the company, or the holder of a power of attorney under an act constituting a hypothec within the meaning of the Civil Code of Quebec that is granted by the company or any person related to the company, or
>
> (ii) related to the trustee, or the holder of a power of attorney, referred to in subparagraph (i).

---

[58] David Baird, "Moral Dilemmas Relating to Accepted Insolvency Practices", (2003, CAIRP Educational Forum) at 9.

[59] *Ibid.* at 10.

Court may replace monitor

(3) On application by a creditor of the company, the court may, if it considers it appropriate in the circumstances, replace the monitor by appointing another trustee, within the meaning of subsection 2(1) of the Bankruptcy and Insolvency Act, to monitor the business and financial affairs of the company.

. . .

23. (1) The monitor shall

(a) except as otherwise ordered by the court, when an order is made on the initial application in respect of a debtor company,

(i) publish, without delay after the order is made, once a week for two consecutive weeks, or as otherwise directed by the court, in one or more newspapers in Canada specified by the court, a notice containing the prescribed information, and

(ii) within five days after the order is made,

(A) send a copy of the order to every known creditor who has a claim against the company of more than $1,000, and

(B) make a list showing the name and address of those creditors publicly available in the prescribed manner;

(b) review the company's cash-flow statement as to its reasonableness and file a report with the court on the monitor's findings;

(c) make, or cause to be made, any appraisal or investigation the monitor considers necessary to determine with reasonable accuracy the state of the company's business and financial affairs and the cause of its financial difficulties or insolvency and file a report with the court on the monitor's findings;

(d) file a report with the court on the state of the company's business and financial affairs, containing prescribed information,

(i) without delay after ascertaining any material adverse change in the company's projected cash-flow or financial circumstances,

(ii) at least seven days before any meeting of creditors under section 4 or 5,

(iii) not later than 45 days, or any longer period that the court may specify, after the end of each of the company's fiscal quarters, and

(iv) at any other times that the court may order;

(e) advise the company's creditors of the filing of the report referred to in any of paragraphs (b) to (d);

(f) file with the Superintendent of Bankruptcy a copy of the documents specified by the regulations and pay the prescribed filing fee;

(g) attend court proceedings held under this Act that relate to the company, and meetings of the company's creditors, if the monitor considers that his or her attendance is necessary for the fulfilment of his or her duties or functions;

(h) if the monitor is of the opinion that it would be more beneficial to the company's creditors if proceedings in respect of the company were taken under the Bankruptcy and Insolvency Act, so advise the court without delay after coming to that opinion;

(i) advise the court on the reasonableness and fairness of any compromise or arrangement that is proposed between the company and its creditors;

(j) unless the court otherwise orders, make publicly available, in the prescribed manner, all documents filed with the court, and all court decisions, relating to proceedings held under this Act in respect of the company and provide the company's creditors with information as to how they may access those documents and decisions; and

(k) carry out any other functions in relation to the company that the court may direct.

Monitor not liable

(2) If the monitor acts in good faith and takes reasonable care in preparing the report referred to in any of paragraphs (1)(b) to (d), the monitor is not liable for loss or damage to any person resulting from that person's reliance on the report.

Right of access

24. For the purposes of monitoring the company's business and financial affairs, the monitor shall have access to the company's property, including the premises, books, records, data, including data in electronic form, and other financial documents of the company, to the extent that is necessary to adequately assess the company's business and financial affairs.

Obligation to act honestly and in good faith

25. In exercising any of his or her powers or in performing any of his or her duties and functions, the monitor must act honestly and in good faith and comply with the Code of Ethics referred to in section 13.5 of the Bankruptcy and Insolvency Act.

Among the changes cited above, the monitor will be required to be a licensed trustee for the first time, although, under current practice, many are already licensed trustees. The amendments would also reverse current practice in that auditors of the debtor corporation will no longer be entitled to be monitors, except under specified conditions set out in the amended section 11.7 of the *CCAA*.

III. INTERIM RECEIVERS IN *CCAA* PROCEEDINGS

The courts have appointed an interim receiver during the course of a *CCAA* proceeding, even though there is nothing in the statute that expressly provides for such an appointment. The monitor continues its role under the statute, pursuant to the order of the court.

The appointment of interim receivers has been made in a *CCAA* proceeding as a means to inject certainty into the situation, address a lack of confidence in the debtor's officers, enable appropriate protective proceedings to be taken and make immediate financing available for current operations.[60] Interim receivers have been appointed during a *CCAA* process to guide and control the debtor company, while still allowing the debtor to continue operating the business, employ employees and remain in possession of its assets.[61]

In *General Electric Capital Canada Inc.* v. *Euro United Corp.,* there was a serious lack of confidence by creditors in the management of the corporation during a *CCAA* proceeding. The Court directed that control vest in the interim receiver instead of the debtor corporation's existing managers. The Court noted that it was not suggesting that the debtor had not acted in good faith and with due diligence; however, the Court was not satisfied that any situation that continued to vest control in existing managers and directors would "neutralize the high level of distrust and the wide ranging lack of confidence" in the governance of the corporation. In the circumstances, the Court concluded that appointment of an interim receiver, while leaving the *CCAA* framework in place, would allow for immediate continued funding and protection of interests.

In *Pangeo Pharma inc.*, the Québec Superior Court appointed an insolvency professional to serve as both monitor and interim receiver; and authorized the offering for sale of assets and subsequently a sale of assets through a vesting order.[62] The Court was satisfied that the security of a creditor was not affected by the sale; and that both the sale process conducted and the sale price were reasonable in the circumstances.

In *Manderley Corp.*, the debtor company brought a concurrent application for appointment of a proposal trustee under the *BIA* and interim receiver and monitor under the *CCAA*, and sought approval for the monitor to arrange DIP financing for either a restructuring or an orderly liquidation.[63] The Ontario Superior Court of Justice granted the order for thirty days and dismissed an application by the bank, which was the debtor's largest secured creditor, to appoint its own agent as receiver for purposes of immediate liquidation. The Ontario Superior Court of Justice in

---

[60] *General Electric Capital Canada Ltd.* v. *Euro United Corp.* (1999), 25 C.B.R. (4th) 250 (Ont. S.C.J. [Commercial List]).

[61] *Royal Oak Mines Inc., Re* (2001), 143 O.A.C. 75 (Ont. C.A.).

[62] *Pangeo Pharma inc.* (August 14, 2003), Doc. C.S. Montréal 500-11-0021037-037 (Que. S.C.).

[63] *Manderley Corp., Re* (2005), 2005 CarswellOnt 1082 (Ont. S.C.J.).

Manderley Corp. held that, despite opposition from a main secured creditor, it was appropriate to grant a "two track approach" under the *BIA* and *CCAA*.[64] The Court held that allowing the debtor company to restructure for at least 30 days provided an opportunity to generate greater value to the stakeholders of the debtor company than an immediate liquidation; the benefits of the proposed DIP financing outweighed the prejudice to the largest secured creditor of the debtor company; and there was a limitation on the draw-down of the DIP financing.[65]

There have also been a number of cases where the court has appointed a receiver after there has been an unsuccessful *CCAA* application. Often, in such circumstances, the receiver may have a role to play in facilitating some sort of workout in terms of an asset sale in order to preserve some value in the firm while maximizing value for creditors. The receiver may operate the business in the period after a failed *CCAA* application and pending a decision about the future of the corporation or it may immediately conduct an orderly shutdown of the operations.

IV. TURNAROUND EXPERTS: COURT OFFICER OR DEBTOR AGENT?

Chapter 5 addressed the role of chief restructuring officers. One policy question that has not been adequately canvassed is whether the CRO is a court-appointed officer such that it has an obligation to act impartially in respect of creditors and other stakeholders. Arguably, as an officer of the debtor corporation, the CRO acquires an obligation to act in the best interests of the corporation.

As discussed in chapter 5, in the context of directors' obligations during bankruptcy, the Supreme Court of Canada in *Peoples Department Stores* has held that the fiduciary obligation of directors and officers is to the corporation and the interests of the corporation are not to be confused with the interests of the creditors or those of any other stakeholders.[66] The Court held that directors and officers must respect the trust and confidence that have been reposed in them to manage the assets of the corporation in pursuit of the realization of the objects of the corporation; they must avoid conflicts of interest with the corporation; and must serve the corporation selflessly, honestly and loyally.[67] The Court held that in using their skills for the benefit of the corporation when it is in troubled waters financially, the directors must be careful to attempt to act in its best interests by creating a "better" corporation, and not to favour the interests of any one group of stakeholders. The Court observed that stakeholders can seek remedies under the oppression remedy provisions of corporations statutes where directors and officers fail to take care of their interests.[68]

---

[64] See the comments made in Chapter 7, part VIII in this text, regarding the transfer of proceedings between *BIA* and *CCAA*.

[65] *Ibid.*

[66] *Peoples Department Stores Ltd. (1992) Inc., Re*, 2004 SCC 68, [2004] 3 S.C.R. 461 (S.C.C.) at para. 43.

[67] *Ibid.* at paras. 35, 36.

[68] *Ibid.* at para. 47.

The Supreme Court also held that directors owe a duty of care to creditors pursuant to section 122(1)(b) of the *CBCA*. Specifically, they must exercise the care, diligence and skill that a reasonably prudent person would exercise in comparable circumstances.[69]

Presumably, CROs acquire the same obligations to act in the best interests of the corporation and owe the same duty of care to creditors. While they may be indemnified by the debtor corporation for their activities during their appointment, they would appear to fall under the same statutory obligations as other corporate managers. At the same time, however, the CRO assumes its functions through a court appointment and the question is whether the CRO acquires any obligations in terms of fairness or impartiality. Greater clarity in respect of the scope of the CRO's obligations could assist parties to a *CCAA* proceeding in their interactions with CROs.

Jean-Daniel Breton has suggested that the dichotomy could be resolved by looking at the court order that addresses the CRO, not in terms of an order appointing the CRO as an officer of the court or otherwise, but as an order approving or ratifying the decision of the debtor company to appoint an officer of the debtor company to oversee the restructuring process.[70] This would place CROs more directly as acquiring the same obligations as directors and officers under corporations statutes.

V. REPRESENTATIVE COUNSEL

There have been a number of cases in which representative counsel have been appointed to represent tort claimants, pensioners and non-unionized employees. Representative counsel are usually paid out of the assets of the debtor corporation. While these representatives are appointed precisely to be advocates for those who are particularly vulnerable or face collective action problems, they are also officers of the court and have an obligation to treat all parties in the proceedings with a degree of respect and impartiality.

This concurrent role of advocate and officer of the court is an important one, but does not really differ from legal counsel representing other parties to the *CCAA* proceeding, in that technically, all counsel are officers of the court, but they also must be advocates for their clients.

Questions for review of materials:

1. In what circumstances is a "skinny monitor" role appropriate; and in what circumstances does it make sense to allow a more robust role for the monitor?

---

[69] *Ibid.* at para. 57.

[70] Jean-Daniel Breton, June 2006, on file with author.

2. How will the proposed amendments under Chapter 47 change the monitor's role?

Questions for discussion:

1. Given the limited resources faced by the insolvent corporation, do you think the current practice of allowing the debtor's auditor to serve as monitor should continue? Why or why not?

2. Considering the discussion in chapters 5 and 6, what is the appropriate way to categorize the obligations of CROs as an officer of the court or as a role more akin to a director and officer? What does this categorization mean in terms of any duties owed?

CHAPTER 9

CROSS-BORDER PROCEEDINGS

I. GROWTH IN CROSS-BORDER CASES

Prior to 1997, Canadian courts relied on the evolving common law principles of comity to recognize and enforce the judicial acts of other jurisdictions. In 1997, both the *BIA* and the *CCAA* were amended to codify cross-border insolvency proceedings.[1] Canadian courts have also endorsed cross-border cooperative initiatives such as the American Law Institute *Guidelines Applicable to Court-to-Court Communications in Cross-Border Cases*, appended as appendix 10 of this text.

There are currently several types of cross-border proceedings that can occur; and those between Canada and the United States are illustrative. There can be a *CCAA* main proceeding and a concurrent Chapter 11 U.S. *Bankruptcy Code* main proceeding, with the courts defining how issues are to be dealt with on either side of the border.[2] In such cases, there are a variety of mechanisms used to facilitate the proceedings, including, cross-border protocols, the courts speaking to each other through their orders and judgments and in some cases, holding joint video-conference hearings. Creditors' claims and the debtor's assets can be addressed in a whole range of ways, in terms of what jurisdiction has carriage of the claims process for particular assets. Typically, a proposed plan must be endorsed by both courts in the concurrent main proceedings. The *Laidlaw* and *Loewen* cases are examples of this type of workout.[3]

Second, there can be a *CCAA* main proceeding and what was previously a §304 U.S. *Bankruptcy Code* ancillary proceeding. The U.S. courts were historically relatively territorial in terms of recognizing ancillary proceedings, but in recent years have recognized such proceedings and the principles of comity. The *Ivaco* and *AT&T* restructurings are examples of a *CCAA* main proceeding and §304 ancillary

[1] Sections 267-275, *BIA* and section 18.6, *CCAA*.

[2] *United States Bankruptcy Code,* 11 U.S.C., Chapter 11 (2000).

[3] *Livent* in Ontario, *Livent Inc., Re* (1998), Court File No. 98-CL-3162 (Ont. Gen. Div. [Commercial List]); *Loewen Group Inc., Re* (2001), Court File No. 99-CL-3384 (Ont. S.C.J. [Commercial List]).

proceeding.[4] Section 304 has now been replaced by Chapter 15 of the U.S. *Bankruptcy Code,* effective October 2005.[5]

Third, there can be a Chapter 11 U.S. *Bankruptcy Code* main proceeding in the U.S., with ancillary proceedings commenced under either section 18.6 of the *CCAA* or section 271 of the *BIA*.[6] There can also be a variety of other proceedings in Canada, with concurrent ancillary proceedings in the U.S. For example, there can be a receivership in Canada under the *BIA*, with Chapter 15 (previously §304) recognition.[7] There can be a bankruptcy proceeding under the *BIA* and recognition of that proceeding under Chapter 15 (previously §304) of the U.S. *Bankruptcy Code*.[8] Similarly, there can be Chapter 11 proceedings in the U.S., with *BIA* interim and/or court-appointed receiverships over Canadian assets, usually where there is a Canadian affiliated company, as opposed to one legal entity in the United States.

Finally, either jurisdiction may have a main proceeding, but no formal proceedings are commenced in the other jurisdiction.[9] For example, there were Canadian assets implicated in the *Enron* U.S. bankruptcy proceedings, but no formal insolvency or bankruptcy proceedings commenced in Canada.[10] Enron Canada was solvent. Another example was Delphi Corporation, which filed in the U.S. but not in Canada, and which obtained an order from the U.S. bankruptcy court permitting it to pay Canadian creditors. This approach has been taken in a number of recent cases involving cross-border businesses.

Canada currently has what could be characterized as a system of modified universalism.[11] Modified universalism reflects the preservation of domestic law, while deferring to cross-border provisions modeled after international law to achieve consistency and uniformity of procedures in insolvency proceedings and to prevent a race to the assets by creditors. While Canada has a traditional history of protecting domestic creditors in their realization of claims, it has recognized the importance of comity and co-operation, and in 1997, codified cross-border provisions, shifting the law from a more territorialist view of insolvency proceedings to reflect a growing recognition by the courts of the principles of comity.

---

4 *Ivaco Inc., Re* (2003), Court File No. 03-CL-5145 (Ont. S.C.J. [Commercial List]); *AT&T Canada Inc., Re* (2002), Court File No. 02-CL-004715 (Ont. S.C.J.).

5 *United States Bankruptcy Code*, 11 U.S.C., Chapter 15, as implemented by section 801 of the *Bankruptcy Abuse and Consumer Protection Act of 2005*, 109th Congress, 1st Session, s. 256.

6 See for example, the proceedings for Delano Technology.

7 For example, *Irwin Toy, TCT Logistics*.

8 See for example, *TriGem Computer*.

9 For example, there was a *CCAA* proceeding for Eagle Precision, but no proceedings in the United States.

10 *Enron Canada Corp.* v. *Cinergy Canada Inc.* (2003), 2003 CarswellAlta 1495, [2003] A.J. No. 1302 (Alta. Q.B.).

11 Universality envisages a system in which all states defer to, and cooperate with, one another in a single proceeding, whether it is liquidation or reorganization, although such a theory does not exist in practice; hence the term modified universalism.

In the United States, adoption of the UNCITRAL Model Law on Cross-Border Insolvency, almost in its entirety, has shifted the U.S. insolvency statute from a largely territorial to a modified universalism model.[12] Professor Jay Westbrook has observed that there was a conscious effort to mirror the Model Law's language when enshrining Chapter 15 into the U.S. *Bankruptcy Code* in order to create uniformity across jurisdictions.[13] He observes that Chapter 15 defines a foreign main proceeding in the exact language of the Model Law, even though the phrase "centre of main interest" (colloquially referred to as COMI) differs considerably from the usual U.S. formulation. Canada's provisions have been closer to the language and objectives of the Model Law for the past decade and hence adoption of Chapter 47 will not bring as large a paradigm shift as may occur in the United States.

Canada already has fairly well developed cross-border procedures, balancing the principles of comity with those of protection of domestic debtors and creditors. The Supreme Court of Canada in *Holt Cargo Systems* held that different jurisdictions have a legitimate and concurrent interest in the conduct of international bankruptcy proceedings and Canada has adopted a pluralist approach. Thus while Canadian courts should be mindful of the principles of comity, they must also do justice to the particular litigants before them.[14] The court has the discretion to enforce or decline to enforce any order made by a foreign court, and is expressly empowered to seek the aid and assistance of a foreign court or other authority where it considers it appropriate. Canadian courts have recognized foreign orders on the basis of comity, where it is not in violation of public policy, although there is considerable debate about the level of deference that should be given to proceedings that do not directly implicate the assets of Canadian corporations.[15]

Under section 18.6 of the *CCAA,* "foreign proceeding" is defined as a judicial or administrative proceeding commenced outside Canada in respect of a debtor under a law relating to bankruptcy or insolvency and dealing with the collective interests of creditors generally.[16] The scope for judicial discretion is broad. The court may make an order and grant relief on such terms and conditions as the court considers appropriate in the circumstances to facilitate, approve or implement arrangements

---

[12] UNCITRAL Model Law on Cross-Border Insolvency, U.N. Doc. A/RES/52/158 (1997) (Model Law).

[13] See Jay Lawrence Westbrook, "Multinational Enterprises in General Default: Chapter 15, the ALI Principles, and the EU Insolvency Regulation" (2002) 76 Am. Bankruptcy L.J. for a general discussion of frameworks at 18-19; See also Jay Lawrence Westbrook, "Chapter 15 at Last" (2005) 79 Am. Bankruptcy L.J. 713.

[14] *Holt Cargo Systems Inc.* v. *ABC Containerline N.V.(Trustees of),* [2001] 3 S.C.R. 907 (S.C.C.) at paras. 80-87.

[15] *Singer Sewing Machine Co. of Canada Ltd., Re* (2000), 18 C.B.R. (4th) 127 (Alta. Q.B.); *Babcock & Wilcox Canada Ltd., Re* (2000), 2000 CarswellOnt 704, [2000] O.J. No. 786 (Ont. S.C.J. [Commercial List]); *Canadian Imperial Bank of Commerce* v. *ECE Group Ltd.* (2001), 2001 CarswellOnt 463, [2001] O.J. No. 535 (Ont. S.C.J.); *Roberts* v. *Picture Butte Municipal Hospital* (1998), 1998 CarswellAlta 646, [1998] A.J. No. 817 (Alta. Q.B.). For a discussion of these issues, see Jacob Ziegel, "Corporate Groups and Canada-US Cross-Border Insolvencies: Contrasting Judicial Visions" (2001) 21 C.B.R. (4th) 161.

[16] Section 18.6(1), *CCAA.*

that will result in a co-ordination of proceedings under the *CCAA* with any foreign proceeding.[17]

Nothing in section 18.6 prevents the court, on the application of a foreign representative or any other interested person, from applying such legal or equitable rules governing the recognition of foreign insolvency orders and assistance to foreign representatives as are not inconsistent with the provisions of the statute. Section 18.6(5) specifies that the court is not required under the cross-border provisions to make any order that is not in compliance with the laws of Canada or to enforce any order made by a foreign court. The court may seek the aid and assistance of a court, tribunal or other authority in a foreign proceeding by order or written request or otherwise as the court considers appropriate.[18] An application to the court by a foreign representative does not submit the foreign representative to the jurisdiction of the court for any other purpose except with regard to the costs of the proceedings, but the court may make any order under this section conditional on the compliance by the foreign representative with any other order of the court.[19]

II. EXPERIENCE WITH THE CURRENT PROVISIONS PRIOR TO U.S. ENACTING CHAPTER 15

The principle of comity permits the court to recognize and enforce in Canada the judicial acts of other jurisdictions, and is a means to enhance co-operation in insolvency proceedings that cross borders.[20] In Canada, the doctrine of comity initially developed through the common law, prior to enactment of the provisions currently in force. Initially, there was considerable uncertainty as to whether the courts in Canada or the U.S. would recognize particular proceedings, although early in its development of cross-border principles, Canadian courts for the most part recognized foreign insolvency proceedings.

The Supreme Court of Canada in *Morguard Investment Ltd.* v. *De Savoye* held that recognition of a foreign legal proceeding hinges on a "real and substantial connection" between the subject matter of the proceeding and the foreign jurisdiction.[21] This decision set out a framework that provided guidance to the development of cross-border law, even though the case dealt with inter-provincial co-operation on enforcement of court orders. Both the *CCAA* and the *BIA* were amended in 1997 to expressly empower the Canadian court to make such orders and grant such relief as it considers appropriate to facilitate, approve or implement arrangements that will

---

[17] Section 18.6(2), *CCAA*. The *BIA* contains language that largely mirrors section 18.6 of the *CCAA*, although arguably, it is slightly narrower as the definition of "debtor" in Part XIII requires that the debtor hold property in Canada; section 267, *BIA*.

[18] Section 18.6(5), *CCAA*.

[19] Section 18.6(7), *CCAA*.

[20] *Babcock & Wilcox Canada Ltd., Re* (2000), 2000 CarswellOnt 704, [2000] O.J. No. 786 (Ont. S.C.J. [Commercial List]). The U.S. caselaw on comity dates back to the 1890s.

[21] *Morguard Investment Ltd.* v. *De Savoye*, [1990] S.C.R. 1077 (S.C.C.).

result in a coordination of proceedings under the *CCAA* with any foreign proceedings.[22]

In *Roberts* v. *Picture Butte Municipal Hospital*, the Court recognized the U.S. Chapter 11 proceedings of Dow Corning and upheld the stay under those proceedings, finding that the appropriate forum to deal with numerous tort claims was the U.S. Bankruptcy Court.[23] The Court noted that steps within the proceedings themselves are also subject to the dictates of comity in recognizing and enforcing a U.S. Bankruptcy Court stay, so as to promote greater efficiency, certainty and consistency in connection with the debtor's restructuring efforts. It held:

> Comity and co-operation are increasingly important in the bankruptcy context. As internationalization increases, more parties have assets and carry on activities in several jurisdictions. Without some coordination there would be multiple proceedings, inconsistent judgments and general uncertainty.
>
> . . . I find that common sense dictates that these matters would be best dealt with by one court, and in the interest of promoting international comity it seems the forum for this case is in the U.S. Bankruptcy Court. Thus, in either case, whether there has been an attornment or not, I conclude it is appropriate for me to exercise my discretion and apply the principles of comity and grant the Defendant's stay application. I reach this conclusion based on all the circumstances, including the clear wording of the U.S. *Bankruptcy Code* provision, the similar philosophies and procedures in Canada and the U.S., the Plaintiff's attornment to the jurisdiction of the U.S. Bankruptcy Court, and the incredible number of claims outstanding ... [24]

One challenge for cross-border recognition is that in Canada, the debtor must be insolvent in order to file a plan of arrangement under the *CCAA*, whereas debtors do not need to be insolvent under Chapter 11 proceedings. Yet the *CCAA* provision defining foreign proceeding does not contain an explicit provision requiring a foreign debtor to be insolvent. While arguably, the provisions are aimed at recognizing the existence of cross-border concurrent proceedings, this lack of definition gave rise to some uncertainty in the court's application of the provision. For example, in *Singer Sewing Machine*, the Alberta Court declined to enforce a stay under U.S. proceedings on the basis that the Canadian subsidiary company was a separate corporate entity and the creditors were only creditors of the Canadian subsidiary, not the parent U.S. corporation.[25] This type of situation is very common. For tax reasons, the Canadian operations of a foreign business are almost always conducted through a separate subsidiary.

In contrast, in *Babcock and Wilcox*, involving mass asbestos tort litigation, the Court applied a U.S. stay order to a solvent Canadian subsidiary. The Canadian subsidiary

---

[22] Section 18.6(5), (6), *CCAA*. For a discussion of the conflicts of laws issues, see Jacob Ziegel, "Ships at Sea, International Insolvencies and Divided Courts" (1998) 29 C.B.L.J. 417.

[23] *Roberts* v. *Picture Butte Municipal Hospital* (1998), 1998 CarswellAlta 646, [1998] A.J. No. 817 (Alta. Q.B.).

[24] *Ibid.* at 6.

[25] *Singer Sewing Machine Co. of Canada Ltd., Re* (2000), 18 C.B.R. (4th) 127 (Alta. Q.B.).

was not part of the Chapter 11 proceedings, although the U.S. Bankruptcy Court judge had noted that it was susceptible to similar claims in Canada and had granted a restraining order against current and potential plaintiffs in ongoing or pending actions against the Canadian subsidiary.[26] The Ontario Court endorsed the recognition of comity and co-operation across borders, specifying that "to the extent reasonably practicable, one jurisdiction should take charge of the principal administration of the enterprise's reorganization, where such principal type approach will facilitate a potential reorganization" and respect the claims of the stakeholders.[27] The judgment prohibited foreign tort claimants from proceeding with claims against the solvent Canadian company, but also acted as a stay on the claims of Canadian creditors in the interests of the foreign proceeding.[28] The Court held that section 18.6(4) specifies that nothing in the section prevents the court from applying legal or equitable rules governing the recognition of foreign insolvency orders and assistance to foreign representatives where they are not inconsistent with the *Act* and here, the application fit within the principles of comity and co-operation.[29]

The Court in *Babcock and Wilcox* held that in granting section 18.6 recognition orders, the court would consider, but not be limited to, the following factors:

- The recognition of comity and co-operation between the courts of various jurisdictions are to be encouraged.

- Respect should be accorded to the overall thrust of foreign bankruptcy and insolvency legislation, unless in substance it is so different from the bankruptcy and insolvency law of Canada, or the legal process that generates the foreign order diverges radically from the process in Canada.

- All stakeholders are to be treated equitably, and to the extent reasonably possible, common or like stakeholders are to be treated equally, regardless of the jurisdiction in which they reside.

- The enterprise is to be permitted to implement a plan so as to reorganize as a global unit, especially where there is an established interdependence on a transnational basis of the enterprise and to the extent reasonably practicable,

---

[26] Madam Justice Sarah Pepall, *Cross-Border Insolvences,* (2004), http://www.iiiglobal.org/country/canada/Cross_Border_Insolvencies_v2.PDF at 19.

[27] *Babcock & Wilcox Canada Ltd., Re* (2000), 2000 CarswellOnt 704, [2000] O.J. No. 786 (Ont. S.C.J. [Commercial List]) at para. 21. See also *Grace Canada Inc., Re* (2001), 2001 CarswellOnt 2886 (Ont. S.C.J. [Commercial List]); *Matlack Inc., Re* (2001), 26 C.B.R. (4th) 45 (Ont. S.C.J. [Commercial List]).

[28] Bruce E. Leonard, "Non-Debtor Protection in an International Case" (2000) 19 American Bankruptcy Institute Journal 28. This judgment was criticized by Professor Ziegel for applying the stay provisions where the Canadian debtor corporation was not insolvent, potentially creating an uneven standard between enforcement of foreign proceedings under the *BIA* and the *CCAA;* Jacob Ziegel, "Corporate Groups and Canada-US Cross-Border Insolvencies: Contrasting Judicial Visions" (2001) 21 C.B.R. (4th) 161.

[29] *Babcock & Wilcox Canada Ltd., Re* (2000), 2000 CarswellOnt 704, [2000] O.J. No. 786 (Ont. S.C.J. [Commercial List]) at para. 16.

one jurisdiction should take charge of the principal administration of the enterprise's reorganization, where such approach will facilitate a potential reorganization, respect the claims of the stakeholders, and not inappropriately detract from the net benefits that may be available from alternative approaches.

- The role of the court and the extent of the jurisdiction it exercises will vary on a case by case basis and depend to a significant degree on the court's nexus to that enterprise; in considering the appropriate level of its involvement, the court will consider:

    (i) the location of the debtor's principal operations, undertaking and assets;

    (ii) the location of the debtor's stakeholders;

    (iii) the development of the law in each jurisdiction to address the specific problems of the debtor and the enterprise;

    (iv) the substantive and procedural law that may be applied so that the aspect of undue prejudice may be analyzed;

    (v) such other factors as may be appropriate in the instant circumstances.

- Where one jurisdiction has an ancillary role,

    (i) the court in the ancillary jurisdiction should be provided with information on an ongoing basis and be kept apprised of developments in respect of that debtor's reorganizational efforts in the foreign jurisdiction;

    (ii) stakeholders in the ancillary jurisdiction should be afforded appropriate access to the proceedings in the principal jurisdiction.

- As effective notice as is reasonably practicable in the circumstances should be given to all affected stakeholders, with an opportunity for such stakeholders to come back into the court to review the granted order with a view, if thought desirable, to rescind or vary the granted order or to obtain any other appropriate relief in the circumstances.[30]

These factors have provided, and will continue to provide, helpful guidance on how Canadian courts should approach foreign recognition orders. The issue of centre of main interest (COMI) is likely to be one that is a key question in the future, given enactment by the United States of Chapter 15 and hence the new requirement under that legislation that there only be one centre of main interest, as discussed below.

Prior to the enactment of Chapter 15 in the United States, §304 of the U.S. *Bankruptcy Code* empowered a foreign representative to commence an ancillary proceeding to assist the foreign insolvency proceeding. Section 304 recognition was discretionary. As such proceedings were ancillary, they did not invoke the full range

---

[30] *Ibid.* at para. 21.

of rights and remedies as parties in a U.S. bankruptcy case; rather, the statute envisioned that if the relief was not sufficient, a full U.S. bankruptcy proceeding could be filed.

Section 304 allowed the court to order an interim or permanent injunction to prevent U.S. creditors from seizing a foreign debtor's assets based in the U.S.; the turnover of a foreign debtor's U.S. assets to a foreign representative for administration in foreign proceedings; and "other appropriate relief." The court exercised its discretion to grant recognition and relief based on: what will best assure an economical and expeditious administration of the foreign debtor's estate, in light of the just treatment of claim and interest holders of the foreign estate; protection of U.S. claim holders against prejudice and inconvenience in the processing of claims in the foreign proceeding; prevention of preferential or fraudulent dispositions of property of the foreign estate; distribution of proceeds of such estate substantially in accordance with the order prescribed by the U.S. *Bankruptcy Code*; comity; and provision of an opportunity for a fresh start for the debtor involved in the foreign proceeding.[31]

Given the territorial nature of the U.S. *Bankruptcy Code*, there was some uncertainty at any given time, as to whether the court would recognize a foreign proceeding. In *Toga Manufacturing Limited*, the debtor was petitioned into bankruptcy, and the trustee in bankruptcy sought an order under §304 for the Michigan court clerk to surrender certain funds. The court rejected the application, holding that the foreign representative had failed to satisfy the criteria established under §304, noting the differential treatment of one creditor under both Canada and U.S. law in terms of whether its claim was secured.[32] The court held that it "must protect United States citizens' claims against foreign judgments inconsistent with this country's well-defined and accepted policies".[33] More recently, however, U.S. courts have granted recognition orders. For example, the U.S. Bankruptcy Court granted ancillary relief in proceedings in Stelco Inc., Canada 3000 Inc., Air Canada, Canadian Airlines International Limited, and Euro United Corporation.[34]

During the 1990s, the courts in Canada and the U.S. developed protocols on cross-border co-operation. These orders have dealt with coordination and co-operation in the administration of proceedings, coordination in ongoing operations, asset sales and distribution, claims filing procedures and choice of law issues, and coordination of development of plans in both countries. Cross-border protocols have reduced the cost of litigation and placed the focus on restructuring issues instead of conflict of laws disputes. These cases involved Canadian debtor corporations with significant operations and asset holdings in the United States, or *vice versa*, and thus the debtor corporations required recourse to protection of insolvency laws in both jurisdictions. A protocol sets out the ground rules by which concurrent insolvency proceedings

[31] J. Robert Stoll and Amy S. Korte, "Cross-Border Insolvency Proceedings Involving Assets Located in the United States of America" (2003) 20 National Insolvency Rev. 53 at 75-76.

[32] *In the Matter of Toga Manufacturing Ltd.*, 28 B.R. 165 (U.S. Mich. Bktcy., 1983) at 166.

[33] *Ibid.* at 170.

[34] *Stelco Inc., Re*, Case Nos. 42402, 42404, and 42403 (U.S. E.D. Mich., January 29, 2004) (Bankruptcy Court for the Eastern District of Michigan).

can be coordinated; honours the sovereignty of the respective courts; harmonizes activities in multi-jurisdictional insolvency proceedings; promotes the orderly and efficient administration of proceedings; promotes international co-operation and respect for comity among the courts; facilitates fair and open processes for insolvency proceedings for the benefit of all parties; and implements a framework of general principles to address basic administration issues arising out of cross-border insolvencies.

The cross-border protocol in the 360Networks case contained as Appendix 9 to this text is an example of a cross-border protocol.[35]

With the amendments in 1997 to the *CCAA* to add section 18.6 in its current form, some practitioners rely more directly on the provisions of the statute and less on protocols than previously.

There have been joint hearings conducted by Canadian and U.S. Courts in restructuring applications.[36] Such hearings allow parties on both sides of the border to have the benefit of making submissions and hearing the concerns of the court without the "filter" of reading their views in foreign judgments. Courts can signal parties regarding restructuring issues that concern the court's particular jurisdiction and they allow the judges to directly communicate instead of only through written judgments.[37] Given the time sensitive nature of restructuring proceedings, they can expedite decisions, cut costs in terms of numbers of court appearances, and facilitate decisions that have pragmatic and practical effect in both jurisdictions.

Section 18.6 also allows the judges in different proceedings internationally to directly communicate with one another under the section 11.6(6) discretion that allows the *CCAA* judge to seek the aid and assistance of a court by written request or otherwise as the court considers appropriate. Canadian courts, through their orders, do directly request information and assistance, and in a number of cases, protocols have allowed direct communication. In the current proceeding of *Muscletech Research and Development Inc.*, the *CCAA* judge and the Chapter 15 U.S. judge are in direct communication in respect of coordination and co-operation.[38]

While protocols for cross-border insolvencies have developed coherent procedural protections for proceedings in multiple jurisdictions, the caselaw continues to be underdeveloped on the level of deference to be accorded to foreign proceedings.

---

[35] Cross-Border Insolvency Protocol in Re 360networks inc. between British Columbia Supreme Court, Vancouver (Mr. Justice D.F. Tysoe), Case No. L011792, (June 28, 2001) and United States Bankruptcy Court for the Southern District of New York (Hon. Allan L. Gropper), Case No. 01-13721-alg, (August 29, 2001).

[36] An example of a joint hearing was *Livent* in Ontario, and in *Solv-x.* in Alberta. Joint hearings were provided for under the *Loewen* protocol. *The Loewen Group,* Initial Order under the *CCAA*, June 1, 1999, (Ont. S.C.J. Commercial List), Court File No. 99-CL3304.

[37] Janis Sarra, *Creditor Rights and the Public Interest, Restructuring Insolvent Corporations* (Toronto: University of Toronto Press, 2003).

[38] *Muscletech Research & Development Inc., Re* (2006), 2006 CarswellOnt 720, [2006] O.J. No. 462 (Ont. S.C.J.) at para. 5.

Teleglobe Inc. and some of its subsidiaries filed for protection under the *CCAA* and the U.S. companies in the Teleglobe group sought ancillary relief under §304 of the U.S. *Bankruptcy Code*. The U.S. Bankruptcy Court for the District of Delaware issued a temporary restraining order.[39] Subsequently, the U.S. Court granted a preliminary injunction with respect to certain of the Teleglobe companies; however, the U.S. Court found that with respect to the U.S. based subsidiaries, that the "petitioner has not demonstrated a reasonable probability of success on the merits of the contention that the domicile, residence, principal place of business, or principal assets of any of the domestic corporations at the commencement of the case give rise to a foreign proceeding within the meaning of 11 U.S.C. s.101(23)".[40] The U.S. bankruptcy court terminated the §304 proceedings with respect to these companies and Chapter 11 proceedings were commenced under the *Bankruptcy Code*.

In *Menegon* v. *Philip Services Corp.*, the Canadian parent corporation had a number of subsidiaries in Canada and the United States.[41] Following the commencement of class-action proceedings in both countries, the parent corporation and its Canadian subsidiaries filed for protection under the *CCAA*, and the parent and its U.S. subsidiaries filed for protection under Chapter 11 of the *Bankruptcy Code*. Separate plans were subsequently filed in the U.S. and Canadian proceedings, and the plans specified that domestic claims would be dealt with in each respective jurisdiction. Certain creditors objected, including a creditor whose claims would have been treated less-favourably under U.S. bankruptcy law than in the Canadian proceedings. The Ontario Superior Court of Justice, in refusing to sanction a cross-border class action settlement in the context of a *CCAA* proceeding, held that approval was premature as the proposed settlement of the class action and the issue of whether the debtor corporation could be successfully restructured were closely linked.[42]

The Court in *Menegon* v. *Philip Services Corp.* held that the fact that a Canadian creditor's rights are to be dealt with by parallel U.S. insolvency proceedings is not in itself sufficient to undermine the fairness and reasonableness of a restructuring plan; however, it is the right to vote on the plan before creditors are bound that is an essential component of the *CCAA* regime. The Court observed that although the company had a substantial connection to the U.S. with respect to the residence of shareholders and the location of the majority of its operating assets, it also had a substantial connection to Canada with company headquarters in Ontario, and 94 locations and 2,000 employees in Canada. It further held that the objective of the protocol was to protect claimants on either side of the border from being swept into the rigours of the other country's regime, where to do so might prevent them from asserting their substantive rights under the applicable laws of their own jurisdictions. Comity does not mean that one court must cede its authority over its own process or over the application of substantive laws of its own jurisdiction. Here, the issue

[39] The U.S. order was made on May 15, 2002. *Teleglobe Inc., Re*, Case No. 02-11404 (MFW) (U.S. Del. Bktcy., 2002).

[40] *Ibid.*

[41] *Menegon* v. *Philip Services Corp.* (1999), 1999 CarswellOnt 3240, [1999] O.J. No. 4080 (Ont. S.C.J. (Commercial List)).

[42] *Ibid.*

was less an issue of comity, but rather, a case where the debtor corporation failed to comply with the statutory requirements of the *CCAA*.[43]

III. U.S. CHAPTER 15 NON-MAIN PROCEEDINGS

One of the first Canadian cases involving a *CCAA* main proceeding and the new U.S. Chapter 15 recognition provisions is *Muscletech Research and Development Inc.*, involving Canadian debtor companies whose products sold in the U.S. have given rise to U.S. product liability class action suits and U.S. consumer class actions.[44] The Canadian Court held that the centre of main interest (COMI) of the applicants was Ontario. The finding of COMI is significant, as under Chapter 15 in the U.S., only one jurisdiction can be the centre of main interest. The Court in *Muscletech Research and Development Inc.* found that Ontario was the COMI on the basis that:

- all the applicant companies were incorporated and registered in Ontario; the principals, directors and officers were Ontario residents;
- all decision-making and control in respect of the applicants takes place at the debtor's premises in Ontario;
- the debtor's principal banking arrangements are conducted in Ontario with a Canadian Bank; and
- all administrative functions and employees performing those functions, including general accounting, financial reporting, budgeting and cash management, are conducted in Ontario.[45]

Hence the indicia of COMI were found to include place of registration, place of control and decision making, as well as the court considering administrative and operational factors. The case is highly fact driven and is still in progress as this text goes to press, so there are not yet many lessons to be drawn from the case.[46] It merits note, however, that there was no issue in respect of the recognition of the foreign main proceeding by the New York U.S. Bankruptcy Court, and while there was considerable debate as to the scope of the order, the U.S. court did not have to rule on the scope. It will be interesting to track the progress of the case, particularly in the area of jurisdiction, both domestically within the U.S. (state versus district jurisdiction), and across borders, as the workout proceeds.

In *Ravelston Corp.*, the Ontario Court of Appeal held that an order of the Ontario Superior Court of Justice that directed a debtor company in receivership and *CCAA* proceedings to attorn to the jurisdiction of a foreign court and plead not guilty to an

[43] *Ibid.* at para. 48.

[44] *Muscletech Research & Development Inc., Re* (2006), 2006 CarswellOnt 264, [2006] O.J. No. 167 (Ont. S.C.J. [Commercial List]) and *Muscletech Research & Development Inc., Re* (2006), 2006 CarswellOnt 720, [2006] O.J. No. 462 (Ont. S.C.J.); Court File No. 06-CL-6241.

[45] *Muscletech Research & Development Inc., Re* (2006), 2006 CarswellOnt 264, [2006] O.J. No. 167 (Ont. S.C.J. [Commercial List]) at para. 4.

[46] See, however, the Court's judgment on the question of torts claims, as discussed in chapter 6.

outstanding criminal indictment does not affect the debtor company's future rights to gain an automatic right of appeal under section 193(a) of the *BIA*, but rather tells the debtor company how it should exercise its present rights. The Court held that a court is entitled to exercise its discretion and follow the recommendations of a monitor regarding the best course of conduct of a debtor company in respect of foreign proceedings where such a decision was within the broad bounds of reasonableness, and the monitor can demonstrate that it fully analyzed the situation at hand before arriving at its decision.[47]

While there is now a high degree of cross-border co-operation, Canadian courts will not make orders that are contrary to domestic law. Kent *et al.* have observed that the complexity of issues and interests in Canadian and U.S. proceedings has necessitated the development of flexible adaptive regimes in order to implement practical solutions that are consistent with each country's legal process and principles, balancing the need for co-operation and comity in cross-border proceedings with the protection of local stakeholders' interests and values.[48]

IV. LEGISLATIVE REFORM

Within the proposed provisions of Chapter 47, Canada has adopted an adapted version of the UNCITRAL Model Law, embracing many of the fundamental objectives of the Model Law, but departing on particular aspects.[49] Adoption could enhance current developments in recognition of stakeholder interests because the Model Law specifies that the court recognizing the foreign proceedings and status of the foreign representative, must impose a stay where compatible with domestic law and restrain disposal of assets without consent. All stakeholders are to be treated equitably, regardless of the jurisdiction in which they reside, and the "enterprise is to be permitted to implement a plan so as to reorganize as a global unity, especially where there is an established interdependence on a transnational basis".[50] Thus while cross-border insolvencies would be facilitated, there would be a level of deference to Canadian law and the court's developing jurisprudence in regard to the public interest. The Chapter 47 cross-border provisions replace Part XIII of the *BIA* and section 18.6 of the *CCAA*, the current cross-border provisions, in their entirety.[51]

---

[47] *Ravelston Corp., Re* (2005), 2005 CarswellOnt 9058 (Ont. C.A.).

[48] Andrew Kent, Stephanie Donaher and Adam Maerov, "UNCITRAL, eh? The Model Law and its Implications for Canadian Stakeholders" in Janis Sarra, ed., *Annual Review of Insolvency Law 2005* (Toronto: Carswell, 2006) at 187.

[49] *Guide to Enactment of the UNCITRAL Model Law on Cross-Border Insolvency 1997*, XXVIII UNCITRAL Y.B, U,N, Doc, A/C.N. 9/442, republished in (1999) 6 Tul. J. Int'l & Comp. Law 415. For a discussion see Ian Fletcher. *Insolvency in Private International Law* (Clarendon Press, 1999); A. Berends, "The UNCITRAL Model Law on Cross-Border Insolvency: A Comprehensive Overview" (1998), 6 Tul. J. Int'l & Comp. Law 309.

[50] *Babcock & Wilcox Canada Ltd., Re* (2000), 2000 CarswellOnt 704, [2000] O.J. No. 786 (Ont. S.C.J. [Commercial List]).

[51] When they are proclaimed in force, the provisions of Chapter 47 will become sections 267-284 of the *BIA*, and sections 44-61 of the *CCAA*.

The Guide to Enactment of the UNCITRAL Model Law on Cross-Border Insolvency noted that in incorporating the text of the model into its system, a state may modify or omit provisions; however, such flexibility can create some uncertainty in harmonization, and hence it recommended that states make as few changes as possible incorporating the Model Law into their legal systems.[52] Canada has taken advantage of the flexibility, but it is unclear yet as to the extent of harmonization that this may work toward or detract from.

The express purpose of the Canadian provisions is to provide mechanisms for dealing with cases of cross-border insolvencies and to promote co-operation between the courts and other competent authorities in Canada with those of foreign jurisdictions in cases of cross-border insolvencies; greater legal certainty for trade and investment; the fair and efficient administration of cross-border insolvencies that protects the interests of creditors, other interested persons and those of debtor companies; the protection and maximization of the value of debtor company's property; and the rescue of financially troubled businesses to protect investment and preserve employment.[53]

Foreign court is defined in Chapter 47 as a judicial or other authority competent to control or supervise a foreign proceeding.[54]

For purposes of the cross-border provisions, if an insolvency, reorganization or similar order has been made in respect of a debtor company in a foreign proceeding, a certified copy of the order is, in the absence of evidence to the contrary, proof that the debtor company is insolvent and proof of the appointment of the foreign representative made by the order.[55] The recognition of a foreign proceeding does not prevent Canadian creditors from initiating or maintaining collection proceedings, although it does stay the proceedings in certain circumstances.

1. Foreign Representative

A key objective of the Canadian provisions is to provide timely and direct access for foreign representatives to Canadian courts, to facilitate both communication and co-operation. Chapter 47 will permit a foreign representative to apply to the court for recognition of a foreign proceeding.[56]

---

[52] *Guide to Enactment of the UNCITRAL Model Law on Cross-Border Insolvency 1997*, XXVIII UNCITRAL Y.B. U.N. Doc. A/C.N. 9/442, republished in (1999) 6 Tul. J. Int'l & Comp. Law 415 at para. 12. A. Berends, "The UNCITRAL Model Law on Cross-Border Insolvency: A Comprehensive Overview" (1998), 6 Tul. J. Int'l & Comp. Law 309.

[53] Section 44, *CCAA*, as modified by Chapter 47. These purposes mirror those of the Model Law, aimed at promoting certainty and predictability in insolvency proceedings. Preamble, Model Law.

[54] Section 45(1), *CCAA*, as modified by Chapter 47; mirroring Article 2, Model Law.

[55] Section 59, *CCAA*, as modified by Chapter 47.

[56] Section 46(1), *CCAA*, as modified by Chapter 47.

Foreign representative under the *CCAA* section of Chapter 47 is defined as a person or body, including one appointed on an interim basis, which is authorized, in a foreign proceeding in respect of a debtor company, to monitor the debtor company's business and financial affairs for the purpose of reorganization; or act as a representative in respect of the foreign proceeding.[57] The provisions under the *CCAA* include authorizing the representative to monitor the debtor company's business and financial affairs for the purpose of reorganization, a provision not expressly included in the Model Law.

Chapter 15 of the U.S. *Bankruptcy Code* specifies that on granting of recognition, the foreign representative may sue or be sued in U.S. courts, subject to any limitations that the court may impose consistent with the policy of Chapter 15.[58] The Canadian provisions do not contain such an express provision, although the new section 51 of the *CCAA* creates a right of the foreign representative to commence and continue proceedings as if the foreign representative were a creditor. The ability to be sued is not expressly included. There is likely to be litigation regarding the scope of potential liability of the foreign representative when filing and receiving a recognition order in the U.S., a matter that may give rise to forum shopping away from the United States, depending on the circumstances of the debtor's financial distress.

An application by a foreign representative for an order does not submit the foreign representative to the jurisdiction of the court for any other purpose except with regard to the costs of the proceedings, but the court may make any order conditional on the compliance by the foreign representative with any other order of the court.[59] As with the Model Law, it constitutes a "safe conduct" rule aimed at ensuring that the court will not assume jurisdiction over all the assets of the debtor corporation solely on the basis of a foreign recognition order, and ensuring that the court does not assume jurisdiction over the foreign representative for matters unrelated to the insolvency.[60]

2. Centre of Main Interest (COMI)

The Canadian provisions specify that in the absence of proof to the contrary, a debtor company's registered office is deemed to be the centre of its main interests, mirroring the Model Law.[61] A "foreign proceeding" under the Canadian provisions is defined as a judicial or an administrative proceeding, including an interim proceeding, in a jurisdiction outside Canada dealing with creditors' collective interests generally under any law relating to bankruptcy or insolvency in which a debtor company's business and financial affairs are subject to control or supervision by a foreign court

[57] Section 45(1), *CCAA*, as modified by Chapter 47.

[58] Section 1509(b)(1) of Chapter 15, U.S. *Bankruptcy Code.*

[59] Section 57, *CCAA*, as modified by Chapter 47.

[60] *Guide to Enactment of the UNCITRAL Model Law on Cross-Border Insolvency 1997*, XXVIII UNCITRAL Y.B. U.N. Doc. A/C.N. 9/442, republished in (1999) 6 Tul. J. Int'l & Comp. Law 415 at para. 94.

[61] Section 45, *CCAA*, as modified by Chapter 47.

for the purpose of reorganization.[62] Foreign main proceeding means a foreign proceeding in a jurisdiction where the debtor company has the centre of its main interests, mirroring the Model Law.[63]

However, foreign non-main proceeding is defined differently than the Model Law. The Canadian provisions define foreign non-main proceeding as a foreign proceeding, other than a foreign main proceeding.[64] In contrast, the Model Law requires that the debtor have an establishment within the jurisdiction of a foreign non-main proceeding, defined as any place of operations where the debtor carries out a non-transitory economic activity with human means and goods or services.[65] Chapter 15 of the U.S. *Bankruptcy Code* also requires an establishment in order to come within the definition of foreign non-main proceedings.[66] In Canada, there will be no requirement to have an establishment in the foreign jurisdiction as a condition of recognition of a foreign non-main proceeding.[67] Hence, arguably, one could have different kinds of foreign non-main proceedings than anticipated by the Model Law or U.S. Chapter 15.

Where the COMI is challenged under the Model Law, the court will determine the matter based on the evidence; however, there is no legislative guidance yet on what proof to contrary might be in terms of establishing a COMI in a jurisdiction other than where the debtor's registered office is located.[68] The UNCITRAL Legislative Guide on Insolvency Law, which is aimed at establishing an effective insolvency framework internationally, defines centre of main interest as "the place where the debtor conducts the administration of its interests on a regular basis and that is therefore ascertainable by third parties".[69] The Guide to Enactment of the Model Law observes that it was not advisable to include more than one criterion of COMI for qualifying a proceeding as a foreign main proceeding because multiple criteria would increase the risk of competing claims from foreign jurisdictions for recognition as the main proceeding.[70] Yet, there will inevitably be contests for control through litigation regarding centre of main interest. Moreover, the single criterion fails to take account of corporate groups.

---

[62] Section 45(1), *CCAA*, as modified by Chapter 47. The definition tracks Article 2 of the Model Law.

[63] Section 45(1), *CCAA*, as modified by Chapter 47. Article 17(2)(a) and Article 2(b), Model Law. See also Section 1502(4), Chapter 15, U.S. *Bankruptcy Code.*

[64] Section 45(1), *CCAA*, as modified by Chapter 47.

[65] Article 2(c) and (f), and 17(2)(b), Model Law. Article 17(4) of the Model Law specifies that the recognition provisions do not prevent modification or termination of recognition if it is shown that the grounds for granting it were fully or partially lacking or have ceased to exist.

[66] Section 1502(5), Chapter 15, U.S. *Bankruptcy Code.*

[67] Section 45(1), *CCAA*, as modified by Chapter 47.

[68] *Guide to Enactment of the UNCITRAL Model Law on Cross-Border Insolvency 1997*, XXVIII UNCITRAL Y.B. U.N. Doc. A/C.N. 9/442, republished in (1999) 6 Tul. J. Int'l & Comp. Law 415 at paras. 72, 122.

[69] *UNCITRAL Legislative Guide on Insolvency Law,* United Nations, New York, 2005, at 4, 41, citing the European Council Regulation No. 1346/2000 of May 2000 on Insolvency Proceedings; http://www.iiiglobal.org/organizations/uncitral/2003_Vienna_Report.PDF.

[70] *Guide to Enactment of the UNCITRAL Model Law on Cross-Border Insolvency 1997*, XXVIII UNCITRAL Y.B. U.N. Doc. A/C.N. 9/442, republished in (1999) 6 Tul. J. Int'l & Comp. Law 415 at para. 127.

The notion of COMI appears grounded for the most part in a single legal entity, and the language reflects the policy intent not to have competing applications for a main proceeding. Yet the reality is that many cross-border insolvencies involve corporate groups, including divisions, subsidiaries, affiliates, and co-venture arrangements, and each of these may have a different registered office, and their own distinct management structure, with little decision-making input from the ultimate parent corporation. Other corporate groups may be highly integrated in their financial and decision making structure. One or more of the parent or subsidiaries may be insolvent. The failure of both the Model Law and Canadian Chapter 47 to deal with the issue of corporate groups and the resultant challenge for determining COMI is significant in Canada, as there are many insolvency proceedings that involve groups of companies carrying on business in more than one jurisdiction.

The issue of COMI has been the key issue in a number of EU insolvency proceedings. The European Court of Justice (Grand Chamber) recently interpreted COMI, specifically, it ruled that where a debtor is a subsidiary company whose registered office and that of its parent company are situated in two different Member States, the presumption laid down in Article 3(1) of Council Regulation (EC) No 1346/2000 on insolvency proceedings, whereby the centre of main interests of that subsidiary is situated in the Member State where its registered office is situated, can be rebutted only if "factors which are both objective and ascertainable by third parties enable it to be established that an actual situation exists which is different from that which location at that registered office is deemed to reflect". The court held that this could occur in the case of a company not carrying out any business in the territory of the Member State where its registered office is situated; however, the mere fact that its economic choices are or can be controlled by a parent company in another Member State is not enough to rebut the presumption laid down by that Regulation.[71] Canadian courts may look to EU law for some direction on how to interpret the COMI rebuttable presumption provisions.

3. Public Policy Exception

The Chapter 47 cross border provisions continue a current provision in the *CCAA* that specifies that the Canadian court is not required to make any order that is not in compliance with the laws of Canada or to enforce any order made by a foreign court.[72] Arguably, this provision provides the Canadian court with jurisdiction to decline to make an order or enforce an order that is contrary to public policy. As noted earlier in this text, Canadian courts have recognized the public interest aspects

[71] *Eurofood IFSC Ltd., Re* (May 2, 2006), Europe Case C-341/04 (European C.J. [Grand Chamber]), at paras. 33-40. The Court further held that a main insolvency proceeding opened by a court of a Member State must be recognized by the courts of the other Member States, without the latter being able to review the jurisdiction of the court of the opening State; however, the court may refuse to recognize insolvency proceedings opened in another Member State where the decision to open the proceedings was taken in flagrant breach of the fundamental right to be heard, which a person concerned by such proceedings enjoys.

[72] Section 61(2), *CCAA*, as modified by Chapter 47.

of restructuring; in particular, the flexibility of the *CCAA* has allowed the court to engage in a balancing of interests and prejudice based on public interest.

4. Application for Recognition

Under the proposed amendments to the *CCAA*, a foreign representative may apply to the court for recognition of the foreign proceeding in respect of which it is a foreign representative.[73] The provisions create a streamlined recognition procedure. The party seeking recognition must file: a certified copy of the instrument that commenced the foreign proceeding or a certificate from the foreign court affirming the existence of the foreign proceeding; a certified copy of the instrument or court order authorizing the foreign representative to act in that capacity; and a statement identifying all foreign proceedings in respect of the debtor company that are known to the foreign representative.[74] The court may, without further proof, accept these documents as evidence that the proceeding to which they relate is a foreign proceeding and that the applicant is a foreign representative in respect of the foreign proceeding.[75] In the absence of the documents referred to, the court may accept any other evidence of the existence of the foreign proceeding and of the foreign representative's authority that it considers appropriate.[76] These provisions closely follow the Model law language.[77] The court may require a translation of documents supplied in support of the application for recognition.[78]

If the court is satisfied that the application for the recognition of a foreign proceeding relates to a foreign proceeding and that the applicant is a foreign representative in respect of that proceeding, the court shall make an order recognizing the foreign proceeding, and shall specify in the order whether the foreign proceeding is a foreign main proceeding or a foreign non-main proceeding.[79] Hence, once the requisite filings are made, the recognition order is automatic and not generally subject to the discretion of the court. Since the provisions mirror both the Model Law and Chapter 15 of the U.S. *Bankruptcy Code*, this will create consistency in respect of recognition of foreign proceedings.[80] In the context of Canada / U.S. cross border proceedings, this should considerably reduce the uncertainty associated with the U.S. court's discretion under former §304 to decline to grant orders in a recognition proceeding. While there has been less uncertainty in Canada as to the exercise of discretion in granting foreign recognition, the mandatory nature of the provision will nevertheless provide greater certainty to debtors in terms of the scope of orders that will be granted on recognition of a foreign main proceeding.

---

[73] Section 46(1), *CCAA*, as modified by Chapter 47, mirroring Article 9, Model Law.

[74] Section 46(2), *CCAA*, as modified by Chapter 47.

[75] Section 46(3), *CCAA*, as modified by Chapter 47.

[76] Section 46(4), *CCAA*, as modified by Chapter 47.

[77] Articles 15 and 16, Model Law. See also sections 1515 and 1516, Chapter 15, U.S. *Bankruptcy Code*.

[78] Section 46(5), *CCAA*, as modified by Chapter 47; Article 15(4), Model Law.

[79] Sections 47(1), (2), *CCAA*, as modified by Chapter 47.

[80] Section 1517, Chapter 15, U.S. *Bankruptcy Code*.

Under the Canadian provisions, the foreign representative must inform the court, without delay, of any substantial change in the status of the recognized foreign proceeding, any substantial change in the status of the foreign representative's authority to act in that capacity, and any other foreign proceeding in respect of the same debtor company that becomes known to the foreign representative.[81] The foreign representative must also publish, without delay after the order is made, once a week for two consecutive weeks, or as otherwise directed by the court, in one or more newspapers in Canada specified by the court, a notice containing the prescribed information.[82]

5. Stay of Proceedings

Once the foreign representative and foreign proceeding are recognized, the stay is mandatory. This stay must be ordered by the court with carriage of the proceeding.[83] Where the court recognizes a foreign main proceeding, the *CCAA* provisions of Chapter 47 specify that the court shall make an order, subject to any terms and conditions it considers appropriate, staying for any period that the court considers necessary, all proceedings taken or that might be taken against the debtor company under the *BIA* or the *WURA;* restraining, until otherwise ordered by the court, further proceedings in any action, suit or proceeding against the debtor company; prohibiting, until otherwise ordered by the court, the commencement or further pursuit of any action, suit or proceeding against the debtor company; and prohibiting the debtor company from selling or otherwise disposing of, outside the ordinary course of its business, any of the debtor company's property or business in Canada.[84]

The stay relief under the Canadian provisions is subject to three conditions. First, the order must be consistent with any order that may be made under the legislation.[85] Second, these provisions do not apply if any proceedings under the *CCAA* or the *BIA* have been commenced in respect of the debtor company at the time the order recognizing the foreign proceeding is made.[86] Third, nothing in the recognition order precludes the debtor company from commencing or continuing proceedings under the *CCAA*, the *BIA* or the *WURA* in respect of the debtor company.[87]

The stay provisions are aimed at an orderly, fair and expeditious conduct of the cross-border proceedings. The mandatory nature of the stay once the court is satisfied that it is appropriate to make a recognition order, facilitates the debtor obtaining operating capital during the workout period by increasing the certainty and predictability of the proceeding. At the same time, the court retains discretion to impose

[81] Section 53, *CCAA*, as modified by Chapter 47. Article 18, Model Law. See also section 1518, Chapter 15, U.S. *Bankruptcy Code*.

[82] Section 53, *CCAA*, as modified by Chapter 47.

[83] Section 48, *CCAA*, as modified by Chapter 47.

[84] Section 48(1), *CCAA*, as modified by Chapter 47. This mirrors Article 20 of the Model Law.

[85] Section 48(2), *CCAA*, as modified by Chapter 47.

[86] Section 48(3), *CCAA*, as modified by Chapter 47.

[87] Section 48(4), *CCAA*, as modified by Chapter 47.

terms and conditions on the order, hence protecting the ability of the court to supervise its own proceedings and advance the public policy objectives of Canadian insolvency law.

The scope of the stay under Chapter 47 is as broad as that under the Model Law. Upon recognition of a foreign main proceeding, an automatic stay of individual creditor actions and proceedings concerning the assets, rights, obligations or liabilities of the debtor takes effect, and the right to execute against, transfer, encumber, or otherwise dispose of assets of the debtor is stayed or suspended.[88] The stay provides the debtor corporation with "breathing space", in terms of preventing creditors from moving to realize on their claims to assets until proper procedures are put into place for reorganization or liquidation or some combination of these strategies. In turn, this is aimed at promoting an orderly and fair cross-border proceeding.[89]

Notably absent from the Canadian provisions is Article 22 of the Model Law, which specifies that in granting or denying relief, the court must be satisfied that the interests of creditors and other interested persons, including the debtor, are adequately protected, allowing the court to impose conditions, modify orders or terminate relief as it considers appropriate.[90] The omission is likely due to the fact that Canadian insolvency law does not currently enshrine a notion of "adequate protection", as currently exists in the U.S. and some other jurisdictions. The court may also, at the request of the foreign representative or a person affected by relief granted, or at its own motion, modify or terminate such relief. Similarly, the Canadian provisions do not contain an express provision similar to Article 23 of the Model Law, titled "actions to avoid acts detrimental to creditors", which specifies that where the foreign representative has standing to initiate actions, the court must be satisfied that the action relates to assets that, under the law of the state, should be administered in the foreign non-main proceeding.

The premise of the adequate protection provisions is that there is a balance between the relief granted to the foreign representative and the interests of creditors and other

---

[88] Article 20(1)(a), (b), and (c), Model Law.

[89] *Guide to Enactment of the UNCITRAL Model Law on Cross-Border Insolvency 1997*, XXVIII UNCITRAL Y.B. U.N. Doc. A/C.N. 9/442, republished in (1999) 6 Tul. J. Int'l & Comp. Law 415 at para. 32.

[90] Article 22, Model Law. See also section 1522, Chapter 15, U.S. *Bankruptcy Code*, which specifies that (a) The court may grant relief under section 1519 or 1521, or may modify or terminate relief under subsection (c), only if the interests of the creditors and other interested entities, including the debtor, are sufficiently protected; (b) The court may subject to relief granted under section 1519 or 1521, or the operation of the debtor's business under section 1520(a)(3), to conditions it considers appropriate, including the giving of security or the filing of a bond; (c) The court may, at the request of the foreign representative or an entity affected by relief granted under section 1519 or 1521, or at its own motion, modify or terminate such relief; (d) Section 1104(d) shall apply to the appointment of an examiner under this chapter. Any examiner shall comply with the qualification requirements imposed on a trustee by section 322.

interested persons that may be affected by the relief granted.[91] However, notwithstanding that there is no such specific provision in Chapter 47, in practice, Canadian courts, in granting relief, engage in a balancing of interests and prejudice in considering the interests of the debtor, creditors, employees and other stakeholders. While this has not been undertaken in the context of strict codification of "adequate protection", it has allowed the court to consider multiple interests in granting relief. Moreover, it merits note that the U.S. *Bankruptcy Code* has long had the concept of adequate protection and Canadian insolvency statutes have not, and this has not acted as a bar to successful cross-border proceedings. Hence this distinction in language should not be a barrier to enhanced cross-border co-operation and coordination.

6. The Court's Discretionary Power to Grant Relief

The Canadian provisions also grant the court discretion to make a number of other orders, similar to the provisions of the Model Law.[92] If a recognition order is granted, the Canadian court may make any order that it considers appropriate, on application by the foreign representative, if it is satisfied that it is necessary for the protection of the debtor company's property or the interests of creditors. If the proceeding is a foreign non-main proceeding, the court has discretion to make orders similar to those available for a main proceeding, such as staying domestic insolvency proceedings or the commencement or pursuit of actions against the debtor company, or disposing of property outside of the ordinary course of business. The court can also order the examination of witnesses; the taking of evidence or the delivery of information concerning the debtor company's property, business and financial affairs, debts, liabilities and obligations; and can authorize the foreign representative to monitor the debtor company's business and financial affairs in Canada for the purpose of reorganization.[93]

Under the Canadian provisions, the restriction on the court's discretion is that if any proceedings under the *CCAA* have been commenced in respect of the debtor company at the time an order recognizing the foreign proceeding is made, an order made under these provisions must be consistent with any order that may be made in any proceedings under the domestic insolvency statute.[94] As with mandatory orders, the making of a discretionary order does not preclude the commencement or the continuation of proceedings under the *CCAA*, the *BIA* or the *WURA* in respect of the debtor company.[95]

---

[91] *Guide to Enactment of the UNCITRAL Model Law on Cross-Border Insolvency 1997*, XXVIII UNCITRAL Y.B. U.N. Doc. A/C.N. 9/442, republished in (1999) 6 Tul. J. Int'l & Comp. Law 415 at para. 161.

[92] Article 21, Model Law.

[93] Section 49(1), *CCAA*, as modified by Chapter 47.

[94] Section 49(2), *CCAA*, as modified by Chapter 47.

[95] Section 49(3), *CCAA*, as modified by Chapter 47.

The foreign representative may commence and continue proceedings under the *BIA* and *CCAA* in respect of a debtor company as if the foreign representative were a creditor of the debtor company, or the debtor company.[96]

7. Obligations

Chapter 47 sets out a series of obligations, including co-operation by the court, other Canadian authorities and the foreign representative. It specifies that if an order recognizing a foreign proceeding is made, the court shall cooperate, to the maximum extent possible, with the foreign representative and the foreign court involved in the foreign proceeding.[97] If any proceedings under the *CCAA* have been commenced in respect of a debtor company, every person who exercises powers or performs duties and functions under Canadian proceedings is required to cooperate, to the maximum extent possible, with the foreign representative and the foreign court involved in the foreign proceeding.[98]

The Canadian provisions do not expressly provide, as the Model Law does, that the court and the person administering the liquidation or reorganization are entitled to communicate directly with, or to request information or assistance directly from, foreign courts or foreign representatives.[99] It is unclear what the significance of this might be, because, as noted above, section 18.6 as currently framed allows this communication. Courts may have to fall back on common law principles of comity and inherent jurisdiction, as well as the discretion under section 11 of the *CCAA* to continue this practice of direct court to court communication.

The Canadian provisions specify that both the court and any person who exercises any powers or performs any duties shall cooperate to the maximum extent possible, as noted above.

In making a compromise or an arrangement of a debtor company, the following shall be taken into account in the distribution of dividends to the company's creditors in Canada as if they were a part of that distribution: (a) the amount that a creditor receives or is entitled to receive outside Canada by way of a dividend in a foreign proceeding in respect of the company; and (b) the value of any property of the company that the creditor acquires outside Canada on account of a provable claim of the creditor or that the creditor acquires outside Canada by way of a transfer that, if it were subject to the *BIA*, would be a preference over other creditors or a transfer at undervalue.[100] The creditor is not entitled to receive a dividend from the distribution in Canada until every other creditor who has a claim of equal rank in the

[96] Section 51 *CCAA*, as modified by Chapter 47. This is similar to Articles 11, 12 and 24, Model Law.

[97] Section 52(1), *CCAA*, as modified by Chapter 47.

[98] Section 52(2), *CCAA*, as modified by Chapter 47. All these provisions are mirrored in proposed amendments to the *BIA*.

[99] Articles 25(2) and 26(2), Model Law.

[100] Section 60(1), *CCAA*, as modified by Chapter 47.

order of priority established under the *BIA* or *CCAA* has received a dividend equal (expressed as a percentage of the claim) to the benefit that the creditor has received or is entitled to receive in the foreign proceedings, for the aggregate of the amount referred to in (a) or (b) above.[101] Moreover, the statute expressly states that nothing prevents the court, on the application of a foreign representative or any other interested person, from applying any legal or equitable rules governing the recognition of foreign insolvency orders and assistance to foreign representatives that are not inconsistent with the provisions of the Act.[102]

8. Coordination of Concurrent Proceedings

Chapter 47 expressly recognizes multiple proceedings, and facilitates coordination between a local proceeding and one or more foreign proceedings. The provisions are aimed at fostering coordination of decision-making, with the ultimate objective of a successful restructuring or maximizing the value of creditors' claims.

Chapter 47 provides for concurrent proceedings, and specifies that if any proceedings under the *CCAA* in respect of a debtor company are commenced at any time after an order recognizing the foreign proceeding is made, the court shall review any order it has made and, if it determines that the order is inconsistent with any orders made in the Canadian proceeding, the court shall amend or revoke the order.[103]

Chapter 47 does not, however, have the Model Law provision that specifies that any relief granted to a representative of a foreign non-main proceeding after recognition of a foreign main proceeding must be consistent with the foreign main proceeding.[104] This Model Law provision has as its object to promote consistency of relief where there are concurrent proceedings; to be achieved by modifying or tailoring of relief, or in some circumstances, terminating relief already granted.[105]

Hence, the statutory language in Canada differs in that it preserves the court's discretion to make orders in the domestic proceeding that perhaps do not align with orders in a foreign main proceeding. Notwithstanding what appears to be a significant difference, it is important to note that there has been a strong willingness by Canadian courts to advance comity and cross-border co-operation, and hence, while there is

[101] Section 60(2), *CCAA*, as modified by Chapter 47.

[102] Section 61(1), *CCAA*, as modified by Chapter 47. Article 32 of the Model Law specifies a rule of payment in concurrent proceedings: Without prejudice to secured claims or rights *in rem*, a creditor who has received part payment in respect of its claim in a proceeding pursuant to a law relating to insolvency in a foreign State may not receive a payment for the same claim in a proceeding under [*identify laws of the enacting State relating to insolvency*] regarding the same debtor, so long as the payment to the other creditors of the same class is proportionately less than the payment the creditor has already received.

[103] Section 54, *CCAA*, as modified by Chapter 47.

[104] Article 30, Model Law.

[105] *UNCITRAL Legislative Guide on Insolvency Law,* United Nations, New York, 2005, at 4, 41, citing the European Council Regulation No. 1346/2000 of May 2000 on Insolvency Proceedings; http://www.iiiglobal.org/organizations/uncitral/2003_Vienna_Report.PDF at para. 193.

not a prohibiting provision in terms of consistency of orders under a domestic proceeding with those of the previously approved foreign main proceeding, Canadian courts are likely to seek to align provisions where they do not conflict with the spirit or requirements of Canadian legislation. Section 61(2) of the proposed changes to the *CCAA* specifies that nothing requires the Canadian court to make any order that is not in compliance with the laws of Canada or to enforce any order made by a foreign court.

If, at any time after a foreign recognition order is made of a foreign non-main proceeding in respect of a debtor company, an order recognizing a foreign main proceeding is made, the Canadian court is required to review any order made in respect of the foreign non-main proceeding and amend or revoke the order if it determines that the order is inconsistent with any orders in respect of the foreign main proceedings.[106]

If a subsequent order recognizing another foreign non-main proceeding is made in respect of the debtor company, the court must review its orders in respect of the first recognized proceeding and amend or revoke the order if it considers it appropriate to facilitate coordination.[107]

There is one key difference between the Model Law and the Canadian Chapter 47. The Model Law specifies that after recognition of a foreign main proceeding, a proceeding under the law of the domestic state may be commenced only if the debtor has assets in the state; and the effects of that proceeding shall be restricted to the assets of the debtor that are located there and, to the extent necessary to implement co-operation and coordination, to other assets of the debtor that, under the domestic law, should be administered in that proceeding.[108] Hence, the Model Law does not prohibit commencement of a local proceeding after recognition of a foreign main proceeding, but it limits the scope of the proceeding normally to assets located in the non-main proceeding jurisdiction.

In contrast, Chapter 47 does not have a provision similar to Article 28 of the Model Law, which appears to effectively preclude commencement of concurrent main proceedings. The Canadian provisions appear to expressly contemplate concurrent main proceedings, as currently exist in some Canadian cross-border proceedings. The language of the Model Law raises several questions. First, if a main proceeding has been recognized in another jurisdiction but not yet granted a recognition order in the domestic state, can the domestic state commence a main proceeding? There is nothing in the language that appears to preclude this. If so, there is likely to be a "race to recognition" and considerable forum shopping. There is no analogous provision that prevents commencement of a domestic proceeding if it precedes

[106] Section 55(1), *CCAA*, as modified by Chapter 47. Articles 11, 12 and 24, Model Law.

[107] Section 55(2), *CCAA*, as modified by Chapter 47. Article 30, Model Law.

[108] Article 28, Model Law; see also Chapter 15.

recognition of a foreign main proceeding.[109] If a recognition order for a foreign main proceeding has been granted, can the domestic court nevertheless approve domestic main proceedings? The Model Law would appear to allow for domestic proceedings, but not main proceedings, as it for the most part restricts the court's jurisdiction to the debtor's assets in the jurisdiction. Yet even such a restriction may not resolve conflicts, given that the domestic jurisdiction may have considerable assets and few creditors' claims. The Model Law is unclear as to how claims are to be realized in such an instance, and which court has jurisdiction over the claims realization process. The impact on a workout strategy is therefore to add an element of uncertainty about the results of liquidation that may impede negotiation for such a strategy.

The Model Law also specifies that when a proceeding in the state is taking place at the time the application for recognition of the foreign proceeding is filed, any relief granted must be consistent with the domestic proceeding; and if the foreign proceeding is recognized in the domestic state as a foreign main proceeding, the Article 20 automatic stay provisions do not apply.[110] When the proceeding in the state commences after filing of an application or recognition of the foreign proceeding, any relief in effect shall be reviewed by the court and is to be modified or terminated if inconsistent with the domestic proceeding.[111] If the foreign proceeding is a foreign main proceeding, the stay and suspension are to be modified or terminated if inconsistent with the domestic proceeding.[112] This language appears broad enough to contemplate a domestic proceeding that could be a main proceeding and a foreign main proceeding, although this would likely be highly contested. Even if it were to be interpreted this way, the language of the Model Law raises the question of whether a third jurisdiction implicated in the debtor's insolvency could recognize two foreign main proceedings.

Under the Canadian provisions, a domestic proceeding may be commenced after recognition of a foreign main proceeding even if the debtor has no assets in Canada, as long as the debtor conducts business in Canada, something that does not appear to be possible under the Model Law.[113] Realistically, however, it is difficult to conduct business in a jurisdiction without some assets, so this may be a distinction without a difference. The Model Law requires that in granting relief to a representative of a foreign non-main proceeding, the court must be satisfied that the relief relates to assets that, under the law of the state, should be administered in the foreign non-main proceeding or concerns information required in that proceeding.[114] Hence, domestic law tempers the scope of relief available under the recognition order, regardless of when the order is sought. The timing of the various recognition orders

---

[109] Marvin Baer, "The Impact of Part XIII of the *BIA* and the UNCITRAL Model Law on Cross-Border Insolvency" (February 1998), online: Government of Canada, http://www.strategis.ic.gc.ca/pics/cl/uncitr_1-2.pdf at 9.

[110] Article 29(a), Model Law.

[111] Article 29(b)(i), Model Law.

[112] Article 29(b)(ii), Model Law.

[113] Section 2 of the current *CCAA* requires that a company within the meaning of the statute is one having assets or doing business in Canada, wherever incorporated.

[114] Article 21(3) and Article 29(3), Model Law.

and commencement of proceedings is likely to place limits on the court's decision to grant particular relief. If proceedings under the *BIA* or *CCAA* have already been commenced, the automatic relief prescribed upon recognition of a foreign main proceeding does not apply.

There continues to be debate in both Canada and the U.S. regarding the scope of concurrent proceedings that may be recognized under section 1528 of Chapter 15. A very liberal interpretation suggests that the courts could recognize a domestic main proceeding and a foreign main proceeding. As with the Model Law, under section 1528 of Chapter 15, the domestic proceeding can extend to assets that are not within the state but are within the jurisdiction of the court and have not been brought under the jurisdiction and control of a foreign proceeding.[115]

The Chapter 47 provisions are codification of many current practices of Canadian courts. Hence while some discretion is removed in the sense of mandatory stay orders once recognition is granted, the reality is that under the current provisions of the *CCAA*, once a court does grant recognition in Canada, these types of orders are almost always granted. While codification will provide greater certainty and predictability for foreign representatives in considering recognition and other applications, in Canada, in practice, the difference may not be significant. This will be clearer after some initial caselaw.

9. Notice

Whereas the Model Law provides detailed notice provisions, the proposed Canadian statutory amendments are for the most part silent.[116] Article 14 of the Model Law

[115] Section 1529 specifies:

> If a foreign proceeding and a case under another chapter of this title are pending concurrently regarding the same debtor, the court shall seek co-operation and coordination under sections 1525, 1526, and 1527, and the following shall apply: (1) If the case in the United States pending at the time the petition for recognition of such foreign proceeding is filed – (A) any relief granted under section 1519 or 1521 must be consistent with the relief granted in the case in the United States; and (B) section 1520 does not apply even if such foreign proceeding is recognized as a foreign main proceeding. (2) If a case in the United States under this title commences after recognition, or after the date of the filing of the petition for recognition, of such foreign proceeding – (A) any relief in effect under section 1519 or 1521 shall be reviewed by the court and shall be modified or terminated if inconsistent with the case in the United States; and (B) if such foreign proceeding is a foreign main proceeding, the stay and suspension referred to in section 1520(a) shall be modified or terminated if inconsistent with the relief granted in the case in the United States. (3) In granting, extending, or modifying relief granted to a representative of a foreign nonmain proceeding, the court must be satisfied that the relief relates to assets that, under the laws of the United States, should be administered in the foreign nonmain proceeding or concerns information required in that proceeding. (4) In achieving co-operation and coordination under sections 1528 and 1529, the court may grant any of the relief authorized under section 305.

[116] Section 1514 of Chapter 15 of the U.S. *Bankruptcy Code* parallels the Model Law notice provisions, except that section 1514(d) does not require the notification to foreign creditors to indicate a reasonable time for filing claims; rather, it specifies that a procedural rule or court order will provide such notice as is "reasonable under the circumstances," consistent with U.S. practice.

specifies that whenever the enacting state's laws require notification of domestic creditors, such notification must be given to known creditors, even where they do not have addresses in the enacting state, and the court may make any order necessary to facilitate the notice to creditors with an unknown address. Notice shall be given to the foreign creditors on an individual basis, provide a reasonable period for filing claims, specify the place of filing, and contain any other information pursuant to the enacting state's laws and the court's orders.[117]

As discussed earlier in this text, there had been criticism of the lack of notice regarding commencement of Canadian insolvency proceedings, particularly in respect of granting priority financing at the initial order stage. However, the court now, for the most part, requires parties to give notice. Chapter 47 enshrines some new notice provisions, for example, in DIP financing applications, but not a more general notice requirement. Greater codification of notice would have facilitated cross-border proceedings. However, the courts in section 18.6 proceedings do typically require that notice be given.

The Court in *Babcock and Wilcox* noted that one factor in granting section 18.6 recognition order is notice:

> As effective notice as is reasonably practicable in the circumstances should be given to all affected stakeholders, with an opportunity for such stakeholders to come back into the court to review the granted order with a view, if thought desirable, to rescind or vary the granted order or to obtain any other appropriate relief in the circumstances.[118]

This suggests some sensitivity by Canadian courts to the issue of notice, even absent the Model Law provision.

10. Corporate Groups

The Canadian economy is heavily dependent on its trading relationship with the U.S., as well as access to U.S. capital markets. There is also a heavily integrated parent-subsidiary relationship among the capital structures and operations of corporations in both jurisdictions. Yet the proposed cross-border provisions fail to adequately address how to deal with corporate groups. As noted above, the structure of the Model Law around the notion of COMI is one that provides an entity based test, failing to address the issue of corporate group. Hence, if a debtor does not file as a single entity and meet the specified tests, the debtor will be dependent on the discretion of the court to address recognition in the context of corporate groups. There is likely to be considerable uncertainty regarding recognition of proceedings for corporate groups in the early years of both U.S. and Canadian versions of the Model Law as the result of failure to seriously address this issue.

---

[117] Article 14, Model Law.

[118] *Babcock & Wilcox Canada Ltd., Re* (2000), 2000 CarswellOnt 704, [2000] O.J. No. 786 (Ont. S.C.J. [Commercial List]) at para. 21.

Where the debtor is a single corporate entity, the filing strategy depends on the location and type of assets, the nature of creditors' claims, the jurisdiction in which assets are situated, and where the head office or centre of main interest is located. The specific objectives of the workout may influence filing choices. For example, if a sale of all or substantially all of the business is anticipated, Canadian *CCAA* proceedings may be more expeditious and less rigid than filing in the U.S. and conducting the sale process there. Similarly, treatment of executory contracts can differ considerably in different jurisdictions and this may affect choice of laws. In the Canadian / U.S. cross-border context, DIP financing is more rule driven in the U.S. and may influence choice of regime.[119] Directors and officers tend to have broader indemnification in Canada than in U.S. restructuring proceedings, and depending on the nature of claims against the debtor and its officers, this may influence where the debtor files.

The question of jurisdiction of filing is complicated when there are corporate groups. In addition to the factors that a single entity considers, there are multiple other considerations regarding the most appropriate forum. The parent and/or some affiliated companies may be insolvent and others are not. The capital structures may be highly integrated across borders. Where management or financing control is centralized, the corporate group may need to file concurrently in multiple jurisdictions in order to continue operating, because a stay in one jurisdiction is not sufficient to allow such a centralized structure to continue during the workout negotiation process. Operations may be quite distinct or highly integrated, particularly where various companies in the corporate group are the critical suppliers for other entities in the group, whatever jurisdiction the corporate group members are located in.

This issue arises in many sectors. In such a case, there may be inter-company flow of assets, which could give rise to claims on a solvent member of the corporate group or reviewable transaction claims where payments have been made in the period leading up to filing. The debt structure may be highly integrated, with inter-company loans that cross borders. There may be guarantees by one entity for another or by the officers of the company for debts of a member of the corporate group. There are many cases in which the corporate group should be reorganized as one proceeding, but definitions of COMI may not easily facilitate such a proceeding. There are also cases where the COMI of the Canadian subsidiary may be in Canada, even if the parent's COMI is elsewhere.

In a cross-border proceeding where there is a corporate group operating in a number of jurisdictions, the facility with which the debtor will be able to restructure will depend to a large measure on the court's willingness to grant relief that facilitates the restructuring but is not inconsistent with domestic legislation. Given that different regimes internationally have different normative conceptions of insolvency, with

---

[119] As discussed in chapter 4, the granting of DIP financing is not currently codified in Canada, but will be when Chapter 47 is proclaimed in force. Even after the implementation of Chapter 47, the granting of DIP financing will be more rule driven in proceedings under the U.S. *Bankruptcy Code* than under the *BIA* or *CCAA*.

particular focus on rehabilitation or liquidation or a mix of both, the ability to restructure as a corporate group may be hampered if the courts narrowly interpret the COMI entity-based test for recognition or are unwilling to grant specific orders because they are not consistent with domestic law. Until there is some interpretation of the meaning of the words "evidence to the contrary" in the test for COMI, there will be considerable transaction costs in litigating such recognition and/or in multiple filings across jurisdictions to prevent prejudice due to unwillingness of courts to recognize corporate group proceedings. Kent *et al.* have raised the issue of whether a parent's control over the subsidiary will be sufficient to rebut the presumption that the location of the subsidiary's registered office constitutes its COMI.[120]

While Chapter 47 will implement a modified version of the Model Law, it continues Canada's regime as one of modified universalism, with a strong commitment to co-operation, coordination and consistency. The feature that would allow concurrent main proceedings borders more on an uneasy balance between territorialism and universalism and is not entirely in sync with the Model Law. Yet a liberal interpretation of both laws may lead to a convergence of interpretive approach, having regard to the express objectives of the cross-border provisions. Evidence to date under section 18.6 *CCAA* recognition orders seems to indicate a generally liberal interpretation of comity and principles of co-operation. However, the contest for control and race to recognition may be heightened if there is not uniformity in interpretive approach by the courts.

Questions for review of materials:

1. What tests does the Canadian court currently apply in recognizing a cross border proceeding?

2. What are the principal criteria in determining centre of main-interest?

Questions for discussion:

1. What do you think the implications will be of Canada retaining the right to have concurrent main proceedings across borders, while the changes in U.S. *Bankruptcy Code* Chapter 15 would appear to preclude this?

2. What criteria should be considered in terms of recognizing centre of main interest where there is a corporate group?

---

[120] Andrew J.F. Kent, Stephanie Donaher and Adam Maerov, "UNCITRAL, eh? The Model Law and its Implications for Canadian Stakeholders" in Janis Sarra, ed., *Annual Review of Insolvency Law 2005* (Toronto: Carswell, 2006) at 187.

CONCLUSION

This text has offered the reader a comprehensive introduction to restructuring under the *CCAA*. It examines design of the Canadian insolvency system, including the court's jurisdiction and how the administration of insolvency proceedings works. It indicates that the statute meets its public policy objective, specifically, that it facilitates the insolvent debtor corporation's ability to negotiate compromises and arrangements with its creditors. However, the text also illustrates that there is an ongoing public policy challenge in thinking about the concurrent needs for flexibility and certainty for parties as they work within the framework of the *CCAA*. The courts have strived for predictability in their judgments through the development of principled approaches to the issues before them.

There are numerous legal, financial and management issues underlying *CCAA* proceedings; and while the technical requirements of the *CCAA* are straight forward, the myriad of decisions that are made under the court's supervision are complex, time sensitive and highly driven by power imbalances at the time of a firm's financial distress. This can increase the costs of proceedings and one issue is whether the current proposed reforms to the *CCAA* will control costs by increasing the predictability of outcomes from use of the statute. The additional codification could have the opposite effect of creating a new wave of litigation as parties sort out their respective rights under the amended statute.

The text also highlights the challenges of financing operations during and after a restructuring, and the rapidly changing dynamic of distressed debt financing and new control challenges for governance of the debtor corporation. These issues become infinitely more complicated as workouts implicate multiple jurisdictions.

Study of the *CCAA* would be greatly enhanced by increasing the transparency of the current system, and it is hoped that the Chapter 47 amendments that provide the OSB with the authority to create a centralized and public database of information, will allow greater numbers of creditors and other stakeholders more access to the decisions and information on the dynamics that have shaped and continue to shape the cases.

The policy objective of the *CCAA* is modest, the facilitating of compromises and arrangements. Arguably the statute has far exceeded that objective, although not without its issues, given that it has been the statutory tool of choice for every major restructuring in the past two decades. The courts play a mediating and supervising role, but ultimately, it is the parties that fashion the workout plan and it is they who need to build sufficient consensus that they can take the full benefit of a going forward strategy for the firm.

APPENDIX 1

Companies' Creditors Arrangement Act

An Act to facilitate compromises and arrangements between companies and their creditors

R.S.C. 1985, c. C-36 as am. R.S.C. 1985, c. 27 (2nd Supp.), ss. 10 (Sched., item 3), 11; S.C. 1990, c. 17, s. 4; 1992, c. 27, s. 90(1)(f); 1993, c. 28, s. 78 (Sched. III, item 20) [Repealed 1999, c. 3, s. 12 (Sched., item 4).]; 1993, c. 34, s. 52; 1996, c. 6, s. 167(1)(d), (2); 1997, c. 12, ss. 120–127; 1998, c. 19, s. 260; 1998, c. 30, s. 14(c); 1999, c. 3, s. 22; 1999, c. 28, s. 154; 2000, c. 30, ss. 156–158; 2001, c. 9, ss. 575–577; 2001, c. 34, s. 33; 2002, c. 7, ss. 133–135; 2004, c. 25, ss. 193–195; 2005, c. 3, ss. 15, 16; 2005, c. 47, ss. 124–131 [Not in force at date of publication.]

Short Title

1. Short title — This Act may be cited as the *Companies' Creditors Arrangement Act*.

Interpretation

2. Definitions — In this Act,

"aircraft objects" has the same meaning as in subsection 2(1) of the *International Interests in Mobile Equipment (aircraft equipment) Act*; *("biens aéronautiques")*

"bond" includes a debenture, debenture stock or other evidences of indebtedness; *("obligation")*

"company" means any company, corporation or legal person incorporated by or under an Act of Parliament or of the legislature of a province and any incorporated company having assets or doing business in Canada, wherever incorporated, except banks, authorized foreign banks within the meaning of section 2 of the *Bank Act*, railway or telegraph companies, insurance companies and companies to which the *Trust and Loan Companies Act* applies; *("compagnie")*

"court" means

(a) in Nova Scotia, British Columbia, and Newfoundland, the Supreme Court,

(a.1) in Ontario, the Superior Court of Justice,

(b) in Quebec, the Superior Court,

(c) in New Brunswick, Manitoba, Saskatchewan and Alberta, the Court of Queen's Bench, and

(c.1) in Prince Edward Island, the Trial Division of the Supreme Court,

(d) in Yukon and the Northwest Territories, the Supreme Court, and in Nunavut, the Nunavut Court of Justice;

("tribunal")

"debtor company" means any company that

(a) is bankrupt or insolvent,

(b) has committed an act of bankruptcy within the meaning of the *Bankruptcy and Insolvency Act* or is deemed insolvent within the meaning of the *Winding-up and Restructuring Act*, whether or not proceedings in respect of the company have been taken under either of those Acts,

(c) has made an authorized assignment or against which a bankruptcy order has been made under the *Bankruptcy and Insolvency Act*, or

(d) is in the course of being wound up under the *Winding-up and Restructuring Act* because the company is insolvent;

("compagnie débitrice")

"secured creditor" means a holder of a mortgage, hypothec, pledge, charge, lien or privilege on or against, or any assignment, cession or transfer of, all or any property of a debtor company as security for indebtedness of the debtor company, or a holder of any bond of a debtor company secured by a mortgage, hypothec, pledge, charge, lien or privilege on or against, or any assignment, cession or transfer of, or a trust in respect of, all or any property of the debtor company, whether the holder or beneficiary is resident or domiciled within or outside Canada, and a trustee under any trust deed or other instrument securing any of those bonds shall be deemed to be a secured creditor for all purposes of this Act except for the purpose of voting at a creditors' meeting in respect of any of those bonds; *("créancier garanti")*

"shareholder" means a shareholder or member of any company to which this Act applies; *("actionnaire")*

"Superintendent of Financial Institutions" means the Superintendent of Financial Institutions appointed under subsection 5(1) of the *Office of the Superintendent of Financial Institutions Act*; *("surintendant des institutions financières")*

"unsecured creditor" means any creditor of a company who is not a secured creditor, whether resident or domiciled within or outside Canada, and a trustee for the holders of any unsecured bonds issue under a trust deed or other instrument running in favour of the trustee shall be deemed to be an unsecured creditor for all purposes of this Act except for the purpose of voting at a creditors' meeting in respect of any of those bonds. *("creancier chirographaire")*

Proposed Amendment — 2

2. (1) Definitions — In this Act,

"aircraft objects" has the same meaning as in subsection 2(1) of the *International Interests in Mobile Equipment (aircraft equipment) Act*; *("biens aéronautiques")*

"bargaining agent" means any trade union that has entered into a collective agreement on behalf of the employees of a company; *("agent négociateur")*

"bond" includes a debenture, debenture stock or other evidences of indebtedness; *("obligation")*

"cash-flow statement", in respect of a company, means the statement referred to in paragraph 10(2)(a) indicating the company's projected cash flow; *("état de l'évolution de l'encaisse")*

"claim" means any indebtedness, liability or obligation of any kind that would be a claim provable within the meaning of section 2 of the *Bankruptcy and Insolvency Act*; *("réclamation")*

"collective agreement", in relation to a debtor company, means a collective agreement within the meaning of the jurisdiction governing collective bargaining between the debtor company and a bargaining agent; *("convention collective")*

"company" means any company, corporation or legal person incorporated by or under an Act of Parliament or of the legislature of a province, any incorporated company having assets or doing business in Canada, wherever incorporated, and any income trust, but does not include banks, authorized foreign banks within the meaning of section 2 of the *Bank Act*, railway or telegraph companies, insurance companies and companies to which the *Trust and Loan Companies Act* applies; *("compagnie")*

"court" means

(a) in Nova Scotia, British Columbia, and Newfoundland, the Supreme Court,

(a.1) in Ontario, the Superior Court of Justice,

(b) in Quebec, the Superior Court,

(c) in New Brunswick, Manitoba, Saskatchewan and Alberta, the Court of Queen's Bench, and

(c.1) in Prince Edward Island, the Trial Division of the Supreme Court,

(d) in Yukon and the Northwest Territories, the Supreme Court, and in Nunavut, the Nunavut Court of Justice;

("tribunal")

"debtor company" means any company that

(a) is bankrupt or insolvent,

(b) has committed an act of bankruptcy within the meaning of the *Bankruptcy and Insolvency Act* or is deemed insolvent within the meaning of the *Winding-up and Restructuring Act*, whether or not proceedings in respect of the company have been taken under either of those Acts,

(c) has made an authorized assignment or against which a bankruptcy order has been made under the *Bankruptcy and Insolvency Act*, or

(d) is in the course of being wound up under the *Winding-up and Restructuring Act* because the company is insolvent;

("compagnie débitrice")

"director", in respect of a company, includes any person, however designated, acting in any capacity that is similar to that of a director of a corporation and, in respect of an income trust, includes its trustee; *("administrateur")*

"income trust" means a trust

(a) that has assets in Canada, and

(b) the units of which are traded on a prescribed stock exchange;

("fiducie de revenu")

"initial application" means the first application made under this Act in respect of a company; *("demande initiale")*

"monitor", in respect of a company, means the person appointed under section 11.7 to monitor the business and financial affairs of the company; *("contrôleur")*

"prescribed" means prescribed by regulation; *("Version anglaise seulement")*

"secured creditor" means a holder of a mortgage, hypothec, pledge, charge, lien or privilege on or against, or any assignment, cession or transfer of, all or any property of a debtor company as security for indebtedness of the debtor company, or a holder of any bond of a debtor company secured by a mortgage, hypothec, pledge, charge, lien or privilege on or against, or any assignment, cession or transfer of, or a trust in respect of, all or any property of the debtor company, whether the holder or beneficiary is resident or domiciled within or outside Canada, and a trustee under any trust deed or other instrument securing any of those bonds shall be deemed to be a secured creditor for all purposes of this Act except for the purpose of voting at a creditors' meeting in respect of any of those bonds; *("créancier garanti")*

"shareholder" means a shareholder, member or holder of any units of any company to which this Act applies; *("actionnaire")*

"Superintendent of Bankruptcy" means the Superintendent of Bankruptcy appointed under subsection 5(1) of the *Bankruptcy and Insolvency Act*; *("surintendant des faillites")*

"Superintendent of Financial Institutions" means the Superintendent of Financial Institutions appointed under subsection 5(1) of the *Office of the Superintendent of Financial Institutions Act*; *("surintendant des institutions financières")*

"unsecured creditor" means any creditor of a company who is not a secured creditor, whether resident or domiciled within or outside Canada, and a trustee for the holders of any unsecured bonds issue under a trust deed or other instrument running in favour of the trustee shall be deemed to be an unsecured creditor for all purposes of this Act except for the purpose of voting at a creditors' meeting in respect of any of those bonds. *("creancier chirographaire")*

(2) Meaning of "related" — For the purpose of this Act, section 4 of the *Bankruptcy and Insolvency Act* applies for the purpose of determining whether a person is related to a company.

2005, c. 47, s. 124 [Not in force at date of publication.]

R.S.C. 1985, c. 27 (2nd Supp.), s. 10 (Sched., item 3); 1990, c. 17, s. 4; 1992, c. 27, s. 90(1)(f); 1993, c. 28, s. 78 (Sched. III, item 20) [Repealed 1999, c. 3, s. 12 (Sched., item 4).]; 1993, c. 34, s. 52; 1996, c. 6, s. 167(1)(d); 1997, c. 12, s. 120; 1998, c. 30, s. 14(c); 1999, c. 3, s. 22; 1999, c. 28, s. 154; 2001, c. 9, s. 575; 2002, c. 7, s. 133; 2004, c. 25, s. 193; 2005, c. 3, s. 15

3. (1) Application — This Act applies in respect of a debtor company or affiliated debtor companies where the total of claims, within the meaning of section 12, against the debtor company or affiliated debtor companies exceeds five million dollars.

Proposed Amendment — 3(1)

(1) Application — This Act applies in respect of a debtor company or affiliated debtor companies if the total of claims against the debtor company or affiliated debtor companies, determined in accordance with section 20, is more than $5,000,000 or any other amount that is prescribed.

2005, c. 47, s. 125 [Not in force at date of publication.]

(2) Affiliated companies — For the purposes of this Act,

(a) companies are affiliated companies if one of them is the subsidiary of the other or both are subsidiaries of the same company or each of them is controlled by the same person; and

(b) two companies affiliated with the same company at the same time are deemed to be affiliated with each other.

(3) Company controlled — For the purposes of this Act, a company is controlled by a person or by two or more companies if

(a) securities of the company to which are attached more than fifty per cent of the votes that may be cast to elect directors of the company are held, other than by way of security only, by or for the benefit of that person or by or for the benefit of those companies; and

(b) the votes attached to those securities are sufficient, if exercised, to elect a majority of the directors of the company.

(4) Subsidiary — For the purposes of this Act, a company is a subsidiary of another company if

(a) it is controlled by

(i) that other company,

(ii) that other company and one ore more companies each of which is controlled by that other company, or

(iii) two or more companies each of which is controlled by that other company; or

(b) it is a subsidiary of a company that is a subsidiary of that other company.

1997, c. 12, s. 121

Part I — Compromises and Arrangements

4. Compromise with unsecured creditors — Where a compromise or an arrangement is proposed between a debtor company and its unsecured creditors or any class of them, the court may, on the application in a summary way of the company, of any such creditor or of the trustee in bankruptcy or liquidator of the company, order a meeting of the creditors or class of creditors, and, if the court so determines, of the shareholders of the company, to be summoned in such manner as the court directs.

5. Compromise with secured creditors — Where a compromise or an arrangement is proposed between a debtor company and its secured creditors or any class of them, the court may, on the application in a summary way of the company or of any such creditor or of the trustee in bankruptcy or liquidator of the company, order a meeting of the creditors or class of creditors, and, if the court so determines, of the shareholders of the company, to be summoned in such manner as the court directs.

5.1 (1) Claims against directors — compromise — A compromise or arrangement made in respect of a debtor company may include in its terms provision for the compromise of claims against directors of the company that arose before the commencement of proceedings under this Act and that relate to the obligations of the company where the directors are by law liable in their capacity as directors for the payment of such obligations.

(2) Exception — A provision for the compromise of claims against directors may not include claims that

(a) relate to contractual rights of one or more creditors; or

(b) are based on allegations of misrepresentations made by directors to creditors or of wrongful or oppressive conduct by directors.

(3) Powers of court — The court may declare that a claim against directors shall not be compromised if it is satisfied that the compromise would not be fair and reasonable in the circumstances.

(4) Resignation or removal of directors — Where all of the directors have resigned or have been removed by the shareholders without replacement, any person who manages or supervises the management of the business and affairs of the debtor company shall be deemed to be a director for the purposes of this section.

1997, c. 12, s. 122

6. Compromises to be sanctioned by court — Where a majority in number representing two-thirds in value of the creditors, or class of creditors, as the case may be, present and voting either in person or by proxy at the meeting or meetings thereof respectively held pursuant to sections 4 and 5, or either of those sections, agree to any compromise or arrangement either as proposed or as altered or modified at the meeting or meetings, the compromise or arrangement may be sanctioned by the court, and if so sanctioned is binding

(a) on all the creditors or the class of creditors, as the case may be, and on any trustee for any such class of creditors, whether secured or unsecured, as the case may be, and on the company; and

(b) in the case of a company that has made an authorized assignment or against which a bankruptcy order has been made under the *Bankruptcy and Insolvency Act* or is in the course of being wound up under the *Winding-up and Restructuring Act*, on the trustee in bankruptcy or liquidator and contributories of the company.

Proposed Amendment — 6

6. (1) — Compromises to be sanctioned by court
Where a majority in number representing two-thirds in value of the creditors, or class of creditors, as the case may be, present and voting either in person or by proxy at the meeting or meetings thereof respectively held pursuant to sections 4 and 5, or either of those sections, agree to any compromise or arrangement either as proposed or as altered or modified at the meeting or meetings, the compromise or arrangement may be sanctioned by the court, and if so sanctioned is binding

(a) on all the creditors or the class of creditors, as the case may be, and on any trustee for any such class of creditors, whether secured or unsecured, as the case may be, and on the company; and

(b) in the case of a company that has made an authorized assignment or against which a bankruptcy order has been made under the *Bankruptcy and Insolvency Act* or is in the course of being wound up under the *Winding-up and Restructuring Act*, on the trustee in bankruptcy or liquidator and contributories of the company.

(2) Restriction — certain Crown claims — Unless Her Majesty agrees otherwise, the court may sanction a compromise or an arrangement only if the compromise or arrangement provides for the payment in full to Her Majesty in right of Canada or a province, within six months after court sanction of the compromise or arrangement, of all amounts that were outstanding at the time of the application for an order under section 11 or 11.02 and that are of a kind that could be subject to a demand under

(a) subsection 224(1.2) of the *Income Tax Act*;

(b) any provision of the *Canada Pension Plan* or of the *Employment Insurance Act* that refers to subsection 224(1.2) of the *Income Tax Act* and provides for the collection of a contribution, as defined in the *Canada Pension Plan*, or an employee's premium, or employer's premium, as defined in the *Employment Insurance Act*, and of any related interest, penalties or other amounts; or

(c) any provision of provincial legislation that has a purpose similar to subsection 224(1.2) of the *Income Tax Act*, or that refers to that subsection, to the extent that it provides for the collection of a sum, and of any related interest, penalties or other amounts, and the sum

(i) has been withheld or deducted by a person from a payment to another person and is in respect of a tax similar in nature to the income tax imposed on individuals under the *Income Tax Act*, or

(ii) is of the same nature as a contribution under the *Canada Pension Plan* if the province is a "province providing a comprehensive pension plan" as defined in subsection 3(1) of the *Canada Pension Plan* and the provincial legislation establishes a "provincial pension plan" as defined in that subsection.

(3) Restriction — default of remittance to Crown — If an order contains a provision authorized by section 11.09, no compromise or arrangement shall be sanctioned by the court if, at the time the court hears the application for sanction, Her Majesty in right of Canada or a province satisfies the court that the company is in default on any remittance of an amount referred to in subsection (2) that became due after the time of the application for an order under section 11.02.

(4) Restriction — employees, etc. — The court may sanction a compromise or an arrangement only if

(a) the compromise or arrangement provides for payment to the employees and former employees of the company, immediately after the court's sanction, of

(i) amounts at least equal to the amounts that they would have been qualified to receive under paragraph 136(1)(d) of the *Bankruptcy and Insolvency Act* if the company had become bankrupt on the date of the filing of initial application in respect of the company, and

(ii) wages, salaries, commissions or compensation for services rendered after that date and before the court's sanction of the compromise or arrangement, together with, in the case of travelling salespersons, disbursements properly incurred by them in and about the company's business during the same period; and

(b) the court is satisfied that the company can and will make the payments as required under paragraph (a).

(5) Restriction — pensions plan — If the company participates in a prescribed pension plan for the benefit of its employees, the court may sanction a compromise or an arrangement in respect of the company only if

(a) the compromise or arrangement provides for payment, immediately after the court sanction, of the following amounts that are unpaid to the fund established for the purpose of the pension plan:

(i) an amount equal to the sum of all amounts that were deducted from the employees' remuneration for payment to the fund,

(ii) if the prescribed pension plan is regulated by an Act of Parliament,

(A) an amount equal to the normal cost, within the meaning of subsection 2(1) of the *Pension Benefits Standards Regulations, 1985*, that was required to be paid by the employer to the fund, and

(B) an amount equal to the sum of all amounts that were required to be paid by the employer to the fund under a defined contribution provision, within the meaning of subsection 2(1) of the *Pension Benefits Standards Act, 1985*; and

(iii) in the case of any other prescribed pension plan,

(A) an amount equal to the amount that would be the normal cost, within the meaning of subsection 2(1) of the *Pension Benefits Standards Regulations, 1985*, that the employer would be required to pay to the fund if the prescribed plan were regulated by an Act of Parliament, and

(B) an amount equal to the sum of all amounts that would have been required to be paid by the employer to the fund under a defined contribution provision, within the meaning of subsection 2(1) of the *Pension Benefits Standards Act, 1985*, if the prescribed plan were regulated by an Act of Parliament; and

(b) the court is satisfied that the company can and will make the payments as required under paragraph (a).

(6) Non-application of subsection (5) — Despite subsection (5), the court may sanction a compromise or arrangement that does not allow for the payment of the amounts referred to in that subsection if it is satisfied that the relevant parties have entered into an agreement, approved by the relevant pension regulator, respecting the payment of those amounts.

2005, c. 47, s. 126 [Not in force at date of publication.]

1992, c. 27, s. 90(1)(f); 1996, c. 6, s. 167(1)(d);
1997, c. 12, s. 123; 2004, c. 25, s. 194

7. Court may give directions — Where an alteration or a modification of any compromise or arrangement is proposed at any time after the court has directed a meeting or meetings to be summoned, the meeting or meetings may be adjourned on such term as to notice and otherwise as the court may direct, and those directions may be given after as well as before adjournment of any meeting or meetings, and the court may in its discretion direct that it is not necessary to adjourn any meeting or to convene any further meeting of any class of creditors or shareholders that in the opinion of the court is not adversely affected by the alteration or modification proposed, and any compromise or arrangement so altered or modified may be sanctioned by the court and have effect under section 6.

8. Scope of Act — This Act extends and does not limit the provisions of any instrument now or hereafter existing that governs the rights of creditors or any class of them and has full force and effect notwithstanding anything to the contrary contained in that instrument.

Part II — Jurisdiction of Courts

9. (1) Jurisdiction of court to receive applications — Any application under this Act may be made to the court that has jurisdiction in the province within which the head office or chief place of business of the company in Canada is situated, or, if the company has no place of business in Canada, in any province within which any assets of the company are situated.

(2) Single judge may exercise powers, subject to appeal — The powers conferred by this Act on a court may, subject to appeal as provided for in this Act, be exercised by a single judge thereof, and those powers may be exercised in chambers during term or in vacation.

10. Form of applications — Applications under this Act shall be made by petition or by way of originating summons or notice of motion in accordance with the practice of the court in which the application is made.

Proposed Amendment — 10

10. (1) Form of applications — Applications under this Act shall be made by petition or by way of originating summons or notice of motion in accordance with the practice of the court in which the application is made.

(2) Documents that must accompany initial application — An initial application must be accompanied by

(a) a statement indicating, on a weekly basis, the projected cash flow of the debtor company;

(b) a report containing the prescribed representations of the debtor company regarding the preparation of the cash-flow statement; and

(c) copies of all financial statements, audited or unaudited, prepared during the year before the application or, if no such statements were prepared in that year, a copy of the most recent such statement.

(3) Publication ban — The court may make an order prohibiting the release to the public of any cash-flow statement, or any part of a cash-flow statement, if it is satisfied that the release would unduly prejudice the debtor company and the making of the order would not unduly prejudice the company's creditors, but the court may, in the order, direct that the cash-flow statement or any part of it be made available to any person specified in the order on any terms or conditions that the court considers appropriate.

2005, c. 47, s. 127 [Not in force at date of publication.]

11. (1) Powers of court — Notwithstanding anything in the *Bankruptcy and Insolvency Act* or the *Winding-up and Restructuring Act*, where an application is made under this Act in respect of a company, the court, on the application of any person interested in the matter, may, subject to this Act, on notice to any other person or without notice as it may see fit, make an order under this section.

(2) Initial application — An application made for the first time under this section in respect of a company, in this section referred to as an **"initial application"**, shall be accompanied by a statement indicating the projected cash flow of the company and copies of all financial statements, audited or unaudited, prepared during the year prior to the application, or where no such statements were prepared in the prior year, a copy of the most recent such statement.

(3) Initial application court orders — A court may, on an initial application in respect of a company, make an order on such terms as it may impose, effective for such period as the court deems necessary not exceeding thirty days,

(a) staying, until otherwise ordered by the court, all proceedings taken or that might be taken in respect of the company under an Act referred to in subsection (1);

(b) restraining, until otherwise ordered by the court, further proceedings in any action, suit or proceeding against the company; and

(c) prohibiting, until otherwise ordered by the court, the commencement of or proceeding with any other action, suit or proceeding against the company.

(4) Other than initial application court orders — A court may, on an application in respect of a company other than an initial application, make an order on such terms as it may impose,

(a) staying, until otherwise ordered by the court, for such period as the court deems necessary, all proceedings taken or that might be taken in respect of the company under an Act referred to in subsection (1);

(b) restraining, until otherwise ordered by the court, further proceedings in any action, suit or proceeding against the company; and

(c) prohibiting, until otherwise ordered by the court, the commencement of or proceeding with any other action, suit or proceeding against the company.

(5) Notice of orders — Except as otherwise ordered by the court, the monitor appointed under section 11.7 shall send a copy of any order made under subsection (3), within ten days after the order is made, to every known creditor who has a claim against the company of more than two hundred and fifty dollars.

(6) Burden of proof on application — The court shall not make an order under subsection (3) or (4) unless

(a) the applicant satisfies the court that circumstances exist that make such an order appropriate; and

(b) in the case of an order under subsection (4), the applicant also satisfies the court that the applicant has acted, and is acting, in good faith and with due diligence.

Proposed Amendment — 11

11. General power of court — Despite anything in the *Bankruptcy and Insolvency Act* or the *Winding-up and Restructuring Act*, if an application is made under this Act in respect of a debtor company, the court, on the application of any person interested in the matter, may, subject to the restrictions set out in this Act, on notice to any other person or without notice as it may see fit, make any order that it considers appropriate in the circumstances.

2005, c. 47, s. 128 [Not in force at date of publication.]

1992, c. 27, s. 90; 1996, c. 6, s. 167(1)(d); 1997, c. 12, s. 124

Proposed Addition — 11.01–11.09

11.01 Rights of suppliers — No order made under section 11 or 11.02 has the effect of

(a) prohibiting a person from requiring immediate payment for goods, services, use of leased or licensed property or other valuable consideration provided after the order is made; or

(b) requiring the further advance of money or credit.

2005, c. 47, s. 128 [Not in force at date of publication.]

11.02 (1) Stays, etc. — initial application — A court may, on an initial application in respect of a debtor company, make an order on any terms that it may impose, effective for the period that the court considers necessary, which period may not be more than 30 days,

(a) staying, until otherwise ordered by the court, all proceedings taken or that might be taken in respect of the company under the *Bankruptcy and Insolvency Act* or the *Winding-up and Restructuring Act*;

(b) restraining, until otherwise ordered by the court, further proceedings in any action, suit or proceeding against the company; and

(c) prohibiting, until otherwise ordered by the court, the commencement of any action, suit or proceeding against the company.

(2) Stays, etc. — other than initial application — A court may, on an application in respect of a debtor company other than an initial application, make an order, on any terms that it may impose,

(a) staying, until otherwise ordered by the court, for any period that the court considers necessary, all proceedings taken or that might be taken in respect of the company under an Act referred to in paragraph (1)(a);

(b) restraining, until otherwise ordered by the court, further proceedings in any action, suit or proceeding against the company; and

(c) prohibiting, until otherwise ordered by the court, the commencement of any action, suit or proceeding against the company.

(3) Burden of proof on application — The court shall not make the order unless

(a) the applicant satisfies the court that circumstances exist that make the order appropriate; and

(b) in the case of an order under subsection (2), the applicant also satisfies the court that the applicant has acted, and is acting, in good faith and with due diligence.

(4) Restriction — Orders doing anything referred to in subsection (1) or (2) may only be made under this section.

2005, c. 47, s. 128 [Not in force at date of publication.]

11.03 (1) Stays — directors — An order made under section 11.02 may provide that no person may commence or continue any action against a director of the company on any claim against directors that arose before the commencement of proceedings under this Act and that relates to obligations of the company if directors are under any law liable in their capacity as directors for the payment of those obligations, until a compromise or an arrangement in respect of the company, if one is filed, is sanctioned by the court or is refused by the creditors or the court.

(2) Exception — Subsection (1) does not apply in respect of an action against a director on a guarantee given by the director relating to the company's obligations or an action seeking injunctive relief against a director in relation to the company.

(3) Persons deemed to be directors — If all of the directors have resigned or have been removed by the shareholders without replacement, any person who manages or supervises the management of the business and affairs of the company is deemed to be a director for the purposes of this section.

2005, c. 47, s. 128 [Not in force at date of publication.]

11.04 Persons obligated under letter of credit or guarantee — No order made under section 11.02 has affect on any action, suit or proceeding against a person, other than the company in respect of whom the order is made, who is obligated under a letter of credit or guarantee in relation to the company.

2005, c. 47, s. 128 [Not in force at date of publication.]

11.05 (1) Eligible financial contracts — No order may be made under section 11.02 staying or restraining the exercise of any right to terminate, amend or claim any accelerated payment, or a forfeiture of the term, under an eligible financial contract.

(2) Existing eligible financial contracts — For greater certainty, if an eligible financial contract entered into before an order is made under section 11.02 is terminated on or after the date of the order, the setting off of obligations between the company and the other parties to the eligible financial contract, in accordance with its provisions, is permitted and, if net termination values determined in accordance with the eligible financial contract are owed by the company to another party to the eligible financial contract, that other party is deemed to be a creditor of the company with a claim against the company in respect of the net termination values.

(3) Definitions — The following definitions apply in this section.

"eligible financial contract" means

(a) a currency or interest rate swap agreement;

(b) a basis swap agreement;

(c) a spot, future, forward or other foreign exchange agreement;

(d) a cap, collar or floor transaction;

(e) a commodity swap;

(f) a forward rate agreement;

(g) a repurchase or reverse repurchase agreement;

(h) a spot, future, forward or other commodity contract;

(i) an agreement to buy, sell, borrow or lend securities, to clear or settle securities transactions or to act as a depository for securities;

(j) any derivative, combination or option in respect of, or agreement similar to, an agreement or contract referred to in paragraphs (a) to (i);

(k) any master agreement in respect of any agreement or contract referred to in paragraphs (a) to (j);

(l) any master agreement in respect of a master agreement referred to in paragraph (k);

(m) a guarantee of the liabilities under an agreement or contract referred to in paragraphs (a) to (l); or

(n) any agreement of a prescribed kind.

("contrat financier admissible")

"net termination value" means the net amount obtained after setting off the mutual obligations between the parties to an eligible financial contract in accordance with its provisions. *("valeur nette due à la date de résiliation")*

2005, c. 47, s. 128 [Not in force at date of publication.]

11.06 Member of the Canadian Payments Association — No order may be made under section 11.02 that has the effect of preventing a member of the Canadian Payments Association established by the *Canadian Payments Act* from ceasing to act as a clearing agent or group clearer for a company in accordance with that Act and the by-laws and rules of that Association.

2005, c. 47, s. 128 [Not in force at date of publication.]

11.07 Aircraft objects — No order may be made under section 11.02 that has the effect of preventing a creditor who holds security on aircraft objects — or a lessor of aircraft objects — under an agreement with a company from taking possession of the aircraft objects

(a) if, after the commencement of proceedings under this Act, the company defaults in protecting or maintaining the aircraft objects in accordance with the agreement;

(b) 60 days after the commencement of proceedings under this Act unless, during that period, the company

(i) remedied the default of every other obligation under the agreement, other than a default constituted by the commencement of proceedings under this Act or the breach of a provision in the agreement relating to the company's financial condition,

(ii) agreed to perform the obligations under the agreement, other than an obligation not to become insolvent or an obligation relating to the company's financial condition, until proceedings under this Act end, and

(iii) agreed to perform all the obligations arising under the agreement after the proceedings under this Act end; or

(c) if, during the period that begins 60 days after the commencement of the proceedings under this Act and ends on the day on which proceedings under this Act end, the company defaults in performing an obligation under the agreement, other than an obligation not to become insolvent or an obligation relating to the company's financial condition.

2005, c. 47, s. 128 [Not in force at date of publication.]

11.08 Restriction — certain powers, duties and functions — No order may be made under section 11.02 that affects

(a) the exercise or performance by the Minister of Finance or the Superintendent of Financial Institutions of any power, duty or function assigned to them by the *Bank Act*, the *Cooperative Credit Associations Act*, the *Insurance Companies Act* or the *Trust and Loan Companies Act*;

(b) the exercise or performance by the Governor in Council, the Minister of Finance or the Canada Deposit Insurance Corporation of any power, duty or function assigned to them by the *Canada Deposit Insurance Corporation Act*; or

(c) the exercise by the Attorney General of Canada of any power, assigned to him or her by the *Winding-up and Restructuring Act*.

2005, c. 47, s. 128 [Not in force at date of publication.]

11.09 (1) Stay — Her Majesty — An order made under section 11.02 may provide that

(a) Her Majesty in right of Canada may not exercise rights under subsection 224(1.2) of the *Income Tax Act* or any provision of the *Canada Pension Plan* or of the *Employment Insurance Act* that refers to subsection 224(1.2) of the *Income Tax Act* and provides for the collection of a contribution, as defined in the *Canada Pension Plan*, or an employee's premium, or employer's premium, as defined in the *Employment Insurance Act*, and of any related interest, penalties or other amounts, in respect of the company if the company is a tax debtor under that subsection or provision, for the period that the court considers appropriate but ending not later than

(i) the expiry of the order,

(ii) the refusal of a proposed compromise by the creditors or the court,

(iii) six months following the court sanction of a compromise or an arrangement,

(iv) the default by the company on any term of a compromise or an arrangement, or

(v) the performance of a compromise or an arrangement in respect of the company; and

(b) Her Majesty in right of a province may not exercise rights under any provision of provincial legislation in respect of the company if the company is a debtor under that legislation and the provision has a purpose similar to subsection 224(1.2) of the *Income Tax Act*, or refers to that subsection, to the extent that it provides for the collection of a sum, and of any related interest, penalties or other amounts, and the sum

(i) has been withheld or deducted by a person from a payment to another person and is in respect of a tax similar in nature to the income tax imposed on individuals under the *Income Tax Act*, or

(ii) is of the same nature as a contribution under the *Canada Pension Plan* if the province is a "province providing a comprehensive pension plan" as defined in subsection 3(1) of the *Canada Pension Plan* and the provincial legislation establishes a "provincial pension plan" as defined in that subsection,

for the period that the court considers appropriate but ending not later than the occurrence or time referred to in whichever of subparagraphs (a)(i) to (v) that may apply.

(2) When order ceases to be in effect — The portions of an order made under section 11.02 that affect the exercise of rights of Her Majesty referred to in paragraph (1)(a) or (b) cease to be in effect if

(a) the company defaults on the payment of any amount that becomes due to Her Majesty after the order is made and could be subject to a demand under

(i) subsection 224(1.2) of the *Income Tax Act*,

(ii) any provision of the *Canada Pension Plan* or of the *Employment Insurance Act* that refers to subsection 224(1.2) of the *Income Tax Act* and provides for the collection of a contribution, as defined in the *Canada Pension Plan*, or an employee's premium, or employer's premium, as defined in the *Employment Insurance Act*, and of any related interest, penalties or other amounts, or

(iii) any provision of provincial legislation that has a purpose similar to subsection 224(1.2) of the *Income Tax Act*, or that refers to that subsection, to the extent that it provides for the collection of a sum, and of any related interest, penalties or other amounts, and the sum

(A) has been withheld or deducted by a person from a payment to another person and is in respect of a tax similar in nature to the income tax imposed on individuals under the *Income Tax Act*, or

(B) is of the same nature as a contribution under the *Canada Pension Plan* if the province is a "province providing a comprehensive pension plan" as defined in subsection 3(1) of the *Canada Pension Plan* and the provincial legislation establishes a "provincial pension plan" as defined in that subsection; or

(b) any other creditor is or becomes entitled to realize a security on any property that could be claimed by Her Majesty in exercising rights under

(i) subsection 224(1.2) of the *Income Tax Act*,

(ii) any provision of the *Canada Pension Plan* or of the *Employment Insurance Act* that refers to subsection 224(1.2) of the *Income Tax Act* and provides for the collection of a contribution, as defined in the *Canada Pension Plan*, or an employee's premium, or employer's premium, as defined in the *Employment Insurance Act*, and of any related interest, penalties or other amounts, or

(iii) any provision of provincial legislation that has a purpose similar to subsection 224(1.2) of the *Income Tax Act*, or that refers to that subsection, to the extent that it provides for the collection of a sum, and of any related interest, penalties or other amounts, and the sum

(A) has been withheld or deducted by a person from a payment to another person and is in respect of a tax similar in nature to the income tax imposed on individuals under the *Income Tax Act*, or

(B) is of the same nature as a contribution under the *Canada Pension Plan* if the province is a "province providing a comprehensive pension plan" as defined in subsection 3(1) of the *Canada Pension Plan* and the provincial legislation establishes a "provincial pension plan" as defined in that subsection.

(3) Operation of similar legislation — An order made under section 11.02, other than the portions of that order that affect the exercise of rights of Her Majesty referred to in paragraph (1)(a) or (b), does not affect the operation of

(a) subsections 224(1.2) and (1.3) of the *Income Tax Act*,

(b) any provision of the *Canada Pension Plan* or of the *Employment Insurance Act* that refers to subsection 224(1.2) of the *Income Tax Act* and provides for the collection of a contribution, as defined in the *Canada Pension Plan*, or an employee's premium, or employer's premium, as defined in the *Employment Insurance Act*, and of any related interest, penalties or other amounts, or

(c) any provision of provincial legislation that has a purpose similar to subsection 224(1.2) of the *Income Tax Act*, or that refers to that subsection, to the extent that it provides for the collection of a sum, and of any related interest, penalties or other amounts, and the sum

(i) has been withheld or deducted by a person from a payment to another person and is in respect of a tax similar in nature to the income tax imposed on individuals under the *Income Tax Act*, or

(ii) is of the same nature as a contribution under the *Canada Pension Plan* if the province is a "province providing a comprehensive pension plan" as defined in subsection 3(1) of the *Canada Pension Plan* and the provincial legislation establishes a "provincial pension plan" as defined in that subsection,

and for the purpose of paragraph (c), the provision of provincial legislation is, despite any Act of Canada or of a province or any other law, deemed to have the same effect and scope against any creditor, however secured, as subsection 224(1.2) of the *Income Tax Act* in respect of a sum referred to in subparagraph (c)(i), or as subsection 23(2) of the *Canada Pension Plan* in respect of a sum referred to in subparagraph (c)(ii), and in respect of any related interest, penalties or other amounts.

2005, c. 47, s. 128 [Not in force at date of publication.]

11.1 (1) Definitions — In this section,

"eligible financial contract" means

(a) a currency or interest rate swap agreement,

(b) a basis swap agreement,

(c) a spot, future, forward or other foreign exchange agreement,

(d) a cap, collar or floor transaction,

(e) a commodity swap,

(f) a forward rate agreement,

(g) a repurchase or reverse repurchase agreement,

(h) a spot, future, forward or other commodity contract,

(i) an agreement to buy, sell, borrow or lend securities, to clear or settle securities transactions or to act as a depository for securities,

(j) any derivative, combination or option in respect of, or agreement similar to, an agreement or contract referred to in paragraphs (a) to (i),

(k) any master agreement in respect of any agreement or contract referred to in paragraphs (a) to (j),

(l) any master agreement in respect of a master agreement referred to in paragraph (k),

(m) a guarantee of the liabilities under an agreement or contract referred to in paragraphs (a) to (l), or

(n) any agreement of a kind prescribed;

"net termination value" means the net amount obtained after setting off the mutual obligations between the parties to an eligible financial contract in accordance with its provisions.

(2) No stay, etc., in certain cases — No order may be made under this Act staying or restraining the exercise of any right to terminate, amend or claim any accelerated payment under an eligible financial contract or preventing a member of the Canadian Payments Association established by the *Canadian Payments Act* from ceasing to act as a clearing agent or group clearer for a company in accordance with that Act and the by-laws and rules of that Association.

(3) Existing eligible financial contracts — For greater certainty, where an eligible financial contract entered into before an order is made under section 11 is terminated on or after the date of the order, the setting off of obligations between the company and the other parties to the eligible financial contract, in accordance with its provisions, is permitted, and if net termination values determined in accordance with the eligible financial contract are owed by the company to another party to the eligible financial contract, that other party shall be deemed to be a creditor of the company with a claim against the company in respect of the net termination values.

Proposed Amendment — 11.1

11.1 (1) Regulatory bodies — Subject to subsection (3), no order made under section

11.02 affects the rights of a regulatory body with respect to any investigation in respect of the company or any action, suit or proceeding taken or to be taken by it against the company, except when it is seeking to enforce any of its rights as a secured creditor or an unsecured creditor.

(2) Declaration that regulatory body is acting as creditor — If there is a dispute as to whether a regulatory body is seeking to enforce any of its rights as a secured creditor or an unsecured creditor, the court may, on application made by the company with notice given to the regulatory body, make an order declaring that the regulatory body is or would be so seeking to enforce its rights.

(3) Exception — compromise or arrangement not viable — Subsection (1) does not apply in respect of any or all actions, suits or proceedings taken or to be taken by a regulatory body if the court, on application made by the company with notice given to the regulatory body, makes an order declaring that a viable compromise or arrangement could not be made in respect of the company if that subsection were to apply.

(4) Restriction — The court shall not make the declaration referred to in subsection (3) if it is of the opinion that it is in the public interest that the regulatory body not be affected by the order made under section 11.02.

(5) Meaning of "regulatory body" — In this section, **"regulatory body"** means any person or body who has powers, duties or functions relating to the enforcement or administration of any Act of Parliament or of the legislature of a province and includes any person or body prescribed to be a regulatory body for the purpose of this Act.

2005, c. 47, s. 128 [Not in force at date of publication.]

1997, c. 12, s. 124; 2001, c. 9, s. 576

11.11 No stay, etc., in certain cases — No order may be made under this Act staying or restraining

(a) the exercise by the Minister of Finance or the Superintendent of Financial Institutions of any power, duty or function assigned to them by the *Bank Act*, the *Cooperative Credit Associations Act*, the *Insurance Companies Act* or the *Trust and Loan Companies Act*;

(b) the exercise by the Governor in Council, the Minister of Finance or the Canada Deposit Insurance Corporation of any power, duty or function assigned to them by the *Canada Deposit Insurance Corporation Act*; or

(c) the exercise by the Attorney General of Canada of any power, assigned to him or her by the *Winding-up and Restructuring Act*.

Proposed Repeal — 11.11

11.11 [Repealed 2005, c. 47, s. 128. Not in force at date of publication.]

2001, c. 9, s. 577

11.2 No stay, etc., in certain cases — No order may be made under section 11 staying or restraining any action, suit or proceeding against a person, other than a debtor company in respect of which an application has been made under this Act, who is obligated under a letter of credit or guarantee in relation to the company.

Proposed Amendment — 11.2

11.2 (1) Interim financing — A court may, on application by a debtor company, make an order, on any conditions that the court considers appropriate, declaring that the property of the company is subject to a security or charge in favour of any person specified in the order who agrees to lend to the company an amount that is approved by the court as being required by the company, having regard to its cash-flow statement,

(a) for the period of 30 days following the initial application in respect of the company if the order is made on the initial application in respect of the company; or

(b) for any period specified in the order if the order is made on any application in respect of a company other than the initial application and notice has been given to the secured creditors likely to be affected by the security or charge.

(2) Restriction — An order may be made under subsection (1) in respect of any period after the period of 30 days following the initial application in respect of the company only if the monitor has reported to the court under paragraph 23(1)(b) that the company's cash-flow statement is reasonable.

(3) Rank — The court may specify in the order that the security or charge ranks in priority over the claim of any secured creditor of the company.

(4) Other orders — The court may specify in the order that the security or charge ranks in priority over any security or charge arising from a previous order made under subsection (1) only with the consent of the person in whose favour the previous order was made.

(5) Factors to be considered — In deciding whether to make an order referred to in subsection (1), the court must consider, among other things,

(a) the period during which the company is expected to be subject to proceedings under this Act;

(b) how the company is to be governed during the proceedings;

(c) whether the company's management has the confidence of its major creditors;

(d) whether the loan will enhance the prospects of a viable compromise or arrangement being made in respect of the company;

(e) the nature and value of the company's assets; and

(f) whether any creditor will be materially prejudiced as a result of the company's continued operations.

2005, c. 47, s. 128 [Not in force at date of publication.]

1997, c. 12, s. 124

11.3 Effect of order — No order made under section 11 shall have the effect of

(a) prohibiting a person from requiring immediate payment for goods, services, use of leased or licensed property or other valuable consideration provided after the order is made; or

(b) requiring the further advance of money or credit.

Proposed Amendment — 11.3

11.3 (1) Assignments — The court may, on the application of a debtor company, make an order assigning the rights and obligations of the company under any agreement to any person, to be specified by the court, who has agreed to the assignment.

(2) Notice — The applicant must give notice of the assignment in the prescribed manner to every party to the agreement.

(3) Exceptions — Subsection (1) does not apply in respect of rights and obligations

(a) under an eligible financial contract within the meaning of subsection 11.05(3);

(b) under a collective agreement; or

(c) that are not assignable by reason of their nature.

(4) Factors to be considered — In deciding whether to make an assignment, the court must consider, among other things,

(a) whether the person to whom the rights and obligations are to be assigned would be able to perform the obligations; and

(b) whether it would be appropriate to assign the rights and obligations to that person.

(5) Restriction — The court may not make an order assigning an agreement unless it is satisfied that all financial defaults in relation to the agreement will be remedied.

2005, c. 47, s. 128 [Not in force at date of publication.]

1997, c. 12, s. 124

11.31 Limitation — aircraft objects — No order made under section 11 prevents a creditor who holds security on aircraft objects — or a lessor of aircraft objects or a conditional seller of aircraft objects — under an agreement with a debtor company in respect of which an application is made under this Act from taking possession of the equipment

(a) if, after the commencement of proceedings under this Act, the company defaults in protecting or maintaining the equipment in accordance with the agreement;

(b) sixty days after the commencement of proceedings under this Act unless, during that period, the company

(i) remedied the default of every other obligation under the agreement, other than a default constituted by the commencement of proceedings under this Act or the breach of a provision in the agreement relating to the company's financial condition,

(ii) agreed to perform the obligations under the agreement, other than an obligation not to become insolvent or an obligation relating to the company's financial condition, until proceedings under this Act end, and

(iii) agreed to perform all the obligations arising under the agreement after the proceedings under this Act end; or

(c) if, during the period that begins on the expiry of the sixty-day period and ends on the day on which proceedings under this Act end, the company defaults in performing an obligation under the agreement, other than an obligation not to become insolvent or an obligation relating to the company's financial condition.

Proposed Repeal — 11.31

11.31 [Repealed 2005, c. 47, s. 128. Not in force at date of publication.]

2005, c. 3, s. 16

11.4 (1) Her Majesty affected — An order made under section 11 may provide that

(a) Her Majesty in right of Canada may not exercise rights under subsection 224(1.2) of the *Income Tax Act* or any provision of the *Canada Pension Plan* or of the *Employment Insurance Act* that refers to subsection 224(1.2) of the *Income Tax Act* and provides for the collection of a contribution, as defined in the *Canada Pension Plan*, or an employee's premium, or employer's premium, as defined in the *Employment Insurance Act*, and of any related interest, penalties or other amounts, in respect of the company if the company is a tax debtor under that subsection or provision, for such period as the court considers appropriate but ending not later than

(i) the expiration of the order,

(ii) the refusal of a proposed compromise by the creditors or the court,

(iii) six months following the court sanction of a compromise or arrangement,

(iv) the default by the company on any term of a compromise or arrangement, or

(v) the performance of a compromise or arrangement in respect of the company; and

(b) Her Majesty in right of a province may not exercise rights under any provision of provincial legislation in respect of the company where the company is a debtor under that legislation and the provision has a similar purpose to subsection 224(1.2) of the *Income Tax Act*, or refers to that subsection, to the extent that it provides for the collection of a sum, and of any related interest, penalties or other amounts, where the sum

(i) has been withheld or deducted by a person from a payment to another person and is in respect of a tax similar in nature to the income tax imposed on individuals under the *Income Tax Act*, or

(ii) is of the same nature as a contribution under the *Canada Pension Plan* if the province is a "province providing a comprehensive pension plan" as defined in subsection 3(1) of the *Canada Pension Plan* and the provincial legislation establishes a "provincial pension plan" as defined in that subsection,

for such period as the court considers appropriate but ending not later than the occurrence or time referred to in whichever of subparagraphs (a)(i) to (v) may apply.

(2) When order ceases to be in effect — An order referred to in subsection (1) ceases to be in effect if

(a) the company defaults on payment of any amount that becomes due to Her Majesty after the order is made and could be subject to a demand under

(i) subsection 224(1.2) of the *Income Tax Act*,

(ii) any provision of the *Canada Pension Plan* or of the *Employment Insurance Act* that refers to subsection 224(1.2) of the *Income Tax Act* and provides for the collection of a contribution, as defined in the *Canada Pension Plan*, or an employee's premium, or employer's premium, as defined in the *Employment Insurance Act*, and of any related interest, penalties or other amounts, or

(iii) under any provision of provincial legislation that has a similar purpose to subsection 224(1.2) of the *Income Tax Act*, or that refers to that subsection, to the extent that it provides for the collection of a sum, and of any related interest, penalties or other amounts, where the sum

(A) has been withheld or deducted by a person from a payment to another person and is in respect of a tax similar in nature to the income tax imposed on individuals under the *Income Tax Act*, or

(B) is of the same nature as a contribution under the *Canada Pension Plan* if the province is a "province providing a comprehensive pension plan" as defined in subsection 3(1) of the *Canada Pension Plan* and the provincial legislation establishes a "provincial pension plan" as defined in that subsection; or

(b) any other creditor is or becomes entitled to realize a security on any property that could be claimed by Her Majesty in exercising rights under

(i) subsection 224(1.2) of the *Income Tax Act*,

(ii) any provision of the *Canada Pension Plan* or of the *Employment Insurance Act* that refers to subsection 224(1.2) of the *Income Tax Act* and provides for the collection of a contribution, as defined in the *Canada Pension Plan*, or an employee's premium, or employer's premium, as defined in the *Employment Insurance Act*, and of any related interest, penalties or other amounts, or

(iii) any provision of provincial legislation that has a similar purpose to subsection 224(1.2) of the *Income Tax Act*, or that refers to that subsection, to the extent that it provides for the collection of a sum, and of any related interest, penalties or other amounts, where the sum

(A) has been withheld or deducted by a person from a payment to another person and is in respect of a tax similar in nature to the income tax imposed on individuals under the *Income Tax Act*, or

(B) is of the same nature as a contribution under the *Canada Pension Plan* if the province is a "province providing a comprehensive pension plan" as defined in subsection 3(1) of the *Canada Pension Plan* and the provincial legislation establishes a "provincial pension plan" as defined in that subsection.

(3) Operation of similar legislation — An order made under section 11, other than an order referred to in subsection (1) of this section, does not affect the operation of

(a) subsections 224(1.2) and (1.3) of the *Income Tax Act*;

(b) any provision of the *Canada Pension Plan* or of the *Employment Insurance Act* that refers to subsection 224(1.2) of the *Income Tax Act* and provides for the collection of a contribution, as defined in the *Canada Pension Plan*, or an employee's premium, or employer's premium, as defined in the *Employment Insurance Act*, and of any related interest, penalties or other amounts; or

(c) any provision of provincial legislation that has a similar purpose to subsection 224(1.2) of the *Income Tax Act*, or that refers to that subsection, to the extent that it provides for the collection of a sum, and of any related interest, penalties or other amounts, where the sum

(i) has been withheld or deducted by a person from a payment to another person and is in respect of a tax similar in nature to the income tax imposed on individuals under the *Income Tax Act*, or

(ii) is of the same nature as a contribution under the *Canada Pension Plan* if the province is a "province providing a comprehensive pension plan" as defined in subsection 3(1) of the *Canada Pension Plan* and the provincial legislation establishes a "provincial pension plan" as defined in that subsection,

and for the purpose of paragraph (c), the provision of provincial legislation is, despite any Act of Canada or of a province or any other law, deemed to have the same effect and scope against any creditor, however secured, as subsection 224(1.2) of the *Income Tax Act* in respect of a sum referred to in subparagraph (c)(i), or as subsection 23(2) of the *Canada Pension Plan* in respect of a sum referred to in subparagraph (c)(ii), and in respect of any related interest, penalties or other amounts.

Proposed Amendment — 11.4

11.4 (1) Critical supplier — On application by a debtor company, the court may make an order declaring a person to be a critical supplier to the company if the court is satisfied that the person is a supplier of goods or services to the company and that those goods or services are critical to the company's continued operation.

(2) Obligation to supply — If the court declares a person to be a critical supplier, the court may make an order requiring the person to supply any goods or services specified by the court to the company on any terms and conditions that are consistent with the supply relationship or that the court considers appropriate.

(3) Security or charge in favour of critical supplier — If the court makes an order under subsection (2), the court shall, in the order, declare that the property of the company is subject to a security or charge in favour of the person declared to be a critical supplier, in an amount equal to the value of the goods or services supplied under the terms of the order.

(4) Rank — The court may specify in the order that the security or charge ranks in priority over the claim of any secured creditor of the company.

2005, c. 47, s. 128 [Not in force at date of publication.]

[Editor's Note: S.C. 2000, c. 30, s. 156(2) provides as follows:

(2) Subsection (1) [which repealed and replaced s. 11.4 of the Act] applies to proceedings commenced under the Act after September 29, 1997.]

[Editor's Note: S.C. 2001, c. 34, s. 33(2) provides as follows:

(2) Subsection (1) [which repealed and replaced the portion of paragraph 11.4(3)(c) before subparagraph (i) of the Act] applies to proceedings commenced under the Act after September 29, 1997.]

1997, c. 12, s. 124; 2000, c. 30, s. 156(1); 2001, c. 34, s. 33

11.5 (1) Stay of proceedings — directors — An order made under section 11 may provide that no person may commence or continue any action against a director of the debtor company on any claim against directors that arose before the commencement of proceedings under this Act and that relates to obligations of the company where directors are under any law liable in their capacity as directors for the payment of such obligations, until a compromise or arrangement in respect of the company, if one is filed, is sanctioned by the court or is refused by the creditors or the court.

(2) Exception — Subsection (1) does not apply in respect of an action against a director on a guarantee given by the director relating to the company's obligations or an action seeking injunctive relief against a director in relation to the company.

(3) Resignation or removal of directors — Where all of the directors have resigned or have been removed by the shareholders without replacement, any person who manages or supervises the management of the business and affairs of the company shall be deemed to be a director for the purposes of this section.

Proposed Amendment — 11.5

11.5 (1) Removal of directors — The court may, on the application of any person interested in the matter, make an order removing from office any director of a debtor company in respect of which an order has been made under this Act if the court is satisfied that the director is unreasonably impairing or is likely to unreasonably impair the possibility of a viable compromise or arrangement being made in respect of the company or is acting or is likely to act inappropriately as a director in the circumstances.

(2) Filling vacancy — The court may, by order, fill any vacancy created under subsection (1).

(3) [Repealed 2005, c. 47, s. 128. Not in force at date of publication.]

2005, c. 47, s. 128 [Not in force at date of publication.]

1997, c. 12, s. 124

Proposed Addition — 11.51, 11.52

11.51 (1) Security or charge relating to director's indemnification — The court may, on the application of a debtor company, make an order declaring that the property of the company is subject to a security or charge, in an amount that the court considers appropriate, in favour of any director or officer of the company to indemnify the director or officer against obligations and liabilities that he or she may incur as a director or an officer of the company after the commencement of proceedings against the company under this Act.

(2) Rank — The court may specify in the order that the security or charge ranks in priority over the claim of any secured creditor of the company.

(3) Restriction — indemnification insurance — The court shall not make the order if, in its opinion, the company could obtain adequate indemnification insurance for the director or officer at a reasonable cost.

(4) Declaration in cases of gross negligence, etc. — The court shall make an order declaring that the security or charge does not apply in respect of a specific obligation or liability incurred by a director or an officer if it is of the opinion that the obligation or liability was incurred as a result of the director's or officer's gross negligence or wilful misconduct or, in the Province of Quebec, the director's gross or intentional fault.

2005, c. 47, s. 128 [Not in force at date of publication.]

11.52 Court may order security or charge to cover certain costs — The court may make an order declaring that property of a debtor company is subject to a security or charge, in an amount that the court considers appropriate, in respect of

(a) the costs of the monitor, including the remuneration and expenses of any financial, legal or other experts engaged by the monitor in the course of the monitor's duties;

(b) the remuneration and expenses of any financial, legal or other experts engaged by the company for the purpose of proceedings under this Act; and

(c) the costs of any interested party in relation to the remuneration and expenses of any financial, legal or other experts engaged by it, if the court is satisfied that the incurring of those costs is necessary for the effective participation of the interested party in the proceedings under this Act.

2005, c. 47, s. 128 [Not in force at date of publication.]

11.6 *Bankruptcy and Insolvency Act* matters — Notwithstanding the *Bankruptcy and Insolvency Act*,

(a) proceedings commenced under Part III of the *Bankruptcy and Insolvency Act* may be taken up and continued under this Act only if a proposal within the meaning of the *Bankruptcy and Insolvency Act* has not been filed under that Part; and

(b) an application under this Act by a bankrupt may only be made with the consent of inspectors referred to in section 116 of the *Bankruptcy and Insolvency Act* but no application may be made under this Act by a bankrupt whose bankruptcy has resulted from

  (i) the operation of subsection 50.4(8) of the *Bankruptcy and Insolvency Act*, or

  (ii) the refusal or deemed refusal by the creditors or the court, or the annulment, of a proposal under the *Bankruptcy and Insolvency Act*.

1997, c. 12, s. 124

11.7 (1) Court to appoint monitor — When an order is made in respect of a company by the court under section 11, the court shall at the same time appoint a person, in this section and in section 11.8 referred to as "the monitor", to monitor the business and financial affairs of the company while the order remains in effect.

(2) Auditor may be monitor — Except as may be otherwise directed by the court, the auditor of the company may be appointed as the monitor.

(3) Functions of monitor — The monitor shall

(a) for the purposes of monitoring the company's business and financial affairs, have access to and examine the company's property, including the premises, books, records, data, including data in electronic form, and other financial documents of the company to the extent necessary to adequately assess the company's business and financial affairs;

(b) file a report with the court on the state of the company's business and financial affairs, containing prescribed information,

(i) forthwith after ascertaining any material adverse change in the company's projected cash-flow or financial circumstances,

(ii) at least seven days before any meeting of creditors under section 4 or 5, or

(iii) at such other times as the court may order;

(c) advise the creditors of the filing of the report referred to in paragraph (b) in any notice of a meeting of creditors referred to in section 4 or 5; and

(d) carry out such other functions in relation to the company as the court may direct.

(4) Monitor not liable — Where the monitor acts in good faith and takes reasonable care in preparing the report referred to in paragraph (3)(b), the monitor is not liable for loss or damage to any person resulting from that person's reliance on the report.

(5) Assistance to be provided — The debtor company shall

(a) provide such assistance to the monitor as is necessary to enable the monitor to adequately carry out the monitor's functions; and

(b) perform such duties set out in section 158 of the *Bankruptcy and Insolvency Act* as are appropriate and applicable in the circumstances.

Proposed Amendment — 11.7

11.7 (1) Court to appoint monitor — When an order is made on the initial application in respect of a debtor company, the court shall at the same time appoint a person to monitor the business and financial affairs of the company. The person so appointed must be a trustee, within the meaning of subsection 2(1) of the *Bankruptcy and Insolvency Act*.

(2) Restrictions on who may be monitor — Except with the permission of the court and on any conditions that the court may impose, no trustee may be appointed as monitor in relation to a company

(a) if the trustee is or, at any time during the two preceding years, was

(i) a director, an officer or an employee of the company,

(ii) related to the company or to any director or officer of the company, or

(iii) the auditor, accountant or legal counsel, or a partner or an employee of the auditor, accountant or legal counsel, of the company; or

(b) if the trustee is

(i) the trustee under a trust indenture issued by the company or any person related to the company, or the holder of a power of attorney under an act constituting a hypothec within the meaning of the *Civil Code of Quebec* that is granted by the company or any person related to the company, or

(ii) related to the trustee, or the holder of a power of attorney, referred to in subparagraph (i).

(3) Court may replace monitor — On application by a creditor of the company, the court may, if it considers it appropriate in the circumstances, replace the monitor by appointing another trustee, within the meaning of subsection 2(1) of the *Bankruptcy and Insolvency Act*, to monitor the business and financial affairs of the company.

(4) [Repealed 2005, c. 47, s. 129. Not in force at date of publication.]

(5) [Repealed 2005, c. 47, s. 129. Not in force at date of publication.]

2005, c. 47, s. 129 [Not in force at date of publication.]

1997, c. 12, s. 124

11.8 (1) Non-liability in respect of certain matters — Notwithstanding anything in any federal or provincial law, where a monitor carries on in that position the business of a debtor company or continues the employment of the company's employees, the monitor is not by reason of that fact personally liable in respect of any claim against the company or related to a requirement imposed on the company to pay an amount where the claim arose before or upon the monitor's appointment.

(2) Status of claim ranking — A claim referred to in subsection (1) shall not rank as costs of administration.

(3) Liability in respect of environmental matters — Notwithstanding anything in any federal or provincial law, a monitor is not personally liable in that position for any environmental condition that arose or environmental damage that occurred

(a) before the monitor's appointment; or

(b) after the monitor's appointment unless it is established that the condition arose or the damage occurred as a result of the monitor's gross negligence or wilful misconduct.

(4) Reports, etc., still required — Nothing in subsection (3) exempts a monitor from any duty to report or make disclosure imposed by a law referred to in that subsection.

(5) Non-liability re certain orders — Notwithstanding anything in any federal or provincial law but subject to subsection (3), where an order is made which has the effect of requiring a monitor to remedy any environmental condition or environmental damage affecting property involved in a proceeding under this Act, the monitor is not personally liable for failure to comply with the order, and is not personally liable for any costs that are or would be incurred by any person in carrying out the terms of the order,

(a) if, within such time as is specified in the order, within ten days after the order is made if no time is so specified, within ten days after the appointment of the monitor, if the order is in effect when the monitor is appointed or during the period of the stay referred to in paragraph (b), the monitor

(i) complies with the order, or

(ii) on notice to the person who issued the order, abandons, disposes of or otherwise releases any interest in any real property affected by the condition or damage;

(b) during the period of a stay of the order granted, on application made within the time specified in the order referred to in paragraph (a) or within ten days after the order is made or within ten days after the appointment of the monitor, if the order is in effect when the monitor is appointed, by

(i) the court or body having jurisdiction under the law pursuant to which the order was made to enable the monitor to contest the order, or

(ii) the court having jurisdiction under this Act for the purposes of assessing the economic viability of complying with the order; or

(c) if the monitor had, before the order was made, abandoned or renounced any interest in any real property affected by the condition or damage.

(6) Stay may be granted — The court may grant a stay of the order referred to in subsection (5) on such notice and for such period as the court deems necessary for the purpose of enabling the monitor to assess the economic viability of complying with the order.

(7) Costs for remedying not costs of administration — Where the monitor has abandoned or renounced any interest in real property affected by the environmental condition or environmental damage, claims for costs of remedying the condition or damage shall not rank as costs of administration.

(8) Priority of claims — Any claim by Her Majesty in right of Canada or a province against a debtor company in respect of which proceedings have been commenced under this Act for costs of remedying any environmental condition or environmental damage affecting real property of the company is secured by a charge on the real property and on any other real property of the company that is contiguous thereto and that is related to the activity that caused the environmental condition or environmental damage, and the charge

(a) is enforceable in accordance with the law of the jurisdiction in which the real property is located, in the same way as a mortgage, hypothec or other security on real property; and

(b) ranks above any other claim, right or charge against the property, notwithstanding any other provision of this Act or anything in any other federal or provincial law.

(9) Claim for clean-up costs — A claim against a debtor company for costs of remedying any environmental condition or environmental damage affecting real property of the company shall be a claim under this Act, whether the condition arose or the damage occurred before or after the date on which proceedings under this Act were commenced.

1997, c. 12, s. 124

12. (1) Definition of "claim" — For the purposes of this Act, **"claim"** means any indebtedness, liability or obligation of any kind that, if unsecured, would be a debt provable in bankruptcy within the meaning of the *Bankruptcy and Insolvency Act*.

(2) Determination of amount of claim — For the purposes of this Act, the amount represented by a claim of any secured or unsecured creditor shall be determined as follows:

(a) the amount of an unsecured claim shall be the amount

(i) in the case of a company in the course of being wound up under the *Winding-up and Restructuring Act*, proof of which has been made in accordance with that Act,

(ii) in the case of a company that has made an authorized assignment or against which a bankruptcy order has been made under the *Bankruptcy and Insolvency Act*, proof of which has been made in accordance with that Act, or

(iii) in the case of any other company, proof of which might be made under the *Bankruptcy and Insolvency Act*, but if the amount so provable is not admitted by the company, the amount shall be determined by the court on summary application by the company or by the creditor; and

(b) the amount of a secured claim shall be the amount, proof of which might be made in respect thereof under the *Bankruptcy and Insolvency Act* if the claim were unsecured, but the amount if not admitted by the company shall, in the case of a company subject to pending proceedings under the *Winding-up and Restructuring Act* or the *Bankruptcy and Insolvency Act*, be established by proof in the same manner as an unsecured claim under the *Winding-up and Restructuring Act* or the *Bankruptcy and Insolvency Act*, as the case may be, and in the case of any other company the amount shall be determined by the court on summary application by the company or the creditor.

(3) Admission of claims — Notwithstanding subsection (2), the company may admit the amount of a claim for voting purposes under reserve of the right to contest liability on the claim for other purposes, and nothing in this Act, the *Winding-up and Restructuring Act* or the *Bankruptcy and Insolvency Act* prevents a secured creditor from voting at a meeting of secured creditors or any class of them in respect of the total amount of a claim as admitted.

Proposed Amendment — 12

12. Fixing of deadline for filing claims — The court may make an order fixing a deadline for creditors to file their claims against a company for the purpose of voting at a creditors' meeting held under section 4 or 5.

2005, c. 47, s. 130 [Not in force at date of publication.]

1992, c. 27, s. 90(1)(f); 1996, c. 6, s. 167(1)(d); 2004, c. 25, s. 195

13. Leave to appeal — Except in Yukon, any person dissatisfied with an order or a decision made under this Act may appeal from the order or decision on obtaining leave of the judge appealed from or of the court or a judge of the court to which the appeal lies and on such terms as to security and in other respects as the judge or court directs.

2002, c. 7, s. 134

14. (1) Court of appeal — An appeal under section 13 lies to the highest court of final resort in or for the province in which the proceeding originated.

(2) Practice — All appeals under section 13 shall be regulated as far as possible according to the practice in other cases of the court appealed to, but no appeal shall be entertained unless, within twenty-one days after the rendering of the order or decision being appealed, or within such further time as the court appealed from, or, in Yukon, a judge of the Supreme Court of Canada, allows, the appellant has taken proceedings therein to perfect his or her appeal, and within that time he or she has made a deposit or given sufficient security according to the practice of the court appealed to that he or she will duly prosecute the appeal and pay such costs as may be awarded to the respondent and comply with any terms as to security or otherwise imposed by the judge giving leave to appeal.

2002, c. 7, s. 135

15. (1) Appeals — An appeal lies to the Supreme Court of Canada on leave therefor being granted by that Court from the highest court of final resort in or for the province or territory in which the proceeding originated.

(2) Jurisdiction of Supreme Court of Canada — The Supreme Court of Canada shall have jurisdiction to hear and to decide according to its ordinary procedure any appeal under subsection (1) and to award costs.

(3) Stay of proceedings — No appeal to the Supreme Court of Canada shall operate as a stay of proceedings unless and to the extent ordered by that Court.

(4) Security for costs — The appellant in an appeal under subsection (1) shall not be required to provide any security for costs, but, unless he provides security for costs in an amount to be fixed by the Supreme Court of Canada, he shall not be awarded costs in the event of his success on the appeal.

(5) Decision final — The decision of the Supreme Court of Canada on any appeal under subsection (1) is final and conclusive.

16. Order of court of one province — Every order made by the court in any province in the exercise of jurisdiction conferred by this Act in respect of any compromise or arrangement shall have full force and effect in all the other provinces and shall be enforced in the court of each of the other provinces in the same manner in all respects as if the order had been made by the court enforcing it.

17. Courts shall aid each other on request — All courts that have jurisdiction under this Act and the officers of those courts shall act in aid of and be auxiliary to each other in all matters provided for in this Act, and an order of a court seeking aid with a request to another court shall be deemed sufficient to enable the latter court to exercise in regard to the matters directed by the order such jurisdiction as either the court that made the request or the court to which the request is made could exercise in regard to similar matters within their respective jurisdictions.

18. (1) Governor in Council may make general rules — The Governor in Council may make, alter or revoke, and may delegate to the judges of the courts exercising jurisdiction under this Act the power to make, alter or revoke, general rules for carrying into effect the objects of this Act.

(2) Limitation — The rules referred to in subsection (1) shall not extend the jurisdiction of the court.

(3) General rules to be laid before Parliament — All general rules as are from time to time made by the Governor in Council shall be laid before Parliament within three weeks after they are made, or, if Parliament is not then sitting, within three weeks after the beginning of the next session.

(4) Judicial notice — All rules referred to in subsection (1) shall be judicially noticed and shall have effect as if enacted by this Act.

Proposed Repeal — 18

18. [Repealed 2005, c. 47, s. 131. Not in force at date of publication.]

18.1 Law of set-off to apply — The law of set-off applies to all claims made against a debtor company and to all actions instituted by it for the recovery of debts due to the company in the same manner and to the same extent as if the company were plaintiff or defendant, as the case may be.

Proposed Repeal — 18.1

18.1 [Repealed 2005, c. 47, s. 131. Not in force at date of publication.]

1997, c. 12, s. 125

18.2 (1) Certain Crown claims — If an order contains a provision authorized by subsection 11.4(1), unless Her Majesty consents, no compromise or arrangement shall be sanctioned by the court that does not provide for the payment in full to Her Majesty in right of Canada or a province, within six months after court sanction of the compromise or arrangement, of all amounts that were outstanding at the time of the application for an order under section 11 and that are of a kind that could be subject to a demand under

(a) subsections 224(1.2) and (1.3) of the *Income Tax Act*;

(b) any provision of the *Canada Pension Plan* or of the *Employment Insurance Act* that refers to subsection 224(1.2) of the *Income Tax Act* and provides for the collection of a contribution, as defined in the *Canada Pension Plan*, or an employee's premium, or employer's premium, as defined in the *Employment Insurance Act*, and of any related interest, penalties or other amounts; or

(c) any provision of provincial legislation that has a similar purpose to subsection 224(1.2) of the *Income Tax Act*, or that refers to that subsection, to the extent that it provides for the collection of a sum, and of any related interest, penalties or other amounts, where the sum

(i) has been withheld or deducted by a person from a payment to another person and is in respect of a tax similar in nature to the income tax imposed on individuals under the *Income Tax Act*, or

(ii) is of the same nature as a contribution under the *Canada Pension Plan* if the province is a "province providing a comprehensive pension plan" as defined in subsection 3(1) of the *Canada Pension Plan* and the provincial legislation establishes a "provincial pension plan" as defined in that subsection.

(2) Default of remittance to Crown — Where an order contains a provision authorized by subsection 11.4(1), no compromise or arrangement shall be sanctioned by the court if, at the time the court hears the application for sanction, Her Majesty in right of Canada or a province satisfies the court that the company is in default on any remittance of an amount referred to in subsection (1) that became due after the time of the application for an order under section 11.

Proposed Repeal — 18.2

18.2 [Repealed 2005, c. 47, s. 131. Not in force at date of publication.]

Note:

S.C. 2000, c. 30, s. 157(2) provides as follows:

(2) Subsection (1) [which replaced s. 18.2(1)] applies to proceedings commenced under the Act after September 29, 1997.

1997, c. 12, s. 125; 2000, c. 30, s. 157(1)

18.3 (1) Deemed trusts — Subject to subsection (2), notwithstanding any provision in federal or provincial legislation that has the effect of deeming property to be held in trust for Her Majesty, property of a debtor company shall not be regarded as held in trust for Her Majesty unless it would be so regarded in the absence of that statutory provision.

(2) Exceptions — Subsection (1) does not apply in respect of amounts deemed to be held in trust under subsection 227(4) or (4.1) of the *Income Tax Act*, subsection 23(3) or (4) of the *Canada Pension Plan* or subsection 86(2) or (2.1) of the *Employment Insurance Act* (each of which is in this subsection referred to as a "federal provision") nor in respect of amounts deemed to be held in trust under any law of a province that creates a deemed trust the sole purpose of which is to ensure remittance to Her Majesty in right of the province of amounts deducted or withheld under a law of the province where

(a) that law of the province imposes a tax similar in nature to the tax imposed under the *Income Tax Act* and the amounts deducted or withheld under that law of the province are of the same nature as the amounts referred to in subsection 227(4) or (4.1) of the *Income Tax Act*, or

(b) the province is a "province providing a comprehensive pension plan" as defined in subsection 3(1) of the *Canada Pension Plan*, that law of the province establishes a "provincial pension plan" as defined in that subsection and the amounts deducted or withheld under that law of the province are of the same nature as amounts referred to in subsection 23(3) or (4) of the *Canada Pension Plan*,

and for the purpose of this subsection, any provision of a law of a province that creates a deemed trust is, notwithstanding any Act of Canada or of a province or any other law, deemed to have the same effect and scope against any creditor, however secured, as the corresponding federal provision.

Proposed Repeal — 18.3

18.3 [Repealed 2005, c. 47, s. 131. Not in force at date of publication.]

1997, c. 12, s. 125; 1998, c. 19, s. 260

18.4 (1) Status of Crown claims — In relation to a proceeding under this Act, all claims, including secured claims, of Her Majesty in right of Canada or a province or any body under an enactment respecting workers' compensation, in this section and in section 18.5 called a "workers' compensation body", rank as unsecured claims.

(2) Exceptions — Subsection (1) does not apply

(a) to claims that are secured by a security or privilege of a kind that can be obtained by persons other than Her Majesty or a workers' compensation body

(i) pursuant to any law, or

(ii) pursuant to provisions of federal or provincial legislation, where those provisions do not have as their sole or principal purpose the establishment of a means of securing claims of Her Majesty or a workers' compensation body; and

(b) to the extent provided in subsection 18.5(2), to claims that are secured by a security referred to in subsection 18.5(1), if the security is registered in accordance with subsection 18.5(1).

(3) Operation of similar legislation — Subsection (1) does not affect the operation of

(a) subsections 224(1.2) and (1.3) of the *Income Tax Act*;

(b) any provision of the *Canada Pension Plan* or of the *Employment Insurance Act* that refers to subsection 224(1.2) of the *Income Tax Act* and provides for the collection of a contribution, as defined in the *Canada Pension Plan*, or an employee's premium, or employer's premium, as defined in the *Employment Insurance Act*, and of any related interest, penalties or other amounts; or

(c) any provision of provincial legislation that has a similar purpose to subsection 224(1.2) of the *Income Tax Act*, or that refers to that subsection, to the extent that it provides for the collection of a sum, and of any related interest, penalties or other amounts, where the sum

(i) has been withheld or deducted by a person from a payment to another person and is in respect of a tax similar in nature to the income tax imposed on individuals under the *Income Tax Act*, or

(ii) is of the same nature as a contribution under the *Canada Pension Plan* if the province is a "province providing a comprehensive pension plan" as defined in subsection 3(1) of the *Canada Pension Plan* and the provincial legislation establishes a "provincial pension plan" as defined in that subsection,

and for the purpose of paragraph (c), the provision of provincial legislation is, despite any Act of Canada or of a province or any other law, deemed to have the same effect and scope against any creditor, however secured, as subsection 224(1.2) of the *Income Tax Act* in respect of a sum referred to in subparagraph (c)(i), or as subsection 23(2) of the *Canada Pension*

Plan in respect of a sum referred to in subparagraph (c)(ii), and in respect of any related interest, penalties or other amounts.

Proposed Repeal — 18.4

18.4 [Repealed 2005, c. 47, s. 131. Not in force at date of publication.]

Note:

S.C. 2000, c. 30, s. 158(2) provides as follows:

> *(2) Subsection (1) [which replaced s. 18.4(3)] applies to proceedings commenced under the Act after September 29, 1997.*

1997, c. 12, s. 125; 2000, c. 30, s. 158(1)

18.5 (1) Statutory Crown securities — In relation to a proceeding under this Act in respect of a debtor company, a security provided for in federal or provincial legislation for the sole or principal purpose of securing a claim of Her Majesty in right of Canada or a province or a workers' compensation body is valid in relation to claims against the company only if the security is registered before the date of the initial application for an order under section 11 pursuant to any system of registration of securities that is available not only to Her Majesty in right of Canada or a province or a workers' compensation body, but also to any other creditor who holds a security, and that is open to the public for information or the making of searches.

(2) Effect of security — A security referred to in subsection (1) that is registered in accordance with that subsection

(a) is subordinate to securities in respect of which all steps necessary to make them effective against other creditors were taken before that registration; and

(b) is valid only in respect of amounts owing to Her Majesty or a workers' compensation body at the time of that registration, plus any interest subsequently accruing on those amounts.

Proposed Repeal — 18.5

18.5 [Repealed 2005, c. 47, s. 131. Not in force at date of publication.]

1997, c. 12, s. 125

International Insolvencies

18.6 (1) Definitions — In this section,

"foreign proceeding" means a judicial or administrative proceeding commenced outside Canada in respect of a debtor under a law relating to bankruptcy or insolvency and dealing with the collective interests of creditors generally;

"foreign representative" means a person, other than a debtor, holding office under the law of a jurisdiction outside Canada who, irrespective of the person's designation, is assigned, under the laws of the jurisdiction outside Canada, functions in connection with a foreign proceeding that are similar to those performed by a trustee in bankruptcy, liquidator or other administrator appointed by the court.

(2) Powers of court — The court may, in respect of a debtor company, make such orders and grant such relief as it considers appropriate to facilitate, approve or implement arrangements that will result in a co-ordination of proceedings under this Act with any foreign proceeding.

(3) Terms and conditions of orders — An order of the court under this section may be made on such terms and conditions as the court considers appropriate in the circumstances.

(4) Court not prevented from applying certain rules — Nothing in this section prevents the court, on the application of a foreign representative or any other interested person, from applying such legal or equitable rules governing the recognition of foreign insolvency orders and assistance to foreign representatives as are not inconsistent with the provisions of this Act.

(5) Court not compelled to give effect to certain orders — Nothing in this section requires the court to make any order that is not in compliance with the laws of Canada or to enforce any order made by a foreign court.

(6) Court may seek assistance from foreign tribunal — The court may seek the aid and assistance of a court, tribunal or other authority in a foreign proceeding by order or written request or otherwise as the court considers appropriate.

(7) Foreign representative status — An application to the court by a foreign representative under this section does not submit the foreign representative to the jurisdiction of the court for any other purpose except with regard to the costs of the proceedings, but the court may make any order under this section conditional on the compliance by the foreign representative with any other order of the court.

(8) Claims in foreign currency — Where a compromise or arrangement is proposed in respect of a debtor company, a claim for a debt that is payable in a currency other than Canadian currency shall be converted to Canadian currency as of the date of the first application made in respect of the company under section 10 unless otherwise provided in the proposed compromise or arrangement.

Proposed Repeal — 18.6

18.6 [Repealed 2005, c. 47, s. 131. Not in force at date of publication.]

1997, c. 12, s. 125

Part III — General

[Heading added 2005, c. 47, s. 131. Not in force at date of publication.]

Claims

[Heading added 2005, c. 47, s. 131. Not in force at date of publication.]

19. Certain sections of *Winding-up and Restructuring Act* do not apply — Sections 65 and 66 of the *Winding-up and Restructuring Act* do not apply to any compromise or arrangement to which this Act applies.

Proposed Amendment — 19

19. (1) Claims that may be dealt with by a compromise or an arrangement — Subject to subsection (2), in addition to deemed claims, the only claims that may be dealt with by a compromise or an arrangement in respect of a debtor company are

(a) claims that relate to debts and liabilities, present or future, to which the company is subject on the earlier of

(i) the day on which the initial application was made in respect of the company, and

(ii) if the company had filed a notice of intention under section 50.4 of the *Bankruptcy and Insolvency Act* or an application under this Act was made by the company with the consent of inspectors referred to in section 116 of the *Bankruptcy and Insolvency Act*, the day that is the date of the initial bankruptcy event within the meaning of subsection 2(1) of that Act; and

(b) claims that relate to debts and liabilities, present or future, to which the company may become subject before the compromise or arrangement is sanctioned by reason of any obligation incurred by the company before the earlier of the days referred to in subparagraphs (a)(i) and (ii).

(2) Exception — A compromise or an arrangement in respect of a debtor company may not deal with any claim that relates to any of the following debts or liabilities unless the compromise or arrangement explicitly provides for the claim's compromise and the relevant creditor has agreed to the compromise or arrangement:

(a) any fine, penalty, restitution order or other order similar in nature to a fine, penalty or restitution order, imposed by a court in respect of an offence;

(b) any award of damages by a court in civil proceedings in respect of

(i) bodily harm intentionally inflicted, or sexual assault, or

(ii) wrongful death resulting from an act referred to in subparagraph (i);

(c) any debt or liability arising out of fraud, embezzlement, misappropriation or defalcation while acting in a fiduciary capacity or, in the Province of Quebec, as a trustee or an administrator of the property of others;

(d) any debt or liability for obtaining property or services by false pretences or fraudulent misrepresentation, other than a debt or liability of the company that arises from the purchase or sale of a share or unit of the company or from the rescission of any such purchase or sale; or

(e) any debt for interest owed in relation to an amount referred to in any of paragraphs (a) to (d).

2005, c. 47, s. 131 [Not in force at date of publication.]

1996, c. 6, s. 167(1)(d)

20. Act to be applied conjointly with other Acts — The provisions of this Act may be applied together with the provisions of any Act of Parliament or of the legislature of any province, that authorizes or makes provision for the sanction of compromises or arrangements between a company and its shareholders or any class of them.

Proposed Amendment — 20

20. (1) Determination of amount of claims — For the purposes of this Act, the amount represented by a claim of any secured or unsecured creditor is to be determined as follows:

(a) the amount of an unsecured claim is the amount

(i) in the case of a company in the course of being wound up under the *Winding-up and Restructuring Act*, proof of which has been made in accordance with that Act,

(ii) in the case of a company that has made an authorized assignment or against which a bankruptcy order has been made under the *Bankruptcy and Insolvency Act*, proof of which has been made in accordance with that Act, or

(iii) in the case of any other company, proof of which might be made under the *Bankruptcy and Insolvency Act*, but if the amount so provable is not admitted by the company, the amount is to be determined by the court on summary application by the company or by the creditor; and

(b) the amount of a secured claim is the amount, proof of which might be made under the *Bankruptcy and Insolvency Act* if the claim were unsecured, but the amount if not admitted by the company is, in the case of a company subject to pending proceedings under the *Winding-up and Restructuring Act* or the *Bankruptcy and Insolvency Act*, to be established by proof in the same manner as an unsecured claim under the *Winding-up and Restructuring Act* or the *Bankruptcy and Insolvency Act*, as the case may be, and, in the case of any other company, the amount is to be determined by the court on summary application by the company or the creditor.

(2) Admission of claims — Despite subsection (1), the company may admit the amount of a claim for voting purposes under reserve of the right to contest liability on the claim for other purposes, and nothing in this Act, the *Winding-up and Restructuring Act* or the *Bankruptcy and Insolvency Act* prevents a secured creditor from voting at a meeting of secured creditors or any class of them in respect of the total amount of a claim as admitted.

(3) Claims acquired after initial application — No person is entitled to vote on a claim acquired after the initial application in respect of the company, unless the entire claim is acquired.

2005, c. 47, s. 131 [Not in force at date of publication.]

21. Act binding on Her Majesty — This Act is binding on Her Majesty in right of Canada or a province.

Proposed Amendment — 21

21. Law of set-off or compensation to apply — The law of set-off or compensation applies to all claims made against a debtor company and to all actions instituted by it for the recovery of debts due to the company in the same manner and to the same extent as if the company were plaintiff or defendant, as the case may be.

2005, c. 47, s. 131 [Not in force at date of publication.]

1997, c. 12, s. 126

Classes of Creditors

[Heading added 2005, c. 47, s. 131. Not in force at date of publication.]

22. (1) Review by Parliament — This Act shall, on the expiration of five years after the coming into force of this section, stand referred to such committee of the Senate, of the House of Commons or of both Houses of Parliament as may be designated or established to review the administration and operation of this Act.

(2) Report — The committee shall, within one year after beginning the review or within such further time as the Senate, the House of Commons or both Houses of Parliaments, as the case may be, may authorize, submit a report on the review to that House or both Houses, including a statement of any changes to this Act that the committee would recommend.

Proposed Amendment — 22

22. (1) Company may establish classes — Subject to subsection (3), a debtor company may divide its creditors into classes for the purpose of a meeting to be held under section 4 or 5 in respect of a compromise or an arrangement relating to a company and, if it does so, it must apply to the court for approval of the division before any meeting is held.

(2) Factors — For the purpose of subsection (1), creditors may be included in the same class if their interests are sufficiently similar to give them a commonality of interest, taking into account

(a) the nature of the debts, liabilities or obligations giving rise to their claims;

(b) the nature and rank of any security in respect of their claims;

(c) the remedies available to the creditors in the absence of the compromise or arrangement being sanctioned, and the extent to which the creditors would recover their claims by exercising those remedies; and

(d) any further criteria, consistent with those set out in paragraphs (a) to (c), that are prescribed.

(3) Claims of shareholders — Creditors having a claim against a debtor company arising from the rescission of a purchase or sale of a share or unit of the company — or a claim for damages arising from the purchase or sale of a share or unit of the company — must be in the same class of creditors in relation to those claims and may not, as members of that class, vote at a meeting to be held under section 4 in respect of a compromise or an arrangement relating to the company.

2005, c. 47, s. 131 [Not in force at date of publication.]

Proposed Addition — 23-63

Monitors

[Heading added 2005, c. 47, s. 131. Not in force at date of publication.]

23. (1) Duties and functions — The monitor shall

(a) except as otherwise ordered by the court, when an order is made on the initial application in respect of a debtor company,

(i) publish, without delay after the order is made, once a week for two consecutive weeks, or as otherwise directed by the court, in one or more newspapers in Canada specified by the court, a notice containing the prescribed information, and

(ii) within five days after the order is made,

(A) send a copy of the order to every known creditor who has a claim against the company of more than $1,000, and

(B) make a list showing the name and address of those creditors publicly available in the prescribed manner;

(b) review the company's cash-flow statement as to its reasonableness and file a report with the court on the monitor's findings;

(c) make, or cause to be made, any appraisal or investigation the monitor considers necessary to determine with reasonable accuracy the state of the company's business and financial affairs and the cause of its financial difficulties or insolvency and file a report with the court on the monitor's findings;

(d) file a report with the court on the state of the company's business and financial affairs, containing prescribed information,

(i) without delay after ascertaining any material adverse change in the company's projected cash-flow or financial circumstances,

(ii) at least seven days before any meeting of creditors under section 4 or 5,

(iii) not later than 45 days, or any longer period that the court may specify, after the end of each of the company's fiscal quarters, and

(iv) at any other times that the court may order;

(e) advise the company's creditors of the filing of the report referred to in any of paragraphs (b) to (d);

(f) file with the Superintendent of Bankruptcy a copy of the documents specified by the regulations and pay the prescribed filing fee;

(g) attend court proceedings held under this Act that relate to the company, and meetings of the company's creditors, if the monitor considers that his or her attendance is necessary for the fulfilment of his or her duties or functions;

(h) if the monitor is of the opinion that it would be more beneficial to the company's creditors if proceedings in respect of the company were taken under the *Bankruptcy and Insolvency Act*, so advise the court without delay after coming to that opinion;

(i) advise the court on the reasonableness and fairness of any compromise or arrangement that is proposed between the company and its creditors;

(j) unless the court otherwise orders, make publicly available, in the prescribed manner, all documents filed with the court, and all court decisions, relating to proceedings held under this Act in respect of the company and provide the company's creditors with information as to how they may access those documents and decisions; and

(k) carry out any other functions in relation to the company that the court may direct.

(2) Monitor not liable — If the monitor acts in good faith and takes reasonable care in preparing the report referred to in any of paragraphs (1)(b) to (d), the monitor is not liable for loss or damage to any person resulting from that person's reliance on the report.

2005, c. 47, s. 131 [Not in force at date of publication.]

24. Right of access — For the purposes of monitoring the company's business and financial affairs, the monitor shall have access to the company's property, including the premises, books, records, data, including data in electronic form, and other financial documents of the company, to the extent that is necessary to adequately assess the company's business and financial affairs.

2005, c. 47, s. 131 [Not in force at date of publication.]

25. Obligation to act honestly and in good faith — In exercising any of his or her powers or in performing any of his or her duties and functions, the monitor must act honestly and in good faith and comply with the Code of Ethics referred to in section 13.5 of the *Bankruptcy and Insolvency Act*.

2005, c. 47, s. 131 [Not in force at date of publication.]

Powers, Duties and Functions of Superintendent of Bankruptcy

[Heading added 2005, c. 47, s. 131. Not in force at date of publication.]

26. (1) Public records — The Superintendent of Bankruptcy must keep, or cause to be kept, in the form that he or she considers appropriate and for the prescribed period, a public record of prescribed information relating to proceedings under this Act. On request, and on payment of the prescribed fee, the Superintendent of Bankruptcy must provide, or cause to be provided, any information contained in that public record.

(2) Other records — The Superintendent of Bankruptcy must keep, or cause to be kept, in the form that he or she considers appropriate and for the prescribed period, any other records relating to the administration of this Act that he or she considers appropriate.

2005, c. 47, s. 131 [Not in force at date of publication.]

27. Applications to court and right to intervene — The Superintendent of Bankruptcy may apply to the court to review the appointment or conduct of a monitor and may intervene, as though he or she were a party, in any matter or proceeding in court relating to the appointment or conduct of a monitor.

2005, c. 47, s. 131 [Not in force at date of publication.]

28. Complaints — The Superintendent of Bankruptcy must receive and keep a record of all complaints regarding the conduct of monitors.

2005, c. 47, s. 131 [Not in force at date of publication.]

29. (1) Investigations — The Superintendent of Bankruptcy may make, or cause to be made, any inquiry or investigation regarding the conduct of monitors that he or she considers appropriate.

(2) Rights — For the purpose of the inquiry or investigation, the Superintendent of Bankruptcy or any person whom he or she appoints for the purpose

(a) shall have access to and the right to examine and make copies of all books, records, data, including data in electronic form, documents and papers in the possession or under the control of a monitor under this Act; and

(b) may, with the leave of the court granted on an *ex parte* application, examine the books, records, data, including data in electronic form, documents and papers relating to any compromise or arrangement to which this Act applies that are in the possession or under the control of any other person designated in the order granting the leave, and for that purpose may under a warrant from the court enter and search any premises.

(3) Staff — The Superintendent of Bankruptcy may engage the services of persons having technical or specialized knowledge, and persons to provide administrative services, to assist the Superintendent of Bankruptcy in conducting an inquiry or investigation, and may establish the terms and conditions of their engagement. The remuneration and expenses of those persons, when certified by the Superintendent of Bankruptcy, are payable out of the appropriation for the office of the Superintendent.

2005, c. 47, s. 131 [Not in force at date of publication.]

30. (1) Powers in relation to licence — If, after making or causing to be made an inquiry or investigation into the conduct of a monitor, it appears to the Superintendent of Bankruptcy that the monitor has not fully complied with this Act and its regulations or that it is in the public interest to do so, the Superintendent of Bankruptcy may

(a) cancel or suspend the monitor's licence as a trustee under the *Bankruptcy and Insolvency Act*; or

(b) place any condition or limitation on the licence that he or she considers appropriate.

(2) Notice to trustee — Before deciding whether to exercise any of the powers referred to in subsection (1), the Superintendent of Bankruptcy shall send the monitor written notice of the powers that the Superintendent may exercise and the reasons why they may be exercised and afford the monitor a reasonable opportunity for a hearing.

(3) Subpoena or summons — The Superintendent of Bankruptcy may, for the purpose of the hearing, issue a subpoena or other request or summons, requiring and commanding any person named in it

(a) to appear at the time and place mentioned in it;

(b) to testify to all matters within his or her knowledge relative to the subject-matter of the inquiry or investigation into the conduct of the monitor; and

(c) to bring and produce any books, records, data, including data in electronic form, documents or papers in the person's possession or under the control of the person relative to the subject-matter of the inquiry or investigation.

(4) Effect throughout Canada — A person may be summoned from any part of Canada by virtue of a subpoena, request or summons issued under subsection (3).

(5) Fees and allowances — Any person summoned under subsection (3) is entitled to receive the like fees and allowances for so doing as if summoned to attend before the Federal Court.

(6) Procedure at hearing — At the hearing, the Superintendent of Bankruptcy

(a) has the power to administer oaths;

(b) is not bound by any legal or technical rules of evidence in conducting the hearing;

(c) shall deal with the matters set out in the notice of the hearing as informally and expeditiously as the circumstances and a consideration of fairness permit; and

(d) shall cause a summary of any oral evidence to be made in writing.

(7) Record — The notice referred to in subsection (2) and, if applicable, the summary of oral evidence referred to in paragraph (6)(d), together with any documentary evidence that the Superintendent of Bankruptcy receives in evidence, form the record of the hearing, and that record and the hearing are public unless the Superintendent of Bankruptcy is satisfied that personal or other matters that may be disclosed are of such a nature that the desirability of avoiding public disclosure of those matters, in the interest of a third party or in the public interest, outweighs the desirability of the access by the public to information about those matters.

(8) Decision — The decision of the Superintendent of Bankruptcy after the hearing, together with the reasons for the decision, must be given in writing to the monitor not later than three months after the conclusion of the hearing, and is public.

(9) Review by Federal Court — A decision of the Superintendent of Bankruptcy given under subsection (8) is deemed to be a decision of a federal board, commission or other tribunal that may be reviewed and set aside under the *Federal Courts Act*.

2005, c. 47, s. 131 [Not in force at date of publication.]

31. (1) Delegation — The Superintendent of Bankruptcy may, in writing, authorize any person to exercise or perform, subject to any terms and conditions that he or she may specify in the authorization, any of the powers, duties or functions of the Superintendent of Bankruptcy under sections 29 and 30.

(2) Notification to monitor — If the Superintendent of Bankruptcy delegates in accordance with subsection (1), the Superintendent or the delegate must give notice of the delegation in the prescribed manner to any monitor who may be affected by the delegation.

2005, c. 47, s. 131 [Not in force at date of publication.]

Agreements

[Heading added 2005, c. 47, s. 131. Not in force at date of publication.]

32. (1) Disclaimer or resiliation of agreements — Subject to subsection (3), a debtor company may disclaim or resiliate any agreement to which it is a party on the day of the filing of the initial application in respect of the company by giving 30 days notice to the other parties to the agreement in the prescribed manner.

(2) Exceptions — Subsection (1) does not apply in respect of

(a) an eligible financial contract within the meaning of subsection 11.05(3);

(b) a collective agreement;

(c) a financing agreement if the debtor is the borrower; and

(d) a lease of real property or an immovable if the debtor is the lessor.

(3) Party may challenge — Within 15 days after being given notice of the disclaimer or resiliation, a party to the agreement may apply to the court for a declaration that subsection (1) does not apply in respect of the agreement, and the court, on notice to any parties that it may direct, shall, subject to subsection (4), make that declaration.

(4) Circumstances for not making declaration — No declaration under subsection (3) shall be made if the court is satisfied that a viable compromise or arrangement could not be made in respect of the company without the disclaimer or resiliation of the agreement and all other agreements that the company has disclaimed or resiliated under subsection (1).

(5) Intellectual property — If the company has, in any agreement, granted the use of any intellectual property to a party to the agreement, the disclaimer or resiliation of the agreement does not affect the party's right to use the intellectual property so long as that party continues to perform its obligations in relation to the use of the intellectual property.

(6) Deemed claim of other party — If an agreement is disclaimed or resiliated by a company, every other party to the agreement is deemed to have a claim for damages as an unsecured creditor.

2005, c. 47, s. 131 [Not in force at date of publication.]

33. (1) Collective agreements — If proceedings under this Act have been commenced in respect of a debtor company, any collective agreement that the company has entered into as the employer remains in force, and may not be altered except as provided in this section or under the laws of the jurisdiction governing collective bargaining between the company and the bargaining agent.

(2) Application for authorization to serve notice to bargain — A debtor company that is a party to a collective agreement and that is unable to reach a voluntary agreement with the bargaining agent to revise any of the provisions of the collective agreement may, on giving five days notice to the bargaining agent, apply to the court for an order authorizing the company to serve a notice to bargain under the laws of the jurisdiction governing collective bargaining between the company and the bargaining agent.

(3) Conditions for issuance of order — The court may issue the order only if it is satisfied that

(a) a viable compromise or arrangement could not be made in respect of the company, taking into account the terms of the collective agreement;

(b) the company has made good faith efforts to renegotiate the provisions of the collective agreement; and

(c) a failure to issue the order is likely to result in irreparable damage to the company.

(4) No delay on vote — The vote of the creditors in respect of a compromise or an arrangement may not be delayed solely because the period provided in the laws of the jurisdiction governing collective bargaining between the company and the bargaining agent has not expired.

(5) Claims arising from termination or amendment — If the parties to the collective agreement agree to revise the collective agreement after proceedings have been commenced under this Act in respect of the company, the bargaining agent that is a party to the agreement is deemed to have a claim, as an unsecured creditor, for an amount equal to the value of concessions granted by the bargaining agent with respect to the remaining term of the collective agreement.

(6) Order to disclose information — On the application of the bargaining agent and on notice to the person to whom the application relates, the court may, subject to any terms and conditions it specifies, make an order requiring the person to make available to the bargaining agent any information specified by the court in the person's possession or control that relates to the company's business or financial affairs and that is relevant to the collective bargaining between the company and the bargaining agent. The court may make the order only after the company has been authorized to serve a notice to bargain under subsection (2).

(7) Parties — For the purpose of this section, the parties to a collective agreement are the debtor company and the bargaining agent that are bound by the collective agreement.

(8) Unrevised collective agreements remain in force — For greater certainty, any collective agreement that the company and the bargaining agent have not agreed to revise remains in force, and the court shall not alter its terms.

2005, c. 47, s. 131 [Not in force at date of publication.]

34. (1) Certain rights limited — No person may terminate or amend any agreement, including a security agreement, with a debtor company, or claim an accelerated payment, or a forfeiture of the term, under any agreement, including a security agreement, with a debtor company by reason only that an order has been made under this Act in respect of the company.

(2) Lease — If the agreement referred to in subsection (1) is a lease, the lessor may not terminate or amend the lease by reason only that an order has been made under this Act in respect of the company or that the company has not paid rent in respect of any period before the filing of the initial application in respect of the company.

(3) Public utilities — No public utility may discontinue service to a debtor company by reason only that an order has been made under this Act in respect of the company or that the company has not paid for services rendered, or for goods provided, before the filing of the initial application in respect of the company.

(4) Certain acts not prevented — Nothing in this section is to be construed as

(a) prohibiting a person from requiring payments to be made in cash for goods, services, use of leased property or other valuable consideration provided after the date of the filing of initial application in respect of the company; or

(b) requiring the further advance of money or credit.

(5) Provisions of section override agreement — Any provision in an agreement that has the effect of providing for, or permitting, anything that, in substance, is contrary to this section is of no force or effect.

(6) Powers of court — The court may, on application by a party to an agreement, declare that this section does not apply, or applies only to the extent declared by the court, if the applicant satisfies the court that the operation of this section would likely cause the applicant significant financial hardship.

2005, c. 47, s. 131 [Not in force at date of publication.]

Obligations and Prohibitions

[Heading added 2005, c. 47, s. 131. Not in force at date of publication.]

35. (1) Obligation to provide assistance — A debtor company shall provide to the monitor the assistance that is necessary to enable the monitor to adequately carry out the monitor's functions.

(2) Obligation to duties set out in section 158 of the *Bankruptcy and Insolvency Act* — A debtor company shall perform the duties set out in section 158 of the *Bankruptcy and Insolvency Act* that are appropriate and applicable in the circumstances.

2005, c. 47, s. 131 [Not in force at date of publication.]

36. (1) Restriction on disposal of certain business assets — A debtor company in respect of which an order has been made under this Act may not sell or dispose of any of its assets outside the ordinary course of its business unless authorized to do so by a court.

(2) Notice to creditors — A company that applies to the court for the authorization must give notice of the application to all secured creditors who are likely to be affected by the proposed sale or disposal of the assets to which the application relates.

(3) Factors to be considered — In deciding whether to grant the authorization, the court must consider, among other things,

(a) whether the process leading to the proposed sale or disposal of the assets to which the application relates was reasonable in the circumstances;

(b) whether the monitor approved the process leading to the proposed sale or disposal of the assets;

(c) whether the monitor has filed with the court a report stating that in his or her opinion the sale or disposal of the assets would be more beneficial to the creditors than if the sale or disposal took place under the *Bankruptcy and Insolvency Act*;

(d) the extent to which the creditors were consulted in respect of the proposed sale or disposal of the assets;

(e) the effects of the proposed sale or disposal on the creditors and other interested parties; and

(f) whether the consideration to be received for the assets is reasonable and fair, taking into account the market value of the assets.

(4) Additional factors — In addition to taking the factors referred to in subsection (3) into account, if the proposed sale or disposal of the assets is to a person who is related to the company, the court may grant the authorization only if it is satisfied that

(a) good faith efforts were made to sell or dispose of the assets to persons who are not related to the company or who are neither directors or officers of the company nor individuals who control it; and

(b) the consideration to be received is superior to the consideration that would be received under all other offers actually received in respect of the assets.

(5) Direction that assets may be sold free of charges, etc. — In granting an authorization for the sale or disposal of assets, the court may order that the assets may be sold or disposed of free and clear of any security, charge or other restriction, but if it so orders, it shall also order that the proceeds realized from the sale or disposal of the assets are subject to a security, charge or other restriction in favour of the creditors whose security, charges or other restrictions are affected by the order.

(6) Related persons — For the purpose of this section, a person who is related to the debtor company includes a person who controls the company, a director or an officer of the company and a person who is related to a director or an officer of the company.

2005, c. 47, s. 131 [Not in force at date of publication.]

Her Majesty

[Heading added 2005, c. 47, s. 131. Not in force at date of publication.]

37. (1) Deemed trusts — Subject to subsection (2), despite any provision in federal or provincial legislation that has the effect of deeming property to be held in trust for Her Majesty, property of a debtor company shall not be regarded as being held in trust for Her Majesty unless it would be so regarded in the absence of that statutory provision.

(2) Exceptions — Subsection (1) does not apply in respect of amounts deemed to be held in trust under subsection 227(4) or (4.1) of the *Income Tax Act*, subsection 23(3) or (4) of the *Canada Pension Plan* or subsection 86(2) or (2.1) of the *Employment Insurance Act* (each of which is in this subsection referred to as a "federal provision"), nor does it apply in respect of amounts deemed to be held in trust under any law of a province that creates a deemed trust the sole purpose of which is to ensure remittance to Her Majesty in right of the province of amounts deducted or withheld under a law of the province if

(a) that law of the province imposes a tax similar in nature to the tax imposed under the *Income Tax Act* and the amounts deducted or withheld under that law of the province are of the same nature as the amounts referred to in subsection 227(4) or (4.1) of the *Income Tax Act*, or

(b) the province is a "province providing a comprehensive pension plan" as defined in subsection 3(1) of the *Canada Pension Plan*, that law of the province establishes a "provincial pension plan" as defined in that subsection and the amounts deducted or withheld under that law of the province are of the same nature as amounts referred to in subsection 23(3) or (4) of the *Canada Pension Plan*,

and for the purpose of this subsection, any provision of a law of a province that creates a deemed trust is, despite any Act of Canada or of a province or any other law, deemed to have the same effect and scope against any creditor, however secured, as the corresponding federal provision.

2005, c. 47, s. 131 [Not in force at date of publication.]

38. (1) Status of Crown claims — In relation to a proceeding under this Act, all claims, including secured claims, of Her Majesty in right of Canada or a province or any body under an enactment respecting workers' compensation, in this section and in section 39 called a "workers' compensation body", rank as unsecured claims.

(2) Exceptions — Subsection (1) does not apply

(a) in respect of claims that are secured by a security or charge of a kind that can be obtained by persons other than Her Majesty or a workers' compensation body

(i) pursuant to any law, or

(ii) pursuant to provisions of federal or provincial legislation if those provisions do not have as their sole or principal purpose the establishment of a means of securing claims of Her Majesty or a workers' compensation body; and

(b) to the extent provided in subsection 39(2), to claims that are secured by a security referred to in subsection 39(1), if the security is registered in accordance with subsection 39(1).

(3) Operation of similar legislation — Subsection (1) does not affect the operation of

(a) subsections 224(1.2) and (1.3) of the *Income Tax Act*,

(b) any provision of the *Canada Pension Plan* or of the *Employment Insurance Act* that refers to subsection 224(1.2) of the *Income Tax Act* and provides for the collection of a contribution, as defined in the *Canada Pension Plan*, or an employee's premium, or employer's premium, as defined in the *Employment Insurance Act*, and of any related interest, penalties or other amounts, or

(c) any provision of provincial legislation that has a purpose similar to subsection 224(1.2) of the *Income Tax Act*, or that refers to that subsection, to the extent that it provides for the collection of a sum, and of any related interest, penalties or other amounts if the sum

(i) has been withheld or deducted by a person from a payment to another person and is in respect of a tax similar in nature to the income tax imposed on individuals under the *Income Tax Act*, or

(ii) is of the same nature as a contribution under the *Canada Pension Plan* if the province is a "province providing a comprehensive pension plan" as defined in subsection 3(1) of the *Canada Pension Plan* and the provincial legislation establishes a "provincial pension plan" as defined in that subsection,

and, for the purpose of paragraph (c), the provision of provincial legislation is, despite any Act of Canada or of a province or any other law, deemed to have the same effect and scope against any creditor, however secured, as subsection 224(1.2) of the *Income Tax Act* in respect of a sum referred to in subparagraph (c)(i), or as subsection 23(2) of the *Canada Pension Plan* in respect of a sum referred to in subparagraph (c)(ii), and in respect of any related interest, penalties or other amounts.

2005, c. 47, s. 131 [Not in force at date of publication.]

39. (1) Statutory Crown securities — In relation to a proceeding under this Act in respect of a debtor company, a security provided for in federal or provincial legislation for the sole or principal purpose of securing a claim of Her Majesty in right of Canada or a province or a workers' compensation body is valid in relation to claims against the company only if the security is registered before the date of the filing of the initial application in respect of the company under any system of registration of securities that is available not only to Her Majesty in right of Canada or a province or a workers' compensation body, but also to any other creditor who holds a security, and that is open to the public for information or the making of searches.

(2) Effect of security — A security referred to in subsection (1) that is registered in accordance with that subsection

(a) is subordinate to securities in respect of which all steps necessary to setting them up against other creditors were taken before that registration; and

(b) is valid only in respect of amounts owing to Her Majesty or a workers' compensation body at the time of that registration, plus any interest subsequently accruing on those amounts.

2005, c. 47, s. 131 [Not in force at date of publication.]

40. Act binding on Her Majesty — This Act is binding on Her Majesty in right of Canada or a province.

2005, c. 47, s. 131 [Not in force at date of publication.]

Miscellaneous

[Heading added 2005, c. 47, s. 131. Not in force at date of publication.]

41. Certain sections of *Winding-up and Restructuring Act* do not apply — Sections 65 and 66 of the *Winding-up and Restructuring Act* do not apply to any compromise or arrangement to which this Act applies.

2005, c. 47, s. 131 [Not in force at date of publication.]

42. Act to be applied conjointly with other Acts — The provisions of this Act may be applied together with the provisions of any Act of Parliament, or of the legislature of any province, that authorizes or makes provision for the sanction of compromises or arrangements between a company and its shareholders or any class of them.

2005, c. 47, s. 131 [Not in force at date of publication.]

43. Claims in foreign currency — If a compromise or an arrangement is proposed in respect of a debtor company, a claim for a debt that is payable in a currency other than Canadian currency is to be converted to Canadian currency as of the date of the initial application in respect of the company unless otherwise provided in the proposed compromise or arrangement.

2005, c. 47, s. 131 [Not in force at date of publication.]

Part IV — Cross-Border Insolvencies

[Heading added 2005, c. 47, s. 131. Not in force at date of publication.]

Purpose

[Heading added 2005, c. 47, s. 131. Not in force at date of publication.]

44. Purpose — The purpose of this Part is to provide mechanisms for dealing with cases of cross-border insolvencies and to promote

(a) cooperation between the courts and other competent authorities in Canada with those of foreign jurisdictions in cases of cross-border insolvencies;

(b) greater legal certainty for trade and investment;

(c) the fair and efficient administration of cross-border insolvencies that protects the interests of creditors and other interested persons, and those of debtor companies;

(d) the protection and the maximization of the value of debtor company's property; and

(e) the rescue of financially troubled businesses to protect investment and preserve employment.

2005, c. 47, s. 131 [Not in force at date of publication.]

Interpretation

[Heading added 2005, c. 47, s. 131. Not in force at date of publication.]

45. (1) Definitions — The following definitions apply in this Part.

"foreign court" means a judicial or other authority competent to control or supervise a foreign proceeding. "tribunal étranger"

"foreign main proceeding" means a foreign proceeding in a jurisdiction where the debtor company has the centre of its main interests. "principale"

"foreign non-main proceeding" means a foreign proceeding, other than a foreign main proceeding. "secondaire"

"foreign proceeding" means a judicial or an administrative proceeding, including an interim proceeding, in a jurisdiction outside Canada dealing with creditors' collective interests generally under any law relating to bankruptcy or insolvency in which a debtor company's business and financial affairs are subject to control or supervision by a foreign court for the purpose of reorganization. "instance étrangère"

"foreign representative" means a person or body, including one appointed on an interim basis, who is authorized, in a foreign proceeding respect of a debtor company, to

(a) monitor the debtor company's business and financial affairs for the purpose of reorganization; or

(b) act as a representative in respect of the foreign proceeding.

("représentant étranger")

(2) Centre of debtor company's main interests — For the purposes of this Part, in the absence of proof to the contrary, a debtor company's registered office is deemed to be the centre of its main interests.

2005, c. 47, s. 131 [Not in force at date of publication.]

Recognition of Foreign Proceeding

[Heading added 2005, c. 47, s. 131. Not in force at date of publication.]

46. (1) Application for recognition of a foreign proceeding — A foreign representative may apply to the court for recognition of the foreign proceeding in respect of which he or she is a foreign representative.

(2) Documents that must accompany application — Subject to subsection (3), the application must be accompanied by

(a) a certified copy of the instrument, however designated, that commenced the foreign proceeding or a certificate from the foreign court affirming the existence of the foreign proceeding;

(b) a certified copy of the instrument, however designated, authorizing the foreign representative to act in that capacity or a certificate from the foreign court affirming the foreign representative's authority to act in that capacity; and

(c) a statement identifying all foreign proceedings in respect of the debtor company that are known to the foreign representative.

(3) Documents may be considered as proof — The court may, without further proof, accept the documents referred to in paragraphs (2)(a) and (b) as evidence that the proceeding to which they relate is a foreign proceeding and that the applicant is a foreign representative in respect of the foreign proceeding.

(4) Other evidence — In the absence of the documents referred to in paragraphs (2)(a) and (b), the court may accept any other evidence of the existence of the foreign proceeding and of the foreign representative's authority that it considers appropriate.

(5) Translation — The court may require a translation of any document accompanying the application.

2005, c. 47, s. 131 [Not in force at date of publication.]

47. (1) Order recognizing foreign proceeding — If the court is satisfied that the application for the recognition of a foreign proceeding relates to a foreign proceeding and that the applicant is a foreign representative in respect of that foreign proceeding, the court shall make an order recognizing the foreign proceeding.

(2) Nature of foreign proceeding to be specified — The court shall specify in the order whether the foreign proceeding is a foreign main proceeding or a foreign non-main proceeding.

2005, c. 47, s. 131 [Not in force at date of publication.]

48. (1) Order relating to recognition of a foreign main proceeding — Subject to subsections (2) to (4), on the making of an order recognizing a foreign proceeding that is specified to be a foreign main proceeding, the court shall make an order, subject to any terms and conditions it considers appropriate,

(a) staying, until otherwise ordered by the court, for any period that the court considers necessary, all proceedings taken or that might be taken against the debtor company under the *Bankruptcy and Insolvency Act* or the *Winding-up and Restructuring Act*;

(b) restraining, until otherwise ordered by the court, further proceedings in any action, suit or proceeding against the debtor company;

(c) prohibiting, until otherwise ordered by the court, the commencement of any action, suit or proceeding against the debtor company; and

(d) prohibiting the debtor company from selling or otherwise disposing of, outside the ordinary course of its business, any of the debtor company's property in Canada that relates to the business and prohibiting the debtor company from selling or otherwise disposing of any of its other property in Canada.

(2) Scope of order — The order made under subsection (1) must be consistent with any order that may be made under this Act.

(3) When subsection (1) does not apply — Subsection (1) does not apply if any proceedings under this Act have been commenced in respect of the debtor company at the time the order recognizing the foreign proceeding is made.

(4) Application of this and other Acts — Nothing in subsection (1) precludes the debtor company from commencing or continuing proceedings under this Act, the *Bankruptcy and Insolvency Act* or the *Winding-up and Restructuring Act* in respect of the debtor company.

2005, c. 47, s. 131 [Not in force at date of publication.]

49. (1) Other orders — If an order recognizing a foreign proceeding is made, the court may, on application by the foreign representative who applied for the order, if the court is satisfied that it is necessary for the protection of the debtor company's property or the interests of a creditor or creditors, make any order that it considers appropriate, including an order

(a) if the foreign proceeding is a foreign non-main proceeding, referred to in subsection 48(1);

(b) respecting the examination of witnesses, the taking of evidence or the delivery of information concerning the debtor company's property, business and financial affairs, debts, liabilities and obligations; and

(c) authorizing the foreign representative to monitor the debtor company's business and financial affairs in Canada for the purpose of reorganization.

(2) Restriction — If any proceedings under this Act have been commenced in respect of the debtor company at the time an order recognizing the foreign proceeding is made, an order made under subsection (1) must be consistent with any order that may be made in any proceedings under this Act.

(3) Application of this and other Acts — The making of an order under paragraph (1)(a) does not preclude the commencement or the continuation of proceedings under this Act, the *Bankruptcy and Insolvency Act* or the *Winding-up and Restructuring Act* in respect of the debtor company.

2005, c. 47, s. 131 [Not in force at date of publication.]

50. Terms and conditions of orders — An order under this Part may be made on any terms and conditions that the court considers appropriate in the circumstances.

2005, c. 47, s. 131 [Not in force at date of publication.]

51. Commencement or continuation of proceedings — If an order is made recognizing a foreign proceeding, the foreign representative may commence and continue proceedings under this Act in respect of a debtor company as if the foreign representative were a creditor of the debtor company, or the debtor company, as the case may be.

2005, c. 47, s. 131 [Not in force at date of publication.]

Obligations

[Heading added 2005, c. 47, s. 131. Not in force at date of publication.]

52. (1) Cooperation — court — If an order recognizing a foreign proceeding is made, the court shall cooperate, to the maximum extent possible, with the foreign representative and the foreign court involved in the foreign proceeding.

(2) Cooperation — other authorities in Canada — If any proceedings under this Act have been commenced in respect of a debtor company and an order recognizing a foreign proceeding is made in respect of the debtor company, every person who exercises powers or performs duties and functions under the proceedings under this Act shall cooperate, to the maximum extent possible, with the foreign representative and the foreign court involved in the foreign proceeding.

2005, c. 47, s. 131 [Not in force at date of publication.]

53. Obligations of foreign representative — If an order recognizing a foreign proceeding is made, the foreign representative who applied for the order shall

(a) without delay, inform the court of

(i) any substantial change in the status of the recognized foreign proceeding,

(ii) any substantial change in the status of the foreign representative's authority to act in that capacity, and

(iii) any other foreign proceeding in respect of the same debtor company that becomes known to the foreign representative; and

(b) publish, without delay after the order is made, once a week for two consecutive weeks, or as otherwise directed by the court, in one or more newspapers in Canada specified by the court, a notice containing the prescribed information.

2005, c. 47, s. 131 [Not in force at date of publication.]

Multiple Proceedings

[Heading added 2005, c. 47, s. 131. Not in force at date of publication.]

54. Concurrent proceedings — If any proceedings under this Act in respect of a debtor company are commenced at any time after an order recognizing the foreign proceeding is made, the court shall review any order made under section 49 and, if it determines that the order is inconsistent with any orders made in the proceedings under this Act, the court shall amend or revoke the order.

2005, c. 47, s. 131 [Not in force at date of publication.]

55. (1) Multiple foreign proceedings — If, at any time after an order is made in respect of a foreign non-main proceeding in respect of a debtor company, an order recognizing a foreign main proceeding is made in respect of the debtor company, the court shall review any order made under section 49 in respect of the foreign non-main proceeding and, if it determines that the order is inconsistent with any orders made under that section in respect of the foreign main proceedings, the court shall amend or revoke the order.

(2) Multiple foreign proceedings — If, at any time after an order is made in respect of a foreign non-main proceeding in respect of the debtor company, an order recognizing another foreign non-main proceeding is made in respect of the debtor company, the court shall, for the purpose of facilitating the coordination of the foreign non-main proceedings, review any order made under section 49 in respect of the first recognized proceeding and amend or revoke the order if it considers it appropriate.

2005, c. 47, s. 131 [Not in force at date of publication.]

Miscellaneous Provisions

[Heading added 2005, c. 47, s. 131. Not in force at date of publication.]

56. Authorization to act as representative of proceeding under this Act — The court may authorize any person or body to act as a representative in respect of any proceeding under this Act for the purpose of having them recognized in a jurisdiction outside Canada.

2005, c. 47, s. 131 [Not in force at date of publication.]

57. Foreign representative status — An application by a foreign representative for any order under this Part does not submit the foreign representative to the jurisdiction of the court for any other purpose except with regard to the costs of the proceedings, but the court may make any order under this Part conditional on the compliance by the foreign representative with any other order of the court.

2005, c. 47, s. 131 [Not in force at date of publication.]

58. Foreign proceeding appeal — A foreign representative is not prevented from making an application to the court under this Part by reason only that proceedings by way of appeal or review have been taken in a foreign proceeding, and the court may, on an application if such proceedings have been taken, grant relief as if the proceedings had not been taken.

2005, c. 47, s. 131 [Not in force at date of publication.]

59. Presumption of insolvency — For the purposes of this Part, if an insolvency or a reorganization or a similar order has been made in respect of a debtor company in a foreign proceeding, a certified copy of the order is, in the absence of evidence to the contrary, proof that the debtor company is insolvent and proof of the appointment of the foreign representative made by the order.

2005, c. 47, s. 131 [Not in force at date of publication.]

60. (1) Credit for recovery in other jurisdictions — In making a compromise or an arrangement of a debtor company, the following shall be taken into account in the distribution of dividends to the company's creditors in Canada as if they were a part of that distribution:

(a) the amount that a creditor receives or is entitled to receive outside Canada by way of a dividend in a foreign proceeding in respect of the company; and

(b) the value of any property of the company that the creditor acquires outside Canada on account of a provable claim of the creditor or that the creditor acquires outside Canada by way of a transfer that, if it were subject to this Act, would be a preference over other creditors or a transfer at undervalue.

(2) Restriction — Despite subsection (1), the creditor is not entitled to receive a dividend from the distribution in Canada until every other creditor who has a claim of equal rank in the order of priority established under this Act has received a dividend whose amount is the same percentage of that other creditor's claim as the aggregate of the amount referred to in paragraph (1)(a) and the value referred to in paragraph (1)(b) is of that creditor's claim.

2005, c. 47, s. 131 [Not in force at date of publication.]

61. (1) Court not prevented from applying certain rules — Nothing in this Part prevents the court, on the application of a foreign representative or any other interested person, from applying any legal or equitable rules governing the recognition of foreign insolvency orders and assistance to foreign representatives that are not inconsistent with the provisions of this Act.

(2) Court not compelled to give effect to certain orders — Nothing in this Part requires the court to make any order that is not in compliance with the laws of Canada or to enforce any order made by a foreign court.

2005, c. 47, s. 131 [Not in force at date of publication.]

Part V — Administration

[Heading added 2005, c. 47, s. 131. Not in force at date of publication.]

62. Regulations — The Minister may make regulations for carrying out the purposes and provisions of this Act, including regulations

(a) specifying documents for the purpose of paragraph 23(1)(f); and

(b) prescribing anything that by this Act is to be prescribed.

2005, c. 47, s. 131 [Not in force at date of publication.]

63. (1) Review of Act — Within five years after the coming into force of this section, the Minister shall cause to be laid before both Houses of Parliament a report on the provisions and operation of this Act, including any recommendations for amendments to those provisions.

(2) Reference to parliamentary committee — The report stands referred to the committee of the Senate, the House of Commons or both Houses of Parliament that is designated or established for that purpose, which shall

(a) as soon as possible after the laying of the report, review the report; and

(b) report to the Senate, the House of Commons or both Houses of Parliament, as the case may be, within one year after the laying of the report of the Minister, or any further time authorized by the Senate, the House of Commons or both Houses of Parliament.

2005, c. 47, s. 131 [Not in force at date of publication.]

Editor's Note: S.C. 1997, c. 12, s. 127, provides as follows:

127. Application — Sections 120, 121, 122, 123, 124, 125 or 126 [which enacted or amended the definition of "company" in s. 120, ss. 3, 5.1, 6, 11, 11.1, 11.2, 11.3, 11.4, 11.5, 11.6, 11.7, 11.8, 18.1, 18.2, 18.3, 18.4, 18.5, 18.6, 21, 22] applies to proceedings commenced under the Companies' Creditors Arrangement Act after that section comes into force. [September 30, 1997, except for s. 22 of the CCAA as enacted by S.C. 1997, c. 12, s. 126, in force April 25, 1997].

1997, c. 12, s. 126

Transitional Provision

— 2005, c. 47, s. 134:

134. The amendments to the *Companies' Creditors Arrangement Act*, as enacted by sections 124 to 131, apply in respect of a debtor company in respect of whom proceedings are commenced under that Act after the coming into force of those sections.

APPENDIX 2

***Air Canada* Initial Stay Order**

Air Canada (Re)
IN THE MATTER OF the Companies' Creditors Arrangement Act,
R.S.C. 1985, c. C-36, as amended
AND IN THE MATTER OF Section 191 of the Canada Business
Corporations Act, R.S.C. 1985, c. C-44, as amended
AND IN THE MATTER OF a plan of compromise or arrangement of
Air Canada and those subsidiaries listed on Schedule "A"
AN APPLICATION UNDER the Companies' Creditors Arrangement
Act, R.S.C. 1985, c. C-36, as amended

I.I.C. Ct. Filing 105734140002
Court File No. 03-CL-4932

Ontario Superior Court of Justice
Commercial List
Farley J.

April 1, 2003.

INITIAL ORDER

¶ 1 **FARLEY J.**:— THIS APPLICATION, made by Air Canada and those subsidiaries listed on Schedule "A" (collectively and together with Air Canada, the "Applicants") for an order substantially in the form attached at Tab 3 of the Application Record herein was heard this day, at 393 University Avenue, Toronto, Ontario.

¶ 2 ON READING the Notice of Application, the Affidavit of M. Robert Peterson sworn April 1, 2003, and the consent of Ernst & Young Inc. as proposed Monitor, filed, and on hearing counsel for the Applicants and counsel to the proposed Monitor, and on being advised that no other person was served with the Application Record herein:

SERVICE

1. THIS COURT ORDERS that the time for service of the Notice of Application and Application Record herein be and is hereby abridged and that this Application is properly returnable today and further that service thereof upon any interested party not served is hereby dispensed with.

APPLICATION

2. THIS COURT ORDERS AND DECLARES that the Applicants are companies to which the Companies' Creditors Arrangement Act, R.S.C. 1985, c. C-36, as amended (the "*CCAA*") applies.

STAY OF PROCEEDINGS

3. THIS COURT ORDERS that, until and including May 1, 2003, or such later date as the Court may order (the "Stay Period"), (a) no suit, action, enforcement process, extra-judicial proceeding or other proceeding (including a proceeding in any court, statutory or otherwise) (a "Proceeding") against or in respect of an Applicant or any present or future property, rights, assets or undertaking of an Applicant wheresoever located, and whether held by an Applicant in whole or in part, directly or indirectly, as principal or nominee, beneficially or otherwise, and without limiting the generality of the foregoing, including only the leasehold interests of the Applicants in any aircraft leased by an Applicant, whether in the possession of an Applicant, or subleased to another entity, any and all real property, personal property and intellectual property of an Applicant, and any and all securities, instruments, debentures, notes or bonds issued to, or held by or on behalf of an Applicant (the "Applicants' Property") shall be commenced and any and all Proceedings against or in respect of an Applicant or the Applicants' Property already commenced be and are hereby stayed and suspended, and (b) all persons are enjoined and restrained from realizing upon or enforcing by court proceedings, private seizure or otherwise, any security of any nature or description held by that person on the Applicants' Property or from otherwise seizing or retaining possession of the Applicants' Property, or from seizing or retaining aircraft operated by the Applicants.

4. THIS COURT ORDERS that all persons, including, without limitation, all employees and union officials or representatives, are hereby restrained from implementing, enforcing or imposing any form of job action, decision, ruling or award resulting from any process, grievance or arbitration pursuant to the provisions of any collective agreement with an Applicant or pursuant to the Canada Labour Code or other similar legislation.

5. THIS COURT ORDERS that during the Stay Period, the right of any person, firm, corporation, governmental authority or other entity to assert, enforce or exercise any right, option or remedy arising by law against an Applicant or the Applicants' Property (including, without limitation, rights under subsection 224(1.2) of the Income Tax Act (Canada) or its provincial equivalents, any right of dilution, registration, attornment, encumbrance, buy-out, divestiture, repudiation, rescission, forced sale, acceleration, set-off, repossession, distress, conversion, possession, termination, suspension, modification or cancellation or right to revoke any qualification or registration) by virtue of any agreement or by any other means, including as a result of any default or non-performance by an Applicant, the making or filing of these proceedings, or any allegation contained in these proceedings be and is hereby restrained.

6. THIS COURT ORDERS that during the Stay Period, no person, firm, corporation, governmental authority, or other entity shall, without leave, discontinue, fail to renew, alter, interfere with or terminate any right, contract, arrangement, agreement, licence or permit in favour of an Applicant or the Applicants' Property or held by or on behalf of an Applicant, including as a result of any default or non-performance by an Applicant, the making or filing of these proceedings or any allegation contained in these proceedings.

7. THIS COURT ORDERS that, during the Stay Period, (a) all persons, firms, corporations, governmental authorities, airport or air navigation authorities or any other entity (including, without limitation, NAV Canada, Office of the Superintendent of Financial Institutions ("OSFI"), IBM Canada Limited and BCE Nexxia Inc.) having written or oral agreements with an Applicant (including, without limitation, leases, pooling or consignment agreements, multilateral interline traffic agreements, codeshare agreements, Tier III Commercial

Agreements, gate access agreements, frequent flyer programs or statutory or regulatory mandates) for the supply of goods and/or services (including, without limitation, computer software and hardware, aircraft parts, aircraft maintenance services and related equipment, ground handling services and equipment, catering, office supplies and equipment, reservations, employee uniforms, crew accommodations, meals and commissary, communication and other data services, accounting and payroll servicing, insurance or indemnity, clearing, banking, cash management, credit cards or credit card processing, transportation, utility or other required services), by or to an Applicant or any of the Applicants' Property are hereby restrained until further order of this Court from discontinuing, failing to renew on terms no more onerous than those existing prior to these proceedings, altering, interfering with or terminating the supply of such goods or services so long as the normal prices or charges for such goods and services received after the date of this order are paid in accordance with present payment practices, or as may be hereafter negotiated from time to time, and (b) subject to section 11.1 of the *CCAA*, all persons being party to fuel consortia agreements, or agreements or arrangements for hedging the price of, or forward purchasing of fuel, are hereby restrained from terminating, suspending, modifying, cancelling, or otherwise interfering with such hedging agreements or arrangements, notwithstanding any provisions in such agreements or arrangements to the contrary.

8. THIS COURT ORDERS that the Applicants shall be entitled to continue to utilize their central cash management system currently in place, including, without limitation, the inter-company flow of funds among Applicants and their affiliates, or replace it with another substantially similar central cash management system provided that such cash management system is permitted under, and otherwise complies with, the terms of the *CCAA* Credit Facility (as hereinafter defined) (the "Cash Management System") and that any present or future bank providing the Cash Management System shall:

a) Not be under any obligation whatsoever to inquire into the propriety, validity or legality of any transfer, payment, collection or other action taken under the Cash Management System, or as to the use or application by the Applicants of funds transferred, paid, collected or otherwise dealt with in the Cash Management System;

b) Be entitled to provide the Cash Management System without any liability, whether statutory, contractual, trust, proprietary or otherwise, in respect thereof to any person, corporation or other entity whatsoever, other than the Applicants or their affiliates and the *CCAA* Lender (as hereinafter defined), pursuant to the terms of the documentation applicable to the Cash Management System; and

c) Be, in its capacity as provider of the Cash Management System, an unaffected creditor with regard to any claims or expenses it may suffer or incur in connection with the provision of the Cash Management System.

9. THIS COURT ORDERS that persons may exercise only such rights of set off as are permitted under section 18.1 of the *CCAA* as of the date of this order. For greater certainty, no person may set off any obligations arising on or after the date of this order against any obligations of an Applicant to such person which arose prior to this order.

10. THIS COURT ORDERS that, without limiting the generality of paragraph 7 hereof, all banks and financial institutions at which an Applicant maintains a bank account are hereby restrained from stopping, withholding, redirecting or otherwise interfering with any amount in such account(s) against any indebtedness owing to that bank or financial institution by an Applicant, or from discontinuing, failing to renew on terms no more onerous than those

existing prior to these proceedings, altering, interfering with or terminating such banking arrangements.

11. THIS COURT ORDERS that, without limiting the generality of paragraph 7 hereof, all credit card companies (including Visa, Mastercard, American Express and Diners Club International) and credit card processing companies (including, without limitation, Global Payments Inc. and Global Payments Direct, Inc.) are hereby restrained from stopping, withholding, redirecting or otherwise interfering with any payments to any of the Applicants or any amount in an Applicant's account(s) against any indebtedness owing to that credit card company by an Applicant or contingent claims not in accordance with past practice, or from discontinuing, failing to renew on terms no more onerous than those existing prior to these proceedings, altering, interfering with or terminating such credit card arrangements.

12. THIS COURT ORDERS that all persons involved in the collection and distribution of monies in connection with passenger and air cargo operations (including, without limitation, travel agents, tour operators, general sales agents, air carriers and all persons who are members of or associated with the International Air Transport Association ("IATA")) are restrained from suspending any Applicant from membership in IATA or any other air carriers or travel organization or from stopping, withholding, redirecting or otherwise interfering with any payments payable to an Applicant whether pursuant to bank settlement plans, Airline Reporting Corporation arrangements, the IATA Clearing House or otherwise, provided that the Applicants shall make all required payments in accordance with the terms of such plans, arrangements and agreements, after the date of this order.

13. THIS COURT ORDERS that during the Stay Period, no action may be commenced or continued against any of the directors or officers of an Applicant with respect to any claim against the directors or officers that relates to any obligation of an Applicant whereby the directors or officers are alleged under any law to be liable in their capacity as directors or officers for the payment or performance of such obligation.

14. THIS COURT ORDERS that no person shall commence or continue any proceeding against any of the Applicants' directors, officers, employees, legal counsel or financial advisors, or the Monitor (as defined herein), for or in respect of the Restructuring (as defined herein) or the creation and implementation of the Plan (as defined herein) without first obtaining leave of this Court, upon seven days' written notice to the Applicants' counsel of record and to all those referred to in this paragraph whom it is proposed be named in such proceedings.

15. THIS COURT ORDERS that, notwithstanding anything else contained herein, an Applicant with the consent of the Monitor and the *CCAA* Lender may, by written consent of its counsel of record herein, agree to waive any of the protections provided to it herein.

EFFECTIVE TIME

16. THIS COURT ORDERS that, from 12:01 a.m. (Toronto time) on the date of this order to the time of the granting of this order, any act or action taken or notice given by any of the Applicants' creditors or other persons in furtherance of their rights to commence or continue realization or to take or enforce any other step or remedy will be deemed not to have been taken or given, as the case may be, subject to the right of any such person to further apply to this Court on seven days' notice to the Applicants, the Monitor and the *CCAA* Lender in respect of such step, act, action or notice given.

17. THIS COURT ORDERS that, to the extent that any statutory limitation periods relating to the Applicants or the Applicants' Property may expire or terminate with the passage of time, the term of such limitation periods shall hereby be deemed to be extended by a period of time equal to the duration of the stay of proceedings effected by this order and any further order of this Court and, for greater certainty, in the event that an Applicant becomes bankrupt or a receiver is appointed in respect of an Applicant within the meaning of section 243(2) of the Bankruptcy and Insolvency Act, R.S.C. 1985, c. B-3 (the "BIA"), the period between the date of this order and the day on which such stay of proceedings is ended shall not be counted in determining the 30-day period referred to in section 81.1 of the *BIA*, provided that this paragraph shall not be construed to extend the term of any lease that expires during the pendency of the Stay Period.

POSSESSION OF PROPERTY AND OPERATIONS

18. THIS COURT ORDERS that the Applicants shall remain in possession and control of the Applicants' Property and shall, except as provided by this order or any subsequent order of this Court, continue to carry on their business (the "Business") in the ordinary course or may discontinue the Business in part, and shall be authorized and empowered to continue to:

a) Contract with other persons and acquire goods and services reasonably necessary or desirable to operate the Business in the ordinary course;

b) Retain and employ the agents, advisors, contractors, servants, solicitors and other assistants, consultants and valuators currently in their employ, with liberty to retain such further agents, advisors, contractors, servants, solicitors, assistants, consultants and valuators as they deem reasonably necessary or desirable in the ordinary course of the Business or the carrying out of the terms of this order, or for the purposes of preparing or effecting the Restructuring or the Plan (as each is defined herein) or otherwise subject to the approval of this Court; and

19. THIS COURT ORDERS that the Applicants shall continue to operate, maintain, insure, inspect, service, repair and overhaul all aircraft, flight simulators, engines and parts, whether for themselves or for third parties, and all of the equipment and facilities in the possession of the Applicants, in the ordinary course (subject to the Restructuring as defined below) and accepted airline industry standards and practice.

20. THIS COURT ORDERS that, after the date hereof and except as otherwise provided to the contrary herein, the Applicants shall be entitled but not required to pay the following expenses incurred by the Applicants in carrying on the Business or discontinuing part of the Business:

a) With the consent of the Monitor, up to $25 million for goods or services actually supplied to an Applicant prior to the date of this order, by a North American supplier, including payments in respect of outstanding documentary credits or deposits, if, in the opinion of the Applicants, the supplier is critical to the Business and ongoing operations of the Applicants;

b) Goods or services actually supplied to an Applicant prior to the date of this order, including payments in respect of outstanding documentary credits or deposits, by trade vendors and suppliers outside North America;

c) All outstanding and future insurance premiums (including directors and officers liability insurance, property and casualty, group insurance or other necessary insurance policy);

d) Expenses and capital expenditures reasonably necessary for the preservation of the Applicants' Property or the Business (including, without limitation, payments on account of insurance, maintenance and security); and

e) All outstanding and future wages, salaries (except group RRSP contributions), disbursements, directors' fees and expenses, employee benefits, severance, termination and other like amounts, vacation pay, and retention payments accruing due to employees or as approved by this Court, and all employee benefits and pension benefits payable to former employees.

21. THIS COURT ORDERS that notwithstanding any other provision of this order or any direction to pay issued by OSFI or any other entity, the Applicants shall immediately cease making contributions to funded pension plans maintained by an Applicant, pending further order of this Court.

22. THIS COURT ORDERS that during the Stay Period, the Applicants shall continue to honour all airline tickets and Aeroplan redemptions in the usual and ordinary course of business until further order of this Court.

23. THIS COURT ORDERS that the Applicants shall remit, in accordance with legal requirements, or pay the following:

a) Goods or services actually supplied to an Applicant after the date of this order, including payments in respect of outstanding documentary credits or deposit;

b) The fees and disbursements of the Monitor (including the fees and disbursements of any counsel retained by the Monitor);

c) The fees and disbursements of any auditor, financial advisor or other professional retained by an Applicant;

d) The fees and disbursements of counsel retained by the Applicants;

e) Any statutory deemed trust amounts in favour of the Crown in right of Canada or of any Province thereof or any other taxation authority which are required to be deducted from employees' wages, including, without limitation, amounts in respect of employment insurance, Canada Pension Plan, Quebec Pension Plan and income taxes;

f) Amounts accruing and payable by an Applicant in respect of employment insurance, Canada Pension Plan, Quebec Pension Plan, workers compensation, employer health taxes and similar obligations of any jurisdiction with respect to employees;

g) All goods and services or other applicable sales taxes payable by an Applicant or its customers in connection with the sale of goods and services by the Applicant to such customers;

h) Amounts accruing and payable by an Applicant in respect of the Air Travellers Security Charge;

i) Any amount payable to the Crown in right of Canada or of any Province thereof or any political subdivision thereof or any other taxation authority in respect of municipal realty, municipal business or other taxes, assessments or levies of any nature or kind which are entitled at law to be paid in priority to claims of secured creditors or lessors and which are attributable to or in respect of the carrying on of the Business by the Applicants; and

j) All amounts accruing to:

   i) Customer programs such as ticket sales, ticket refunds, ticket re-issues, baggage claims, cargo claims (excluding payments to those entities with which an Applicant is currently in dispute or litigation), frequent flyer programs and barter arrangements;

   ii) Bilateral and multi-lateral interline agreements;

   iii) Clearing house agreements such as Airline Clearing House and International Air Transport Association;

   iv) Airline Reporting Corporation Agreements;

   v) Alliance Agreements;

   vi) Computer Reservation Agreements;

   vii) Travel Agency Agreements, and Corporate Accounts Agreements;

   viii) Cargo Agreements;

   ix) Universal Air Travel Plan Agreements;

   x) Airline Tariff Publishing Company Agreements;

   xi) Bank Settlement Plan Agreements;

   xii) General Service Agent Agreements;

   xiii) Cargo Network Services Corp.; and

   xiv) Cargo Agency Settlement System.

k) All ticket refunds, customer claims, travel agent commissions, interline, codeshare, Tier III Commercial Agreements, frequent flyer and similar obligations with other airlines;

l) All amounts payable as fees to any airport or air navigation authority after the date hereof (subject to paragraph 19(b) hereof with respect to foreign airport authorities);

m) All amounts payable under bank settlement plans, Airline Reporting Corporation and similar arrangements; and

n) Subject to further order of this Court, all amounts owing by an Applicant under any credit card arrangements.

RESTRUCTURING

24. THIS COURT ORDERS that the Applicants shall have the right to:

a) With the consent of the Monitor, permanently or temporarily cease, downsize or shut down any part or location of the Business or their operations and to sell or otherwise dispose of redundant or non-material assets not exceeding $25 million in any one transaction or series of connected transactions without Court approval;

b) With the consent of the Monitor, wind down or bankrupt any direct or indirect subsidiary of Air Canada;

c) Notwithstanding any collective agreement to which an Applicant is a party, upon seven days' notice to the employee and the applicable trade union, terminate the employment of such of their employees or temporarily lay off such of their employees as they deem appropriate on such terms as may be agreed upon between the Applicants and such employee, or failing such agreement, to deal with the consequences thereof in the Plan;

d) Terminate or amend any funded or unfunded pension and benefit plans maintained by an Applicant on such terms as this Court may direct;

e) With the consent of the Monitor, vacate, abandon or quit any leased premises and/or terminate or repudiate any lease and any ancillary agreements relating to any leased premises, on not less than four days' written notice to the relevant landlord on such terms as may be agreed upon between the Applicants and such landlord, or failing such agreement, to deal with the consequences thereof in the Plan;

f) Terminate or suspend such of their arrangements or agreements of any nature whatsoever (including, without limitation, aircraft and equipment leases), whether oral or written, as the Applicants deem appropriate on such terms as may be agreed upon between the Applicants and such counter-parties, or failing such agreement, to deal with the consequences thereof in the Plan;

g) Pursue all avenues of refinancing and to market and sell, in conjunction with the Monitor, material parts of the Business or Applicants' Property, in whole or part, subject to prior approval of this Court being obtained before any sale exceeding $25 million in any one transaction or series of connected transactions;

h) Engage in usual and ordinary course transactions with other Applicants and non-Applicants; and

i) With the consent of the Monitor, continue to fund in the ordinary course, through the provision of cash or credit, non-Applicant affiliates;

all of the foregoing to permit the Applicants to proceed with an orderly restructuring of the Business (the "Restructuring").

25. THIS COURT ORDERS that the Applicants are authorized to conduct a review of their aircraft leases, with the assistance of the Monitor, to determine which leases are true operating leases and which are financing leases, and to request that its aircraft lessors agree to a 60-day payment moratorium prior to the due date of a lease payment, and with respect to any lessor who refuses to agree to such moratorium, either return such aircraft to the lessor or to make such payment to the lessor as this Court may direct in order to retain the aircraft for such period of time as is necessary to obtain a replacement.

26. THIS COURT ORDERS that the Applicants shall provide each of the relevant landlords with notice of an intention to remove any fixtures from a leased location closed and abandoned by an Applicant at least four days prior to the date of the intended removal. The relevant landlord shall be entitled to have a representative present in the leased location to observe such removal and, if the landlord disputes the Applicant's entitlement to remove any such fixture under the provisions of the lease, such fixture shall remain on the premises and shall be dealt with as agreed between any applicable secured creditors, such landlord and the Applicant, or by further order of this Court upon application by the Applicant on at least

four days' notice to such landlord and any such secured creditor. If an Applicant has otherwise vacated any such leased location, it shall not be considered to be in occupation thereof pending resolution of any such dispute.

27. THIS COURT ORDERS that, if a leased location is quit, vacated or abandoned by an Applicant the relevant landlord shall be entitled to take possession of any such leased location without waiver of or prejudice to any claims or rights such landlord may have against the Applicant in respect of the quitting, vacating or abandonment of such leased location and such landlord shall be entitled to notify the Applicant of the basis on which it is taking possession and to gain possession of and re-lease such leased location to any third party or parties on such terms as such landlord considers advisable, provided that nothing herein shall relieve such landlord of its obligation to mitigate any damages claimed in connection therewith.

28. THIS COURT ORDERS that the existing subscription letter (the "Subscription Letter") dated January 24, 2003 and related documentation among Air Canada, Aeroplan Limited Partnership ("Aeroplan"), 3913368 Canada Inc. and Onex Corporation relating to a proposed investment by Onex Corporation or one of its affiliates in the business currently conducted by Aeroplan is hereby terminated.

29. THIS COURT ORDERS that the letter of intent (the "Onex Letter of Intent") dated March 31, 2003 between Air Canada and Onex Corporation is hereby approved and that: (i) Onex Corporation shall have the exclusive right to negotiate with Air Canada for a definitive agreement relating to a proposed investment in Aeroplan as contemplated by the Letter of Intent, which proposed investment would close on implementation of a plan of arrangement submitted by Air Canada to all or certain of its creditors; (ii) Onex Corporation's exclusive right shall remain in place for a period of 30 days from this Order or such longer period of as may be mutually agreed by Air Canada and Onex Corporation; and (iii) Air Canada shall comply with the exclusivity and confidentiality provisions of the Onex Letter of Intent.

POWER TO BORROW

30. THIS COURT ORDERS that Air Canada is hereby authorized and empowered to borrow from General Electric Capital Canada Inc., together with any participant in a syndication of the *CCAA* Credit Facility (as hereinafter defined) and the agent thereof (collectively, the "*CCAA* Lender") such monies from time to time as Air Canada may consider necessary or desirable, pursuant to a credit facility up to the principal sum of $700,000,000 (U.S.) substantially on the terms and conditions set forth in the commitment letter between Air Canada and the *CCAA* Lender dated as of April 1, 2003 (the "*CCAA* Term Sheet") annexed hereto as Schedule "B", which *CCAA* Term Sheet is hereby approved, to fund the ongoing operations, capital expenditures and working capital for the preservation of the Applicants' Property, and to pay such other amounts as are permitted by the terms of this Order, the *CCAA* Term Sheet and the definitive documents contemplated thereby (the "*CCAA* Credit Facility").

31. THIS COURT ORDERS that the Applicants shall pay when due all principal and interest, and fees and expenses, including without limiting the generality of the foregoing, all fees and disbursements of counsel, on a full indemnity basis, and all other advisors to or agents of the *CCAA* Lender (the "*CCAA* Credit Facility Expenses") under the *CCAA* Credit Facility.

32. THIS COURT ORDERS that each of the Applicants that are not borrowers under the *CCAA* Credit Facility are hereby deemed to guarantee repayment of all amounts owing under the *CCAA* Credit Facility from all other Applicants and the performance of all obligations of such Applicants thereunder.

33. THIS COURT ORDERS that the *CCAA* Lender and GECAS (as defined in the *CCAA* Credit Facility) are hereby granted a charge over all of the Applicants' Property to secure the repayment of all amounts owing by any of the Applicants, including principal and interest and *CCAA* Credit Facility Expenses under the *CCAA* Credit Facility and the performance of all obligations of any of the Applicants under the *CCAA* Credit Facility or under any amounts owing now or in the future in connection with the GECAS Obligations (as defined in the *CCAA* Credit Facility) (the "*CCAA* Lender's Charge").

34. THIS COURT ORDERS that each of the Applicants is hereby authorized and directed to execute any and all security documents and guarantees required by the *CCAA* Credit Facility or this Order in favour of the *CCAA* Lender and any and all ancillary documents in connection therewith (collectively, the "*CCAA* Lender's Security").

35. THIS COURT ORDERS that any fixed or floating lien, charge, mortgage, hypothec, security interest, pledge or encumbrance (collectively, "Encumbrances") created or granted under the *CCAA* Lender's Security and the *CCAA* Lender's Charge shall attach as of the effective time of this Order, to the Applicants' Property, including, without limiting the generality of the foregoing, any lease, license, occupation permit, landing right, spare parts, slots, gates or other contract, notwithstanding any requirement for the consent of the lessor, licensor or other party to any such contract, license, occupation permit, landing right, spare parts, slot, gate or any other Person.

36. THIS COURT ORDERS that the necessity for the giving of any consent referred to in the preceding paragraph is hereby dispensed with, and that the absence of any such consent shall not constitute a breach of or default under any such lease, license, occupation permit, landing right, spare parts, slot, gate or other contract except to the extent that such consent may be required from Transport Canada in respect of the charge over any such license, landing right, slot or gate.

37. THIS COURT ORDERS that before and after an event of default occurs under the *CCAA* Credit Facility, (a) the beneficiaries of the Administrative Charge in respect of amounts owing up to $10,000,000 shall be entitled to enforcement remedies irrespective of whether or not the *CCAA* Lender has received any payments under the *CCAA* Credit Facility, and (b) the beneficiaries of the Administrative Charge in respect of amounts owing greater than $10,000,000 and the Directors' Charge shall not be entitled to any enforcement remedies until the *CCAA* Lender has been paid in full.

38. THIS COURT ORDERS that there shall be no Encumbrances and none of the Applicants shall grant or allow any Encumbrances over the Applicants' Property ranking pari passu with or in priority to the *CCAA* Lender's Charge or the *CCAA* Lender's Security, except as specifically contemplated under the provisions of this Order or the *CCAA* Credit Facility, without the prior written consent of the *CCAA* Lender, and any Encumbrances granted or allowed by the Applicants contrary to this Order shall be subordinate in all respects to the *CCAA* Lender's Charge and the *CCAA* Lender's Security.

39. THIS COURT ORDERS that, notwithstanding (a) the pendency of these proceedings and the declarations of insolvency made herein, (b) the pendency of any petitions for receiving orders hereafter issued pursuant to the *BIA* in respect of any of the Applicants and any receiving orders issued pursuant to any such petitions and, (c) the provisions of any federal or provincial statute, the obligations and all security constituted by the *CCAA* Credit Facility, the *CCAA* Lender's Charge and the *CCAA* Lender's Security (i) constitute legal, valid and binding obligations of the Applicants enforceable against them in accordance with the terms thereof, and (ii) do not constitute conduct meriting an oppression remedy, settlements, fraudulent preferences, fraudulent conveyances or other challengeable or reviewable transactions under any applicable law, federal, provincial or otherwise.

40. THIS COURT ORDERS that the *CCAA* Lender's Charge and the *CCAA* Lender's Security shall be deemed to be valid and effective notwithstanding any negative covenants, prohibitions or other similar provisions with respect to incurring debt or the creation of liens or security contained in any existing agreement between the Applicants and any lender, including, without limitation, the existing credit agreements between Air Canada and Visa, Mastercard, American Express and Diners Club International, and that, notwithstanding any provision to the contrary in such agreements, (a) neither the creation of the *CCAA* Lender's Charge, nor the execution, delivery, registration or perfection of the *CCAA* Lender's Security shall create or be deemed to constitute a breach by any one of the Applicants of any agreement to which it is a party, and (b) the *CCAA* Lender shall have no liability to any Person whatsoever as a result of any breach of any agreement caused by or resulting from the Applicants entering into the *CCAA* Term Sheet and the *CCAA* Credit Facility, the creation of the *CCAA* Lender's Charge or the execution and delivery of the *CCAA* Lender's Security.

41. THIS COURT ORDERS that the *CCAA* Lender shall be treated as an unaffected creditor in these proceedings and in any plan of compromise, arrangement or reorganization filed pursuant thereto and, subject to the *CCAA* Credit Facility, nothing impairs the right of the Applicants to treat GECAS as an affected creditor in these proceedings and in any plan of compromise, arrangement or reorganization filed pursuant thereto.

42. THIS COURT ORDERS that, except as provided for in the *CCAA* Credit Facility, nothing herein shall oblige the *CCAA* Lender to make any advance to the Applicants.

43. THIS COURT ORDERS that the *CCAA* Lender shall not take any enforcement steps under the *CCAA* Lender's Charge or *CCAA* Lender's Security without providing at least three days written notice (the "Notice Period") of a default thereunder to the Applicants with a copy to the Monitor. Upon expiry of such Notice Period, the *CCAA* Lender shall be entitled (with leave of the Court) to take any and all steps under the *CCAA* Lender's Charge or *CCAA* Lender's Security without the requirement of sending any demands, statutory or otherwise, including without limiting the generality of the foregoing, under section 244 of the *BIA*.

44. THIS COURT ORDERS that, in addition to any rights under the *CCAA* Lender's Security, at law or in equity, after the expiry of the Notice Period, the *CCAA* Lender shall be entitled to apply to this Court for the appointment of an interim receiver, receiver, receiver and manager, for the appointment of a trustee in bankruptcy, and (with leave of the Court), shall have the right to receive all cash flows under the cash concentration and block account regime contemplated by the *CCAA* Term Sheet, provided the *CCAA* Lender shall respect the priority of the first $10,000,000 of the Administrative Charge.

45. THIS COURT ORDERS that Air Canada on behalf of the Applicants, and the Monitor to the extent that it becomes aware, shall notify the *CCAA* Lender from time to time of: (a) any Encumbrances, other than any Permitted Encumbrances under the *CCAA* Term Sheet or the *CCAA* Credit Facility, that are registered, preserved, perfected or become enforceable subsequent to the date of this Order over any of the Applicants' Property; (b) any exercise of the Applicants' right under paragraph 24 of this Order; (c) any actual or threatened seizures or detentions of any aircraft by any Person, including, without limitation, any air navigation, airport, or other aviation authority; and (d) with respect to paragraph 24 of this Order any contemplated sale of real property which would exceed the sum of $2,500,000.

46. THIS COURT ORDERS that in the event that the *CCAA* Credit Facility provided for in the *CCAA* Term Sheet is syndicated, the *CCAA* Term Sheet, the *CCAA* Lender's Charge and the *CCAA* Lender's Security shall be administered by the Agent (as defined in the *CCAA* Term Sheet) on behalf of all syndicate members and all consents contemplated in this Order or in the *CCAA* Term Sheet shall be given by the Agent.

47. THIS COURT ORDERS that the *CCAA* Lender is hereby authorized to take such steps as it may deem appropriate to register, record or perfect the *CCAA* Lender's Security in all such jurisdictions as the *CCAA* Lender may consider appropriate, and that the Applicants are hereby authorized and directed to cooperate and give assistance to the *CCAA* Lender in that regard, notwithstanding any stay of proceedings provided for herein or in any foreign jurisdiction.

48. THIS COURT ORDERS that the *CCAA* Lender shall not be require to file, register, record or perfect the *CCAA* Lender's Charge and such *CCAA* Lender's Charge shall be binding on all Persons, including any trustee in bankruptcy, receiver, receiver and manager or interim receiver of any or all of the Applicants and the *CCAA* Lender's Charge shall retain its full perfection and priority pursuant to the terms of this Order.

49. THIS COURT ORDERS that the Monitor together with the Applicants shall prepare the Cash Flow Budget in accordance with the *CCAA* Term Sheet.

50. THIS COURT ORDERS that notwithstanding any other provision hereof, the *CCAA* Lender's Charge shall be subject to Permitted Encumbrances as defined in the *CCAA* Credit Facility other than the charges and amounts set out in paragraph 63(c) (d) and (e) hereof.

DIRECTORS' CHARGE

51. THIS COURT ORDERS that, in addition to any existing indemnity, the Applicants shall indemnify its directors (or any person deemed to be a director under applicable law) and officers from:

a) all costs (including, without limitation, defence costs), charges, expenses, claims, liabilities and obligations (other than those asserted by the Applicants) ("Claim" or "Claims") of any nature whatsoever which may arise out of their acting as directors or officers of the Applicants (including, without limitation, an amount paid to settle an action or satisfy a judgment in a civil, criminal or administrative action or proceeding to which such director or officer may be made a party by reason of being or having been an officer or director, provided that the director or officer (i) acted honestly and in good faith with a view to the best interests of the relevant Applicant and (ii) in the case of a criminal or administrative action, the director or officer had reasonable grounds for believing his or her conduct was lawful) except to the extent that, with respect to any officer or director, such officer or director has actively participated in the breach of any related fiduciary duties or has been grossly negligent or guilty of wilful misconduct; and

b) all Claims relating to the failure of the Applicants to at any time make payments of the nature referred to in sub-paragraphs 22(a), (b), (c) and (d) of this order or to pay amounts in respect of employee or former employee entitlements to wages, vacation pay, severance payments, pensions and benefits which they sustain or incur by reason of or in relation to their respective capacities as directors and officers of an Applicant except to the extent that, with respect to any director or officer, such director or officer has actively participated in the breach of any related fiduciary duties or has been grossly negligent or guilty of wilful misconduct.

52. THIS COURT ORDERS that the directors (or any person deemed to be a director under applicable law) and officers of any of the Applicants shall be entitled to the benefit of and are hereby granted a charge (the "Directors' Charge") on the Applicant's Property in the aggregate amount of $170 million as security for the indemnity provided in paragraph 51 of this order, but such Directors' Charge shall only apply to the extent that the directors and officers do not have full coverage under the provisions of any applicable directors' and officers' insurance for any reason including, without limitation, the limits of the policy. In respect of any Claim which is asserted against the directors and/or officers of an Applicant, if the directors and/or officers against whom the Claim is asserted (collectively "Respondent Directors") do not receive satisfactory confirmation from the applicable insurer within 21 days of delivery of notice of the Claim to the applicable insurer confirming that the applicable insurer will provide coverage for and indemnify the Respondent Directors against the entire amount of the Claim, then, without prejudice to the subrogation rights hereinafter referred to, all such Claims shall be paid proportionately by the Applicants and by the trustee under the Directors' Trust (as described in the Affidavit of M. Robert Peterson sworn on April 1, 2003) based on the amount of the Directors' Charge and the amount held in the Directors' Trust at the time of the payment of the Claims, provided that:

a) No payment shall be made on account of any Claim unless and until the Monitor is satisfied that the Directors' Charge and Directors' Trust are sufficient to pay all proven Claims and all costs permitted thereunder failing which distribution on account of the Claims shall be subject to further order of this Court;

b) The Court has ordered that a claimant wishing to assert a Claim shall deliver to the Monitor a claim notice on or before a specific date (the "Claims Bar Date"); and

c) The Court has ordered that the Claims of all claimants who do not deliver to the Monitor a claim notice by the Claims Bar Date shall be forever extinguished and barred from and after the Claims Bar date and that all such claimants shall be deemed to have fully and finally released all Claims.

If the Applicants fail to make any payment on account of a Claim, the Respondent Directors shall be entitled to enforce the Directors' Charge, provided that the Respondent Directors shall reimburse the Applicant to the extent that they subsequently receive insurance proceeds in respect of a Claim paid by the Applicants and provided further that the Applicants shall, in the event that such payment is made, be subrogated to the rights of the Respondent Directors to pursue recovery thereof from the applicable insurer as if no such payment has been made. Any claim by an Applicant under the provisions of any insurance policy providing coverage to a Respondent Director shall be subordinated to any Claim asserted by a Respondent Director under the provisions of that policy. The Directors' Charge shall not constitute a contract of insurance.

53. THIS COURT ORDERS that the Applicants shall and do hereby indemnify legal counsel and the financial advisors to the Applicants and the Monitor, of and from all claims, liabilities and obligations of any nature whatsoever, including, without limitation, legal fees and disbursements, which may arise out of their involvement with the Applicants, the Restructuring or the Plan, from and after the date hereof in the above-mentioned capacities, save and except such as may arise from wilful misconduct or gross negligence on the part of any of them.

MONITOR

54. THIS COURT ORDERS that, until further order of this Court, Ernst & Young Inc. (the "Monitor") shall be and is hereby appointed as an officer of this Court to monitor the business and affairs of the Applicants with the powers and obligations set forth in the *CCAA* and hereinafter, and that the Applicants and all other persons upon whom this order is served shall cooperate fully with the Monitor in the exercise of its powers and discharge of its obligations. Without limiting the generality of the foregoing, all persons upon whom this order is served shall provide the Monitor with such access to the Applicants' books, records, property and premises as the Monitor requires to exercise its powers and perform its obligations under this order.

55. THIS COURT ORDERS that the Monitor shall:

a) Advise the Applicants in connection with the development of cash flow statements, the Plan and any amendments thereto, and the implementation of the Plan and shall together with the Applicants prepare the Cash Flow Budget in accordance with the *CCAA* Term Sheet;

b) Monitor the Applicants' receipts and disbursements;

c) Assist the Applicants in negotiations with creditors and, with the holding and administering of any meetings for voting on the Plan;

d) Deliver to the Applicants and file with the Court such reports as the Monitor considers appropriate or relevant to the proceedings;

e) Be at liberty to engage legal counsel to advise and to represent the Monitor in relation to the exercise of its powers and discharge of its obligations under this order;

f) Be at liberty to engage such other persons as the Monitor deems necessary or advisable respecting the exercise of its powers and performance of its obligations under this order; and

g) Perform such other duties as are required by this order or further order of this Court.

56. THIS COURT ORDERS that, in response to any reasonable request for information made in writing by any of the Applicants' creditors addressed to the Monitor, the Monitor shall request such information from the Applicants and shall provide such creditor with such information as may be supplied by the Applicants in response to the request. In the case of information which the Monitor has been advised by an Applicant is confidential, the Monitor

shall not provide such information to the requesting creditor unless otherwise directed by this Court or consented to by the Applicants.

57. THIS COURT ORDERS that the Monitor is not empowered to take possession of any of the Applicants' Property or to manage any part of the Business and shall not, by fulfilling its obligations hereunder, be deemed to have taken or maintained possession or control of the Applicants' Property, or any part thereof, and shall not occupy any premises except in such circumstances as the Monitor deems necessary.

58. THIS COURT ORDERS that the Monitor and counsel to the Monitor shall be paid their reasonable fees and disbursements by the Applicants as part of the cost of these proceedings, whether incurred before or after the making of this order.

59. THIS COURT ORDERS that:

a) The Monitor shall not be liable for any act or omission on its part, including with respect to any reliance thereon, including without limitation, any act or mission pertaining to the discharge of its duties under the *CCAA* or this order, save and except for gross negligence or wilful misconduct on its part, nor shall the Monitor be liable for any debt incurred by an Applicant whether before or after the date of this order; and

b) The mere appointment of the Monitor shall not disqualify it from being appointed by this Court as receiver and manager of the Applicants' Property or as trustee in bankruptcy of an Applicant, should it consent to such appointment(s).

60. THIS COURT ORDERS that, if required by the Applicants and consented to by the Monitor, the Applicants may pay to the Monitor funds necessary (up to a limit of $25 million) for payment of goods or services supplied or to be supplied by critical suppliers to the Applicant after the date of this order, and the Monitor shall have the right and authority to make reasonable arrangements (including without limitation, trust or escrow arrangements) in exchange for the delivery of goods or services supplied to the Applicants and, for greater certainty, the Monitor shall not be liable for any obligations or liabilities for the supply of any such goods or services.

61. THIS COURT ORDERS that the Monitor shall not, solely as a result of the making of this order, for any purpose whatsoever, be held to be an employer, successor employer, sponsor, or payor with respect to an Applicant under any collective agreement or other contract between the Applicant and any of its present or former employees, or within the meaning of any legislation governing employment or labour standards or pensions or benefits or within the meaning of any other statute, regulation or rule of law or equity and further, that the Monitor shall not, solely as a result of the making of this order, for any purpose whatsoever, be held to be an owner or in possession, control or management of the property or of the business and affairs of an Applicant whether pursuant to any legislation enacted for the protection of the environment, the transportation of hazardous goods, health and safety or pursuant to any other statute or regulation of any federal, provincial or other jurisdiction or under any rule of law or equity.

ADMINISTRATIVE CHARGE

62. THIS COURT ORDERS that the Monitor, counsel to the Monitor, and counsel to the Applicants, shall be paid their fees and disbursements (whether in its capacity as Monitor

or foreign representative) by the Applicants as part of the costs of these proceedings. The Applicants are hereby authorized and directed to pay the Monitor, any counsel to the Monitor and the Applicants' own counsel on a weekly basis and to pay retainers to the Monitor and to the Applicants' own counsel in the amount of up to $1 million each as security for payment of their fees and disbursements from time to time. The indemnity provided in paragraph 55 of this order and the fees and disbursements of the Monitor, counsel to the Monitor and counsel to the Applicants shall be secured by a charge on the Applicants' Property, present and future (the "Administrative Charge"), without the requirement to file, register, record or perfect the charge.

PRIORITY OF CHARGES

63. THIS COURT ORDERS that the Administrative Charge, the *CCAA* Lender's Charge and the Directors' Charge shall have priority over all present and future charges, encumbrances and security in the Applicants' Property, in the following priority:

a) First, the Administrative Charge up to a maximum of $10 million;

b) Second, the *CCAA* Lender's Charge, up to a maximum of U.S. $700 million;

c) Third, the Directors' Charge up to a maximum of $70 million;

d) Fourth, the Administrative Charge for any amount in excess of $10 million; and

e) Fifth, the Directors' Charge for any amount in excess of $70 million, up to $170 million or such other amount fixed by the Court.

PLAN OF COMPROMISE OR ARRANGEMENT

64. THIS COURT ORDERS that the Applicants are hereby authorized and permitted to file with this Court one or more plans of compromise or arrangement regarding the Applicants pursuant to the *CCAA* (the "Plan").

GENERAL PROVISIONS

65. THIS COURT ORDERS that notwithstanding section 11(5) of the *CCAA*, the Monitor shall, within ten (10) business days of the date of this order, send a copy of this order to those creditors with claims in excess of $50,000 and to all parties filing a Notice of Appearance in respect of this Application and, if requested by them, to any other creditor or potential creditor of the Applicants. The Applicants and the Monitor are relieved of their obligations to give notice to any other person other than as provided herein.

66. THE COURT ORDERS that the Applicants may:

a) Serve this order, any other orders in these proceedings, all motions, the Plan, any notices of meetings and all other notices, letters to creditors, information circulars, proofs of claim, proxies and disallowances of claims, by forwarding true copies thereof by prepaid ordinary mail, courier, personal delivery or electronic transmission to the Applicants' creditors at their respective addresses as last shown on the records of the Applicants and that any such service or notice by courier, personal delivery or electronic transmission shall be deemed to be received on the next business day following the date of forwarding thereof, or if sent by ordinary mail, on the fourth business day after mailing;

b) With the concurrence of the Monitor, take such proceedings under the *BIA* as the Applicants at any time deem appropriate;

c) With the concurrence of the Monitor, at any time consent to the appointment of a receiver and/or receiver and manager over any of the Applicants' Property; and

d) Register this order against title to any of the Applicants' Property.

67. THIS COURT ORDERS that, notwithstanding any other provision of this order, the Applicants may apply at any time to this Court to vary this order or seek any further relief.

68. THIS COURT ORDERS that any other interested person may apply to this Court on April 22, 2003 or such later date as this Court may direct, to vary or rescind this order or seek other relief on seven days' written notice to the Applicants, the Monitor, and to any other person likely to be affected by the order sought or on such other notice as this Court may order, provided that nothing in this section shall act to extend any applicable appeal period.

69. THIS COURT ORDERS that the Applicants or the Monitor may, from time to time, apply to this Court for directions regarding the discharge of their powers and duties hereunder or in respect of the proper execution of this order.

70. THIS COURT REQUESTS the aid and recognition of any court or any judicial, regulatory or administrative body in any province or territory of Canada (including the assistance of any court in Canada pursuant to section 17 of the *CCAA*) and the Federal Court of Canada and any judicial, regulatory or administrative tribunal or other court constituted pursuant to the Parliament of Canada or the legislature of any province and any court or any judicial, regulatory or administrative body of the United States of America and the states or other subdivisions of the United States and any other nation or state to act in aid of and to be complementary to this Court in carrying out the terms of this order.

71. THIS COURT ORDERS that the Monitor be at liberty and is hereby authorized, directed and empowered to apply to any other court in any other jurisdiction, whether in Canada or elsewhere, for an order recognizing this proceeding or to take such steps, actions or proceedings as may be necessary or desirable for the receipt, preservation, protection, maintenance or liquidation of all or any part of the Applicants' Property, including acting as foreign representative of the Applicants. All courts of all other jurisdictions are hereby respectfully requested to make such orders and provide such other aid and assistance to the Monitor, as an officer of this Court, as they may deem necessary or appropriate in furtherance of this order, and it is specifically respectfully requested that the United States Bankruptcy Court for the Southern District of New York recognize the within proceedings for the purposes of section 304 of the United States Bankruptcy Code and recognize Ernst & Young Inc. in its capacity as Monitor as a foreign representative for the purposes of section 304 of the United States Bankruptcy Code.

72. THIS COURT ORDERS that the directors of the Applicants are hereby permitted to authorize the commencement of proceedings under section 304 of the United States Bankruptcy Code or such other relief under the code as may be appropriate and to which the Monitor consents.

73. THIS COURT ORDERS that for the purposes of seeking the aid and recognition of any court or any judicial, regulatory or administrative body outside of Canada, the Monitor shall act as and be deemed to be the foreign representative of the Applicants.

SCHEDULE "A"

3838722 Canada Inc.
Air Canada Capital Ltd.
Jazz Air Inc.
Manoir Int'l Finance Inc.
Simco Leasing Ltd.
Wingco Leasing Inc.
Zip Air Inc.

SCHEDULE "B"

April 1, 2003

CONFIDENTIAL

Air Canada
Air Canada Headquarters Building
Air Canada Centre
7373 Côte Vertu Boulevard West
Saint-Laurent, Québec
H4Y 1H4

Attention: Pat Iaconi and David Shapiro

Re: Commitment for Financing During *CCAA* Proceedings

Ladies and Gentlemen:

You have advised us that Air Canada ("AC"), and its subsidiaries listed in Schedule I (collectively, the "Applicants"), intend to apply to the Ontario Superior Court of Justice (Commercial List) sitting at Toronto, Ontario (the "*CCAA* Court") for an order that the Applicants are entitled to relief (as amended or modified without resulting in an event of default under the DIP Facility, the "Original Order") under the Companies' Creditors Arrangement Act (Canada) ("*CCAA*"), which order also will contain the terms contained in Schedule II, and make a concurrent petition under section 304 of the U.S. Bankruptcy Code in the United States Bankruptcy Court for the Southern District of New York (the "U.S. Bankruptcy Court"). You have further advised us that it is the Applicants' intention to remain in possession and control of their assets and business during the course of the *CCAA* proceeding (the "*CCAA* Proceeding"). General Electric Capital Canada Inc. ("GECC") is pleased to offer its commitment to provide to the Applicants, up to an aggregate of U.S. $700 million (or an equivalent amount thereof in Canadian dollars not to exceed C$1.05 billion) of senior secured financing during the *CCAA* Proceeding, subject to the terms and conditions of this Commitment Letter (the "DIP Facility").

SUMMARY OF TERMS
FOR DIP FACILITY

BORROWER: AC, as an applicant in the *CCAA* Proceeding.

ADMINISTRATIVE AGENT OR AGENT: GECC

COLLATERAL AGENT: GECC

LENDERS: GECC and, if the DIP Facility is syndicated, other lenders acceptable to GECC.

FACILITIES AND AMOUNTS:

1) A revolving term credit facility (the "Tranche A Facility") in a principal amount not to exceed U.S. $300 million (or the equivalent amount thereof in Canadian dollars; for purposes of this Commitment Letter, references to financing in U.S. dollars shall include the equivalent amount thereof in Canadian dollars), including a Letter of Credit Subfacility of up to an amount to be agreed between Borrower and GECC. Letters of Credit will be issued by a bank on terms acceptable to Agent, and will be guaranteed by GECC. The Tranche A Facility will be available subject to the satisfaction of the Stage One and Stage Two Conditions set out opposite OTHER TERMS AND CONDITIONS below.

2) A non-revolving term loan facility (the "Tranche B Facility") in a principal amount of up to U.S. $400 million. The Tranche B Facility will be available subject to the satisfaction of the Stage One Conditions set out opposite OTHER TERMS AND CONDITIONS below. Any Lender under the Tranche B Facility may decline any voluntary prepayment by Borrower thereunder.

TERM:

The earlier of (i) 18 months from closing or (ii) the effective date of a plan of arrangement in the *CCAA* Proceeding.

AVAILABILITY ADVANCE RATES:

Tranche A

Facility: The availability of the Tranche A Facility will be subject to the maintenance of a maximum loan to collateral ratio. For the purpose of such ratio, the collateral will include the orderly liquidation value of the Applicants' aircraft; the fair market value of the Applicants' fee simple real estate; the orderly liquidation value of the Applicants' equipment (which, for greater certainty, shall not include any of the Applicants' aircraft spare parts inventory ("Spare Parts") which consists of rotable components that have been restored to airworthy status), each valued on a basis, and with each such valuation being evidenced in a manner, satisfactory to the Collateral Agent, less reserves established by the Collateral Agent in its reasonable credit judgment. Collateral Agent, GE Capital Aviation Services, Inc. or such other valuer or appraiser acceptable to Collateral Agent shall determine or perform such valuations. The Collateral Agent will retain the right from time to time to update its valuations of the collateral for purposes of the loan to collateral ratio and to establish and modify reserves against the valuations of collateral in its reasonable credit judgment. The face amount of all letters of credit issued under the Letter of Credit Subfacility will constitute a loan for purposes of the loan to collateral ratio.

Tranche B

Facility: The outstanding amount of the Tranche B Facility will be subject to the maintenance of maximum loan to collateral ratios. For the purposes of such ratios, the collateral will include Applicants' accounts receivable and Spare Parts. The initial valuation of Spare Parts and updates thereof shall be performed by the Collateral Agent, GECAS or such other valuer or appraiser acceptable to Collateral Agent, on a basis and evidenced in a form acceptable to Collateral Agent. The initial and periodic audits of Applicants' accounts receivable shall be performed by Collateral Agent or on its behalf by an auditor selected by it.

USE OF PROCEEDS:

For funding the ordinary course operations of the Applicants during the *CCAA* Proceeding, expenses arising in the *CCAA* Proceeding as may be approved by the Original Order or otherwise by the *CCAA* Court, and such other obligations as may be agreed to by Agent and approved by the *CCAA* Court, all subject to certain restrictions to be set forth in the final DIP Facility documents.

BORROWING AND INTEREST OPTIONS:

At Borrower's option, the Tranche A Facility and the Tranche B Facility will be available (A) in U.S. dollars, (i) at a floating rate equal to the U.S.$ Index Rate plus the Applicable U.S.$ Index Margin or (ii) absent a default, a 1, 2 or 3-month LIBOR Rate plus the Applicable LIBOR Margin; or (B) in Canadian dollars at (i) a floating rate equal to the Cdn.$ Index Rate plus the Applicable Cdn.$ Index Margin or (ii) absent a default, a 30, 60 or 90 day BA Rate plus the Applicable BA Margin.

The term "LIBOR Rate" will be defined as the rate per annum equal to the offered rate for deposits in U.S. dollars for the applicable interest period that appears on Telerate Page 3750 as of 11:00 a.m. (London time) two (2) Eurodollar business days prior to the beginning of such interest period. Interest on LIBOR loans will be payable and adjusted at the end of each applicable LIBOR period. LIBOR breakage fees and borrowing mechanics will be set forth in the final DIP Facility documents.

The term "U.S.$ Index Rate" will be defined as the higher of (i) the prime rate per annum as most recently reported in the "Money Rates" column of The Wall Street Journal or (ii) the overnight Federal funds rate per annum plus 50 basis points. Interest on U.S.$ Index Rate loans will be payable monthly in arrears and will be adjusted as of each change in the U.S.$ Index Rate.

The term "BA Rate" will be defined as the rate per annum determined by Agent by reference to the average rate quoted on the Reuters Monitor Screen Page CDOR (displaying Canadian interbank bid rates for Canadian dollar bankers' acceptances) applicable to bankers' acceptances for the applicable term as of 11:00 a.m. (Toronto time) two (2) business days prior to the beginning of such term. Interest on BA Rate loans will be payable at the end of each applicable BA period. BA Rate loan breakage fees and borrowing mechanics will be set forth in the final DIP Facility documents.

The term "Cdn.$ Index Rate" will be defined as the higher of (i) the annual rate of interest quoted from time to time in the "Report on Business" section of The Globe and Mail as being "Canadian prime", "chartered bank prime rate" or words of similar description and (ii) the

BA Rate in respect of a BA period for 30 days, plus, 1.75%. Interest on Cdn.$ Index Rate loans will be payable monthly in arrears and will be adjusted as of each change in the Cdn.$ Index Rate.

All interest and fees will be calculated on the basis of a 360-day year and actual days elapsed.

APPLICABLE MARGINS:

The following applicable margins will apply so long as any loan remains outstanding:

Applicable U.S.$ Index Margin	5.0%
Applicable LIBOR Margin	6.5%
Applicable Cdn.$ Index Margin	5.0%
Applicable BA Margin	6.5%
Applicable L/C Margin	4.0%
Applicable Unused Facility Fee Margin:	

Aggregate Unused Tranche A Facility Level	[less than or equal to] U.S. $100 million	[greater than] U.S. $100 million and [less than or equal to] U.S. $200 million	[greater than or equal to] U.S. $200 million
Applicable Unused Facility Fee Margin	.50%	.75%	1.0%

FEES:

Commitment Fee of U.S. $5 million due and payable to GECC in U.S. dollars upon acceptance of this Commitment Letter, which fee shall be fully earned and non-refundable when due and payable.

Closing Fee of U.S. $35 million due and payable to GECC in U.S. dollars at the time that the conditions precedent to the Tranche B Facility have been satisfied and the Tranche B Facility is available for usage, which fee shall be fully earned and non-refundable when due and payable.

Letter of Credit Fee equal to the Applicable L/C Margin on the face amount of letters of credit, payable to Agent monthly in arrears, plus any charges assessed by the issuing bank.

Unused Facility Fee equal to the Applicable Unused Facility Fee Margin on the average unused daily balance of the DIP Facility, payable to Agent monthly in arrears.

Collateral Monitoring Fee of U.S. $500,000 per year, payable to Agent yearly in advance on the closing date and on the first anniversary date thereof; provided, that if a plan of arrangement in the *CCAA* Proceeding becomes effective during the 12-month period in respect of which such fee has been paid, Collateral Agent will refund (by credit or payment) an amount of such fee that has been paid based on the number of days in the year following the effective date of such plan.

DEFAULT RATES:

Interest rates and the Letter of Credit Fee, otherwise applicable, will increase by 2% upon the occurrence and during the continuance of an Event of Default.

SECURITY AND PRIORITY:

To secure all existing and future obligations of the Applicants and their subsidiaries under or in connection with the Tranche A Facility and the Tranche B Facility, and all existing and future obligations owed in respect of agreements to which any of the Applicants or any of their affiliates are party and that are managed or serviced by GE Capital Aviation Services, Inc. or any of its affiliates (collectively, "GECAS") in respect of the assets listed on Schedule III (collectively, the "GECAS Obligations"). Collateral Agent, on behalf of itself, Lenders and GECAS, on behalf of itself and the Lease Obligees, will receive through the Original Order and the final DIP Facility documents, a fully perfected first priority security interest in, and first ranking charge on (or applicable equivalents thereto outside the Province of Ontario; such security interests and charge, together with the pledges referred to in the immediately following paragraph, collectively, the "Liens"), subject only to, in terms of priority, Permitted Liens (as defined in the second following paragraph) that pursuant to the Original Order are stated to have priority over the Liens and those Permitted Liens described in paragraph (2) of the second following paragraph, all of the existing and after acquired real and personal, tangible and intangible, property of the Applicants and their subsidiaries including, without limitation, all cash, cash equivalents, bank accounts, accounts, chattel paper, contract rights, inventory, instruments, documents, securities (whether or not marketable), equipment, fixtures, real property interests, patents, tradenames, trademarks, copyrights, industrial designs, intangibles, commercial tort claims, causes of action and all substitutions, accessions and proceeds of the foregoing, wherever located, including insurance or other proceeds, (collectively, the "Collateral").

All subsidiaries of the Borrower will guarantee the obligations of the Borrower under the DIP Facility and the GECAS Obligations, and the Collateral Agent will receive a first ranking pledge of all of the issued and outstanding capital stock of each subsidiary and affiliate of the Applicants. For the purpose of this Commitment Letter, subsidiaries will include limited partnerships and general partnerships and capital stock will include limited partnership and general partnership interests.

All Collateral will be free and clear of other liens, encumbrances and claims, except for (1) liens created under the Original Order and to be set forth in the final DIP Facility documents, the amount secured by, and the priority of, each of which to be acceptable to the Collateral Agent, and (2) existing validly perfected liens granted by the Applicants prior to the date hereof; provided, that none of the Applicants' property that is the subject of any valuation or appraisal and that supports any loan to be made available under the DIP Facility, will be subject to such existing liens (collectively, "Permitted Liens").

The Agent will have the discretion to determine, as between the Tranche A Facility and the Tranche B Facility, the relative priorities of the Liens on the Collateral securing such facilities.

Notwithstanding any other provision hereof, if Borrower receives from Canadian Imperial Bank of Commerce ("CIBC") up to C$350 million cash as a prepayment of accounts payable by CIBC for Aeroplan points in respect of the Aerogold feature of Aeroplan, and Borrower grants to CIBC a security interest in revenues receivable for 12 months under Borrower's agreements with CIBC regarding Aerogold and the licences and trademarks used by CIBC in connection with Aerogold, those revenues (not to exceed those covering such 12 month period), licences and trademarks will not be subject to the Lien; provided, that prior to receiving any such cash from CIBC, the Borrower shall provide to the Collateral Agent updated advice from Solomon Smith Barney (in a form and premised on a basis satisfactory to the Collateral Agent, acting reasonably) showing increased annual revenue to the Borrower pursuant to the Borrower's amended agreements with CIBC regarding Aerogold of an amount not less than C$50 million as a result of amendments to such agreements.

MANDATORY PREPAYMENTS:

The following prepayments in the following amounts will be required: (a) all net proceeds (after satisfying prior-ranking liens and court ordered charges) of any sale or other disposition of any assets of the Applicants; and (b) subject to exceptions for repairs and replacements and satisfaction of prior-ranking liens and court ordered charges, all net insurance proceeds or other awards payable in connection with the loss, destruction or condemnation of any assets of the Applicants. All prepayments will be applied in accordance with the priorities of the Liens securing the Collateral from which the proceeds are derived that must be used for the applicable prepayment.

DOCUMENTATION:

The final DIP Facility documents will be mutually acceptable to all parties and will contain representations and warranties; conditions precedent; affirmative, negative and financial covenants (which shall only include minimum monthly EBITDA and cash balance requirements that are based on the annual monthly projections (consistently prepared and applied) provided by Borrower to Agent and only be applicable on and after the satisfaction of the Second Stage Conditions); indemnities; and events of default and remedies as required by Agent. Relevant documents, such as transaction documents, subordination agreements, intercreditor agreements, equity or stockholder agreements, incentive and employment agreements, tax agreements, and other material agreements, to be acceptable to Agent. All orders of the *CCAA* Court and U.S. Bankruptcy Court, and all motions relating thereto, shall be in form and substance acceptable to Agent. Without limiting the foregoing, the Original Order will include the terms set out in Schedule II, unless otherwise agreed in writing by Agent.

FINANCIAL AND OTHER REPORTING:

The final DIP Facility documents will require Borrower, on a monthly basis, to provide to Agent internally prepared financial statements and the monitor for the Applicants in the *CCAA* Proceeding (the "Monitor") to provide to Agent a cash flow budget for the Applicants for the first 13 weeks following the date of the Original Order which shall be updated by the Monitor on a weekly basis. Annually, Borrower will be required to provide audited financial statements and a board approved operating plan for the subsequent year. Borrower will provide, on an as requested basis, borrowing base certificates and other information reasonably requested by Agent including, without limitation, as promptly as practicably possible, notice of any threatened or actual seizures or detentions of aircraft or other assets by any person, including any air navigation, airport or other aviation authority. All financial statements and the cash flow budget shall be prepared on a consolidated and consolidating basis. In addition, copies of all pleadings, motions, applications, judicial information, financial information and other documents filed by or on behalf of the Applicants or the Monitor with the *CCAA* Court or the U.S. Bankruptcy Court, and such other reports and information respecting the Applicants' business, financial condition or prospects as Agent may, from time to time, reasonably request shall be provided to Agent. Borrower shall provide to Agent copies of letters that it will send to air navigation and airport authorities designated by Agent irrevocably authorizing those authorities to provide Agent with information relating to the Applicants and their subsidiaries requested by Agent from such authorities.

LOAN TO COLLATERAL RATIOS AND FINANCIAL COVENANTS

Collateral Agent agrees to establish the loan to collateral ratios and applicable financial covenants (including under the Stage Two Conditions) as soon as practically possible and, in any event, within 30 days hereof provided that Borrower has delivered to Collateral Agent on a timely basis the information that Collateral Agent requests for the purpose of doing so, recognizing that Collateral Agent requires a reasonable period of time to evaluate and analyze such information for these purposes.

SYNDICATION:

Upon acceptance of this Commitment Letter, GECC Capital Markets Group, Inc. ("GECMG") may initiate discussions with potential lenders regarding their participation in the DIP Facility. The success of such syndication will not be a condition precedent to the DIP Facility being made available.

If GECMG initiates syndication of the transaction, Borrower and its management will assist GECMG on such syndication. Such assistance will include, but not be limited to: (i) prompt assistance in the preparation of an Information Memorandum and verification of the accuracy and completeness of the information contained therein; and (ii) participation of Borrower's senior management in meetings and conference calls with potential lenders at such times and places as GECMG may reasonably request.

GECMG reserves the right to provide to industry trade organizations information necessary and customary for inclusion in league table measurements.

OTHER TERMS AND CONDITIONS

(All to be acceptable to Agent)

1. General (Including Stage One Conditions):

* Satisfactory completion of all business, environmental and legal due diligence relating to the Collateral including, without limitation, satisfactory completion of the valuation and audit of the Collateral supporting the Tranche B Facility.

* Entry of the Original Order by the *CCAA* Court and the 304 Order by the U.S. Bankruptcy Court in form and substance satisfactory to Agent and its counsel approving the DIP Facility.

* Agent's rights of inspection; access to facilities, management and auditors.

* Cash management system for the Applicants, Agent will have full cash dominion by means of lock boxes and blocked account agreements.

* Agent shall be satisfied that the Liens are prior to any lien securing any amount, and are not subject to any amount in trust, owing by or on behalf of the Applicants in respect of its pension plans.

* Commercially reasonable insurance protection for the Applicants' industry, size, and risk and the protection of the Collateral (terms, underwriter, scope, and coverage to be acceptable to Agent); Agent named as loss payee (property/casualty) and Collateral Agent, Agent and Lenders additional insureds (liability); and non-renewal/cancellation/amendment riders to provide 30 days advance notice to Agent.

* Receipt of all necessary or appropriate third party and governmental waivers and consents.

* Customary corporate and estoppel certificates; landlord/mortgagee/bailee waivers.

* Limitations on commercial transactions, management agreements, service agreements, and borrowing transactions between the Applicants and their subsidiaries and their officers, directors, employees and affiliates other than as expressly permitted by the Original Order.

* Limitations on, or prohibitions of, cash dividends, other distributions to equity holders, payments in respect of subordinated debt, payment of management fees to affiliates and redemption of common or preferred shares other than as expressly permitted by the Original Order.

* Prohibitions of amalgamations, mergers, acquisitions, the sale of any Applicant, their shares or a material portion of their assets.

* Prohibitions of a direct or indirect change in senior management of the Borrower.

* Capital expenditures in accordance with Applicants' projections.

* Customary yield protection provisions, including, without limitation, provisions as to capital adequacy, illegality, changes in circumstances and withholding taxes.

* Satisfactory opinions of counsel from the Applicants' counsel (including local counsel as requested) reasonably acceptable to Agent.

* The Original Order approving the DIP Facility to be entered on the commencement of the *CCAA* Proceeding, and to include, all of the provisions attached hereto as Schedule II, unless otherwise agreed by the Agent.

* Events of default will include, but not be limited to, (i) the appointment of a receiver, interim receiver, receiver and manager or trustee in bankruptcy with powers to operate or manage the affairs of any Applicant; (ii) the dismissal or conversion of *CCAA* Proceeding, or granting relief from the stay in favour of third parties except as contemplated by the definitive DIP Facility documentation; (iii) a post-*CCAA* Proceeding judgment liability or event that will, in Agent's judgment, significantly impair the Applicants' financial condition, operations, or ability to perform under the DIP Facility or any order of the *CCAA* Court or U.S. Bankruptcy Court; (iv) threatened seizure or detention of any aircraft by any airport or navigation authority (subject to cure periods to be negotiated) or actual seizure or detention of any aircraft by any such authority or airline or airport related servicer or other material property of the Applicants; (v) any violation or breach of any representation or warranty in any material respect, or covenant (subject to cure periods to be negotiated); or (vi) any amendment or modification of the Original Order that adversely affects Agent's, Collateral Agent's or Lenders' rights without Agent's prior consent.

* As of the closing date, there will have been no litigation commenced which has not been stayed by the *CCAA* Court or the U.S. Bankruptcy Court, as applicable and which, if successful, will have a material adverse impact on the Applicants, their business or Borrower's ability to repay the loans, or which will challenge the transactions under consideration.

* Compliance with applicable laws and decrees, and agreements, licences, authorizations and permits material to the operation of the Applicants' businesses.

* Agent shall have received the current terms and conditions of Applicants' agreements with CIBC regarding Aerogold.

* Lender syndication/assignment rights.

* Governing law: Ontario.

2. Stage Two Conditions:

* With respect to any real estate collateral, receipt of title insurance policies, at the Collateral Agent's discretion, in amount, form, and from an issuer satisfactory to Agent.

* If and to the extent requested by Agent, environmental surveys, reviews or audits in scope and form, by firms, and with results acceptable to Agent.

* Appraisals in form and substance acceptable to Agent reflecting asset values at levels acceptable to Agent.

The appraisals will be performed by GECAS or another qualified person acceptable to Agent.

* Presentation by the Borrower of a business plan for the next 12 months in form and substance satisfactory to the Agent.

* Achievement of monthly EBITDA amounts and minimum cash balances.

* Borrower shall have delivered to Agent the Solomon Smith Barney investment banking report prepared for Borrower confirming a valuation of Aeroplan in an amount of at least $700 million, such valuation to be in a form and on a basis reasonably satisfactory to Agent.

GECC's commitment hereunder is subject to execution and delivery of final legal documentation acceptable to GECC and its counsel incorporating, without limitation, the terms set forth herein. Moreover, the preceding summary of terms and conditions is not intended to be all-inclusive. Any terms and conditions that are not specifically addressed above will be subject to future negotiations.

You agree that GECMG will act as the sole syndication agent for the DIP Facility and that no additional agents, co-agents or arrangers will be appointed, or other titles conferred, without GECMG's consent. You agree that no Lender will receive any compensation of any kind for its participation in the DIP Facility, except as expressly provided in this Commitment Letter.

To ensure an orderly and effective syndication of the DIP Facility, you agree that until the termination of the syndication, as determined by GECMG, you will not, and will not permit any of your affiliates to, syndicate or issue, or attempt to syndicate or issue, announce or authorize the announcement of the syndication or of issuance of, or engage in discussion concerning the syndication or issuance of, any debt facility or debt security (including any renewals thereof), without the prior written consent of GECMG.

By signing this Commitment Letter, each party acknowledges that this Commitment Letter supersedes any and all discussions and understandings, written or oral, between or among GECC (and/or GECC's affiliates and any other person as to the subject matter hereof (collectively, the "Prior Communications"). No amendments, waivers or modifications of this

Commitment Letter or any of its contents shall be effective unless expressly set forth in writing and executed by the parties hereto.

This Commitment Letter is being provided to you on the condition that, except as required by law, neither it, the Prior Communications nor their contents will be disclosed publicly or privately except to those individuals who are your officers, employees or advisors who have a need to know as a result of being involved in the DIP Facility and then only on the condition that such matters may not be further disclosed. No person, other than the parties hereto, is entitled to rely upon this Commitment Letter or any of its contents. No one shall, except as required by law, use the name of, or refer to, GECC, or any of its affiliates (including GECMG), in any correspondence, discussions, advertisement or disclosure made in connection with the DIP Facility without the prior consent of GECC. GECC hereby consents to the delivery of this Commitment Letter after your acceptance hereof to the *CCAA* Court and the U.S. Bankruptcy Court solely for the purpose of obtaining the Letter Approval (defined below).

Regardless of whether the commitment herein is terminated or the DIP Facility closes, the Borrower agrees to pay upon request to GECC and GECMG all out-of-pocket expenses (including all reasonable legal, environmental, appraisal and valuation and other consultant costs and fees) incurred in connection with this Commitment Letter, the Prior Communications, the DIP Facility, and a field examination fee per person per diem plus actual out-of-pocket expenses in connection with the conduct of GECC's field audit and the evaluation and documentation of the DIP Facility. Borrower agrees to deliver to Agent U.S. $1,000,000 as an underwriting deposit (the "Underwriting Deposit"). At GECC's request from time to time, prior to the closing, Borrower shall further increase the Underwriting Deposit so that at all times prior to the closing, an unused balance thereof remains of at least U.S. $100,000. GECC will charge the Underwriting Deposit for fees and expenses to be reimbursed as outlined above. If GECC should close the DIP Facility, your remaining Underwriting Deposit (net of fees and expenses) will be applied toward fees due at closing. If the DIP Facility does not close, GECC will return any unapplied amount of the Underwriting Deposit. Regardless of whether the commitment herein is terminated or the DIP Facility closes, the Borrower agrees to indemnify and hold GECC, its affiliates (including GECMG), and the directors, officers, employees, and representatives of any of them (each, an "Indemnified Person"), harmless from and against all suits, actions, proceedings, claims, damages, losses, liabilities and expenses (including, but not limited to, attorneys' fees) of any kind which may be incurred by, or asserted against, any such person in connection with, or arising out of, this Commitment Letter, the Prior Communications, the DIP Facility, any other related financing, documentation, disputes or environmental liabilities, or any related investigation, litigation, or proceeding. Notwithstanding the preceding sentence, the indemnitors under this paragraph shall not be liable for any indemnification to any Indemnified Person to the extent that any such suit, action, proceeding, claim, damage, loss, liability or expense results from such Indemnified Person's gross negligence or willful misconduct. Under no circumstances shall GECC or any of its affiliates (including GECMG) be liable for any punitive, exemplary, consequential or indirect damages which may be alleged to result in connection with this Commitment Letter, the Prior Communications, the DIP Facility, the documents related thereto, or any other financing, regardless of whether the commitment herein is terminated or the DIP Facility closes.

By signing this Commitment Letter, Borrower agrees to proceed in good faith and expeditiously to obtain, as soon as possible, all necessary *CCAA* Court and U.S. Bankruptcy Court approvals in connection with Borrower's execution hereof and the Applicants' obligations hereunder; (the "Letter Approval").

This Commitment Letter is governed by and shall be construed in accordance with the laws of the Province of Ontario applicable to contracts made and performed in Ontario.

GECC shall have access to all relevant facilities, personnel and accountants, and copies of all documents that GECC may request, including business plans, financial statements (actual and pro forma), book, records and other documents.

This Commitment Letter shall be of no force and effect unless and until (a) Borrower executes this Commitment Letter and delivers it to the undersigned care of GE Capital Commercial Finance, Inc., 800 Connecticut Avenue, Two North, Norwalk, CT 06854, Attention: Stuart Armstrong on or before April 1, 2003, and (b) receipt by the Agent on April 1, 2003 of the Commitment Fee and the Underwriting Deposit by way of wire transfer to the following account of the Agent:

GECCI - Commercial Finance
Royal Bank of Canada
Account Number: 4002739
Transit Number: 00002
Bank Number: 003
200 Bay Street
Main Branch
Toronto, Ontario
Reference: Air Canada

Once effective, GECC's commitment to provide financing in accordance with the terms of this Commitment Letter shall cease if the Tranche B Facility is not funded for any reason, on or before May 15, 2003, and neither GECC nor any of its affiliates shall have liability to any person in connection with its refusal to fund the DIP Facility or any portion thereof after such date.

GECC agrees to work reasonably with existing senior management of the Borrower to convert a minimum of U.S. $200 million and up to U.S. $300 million principal amount of the obligations outstanding under the DIP Facility into a senior secured credit facility for the Borrower upon emerging from the *CCAA* Proceeding and the U.S. Bankruptcy proceeding on terms and conditions to be reasonably acceptable to GECC, including the values of Spare Parts and accounts receivable that are included in the collateral securing such a facility. At GECC's option, GECAS shall purchase at par the obligations under such senior secured credit facility.

GECAS agrees to work reasonably with existing senior management of Borrower by assisting in the facilitation of a consensual restructuring of leases to the Applicants, including leases managed or serviced by GECAS, so that the Applicants may emerge successfully from the *CCAA* Proceeding. For greater certainty, if after such a consensual restructuring, a deficiency claim remains under any such lease, that deficiency claim shall not constitute a GECAS Obligation.

EACH PARTY HEREBY WAIVES ANY RIGHT TO A TRIAL BY JURY OR ANY CLAIM OR CAUSE OF ACTION ARISING IN CONNECTION WITH THIS COMMITMENT

LETTER, THE DIP FACILITY OR ANY OTHER RELATED FINANCING, WHETHER ARISING IN CONTRACT, TORT OR OTHERWISE.

Our business is helping yours. We look forward to continuing to work with you toward completing this transaction.

Sincerely,

GENERAL ELECTRIC CAPITAL CANADA INC.

By: ______________________ Stephen Smith

Duly Authorized Signatory

GE CAPITAL AVIATION SERVICES, INC.

By: ______________________

Agreed and accepted as of this ________ day of April, 2003
AIR CANADA

By: ______________________

Its: ______________________

[Schedules 1 and 2 omitted]

APPENDIX 3

ONTARIO MODEL INITIAL ORDER

Court File No. ________

ONTARIO
SUPERIOR COURT OF JUSTICE
COMMERCIAL LIST

THE HONOURABLE ____________	)	________ DAY, THE ____
____________________________	)	
JUSTICE ____________________	)	DAY OF ________, 200 __

IN THE MATTER OF THE *COMPANIES' CREDITORS ARRANGEMENT ACT*, R.S.C. 1985, c. C-36, AS AMENDED

AND IN THE MATTER OF A PLAN OF COMPROMISE OR ARRANGEMENT OF [APPLICANT'S NAME] (the "Applicant")

INITIAL ORDER[1]
(Long Form)

THIS APPLICATION, made by the Applicant, pursuant to the *Companies' Creditors Arrangement Act*, R.S.C. 1985, c. C-36, as amended (the "CCAA") was heard this day at 393 University Avenue, Toronto, Ontario.

ON READING the affidavit of [NAME] sworn [DATE] and the Exhibits thereto and on hearing the submissions of counsel for [NAMES], no one appearing for [NAME] although duly served as appears from the affidavit of service of [NAME] sworn [DATE] and on reading the consent of [MONITOR'S NAME] to act as the Monitor,

SERVICE

1. THIS COURT ORDERS that the time for service of the Notice of Application and the Application Record is hereby abridged so that this Application is properly returnable today and hereby dispenses with further service thereof.

APPLICATION

2. THIS COURT ORDERS AND DECLARES that the Applicant is a company to which the CCAA applies.

[1] The CLUC Subcommittee has proceeded to draft this Model Order without incorporating specific changes mandated by Bill C-55. When Bill C-55 (or a version thereof) is declared to be in force, the CLUC Subcommittee will update this and other Model Orders to make the necessary changes.

PLAN OF ARRANGEMENT

3. THIS COURT ORDERS that the Applicant shall have the authority to file and may, subject to further order of this Court, file with this Court a plan of compromise or arrangement (hereinafter referred to as the "Plan") between, *inter alia*, the Applicant and one or more classes of its secured and/or unsecured creditors as it deems appropriate.

POSSESSION OF PROPERTY AND OPERATIONS

4. THIS COURT ORDERS that the Applicant shall remain in possession and control of its current and future assets, undertakings and properties of every nature and kind whatsoever, and wherever situate including all proceeds thereof (the "Property"). Subject to further Order of this Court, the Applicant shall continue to carry on business in a manner consistent with the preservation of its business (the "Business") and Property. The Applicant shall be authorized and empowered to continue to retain and employ the employees, consultants, agents, experts, accountants, counsel and such other persons (collectively "Assistants") currently retained or employed by it, with liberty to retain such further Assistants as it deems reasonably necessary or desirable in the ordinary course of business or for the carrying out of the terms of this Order.

5. [Note: This provision should only be utilized where necessary, in view of the fact that central cash management systems often operate in a manner that consolidates the cash of applicant companies] THIS COURT ORDERS that the Applicant shall be entitled to continue to utilize the central cash management system currently in place as described in the Affidavit of [NAME] sworn [DATE] or replace it with another substantially similar central cash management system (the "Cash Management System") and that any present or future bank providing the Cash Management System shall not be under any obligation whatsoever to inquire into the propriety, validity or legality of any transfer, payment, collection or other action taken under the Cash Management System, or as to the use or application by the Applicant of funds transferred, paid, collected or otherwise dealt with in the Cash Management System, shall be entitled to provide the Cash Management System without any liability in respect thereof to any Person (as hereinafter defined) other than the Applicant, pursuant to the terms of the documentation applicable to the Cash Management System, and shall be, in its capacity as provider of the Cash Management System, an unaffected creditor under the Plan with regard to any claims or expenses it may suffer or incur in connection with the provision of the Cash Management System.

6. THIS COURT ORDERS that the Applicant shall be entitled but not required to pay the following expenses whether incurred prior to or after this Order:

(a) all outstanding and future wages, salaries, employee and pension benefits, vacation pay, bonuses and expenses payable on or after the date of this Order, in each case incurred in the ordinary course of business and consistent with existing compensation policies and arrangements; and

(b) the fees and disbursements of any Assistants retained or employed by the Applicant in respect of these proceedings, at their standard rates and charges.

7. THIS COURT ORDERS that, except as otherwise provided to the contrary herein, the Applicant shall be entitled but not required to pay all reasonable expenses incurred by the Applicant in carrying on the Business in the ordinary course after this Order, and in carrying out the provisions of this Order, which expenses shall include, without limitation:

(a) all expenses and capital expenditures reasonably necessary for the preservation of the Property or the Business including, without limitation, payments on account of insurance (including directors and officers insurance), maintenance and security services; and

(b) payment for goods or services actually supplied to the Applicant following the date of this Order.

8. THIS COURT ORDERS that the Applicant shall remit, in accordance with legal requirements, or pay:

(a) any statutory deemed trust amounts in favour of the Crown in right of Canada or of any Province thereof or any other taxation authority which are required to be deducted from employees' wages, including, without limitation, amounts in respect of (i) employment insurance, (ii) Canada Pension Plan, (iii) Quebec Pension Plan, and (iv) income taxes;

(b) all goods and services or other applicable sales taxes (collectively, "Sales Taxes") required to be remitted by the Applicant in connection with the sale of goods and services by the Applicant, but only where such Sales Taxes are accrued or collected after the date of this Order, or where such Sales Taxes were accrued or collected prior to the date of this Order but not required to be remitted until on or after the date of this Order, and

(c) any amount payable to the Crown in right of Canada or of any Province thereof or any political subdivision thereof or any other taxation authority in respect of municipal realty, municipal business or other taxes, assessments or levies of any nature or kind which are entitled at law to be paid in priority to claims of secured creditors and which are attributable to or in respect of the carrying on of the Business by the Applicant.

9. THIS COURT ORDERS that until such time as the Applicant repudiates a real property lease in accordance with paragraph **[11(c)]** of this Order, the Applicant shall pay all amounts constituting rent or payable as rent under real property leases (including, for greater certainty, common area maintenance charges, utilities and realty taxes and any other amounts payable to the landlord under the lease) or as otherwise may be negotiated by the Applicant from time to time ("Rent"), for the period commencing from and including the date of this Order, bi-weekly, in advance (but not in arrears).

10. THIS COURT ORDERS that, except as specifically permitted herein, the Applicant is hereby directed, until further Order of this Court: (a) to make no payments of principal, interest thereon or otherwise on account of amounts owing by the Applicant to any of its creditors as of this date; (b) to grant no security interests, trust, liens, charges or encumbrances upon or in respect of any of its Property; and (c) to not grant credit or incur liabilities except in the ordinary course of the Business.

RESTRUCTURING

11. THIS COURT ORDERS that the Applicant shall, subject to such covenants as may be contained in the Definitive Documents (as hereinafter defined), have the right to:

(a) permanently or temporarily cease, downsize or shut down any of its business or operations and to dispose of redundant or non-material assets not exceeding $■ in any one transaction or $■ in the aggregate, subject to paragraph **[11(c)]**, if applicable;

(b) terminate the employment of such of its employees or temporarily lay off such of its employees as it deems appropriate on such terms as may be agreed upon between the Applicant and such employee, or failing such agreement, to deal with the consequences thereof in the Plan;

(c) in accordance with paragraphs **[12]** and **[13]**, vacate, abandon or quit any leased premises and/or repudiate any real property lease and any ancillary agreements relating to any leased premises, on not less than seven (7) days' notice in writing to the relevant landlord on such terms as may be agreed upon between the Applicant and such landlord, or failing such agreement, to deal with the consequences thereof in the Plan;

(d) repudiate such of its arrangements or agreements of any nature whatsoever, whether oral or written, as the Applicant deems appropriate on such terms as may be agreed upon between the Applicant and such counter-parties, or failing such agreement, to deal with the consequences thereof in the Plan; and

(e) pursue all avenues of refinancing and offers for material parts of its Business or Property, in whole or part, subject to prior approval of this Court being obtained before any material refinancing or any sale (except as permitted by subparagraph ■, above),

all of the foregoing to permit the Applicant to proceed with an orderly restructuring of the Business (the "Restructuring").

12. THIS COURT ORDERS that the Applicant shall provide each of the relevant landlords with notice of the Applicant's intention to remove any fixtures from any leased premises at least seven (7) days prior to the date of the intended removal. The relevant landlord shall be entitled to have a representative present in the leased premises to observe such removal and, if the landlord disputes the Applicant's entitlement to remove any such fixture under the provisions of the lease, such fixture shall remain on the premises and shall be dealt with as agreed between any applicable secured creditors, such landlord and the Applicant, or by further Order of this Court upon application by the Applicant on at least two (2) days' notice to such landlord and any such secured creditors. If the Applicant repudiates the lease governing such leased premises in accordance with paragraph **[11(c)]** of this Order, it shall not be required to pay Rent under such lease pending resolution of any such dispute, and the repudiation of the lease shall be without prejudice to the Applicant's claim to the fixtures in dispute.

13. THIS COURT ORDERS that if a lease is repudiated by the Applicant in accordance with paragraph **[11(c)]** of this Order, then (a) during the notice period prior to the effective time of the repudiation, the landlord may show the affected leased premises to prospective tenants during normal business hours, on giving the Applicant and the Monitor 24 hours' prior written notice, and (b) at the effective time of the repudiation, the relevant landlord shall be entitled to take possession of any such leased premises without waiver of or prejudice to any claims or rights such landlord may have against the Applicant in respect of such lease or leased premises and such landlord shall be entitled to notify the Applicant of the basis on which it is taking possession and to gain possession of and re-lease such leased premises to any third party or parties on such terms as such landlord considers advisable, provided that

nothing herein shall relieve such landlord of its obligation to mitigate any damages claimed in connection therewith.

14. THIS COURT ORDERS that, subject to the other provisions of this Order (including the payment of Rent as herein provided) and any further Order of this Court, the Applicant shall be permitted to dispose of any or all of the Property located (or formerly located) at such leased premises without any interference of any kind from landlords (notwithstanding the terms of any leases) and, for greater certainty, the Applicant shall have the right to realize upon the Property and other assets in such manner and at such locations, including leased premises, as it deems suitable or desirable for the purpose of maximizing the proceeds and recovery therefrom.

NO PROCEEDINGS AGAINST THE APPLICANT OR THE PROPERTY

15. THIS COURT ORDERS that until and including [DATE – MAX. 30 DAYS], or such later date as this Court may order (the "Stay Period"), no proceeding or enforcement process in any court or tribunal (each, a "Proceeding") shall be commenced or continued against or in respect of the Applicant or the Monitor, or affecting the Business or the Property, except with the written consent of the Applicant and the Monitor, or with leave of this Court, and any and all Proceedings currently under way against or in respect of the Applicant or affecting the Business or the Property are hereby stayed and suspended pending further Order of this Court.

NO EXERCISE OF RIGHTS OR REMEDIES

16. THIS COURT ORDERS that during the Stay Period, all rights and remedies of any individual, firm, corporation, governmental body or agency, or any other entities (all of the foregoing, collectively being "Persons" and each being a "Person") against or in respect of the Applicant or the Monitor, or affecting the Business or the Property, are hereby stayed and suspended except with the written consent of the Applicant and the Monitor, or leave of this Court, provided that nothing in this Order shall (i) empower the Applicant to carry on any business which the Applicant is not lawfully entitled to carry on, (ii) exempt the Applicant from compliance with statutory or regulatory provisions relating to health, safety or the environment, (iii) prevent the filing of any registration to preserve or perfect a security interest, or (iv) prevent the registration of a claim for lien.

NO INTERFERENCE WITH RIGHTS

17. THIS COURT ORDERS that during the Stay Period, no Person shall discontinue, fail to honour, alter, interfere with, repudiate, terminate or cease to perform any right, renewal right, contract, agreement, licence or permit in favour of or held by the Applicant, except with the written consent of the Applicant and the Monitor, or leave of this Court.

CONTINUATION OF SERVICES

18. THIS COURT ORDERS that during the Stay Period, all Persons having oral or written agreements with the Applicant or statutory or regulatory mandates for the supply of goods and/or services, including without limitation all computer software, communication and other data services, centralized banking services, payroll services, insurance, transportation, services, utility or other services to the Business or the Applicant, are hereby restrained

until further Order of this Court from discontinuing, altering, interfering with or terminating the supply of such goods or services as may be required by the Applicant, and that the Applicant shall be entitled to the continued use of its current premises, telephone numbers, facsimile numbers, internet addresses and domain names, provided in each case that the normal prices or charges for all such goods or services received after the date of this Order are paid by the Applicant in accordance with normal payment practices of the Applicant or such other practices as may be agreed upon by the supplier or service provider and each of the Applicant and the Monitor, or as may be ordered by this Court.

NON-DEROGATION OF RIGHTS

19. THIS COURT ORDERS that, notwithstanding anything else contained herein, no creditor of the Applicant shall be under any obligation after the making of this Order to advance or re-advance any monies or otherwise extend any credit to the Applicant. Nothing in this Order shall derogate from the rights conferred and obligations imposed by the CCAA.

PROCEEDINGS AGAINST DIRECTORS AND OFFICERS

20. THIS COURT ORDERS that during the Stay Period, and except as permitted by subsection 11.5(2) of the CCAA, no Proceeding may be commenced or continued against any of the former, current or future directors or officers of the Applicant with respect to any claim against the directors or officers that arose before the date hereof and that relates to any obligations of the Applicant whereby the directors or officers are alleged under any law to be liable in their capacity as directors or officers for the payment or performance of such obligations, until a compromise or arrangement in respect of the Applicant, if one is filed, is sanctioned by this Court or is refused by the creditors of the Applicant or this Court.

DIRECTORS' AND OFFICERS' INDEMNIFICATION AND CHARGE

21. THIS COURT ORDERS that the Applicant shall indemnify its directors and officers from all claims, costs, charges and expenses relating to the failure of the Applicants, after the date hereof, to make payments of the nature referred to in subparagraphs **[6(a)]**, **[8(a)]**, **[8(b)]** and **[8(c)]** of this Order which they sustain or incur by reason of or in relation to their respective capacities as directors and/or officers of the Applicants except to the extent that, with respect to any officer or director, such officer or director has actively participated in the breach of any related fiduciary duties or has been grossly negligent or guilty of wilful misconduct.

22. THIS COURT ORDERS that the directors and officers of the Applicant shall be entitled to the benefit of and are hereby granted a charge (the "Directors' Charge") on the Property, which charge shall not exceed an aggregate amount of **$■**, as security for the indemnity provided in paragraph **[21]** of this Order. The Directors' Charge shall have the priority set out in paragraphs **[39]** and **[41]** herein.

23. THIS COURT ORDERS that, notwithstanding any language in any applicable insurance policy to the contrary, (a) no insurer shall be entitled to be subrogated to or claim the benefit of the Directors' Charge, and (b) the Applicant's directors and officers shall only be entitled to the benefit of the Directors' Charge to the extent that they do not have coverage under any directors' and officers' insurance policy, or to the extent that such coverage is insufficient to pay amounts indemnified in accordance with paragraph **[21]** of this Order.

APPOINTMENT OF MONITOR

24. THIS COURT ORDERS that [MONITOR'S NAME] is hereby appointed pursuant to the CCAA as the Monitor, an officer of this Court, to monitor the Property and the Applicant's conduct of the Business with the powers and obligations set out in the CCAA or set forth herein and that the Applicant and its shareholders, officers, directors, and Assistants shall advise the Monitor of all material steps taken by the Applicant pursuant to this Order, and shall co-operate fully with the Monitor in the exercise of its powers and discharge of its obligations.

25. THIS COURT ORDERS that the Monitor, in addition to its prescribed rights and obligations under the CCAA, is hereby directed and empowered to:

(a) monitor the Applicant's receipts and disbursements;

(b) report to this Court at such times and intervals as the Monitor may deem appropriate with respect to matters relating to the Property, the Business, and such other matters as may be relevant to the proceedings herein;

(c) assist the Applicant, to the extent required by the Applicant, in its dissemination, to the DIP Lender and its counsel on a [TIME INTERVAL] basis of financial and other information as agreed to between the Applicant and the DIP Lender which may be used in these proceedings including reporting on a basis to be agreed with the DIP Lender;

(d) advise the Applicant in its preparation of the Applicant's cash flow statements and reporting required by the DIP Lender, which information shall be reviewed with the Monitor and delivered to the DIP Lender and its counsel on a periodic basis, but not less than [TIME INTERVAL], or as otherwise agreed to by the DIP Lender;

(e) advise the Applicant in its development of the Plan and any amendments to the Plan;

(f) advise the Applicant, to the extent required by the Applicant, with the holding and administering of creditors' or shareholders' meetings for voting on the Plan;

(g) have full and complete access to the books, records and management, employees and advisors of the Applicant and to the Business and the Property to the extent required to perform its duties arising under this Order;

(h) be at liberty to engage independent legal counsel or such other persons as the Monitor deems necessary or advisable respecting the exercise of its powers and performance of its obligations under this Order;

(i) consider, and if deemed advisable by the Monitor, prepare a report and assessment on the Plan; and

(j) perform such other duties as are required by this Order or by this Court from time to time.

26. THIS COURT ORDERS that the Monitor shall not take possession of the Property and shall take no part whatsoever in the management or supervision of the management of the Business and shall not, by fulfilling its obligations hereunder, be deemed to have taken or maintained possession or control of the Business or Property, or any part thereof.

27. THIS COURT ORDERS that nothing herein contained shall require the Monitor to occupy or to take control, care, charge, possession or management (separately and/or collectively, "Possession") of any of the Property that might be environmentally contaminated, might be a pollutant or a contaminant, or might cause or contribute to a spill, discharge, release or deposit of a substance contrary to any federal, provincial or other law respecting the protection, conservation, enhancement, remediation or rehabilitation of the environment or relating to the disposal of waste or other contamination including, without limitation, the *Canadian Environmental Protection Act*, the Ontario *Environmental Protection Act*, the Ontario *Water Resources Act*, or the Ontario *Occupational Health and Safety Act* and regulations thereunder (the "Environmental Legislation"), provided however that nothing herein shall exempt the Monitor from any duty to report or make disclosure imposed by applicable Environmental Legislation. The Monitor shall not, as a result of this Order or anything done in pursuance of the Monitor's duties and powers under this Order, be deemed to be in Possession of any of the Property within the meaning of any Environmental Legislation, unless it is actually in possession.

28. THIS COURT ORDERS that that the Monitor shall provide any creditor of the Applicant and the DIP Lender with information provided by the Applicant in response to reasonable requests for information made in writing by such creditor addressed to the Monitor. The Monitor shall not have any responsibility or liability with respect to the information disseminated by it pursuant to this paragraph. In the case of information that the Monitor has been advised by the Applicant is confidential, the Monitor shall not provide such information to creditors unless otherwise directed by this Court or on such terms as the Monitor and the Applicant may agree.

29. THIS COURT ORDERS that, in addition to the rights and protections afforded the Monitor under the CCAA or as an officer of this Court, the Monitor shall incur no liability or obligation as a result of its appointment or the carrying out of the provisions of this Order, save and except for any gross negligence or wilful misconduct on its part. Nothing in this Order shall derogate from the protections afforded the Monitor by the CCAA or any applicable legislation.

30. THIS COURT ORDERS that the Monitor, counsel to the Monitor and counsel to the Applicant shall be paid their reasonable fees and disbursements, in each case at their standard rates and charges, by the Applicant as part of the costs of these proceedings. The Applicant is hereby authorized and directed to pay the accounts of the Monitor, counsel for the Monitor and counsel for the Applicant on a [TIME INTERVAL] basis and, in addition, the Applicant is hereby authorized to pay to the Monitor, counsel to the Monitor, and counsel to the Applicant, retainers in the amount[s] of $■ [, respectively,] to be held by them as security for payment of their respective fees and disbursements outstanding from time to time

31. THIS COURT ORDERS that the Monitor and its legal counsel shall pass their accounts from time to time, and for this purpose the accounts of the Monitor and its legal counsel are hereby referred to a judge of the Commercial List of the Ontario Superior Court of Justice.

32. THIS COURT ORDERS that the Monitor, counsel to the Monitor, if any, and the Applicant's counsel shall be entitled to the benefits of and are hereby granted a charge (the "Administration Charge") on the Property, which charge shall not exceed an aggregate amount of $■, as security for their professional fees and disbursements incurred at the normal rates and charges of the Monitor and such counsel, both before and after the making of this Order

in respect of these proceedings. The Administration Charge shall have the priority set out in paragraphs **[39]** and **[41]** hereof.

DIP FINANCING

33. THIS COURT ORDERS that the Applicant is hereby authorized and empowered to obtain and borrow under a credit facility from [DIP LENDER'S NAME] (the "DIP Lender") in order to finance the Applicant's working capital requirements and other general corporate purposes and capital expenditures, provided that borrowings under such credit facility shall not exceed $■ unless permitted by further Order of this Court.

34. THIS COURT ORDERS THAT such credit facility shall be on the terms and subject to the conditions set forth in the commitment letter between the Applicant and the DIP Lender dated as of [DATE] (the "Commitment Letter"), filed.

35. THIS COURT ORDERS that the Applicant is hereby authorized and empowered to execute and deliver such credit agreements, mortgages, charges, hypothecs and security documents, guarantees and other definitive documents (collectively, the "Definitive Documents"), as are contemplated by the Commitment Letter or as may be reasonably required by the DIP Lender pursuant to the terms thereof, and the Applicant is hereby authorized and directed to pay and perform all of its indebtedness, interest, fees, liabilities and obligations to the DIP Lender under and pursuant to the Commitment Letter and the Definitive Documents as and when the same become due and are to be performed, notwithstanding any other provision of this Order.

36. THIS COURT ORDERS that the DIP Lender shall be entitled to the benefits of and is hereby granted a charge (the "DIP Lender's Charge") on the Property, which charge shall not exceed the aggregate amount owed to the DIP Lender under the Definitive Documents. The DIP Lender's Charge shall have the priority set out in paragraphs **[39]** and **[41]** hereof.

37. THIS COURT ORDERS that, notwithstanding any other provision of this Order:

(a) the DIP Lender may take such steps from time to time as it may deem necessary or appropriate to file, register, record or perfect the DIP Lender's Charge or any of the Definitive Documents;

(b) upon the occurrence of an event of default under the Definitive Documents or the DIP Lender's Charge, the DIP Lender, upon ■ days notice to the Applicant and the Monitor, may exercise any and all of its rights and remedies against the Applicant or the Property under or pursuant to the Commitment Letter, Definitive Documents and the DIP Lender's Charge, including without limitation, to cease making advances to the Applicant and set off and/or consolidate any amounts owing by the DIP Lender to the Applicant against the obligations of the Applicant to the DIP Lender under the Commitment Letter, the Definitive Documents or the DIP Lender's Charge, to make demand, accelerate payment and give other notices, or to apply to this Court for the appointment of a receiver, receiver and manager or interim receiver, or for a bankruptcy order against the Applicant and for the appointment of a trustee in bankruptcy of the Applicant, and upon the occurrence of an event of default under the terms of the Definitive Documents, the DIP Lender shall be entitled to seize and retain proceeds from the sale of the Property and the cash flow of the Applicant to repay amounts owing to the DIP Lender in accordance with the Definitive Documents and the DIP Lender's Charge, but subject to the priorities as set out in paragraphs **[39]** and **[41]** of this Order; and

(c) the foregoing rights and remedies of the DIP Lender shall be enforceable against any trustee in bankruptcy, interim receiver, receiver or receiver and manager of the Applicant or the Property.

38. THIS COURT ORDERS AND DECLARES that the DIP Lender shall be treated as unaffected in any plan of arrangement or compromise filed by the Applicant under the CCAA, or any proposal filed by the Applicant under the *Bankruptcy and Insolvency Act* of Canada (the "BIA"), with respect to any advances made under the Definitive Documents.

VALIDITY AND PRIORITY OF CHARGES CREATED BY THIS ORDER

39. THIS COURT ORDERS that the priorities of the Directors' Charge, the Administration Charge and the DIP Lender's Charge, as among them, shall be as follows:

First – Administration Charge (to the maximum amount of $■);

Second – DIP Lender's Charge; and

Third – Directors' Charge (to the maximum amount of $■).

40. THIS COURT ORDERS that the filing, registration or perfection of the Directors' Charge, the Administration Charge or the DIP Lender's Charge (collectively, the "Charges") shall not be required, and that the Charges shall be valid and enforceable for all purposes, including as against any right, title or interest filed, registered, recorded or perfected subsequent to the Charges coming into existence, notwithstanding any such failure to file, register, record or perfect.

41. THIS COURT ORDERS that each of the Directors' Charge, the Administration Charge and the DIP Lender's Charge (all as constituted and defined herein) shall constitute a charge on the Property and such Charges shall rank in priority to all other security interests, trusts, liens, charges and encumbrances, statutory or otherwise (collectively, "Encumbrances") in favour of any Person.

42. THIS COURT ORDERS that except as otherwise expressly provided for herein, or as may be approved by this Court, the Applicant shall not grant any Encumbrances over any Property that rank in priority to, or *pari passu* with, any of the Directors' Charge, the Administration Charge or the DIP Lender's Charge, unless the Applicant also obtains the prior written consent of the Monitor, the DIP Lender and the beneficiaries of the Directors' Charge and the Administration Charge, or further Order of this Court.

43. THIS COURT ORDERS that the Directors' Charge, the Administration Charge, the Commitment Letter, the Definitive Documents and the DIP Lender's Charge shall not be rendered invalid or unenforceable and the rights and remedies of the chargees entitled to the benefit of the Charges (collectively, the "Chargees") and/or the DIP Lender thereunder shall not otherwise be limited or impaired in any way by (a) the pendency of these proceedings and the declarations of insolvency made herein; (b) any application(s) for bankruptcy order(s) issued pursuant to BIA, or any bankruptcy order made pursuant to such applications; (c) the filing of any assignments for the general benefit of creditors made pursuant to the BIA; (d) the provisions of any federal or provincial statutes; or (e) any negative covenants, prohibitions

or other similar provisions with respect to borrowings, incurring debt or the creation of Encumbrances, contained in any existing loan documents, lease, sublease, offer to lease or other agreement (collectively, an "Agreement") which binds the Applicant, and notwithstanding any provision to the contrary in any Agreement:

(a) neither the creation of the Charges nor the execution, delivery, perfection, registration or performance of the Commitment Letter or the Definitive Documents shall create or be deemed to constitute a breach by the Applicant of any Agreement to which it is a party;

(b) none of the Chargees shall have any liability to any Person whatsoever as a result of any breach of any Agreement caused by or resulting from the Applicant entering into the Commitment Letter, the creation of the Charges, or the execution, delivery or performance of the Definitive Documents; and

(c) the payments made by the Applicant pursuant to this Order, the Commitment Letter or the Definitive Documents, and the granting of the Charges, do not and will not constitute fraudulent preferences, fraudulent conveyances, oppressive conduct, settlements or other challengeable, voidable or reviewable transactions under any applicable law.

SERVICE AND NOTICE

44. THIS COURT ORDERS that the Applicant shall, within ten (10) business days of the date of entry of this Order, send a copy of this Order to its known creditors, other than employees and creditors to which the Applicant owes less than $■, at their addresses as they appear on the Applicant's records, and shall promptly send a copy of this Order (a) to all parties filing a Notice of Appearance in respect of this Application, and (b) to any other interested Person requesting a copy of this Order, and the Monitor is relieved of its obligation under Section 11(5) of the CCAA to provide similar notice, other than to supervise this process.

45. THIS COURT ORDERS that the Applicant and the Monitor be at liberty to serve this Order, any other materials and orders in these proceedings, any notices or other correspondence, by forwarding true copies thereof by prepaid ordinary mail, courier, personal delivery or electronic transmission to the Applicant's creditors or other interested parties at their respective addresses as last shown on the records of the Applicant and that any such service or notice by courier, personal delivery or electronic transmission shall be deemed to be received on the next business day following the date of forwarding thereof, or if sent by ordinary mail, on the third business day after mailing.

46. THIS COURT ORDERS that the Applicant, the Monitor, and any party who has filed a Notice of Appearance may serve any court materials in these proceedings by e-mailing a PDF or other electronic copy of such materials to counsels' email addresses as recorded on the Service List from time to time, in accordance with the E-filing protocol of the Commercial List to the extent practicable, and the Monitor may post a copy of any or all such materials on its website at [INSERT WEBSITE ADDRESS].

GENERAL

47. THIS COURT ORDERS that the Applicant or the Monitor may from time to time apply to this Court for advice and directions in the discharge of its powers and duties hereunder.

48. THIS COURT ORDERS that nothing in this Order shall prevent the Monitor from acting as an interim receiver, a receiver, a receiver and manager, or a trustee in bankruptcy of the Applicant, the Business or the Property.

49. THIS COURT HEREBY REQUESTS the aid and recognition of any court, tribunal, regulatory or administrative body having jurisdiction in Canada or in the United States, to give effect to this Order and to assist the Applicant, the Monitor and their respective agents in carrying out the terms of this Order. All courts, tribunals, regulatory and administrative bodies are hereby respectfully requested to make such orders and to provide such assistance to the Applicant and to the Monitor, as an officer of this Court, as may be necessary or desirable to give effect to this Order, to grant representative status to the Monitor in any foreign proceeding, or to assist the Applicant and the Monitor and their respective agents in carrying out the terms of this Order.

50. THIS COURT ORDERS that each of the Applicant and the Monitor be at liberty and is hereby authorized and empowered to apply to any court, tribunal, regulatory or administrative body, wherever located, for the recognition of this Order and for assistance in carrying out the terms of this Order.

51. THIS COURT ORDERS that any interested party (including the Applicant and the Monitor) may apply to this Court to vary or amend this Order on not less than seven (7) days' notice to any other party or parties likely to be affected by the order sought or upon such other notice, if any, as this Court may order.

52. THIS COURT ORDERS that this Order and all of its provisions are effective as of 12:01 a.m. Eastern Standard Time on the date of this Order.

APPENDIX 4

ONTARIO MODEL INITIAL ORDER- SHORT FORM

Court File No. ________

ONTARIO
SUPERIOR COURT OF JUSTICE
COMMERCIAL LIST

THE HONOURABLE ____________	)	__________ DAY, THE _____
______________________________	)	
JUSTICE ______________________	)	DAY OF __________, 200 __

IN THE MATTER OF THE *COMPANIES' CREDITORS ARRANGEMENT ACT,* R.S.C. 1985, c. C-36, AS AMENDED

AND IN THE MATTER OF A PLAN OF COMPROMISE OR ARRANGEMENT OF [APPLICANT'S NAME] (the "Applicant")

INITIAL ORDER[1]
(Short Form)

THIS APPLICATION, made by the Applicant, pursuant to the *Companies' Creditors Arrangement Act*, R.S.C. 1985, c. C-36, as amended (the "CCAA") was heard this day at 393 University Avenue, Toronto, Ontario.

ON READING the affidavit of [NAME] sworn [DATE] and the Exhibits thereto and on hearing the submissions of counsel for [NAMES], no one appearing for [NAME] although duly served as appears from the affidavit of service of [NAME] sworn [DATE] and on reading the consent of [MONITOR'S NAME] to act as the Monitor,

SERVICE

53. THIS COURT ORDERS that the time for service of the Notice of Application and the Application Record is hereby abridged so that this Application is properly returnable today and hereby dispenses with further service thereof.

APPLICATION

54. THIS COURT ORDERS AND DECLARES that the Applicant is a company to which the CCAA applies.

---

[1] The CLUC Subcommittee has proceeded to draft this Model Order without incorporating specific changes mandated by Bill C-55. When Bill C-55 (or a version thereof) is declared to be in force, the CLUC Subcommittee will update this and other Model Orders to make the necessary changes.

FURTHER HEARING

55. THIS COURT ORDERS that a further hearing in this Application shall be held on [DATE – WITHIN INITIAL STAY PERIOD] or such alternate date as this Court may fix, at which time this Order may be supplemented or otherwise varied, and the Stay Period (as herein defined) extended or terminated. The Applicant and the Monitor shall serve their materials for this further hearing on all parties who serve a Notice of Appearance on the Applicant and the Monitor, such materials to be served by no later than [FIVE] days prior to the date scheduled for the further hearing.

POSSESSION OF PROPERTY AND OPERATIONS

56. THIS COURT ORDERS that the Applicant shall remain in possession and control of its current and future assets, undertakings and properties of every nature and kind whatsoever, and wherever situate including all proceeds thereof (the "Property"). Subject to further Order of this Court, the Applicant shall continue to carry on business in a manner consistent with the preservation of its business (the "Business") and Property. The Applicant shall be authorized and empowered to continue to retain and employ the employees, consultants, agents, experts, accountants, counsel and such other persons (collectively "Assistants") currently retained or employed by it, with liberty to retain such further Assistants as it deems reasonably necessary or desirable in the ordinary course of business or for the carrying out of the terms of this Order.

57. THIS COURT ORDERS that the Applicant shall be entitled but not required to pay the following expenses whether incurred prior to or after this Order:

(a) all outstanding and future wages, salaries, employee and pension benefits, vacation pay, bonuses and expenses payable on or after the date of this Order, in each case incurred in the ordinary course of business and consistent with existing compensation policies and arrangements; and

(b) the fees and disbursements of any Assistants retained or employed by the Applicant in respect of these proceedings, at their standard rates and charges.

58. THIS COURT ORDERS that, except as otherwise provided to the contrary herein, the Applicant shall be entitled but not required to pay all reasonable expenses incurred by the Applicant in carrying on the Business in the ordinary course after this Order, and in carrying out the provisions of this Order, which expenses shall include, without limitation:

(a) all expenses and capital expenditures reasonably necessary for the preservation of the Property or the Business including, without limitation, payments on account of insurance (including directors and officers insurance), maintenance and security services; and

(b) payment for goods or services actually supplied to the Applicant following the date of this Order.

59. THIS COURT ORDERS that the Applicant shall remit, in accordance with legal requirements, or pay:

(a) any statutory deemed trust amounts in favour of the Crown in right of Canada or of any Province thereof or any other taxation authority which are required to be deducted from employees' wages, including, without limitation, amounts in respect of (i) employment insurance, (ii) Canada Pension Plan, (iii) Quebec Pension Plan, and (iv) income taxes;

(b) all goods and services or other applicable sales taxes (collectively, "Sales Taxes") required to be remitted by the Applicant in connection with the sale of goods and services by the Applicant, but only where such Sales Taxes are accrued or collected after the date of this Order, or where such Sales Taxes were accrued or collected prior to the date of this Order but not required to be remitted until on or after the date of this Order, and

(c) any amount payable to the Crown in right of Canada or of any Province thereof or any political subdivision thereof or any other taxation authority in respect of municipal realty, municipal business or other taxes, assessments or levies of any nature or kind which are entitled at law to be paid in priority to claims of secured creditors and which are attributable to or in respect of the carrying on of the Business by the Applicant.

60. THIS COURT ORDERS that, except as specifically permitted herein, the Applicant is hereby directed, until further Order of this Court: (a) to make no payments of principal, interest thereon or otherwise on account of amounts owing by the Applicant to any of its creditors as of this date; (b) to grant no security interests, trust, liens, charges or encumbrances upon or in respect of any of its Property; and (c) to not grant credit or incur liabilities except in the ordinary course of the Business.

NO PROCEEDINGS AGAINST THE APPLICANT OR THE PROPERTY

61. THIS COURT ORDERS that until and including [DATE – MAX. 30 DAYS], or such later date as this Court may order (the "Stay Period"), no proceeding or enforcement process in any court or tribunal (each, a "Proceeding") shall be commenced or continued against or in respect of the Applicant or the Monitor, or affecting the Business or the Property, except with the written consent of the Applicant and the Monitor, or with leave of this Court, and any and all Proceedings currently under way against or in respect of the Applicant or affecting the Business or the Property are hereby stayed and suspended pending further Order of this Court.

NO EXERCISE OF RIGHTS OR REMEDIES

62. THIS COURT ORDERS that during the Stay Period, all rights and remedies of any individual, firm, corporation, governmental body or agency, or any other entities (all of the foregoing, collectively being "Persons" and each being a "Person") against or in respect of the Applicant or the Monitor, or affecting the Business or the Property, are hereby stayed and suspended except with the written consent of the Applicant and the Monitor, or leave of this Court, provided that nothing in this Order shall (i) empower the Applicant to carry on any business which the Applicant is not lawfully entitled to carry on, (ii) exempt the Applicant from compliance with statutory or regulatory provisions relating to health, safety or the environment, (iii) prevent the filing of any registration to preserve or perfect a security interest, or (iv) prevent the registration of a claim for lien.

NO INTERFERENCE WITH RIGHTS

63. THIS COURT ORDERS that during the Stay Period, no Person shall discontinue, fail to honour, alter, interfere with, repudiate, terminate or cease to perform any right, renewal right, contract, agreement, licence or permit in favour of or held by the Applicant, except with the written consent of the Applicant and the Monitor, or leave of this Court.

CONTINUATION OF SERVICES

64. THIS COURT ORDERS that during the Stay Period, all Persons having oral or written agreements with the Applicant or statutory or regulatory mandates for the supply of goods and/or services, including without limitation all computer software, communication and other data services, centralized banking services, payroll services, insurance, transportation, services, utility or other services to the Business or the Applicant, are hereby restrained until further Order of this Court from discontinuing, altering, interfering with or terminating the supply of such goods or services as may be required by the Applicant, and that the Applicant shall be entitled to the continued use of its current premises, telephone numbers, facsimile numbers, internet addresses and domain names, provided in each case that the normal prices or charges for all such goods or services received after the date of this Order are paid by the Applicant in accordance with normal payment practices of the Applicant or such other practices as may be agreed upon by the supplier or service provider and each of the Applicant and the Monitor, or as may be ordered by this Court.

NON-DEROGATION OF RIGHTS

65. THIS COURT ORDERS that, notwithstanding anything else contained herein, no creditor of the Applicant shall be under any obligation after the making of this Order to advance or re-advance any monies or otherwise extend any credit to the Applicant. Nothing in this Order shall derogate from the rights conferred and obligations imposed by the CCAA.

PROCEEDINGS AGAINST DIRECTORS AND OFFICERS

66. THIS COURT ORDERS that during the Stay Period, and except as permitted by subsection 11.5(2) of the CCAA, no Proceeding may be commenced or continued against any of the former, current or future directors or officers of the Applicant with respect to any claim against the directors or officers that arose before the date hereof and that relates to any obligations of the Applicant whereby the directors or officers are alleged under any law to be liable in their capacity as directors or officers for the payment or performance of such obligations, until a compromise or arrangement in respect of the Applicant, if one is filed, is sanctioned by this Court or is refused by the creditors of the Applicant or this Court.

DIRECTORS' AND OFFICERS' INDEMNIFICATION AND CHARGE

67. THIS COURT ORDERS that the Applicant shall indemnify its directors and officers from all claims, costs, charges and expenses relating to the failure of the Applicants, after the date hereof, to make payments of the nature referred to in subparagraphs **[5(a)]**, **[7(a)]**, **[7(b)]** and **[7(c)]** of this Order which they sustain or incur by reason of or in relation to their respective capacities as directors and/or officers of the Applicants except to the extent that, with respect to any officer or director, such officer or director has actively participated in the

breach of any related fiduciary duties or has been grossly negligent or guilty of wilful misconduct.

68. THIS COURT ORDERS that the directors and officers of the Applicant shall be entitled to the benefit of and are hereby granted a charge (the "Directors' Charge") on the Property, which charge shall not exceed an aggregate amount of $■, as security for the indemnity provided in paragraph **[15]** of this Order. The Directors' Charge shall have the priority set out in paragraphs **[32]** and **[34]** herein.

69. THIS COURT ORDERS that, notwithstanding any language in any applicable insurance policy to the contrary, (a) no insurer shall be entitled to be subrogated to or claim the benefit of the Directors' Charge, and (b) the Applicant's directors and officers shall only be entitled to the benefit of the Directors' Charge to the extent that they do not have coverage under any directors' and officers' insurance policy, or to the extent that such coverage is insufficient to pay amounts indemnified in accordance with paragraph **[15]** of this Order.

APPOINTMENT OF MONITOR

70. THIS COURT ORDERS that [MONITOR'S NAME] is hereby appointed pursuant to the CCAA as the Monitor, an officer of this Court, to monitor the Property and the Applicant's conduct of the Business with the powers and obligations set out in the CCAA or set forth herein and that the Applicant and its shareholders, officers, directors, and Assistants shall advise the Monitor of all material steps taken by the Applicant pursuant to this Order, and shall co-operate fully with the Monitor in the exercise of its powers and discharge of its obligations.

71. THIS COURT ORDERS that the Monitor, in addition to its prescribed rights and obligations under the CCAA, is hereby directed and empowered to:

(a) monitor the Applicant's receipts and disbursements;

(b) report to this Court at such times and intervals as the Monitor may deem appropriate with respect to matters relating to the Property, the Business, and such other matters as may be relevant to the proceedings herein;

(c) assist the Applicant, to the extent required by the Applicant, in its dissemination, to the DIP Lender and its counsel on a [TIME INTERVAL] basis of financial and other information as agreed to between the Applicant and the DIP Lender which may be used in these proceedings including reporting on a basis to be agreed with the DIP Lender;

(d) advise the Applicant in its preparation of the Applicant's cash flow statements and reporting required by the DIP Lender, which information shall be reviewed with the Monitor and delivered to the DIP Lender and its counsel on a periodic basis, but not less than [TIME INTERVAL], or as otherwise agreed to by the DIP Lender;

(e) have full and complete access to the books, records and management, employees and advisors of the Applicant and to the Business and the Property to the extent required to perform its duties arising under this Order;

(f) be at liberty to engage independent legal counsel or such other persons as the Monitor deems necessary or advisable respecting the exercise of its powers and performance of its obligations under this Order; and

(g) perform such other duties as are required by this Order or by this Court from time to time.

72. THIS COURT ORDERS that the Monitor shall not take possession of the Property and shall take no part whatsoever in the management or supervision of the management of the Business and shall not, by fulfilling its obligations hereunder, be deemed to have taken or maintained possession or control of the Business or Property, or any part thereof.

73. THIS COURT ORDERS that nothing herein contained shall require the Monitor to occupy or to take control, care, charge, possession or management (separately and/or collectively, "Possession") of any of the Property that might be environmentally contaminated, might be a pollutant or a contaminant, or might cause or contribute to a spill, discharge, release or deposit of a substance contrary to any federal, provincial or other law respecting the protection, conservation, enhancement, remediation or rehabilitation of the environment or relating to the disposal of waste or other contamination including, without limitation, the *Canadian Environmental Protection Act*, the Ontario *Environmental Protection Act*, the Ontario *Water Resources Act*, or the Ontario *Occupational Health and Safety Act* and regulations thereunder (the "Environmental Legislation"), provided however that nothing herein shall exempt the Monitor from any duty to report or make disclosure imposed by applicable Environmental Legislation. The Monitor shall not, as a result of this Order or anything done in pursuance of the Monitor's duties and powers under this Order, be deemed to be in Possession of any of the Property within the meaning of any Environmental Legislation, unless it is actually in possession.

74. THIS COURT ORDERS that, in addition to the rights and protections afforded the Monitor under the CCAA or as an officer of this Court, the Monitor shall incur no liability or obligation as a result of its appointment or the carrying out of the provisions of this Order, save and except for any gross negligence or wilful misconduct on its part. Nothing in this Order shall derogate from the protections afforded the Monitor by the CCAA or any applicable legislation.

III. THIS COURT ORDERS that the Monitor, counsel to the Monitor and counsel to the Applicant shall be paid their reasonable fees and disbursements, in each case at their standard rates and charges, by the Applicant as part of the costs of these proceedings. The Applicant is hereby authorized and directed to pay the accounts of the Monitor, counsel for the Monitor and counsel for the Applicant on a [TIME INTERVAL] basis and, in addition, the Applicant is hereby authorized to pay to the Monitor, counsel to the Monitor, and counsel to the Applicant, retainers in the amount[s] of $■ [, respectively,] to be held by them as security for payment of their respective fees and disbursements outstanding from time to time.

75. THIS COURT ORDERS that the Monitor and its legal counsel shall pass their accounts from time to time, and for this purpose the accounts of the Monitor and its legal counsel are hereby referred to a judge of the Commercial List of the Ontario Superior Court of Justice.

76. THIS COURT ORDERS that the Monitor, counsel to the Monitor, if any, and the Applicant's counsel shall be entitled to the benefits of and are hereby granted a charge (the "Administration Charge") on the Property, which charge shall not exceed an aggregate amount of $■, as security for their professional fees and disbursements incurred at the normal rates and charges of the Monitor and such counsel, both before and after the making of this Order

in respect of these proceedings. The Administration Charge shall have the priority set out in paragraphs **[32]** and **[34]** hereof.

DIP FINANCING

77. THIS COURT ORDERS that the Applicant is hereby authorized and empowered to obtain and borrow under a credit facility from **[DIP LENDER'S NAME]** (the "DIP Lender") in order to finance the Applicant's working capital requirements and other general corporate purposes and capital expenditures, provided that borrowings under such credit facility shall not exceed $■ unless permitted by further Order of this Court.

78. THIS COURT ORDERS THAT such credit facility shall be on the terms and subject to the conditions set forth in the commitment letter between the Applicant and the DIP Lender dated as of [DATE] (the "Commitment Letter"), filed.

79. THIS COURT ORDERS that the Applicant is hereby authorized and empowered to execute and deliver such credit agreements, mortgages, charges, hypothecs and security documents, guarantees and other definitive documents (collectively, the "Definitive Documents"), as are contemplated by the Commitment Letter or as may be reasonably required by the DIP Lender pursuant to the terms thereof, and the Applicant is hereby authorized and directed to pay and perform all of its indebtedness, interest, fees, liabilities and obligations to the DIP Lender under and pursuant to the Commitment Letter and the Definitive Documents as and when the same become due and are to be performed, notwithstanding any other provision of this Order.

80. THIS COURT ORDERS that the DIP Lender shall be entitled to the benefits of and is hereby granted a charge (the "DIP Lender's Charge") on the Property, which charge shall not exceed the aggregate amount owed to the DIP Lender under the Definitive Documents. The DIP Lender's Charge shall have the priority set out in paragraphs **[32]** and **[34]** hereof.

81. THIS COURT ORDERS that, notwithstanding any other provision of this Order:

(a) the DIP Lender may take such steps from time to time as it may deem necessary or appropriate to file, register, record or perfect the DIP Lender's Charge or any of the Definitive Documents;

(b) upon the occurrence of an event of default under the Definitive Documents or the DIP Lender's Charge, the DIP Lender, upon ■ days notice to the Applicant and the Monitor, may exercise any and all of its rights and remedies against the Applicant or the Property under or pursuant to the Commitment Letter, Definitive Documents and the DIP Lender's Charge, including without limitation, to cease making advances to the Applicant and set off and/or consolidate any amounts owing by the DIP Lender to the Applicant against the obligations of the Applicant to the DIP Lender under the Commitment Letter, the Definitive Documents or the DIP Lender's Charge, to make demand, accelerate payment and give other notices, or to apply to this Court for the appointment of a receiver, receiver and manager or interim receiver, or for a bankruptcy order against the Applicant and for the appointment of a trustee in bankruptcy of the Applicant, and upon the occurrence of an event of default under the terms of the Definitive Documents, the DIP Lender shall be entitled to seize and retain proceeds from the sale of the Property and the cash flow of the Applicant to repay amounts owing to the DIP Lender in accordance with the Definitive Documents and the DIP Lender's Charge, but subject to the priorities as set out in paragraphs **[32]** and **[34]** of this Order; and

(c) the foregoing rights and remedies of the DIP Lender shall be enforceable against any trustee in bankruptcy, interim receiver, receiver or receiver and manager of the Applicant or the Property.

82. THIS COURT ORDERS AND DECLARES that the DIP Lender shall be treated as unaffected in any plan of arrangement or compromise filed by the Applicant under the CCAA, or any proposal filed by the Applicant under the *Bankruptcy and Insolvency Act* of Canada (the "BIA"), with respect to any advances made under the Definitive Documents.

VALIDITY AND PRIORITY OF CHARGES CREATED BY THIS ORDER

83. THIS COURT ORDERS that the priorities of the Directors' Charge, the Administration Charge and the DIP Lender's Charge, as among them, shall be as follows:

First – Administration Charge (to the maximum amount of $■);

Second – DIP Lender's Charge; and

Third – Directors' Charge (to the maximum amount of $■).

84. THIS COURT ORDERS that the filing, registration or perfection of the Directors' Charge, the Administration Charge or the DIP Lender's Charge (collectively, the "Charges") shall not be required, and that the Charges shall be valid and enforceable for all purposes, including as against any right, title or interest filed, registered, recorded or perfected subsequent to the Charges coming into existence, notwithstanding any such failure to file, register, record or perfect.

85. THIS COURT ORDERS that each of the Directors' Charge, the Administration Charge and the DIP Lender's Charge (all as constituted and defined herein) shall constitute a charge on the Property and such Charges shall rank in priority to all other security interests, trusts, liens, charges and encumbrances, statutory or otherwise (collectively, "Encumbrances") in favour of any Person.

86. THIS COURT ORDERS that except as otherwise expressly provided for herein, or as may be approved by this Court, the Applicant shall not grant any Encumbrances over any Property that rank in priority to, or *pari passu* with, any of the Directors' Charge, the Administration Charge or the DIP Lender's Charge, unless the Applicant also obtains the prior written consent of the Monitor, the DIP Lender and the beneficiaries of the Directors' Charge and the Administration Charge, or further Order of this Court.

87. THIS COURT ORDERS that the Directors' Charge, the Administration Charge, the Commitment Letter, the Definitive Documents and the DIP Lender's Charge shall not be rendered invalid or unenforceable and the rights and remedies of the chargees entitled to the benefit of the Charges (collectively, the "Chargees") and/or the DIP Lender thereunder shall not otherwise be limited or impaired in any way by (a) the pendency of these proceedings and the declarations of insolvency made herein; (b) any application(s) for bankruptcy order(s) issued pursuant to BIA, or any bankruptcy order made pursuant to such applications; (c) the filing of any assignments for the general benefit of creditors made pursuant to the BIA; (d) the provisions of any federal or provincial statutes; or (e) any negative covenants, prohibitions

or other similar provisions with respect to borrowings, incurring debt or the creation of Encumbrances, contained in any existing loan documents, lease, sublease, offer to lease or other agreement (collectively, an "Agreement") which binds the Applicant, and notwithstanding any provision to the contrary in any Agreement:

(a) neither the creation of the Charges nor the execution, delivery, perfection, registration or performance of the Commitment Letter or the Definitive Documents shall create or be deemed to constitute a breach by the Applicant of any Agreement to which it is a party;

(b) none of the Chargees shall have any liability to any Person whatsoever as a result of any breach of any Agreement caused by or resulting from the Applicant entering into the Commitment Letter, the creation of the Charges, or the execution, delivery or performance of the Definitive Documents; and

(c) the payments made by the Applicant pursuant to this Order, the Commitment Letter or the Definitive Documents, and the granting of the Charges, do not and will not constitute fraudulent preferences, fraudulent conveyances, oppressive conduct, settlements or other challengeable, voidable or reviewable transactions under any applicable law.

SERVICE AND NOTICE

88. THIS COURT ORDERS that the Applicant shall, within ten (10) business days of the date of entry of this Order, send a copy of this Order to its known creditors, other than employees and creditors to which the Applicant owes less than $■, at their addresses as they appear on the Applicant's records, and shall promptly send a copy of this Order (a) to all parties filing a Notice of Appearance in respect of this Application, and (b) to any other interested Person requesting a copy of this Order, and the Monitor is relieved of its obligation under Section 11(5) of the CCAA to provide similar notice, other than to supervise this process.

89. THIS COURT ORDERS that the Applicant and the Monitor be at liberty to serve this Order, any other materials and orders in these proceedings, any notices or other correspondence, by forwarding true copies thereof by prepaid ordinary mail, courier, personal delivery or electronic transmission to the Applicant's creditors or other interested parties at their respective addresses as last shown on the records of the Applicant and that any such service or notice by courier, personal delivery or electronic transmission shall be deemed to be received on the next business day following the date of forwarding thereof, or if sent by ordinary mail, on the third business day after mailing.

90. THIS COURT ORDERS that the Applicant, the Monitor, and any party who has filed a Notice of Appearance may serve any court materials in these proceedings by e-mailing a PDF or other electronic copy of such materials to counsels' e-mail addresses as recorded on the Service List from time to time, in accordance with the E-filing protocol of the Commercial List to the extent practicable, and the Monitor may post a copy of any or all such materials on its website at [INSERT WEBSITE ADDRESS].

GENERAL

91. THIS COURT ORDERS that the Applicant or the Monitor may from time to time apply to this Court for advice and directions in the discharge of its powers and duties hereunder.

92. THIS COURT ORDERS that nothing in this Order shall prevent the Monitor from acting as an interim receiver, a receiver, a receiver and manager, or a trustee in bankruptcy of the Applicant, the Business or the Property.

93. THIS COURT HEREBY REQUESTS the aid and recognition of any court, tribunal, regulatory or administrative body having jurisdiction in Canada or in the United States, to give effect to this Order and to assist the Applicant, the Monitor and their respective agents in carrying out the terms of this Order. All courts, tribunals, regulatory and administrative bodies are hereby respectfully requested to make such orders and to provide such assistance to the Applicant and to the Monitor, as an officer of this Court, as may be necessary or desirable to give effect to this Order, to grant representative status to the Monitor in any foreign proceeding, or to assist the Applicant and the Monitor and their respective agents in carrying out the terms of this Order.

94. THIS COURT ORDERS that each of the Applicant and the Monitor be at liberty and is hereby authorized and empowered to apply to any court, tribunal, regulatory or administrative body, wherever located, for the recognition of this Order and for assistance in carrying out the terms of this Order.

95. THIS COURT ORDERS that any interested party (including the Applicant and the Monitor) may apply to this Court to vary or amend this Order on not less than seven (7) days' notice to any other party or parties likely to be affected by the order sought or upon such other notice, if any, as this Court may order.

96. THIS COURT ORDERS that this Order and all of its provisions are effective as of 12:01 a.m. Eastern Standard Time on the date of this Order.

APPENDIX 5

THE NEW STANDARD FORM TEMPLATE CCAA FIRST-DAY ORDERS Explanatory Notes for Long Form and Short Form CCAA Orders, Versions dated July 25, 2006

These notes are to be read in conjunction with the new standard form template *Companies' Creditors Arrangement Act* ("CCAA") orders developed by a subcommittee (the "Committee") of the Commercial List Users' Committee of the Ontario Superior Court of Justice (the "Users' Committee"). These notes apply to both the "Short" form of CCAA Initial Order, and the "Long" form, both of which were released by the Committee at the same time. The main differences between the Short and Long forms are noted below.

Introduction

The Committee previously developed a standard form template receivership order, which has been widely used in Ontario and has been adopted in many respects by other Canadian jurisdictions, notably Alberta and British Columbia. Explanatory Notes with respect to the standard form template receivership order are also available on the Ontario Superior Court Commercial List website at "ontariocourts.on.ca/superior court justice/commercial", and provide more detail as to the theory and approach taken by the Committee in developing that standard form order.

The theory and approach behind the CCAA orders is the same, that is, to give the Courts and practitioners a guide for first-day or initial CCAA orders, while recognizing that such orders can and must be tailored to suit the circumstances of the case before the Court.

The Committee and the Users' Committee discussed whether the model orders should specifically take into account the provisions of Bill C-55. Given the current uncertainty as to when Bill C-55 will be proclaimed, and whether the legislation will be subject to amendment before its proclamation, the Committee decided that it did not make sense to prepare the model orders in accordance with Bill C-55 at this time.

The Committee also notes, as it did in the explanatory notes for the standard form template receivership order, that the process of developing standard form template orders is a dynamic one. These standard form orders will be reviewed from time to time (and certainly on the implementation of Bill C-55), to ensure that they keep pace with legislative and practice developments. The Committee invites comments with respect to any of the standard form orders, which comments can be directed to any member of the Committee, as listed at the end of these notes.

Despite the proliferation of cross-border proceedings in recent years, the Committee decided not to include specific clauses for recognition of concurrent proceedings under a foreign statute, such as Chapter 11 of the *U.S. Bankruptcy Code*. Rather, practitioners who seek approval or recognition of a foreign proceeding (and any related court-to-court communication guidelines or protocols) are encouraged to add the necessary provisions to the appropriate form of model order and bring the changes to the attention of the presiding judge.

If it is necessary to have the Order recognized in a foreign jurisdiction, a clause should be added authorizing the Monitor to act as the Applicant's "foreign representative" in any such jurisdiction.

The Committee has also taken care to ensure that the provisions of the standard form template CCAA orders are as consistent as possible with each other, and with similar provisions in the standard form template receivership order. Accordingly, many of the provisions related to service, stays of proceedings, notices, etcetera are identical, or at least similar in many respects – both as between the receivership order and the CCAA orders, and as between the two CCAA orders.

The Committee received numerous comments on the Model Order from representatives of the Office of the Attorney-General (Ontario) and the Department of Justice (collectively, the "Crown") with respect to the impact of the stay of proceedings and restructuring provisions on various aspects of legislative and regulatory authority. In reviewing the comments, the Committee felt that the specific amendments requested by the Crown were not appropriate for a Model Order given that different regulatory regimes and legislative schemes come into play depending on the nature of the Applicant's business. In addition, the Committee felt that most of the concerns expressed by the Crown were addressed by the language included in paragraph 10 (short form) and paragraph 16 (long form) which each create a carve-out from the stay of proceedings with respect to compliance with statutory or regulatory provisions relating to health, safety or the environment. The Committee does suggest, as recommended by the Crown, that parties seeking relief under the CCAA ensure that proper notice of the application is delivered to representatives of the Office of the Attorney-General (Ontario) and Department of Justice (Canada) where it is appropriate to do so. Once the Crown has notice of the proceedings, they may seek specific relief with respect to legislative or regulatory aspects of a particular proceeding if needed.

In an effort to assist the profession, the members of the Committee felt that it would be useful to identify some of the issues that were discussed during the process of creating the standard form template CCAA orders. What follows therefore is a discussion of substantive and other legal issues but in no way reflects any determination of the Committee on any of these issues. In fact, in keeping with the determination that standard form template orders would not resolve substantive issues, the Committee expressly refrained from seeking to resolve issues that ought properly be heard in Court.

The "Short" and "Long" Forms of CCAA Initial Orders

The Committee started with the premise that first-day CCAA orders should be somewhat minimalistic in terms of the substantive rights altered on that first day, especially in cases where little or no notice of the first hearing is given. Initially, the Committee attempted to draft a "lights-on" type of order, of the nature referred to by Justice Blair in *Royal Oak Mines Inc., Re* (1999), 6 C.B.R. (4th) 314 (Ont. Gen. Div. [Commercial List]). However, a consensus quickly developed that some provisions (such as basic DIP financing and a charge in favour or directors and officers) might typically be part of even the shorter form of a first-day order, and accordingly the Committee included these types of provisions in the "Short" form or order. As a result, the "Short" order is in reality not that brief.

The main difference between the two forms of orders is that the "Short" form of CCAA Initial Order does not contain the restructuring powers and some of the corresponding powers and duties of the Monitor found in the "Long" form. These restructuring powers are quite intrusive and alter substantive legal rights; the Committee's view is therefore that in cases where no notice, or short notice, of the initial hearing is given, the "Short" form of order should be sought with a date set for a further hearing to obtain additional substantive relief, which can take place on ample notice to affected parties such as landlords.

Clause by Clause Review of the Standard Form Template CCAA Orders

Parties, Recitals and Service

The Committee assumes that both forms of CCAA orders will be sought on notice to affected parties, if this is possible. Where service is not possible as a result of constraints imposed on public companies, or due to other valid reasons, then the Committee is of the view that the "Short" form of order is the appropriate form to be sought at the first-day hearing. As with the standard form template receivership order, these CCAA orders work on the assumption that the identities and the appearance or non-appearance of parties served with notice of the application are included in the draft order requested, as required by the Ontario *Rules of Civil Procedure*.

Paragraph 3 – Further Hearing / Plan of Arrangement

The Short form of order calls for a further hearing to be held within the initial stay period, and suggests that parties should receive the Applicant's materials and the Monitor's materials no less than five days prior to this 'comeback' hearing.

Since the Long form of order assumes appropriate notice prior to the initial hearing, paragraph 3 of the Long form jumps forward to the Plan of Arrangement phase, by permitting the Applicant to file a Plan.

Debtor in Possession – Paragraphs 4 to 8 (Short order) and 4 to 10 (Long order)

Most of these paragraphs are similar in each of the two CCAA orders. They authorize the Applicant to remain in possession of its assets, to continue its business, to continue the employment of its employees, and to continue and supplement its advisors as necessary in order to move forward in the CCAA process.

The Long form of order contains (in paragraph 5) a "central cash management" system, which might be necessary where the Applicant carries on business in common with other related companies, whether or not they are also Applicants. As noted in this provision, a "central cash management" system may alter substantive rights inasmuch as it may blur the separation of the affairs of various corporate entities. Therefore, it is (a) to be used with caution, (b) where possible, only sought on notice to affected parties, and (c) to be fully described in the affidavit filed in support of the order.

Three paragraphs in each order deal first with permitted payments of liabilities whether incurred *before or after* the making of the initial order, and second with the payment of liabilities incurred only *after* the making of the initial order. The category of permitted payments for pre-filing liabilities is intentionally limited, on the general theory (expressed in paragraph 8 of the Short order and paragraph 10 of the Long order) that all pre-filing payments should be treated equally pending the filing and approval of a Plan – which usually means that payments regarding pre-filing liabilities are suspended until the Plan is approved, and that such payments are then made only in accordance with an approved Plan. These forms of

CCAA orders permit payment of some pre-filing liabilities simply to avoid the administrative issues which would otherwise arise from the halting of payments which relate to 'stub periods' for regular and frequent payments such as wages. The Committee discussed the need to have a clause allowing the payment of pre-filing "critical" supplier accounts, either with a cap or some form of Monitor approval (or both). The Committee decided that the authorization to pay specific pre-filing creditors should be addressed on a case-by-case basis and that it would be appropriate for such a clause to be highlighted to the Court in a blackline to the model order.

Paragraph 9 of the Long form of order deals with the continuation of rental payments related to real property. This provision is not found in the Short form of order because the power to repudiate real property leases is not found in the Short form of order; the Short form of order assumes that all post-filing rent will be paid unless and until the Court permits otherwise.

The Stay – Paragraphs 9 to 15 (Short form) and 15 to 21 (Long Form)

Some background with respect to the evolution of stay provisions may be found in the Explanatory Notes related to the standard form template receivership order.

These provisions are very similar as between the two template CCAA orders. In addition, they are similar as between the template receivership order and the two CCAA orders, except that the CCAA orders also contains a stay of proceedings in favour of officers and directors. This stay is incorporated for three reasons: first, a Plan may compromise the claims against officers and directors; second, the directors and officers are typically protected by a court-ordered charge in a CCAA proceeding; and, third, officers and directors typically continue to play a role in a CCAA proceeding, unlike a receivership, and therefore will require some protection during CCAA proceedings.

It should be noted that there is no specific stay of any person's right to set off pre-filing claims against the Applicant in response to post-filing claims by the Applicant. The standard form template orders permit the filing of notice of security interests and the registration of claims for liens under the provisions of provincial personal property regimes. This seems to accord with the statutes and the most recent case law on these topics. However, lien claimants continue to require the consent of the Applicant and the Monitor or leave of the Court in order to commence actions to enforce lien rights. It remains open to anyone seeking to prohibit setoff or the registration of security or claims for lien, to ask the Court to do so by blacklining the standard form template order and bringing the matter to the attention of the presiding judge.

Some CCAA orders contain a provision supplementary to paragraph 10 of the Short form of Order (paragraph 16 of the Long form), which states that the "rights and remedies hereby stayed shall include all rights and remedies relating to the securities, instruments, debentures, notes or bonds issued by or on behalf of the Applicant". This provision, or a tailored version of it, may often be appropriate. However, the Committee elected not to include it in the standard form CCAA orders because of its breadth and the risk that it would be included in orders as a default, without specific thought being given to its implications.

In some CCAA orders made, there has been a specific clause (referred to as a tolling clause) utilized to seek to suspend the time from running under s. 81.1 of the *Bankruptcy and Insolvency Act* (the "BIA") and thereby to preserve the ability of suppliers of goods to seek to enforce their rights to re-possess their goods at the end of the CCAA process. Some question the usefulness of this provision because, in most cases, the suppliers' rights are compromised in the proceeding or else the goods are sold or consumed before the proceeding ends. In other cases, elaborate clauses have been developed to seek to extend limitation periods that might expire during a Court-ordered stay. It certainly seems fair to ensure that a party facing the expiry of a limitation period, contractual or statutory, who is prevented by a stay from taking the steps required to perfect its rights, should be given an opportunity to take these steps once the stay is lifted. However, this rationale does not fit well with every time period that may be affected by a stay. For example, there is no case law suggesting that a lease of real property ought to be automatically extended if it were otherwise to expire during the course of a stay. The model order likewise does not exempt parties who are subject to an impending expiry of a limitation period from the application of the stay and anyone seeking to enforce a remedy consequent on the lapse of time will continue to require leave of the Court as is the case with all other stakeholders. Accordingly, the standard form template orders simply continue to enjoin the exercise of rights and "suspend" all rights and remedies. The specific effect of any suspension will remain to be dealt with in individual cases either by amendments to the standard form template order or by subsequent proceedings.

There has been some controversy in the development of stay orders concerning the appropriateness and the jurisdiction of the Court to order counter-parties to renew contracts with the debtor. For the purpose of the standard form template orders, the "No Interference with Rights" stay provision prohibits third parties from failing to "honour renewal rights". To the extent anyone wishes to seek to force a renewal in the absence of a contractual renewal right, the matter will have to be brought to the attention of the Court.

Although paragraphs 13 and 14 of the Short form of order, and paragraphs 19 and 20 of the Long form, protect suppliers and others from forced supply in the face of non-payment, these provisions are limited in that they do not necessarily ensure payment for goods or services supplied. Suppliers must be mindful of this, and satisfy themselves that payment from the Applicant is assured once the supply is made.

Paragraph 14 of the Short form of order, and paragraph 20 of the Long form, repeat the concept found in the CCAA that nothing in these orders obligates any person to advance or re-advance monies or extend credit to the Applicant. These paragraphs also provide that nothing in these orders derogates from the rights conferred and obligations imposed by the CCAA. In other words, the mandatory provisions of the CCAA still govern, and any conflicts between these orders and the CCAA will be resolved in favour of the relevant CCAA provision. The Committee opted to use a general non-derogation clause rather than repeat specific provisions in the CCAA (i.e. no prohibition of set-off; stay does not apply to "eligible financial contracts"; etc.). The Committee notes that recently-enacted changes to the BIA and CCAA place limits on the stay of proceedings as it affects aircraft. Reference is made to the *International Interests in Mobile Equipment (aircraft equipment) Act*, S.C. 2005, c. 3.

Directors' and Officers' Indemnification and Charge

These provisions recognize that the Applicant may need to provide directors and officers with some assurances and protections, in order that these people remain to govern the Applicant during the CCAA process. Accordingly, both a limited indemnification and a corresponding charge on the Applicant's property are created. The quantum of this charge (and the other charges) is capped, but will increase if certain obligations (including wages) are not paid. Each order also contains provisions specifying that directors and officers only have recourse to this charge to the extent that they do not have insurance coverage, and provides that insurers are not entitled to be subrogated to or claim the benefit of this charge. Reference is made to the decision of Mr. Justice Ground in *General Publishing Co., Re* (2002), 39 C.B.R. (4th) 216 (Ont. S.C.J.), affirmed (2004), 1 C.B.R. (5th) 202 (Ont. C.A.).

Restructuring Powers (Paragraph 11 – 14, Long form only)

These provisions give the Applicant broad powers to restructure its business, and for this reason these restructuring powers are found only in the Long form of order, and the Committee expects that broad restructuring powers such as this will only be sought on ample notice to affected parties.

Subparagraph 11(b) does not resolve the ongoing debate as to whether employee terminations can only be carried out in accordance with a governing collective agreement. This is an issue which will have to be addressed by the Court, or legislatively with the passage of Bill C-55 or other legislation.

The standard Long form of order has adopted what the Committee believes is a clearer and simpler approach to real property leases. Previous forms of orders sometimes required the payment of rent based on concepts of "occupation", "abandonment", or the "quitting" of leased premises. To avoid confusion and interpretational difficulties, the Committee has adopted the simple approach that the Applicant either delivers a written notice of repudiation to the Landlord (in which case certain events follow), or it does not (in which case the Applicant continues to pay rent).

The standard form CCAA orders do not provide for the payment of percentage rent, merely because the members of the Committee concluded that this level of detail was unnecessary in the template order. More detail in this regard could be inserted into a first-day order, in appropriate circumstances.

Some orders have provided that landlords are exempted from the stay of proceedings, if the Applicant defaults in the performance of its lease terms. The Committee is of the view that this type of 'automatic' exemption was not appropriate, given the potential consequences for the Applicant and the CCAA proceedings, and that therefore the landlord, like most other parties, should only be exempted from the stay of proceedings by the consent of the Applicant and the Monitor or with leave of the Court.

Paragraph 14 of the Long form of CCAA order provides that the Applicant is permitted to dispose of property located at leased premises without interference of any kind from landlords, and "notwithstanding the terms of any leases". This language clearly alters the *status quo ante* in favour of the Applicant, and therefore (as noted above), it is assumed that this provision would only be sought on notice to affected parties – in this case landlords. The Committee was divided as to whether this provision is appropriate, and notes that there may be quite distinct concerns arising, depending on whether the Applicant is involved in retail businesses (where "use" clauses are common) or non-retail businesses. While the language referred to above may assist in a restructuring, it also overrides landlord rights. The position of commercial landlords is that this paragraph should specifically direct the Applicant to abide by the terms of all leases, including in the context of a sale of assets.

Paragraph 14 of the Long form of CCAA order also does not deal with any "Agent" (liquidator) that might be appointed. It is expected that any Agency Agreement would be subject to approval by the Court, and, if so approved, provisions dealing with the "Agent" would be inserted into an order at that time.

The standard form template CCAA orders do not contain a "PIPEDA" clause such as the provision found at paragraph 14 of the standard form template receivership order. The Long form of the model CCAA order does allow the Applicant to "pursue . . . offers for material parts of its Business or Property". If the Applicant believes that any such sale might progress to the point where personal information of the type protected by the Canada *Personal Information Protection and Electronic Documents Act* will be made available to potential buyers, then a PIPEDA clause could be added to the initial CCAA order.

Paragraph 16 – Appointment of Monitor

The Monitor's duties and powers are somewhat more enlarged in the Long form of order since it, unlike the Short form or order, contains restructuring powers, and the power to present a Plan and conduct creditors' meetings.

The Monitor in these standard form template orders is a 'monitor' in the true sense. It has full rights to information but does not, by way of example, have the power to take possession or control of the Applicant's business. For this reason, some provisions found in the standard form receivership order, such as protection from environmental liabilities, and protection from employee-related liabilities, are not found in the standard form template CCAA orders, as it is not expected that the Monitor will either 'occupy' the Applicant's business or premises, or 'employ' the Applicant's employees.

The Committee accepted the suggestion of the Ontario Bar Association, Insolvency Section that the consent of the Monitor, in addition to the consent of the Applicant, should generally be required when a person is being exempted from a stay of proceedings under the order. This will help to keep track of what exemptions are given, and perhaps prevent inconsistencies or favouritism, recognizing that the Monitor has the right to seek directions from the Court if it has any concerns about giving its consent to a particular request.

The Committee did not include provisions in these standard form orders that would mandate the collection and distribution of information by the Monitor. Paragraph 29 of the Long form of order provides only that the Monitor shall provide information provided to it by the Applicant, and shall not distribute information which the Applicant has advised is confidential, unless otherwise directed by the Court. The Monitor is also relieved of any liability with respect to the information disseminated by it in accordance with this paragraph. The Committee recognizes that this approach to the collection and distribution of information may be too restrictive in some situations, and that regular financial reporting and/or additional disclosure may be quite appropriate in some cases.

The standard form template CCAA orders contemplate that the Monitor's fees, and those of its counsel, are subject to approval by the Court. As with other provisions of the standard form template CCAA orders, this may be altered in appropriate cases.

The Orders provide that the Monitor, along with its counsel and counsel to the Applicants, is granted a charge to secure its fees and disbursements.

DIP Financing

The standard form template CCAA orders each contain relatively straightforward DIP financing provisions, since DIP financing seems to be very common in most CCAA filings, and is clearly essential in many. These provisions allow DIP financing to a pre-determined maximum amount, and also envision the attachment of a Commitment Letter, so that the Court and the affected parties can turn their minds to the details of the proposed DIP financing. While both forms of order contemplate a cap on the amount of DIP funding that is permitted, it is anticipated that the cap employed for the Short form of order will be the minimum amount needed for the first 30-day period to "keep the lights on", with a more comprehensive amount being requested on the "comeback" hearing.

These orders also exempt the DIP lender from the stay of proceedings, in the event of a default by the Applicant under the DIP lending documents, but provide that notice must be given to both the Applicant and the Monitor before the DIP lender exercises its rights and remedies. The Committee believes that the notice requirement gave the Applicant sufficient protection as it would allow the Applicant to seek specific relief with respect to the DIP Lender if so warranted. Finally, these orders provide that the DIP lender cannot be affected by the Plan. This is common in CCAA orders made to date.

The standard form CCAA orders do not attempt to spell out what must be in the "Definitive Documents", but the terms of these "Definitive Documents", once available, must clearly be reviewed by stakeholders to ensure that their respective interests are protected. Among other things, these Definitive Documents may propose altering the rights of lenders, equipment lessors, and other secured creditors, by securing pre-filing advances with the DIP Lender's Charge or by otherwise altering priorities. The appropriateness of the Definitive Documents should be judged in the context of the specific facts before the Court.

Validity and Priority of Charges

These provisions are typical in the sense that they do not require the Court-ordered charges to be registered under any system of registration such as the Ontario *Personal Property Security Act*.

The ranking of the Court-ordered charges is also spelled out in these standard form orders. The ranking set out in the model orders is not meant to be determinative, but rather reflects the most common ranking found in orders to date. This ranking, of course, may be subject to negotiation, and should be tailored to the circumstances of the case before the Court. Similarly, the quantum of each charge may be negotiated and be either unlimited or limited to a maximum amount.

It should be noted that the charges created by these orders is declared to "rank in priority to all other security interests, trusts, liens, charges and encumbrances, statutory or otherwise". The Committee is of the view that it was desirable that the template orders grant as broad a charge as was possible, and with as high a priority as possible. The Committee recognizes, however, that the 'super-priority' of the charges created may be limited by other variables, such as lack of notice to certain secured or statutory creditors over whom priority is being asserted, and by specific statutory terms which do not permit the granting of a priority charge over certain statutory-based charges.

Notice of CCAA proceedings, and General Provisions

The provisions in these standard form template CCAA orders are fairly typical, and require that the Applicant send a copy of the Initial Order to most of its creditors within 10 business days of the entry of the order. These provisions also allow service by e-mail in accordance with the Commercial List's E-filing protocol, and for the posting of materials on the Monitor's website, each now a common feature of CCAA proceedings.

These orders give the Monitor broad powers to seek recognition in domestic or foreign jurisdictions, and request the aid of all courts, tribunals, regulatory and administrative bodies.

Finally, these orders provide that they are each effective as of 12:01 a.m. Eastern Standard Time, on the date on which the order is made.

Concluding Notes

It is hoped that the use of templates will simplify cases by providing a well-understood starting point and by focusing counsel and the Court upon the rationales for customizations required in the particular circumstances of each case before the Court. This area is not a simple one and many of the clauses which are now seen as "standard" have long histories involving valid arguments pro and con.

Tony Reyes, Ogilvy Renault LLP, and
Scott Bomhof, Torys LLP
for: Standard Form Template Order Sub-committee:
Scott Bomhof, Torys LLP (Co-Chair)
Gus Camelino, McLean & Kerr LLP
Paul Casey, Deloitte & Touche LLP
Richard Conway, Torys LLP
Richard Howell, Clark, Farb, Fiksel
Alex MacFarlance, McMillan Binch Mendelsohn LLP
Murray McDonald, Ernst & Young Inc.
Fred Myers, Goodmans LLP
A. John Page, A. John Page & Associates Inc.
Elizabeth Pillon, Stikeman Elliott LLP
Tony Reyes, Ogilvy Renault LLP (Co-Chair)
Derrick Tay, Ogilvy Renault LLP

The Sub-committee would like to acknowledge the valuable input and consultation provided by the following individuals or organizations:

Ontario Association of Insolvency and Restructuring Professionals

The Honourable Mr. James M. Farley

The Honourable Mr. Justice J. Ground

The Honourable Mr. Justice Geoffrey Morawetz

Bruce E. Leonard, Cassels Brock & Blackwell LLP

Ontario Bar Association, Insolvency Section

Office of the Attorney-General (Ontario)

Department of Justice (Canada)

Commercial List Users' Committee of the Ontario Superior Court of Justice

APPENDIX 6

QUÉBEC SUPERIOR COURT MODEL INITIAL ORDER

Short Form January 2005

CANADA

PROVINCE OF QUEBEC
DISTRICT OF MONTREAL

SUPERIOR COURT
Commercial Division

File: No: 500-11-●

Montreal, ●, 200●

Present: The Honourable ●,

j.s.c.

IN THE MATTER OF THE *COMPANIES' CREDITORS ARRANGEMENT ACT,* R.S.C. 1985, c. C-36, AS AMENDED:

●
Petitioner
And

●
Monitor

INITIAL ORDER

SEEING ●'s petition for an initial order pursuant to Sections 4, 5 and 11 of the Companies' Creditors Arrangement Act, R.S.C. 1985, C-36, as amended (the "*CCAA*") and the exhibits, and the affidavit of ● filed in support thereof (the "Petition"), the consent of ● to act as monitor (the "Monitor") and the submissions of counsel for ●;

GIVEN the provisions of the *CCAA;*

WHEREFORE, THE COURT:

1. GRANTS the Petition.

2. ISSUES an order pursuant to Sections 4, 5 and 11 of the *CCAA* (the "Order"), divided under the following headings:

   - Service
   - Application of the *CCAA*
   - Effective Time
   - Plan of Arrangement
   - Stay of Proceedings against the Petitioner, the Property, the Directors or others
   - Possession of Property and Carrying on Business
   - Restructuring
   - Directors Indemnification and Charge
   - Powers of the Monitor
   - Priorities and General Provisions Relating to *CCAA* Charges
   - General

Service

3. EXEMPTS ● (the "Petitioner") from having to serve the Petition and from any notice of presentation.

Application of the *CCAA*

4. DECLARES that Petitioner is a debtor company to which the *CCAA* applies.

Effective time

5. DECLARES that from immediately after midnight (Montreal time) on the day prior to the Order (the "Effective Time") to the time of the granting of the Order, any act or action taken or notice given by any Person in respect of Petitioner, the Directors or the Property (as those terms are defined hereinafter), are deemed not to have been taken or given, as the case may be, to the extent such act, action or notice would otherwise be stayed after the granting of the Order.

Plan of Arrangement

6. ORDERS that Petitioner shall file with this Court and submit to its creditors one or more plans of compromise or arrangement under the *CCAA* (collectively, the "Plan") between, among others, Petitioner and one or more classes of its creditors as Petitioner may deem appropriate, on or before the Stay Termination Date (as defined hereinafter) or such other time or times as may be allowed by this Court.

Stay of Proceedings against the Petitioner, the Property, the Directors or others

7. ORDERS that, until and including ●, or such later date as the Court may order (the "Stay Termination Date", the period from the date of the Order to the Stay Termination Date being referred to as the "Stay Period"), no right, legal or conventional, may be exercised and no proceeding, at law or under a contract, by reason of this Order or

otherwise, however and wherever taken (collectively the "Proceedings") may be commenced or proceeded with by anyone, whether a person, firm, partnership, corporation, stock exchange, government, administration or entity exercising executive, legislative, judicial, regulatory or administrative functions (collectively, "Persons" and, individually, a "Person") against or in respect of Petitioner, or any of the present or future property, assets, rights and undertakings of Petitioner, of any nature and in any location, whether held directly or indirectly by Petitioner, in any capacity whatsoever, or held by others for Petitioner (collectively, the "Property"), and all Proceedings already commenced against Petitioner or any of the Property, are stayed and suspended until the Court authorizes the continuation thereof, the whole subject to the provisions of the *CCAA*.

8. ORDERS that, without limiting the generality of the foregoing, during the Stay Period, all Persons having agreements, contracts or arrangements with Petitioner or in connection with any of the Property, whether written or oral, for any subject or purpose:

   a) are restrained from accelerating, terminating, cancelling, suspending, refusing to modify or extend on reasonable terms such agreements, contracts or arrangements or the rights of Petitioner or any other Person thereunder;

   b) are restrained from modifying, suspending or otherwise interfering with the supply of any goods, services, or other benefits by or to such Person thereunder (including, without limitation, any directors' and officers' insurance, any telephone numbers, any form of telecommunications service, any oil, gas, electricity or other utility supply); and

   c) shall continue to perform and observe the terms and conditions contained in such agreements, contracts or arrangements, so long as Petitioner pays the prices or charges for such goods and services received after the date of the Order as such prices or charges become due in accordance with the law or as may be hereafter negotiated (other than deposits whether by way of cash, letter of credit or guarantee, stand-by fees or similar items which Petitioner shall not be required to pay or grant), unless the prior written consent of Petitioner and the Monitor is obtained or the leave of this Court is granted;

9. ORDERS that, without limiting the generality of the foregoing and subject to Section 18.1 of the *CCAA*, if applicable, cash or cash equivalents placed on deposit by Petitioner with any Person during the Stay Period, whether in an operating account or otherwise for itself or for another entity, shall not be applied by such Person in reduction or repayment of amounts owing to such Person as of the date of the Order or due on or before the expiry of the Stay Period or in satisfaction of any interest or charges accruing in respect thereof; however, this provision shall not prevent any financial institution from: (i) reimbursing itself for the amount of any cheques drawn by Petitioner and properly honoured by such institution, or (ii) holding the amount of any cheques or other instruments deposited into Petitioner's account until those cheques or other instruments have been honoured by the financial institution on which they have been drawn.

10. ORDERS that, notwithstanding the foregoing, any Person who provided any kind of letter of credit, bond or guarantee (the "Issuing Party") at the request of Petitioner shall be required to continue honouring any and all such letters, bonds and guarantees, issued on or before the date of the Order; however, the Issuing Party shall be entitled, where

applicable, to retain the bills of lading or shipping or other documents relating thereto until paid therefore.

11. DECLARES that, to the extent any rights, obligations, or time or limitation periods, including, without limitation, to file grievances, relating to Petitioner or any of the Property may expire, other than the term of any lease of real property, the term of such rights or obligations, or time or limitation periods shall hereby be deemed to be extended by a period equal to the Stay Period. Without limitation to the foregoing, in the event that Petitioner becomes bankrupt or a receiver within the meaning of paragraph 243(2) of the Bankruptcy and Insolvency Act (Canada) (the "BIA") is appointed in respect of Petitioner, the period between the date of the Order and the day on which the Stay Period ends shall not be calculated in respect of Petitioner in determining the 30-day periods referred to in Sections 81.1 and 81.2 of the *BIA*.

12. ORDERS that no Person may commence, proceed with or enforce any Proceedings against any former, present or future director or officer of Petitioner or any person that, by applicable legislation, is treated as a director of Petitioner or that will manage in the future the business and affairs of Petitioner (each, a "Director", and collectively the "Directors") in respect of any claim against such Director that arose before this Order was issued and that relates to obligations of Petitioner for which such Director is or is alleged to be liable (as provided under Section 5.1 of the *CCAA*) until further order of this Court or until the Plan, if one is filed, is refused by the creditors or is not sanctioned by the Court.

13. ORDERS that no Person shall commence, proceed with or enforce any Proceedings against any of the Directors, officers, employees, legal counsel or financial advisers of Petitioner, or the Monitor, for or in respect of the Restructuring (as defined hereinafter) or the formulation and implementation of the Plan without first obtaining leave of this Court, upon seven days written notice to Petitioner's ad litem counsel and to all those referred to in this paragraph whom it is proposed be named in such Proceedings.

Possession of Property and Carrying on Business

14. ORDERS that, subject to the terms of the Order, Petitioner shall remain in possession of the Property until further order in these proceedings.

15. ORDERS that Petitioner shall continue to carry on its business and financial affairs in a manner consistent with the commercially reasonable preservation thereof.

Restructuring

16. DECLARES that, to facilitate the orderly restructuring of its business and financial affairs (the "Restructuring"), Petitioner shall have the right, subject to approval of the Monitor or further order of the Court, to:

    a) permanently or temporarily cease, downsize or shut down any of its operations or locations as it deems appropriate and make provision for the consequences thereof in the Plan;

    b) pursue all avenues to market and sell, subject to subparagraph (c), the Property, in whole or part;

c) convey, transfer, assign, lease, or in any other manner dispose of the Property, in whole or in part, provided that the price in each case does not exceed $■ or $■ in the aggregate;

d) terminate the employment of such of its employees or temporarily or permanently lay off such of its employees as it deems appropriate and, to the extent any amounts in lieu of notice, termination or severance pay or other amounts in respect thereof are not paid in the ordinary course, make provision for any consequences thereof in the Plan, as Petitioner may determine;

e) subject to paragraphs 18 and 19 hereof, vacate or abandon any leased real property or repudiate any lease and ancillary agreements related to any leased premises as it deems appropriate, provided that Petitioner gives the relevant landlord at least seven days prior written notice, on such terms as may be agreed between Petitioner and such landlord, or failing such agreement, to make provision for any consequences thereof in the Plan; and

f) repudiate such of its agreements, contracts or arrangements of any nature whatsoever, whether oral or written, as it deems appropriate, on such terms as may be agreed between Petitioner and the relevant party, or failing such agreement, to make provision for the consequences thereof in the Plan and to negotiate any amended or new agreements or arrangements.

17. DECLARES that, in order to facilitate the Restructuring, Petitioner may, subject to approval of the Monitor:

a) settle claims of customers and suppliers that are in dispute; and

b) establish a plan for the retention of key employees and the making of retention payments or bonuses in connection therewith.

18. DECLARES that, if leased premises are vacated or abandoned by Petitioner pursuant to subparagraph 16 e), the landlord may take possession of any such leased premises without waiver of, or prejudice to, any claims or rights of the landlord against Petitioner, provided the landlord mitigates its damages, if any, and re-leases any such leased premises to third parties on such terms as any such landlord may determine.

19. ORDERS THAT Petitioner shall provide to any relevant landlord notice of Petitioner's intention to remove any fixtures or leasehold improvements at least seven days in advance. If Petitioner has already vacated the leased premises, it shall not be considered to be in occupation of such location pending the resolution of any dispute.

20. DECLARES that, pursuant to sub-paragraph 7(3)(c) of the Personal Information Protection and Electronic Documents Act, S.C. 2000, c.5, Petitioner is permitted, in the course of these proceedings, to disclose personal information of identifiable individuals in its possession or control to stakeholders or prospective investors, financiers, buyers or strategic partners and to its advisers (individually, a "Third Party"), but only to the extent desirable or required to negotiate and complete the Restructuring or the preparation and implementation of the Plan or a transaction for that purpose, provided that the Persons to whom such personal information is disclosed enter into confidentiality agreements with Petitioner binding them to maintain and protect the privacy of such information and to limit the use of such information to the extent necessary to complete the transaction or Restructuring then under negotiation. Upon the completion of the

use of personal information for the limited purpose set out herein, the personal information shall be returned to Petitioner or destroyed. In the event that a Third Party acquires personal information as part of the Restructuring or the preparation and implementation of the Plan or a transaction in furtherance thereof, such Third Party may continue to use the personal information in a manner which is in all respects identical to the prior use thereof by Petitioner.

Directors Indemnification and Charge

21. ORDERS that, in addition to any existing indemnities, Petitioner shall indemnify each of the Directors from and against the following (collectively, "D&O Claims"):

    a) all costs (including, without limitation, full defence costs), charges, expenses, claims, liabilities and obligations, of any nature whatsoever, which may arise on or after the date of the Order (including, without limitation, an amount paid to settle an action or a judgment in a civil, criminal, administrative or investigative action or proceeding to which a Director may be made a party), provided that any such liability relates to such Director in that capacity, and, provided that such Director (i) acted honestly and in good faith in the best interests of Petitioner and (ii) in the case of a criminal or administrative action or proceeding in which such Director would be liable to a monetary penalty, such Director had reasonable grounds for believing his or her conduct was lawful, except if such Director has actively breached any fiduciary duties or has been grossly negligent or guilty of wilful misconduct; and

    b) all costs, charges, expenses, claims, liabilities and obligations relating to the failure of Petitioner to make any payments or to pay amounts in respect of employee or former employee entitlements to wages, vacation pay, termination pay, severance pay, pension or other benefits, or any other amount for services performed on or after the date of the Order and that such Directors sustain, by reason of their association with Petitioner as a Director, except to the extent that they have actively breached any fiduciary duties or have been grossly negligent or guilty of wilful misconduct.

    The foregoing shall not constitute a contract of insurance or other valid and collectible insurance, as such term may be used in any existing policy of insurance issued in favour of Petitioner or any of the Directors.

22. DECLARES that, as security for the obligation of Petitioner to indemnify the Directors pursuant to paragraph 21 hereof, the Directors are hereby granted a hypothec on, mortgage of, lien on and security interest in the Property to the extent of the aggregate amount of $● (the "D&O Charge"), having the priority established by paragraphs 30 and 31 hereof. Such D&O Charge shall not constitute or form a trust. Such D&O Charge, notwithstanding any language in any applicable policy of insurance to the contrary, shall only apply to the extent that the Directors do not have coverage under any directors' and officers' insurance, which shall not be excess insurance to the D&O Charge. In respect of any D&O Claim against any of the Directors (collectively, the "Respondent Directors"), if such Respondent Directors do not receive confirmation from the applicable insurer within 21 days of delivery of notice of the D&O Claim to the applicable insurer, confirming that the applicable insurer will provide coverage for and indemnify the Respondent Directors, then, without prejudice to the subrogation rights hereinafter referred to, Petitioner shall pay the amount of the D&O Claim upon

expiry. Failing such payment, the Respondent Directors may enforce the D&O Charge provided that the Respondent Directors shall reimburse Petitioner to the extent that they subsequently receive insurance benefits for the D&O Claim paid by Petitioner, and provided further that Petitioner shall, upon payment, be subrogated to the rights of the Respondent Directors to recover payment from the applicable insurer as if no such payment had been made.

Powers of the Monitor

23. ORDERS that ● is hereby appointed to monitor the business and financial affairs of Petitioner as an officer of this Court (the "Monitor") and that the Monitor shall, in addition to the duties and functions referred to in Section 11.7 of the *CCAA*:

a) send notice of the Order, within 10 days, to every known creditor of Petitioner having a claim of more than $250 against it, advising that such creditor may obtain a copy of the Order on the internet at the website of the Monitor (the "Website") or, failing that, from the Monitor and the Monitor shall so provide it. Such notice shall be sufficient in accordance with Subsection 11(5) of the *CCAA*;

b) assist Petitioner, to the extent required by Petitioner, in dealing with its creditors and other interested Persons during the Stay Period;

c) assist Petitioner, to the extent required by Petitioner, with the preparation of its cash flow projections and any other projections or reports and the development, negotiation and implementation of the Plan;

d) advise and assist Petitioner, to the extent required by Petitioner, to review Petitioner's business and assess opportunities for cost reduction, revenue enhancement and operating efficiencies;

e) assist Petitioner, to the extent required by Petitioner, with the Restructuring and in its negotiations with its creditors and other interested Persons and with the holding and administering of any meetings held to consider the Plan;

f) report to the Court on the state of the business and financial affairs of Petitioner or developments in these proceedings or any related proceedings within the time limits set forth in the *CCAA* and at such time as considered appropriate by the Monitor or as the Court may order;

g) report to this Court and interested parties, including but not limited to creditors affected by the Plan, with respect to the Monitor's assessment of, and recommendations with respect to, the Plan;

h) retain and employ such agents, advisers and other assistants as are reasonably necessary for the purpose of carrying out the terms of the Order, including, without limitation, one or more entities related to or affiliated with the Monitor;

i) engage legal counsel to the extent the Monitor considers necessary in connection with the exercise of its powers or the discharge of its obligations in these proceedings and any related proceeding, under the Order or under the *CCAA*;

j) may act as a "foreign representative" of Petitioner in any proceedings outside of Canada;

k) may give any consent or approval as are contemplated by the Order; and

l) perform such other duties as are required by the Order, the *CCAA* or this Court from time to time.

The Monitor shall not otherwise interfere with the business and financial affairs carried on by Petitioner, and the Monitor is not empowered to take possession of the Property nor to manage any of the business and financial affairs of Petitioner.

24. ORDERS that Petitioner and its directors, officers, employees and agents, accountants, auditors and all other Persons having notice of the Order shall forthwith provide the Monitor with unrestricted access to all of the Property, including, without limitation, the premises, books, records, data, including data in electronic form, and all other documents of Petitioner in connection with the Monitor's duties and responsibilities hereunder.

25. DECLARES that the Monitor may provide creditors and other relevant stakeholders of Petitioner with information in response to requests made by them in writing addressed to the Monitor and copied to Petitioner's counsel. The Monitor shall not have any duties or liabilities in respect of such information disseminated by it pursuant to the provisions of the Order or the *CCAA*, other than as provided in paragraph 27 hereof. In the case of information that the Monitor has been advised by Petitioner is confidential, proprietary or competitive, the Monitor shall not provide such information to any Person without the consent of Petitioner unless otherwise directed by this Court.

26. DECLARES that the Monitor shall not be, nor be deemed to be, an employer or a successor employer of the employees of Petitioner or a related employer in respect of Petitioner within the meaning of any federal, provincial or municipal legislation governing employment, labour relations, pay equity, employment equity, human rights, health and safety or pensions or any other statute, regulation or rule of law or equity for any similar purpose and, further, that the Monitor shall not be, nor be deemed to be, in occupation, possession, charge, management or control of the Property or business and financial affairs of Petitioner pursuant to any federal, provincial or municipal legislation, statute, regulation or rule of law or equity which imposes liability on the basis of such status, including, without limitation, the *Environment Quality Act* (Québec), the *Canadian Environmental Protection Act*, 1999 or the *Act Respecting Occupational Health and Safety* (Québec) or similar other federal or provincial legislation.

27. DECLARES that, in addition to the rights and protections afforded to the Monitor by the *CCAA*, the Order or its status as an officer of the Court, the Monitor shall not incur any liability or obligation as a result of its appointment and the fulfilment of its duties or the provisions of the Order, save and except any liability or obligation arising from the gross negligence or wilful misconduct, and no action or other proceedings shall be commenced against the Monitor relating to its appointment, its conduct as Monitor or the carrying out the provisions of any order of this Court, except with prior leave of this Court, on at least seven days notice to the Monitor and its counsel. The entities related to or affiliated with the Monitor referred to in subparagraph 23.h) hereof shall also be entitled to the protection, benefits and privileges afforded to the Monitor pursuant to this paragraph.

28. ORDERS that Petitioner shall pay the fees and disbursements of the Monitor, the Monitor's legal counsel, Petitioner's legal counsel and other advisers, incurred in connection with or with respect to the Restructuring, whether incurred before or after

the Order, and shall provide each with a reasonable retainer in advance on account of such fees and disbursements, if so requested.

29. DECLARES that the Monitor, the Monitor's legal counsel, the Petitioner's legal counsel and other advisers, as security for the professional fees and disbursements incurred both before and after the making of the Order in respect of these proceedings, the Plan and the Restructuring, in addition to the retainers referred to paragraph 28 hereof, be entitled to the benefit of and are hereby granted a hypothec on, mortgage of , lien on, and security interest in the Property to the extent of the aggregate amount of $● (the "Administration Charge"), having the priority established by paragraphs 30 and 31 hereof.

Priorities and General Provisions Relating to *CCAA* Charges

30. DECLARES that the priorities of the Administration Charge and D&O Charge (collectively, the "*CCAA* Charges"), as between them with respect to any Property to which they apply, shall be as follows:

    first, the Administration Charge;
    second, the D&O Charge; and
    third, ●.

31. DECLARES that each of the *CCAA* Charges shall rank in priority to any and all other hypothecs, mortgages, liens, security interests, priorities, conditional sale agreements, financial leases, charges, encumbrances or security of whatever nature or kind (collectively, "Encumbrances") affecting any of the Property.

32. ORDERS that, except as otherwise expressly provided for herein, Petitioner shall not grant any Encumbrances in or against any Property that rank in priority to, or pari passu with, any of the *CCAA* Charges unless Petitioner obtain the prior written consent of the Monitor and the prior approval of the Court.

33. DECLARES that each of the *CCAA* Charges shall attach, as of the Effective Time of the Order, to all present and future Property of Petitioner, notwithstanding any requirement for the consent of any party to any such charge or to comply with any condition precedent.

34. DECLARES that the *CCAA* Charges and the rights and remedies of the beneficiaries of such Charges, as applicable, shall be valid and enforceable and shall not otherwise be limited or impaired in any way by: (i) these proceedings and the declaration of insolvency made herein; (ii) any petition for a receiving order filed pursuant to the *BIA* in respect of Petitioner or any receiving order made pursuant to any such petition or any assignment in bankruptcy made or deemed to be made in respect of Petitioner; or (iii) any negative covenants, prohibitions or other similar provisions with respect to borrowings, incurring debt or the creation of Encumbrances, contained in any agreement, lease, sub-lease, offer to lease or other arrangement which binds Petitioner (a "Third Party Agreement"), and notwithstanding any provision to the contrary in any Third Party Agreement:

    a) the creation of any of the *CCAA* Charges shall not create or be deemed to constitute a breach by Petitioner of any Third Party Agreement to which it is a party; and

b) any of the beneficiaries of the *CCAA* Charges shall not have liability to any Person whatsoever as a result of any breach of any Third Party Agreement caused by or resulting from the creation of the *CCAA* Charges.

35. DECLARES that notwithstanding: (i) these proceedings and any declaration of insolvency made herein, (ii) any petition for a receiving order filed pursuant to the *BIA* in respect of Petitioner and any receiving order allowing such petition or any assignment in bankruptcy made or deemed to be made in respect of Petitioner, and (iii) the provisions of any federal or provincial statute, the payments or disposition of Property made by Petitioner pursuant to the Order and the granting of the *CCAA* Charges, do not and will not constitute settlements, fraudulent preferences, fraudulent conveyances or other challengeable or reviewable transactions or conduct meriting an oppression remedy under any applicable law.

36. DECLARES that the *CCAA* Charges shall be valid and enforceable as against all Property of Petitioner and against all Persons, including, without limitation, any trustee in bankruptcy, receiver, receiver and manager or interim receiver of Petitioner, for all purposes.

General

37. DECLARES that the Order and any proceeding or affidavit leading to the Order, shall not, in and of themselves, constitute a default or failure to comply by Petitioner under any statute, regulation, licence, permit, contract, permission, covenant, agreement, undertaking or other written document or requirement.

38. DECLARES that, except as otherwise specified herein, Petitioner is at liberty to serve any notice, proof of claim form, proxy, circular or other document in connection with these proceedings by forwarding copies by prepaid ordinary mail, courier, personal delivery or electronic transmission to Persons or other appropriate parties at their respective given addresses as last shown on the records of Petitioner and that any such service shall be deemed to be received on the date of delivery if by personal delivery or electronic transmission, on the following business day if delivered by courier, or three business days after mailing if by ordinary mail.

39. DECLARES that Petitioner may serve any court materials in these proceedings on all represented parties electronically, by emailing a PDF or other electronic copy of such materials to counsels' email addresses, provided that Petitioner shall deliver "hard copies" of such materials upon request to any party as soon as practicable thereafter.

40. DECLARES that any party in these proceedings, other than Petitioner, may serve any court materials electronically, by emailing a PDF or other electronic copy of all materials to counsels' email addresses, provided that such party shall deliver both PDF or other electronic copies and "hard copies" of all materials to counsel to Petitioner and the Monitor and to any other party requesting same.

41. DECLARES that, unless otherwise provided herein or ordered by this Court, no document, order or other material need be served on any Person in respect of these proceedings, unless such Person has served a Notice of Appearance on the solicitors for Petitioner and the Monitor and has filed such notice with this Court.

42. DECLARES that Petitioner or the Monitor may, from time to time, apply to this Court for directions concerning the exercise of their respective powers, duties and rights hereunder or in respect of the proper execution of the Order on notice only to each other.

43. DECLARES that any interested Person may apply to this Court to vary or rescind the Order or seek other relief upon seven days notice to Petitioner, the Monitor and to any other party likely to be affected by the order sought or upon such other notice, if any, as this Court may order.

44. DECLARES that the Order and all other orders in these proceedings shall have full force and effect in all provinces and territories in Canada.

45. DECLARES that the Monitor, with the prior consent of Petitioner, shall be authorized to apply as it may consider necessary or desirable, with or without notice, to any other court or administrative body, whether in Canada, the United States of America or elsewhere, for orders which aid and complement the Order and any subsequent orders of this Court and, without limitation to the foregoing, an order under section 304 of the U.S. Bankruptcy Code, for which the Monitor shall be the foreign representative of Petitioner. All courts and administrative bodies of all such jurisdictions are hereby respectively requested to make such orders and to provide such assistance to the Monitor as may be deemed necessary or appropriate for that purpose.

46. REQUESTS the aid and recognition of any Court or administrative body in any Province of Canada and any Canadian federal court or administrative body and any federal or state court or administrative body in the United States of America and any court or administrative body elsewhere, to act in aid of and to be complementary to this Court in carrying out the terms of the Order.

47. ORDERS the provisional execution of the Order notwithstanding any appeal and without the necessity of furnishing any security.

________ , ____ , 20 ______

____

Honourable ____

APPENDIX 7

BC MODEL CCAA INITIAL ORDER – VERSION #1 dated August 8, 2006

No. __________________
Vancouver Registry

IN THE SUPREME COURT OF BRITISH COLUMBIA

IN THE MATTER OF THE *COMPANIES' CREDITORS ARRANGEMENT ACT*, R.S.C. 1985, c. C-36

AND

IN THE MATTER OF THE [*CANADA BUSINESS CORPORATIONS ACT* or applicable Provincial statute]

AND

IN THE MATTER OF [Petitioner(s)]

PETITIONER(S)

<u>O R D E R</u>

BEFORE THE HONOURABLE	)	______________, THE ____ DAY
	)	
__________________________	)	OF __________________, 200 __

THE APPLICATION of the Petitioner coming on for hearing *ex parte* at Vancouver, British Columbia, on the _______ day of _____________, 200 __ (the "Filing Date"); AND ON HEARING ______________, counsel for the Petitioner and other counsel as listed on Schedule "A" hereto; AND UPON READING the material filed, including the Affidavit #1 of ____________ sworn _____________, 200 _____; AND pursuant to the *Companies' Creditors Arrangement Act*, R.S.C. 1985 c. C-36 (the "CCAA"), Rules 3, 10, 12, 13(1), 13(6), 14 and 44 of the Rules of Court and the inherent jurisdiction of this Honourable Court:

JURISDICTION

1. THIS COURT ORDERS AND DECLARES that the Petitioner is a company to which the CCAA applies.

PETITION HEARING

2. THIS COURT ORDERS that the hearing of the Petition in this proceeding be held at the Courthouse at 800 Smithe Street, Vancouver, British Columbia at _____ a.m. on ___

, the ________ day of ______________ , 200 ___, provided that the service referred to in paragraph 44 of this Order occur no later than ______________ , 200 ___ .

3. THIS COURT ORDERS that all of the relief provided for in the subsequent paragraphs of this Order is granted to the Petitioner on an interim basis only, and that the relief made in the subsequent paragraphs will expire at 11:59 p.m. (local Vancouver time) on ___ , 200 ___ , unless extended by this Court at the hearing of the Petition which will occur on that date.

POSSESSION OF PROPERTY AND OPERATIONS

4. THIS COURT ORDERS that, subject to this Order and any further Order of this Court, the Petitioner shall remain in possession and control of its current and future assets, undertakings and properties of every nature and kind whatsoever, and wherever situate including all proceeds thereof (the "Property"), and continue to carry on its business in the ordinary course and in a manner consistent with the preservation of its business (the "Business") and Property. The Petitioner shall be authorized and empowered to continue to retain and employ the employees, consultants, agents, experts, accountants, counsel and such other persons (collectively "Assistants") currently retained or employed by it, with liberty to retain such further Assistants as it deems reasonably necessary or desirable in the ordinary course of business or for carrying out the terms of this Order.

5. THIS COURT ORDERS that the Petitioner shall be entitled, but not required, to pay the following expenses which may have been incurred prior to the Filing Date: **[1]**

(a) all outstanding wages, salaries, employee and pension benefits (including long and short term disability payments), vacation pay, bonuses and expenses (but excluding severance pay) payable before or after the Filing Date, in each case incurred in the ordinary course of business and consistent with the relevant compensation policies and arrangements existing at the time incurred (collectively "Wages");**[2]** and

(b) the fees and disbursements of any Assistants retained or employed by the Petitioner in respect of these proceedings, at their standard rates and charges, including payment of the fees and disbursements of legal counsel retained by the Petitioner, whenever and wherever incurred, in respect of:

(i) these proceedings or any other similar proceedings in other jurisdictions in which the Petitioner or any subsidiaries or affiliated companies of the Petitioner are domiciled;

(ii) any litigation in which the Petitioner is named as a party, whether commenced before or after the Filing Date; and

(iii) any related corporate matters;

necessary to assist in the restructuring of the Petitioner.

6. THIS COURT ORDERS that, except as otherwise provided herein, the Petitioner shall be entitled to pay all expenses reasonably incurred by the Petitioner in carrying on the Business in the ordinary course following the Filing Date, and in carrying out the provisions of this Order, which expenses shall include, without limitation:

(a) all expenses reasonably incurred for the preservation of the Property or the Business including, without limitation, payments on account of insurance (including directors' and officers' insurance), maintenance and security services;

(b) all capital expenditures reasonably incurred for the preservation of the Property or the Business as approved by the Monitor, as hereinafter defined in paragraph **[30]**; **[3]**

(c) all obligations incurred by the Petitioner after the Filing Date, including without limitation, with respect to goods and services actually supplied to the Petitioner following the date of this Order (including those under purchase orders outstanding at the Filing Date but excluding any interest on the Petitioner's obligations incurred prior to the Filing Date);

(d) amounts outstanding to creditors for goods and services provided prior to the Filing Date where expressly authorized by this Order or any further Order of this Court; and

(e) fees and disbursements of the kind referred to in paragraph **[5(b)]** which may be incurred after the Filing Date.

7. THIS COURT ORDERS that the Petitioner is authorized to remit, in accordance with legal requirements, or pay:

(a) any statutory deemed trust amounts in favour of the Crown in right of Canada or of any Province thereof or any other taxation authority which are required to be deducted from Wages, including, without limitation, amounts in respect of (i) employment insurance, (ii) Canada Pension Plan, (iii) Quebec Pension Plan, and (iv) income taxes or any such claims which are to be paid pursuant to Section 18.2 of the CCAA; **[4]**

(b) all goods and services or other applicable sales taxes (collectively, "Sales Taxes") required to be remitted by the Petitioner in connection with the sale of goods and services by the Petitioner, but only where such Sales Taxes are accrued or collected after the date of this Order, or where such Sales Taxes were accrued or collected prior to the date of this Order but not required to be remitted until on or after the date of this Order; and

(c) any amount payable to the Crown in right of Canada or of any Province thereof or any political subdivision thereof or any other taxation authority in respect of municipal property taxes, municipal business taxes or other taxes, assessments or levies of any nature or kind which may at law be payable in priority to claims of secured creditors and which are attributable to or in respect of the carrying on of the Business by the Petitioner.

8. THIS COURT ORDERS that until such time as the Petitioner repudiates a real property lease in accordance with paragraph **[12(b)(iv)]** of this Order, the Petitioner may pay all amounts constituting rent or payable as rent under real property leases (including, for greater certainty, common area maintenance charges, utilities and realty taxes and any other amounts payable as rent to the landlord under the lease) based on the terms of existing lease arrangements or as otherwise may be negotiated by the Petitioner from time to time, for the period commencing from and including the date of this Order ("Rent"), but shall not pay any rent in arrears. **[5]**

9. THIS COURT ORDERS that until such time as the Petitioner repudiates any equipment lease in accordance with paragraph **[12(b)(v)]** of this Order, and provided that the equipment lease is a true lease and not a financing lease creating a security interest, the Petitioner may pay all amounts or payable under such leases based on the terms of existing lease arrangements or as otherwise may be negotiated by the Petitioner from time to time, for the period commencing from and including the date of this Order, but shall not pay any amount with respect to pre-Filing Date arrears.

10. THIS COURT ORDERS that, except as specifically permitted herein, the Petitioner is hereby directed, until further Order of this Court:

(a) to make no payments of principal, interest or otherwise on account of amounts owing by the Petitioner to any of its creditors as of the Filing Date except as authorized by this Order;

(b) to grant no security interests, trust, mortgages, liens, charges or encumbrances upon or in respect of any of its Property, nor become a guarantor or surety, nor otherwise become liable in any manner with respect to any other person or entity except as authorized by this Order; and **[6]**

(c) to grant credit only to the customers of its business and then only for goods and services actually supplied to those customers and on payment terms ordinarily granted by the Petitioner in the usual course of its business, and only upon the customer agreeing that there is no right of set-off in respect of amounts owing for such goods and services against any debt owing by the Petitioner to such customers as of the Filing Date.

FINANCIAL ARRANGEMENTS

11. THIS COURT ORDERS that notwithstanding any other provision in this Order:

(a) the Petitioner is hereby authorized and empowered to borrow, repay and reborrow from ______________ (the "Lender") such amounts from time to time as the Petitioner considers necessary, and the Lender shall be entitled to revolve its operating loan facility (the "Lender Loan Facility") and collect interest, fees and costs on the Lender Loan Facility, subject to such amendments as are agreed between the Lender and the Petitioner;

(b) the Lender Loan Facility shall be secured by the same charge (the "Lender Charge") as secured the Lender Loan Facility as at the Filing Date; and

(c) the Petitioner is authorized to deal with the Lender in respect of the Lender Loan Facility on such terms as may be negotiated and agreed upon between the Petitioner and the Lender.

RESTRUCTURING

12. THIS COURT ORDERS that, subject to the terms of this Order, the Petitioner shall remain in possession of its Property and Business, provided that:

(a) it shall not sell or otherwise dispose of any of its Property or Business outside of the ordinary course of business except pursuant to this paragraph or as may be authorized by an Order of the Court; and

(b) it shall have the right, subject to the consent of the Monitor, to proceed with an orderly downsizing of the Business and operations, including without limitation, the right to:

(i) permanently or temporarily cease, downsize or shut down any of its Business or operations, and to dispose of redundant or non-material assets not exceeding a value of $______ in any one transaction or $______ in the aggregate;

(ii) terminate the employment of such of its employees or temporarily lay off such of its employees as it deems appropriate on such terms as may be agreed upon between the Petitioner and such employee, or failing such agreement, to deal with the consequences thereof in the Plan;

(iii) terminate such of its supplier arrangements as it deems appropriate;

(iv) in accordance with paragraphs **[13 and 14]** of this Order, vacate, abandon or quit any leased premises and/or repudiate any real property lease and any ancillary agreements relating to any leased premises, on such terms as may be agreed upon between the Petitioner and such landlord, or failing such agreement, to deal with the consequences thereof in the Plan;

(v) repudiate such leases of equipment as it deems to be unnecessary for its business, on such terms as may be agreed upon between the Petitioner and the lessor of such equipment, or failing such agreement, to deal with the consequences thereof in the Plan;

(vi) terminate or repudiate such of its arrangements or agreements of any nature whatsoever as the Petitioner deems appropriate, on such terms as may be agreed upon between the Petitioner and such counter-parties, or failing such agreement, to deal with the consequences thereof in the Plan; and

(vii) pursue all sources of refinancing and offers for material parts of its Business or Property, in whole or part, subject to prior approval of this Court being obtained before any material refinancing or any sale, except as permitted by subparagraph (b)(i), above;

all of the foregoing to permit the Petitioner to proceed with an orderly restructuring of the Business (the "Restructuring").

13. THIS COURT ORDERS that the Petitioner shall provide each of the relevant landlords with notice of the Petitioner's intention to remove any fixtures from any leased premises at least seven (7) days prior to the date of the intended removal. The relevant landlord shall be entitled to have a representative present on the leased premises to observe such removal and, if the landlord disputes the Petitioner's entitlement to remove any such fixture under the provisions of the lease, such fixture shall remain on the premises and shall be dealt with as agreed between any secured creditors who claim a security interest in the fixtures, such landlord and the Petitioner, or by further Order of this Court upon application by the Petitioner on at least two (2) clear days' notice to such landlord and any such secured creditors. If the Petitioner repudiates the lease governing such leased premises in accordance with paragraph **[12(b)(iv)]** of this Order, it shall not be required to pay Rent under such lease pending resolution of any such dispute with respect to the fixtures, and the repudiation of the lease shall be without prejudice to the Petitioner's claim to the fixtures in dispute.

14. THIS COURT ORDERS that if a lease is repudiated by the Petitioner in accordance with paragraph **[12(b)(iv)]** of this Order, then at the effective time of the repudiation, the

relevant landlord shall be entitled to take possession of any such leased premises without waiver of or prejudice to any claims or rights such landlord may have against the Petitioner in respect of such lease or leased premises and such landlord shall be entitled to notify the Petitioner of the basis on which it is taking possession and to gain possession of and re-lease such leased premises to any third party or parties on such terms as such landlord considers advisable, provided that nothing herein shall relieve such landlord of its obligation to mitigate any damages claimed in connection therewith.

15. THIS COURT ORDERS that, subject to the other provisions of this Order (including the payment of Rent as herein provided) and any further Order of this Court, the Petitioner shall be permitted to dispose of any or all of the Property located (or formerly located) on such leased premises without any interference of any kind from the landlord (notwithstanding the terms of any leases) and, for greater certainty, the Petitioner shall have the right to realize upon the Property in such manner and at such leased premises, as it deems suitable or desirable for the purpose of maximizing the proceeds and recovery therefrom.

16. THIS COURT DECLARES that, pursuant to Section 7(3)(c) of the *Personal Information Protection and Electronics Documents Act*, S.C. 2000, c. 5 and Section 18(1)(o) of the *Personal Information Protection Act*, S.B.C. 2003, c. 63, and any regulations promulgated under authority of either Act, as applicable (the "Relevant Enactment"), the Petitioner is permitted, in the course of these proceedings, to disclose personal information of identifiable individuals in its possession or control to stakeholders, its advisors, prospective investors, financiers, buyers or strategic partners (collectively, "Third Parties"), but only to the extent desirable or required to negotiate and complete the Restructuring or to prepare and implement the Plan or transactions for that purpose; provided that the Third Parties to whom such personal information is disclosed enter into confidentiality agreements with the Petitioner binding them in the same manner and to the same extent with respect to the collection, use and disclosure of that information as if they were an organization as defined under the Relevant Enactment, and limiting the use of such information to the extent desirable or required to negotiate and complete the Restructuring or to prepare and implement the Plan or transactions for that purpose, and attorning to the jurisdiction of this Court for the purposes of that agreement. Upon the completion of the use of personal information for the limited purposes set out herein, the Third Parties shall return the personal information to the Petitioner or destroy it. If the Third Parties acquire personal information as part of the Restructuring or the preparation and implementation of the Plan or transactions in furtherance thereof, such Third Parties may, subject to this paragraph and any Relevant Enactment, continue to use the personal information in a manner which is in all respects identical to the prior use thereof by the Petitioner.

NO PROCEEDINGS AGAINST THE PETITIONER OR MONITOR

17. THIS COURT ORDERS that until and including **[DATE – MAX. 30 DAYS FROM FILING DATE]**, or such later date as this Court may order (the "Stay Period"), no action, suit or proceeding in any court or tribunal (each, a "Proceeding") shall be commenced or continued against or in respect of the Petitioner, or affecting the Business or the Property, except with the written consent of the Petitioner or with leave of this Court, and any and all Proceedings currently under way against or in respect of the Petitioner or affecting the Business or the Property are hereby stayed and suspended during the Stay Period pending further Order of this Court.

18. THIS COURT ORDERS that during the Stay Period, no Proceeding shall be commenced against or in respect of the Monitor, in its capacity as Monitor, except with the written consent of the Monitor or with leave of this Court.

NO EXERCISE OF RIGHTS OR REMEDIES

19. THIS COURT ORDERS that during the Stay Period, all rights and remedies of any individual, firm, corporation, governmental body or agency, or any other persons or entities having notice of this Order (all of the foregoing, collectively being "Persons" and each being a "Person") against or in respect of the Petitioner or the Monitor, or affecting the Business or the Property, are hereby stayed and suspended except with the written consent of the Petitioner and the Monitor or leave of this Court, provided that nothing in this paragraph shall (i) empower the Petitioner to carry on any business which the Petitioner is not lawfully entitled to carry on, (ii) affect the rights and remedies of a regulatory body with respect to any investigation in respect of the Petitioner, Property or the Business or Proceeding taken or to be taken by a regulatory body against the Petitioner or with respect to the Property or Business, except when it is seeking, directly or indirectly, to enforce any of its rights as a secured creditor or an unsecured creditor, (iii) prevent the filing of any registration to preserve or perfect a mortgage, charge or security interest (subject to the provisions of Section 18.5 of the CCAA relating to the priority of statutory Crown securities) or (iv) prevent the registration or filing of a lien or claim for lien or the commencement of a Proceeding to protect lien or other rights that might otherwise be barred or extinguished by the effluxion of time, provided that no further step shall be taken in respect of such lien, claim for lien or Proceeding except for service of the initiating documentation on the Petitioner. **[7] [8]**

20. THIS COURT ORDERS that the rights and remedies hereby stayed shall include all rights or remedies relating to mortgages, charges, trusts, security interests, securities, instruments, debentures, notes or bonds issued by or on behalf of the Petitioner.

NO INTERFERENCE WITH RIGHTS

21. THIS COURT ORDERS that during the Stay Period, no Person shall discontinue, fail to honour, alter, interfere with, repudiate, terminate or cease to perform any right, renewal right, contract, agreement, licence or permit in favour of or held by the Petitioner, except with the written consent of the Petitioner and the Monitor or leave of this Court. **[9]**

CONTINUATION OF SERVICES

22. THIS COURT ORDERS that during the Stay Period, all Persons having agreements with the Petitioner or mandates under an enactment for the supply of goods and/or services, including without limitation all computer software, communication and other data services, centralized banking services, payroll services, insurance, transportation, services, utility or other services to the Business or the Petitioner, are hereby restrained until further Order of this Court from discontinuing, altering, interfering with, breaching or terminating any such agreement for the supply of such goods or services as may be required by the Petitioner, and that the Petitioner shall be entitled to the continued use of its current premises, telephone numbers, facsimile numbers, internet addresses and domain names, provided in each case that the normal prices or charges (excluding amounts outstanding as at the Filing Date) for all such goods or services received by the Petitioner after the date of this Order are paid by the Petitioner in accordance with normal payment practices of the Petitioner or such other

arrangements as may be agreed upon by the supplier or service provider and the Petitioner, or as may be ordered by this Court.

23. THIS COURT ORDERS that during the Stay Period and subject to the other provisions of this Order, no creditor of or other person who has dealt or may deal with the Petitioner shall be under any obligation after the date of this Order to enter into new or renewed arrangements with the Petitioner except that:

(a) any person who has provided policies of insurance or indemnity at the request of the Petitioner shall be required to continue or to renew such policies of insurance or indemnities following the date of this Order provided that the Petitioner makes payment of the premiums (other than premiums outstanding as at the Filing Date) on the usual commercial terms (as if these proceedings had not been commenced) and otherwise complies with the provisions of such policies; and

(b) any person who has supplied goods and/or services to the Petitioner essential to the operations of the Petitioner shall be required to continue or to renew any contracts or agreements or otherwise continue the arrangement for the provision of such supply or service, provided that the Petitioner pays the prices or charges under the agreements for such goods or services (excluding amounts outstanding as at the Filing Date) incurred after the Filing Date concurrently with such supply, or alternatively when the same become due in accordance with the payment terms negotiated between the Petitioner and such person subsequent to the Filing Date, and provided that such terms shall be the usual or common commercial terms charged by such person to others for the same or similar supplies and services and, in any event, such terms to be no more onerous than those which applied to the Petitioner before these proceedings had been commenced for such supplies and services.

24. THIS COURT ORDERS that, notwithstanding any provision in this Order, no creditor of the Petitioner shall be under any obligation after the making of this Order to advance or re-advance any monies or otherwise extend any credit to the Petitioner.

25. The Petitioner may, by written advice from its counsel of record herein and with the written consent of the Monitor, agree to waive any of the protections provided to it herein.

PROCEEDINGS AGAINST DIRECTORS AND OFFICERS

26. THIS COURT ORDERS that during the Stay Period, and except as permitted by subsection 11.5(2) of the CCAA, no Proceeding may be commenced or continued against any of the current or future directors and officers of the Petitioner with respect to any claim against the directors and officers that arose before the date hereof and that relates to any obligations of the Petitioner whereby the directors and officers are alleged under any law to be liable in their capacity as directors and officers for the payment or performance of such obligations.

DIRECTORS AND OFFICERS INDEMNIFICATION AND CHARGE [10]

27. THIS COURT ORDERS that the Petitioner is permitted to indemnify its present and future directors and officers and each of them from all claims, costs, charges and expenses relating to the failure of the Petitioner, after the date hereof, to make payments of such

obligations which they sustain or incur by reason of or in relation to their respective capacities as directors and officers of the Petitioner (and irrespective of whether such obligations of the Petitioner arose before or after the Filing Date), provided that such indemnity shall apply only to the extent that the directors and officers have acted honestly and in good faith with a view to the best interests of the Petitioner, have not committed wilful misconduct or gross negligence, have not breached their related fiduciary duties, and have not authorized actions or conduct inconsistent with the terms of this Order or any other order subsequently pronounced in these proceedings.

28. THIS COURT ORDERS that the directors and officers of the Petitioner shall be entitled to the benefit of and are hereby granted a charge (the "Directors' Charge") on the Property, which charge shall not exceed an aggregate amount of $ _______ , as security for the indemnity provided in paragraph **[27]** of this Order. The Directors' Charge shall have the priority set out in paragraphs **[39 and 41]** herein.

29. THIS COURT ORDERS that, notwithstanding any language in any applicable insurance policy to the contrary, (a) no insurer shall be entitled to be subrogated to or claim the benefit of the Directors' Charge, and (b) the Petitioner's directors and officers shall only be entitled to the benefit of the Directors' Charge to the extent that they do not have coverage under any directors' and officers' insurance policy, or to the extent that such coverage is insufficient to pay amounts indemnified in accordance with paragraph **[27]** of this Order. The Petitioner shall not allow such directors and officers insurance, if any, to lapse, or reduce coverage under or fail to renew such insurance, save with the consent of the Monitor.

APPOINTMENT OF MONITOR

30. THIS COURT ORDERS that _______________ is hereby appointed pursuant to the CCAA as the monitor (the "Monitor"), an officer of this Court, to monitor the Property and the Petitioner's conduct of the Business with the powers and obligations set out in the CCAA or set forth herein, and that the Petitioner and its shareholders, officers, directors, and Assistants shall cooperate fully with the Monitor in the exercise of its powers and rights and discharge of its obligations.

31. THIS COURT ORDERS that the Monitor, in addition to its rights and obligations specifically set out in the CCAA, is hereby directed and empowered to:

(a) monitor the Petitioner's receipts and disbursements;

(b) report to this Court and the creditors at such times and intervals as the Monitor may deem appropriate with respect to matters relating to the Property, the Business, the Restructuring and such other matters as may be relevant to the proceedings herein;

(c) advise the Petitioner as to the preparation of the Petitioner's cash flow statements and reporting and such financial and other information as required by the Lender;

(d) advise the Petitioner as to the development of any Plan authorized to be presented to the creditors, and any amendments to the Plan;

(e) have full and complete access to the Property, books, records and management, employees and advisors of the Petitioner, to the extent required to perform its duties arising under this Order;

(f) be at liberty to engage independent legal counsel or such other persons as the

Monitor deems necessary or advisable respecting the exercise of its powers and performance of its obligations under this Order;

(g) perform such other duties as are required by this Order or by this Court from time to time;

(h) take all reasonable steps to ensure that the Petitioner makes payment of all required amounts from its bank accounts or otherwise in the manner directed in this Order; and

(i) provide assistance to the Petitioner with respect to the Restructuring and the downsizing.

32. THIS COURT ORDERS that the Monitor shall not take possession of the Property and shall take no part whatsoever in the management or supervision of the management of the Business and shall not, by fulfilling its obligations hereunder, or by inadvertence in relation to the due exercise of powers or performance of duties under this Order, be deemed to have taken or maintained possession or control of the Business or Property, or any part thereof, and nothing in this Order shall be construed as resulting in the Monitor being an employer or a successor employer, within the meaning of any statute, regulation or rule of law or equity, for any purpose whatsoever.

33. THIS COURT ORDERS that the Monitor shall provide the Lender and any other creditor of the Petitioner with information provided by the Petitioner in response to reasonable requests for information made in writing by the Lender or such creditor addressed to the Monitor. The Monitor shall not have any responsibility or liability with respect to the information provided by it pursuant to this paragraph. In the case of information that the Monitor has been advised by the Petitioner is confidential, the Monitor shall not provide such information to the Lender or the creditors unless otherwise directed by this Court or on such terms as the Monitor and the Petitioner may agree.

34. THIS COURT ORDERS that, in addition to the rights and protections specifically afforded to the Monitor under the CCAA or which the Monitor possesses as an officer of this Court, the Monitor shall incur no liability or obligation as a result of its appointment or the carrying out of the provisions of this Order, save and except for any gross negligence or wilful misconduct on its part. Nothing in this Order shall derogate from the rights and protections given to the Monitor by any applicable legislation. **[11]**

35. THIS COURT ORDERS that the Monitor need not file security with this Court for the due and proper exercise and performance of its powers and duties as Monitor.

36. THIS COURT ORDERS that the Monitor shall be at liberty to post any report relating to the subject matter of this proceeding on the Monitor's web site at www.________ in lieu of mailing such reports to creditors of the Petitioner or to any other interested parties.

ADMINISTRATION CHARGE

37. THIS COURT ORDERS that the Monitor, counsel to the Monitor, if any, and counsel to the Petitioner shall be paid their reasonable fees and disbursements, in each case at their standard rates and charges, by the Petitioner as part of the cost of these proceedings. The Petitioner is hereby authorized and directed to pay the accounts of the Monitor, counsel to the Monitor and counsel to the Petitioner on a periodic basis and, in addition, the Petitioner

is hereby authorized to pay to the Monitor, counsel to the Monitor, and counsel to the Petitioner, retainers in the amount[s] of $ _______ [respectively] to be held by them as security for payment of their respective fees and disbursements outstanding from time to time.

38. THIS COURT ORDERS that the Monitor and its legal counsel shall pass their accounts from time to time, and for this purpose the accounts of the Monitor and its legal counsel are hereby referred to a judge of the British Columbia Supreme Court and may be heard on a summary basis.

39. THIS COURT ORDERS that the Monitor, counsel to the Monitor, if any, and counsel to the Petitioner shall be entitled to the benefits of, and are hereby granted, a charge (the "Administration Charge") on the Property, which charge shall not exceed an aggregate amount of $ _______ , as security for payment of their respective fees and disbursements incurred at the standard rates and charges of the Monitor and such counsel, both before and after the making of this Order in respect of these proceedings. The Administration Charge shall have the priority set out in paragraphs **[40 and 42]** hereof. **[12]**

[DIP FINANCING] [13]

VALIDITY AND PRIORITY OF CHARGES CREATED BY THIS ORDER

40. THIS COURT ORDERS that the priorities of the Administration Charge and the Directors' Charge, as between them, shall be as follows:

First – Administration Charge (to the maximum amount of $ _______);

Second – Directors' Charge (to the maximum amount of $ _______). **[14]**

41. THIS COURT ORDERS that the filing, recording, registration or perfection of the Administration Charge and the Directors' Charge (collectively, the "Charges") shall not be required, and the Charges shall, notwithstanding any lack of filing, recording, registering or perfection, be valid and enforceable for all purposes, including as against any right, title or interest filed, recorded, registered or perfected before or after the Charges come into existence.

42. THIS COURT ORDERS that each of the Administration Charge and the Directors' Charge (as constituted and defined herein) shall constitute a charge on the Property and such Charges shall rank in priority to all other security interests, trusts, liens, mortgages, charges and encumbrances, statutory or otherwise (collectively, "Encumbrances"), in favour of any Person.

43. THIS COURT ORDERS that except as otherwise expressly provided herein, or as may be approved by this Court, the Petitioner shall not grant any Encumbrances over any Property that rank in priority to, or *pari passu* with the Charges, unless the Petitioner obtains the prior written consent of the Monitor and the beneficiaries of the Charges (collectively, the "Chargees").

44. THIS COURT ORDERS that the Charges shall not be rendered invalid or unenforceable and the rights and remedies of the Chargees shall not otherwise be limited or impaired in any way by (a) the pendency of these proceedings and the declarations of insolvency made herein; (b) any application(s) for bankruptcy order(s) issued pursuant to *Bankruptcy and Insolvency Act* ("BIA"), or any bankruptcy order made pursuant to such applications; (c) the filing of any assignments for the general benefit of creditors made pursuant to the BIA; or

(d) any negative covenants, prohibitions or other similar provisions or lack of consent with respect to borrowings, incurring debt or the creation of Encumbrances, contained in any existing loan document, lease, mortgage, security agreement, debenture, sublease, offer to lease or other agreement (collectively, an "Agreement") which binds the Petitioner; and notwithstanding any provision to the contrary in any Agreement:

(a) neither the creation of the Charges nor the execution, delivery, perfection, registration or performance of any documents relating thereto shall create or be deemed to constitute a breach by the Petitioner of any Agreement to which it is a party; and

(b) none of the Chargees shall have any liability to any Person whatsoever as a result of any breach of any Agreement caused by or resulting from the creation of the Charges.

SERVICE AND NOTICE

45. THIS COURT ORDERS that the Petitioner be at liberty to serve this Order, the Petition, the Notice of Hearing of Petition, the Affidavit #1 of ______________ and any other pleadings in this proceeding on any creditor or shareholder of the Petitioner, or any other interested party, other than employees and creditors to which the Petitioner owes less than $250.00:

(a) by delivering a copy of same to the last address known to the Petitioner, if any, communicated by such creditor, shareholder or party to the Petitioner; and

(b) by causing an advertisement to be placed in one edition of each of the __________ and the ______________ describing these proceedings; and

(c) by posting a copy of the pleadings on the Monitor's website.

The Monitor is relieved of its obligation under Section 11(5) of the CCAA to provide similar notice, other than to supervise this process.

46. THIS COURT ORDERS that counsel of record who provide an email address in an Appearance filed in these proceedings shall be deemed to have consented to delivery of documents by any party by email unless objection is made before or at the time of the hearing of the Petition.

47. THIS COURT ORDERS that the Petitioner and the Monitor be at liberty to serve the documents referred to in paragraph **[45]** of this Order, any other materials and orders in these proceedings, any notices or other correspondence, by forwarding true copies thereof by prepaid ordinary mail, courier, personal delivery or fax transmission to the Petitioner's creditors at their respective addresses as last shown on the records of the Petitioner, and any such service or notice by courier, personal delivery or fax transmission shall be deemed to be received on the next business day following the date of forwarding thereof, or if sent by ordinary mail, on the third business day after mailing.

48. THIS COURT ORDERS that notwithstanding paragraphs **[45 and 47]** of this Order, service of the Petition, the Notice of Hearing, the Affidavit #1 of ______________ this Order and any other pleadings in this proceeding, shall be made on the federal and British Columbia Crowns in accordance with the *Crown Liability and Proceedings Act*, R.S.C. 1985, c. C-50, and regulations thereto, in respect of the federal Crown, and the *Crown Proceeding Act*, R.S.B.C. 1996, c. 89, in respect of the British Columbia Crown. **[15]**

GENERAL

49. THIS COURT ORDERS that the Petitioner or the Monitor may from time to time apply to this Court for advice and directions in the discharge of their respective powers, duties and obligations hereunder.

50. THIS COURT ORDERS that nothing in this Order shall prevent the Monitor from acting as an interim receiver, a receiver, a receiver and manager, or a trustee in bankruptcy of the Petitioner, the Business or the Property.

51. THIS COURT ORDERS that this Order and any other orders in these proceedings shall have full force and effect in all provinces and territories of Canada and shall be binding on all creditors of the Petitioners(s), wherever situate. This Court seeks and requests the aid and recognition of other Canadian and foreign Courts and administrative bodies including any Court or administrative tribunal of any Federal or State Court or administrative body in the United States of America, to act in aid of and to be complementary to this Court in carrying out the terms of this Order where required.

52. THIS COURT ORDERS that each of the Petitioner and the Monitor be at liberty and is hereby authorized and empowered to apply to any court, tribunal, regulatory or administrative body, wherever located, for the recognition of this Order and for assistance in carrying out the terms of this Order. In particular, the Monitor shall be authorized as a foreign representative of the Petitioner to apply to the United States Bankruptcy Court for relief pursuant to Chapter 15 of the *United States Bankruptcy Code*, 11 U.S.C. §§ 101-1330, as amended, if required.

53. THIS COURT FURTHER ORDERS that the Petitioner may (subject to the provisions of the CCAA and the BIA) at any time file a voluntary assignment in bankruptcy or a proposal pursuant to the commercial reorganization provisions of the BIA if and when the Petitioner determines that such a filing is appropriate.

54. THIS COURT FURTHER ORDERS that the Petitioner is hereby at liberty to apply for such further interim or interlocutory relief as to it may be advisable within the time for the filing of an Appearance by the creditors of the Petitioner in this proceeding.

55. THIS COURT FURTHER ORDERS that any interested Person or creditor of the Petitioner may file an Appearance in this proceeding and the time limited for filing such an Appearance for such person or creditor of the Petitioner outside of British Columbia shall be 14 days from the date of service upon such Person or creditor.

56. THIS COURT FURTHER ORDERS that liberty is reserved to any interested person or party to apply to this Court on two (2) clear days' notice to the Petitioner and such persons who have filed Appearances for such further Order of this Court or for variation of this Order or otherwise as may be advised.

57. THIS COURT FURTHER ORDERS that short leave is hereby granted to allow the hearing of an application on two (2) clear days' notice after delivery of the Notice of Motion, affidavits in support and Notice of Hearing, subject to the Court in its discretion further abridging or extending the time for service. Outlines, Responses and Chambers Records shall not be required to be exchanged by counsel or filed in this proceeding.

58. THIS COURT FURTHER ORDERS that endorsement of this Order by counsel appearing on this application is hereby dispensed with. **[16]**

59. THIS COURT ORDERS that this Order and all of its provisions are effective as of 12:01 a.m. local Vancouver time, the date of this Order. **[17]**

BY THE COURT

____

DISTRICT REGISTRAR

APPROVED AS TO FORM:

____

Counsel for the Petitioner

Schedule "A"

(List of Counsel)

No.
Vancouver Registry

IN THE SUPREME COURT OF BRITISH COLUMBIA

IN THE MATTER OF THE *COMPANIES' CREDITORS ARRANGEMENT ACT*, R.S.C. 1985, c. C-36

AND IN THE MATTER OF

____

PETITIONER

____

ORDER

____

____

Counsel: ______________
Matter No: ______________

EXPLANATORY NOTES

[1] Paragraphs 5 and 6 were separated to make it clear that only very limited payments may be made on account of pre-filing accruals and expenses. The Petitioner may consider seeking authority to make other payments during the stay, such as an amendment to paragraph 6 allowing certain payments to creditors, including critical supplier payments, on the following terms:

"...... with the written consent of the Monitor:

(i) pay the entire amount of its obligations to any creditor if the amount of such obligations, as agreed between the Petitioner and the creditor, is $ ______ or less as at the Filing Date;

(ii) pay $ ______ to any other creditor to which the outstanding obligations of the Petitioner are greater than $ ______ as at the Filing Date, provided such creditor agrees to accept that amount in full satisfaction of all obligations of the Petitioner to such creditor as at the Filing Date;

(iii) pay amounts owing to creditors who hold possessory or statutory liens against any asset of the Petitioner where the value of such asset exceeds the amount of the possessory or statutory liens or where the asset is deemed critical by the Petitioner and the Monitor to the business operations of the Petitioner;

(iv) pay an amount not exceeding $ ______ to a supplier deemed to be critical to the ongoing operations of the Petitioner."

[2] The Petitioner may wish to specifically apply to pay severance pay outstanding as at the Filing Date.

[3] The Petitioner may wish to consider a limit on this prohibition to allow for flexibility: ". . . . provided that any capital expenditure exceeding $ ______ shall be approved by the Monitor."

[4] The definition of Wages in paragraph 5(a) is intended to allow payment of these amounts even if owed prior to the Filing Date in recognition of the fact that Wages are paid at the end of a stub period and that continued employment is critical to the ongoing operations of the Petitioner. The extension of the payment beyond Wages in this paragraph is intended to address (a) protection of directors and officers from statutory claims and (b) that Section 18.2 of the CCAA provides for the payment of some of these amounts in any event in a restructuring. It is anticipated that the magnitude of such obligations will be brought to the attention of the Court if significant.

[5] Counsel may wish to address specific situations involving landlords where security deposits or other security (such as letters of credit) are held.

[6] Counsel may wish to consider adding a provision allowing the granting of PMSI security after the Filing Date.

[7] In keeping with the underlying philosophy of the Model Order, this provision contains a succinct stay provision without the extensive additional provisions found in previous CCAA initial orders. Nevertheless, the intention is to encapsulate the very broad stay provisions found in those previous orders and is, in no way, intended to restrict the breadth of the stay that will typically be granted on an initial application.

In particular, this provision clarifies that the stay is not intended to, for example, prevent a secured creditor from filing a financing statement in the Personal Property Registry since such a filing does not normally affect the Petitioner's ability to restructure. If a case can be made out that in a particular fact pattern it does, then the Model Order can be amended based on those facts. Some lien proceedings are commenced by filing a writ and some claims against the Petitioner may be subject to a limitation issue. BCMIOC was of the view that there is no harm in allowing these proceedings to be commenced provided no further steps are taken.

[8] In addition, counsel should consider clauses dealing with Section 81.1 and 81.2 of the BIA, as follows:

> Re 81.1: "Notwithstanding anything to the contrary herein, if the Petitioner subsequently becomes bankrupt or a receiver is appointed in respect of the Petitioner within the meaning of section 243(2) of the BIA, the period between the date of this Order and the day on which the Stay Period is terminated shall not be counted in determining the 30-day period referred to in section 81.1 of the BIA."
>
> Re 81.2: "Notwithstanding anything to the contrary herein, if the Petitioner subsequently becomes bankrupt or a receiver is appointed in respect of the Petitioner within the meaning of section 243(2) of the BIA, the period between the date of this Order and the day on which the Stay Period is terminated shall not be counted in determining the 15-day and 30-day periods referred to in section 81.2 of the BIA."

[9] The Petitioner may wish to consider whether an application should be made relating to the ongoing entitlement/benefit of any applicable volume rebates or discounts based upon volumes supplied during the period prior to the Filing Date.

[10] Counsel should be aware that the provisions relating to Directors/Officers/Employees Indemnification and Charge may not be appropriate in all circumstances.

[11] Counsel should be aware that the provision exempting the Monitor in situations except for gross negligence may not be appropriate in all circumstances.

[12] Counsel should be aware that the provision allowing for an Administration Charge in favour of the Petitioner's counsel may not be appropriate in all circumstances.

[13] In accordance with existing jurisprudence, the imposition of a DIP Charge at the time of the Initial Order will be rare. In those circumstances, or in any Comeback Order, these provisions may be appropriate:

DIP CHARGE

THIS COURT ORDERS that the Petitioner is hereby authorized and empowered, with the consent of the Monitor, to obtain and borrow under a credit facility (the "DIP Facility") from [DIP LENDER'S NAME] (the "DIP Lender") in order to finance the Petitioner's working capital requirements and other general corporate purposes and capital expenditures, provided that borrowings under such credit facility shall not exceed $ ______ unless permitted by further Order of this Court.

THIS COURT ORDERS that the DIP Facility shall be on the terms and subject to the conditions set forth in the commitment letter between the Petitioner and the DIP Lender dated as of [DATE] (the "Commitment Letter"), filed as Exhibit " ______ " to the Affidavit # ____ of ______________ .

THIS COURT ORDERS that the Petitioner is hereby authorized and empowered to execute and deliver such credit agreements, mortgages, charges, hypothecs and security documents, guarantees and other definitive documents (collectively, the "DIP Documents"), as are contemplated by the Commitment Letter or as may be reasonably required by the DIP Lender pursuant to the terms thereof, and the Petitioner is hereby authorized and directed to pay and perform all of its indebtedness, interest, fees, liabilities and obligations to the DIP Lender under and pursuant to the Commitment Letter and the DIP Documents as and when the same become due and are to be performed, notwithstanding any other provision of this Order.

THIS COURT ORDERS that the DIP Lender shall be entitled to the benefits of, and is hereby granted, a charge (the "DIP Lender's Charge") on the Property, which charge shall not exceed the aggregate amount owed to the DIP Lender under the DIP Documents. The DIP Lender's Charge shall have the priority set out in paragraphs ______ and ______ hereof.

THIS COURT ORDERS that, notwithstanding any other provision of this Order:

(a) the DIP Lender may take such steps from time to time as it may deem necessary or appropriate to file, register, record or perfect the DIP Lender's Charge or any of the DIP Documents;

(b) upon the occurrence of an event of default under the DIP Documents or the DIP Lender's Charge, the DIP Lender, upon ______ days' notice to the Petitioner and the Monitor, may exercise any and all of its rights and remedies against the Petitioner or the Property under or pursuant to the Commitment Letter, DIP Documents and the DIP Lender's Charge, including without limitation, to cease making advances to the Petitioner and set off and/or consolidate any amounts owing by the DIP Lender to the Petitioner against the obligations of the Petitioner to the DIP Lender under the Commitment Letter, the DIP Documents or the DIP Lender's Charge, to make demand, accelerate payment and give other notices, or to apply to this Court for the appointment of a receiver, receiver and manager or interim receiver, or for a bankruptcy order against the Petitioner and for the appointment of a trustee in bankruptcy of the Petitioner and, for greater certainty, upon the occurrence of an event of default under the terms of the DIP Documents, the DIP Lender shall be entitled to seize and retain proceeds from the sale of the Property and the cash flow of the Petitioner to repay amounts owing to the DIP Lender in accordance with the DIP Documents and the DIP Lender's Charge, but subject to the priorities as set out in paragraphs _____ and _____ of this Order; and

(c) the foregoing rights and remedies of the DIP Lender shall be enforceable against any trustee in bankruptcy, interim receiver, receiver or receiver and manager of the Petitioner or the Property.

THIS COURT ORDERS AND DECLARES that the DIP Lender shall be treated as unaffected in any plan of arrangement or compromise filed by the Petitioner under the CCAA, or any proposal filed by the Petitioner under the BIA.

[14] The priority of the Administration Charge may be subject to negotiation between those entitled to the Charges and any secured creditors, including the Lender. The results of those negotiations may be incorporated in the Initial Order as the parties see fit.

[15] *The Crown Proceeding Act*, R.S.B.C. 1996, c. 89, s. 8 provides for service on the British Columbia Crown, as follows:

"A document to be served on the government

(a) must be served on the Attorney General at the Ministry of the Attorney General in the City of Victoria, and

(b) is sufficiently served if

(i) left there during office hours with a solicitor on the staff of the Attorney General at Victoria, or

(ii) mailed by registered mail to the Deputy Attorney General at Victoria.

A similar provision relating to the federal Crown is found at s. 23(2) of the *Crown Liability and Proceeding Act*, R.S. 1985, c. C-50, which provides for service on the Deputy Attorney General of Canada or the chief executive officer of the agency in whose name the proceedings are taken, as the case may be.

[16] Counsel should be aware that the final form of the Order may be modified before entry at the discretion of the Chambers Judge.

[17] For a provision of this or any subsequent order in these proceedings to make any provincial law inapplicable or inoperative, notice must be given under s. 8 of the *Constitutional Question Act* R.S.B.C. 1996, c. 68. If notice is not given, the provision could later be challenged and set aside.

SCHEDULE "A"

British Columbia Model Insolvency Order Committee

Bench
Tysoe J.
Brown J.
Burnyeat J.

Bar/Trustee
Shelley Fitzpatrick, Chair
Craig Bushell
Richard Butler
Michael Fitch, Q.C.
John Grieve
David Hatter
Douglas Knowles, Q.C.
Raymond Leong
John McLean

APPENDIX 8

Plan Sanction Judgment in *Uniforêt* and Example of a *CCAA* Plan

Uniforêt inc., Re

In the matter of the arrangement of: Uniforêt Inc., Uniforêt Scierie-Pâte Inc. and Foresterie Port-Cartier Inc. (collectively, Uniforêt), and Richter & Associés (Monitor), Monitor/mis en cause and Jolina Capital Inc. (Jolina), mise en cause c. Highland Capital Management, L.P. (Highland), ML CBO IV (Cayman) Ltd., Pamco Cayman, Ltd., Highland Legacy, Ltd., Pam Capital Funding, L.P., Prospect Street High Income and Portfolio Inc. (Prospect), Opposing creditors

Québec Superior Court

Tingley J.C.S.

Docket: C.S. Qué. Montréal 500-05-064436-015
2003 CarswellQue 3404

JUDGMENT

(On a motion to Sanction a Plan of Arrangement)

THE ISSUES

¶ 1 Uniforêt asks the Court to sanction a Second Amended Plan of Arrangement (Plan) made after proof was completed on May 6, 2003 pursuant to the Companies' Creditors Arrangement Act (Act) [See Note 1 below]. An Amended Plan (First Plan) was approved by each of seven classes of creditors to the extent of at least 92% in number and 72% in value. Six secured creditors from a class (Class 2) of some 125 noteholders (or 4.79% of all noteholders), representing almost 28% in value of the class, oppose the sanction application, alleging amongst other things, manipulation and irregularities of the voting process [See Note 2 below], oppression of the minority (the Opposing Creditors) of the Class 2 creditors by the majority (Jolina), unfair and confiscatory treatment of the class 2 claims and the existence of preferential payments made to so-called "unaffected creditors" prejudicial to the mass of creditors. They add that the Plan is unreasonable, unfair and confiscatory. They conclude in their written contestation that the Court should accordingly refuse to sanction it and should instead order the sale of the assets and undertakings subject to the security [See Note 3 below] of Class 2 claims "as a going concern" or, subsidiarily, that the Class 2 creditors be given a single class of new notes in the aggregate amount of $100 million and 90% of the equity of Uniforêt [See Note 4 below], rather than the 55% that is offered as a conversion feature tied to $40 million of the new debt or B Notes [See Note 5 below].

Note 1: R.S.C., 1985, c.C-36, section 6 which provides that: 6. [Compromises to be sanctioned by court] Where a majority in number representing two-thirds in value of the creditors, or class of creditors, as the case may be, present and voting either in person or by proxy at the meeting or meetings thereof respectively held pursuant to sections 4 and 5, or either of those sections, agree to any compromise or arrangement either as proposed or as altered or modified at the meeting or meetings, the compromise or arrangement may be sanctioned by the court, and if so sanctioned is binding (a) on all the creditors or the class of creditors, as the case may be, and on any trustee for any such class of creditors, whether secured or unsecured, as the case may be, and on the company, and (b) in the case of a company that has made an authorized assignment or against which a receiving order has been made under the *Bankruptcy and Insolvency Act* or is in the course of being wound up under the *Winding-up and Restructuring Act*, on the trustee in bankruptcy or liquidator and contributories of the company.

Note 2: Addressed in large part in the Court's judgment of October 23, 2002 rendered by Madame Justice Zerbisias dealing primarily with classification issues.

Note 3: Essentially all the assets and undertakings of Uniforêt's operating companies excluding receivables and inventory and specified equipment under capital leases.

Note 4: Contemplating a reorganization of the capital structure of Uniforêt pursuant to the provisions of Section 191 of the *Canada Business Corporations Act*, R.S.C., 1985, c. C-44, as amended.

Note 5: Infra, paragraph [9]. See paragraph 4.2.2 of the Plan.

¶ 2 Uniforêt denies any irregularities in the voting process or oppression of the Opposing Creditors by it or Jolina and relies on the Monitor's opinion that its Plan is both fair and reasonable. It adds that as all the classes of creditors have approved the Plan, in most cases overwhelmingly, the Court should sanction it. As to the request to sell the business as part of an orderly liquidation, Uniforêt stresses that such an alternative proposal (a) was considered and rejected by its management for lack of interest prior to the presentation of the First Plan, (b) comes far too late in the day and (c) poses a serious risk of prejudicing the implementation of the Plan and the expectations of the creditors who approved the First Plan in October, 2001.

THE FACTS

¶ 3 Uniforêt first obtained protection under the Act on April 17, 2001. It filed an amended plan of arrangement (First Plan) with the Court on July 23, 2001 contemplating seven classes of creditors with potential claims aggregating in excess of $250,000,000. This Plan proposed the following arrangements:

Class	Description	Plan of Arrangement
1	The Municipalities of Port-Cartier and of l'Ascension (for Municipal taxes)	Pursuant to existing agreements

2	US Noteholders [which include the Opposing creditors and Jolina]	First US $25,000 cash with remaining balance, if any, exchanged for two new US Secured Notes: Note "A" 9% due on March 15, 2009; Note "B" convertible due on September 15, 2008; the whole for a total of $100,000,000 CDN
3	Holders of Capital Leases	Pursuant to existing agreements and contracts
4	Forestry Contractors	75% of proven claims
5	Unsecured Creditors	The lesser of $2,500 and the proven claim or a prorata share of a fund of $5,000,000
6	Canadian Debentureholders	Choice of receiving 8% of face value in cash or conversion into voting common shares of Uniforêt at a conversion rate of $6.00 per share
7	[Jolina]'s unsecured shareholder loan	Repayable on March 15, 2009 without interest

¶ 4 The Opposing Creditors, members of Class 2 holding secured U.S. Notes in the face amount of $33.5 million U.S., applied to the Court on July 17, 2001 to modify the proposed Class 2. They asked amongst other things to be placed in a separate class from Jolina, a major shareholder of Uniforêt and the holder of more than two-thirds of the other U.S. Notes. A vote on the First Plan by Class 2 creditors was suspended pending the outcome of the Opposing Creditor's application. All of the other creditors approved the First Plan at meetings of creditors duly called and held on August 15, 2001. The Opposing Creditors' application was heard by Madame Justice Zerbisias over some 20 days. She rendered a lengthy judgment on October 23, 2002 dismissing the application and:

2) AUTHORIZED [Uniforêt] to call a meeting of creditors concerning Class 2 (U.S. Noteholders) to submit to them the amended plan (D-1) for voting purposes;

3) ORDERED [Uniforêt] and the Monitor to furnish to [the Opposing Creditors] whatever information they may possess as to the names, addresses, telephone and telecopier numbers of all beneficial owners of the U.S. notes within 5 days of this Judgment;

4) ORDERED provisional execution [...] notwithstanding appeal; [...]

¶ 5 Leave to appeal from this judgment was sought and refused on November 21, 2002 by Mr. Justice Nuss of the Court of Appeal who observed:

> [8] The issues of fairness and reasonableness of the plan can be fully canvassed and debated at the hearing before the [Superior] Court to consider the sanctioning of the plan once the vote of all the Classes of [creditors] has taken place. Indeed, [the Opposing Creditors] acknowledge, and urged during the hearing before me, that most of the issues raised in the Motion for leave to appeal deal with the fairness and reasonableness of the plan and that the proper time for considering them will be at the hearing before the Court for the sanctioning of the plan.

¶ 6 Four days later, the Class 2 creditors voted on the Plan. The results were as follows:

Cat.	Montant total en capital des réclamations (US $)		% en nombre		% en valeur	
	Oui	Non	Oui	Non	Oui	Non
2	87,918,000.00	33,505,000.00	95.21	4.79	72.41	27.59

¶ 7 Uniforêt's Motion to Sanction the First Plan was first presented to the Court on December 11, 2002. The Opposing Creditors appeared to oppose its approval. Mr. Justice Lévesque was designated to manage the dossier and bring the matter on for hearing. He responded to requests for the production of additional documents and expertises and heard opposing counsel on a variety of pre-trial issues, including a request by Uniforêt to strike certain allegations of the amended, particularized contestation of the Opposing Creditors. As this request came shortly before the scheduled hearing, Mr. Justice Lévesque judiciously referred it, amongst other requests, to the trial judge.

¶ 8 The Motion to Strike seems intended to prevent the reventilation of matters or issues already decided by Madame Justice Zerbisias in her judgment of October 23, 2002. The Court resisted the temptation to limit the debate to new issues. It informed counsel that objections to the introduction of "old" or repeat evidence would, for the most part, be taken under reserve and the legal issues arising from the Motion to Strike would if necessary be considered by this judgment. These issues were not addressed during oral argument and accordingly they will not be considered by this judgment.

¶ 9 The Plan, as twice amended, provides in part that:

ARTICLE 2

PURPOSE AND EFFECT OF PLAN

2.1 Purpose

The purpose of this Plan is to effect a reorganization of the liabilities, business and affairs of Uniforêt in order to enable its business to continue, in the expectation that all Persons with an interest in Uniforêt will derive a greater benefit from its continued operation than would result from the immediate forced liquidation of Uniforêt's assets and business.

2.2 Joint Plan

As explained in Uniforêt's Petition for the issuance of the Initial Order pursuant to the [Act], most of the financing of Uniforêt's business is with Uniforêt Inc., while the operations and fixed assets are with Uniforêt Scierie-Pâte Inc. and Foresterie Port-Cartier Inc. who, in many instances, guaranteed the debts and obligations of Uniforêt Inc. Therefore, the related operations of Petitioners justify [...] presenting a joint Plan, the whole as permitted by the *CCAA* and the Initial Order. None of Uniforêt's Creditors will be prejudiced by such a joint Plan.

2.3 Persons Affected

This Plan shall become effective on the Plan Implementation Date and shall, on and after the Plan Implementation Date, bind Uniforêt and all Uniforêt's Creditors affected by the Plan.

2.4 Obligations Not affected

This Plan shall not affect any Unaffected Obligations [See Note 6 below].

Note 6: Defined in the Plan as: a. Interim Period Debts, which shall be paid by Uniforêt in accordance with terms previously agreed upon with the respective Interim Creditors; b. Uniforêt Scierie-Pâte Inc.'s obligations towards the Municipalité Régionale de Comté de Sept-Rivières to build and maintain roads, as provided in the agreement dated April 3, 2001, and the related Hydro-Québec's claim in the amount of $5,000,000 referred to therein; c. Claims of legal, accounting and financial advisors to Uniforêt, including the Monitor and its counsel, in respect of any debt incurred or to be incurred by Uniforêt for the purposes of reorganizing Uniforêt's liabilities, business and affairs including, without limitation, pursuant to the Plan, which monies shall be paid by Uniforêt in accordance with the Initial Order; d. Claims for indemnity pursuant to the indemnities provided by Uniforêt to directors or officers of Uniforêt; e. Claims of Employee Creditors, which monies shall be paid by Uniforêt in the ordinary course of business; f. [...] g. Dues owing to the Quebec Minister of Natural Resources pursuant to the *Forests Act*, R.S.Q., c. F-4.1, which shall be paid by Uniforêt in accordance with terms previously agreed upon with the Quebec Minister of Natural Resources; h. Monies, if any, owing to National Bank of Canada, Bank of Montreal and La Société d'hypothèque CIBC, which shall be paid by Uniforêt in accordance with existing agreements and contracts, or as may be agreed between each of them; i. Claims for goods on consignment, which monies shall be paid by Uniforêt in accordance with terms previously agreed upon with the Creditors of such Claims; and j. Claims for warehousing contracts, which monies shall be paid by Uniforêt in accordance with terms previously agreed upon with the Creditors of such Claims.

ARTICLE 3

CLASSIFICATION OF CREDITORS, VALUATION OF CLAIMS AND PROCEDURAL MATTERS

3.1 Classification of Creditors

The Claims of the Creditors shall be grouped into the following Classes, and each Creditor in a designated Class shall, to the extent provided herein, be entitled to vote on the Plan as part of such Class:

Class 1	The Cities of Port-Cartier and l'Ascension (municipal taxes);

Class 2	US Noteholders;
Class 3	Holders of Capital Leases;
Class 4	Forestry Contractors;
Class 5	Unsecured Creditors;
Class 6	Canadian Debentureholders; and
Class 7	Jolina Capital Inc.'s unsecured shareholder loan.

3.2 Creditors Meetings

Following the filing of the Plan with the Court, Uniforêt will hold the necessary Creditors Meetings to vote on the Plan, the whole in accordance with the Initial Order. [...]

3.3 Creditors Votes Required

In order that the Plan be binding on all the Creditors of Uniforêt affected by the Plan, it must first be accepted within each and every Class of Creditors as prescribed by the Plan by a majority in number of the Creditors in such Class who actually vote on the Plan (in person, by voting letter or by proxy) at the Creditors Meeting held in respect of such Class, representing two-thirds in value of the Accepted Claims for Voting Purposes of the Creditors in such Class who actually vote on the Plan (in person, by voting letter or by proxy) at such Creditors Meeting. [...]

3.4 Valuation of Claims for Voting and Distribution Purposes

Each Creditor having a Proven Claim in a Class shall be entitled to attend and to vote at the Creditors Meeting for such Class. Each Creditor of a Class who is entitled to vote shall be entitled to that number of votes at the Creditors Meeting for such Class as is equivalent to the dollar amount of its Proven Claim. In the event that the Proven Claim of a Creditor is not finally determined prior to the Date of the Creditors Meeting for any Class in accordance with this Plan and any Order of the Court, the Creditor shall be entitled to vote at the Creditors Meeting for such Class based on its Accepted Claim for Voting Purposes as determined by the Monitor, without prejudice to Uniforêt's right or the Creditor's right to require the final determination by the Court of the Creditor's Proven Claim, which Proven Claim shall apply for all purposes in connection with the Plan, including, without limitation, the Creditor's entitlement to participate in distributions under the Plan.

3.5 Participation in Different Capacities

Creditors whose Claims are affected by this Plan may be affected in more than one capacity. Each such Creditor shall be entitled to participate hereunder separately in each such capacity, unless otherwise specified. Any action taken by a Creditor in any one capacity shall not affect the Creditor in any other capacity unless the Creditor agrees to otherwise in writing.

3.6 Confirmation of Plan by the Final Order

In the event that the Plan is approved by the required majority of Creditors provided in Section 3.3, Uniforêt will seek the Final Order for the sanction and approval of the Plan. Subject only to the Final Order being granted and the satisfaction of the conditions of the Plan described in Section 5.1, the Plan will be implemented by Uniforêt and will be binding on all Uniforêt's Creditors affected by the Plan.

ARTICLE 4

THE COMPROMISE AND ARRANGEMENT

4.1 Class 1: Treatment of the Cities of Port-Cartier and l'Ascension (municipal taxes)

Uniforêt proposes to pay to the Cities of Port-Cartier and l'Ascension the full amounts which are due to them as municipal taxes pursuant to existing agreements, or as may be agreed between them.

4.2 Class 2: Treatment of US Noteholders

Uniforêt proposes to all US Noteholders, holding US Secured Notes totalling approximately CDN $190,000,000, as final compromise and arrangement, the following:

4.2.1 Uniforêt will pay, on the Plan Implementation Date [See Note 7 below], to each US Noteholder the lesser of US $25,000 or the amount of the US Secured Note held by such US Noteholder; and

---

Note 7: Described in the Plan as: the date on which all conditions contained in Section 5.1 of this Plan are satisfied. These conditions, save those subject to the discretion of the Court, have all been satisfied.

4.2.2 Uniforêt will exchange, on the Plan Implementation Date, all outstanding US Secured Notes, after payment of the amounts provided in Section 4.2.1 for two (2) new secured notes for each outstanding US Secured Note, namely (1) 9% Note "A" due March 15, 2009 and one (1) Convertible Note "B" due September 15, 2008, to be issued under an indenture providing for the issuance of 9% Notes "A" due March 15, 2009, in an aggregate principal amount of CDN $60,000,000, and Convertible Notes "B" due September 15, 2008, in an aggregate principal amount of CDN $40,000,000, both Notes "A" and "B" totalling an aggregate principal amount of CDN $100,000,000, to be issued under commercially acceptable terms and having similar secured rights on Uniforêt's assets as those held by the US Noteholders under the US Indenture, the whole, on a pro rata pari passu basis. These Notes "A" and "B" will be subject to the following terms and conditions:

9% Notes "A":

from the Plan Implementation Date, 9% Notes "A" will bear an annual interest rate of 9%, payable in arrears on a semi-annual basis, on March 15 and September 15 of each year, with the first interest payment date being on March 15, 2002, and will provide for annual principal repayment on March 15 of each year, commencing on March 15, 2003, always on a pro rata pari passu basis, equal to 50% of Available Cash Flow for fiscal years 2002 and 2003, and 75% of Available Cash Flow for subsequent fiscal years until the earlier of the maturity date, namely March 15, 2009, at which time the balance thereof will be fully repaid, or refinancing thereof;

furthermore, at its sole discretion, Uniforêt can make, on any interest payment date, without penalty, additional principal repayments on the 9% Notes "A" and

Convertible Notes "B":

will bear no interest until September 15, 2004 and, thereafter, will bear an annual interest rate of 7.5%, payable in arrears on a semi-annual basis, on March 15 and September 15 of each year, with the first interest payment date being on March 15, 2005, and will provide for no annual principal repayment prior to September 15, 2008 and the full repayment of the principal thereof at maturity, namely on September 15, 2008;

furthermore, Convertible Notes "B" will, from the Plan Implementation Date until September 15, 2008, be convertible at any time into Class A Subordinate Voting Shares of Uniforêt Inc. (listed on The Toronto Stock Exchange under the trading symbol UNF.A) at a conversion price of $0.50 per share, such conversion right to expire at the close of business on September 15, 2008 and to be subject to a thirty (30) days prior written conversion notice to Uniforêt, which may then offer, prior to the expiry of such thirty (30) day period, to pay in cash to the noteholder, who will not be obliged to accept any such offer, an amount equal to the Market Value of the Class A Subordinate Voting Shares of Uniforêt Inc. issuable upon conversion instead of delivering shares to the noteholder [See Note 8 below];

Note 8: The highlighted portions represent the changes made to the First Plan on May 6, 2003. Prior to these changes, this paragraph read: furthermore, Convertible Notes "B" will, from the Plan Implementation Date until September 15, 2004, be convertible at any time into Class A Subordinate Voting Shares of Uniforêt Inc. (listed on The Toronto Stock Exchange under the trading symbol UNF.A) at a conversion price of $0.50 per share, such conversion right to expire at the close of business of September 15, 2004 and to be subject to a thirty (30) days prior written conversion notice to Uniforêt, which may then elect, prior to the expiry of such thirty (30) day period, to pay in cash to the noteholder an amount equal to the Market Value of the Class A Subordinate Voting Shares of Uniforêt Inc. issuable upon conversion instead of delivering shares to the noteholder; effectively giving to Uniforêt a repurchase option.

"Market Value" of the Class A Subordinate Voting Shares of Uniforêt Inc. shall mean the weighted average trading price of the Class A Subordinate Voting Shares of Uniforêt Inc. on the Toronto Stock Exchange during the twenty (20) consecutive trading days preceding the date on which the conversion notice is given to Uniforêt.

US Noteholders have no Claim for interest outstanding as of the Plan Implementation Date under US Secured Notes and are not entitled to participate in any other Class for Claims related, in any manner whatsoever, to US Secured Notes.

4.3 Class 3: Treatment of Holders of Capital Leases

Uniforêt proposes to pay to holders of Capital Leases the full amount which is due to them pursuant to existing agreements and contracts, or as may be agreed between them.

4.4 Class 4: Treatment of Forestry Contractors

Uniforêt proposes to pay, at the latest on the Plan Implementation Date, to each Forestry Contractor, as final compromise and arrangement of their respective Proven Claim, 75% thereof.

4.5 Class 5: Treatment of Unsecured Creditors

Uniforêt proposes to pay to Unsecured Creditors, as final compromise and arrangement of their respective Proven Claim, on the Plan Implementation Date, in accordance with their respective election, the following

4.5.1 the lesser of $2,500 or the Unsecured Creditor's Proven Claim;

or

4.5.2 a pro rata pari passu share in the Unsecured Creditors Fund for those Unsecured Creditors with Proven Claims as of the Plan Implementation Date who will not have elected to be paid in accordance with Section 4.5.1 of this Plan.

4.6 Class 6: Treatment of Canadian Debentureholders

Uniforêt proposes to Canadian Debentureholders, as final compromise and arrangement, in accordance with their respective election, the following: On the Plan Implementation Date,

4.6.1 payment of an amount equal to 8% of the outstanding balance of the Canadian 8% Convertible Unsecured Subordinated Debentures held; or

4.6.2 conversion of Canadian 8% Convertible Unsecured Subordinated Debentures held by a Canadian Debentureholder into Class A Subordinate Voting Shares of Uniforêt Inc. (listed on The Toronto Stock Exchange under the trading symbol UNF.A) at a conversion price of $6.00 per share, being a rate of 16.667 Class A Subordinate Voting Shares per $100 principal amount of Canadian 8% Convertible Unsecured Subordinated Debentures held by a Canadian Debentureholder, for those Canadian Debentureholders who have not elected to be paid in accordance with Section 4.6.1 of this Plan.

Canadian Debentureholders have no Claim for interest outstanding as of the Plan Implementation Date under Canadian 8% Convertible Unsecured Subordinated Debentures and are not entitled to participate in any other Class for Claims related, in any manner whatsoever, to Canadian 8% Convertible Unsecured Subordinated Debentures.

4.7 Class 7: Treatment of Jolina Capital Inc.'s unsecured shareholder loan

Uniforêt proposes to pay Jolina Capital Inc.'s unsecured shareholder loan in the amount of $5,405,000, as final compromise and arrangement thereof, by issuing, on the Plan Implementation Date, a promissory note for the same amount, bearing no interest and providing for the full repayment thereof on March 15, 2009.

¶ 10 Between July 23, 2001 and February 27, 2003, the Monitor produced four reports, two addressed to the creditors prior to their voting on the First Plan and two addressed to the Court in connection with the Motion to Sanction. These latter reports express the following opinions:

E) Analyse de Plan

23. L'acceptation du Plan par toutes les catégories de créanciers permettra à Uniforêt de restructurer son endettement ainsi que de poursuivre ses activités.

24. Le Contrôleur est d'avis que les Débitrices ont agi et continuent d'agir de bonne foi, avec toute la diligence voulue dans les circonstances. Aussi, le Contrôleur n'a constaté aucun fait qui nous porterait à croire que la conduite des Débitrices est ou a été répréhensible.

25. Le Contrôleur est d'avis que le Plan proposé fut préparé de façon sérieuse et diligente par Uniforêt.

26. Le Contrôleur est d'avis que le Plan d'Uniforêt est juste et raisonnable envers les créanciers en général et envers chacune des catégories de créanciers.

27. Le Contrôleur est d'avis que le Plan tient compte de la capacité financière d'Uniforêt de respecter les termes dudit Plan advenant son homologation par la Cour et sa mise en oeuvre.

28. Le Contrôleur, avec l'assistance d'autres conseillers professionnels et en se basant sur son expérience, a procédé à une analyse de la valeur probable des éléments d'actif d'Uniforêt dans un contexte de liquidation ordonnée.

29. Tel que déclaré dans le Premier Rapport du Contrôleur, le Contrôleur est d'avis que, dans un contexte de liquidation ordonnée, la valeur estimative des immobilisations d'Uniforêt pourrait se situer entre 60 000 000 $ et 80 000 000 $ après déduction des coûts de liquidation et des charges prioritaires (employés, droits de coupe impayés, etc.). Le montant ainsi réalisé ne serait suffisant pour assurer le remboursement intégral des sommes dues aux créanciers garantis qui totalisent 125 000 000 $ US (approximativement 200 000 000 $ CDN).

30. Tel que déclaré dans le Second Rapport du Contrôleur, le Contrôleur est d'avis que, dans un contexte de liquidation ordonnée, même en considérant la valeur aux livres en date du 30 septembre 2002, de l'encaisse, des comptes à recevoir, ainsi que des inventaires totalisant approximativement 43 000 000 $ la valeur des éléments d'actif d'Uniforêt ne s'est pas améliorée depuis juillet 2001. En fait, en tenant compte de l'état actuel du marché, des conditions de l'industrie ainsi que des facteurs externes qui sont hors du contrôle d'Uniforêt, nous sommes d'avis que les chances d'obtenir la valeur nette de réalisation estimative discutée au paragraphe 29 ont diminué.

31. Le Contrôleur est d'avis que, dans le cadre d'une liquidation forcée, la valeur estimative des immobilisations d'Unifôret serait réduite de 50 %. Il semble que, dans le contexte actuel, une liquidation forcée serait plus vraisemblable.

32. Le Contrôleur est d'avis que l'acceptation du Plan est plus avantageuse pour les créanciers que la liquidation des éléments d'actif d'Uniforêt dont l'analyse se résume comme suit :

	Montant dû		Plan d'arrangement			Liquidation ordonnée (Valeur nette de réalisation estimée (a)			Liquidation ordonnée (Valeur nette de réalisation estimée (b)	
1	298 971 $		298 271 $	100%		300 000 $	100%		300 000 $	100%
2	195 337 500	(c)	100 000 000	51%		65 000 000	33%		30 000 000	15%
					(e)	16 000 000	8%	(e)	16 700 000	9%
3	5 135 924		5 135 924	100%	(d)	5 150 000	100%	(d)	5 100 100	100%
4	2 534 190	(f)	1 900 642	75%	(e)	300 000	12%	(e)	250 000	10%
5	24 849 498	(g)	5 700 000	23%	(e)	3 000 000	12%	(e)	2 500 000	10%
6	16 554 904	(h)	1 324 392	8%		néant	—%		néant	—%
7	5 405 000	(i)	1 104 858	20%	(e)	650 000	12%	(e)	550 000	10%
	250 115 987 $		115 464 087 $	46%		90 400 000 $	36%		55 400 000 $	22%

(a) Assumant une valeur de liquidation de 20 000 000 $ pour les comptes à recevoir et les stocks et une valeur nette de 70 000 000 $ pour les immobilisations.
(b) Assumant une valeur de liquidation de 20 000 000 $ pour l'encaisse, les comptes à recevoir et les stocks et une valeur nette de 35 000 000 $ pour les immobilisations.
(c) Excluant le montant du premier 38 500 $ (25 000 US) à être reçu par chaque Porteur de Billets Américains.
(d) En assumant que les créanciers de premier rang paient les soldes dus en vertu des Contrats de Location-Acquisition afin de libérer les actifs visés.
(e) Calculé en partageant la valeur estimée de liquidation des comptes clients et des stocks entre les créanciers des catégories 2 (perte excédentaire seulement), 4, 5 et 7, sur la base prorata et pari passu.
(f) 75 % du montant dû.
(g) Incluant un estimé des créanciers qui choisiront de recevoir le paiement comptant de 2 500 $.
(h) Assumant que la totalité de la catégorie choisit de recevoir un paiement comptant.
(i) Valeur actualisée du montant dû à un taux d'escompte de 18%.

33. Le Contrôleur est d'avis que l'acceptation et l'homologation du Plan est plus avantageuse pour les créanciers que la liquidation des actifs d'Uniforêt.

34. Le Contrôleur est d'avis que la continuité des opérations d'Uniforêt permettra à la majorité des créanciers d'avoir l'opportunité de poursuivre des relations avec Uniforêt qui, entre autres, vont permettre également le maintien d'emplois et d'une activité économique importante pour les municipalités de Péribonka et de Port-Cartier. De plus, certaines catégories de créanciers (catégories 2 et 3) pourront bénéficier d'un rendement continu de leurs investissements nonobstant la réduction de la valeur nominale de leur créance prévue par le Plan.

35. Le Contrôleur est d'avis qu'il est dans l'intérêt de l'ensemble des créanciers d'Uniforêt que le Plan soit homologué et approuvé par cette Cour.

¶ 11 The Monitor relied for some of its opinions upon the expertise of CIB World Markets Inc. prepared as of February 24, 2003. The key conclusions of this expertise are:

1. The current environment for selling assets in the pulp and lumber industry is poor. There are only a limited number of buyers, but numerous mills for sale.

2. With regard to the BCTMP mill, the lack of transactions at any meaningful price over the past several years is the best indicator of [...] poor market conditions – the market has spoken for itself.

3. With regard to the sawmills, even if a temporary resolution to the on-going trade dispute with the U.S. is negotiated, the economic fundamentals underlying the Canadian industry remain troubling. Once the uncertainty associated with the trade barriers is added to the oversupply situation, it is unlikely that reasonable bids could be expected for the sawmill over at least the next 12-18 months. This problem is compounded by the volume of sawmill capacity currently being offered for sale in Quebec (or deemed "non-core") by companies other than Uniforêt.

¶ 12 The Opposing Creditors retained Houlihan, Lokey Award & Zukin Financial Advisors Inc. (Houlihan) of New York to review the First Plan and the Monitor's report of July 23, 2001 and comment on the fairness of that plan to the Opposing Creditors. Houlihan concluded that the First Plan was "not fair and reasonable to the creditors in general or in relation to each other for [...] the following reasons:

The Plan preserves the existing common equity ownership of [Uniforêt], and thereby allows common shareholders to maintain control [...] and to benefit from a significant de-leveraging. [...] This is unfair to secured creditors who receive less than a 100% recovery.

The Plan provides for substantial recoveries to unsecured creditors that have claims that rank junior in priority to the secured creditors. This is unfair to secured creditors who receive less than a 100% recovery.

The Plan provides for 100% recoveries in cash for the Class 3 secured creditors, but the Class 2 secured creditors will receive new debt securities with a face value of $100.0 million that approximates 51.2% of the Class 2 secured creditors claims of $195.5 million. This is unfair to the Class 2 Claimholders.

The Plan provides an inadequate amount of value to the Class 2 Claimholders because the debt securities that are being offered in satisfaction of the Class 2 Claims will trade at a significant discount to face value. This is unfair to the Class 2 Claimholders.

The Plan provides less value to the Class 2 Claimholders than they would receive in a liquidation based on the liquidation values provided in the Monitor's Report. This is unfair to the Class 2 Claimholders.

The Plan deprives the Class 2 Claimholders of the value of the unsecured portion of their claim. This is unfair to the Class 2 Claimholders.

The Plan is being proposed under the assumption that the Port-Cartier pulp Mill [...] on which the Class 2 Claimholders have a first lien), will not be in operation. [This] mill is a significant asset of [Uniforêt] in which over $200 million of capital expenditures have been invested since 1988. The Plan inhibits the Class 2 Claimholders from benefiting in the value that might be created in the event that the pulp mill is restarted, converted, sold or liquidated and transfers a majority of such benefits to junior creditors and common equity holders. This is unfair to the Class 2 Claimholders.

The Plan provides for a highly leveraged capital structure that is sub-optimal from a corporate finance perspective. As a result, it is likely that both the debt and equity securities of [Uniforêt] will trade with limited liquidity and at significant discounts to their intrinsic values. This is unfair to the Class 2 Claimholders.

The Plan consolidates all U.S. Noteholders in Class 2 for voting purposes. The purported holder of approximately 66.9% of the Class 2 Claims (Jolina Capital) is also a holder of a majority of the Class 3 Claims, certain Class 5 Claims, 100% of the Class 7 Claims and is also the largest shareholder of [Uniforêt]. [Thus], Jolina will recover a portion of the value that the Plan transfers from the Class 2 Claimholders to holders of Class 3, Class 5 and Class 7 Claims as well as the equity. Accordingly, Jolina has a different recovery profile than other Class 2 Claimholders and an economic conflict of interest with respect to voting as a Class 2 Claimholder. This is unfair to the non-Jolina Class 2 Claimholders.

¶ 13 This report, prepared on October 8, 2001, was filed at the hearing before Madam Justice Zerbisias together with a previous report Houlihan had submitted dated May 15, 2000. Mr. Slonecker, one of their authors, spoke to them. Madam Justice Zerbisias had this to say about those parts of the Houlihan reports that concerned her:

[72] Houlihan's first report, of May 15, 2000, assesses the value of the assets of Uniforêt at U.S. $123 to $134 million, excluding the assets of Tripap, but including the Port Cartier pulpmill whose assets are therein evaluated at U.S. $38 to 41 million. On that basis, the report and Mr. Slonecker concluded that the recovery rate relative to the face value of the notes is approximately 49 to 56%, compared to the current market trading price between 27 to 30%.

[73] Houlihan's second report, of October 8, 2001, was prepared by Houlihan at Petitioner's request as a reply to the Report of the Monitor on the Debtor's financial affairs and on the fairness of the plan. Mr. Slonecker and the report re-evaluate the assets of Uniforêt at CND $90 million. No value whatsoever is attributed to the assets of the Port Cartier pulpmill because it was not operating. Mr. Slonecker in his report, then evaluates the new securities, redeemable or convertible at a future date being provided to the Class 2 noteholders under the plan, at CDN $56.4 million, which implies a recovery rate of 51.2% of the total face value of the Class 2 claims. After discounting for the delay in payment, he concludes that this implies a real recovery rate of only 28.9%. He adds that the trading value of the Class A notes is 74% of face value, whereas the trading value of the class B notes is 31% of face value.

[74] Jolina, as a Class 2 creditor is affected by the same determinations as to its potential recovery on its U.S. notes. In addition, Houlihan and Mr. Slonecker evaluate the trading value of Jolina's new note under the plan in payment of its claim for its shareholder loan of CND $5.4 million at 18.8% of face value, i.e. worth approximately $1 million Canadian when discounted, for the delay in payment.

[75] Thus, Houlihan and Mr. Slonecker conclude on the basis of two completely different scenarios as set forth in the two reports, that the recovery rate on the U.S. notes is approximately the same: 49 to 56% on the first report and 51.2% on the second report, without attributing any value to the Port Cartier pulpmill, absent any discount for delays in payment. Similarly, the Monitor concludes that the recovery rate for Class 2 claimants

is 51% under the plan, or 33% on a forced liquidation. Thus it appears that Petitioners will gain more under the plan and less on liquidation.

¶ 14 The Opposing Creditors obtained Court permission to produce another expertise prepared by Price Waterhouse Coopers (PWC). Completed on February 7, 2003, this expertise concludes that:

141. In summary, in our view, the Plan:

(i) Does not treat secured creditors in accordance with their existing rights and priorities;

(ii) Provides significantly higher recoveries to certain unsecured creditors than is being offered to the secured US Noteholders, including the ultimate payment of 100 cent(s) on the dollar in respect of Jolina's unsecured shareholder loan;

(iii) Requires Class 5 creditors to make an election in respect of their treatment under the Plan without being able to assess the economic impact of the alternatives available;

(iv) Provides for a recovery to Class 6 creditors, notwithstanding that such creditors have contractually subordinated themselves to all other creditors;

(v) Treats the claim of Bank of Montreal (BoM) as an Unaffected Obligation [See Note 9 below], with no benefit or advantage to [Uniforêt or its] arms-length creditors, but with the significant disadvantage that $4 million that would otherwise be available for the purposes of making additional payments to Affected Creditors, funding operations or servicing debt will be paid to this unsecured creditor; and;

Note 9: Supra, Note 6, paragraph (h).

(vi) Contrary to established practice in *CCAA* restructurings, leaves substantially all of the post-restructuring equity in [Uniforêt] in the hands of the existing shareholders without any additional funding or support being provided by such shareholders, with the result that the consequences of [Uniforêt's involvency] are being suffered by the creditors, while the benefits of the compromises by creditors and a successful restructuring will accrue to the existing shareholders.

142. The Plan was approved by the Class 2 creditors only as a result of Jolina, the largest shareholder of Uniforêt, voting in favour of the Plan. Based on the Monitor's records, the Plan would not have been approved if 373 [See Note 10 below] had been included in the *CCAA* filing and Jolina, as a result, had been prevented from exercising its hypothecary rights over the US Notes held by 373. Furthermore, based on our experience, we believe it is unlikely that an arm's length creditor holding the majority of the Class 2 claims would have voted in favour of the Plan.

Note 10: Infra, see paragraph [18] below. A wholly owned subsidiary of Uniforêt Inc., 3735061 Canada Inc. (373) offered to purchase all the U.S. Notes for 30% of their principal amounts. The funds to satisfy this offer were borrowed from a bank syndicate and the syndicate loans were guaranteed by Jolina. 373 defaulted under the syndicate loans. Jolina stepped into the shoes of the bank syndicate and took the U.S. Notes acquired by 373 in lieu of payment of the syndicate loan.

---

143. The sale of the business as a going concern appears to be a commercially viable alternative to the Plan that could improve overall recoveries available to creditors by approximately $26.4 million to $42.4 million, representing an increase of approximately 31.7% to 50.6%.

144. The creditors most prejudiced by the Plan are the Class 2 creditors that would share in Notes A and Notes B, primarily Jolina and the minority US Noteholders. If the business were sold as a going concern and the proceeds distributed in the same manner as the cash payments that would be made to affected creditors under the plan, we estimate that such Class 2 creditors would recover $26.4 million to $42.4 million, more than they will recover under the Plan. These amounts would be reduced by any amount that would be needed to make a fair and reasonable distribution on account of the Class 7 Jolina shareholder loan. Under the Plan, Jolina retains its existing equity in Uniforêt while no equity is offered to the Minority US Noteholders. In these circumstances, the compromise being required of the Minority U.S. Noteholders is disproportionately large and cannot be considered reasonable.

145. As previously noted, the Monitor, in its July 23 Report, its October 28 Report and its December 11 Report, concluded that the Plan was fair and reasonable. Having given due consideration to the foregoing issues, the other matters discussed in this report, and all of the considerations outlined by Madam Justice Paperny in Re. Canadian Airlines, [See Note 11 below] we respectfully disagree with the conclusion of the Monitor and we have concluded that the Plan is not fair and reasonable.

Note 11: (2000) 20 C.B.R. (4th) 1, at page 36: Where a company is insolvent, only the creditors maintain a meaningful stake in its assets. Through the mechanism of liquidation or insolvency legislation, the interests of shareholders are pushed to the bottom rung of the priority ladder. The expectations of creditors and shareholders must be viewed and measured against an altered financial and legal landscape. Shareholders cannot reasonably expect to maintain a financial interest in an insolvent company where creditors' claims are not being paid in full. It is through the lens of insolvency that the court must consider whether the acts of the company are in fact oppressive, unfairly prejudicial or unfairly disregarded. *CCAA* proceedings have recognized that shareholders may not have "a true interest to be protected" because there is no reasonable prospect of economic value to be realized by the shareholders given the existing financial misfortunes of the company: Royal Oak Mines Ltd., supra, para. 4., Re Cadillac Fairview Inc. [1995] O.J. No. 707 (March 7, 1995), Doc. B28/95 (Ont. Gen. Div. [Commercial List]), and T. Eaton Company, supra. To avail itself of the protection of the *CCAA*, a company must be insolvent. The *CCAA* considers the hierarchy of interests and assesses fairness and reasonableness in that context. The court's mandate not to sanction a plan in the absence of fairness necessitates the determination as to whether the complaints of dissenting creditors and shareholders are legitimate, bearing in mind the company's financial state. The articulated purpose of the Act and the jurisprudence interpreting it, "widens the lens" to balance a broader range of interests that includes creditors and shareholders and beyond the company, the employees and the public, and tests the fairness of the plan with reference to its impact on all of its constituents. It is through the lens of insolvency legislation that the rights and interests of both shareholders and creditors must be considered. The reduction or elimination of rights of both groups is a function of the insolvency and not of oppressive conduct in the operation of the *CCAA*. The antithesis of oppression is fairness, the guiding test for judicial sanction. If a plan unfairly disregards or is unfairly prejudicial it will not be approved. However, the court retains the power to compromise or prejudice rights to effect a broader purpose, the restructuring of an insolvent company, provided that the plan does so in a fair manner.

¶ 15 Following completion of most of the proof on May 2nd, 2003, the Court shared with the parties and their counsel its principal preoccupation concerning the fairness of the Plan in circumstances where, as here, secured creditors are asked to reduce the face amount of their notes by almost half and to accept, eventually, reduced interest on these reduced notes. The Court asked why the Plan failed to replace what was to be taken from them by equity [See Note 12 below], unencumbered by a repurchase option [See Note 13 below]. Uniforêt responded to this enquiry on May 6, 2003 by further amending the Plan to effectively remove the repurchase option and to extend the delay during which a noteholder can exercise the conversion rights attaching to the B Notes from 2004 to 2008, coincidental with the maturity date of such notes. If exercised, the Class 2 creditors would hold 55% of the equity of Uniforêt.

Note 12: As was done for example in Plans approved in Re Skeena Cellulose Inc., (100% of the equity offered to the secured creditors) R Silcorp Limited, (75%); Re Pioneer Companies Inc., (57%); Re Microcell Telecommunications Inc., 500-11-019761-036; 2003-04-30 (99.9% to the creditors); Re White Rose, (94.4%); Re Royal Oak Mines Inc., 14 C.B.R. (4th) 279 (99%); Re Eagle Precision, (90.3%); Bluestar Battery, (83%); Re Algoma Steel Inc., 30 C.B.R. (4th) 1 (100%); Re McWatters Mining (2002), (75% to unsecured creditors); Re 360 Networks, (100%); Re Kmart, (50% to secured creditors). See as well Jolina's Exhibits J-28 and 29 and the Monitor's Exhibit M-1.

Note 13: Supra, Note 8.

¶ 16 On the same morning, the Opposing Creditors submitted a "Re-Amended Particularized Contestation" to further amend their conclusions to ask for an "Alternate Plan" in the event a "going concern sale" cannot profitably be concluded. The Alternate Plan would differ from the Plan in that:

(a) Class 2 creditors would receive one class of New Notes in an aggregate amount of $100 million having the same repayment and interest terms as Notes A under the Plan and 90% of the equity of Uniforêt following a reorganization of its capital structure pursuant to S.191 of the *Canada Business Corporations Act* (CBCA) [See Note 14 below], and

---

Note 14: Supra, Note 4.

(b) Jolina's claim as a Class 3 creditor would be disallowed and put into Class 5. The Bank of Montreal claim would also be added to Class 5 and disallowed as an "unaffected obligation".

LEGAL PRINCIPLES

¶ 17 Counsel for the Opposing Creditors remind the Court that shareholders do not have an economic stake in an insolvent company seeking relief under the *CCAA* [See Note 15 below]. They add that a plan of arrangement should offer more to creditors than would be available to them under a liquidation [See Note 16 below]. In assessing fairness of a plan, the Court must consider alternatives to it that are commercially available [See Note 17 below], in particular a sale of the enterprise as a going concern. Moreover, they point to the inherent jurisdiction of the Court either to amend the plan for compelling reasons [See Note 18 below] or to order a sale of assets before a plan is presented to the creditors [See Note 19 below].

Note 15: Supra, Note 11, and see Re Central Capital Corp., 38 C.B.R. (3d) 1 (Ont. C.A.), at page 37, paragraph 90 where Mr. Justice Finlayson observed that: In the case of an insolvency where the debts to creditors clearly exceed the assets of the company, the policy of federal insolvency legislation appears to be clear that shareholders do not have the right to look to the assets of the corporation until the creditors have been paid.; Re T. Eaton Co., 15 C.B.R. (4th) 311 (Ont. S.C.J.), at page 314, paragraphs 9 to 13 inclusive and Re Royal Oak Mines Inc., 14 C.B.R. (4th) 279 (Ont. S.C.J.), at page 281, paragraph 2 where Mr. Justice Farley, prior to approving a proposal contemplating the sale of a business, observed that: [...] the shareholders would have to appreciate that, when viewed as to the hierarchy of interests to receive value in a liquidation related transaction, they are at the bottom. Further in these particular circumstances there are, in relation to the available tax losses (which is in itself a conditional asset), very substantial amounts of unsecured debt standing on the shareholders' shoulders. That is, the shareholders, even assuming an ongoing operation achieving a turnaround to profitability without restructuring, would have to wait a long while before their interests saw the light of day.

Note 16: Supra, Note 1, at page 26, paragraph 96, where Madam Justice Paperny reminds us that: The sanction of the court of a creditor-approved plan is not to be considered as a rubber stamp process. Although the majority vote that brings the plan to a sanction hearing plays a significant role in the court's assessment, the court will consider other matters as are appropriate in light of its discretion. In the unique circumstances of this case, it is appropriate to consider a number of additional matters: a. The composition of the unsecured vote; b. What creditors would receive on liquidation or bankruptcy as compared to the Plan; c. Alternatives available to the Plan and bankruptcy; d. Oppression; e. Unfairness to Shareholders of CAC; and f. The public interest.

Note 17: See Re T. Eaton Co., Supra, Note 15, at page 314, paragraphs 8 and 9.

Note 18: See Ontario v. Canadian Airlines Corp., (2001) 29 C.B.R. (4th) 236 (Alb. Q.B.), at paragraph 61.

Note 19: See Re Canadian Red Cross Society, 5 C.B.R. (4th) 299 (Ont. S.C.J.), at page 315, paragraphs 43 and 45.

¶ 18 Counsel for Uniforêt and the Monitor acknowledged that generally, a plan of arrangement is consensual and results from negotiations leading to agreement [See Note 20 below]. They remind the Court that its role on a sanction hearing "is to consider whether the plan fairly balances the interests of all the stakeholders" [See Note 21 below] including the public interest. [See Note 22 below] Perfection is not required. [See Note 23 below] They add that there is a heavy burden upon Opposing Creditors in their quest to upset the Plan [See Note 24 below] and conclude that the Court should be reluctant to interfere with the business decisions of a majority of creditors "reached as a body" [See Note 25 below].

Note 20: See Algoma Steel Corp. v. Royal Bank, (1992) 11 C.B.R. (3d) 11 (Ont. C.A.), at page 14, paragraph 7.

Note 21: Supra, Note 11, at page 5, paragraph 3, where Madam Justice Paperny adds: Faced with an insolvent organization, its role is to look forward and ask: does this plan represent a fair and reasonable compromise that will permit a viable commercial entity to emerge? It is also an exercise in assessing current reality by comparing available commercial alternatives to what is offered in the proposed plan.

Note 22: Ibid, at pages 42 to 44 inclusive, paragraphs 171 to 177.

Note 23: Ibid, at page 44, pages 178 and 179, citing with approval the remarks of Mr. Justice Farley in Re Sammi Atlas Inc., (1998), 3 C.B.R. (4th) 171 (Ont. Gen. Div.), at page 173: A plan under the *CCAA* is a compromise; it cannot be expected to be perfect. It should be approved if it is fair, reasonable and equitable. Equitable treatment is not necessarily equal treatment. Equal treatment may be contrary to equitable treatment. And see Re Quintette Coal Ltd., (1992) 13 C.B.R. (3d) 146, at page 165, paragraph 93.

Note 24: See Re Central Guaranty Trustco Ltd., (1993), 21 C.B.R. (3d) 139, at page 141, where Mr. Justice Farley observed that: The Revised Plan of Arrangement had required that there be a vote on the proposed compromise re these Claims (with a majority in number representing three-quarters in value of the proven Claims). That vote was even more overwhelming as only FSTQ voted against. 92.54% by number (96.16% by value) were in favour and 7.46% by number (3.84% by value) were opposed. This on either basis is well beyond the specific majority requirement of *CCAA*. Clearly there is a very heavy burden on parties seeking to upset a plan that the required majority have found that they could vote for; given the overwhelming majority this burden is no lighter. This vote by sophisticated lenders speaks volumes as to fairness and reasonableness. But see also Re Quintette Coal Ltd., ibid, at pages 168 and 169, paragraphs 108 to 116.

Note 25: See Re Sammi Atlas Inc., supra, Note 23, at page 174, paragraph 5.

DISCUSSION

A. The Plan is prejudicial to the Class 2 Creditors

1. Two Fundamental Reasons

¶ 19 The Opposing Creditors and their experts criticize the First Plan on several fronts. On the one hand they assert that the First Plan treats some unsecured creditors more favourably than the Class 2 secured creditors. They point out that Jolina will receive the entire amount of both its $5.4 million shareholder loan (Class 7) and its $3.5 million advance towards the acquisition and installation of a planer in the Peribonka sawmill (Class 3) and that the forestry contractors will realize 75% of their claims (Class 4). On the other hand, they argue that the Plan is confiscatory in that the Class 2 creditors will only receive 51% of the face amount of their old U.S. notes two years later than promised at a lower interest rate while they wait to be paid and they will not receive any meaningful equity to replace what has been taken from them, nor are they entitled to recover unpaid interest accrued on the U.S. Notes.

2. Too fair to other creditors, especially Jolina

¶ 20 There is no doubt Jolina has been relatively well treated under both the First Plan and the Plan. Jolina is Uniforêt's White Knight. [See Note 26 below] It has been a shareholder and involved in the affairs of Uniforêt since 1994. It financed a new planer for the Péribonka sawmill in late 1999. It ultimately provided the funding to acquire the majority of the U.S. Notes in Uniforêt's initial attempt to rationalize its debt through a public offering for all the U.S. Notes at 30% of their principal amount in early 2000. This initiative attracted about 50% of the U.S. Notes at a cost of $33 million, or 53 cent(s). Jolina then acquired another 16% of the U.S. Notes in the market, enough to control the outcome of the vote by the Class 2 creditors. It helped to backstop an $11M short term or bridge loan from the Bank of Montreal to pay wages and other pressing payables. Uniforêt repaid over $6 million of this loan and shortly thereafter applied to the Court for relief under the C.C.A.A. The balance due on this loan is treated as an "unaffected obligation [See Note 27 below]. Accordingly, the White Knight's several claims have received generous treatment under the Plan, as well they should. After all, Jolina is Uniforêt's largest and most important creditor, quite apart from being a major shareholder. Plans of arrangement cannot hope to succeed without the approval of such a creditor. The Plan proposes, in effect, to make Jolina more or less whole, at least eventually [See Note 28 below].

Note 26: Defined in Dictionary of Finance and Investment Terms, Barron's, 1985, at p. 470 as: WHITE KNIGHT acquirer sought by the target of an unfriendly TAKEOVER to rescue it from the unwanted bidder's control. The white knight strategy is an alternative to SHARK REPELLENT tactics and is used to avert an extended or bitter fight for control.

Note 27: Supra, Note 6 (h).

Note 28: Ignoring any discount for projected delays in payment.

¶ 21 For a plan of arrangement to succeed, an insolvent company must secure the approval of all classes of its creditors, even those who have subordinated their claims to all other creditors, as is the case with the debentureholders (Class 6). It does not necessarily follow that a plan generous to some creditors must therefore be unfair to others. A plan can be more generous to some creditors and still fair to all creditors [See Note 29 below]. A creditor like Jolina that has stepped into the breach on several occasions to keep Uniforêt afloat in the 4 years preceding the filing of the First Plan warrants special treatment.

Note 29: See Algoma Steel v. Royal Bank, Supra, Note 20, at page 9 where Mr. Justice Farley notes: What might appear on the surface to be unfair to one party when viewed in relation to all other parties may be considered to be quite appropriate.

¶ 22 The Forresters' claims, although unsecured, are another special case. The Forresters had to be encouraged to bring their equipment back into the bush after the winter thaw. Without logs, the sawmills have nothing to cut. Similarly, if government permits (stumpage duties) are not paid in one year, they will not be issued in a subsequent year [See Note 30 below]. This explains why the cost of permits are quite properly treated in the Plan as "unaffected obligations".

Note 30: See Section 7 of the Forest Act, supra, Note 6 (g).

---

3. Unfair to Class 2 Creditors

¶ 23 The minority Class 2 creditors complain that Jolina wears too many hats in this dossier. They argue that if Jolina, like them [See Note 31 below], was nothing more than a holder of U.S. Notes, it would not have voted in favour of the proposed treatment for Class 2 creditors. It did so, they add, only because of the generous treatment proposed for its unsecured claims under classes 3, 5 and 7 and the fact it was already a major shareholder. This is, of course, a purely hypothetical argument that nevertheless invites an analysis of the treatment actually accorded to the Class 2 creditors.

Note 31: That is, the proverbial "reasonable person".

¶ 24 The experts and Uniforêt agree that the "enterprise" or "going concern" values of the businesses of Uniforêt lie somewhere between $90 million (Houlihan in 2001) and $112 million (PWC in 2003) [See Note 32 below]. There is also general agreement that Uniforêt cannot support debt in excess of $60 million from its current and projected cash flows [See Note 33 below]. This explains why the old U.S. Notes are to be exchanged for two classes of notes, $60 million of "A" notes and $40 million of "B" notes ($100 million in the aggregate) and why there is a conversion feature into shares attached to the "B" notes.

Note 32: This is the top of a range of between $90 and $112 million.

Note 33: Or more accurately, its earnings before interest, taxes, depreciation and amortisation (EBITDA).

¶ 25 Thus, Uniforêt proposes to give the Class 2 creditors its assessment of its entire enterprise value backed by the same security the U.S. noteholders enjoyed under their Trust Indenture [See Note 34 below]. If the workout over the next four to five years is successful, the holders of "B" notes will be able to share, to the extent of 55%, any future equity accruing to the shares of Uniforêt, in excess of $40 million. Mathematically, 55% of nothing is no different than 90% of nothing. However, a successful workout combined with improved economic conditions for the Canadian forestry industry - capital intensive, highly cyclical and beetle infested - may permit the "B" noteholders to recover something of what has been lost from the face amount of their old U.S. notes.

Note 34: Supra, Note 3.

¶ 26 The experts further agree that the orderly liquidation values of the assets of Uniforêt in a bankruptcy scenario will not realize more than $90.4 million at best [See Note 35 below]. Most estimates are well below this figure, including that of PWC. The one area where the experts differ is what they think might be realized, and when, if the enterprise were offered for sale "as a going concern" while under the protection of the *CCAA*. The Monitor and Mr. Roberts of CIB World Markets doubt such a sale would attract a price any more favourable than what is offered in the Plan anytime sooner than 18 months, if ever. Mr. Meakin of PWC thinks a carefully orchestrated sale culminating in an auction while under the umbrella of the *CCAA* could result in a return to the Class 2 creditors in the next 6 months of up to $42 million more than what they are to receive under the Plan. The Monitor views any such result as entirely "illusoire, irréaliste et utopique". His views are shared by Mr. Moreau, the president and chief executive officer of Uniforêt, expressed even more succinctly. Mr. Roberts observed that ever since Uniforêt applied for relief from the Court, competitors in the industry have considered it to be "for sale", yet no serious buyer has as yet surfaced. He suggests that competitors are waiting to acquire a bargain in an industry beset with overcapacity compounded by punishing countervailing duties imposed by our southern neighbours. Worse, one such competitor holds a right of first refusal affecting a key asset.

Note 35: Estimated by the Monitor in paragraph 32 of his February 27, 2003 report reproduced above in paragraph [10] and based on the rosiest of assumptions.

¶ 27 Mr. Meakin's "utopian" views as to a possible outcome from a sale of the enterprise fails to account for some $19.5 million of payments due to the creditors of unaffected obligations, presupposes that (a) the payment of $6 million to the Bank of Montreal is an avoidable transaction, (b) the balance of $4 million due on its loan is a Class 5 claim and (c) omits contracts that would have to be assumed by a buyer of at least $2.3 million. This reduces a best case scenario from a sale of the business to less than a possible $10 million improvement for the Class 2 Creditors, before expenses. The Opposing Creditors' share of this theoretical sum would not exceed $2.8 million before expenses. Further, Mr. Meakin's proposal to sidestep the right of first refusal is unconvincing. This right, together with long term fiber procurement contracts, if not revoked, "would hamper significantly any kind of divestiture process" according to Mr. Meakin's partner, Mr. Leblanc.

¶ 28 There are serious risks associated with any attempted sale of an insolvent enterprise over an unspecified period of time. Employees who are key to Uniforêt's business operations but not necessarily to a buyer's operations will almost certainly begin looking for safe havens. Customers will look to other sources for their wood products. Suppliers will tighten credit facilities and look for other customers. There will almost certainly be erosion on several fronts. Added to all this, it should not be forgotten that those creditors of Uniforêt who have voted in favour of the First Plan have implicitly agreed that current management and direction should remain unchanged.

¶ 29 Given all of these factors, the Court concludes that it would be folly to attempt a sale of Uniforêt's businesses – even to test the market – almost 2 years after the First Plan was filed for so small a possible yet unlikely gain. Uniforêt has so far managed to survive under *CCAA* protection in weak and difficult market conditions all the while fighting this litigation. It deserves a chance to prove to its stakeholders that it can both survive and return to profitability. This is what the *CCAA* was designed to encourage and facilitate.

B. Who really gets hurt

¶ 30 For those Opposing Creditors who acquired their notes for 28 cent(s) in the dollar like Prospect, there will be no "haircut". Rather, the issue for them is the size of their gain and the yield on their investment to maturity. Only those U.S. noteholders who paid more in the after market for their U.S. Notes than they stand to receive from the Plan will suffer any loss under it. Jolina's average cost for the U.S. Notes it holds amounts to about 53 cent(s) in the dollar. Its haircut will be modest. Accordingly it should come as no surprise to anyone that it does not insist on equity in circumstances where it will recover almost all it had to pay for its U.S. Notes. Add to this the fact it already holds 40% of the existing equity in Uniforêt. If it converts the "B" Notes it will receive under the Plan, it will increase its equity position in Uniforêt to about 63%, allowing for dilution.

¶ 31 Highland acquired its U.S. Notes from Prospect, one of the funds it manages, at a cost of 80 cent(s), after Uniforêt had applied for relief under the *CCAA*. The market at the time for the U.S. Notes was in the region of 28 cent(s). Thus, Prospect has already realized a tidy gain on the sale of $3 million of the principal amount of the U.S. Notes it then held. It is left with $20 million of U.S. Notes. The explanation for this generous transaction – at a price more than twice the market price – leaves as many questions unanswered as were answered. Without any U.S. Notes, Highland would have no standing in these proceedings as a Class 2 creditor. The price Highland elected to pay for its U.S. Notes reflects what it hoped to achieve for all its clients in its forthcoming negotiations with Uniforêt. Highland believed that its group would control the claims of the U.S. noteholders in any Chapter 11 type proceedings and assumed that Jolina, being a shareholder of Uniforêt, would not be permitted to vote on any of its claims as Uniforêt's creditor. In this it was mistaken, as Highland's President, Mr. Dondero, readily conceded. Canadian rules do not prevent a shareholder of an insolvent company from voting on its claims as a creditor.

¶ 32 Thus, only four of the six Opposing Creditors will sustain a real loss if the Plan is approved. Together they hold $12.5 million of U.S. Notes purchased at prices ranging from 96 cent(s) to 66 cent(s). Highland's loss is self inflicted. It is also Prospect's initial gain. In addition, Prospect will gain from the Plan itself, having purchased its $20 million U.S. Notes for only about 28 cent(s). In the giant scheme of things, four holders of 10%

of the $125 million U.S. Notes will sustain a legitimate loss if the Plan is approved. They will lose much more in a bankruptcy.

¶ 33 Arguably, the question the Court might ask is whether a Plan thought by the Monitor to be both fair and reasonable – feasible and workable – and to have been approved by the required majority of all the creditors of Uniforêt should nevertheless be sacrificed to please four speculators [See Note 36 below]. Of course not. Their actual losses will not exceed 45 cent(s) in the dollar [See Note 37 below] if the Plan succeeds, perhaps less if the conversion option is exercised. Absent bad faith, the *CCAA* should not be employed to permit a cranky minority creditor to frustrate a feasible and fair plan that has been blessed by an overwhelming majority of all the creditors of a debtor [See Note 38 below].

Note 36: That is, investors in below investment grade securities acquired in the after market.

Note 37: In most cases, much less.

Note 38: Supra, Note 24.

C. The Equity Issue

¶ 34 It became evident during the hearing that a serious bone of contention between the Opposing Creditors and Uniforêt centered on the unwillingness of the latter to give sufficient equity to the former. While the First Plan provided for a conversion option exercisable before September 15, 2004, it came with a very short fuse, or repurchase option [See Note 39 below]. By the amendments made to the Plan on May 6, 2003, the repurchase option has been dropped and the conversion of the "B" Notes may be exercised anytime before September 15, 2008. This puts a serious dent into the oppression argument advanced by the Opposing Creditors concerning the lack of an equity kicker for the Class 2 creditors.

Note 39: Supra, Note 8.

¶ 35 Arguably, the issue now becomes how much equity ought to have been made available to the Class 2 creditors. Jolina accepted its share of a potential 55% of the equity subject to the repurchase option. Uniforêt has removed that option and extended the conversion period by 4 years. The shareholders of Uniforêt, qua shareholders, are not involved in the Plan. Nothing was offered to them and one consequence of the Plan is that whatever interest they now have is going to be diluted. In all the circumstances of this case, the Court concludes that the offer of equity, while perhaps not overly generous when compared to some other recently sanctioned plans [See Note 40 below], is nevertheless adequate and fair.

Note 40: Supra, Note 12.

D. Bad Faith

¶ 36 The good faith of the Opposing Creditors has been called into question by Madam Justice Zerbisias [See Note 41 below]. The Opposing Creditors assert that Uniforêt "and its allies [...] have shown bad faith of the kind which should convince any reasonable observer that the Plan is neither fair nor reasonable". They point to the treatment accorded the Bank of Montreal $11 million loan, the repayment of part of it [See Note 42 below], a loan by Jolina of $1.1 million [See Note 43 below] repaid by Uniforêt on March 6, 2001 and Jolina's claim for the purchase of the planer (Class 3) [See Note 44 below].

Note 41: Supra, Note 2, at pages 29 and 30; paragraphs 95 and 96.

Note 42: Which the Opposing Creditors say is a $6 million preferential payment.

Note 43: Used to settle wage claims of an affiliate company for which Messrs Perron and Mercier, as directors of the affiliate, were legally liable.

Note 44: Jolina's security position in respect of its advances to acquire the planer is in some doubt.

¶ 37 Suffice it to say that there has been aggressive behaviour displayed by all the parties in the course of this affair, at least some of the time. The Court has already commented on the transactions impugned by the Opposing Creditors [See Note 45 below]. Absent a bankruptcy, these claims will all be resolved eventually, just like the claims of the Opposing Creditors, either in accordance with their terms or subject to the Plan. Again, absent a bankruptcy, the impugned claims don't add any value to the Petitioners' enterprise. However, had the planer never been acquired, the Peribonka mill would not have been as profitable as it was in the 18 months preceding the *CCAA* filing.

Note 45: See paragraphs [19], [20], [22] and [23] above.

¶ 38 Aggressive behaviour is to be expected in proceedings of this kind [See Note 46 below]. The *CCAA* favours the survival of businesses and the jobs that go with them. Where, as here, it has been amply demonstrated that the creditors as a whole will fare much better under the Plan than in a liquidation, the solution is obvious. The issue in this case was to decide if a minority group of secured creditors has been materially oppressed by the behaviour of the majority. That case has not been made out. The U.S. noteholders are offered the entire enterprise value of Uniforêt in the form of reconstituted notes and they will receive annual yields on these notes for the next five years varying between some 10% and 17%.

Note 46: See Re T. Eaton Co., Supra, Note 15, where at page 258, paragraph 6, Mr. Justice Farley observed: "The Act clearly contemplates rough-and tumble negotiations between debtor companies desperately seeking a chance to survive and creditors willing to keep them afloat, but on the best terms they can get, [...]".

E. The Alternate Plan

¶ 39 While the Court may have the authority to adopt a Plan different from that sought to be sanctioned, it should only exercise that authority if it is satisfied that the proposed Plan is unfair. Moreover, the Alternate Plan proposed by the Opposing Creditors calls for a reorganization of the capital structure of Uniforêt Inc. requiring confiscation of the rights of existing shareholders without their approval being required. The Court has qualified the Plan as both fair and reasonable. The shareholders of Uniforêt have already offered control of their company to the U.S. noteholders. That is quite enough in the circumstances of this case.

¶ 40 FOR THESE REASONS, THE COURT:

¶ 41 MAINTAINS Petitioners' Motion to Sanction a Plan of Arrangement;

¶ 42 DISMISSES the Opposing Creditors Re-Amended Particularized Contestation;

¶ 43 SANCTIONS and APPROVES the Second Amended Plan of Compromise and Arrangement (Plan);

¶ 44 PERMITS Petitioners to replace the U.S. Secured Notes, as defined in paragraph 1.1 of the Plan, by two new secured notes for each unpaid U.S. Note, a Note "A" and a Note "B" as described in paragraph 4.2 of the Plan and in virtue of two Trust Agreements previously approved by the Securities and Exchange Commissions of the United States;

¶ 45 DECLARES that the American Trust Indenture, as defined in paragraph 1.1 of the Plan, be amended and updated by the said two Trust Agreements;

¶ 46 DECLARES that all of the Executory Contracts, as defined in paragraph 1.1 of the Plan, save those terminated or repudiated by Petitioners before the "Plan Implementation Date", are in full force and effect as at the Plan Implementation Date, notwithstanding:

a) that Petitioners have obtained relief under the *CCAA*;

b) the effect on Petitioners of the completion of any one of the transactions contemplated by the Plan;

c) any compromises or arrangements effected pursuant to the Plan;

d) any default with respect to such a contract by Petitioners prior to the Plan Implementation Date; or

e) any automatic termination of any such contract or any purported termination thereof by any Person other than Petitioners

the whole in conformity with paragraph 6.7 of the Plan.

¶ 47 DECLARES that no party to an Executory Contract, as defined in paragraph 1.1 of the Plan, shall be entitled to accelerate the obligations of Petitioners or terminate, rescind or repudiate such other party's obligations under an Executory Contract following the Plan Implementation Date on the sole ground:

a) of any event that occurred on or prior to the Plan Implementation Date which would have entitled such party to accelerate Petitioners' obligations under such Executory Contract;

b) that Petitioners have obtained relief under the *CCAA*;

c) of the effect on Petitioners of the completion of any of the transactions contemplated by the Plan; or

d) of any compromises or arrangements effected pursuant to the Plan.

the whole in conformity with paragraph 6.7 of the Plan.

¶ 48 DECLARES that the date for the implementation of the Plan will be deemed to be the date specified in a Certificate to be filed in the Court record by Petitioners and the Monitor as soon as all the conditions specified in paragraph 5.1 of the Plan have been fulfilled or satisfied.

¶ 49 EXEMPTS Petitioners from furnishing any security;

¶ 50 ORDERS provisional execution of this judgment notwithstanding appeal;

¶ 51 THE WHOLE with costs against the Opposing Creditors and in favour of Petitioners, the Monitor and Jolina Capital Inc.

DANIEL H. TINGLEY J.S.C.

APPENDIX 9

Cross-Border Insolvency Protocol in Re 360networks inc.

between British Columbia Supreme Court, Vancouver (Mr. Justice D.F. Tysoe), Case No. L011792, (June 28, 2001) and United States Bankruptcy Court for the Southern District of New York (Hon. Allan L. Gropper), Case No. 01-13721-alg, (August 29, 2001)

CROSS-BORDER INSOLVENCY PROTOCOL FOR 360NETWORKS INC. AND ITS AFFILIATED COMPANIES

1. Certain defined terms used in this Protocol shall have the meanings assigned to them in Appendix "A".

2. The 360 Group has developed this Protocol which when approved by the Canadian Court and the U.S. Court shall govern the conduct of all parties in interest in the Insolvency Proceedings.

3. The Parent is a Nova Scotia company extra provincially registered in British Columbia and is the ultimate parent company of an enterprise that operates through its various subsidiaries and affiliates, in Canada, the United States and various other countries throughout the world.

4. The Parent and the 360 Canada Group have commenced the Canadian Proceedings by filing an application under the applicable provisions of the *Companies' Creditors Arrangement Act* in the British Columbia Supreme Court. The Parent and the 360 Canada Group have sought the CCAA Order pursuant to which:

(a) the Parent and the 360 Canada Group have been determined to be entities to which the *CCAA* applies, all proceedings in Canada have been stayed as against them and they have been authorized to continue reorganization steps under the *CCAA*; and

(b) the Monitor was appointed as monitor of the Parent and the 360 Canada Group, with the rights, powers, duties and limitations upon liabilities set forth in the *CCAA* Order.

5. The 360 US Group have commenced the U.S. Proceedings under chapter 11 of the United States Bankruptcy Code, 11 U.S.C. § 101-1330 in the United States Bankruptcy Court for the Southern District of New York. The members of the 360 U.S. Group are continuing in possession of their respective properties managing their respective businesses as debtors in possession, pursuant to sections 1107 and 1108 of the Bankruptcy Code. The U.S. Trustee has not yet appointed any official U.S. Committee in the U.S. Proceedings.

Purpose and Goals

6. While the Insolvency Proceedings are pending in Canada, the United States and elsewhere for the 360 Group, the implementation of basic administrative procedures is necessary to coordinate certain activities in the Insolvency Proceedings, protect the rights of

parties thereto and ensure the maintenance of the Court's independent jurisdiction and comity. Accordingly, this Protocol has been developed to promote the following mutually desirable goals and objectives in both the U.S. Proceedings and the Canadian Proceedings and, to any extent necessary, the Foreign Proceedings:

(a) harmonize and coordinate activities in the Insolvency Proceedings before the Canadian Court, the U.S. Court and any foreign court;

(b) promote the orderly and efficient administration of the Insolvency Proceedings to, among other things, maximize the efficiency of the Insolvency Proceedings, reduce the costs associated therewith and avoid duplication of effort;

(c) honour the independence and integrity of the Courts and other courts and tribunals of Canada, the United States or other countries;

(d) promote international cooperation and respect for comity among the Courts, the 360 Group, the Committees, the Estate representatives and other creditors and interested parties in the Insolvency Proceedings;

(e) facilitate the fair, open and efficient administration of the Insolvency Proceedings for the benefit of all of the creditors of the 360 Group and other interested parties, wherever located; and

(f) implement a framework of general principles to address basic administrative issues arising out of the cross-border and international nature of the Insolvency Proceedings.

Comity and Independence of the Courts

7. The approval and implementation of this Protocol shall not divest or diminish the U.S. Court's and the Canadian Court's independent jurisdiction over the subject matter of the U.S. Proceedings and the Canadian Proceedings, respectively. By approving and implementing this Protocol, neither the U.S. Court, the Canadian Court, the 360 Group nor any creditors or interested parties shall be deemed to have approved or engaged in any infringement on the sovereignty of the United States or Canada.

8. The U.S. Court shall have sole and exclusive jurisdiction and power over the conduct and hearing of the U.S. Proceedings. The Canadian Court shall have sole and exclusive jurisdiction and power over the conduct and hearing of the Canadian Proceedings.

9. In accordance with the principles of comity and independence established in the two preceding paragraphs, nothing contained herein shall be construed to:

(a) increase, decrease or otherwise modify the independence, sovereignty or jurisdiction of the U.S. Court, the Canadian Court or any other court or tribunal in the United States or Canada, including the ability of any such court or tribunal to provide appropriate relief under applicable law on an ex parté or "limited notice" basis;

(b) require the 360 Group, the Committee or the Estate Representatives to take any action or refrain from taking any action that would result in a breach of any duty imposed on them by any applicable law;

(c) authorize any action that requires the specific approval of one or both of the Courts under the Bankruptcy Code or the CCAA after appropriate notice and a hearing (except to the extent that such action is specifically described in this Protocol); or

(d) preclude any creditor or other interested party from asserting such party's substantive rights under the applicable laws of the United States, Canada or any other jurisdiction including, without limitation, the rights of interested parties or affected persons to appeal from the decisions taken by one or both of the Courts.

10. The 360 Group, the Committee, the Estate Representatives and their respective employees, members, agents and professionals shall respect and comply with the independent, non-delegable duties imposed upon them by the Bankruptcy Code, the CCAA, the CCAA Order and other applicable laws.

Cooperation

11. To assist in the efficient administration of the Insolvency Proceedings, the 360 Group, the Committee and the Estate Representatives shall:

(a) reasonably cooperate with each other in connection with actions taken in both the U.S. Court and the Canadian Court; and

(b) take any other reasonable steps to coordinate the administration of the U.S. Proceedings and the Canadian Proceedings for the benefit of the 360 Group's respective estates and stakeholders.

12. To harmonize and coordinate the administration of the Insolvency Proceedings, the U.S. Court and the Canadian Court each shall use its best efforts to coordinate activities with and defer to the judgment of the other Court, where appropriate and feasible. The U.S. Court and the Canadian Court may communicate with one another with respect to any matter relating to the Insolvency Proceedings and may conduct joint hearings with respect to any matter relating to the conduct, administration, determination or disposition of any aspect of the U.S. Proceedings and the Canadian Proceedings, in circumstances where both Courts consider such joint hearings to be necessary or advisable and, in particular, to facilitate or coordinate with the proper and efficient conduct of the U.S. Proceedings and the Canadian Proceedings. With respect to any such hearing, unless otherwise ordered, the following procedures will be followed:

(a) a telephone or video link shall be established so that both the U.S. Court and the Canadian Court shall be able to simultaneously hear the proceedings in the other Court;

(b) any party intending to rely on any written evidentiary materials in support of a submission to the U.S. Court or the Canadian Court in connection with any joint hearing shall file such materials, which shall be identical insofar as possible and shall be consistent with the procedure and evidentiary rules and requirements of each Court, in advance of the time of such hearing or the submissions of such application. If a party has not previously appeared in or attorned or does not wish to attorn to the jurisdiction of either court, it shall be entitled to file such materials without, by the act of filing, being deemed to have attorned to the jurisdiction of the Court in which such material is filed, so long as it does not request in its materials or submissions any affirmative relief from the Court to which it does not wish to attorn;

(c) submissions or applications by any party shall be made only to the Court in which such party is appearing, unless specifically given leave by the other Court to make submissions or applications to it;

(d) the Judge of the U.S. Court and the Justice of the Canadian Court who will hear any such application shall be entitled to communicate with each other in advance of the hearing on the application, with or without counsel being present, to establish guidelines for the orderly submission of pleadings, papers and other materials and the rendering of decisions by the U.S. Court and the Canadian Court, and to deal with any related procedural, administrative or preliminary matters; and

(e) the Judge of the U.S. Court and the Justice of the Canadian Court, having heard any such application, shall be entitled to communicate with each other after the hearing on such application, without counsel present, for the purpose of determining whether consistent rulings can be made by both Courts, and the terms upon which such rulings shall be made, as well as to address any other procedural or non-substantive matter relating to such applications.

13. Notwithstanding the terms of the preceding paragraph, the Protocol recognizes that the U.S. Court and the Canadian Court are independent courts. Accordingly, although the Courts will seek to cooperate and coordinate with each other in good faith, each of the Courts shall be entitled at all times to exercise its independent jurisdiction and authority with respect to:

(a) matters presented to such Court; and

(b) the conduct of the parties appearing in such matters.

Retention and Compensation of Estate Representatives and Professionals

14. The Monitor, the Affiliated Professionals, the Canadian Representatives and Canadian Professionals appointed in the Canadian Proceedings shall all be subject to the sole and exclusive jurisdiction of the Canadian Court with respect all matters, including:

(a) their tenure in office;

(b) their retention and compensation;

(c) their liability, if any, to any person or entity, including the 360 Canada Group and any third parties, in connection with the Insolvency Proceedings; and

(d) the hearing and determination of any matters relating to them arising in the Canadian Proceedings under the CCAA or other applicable Canadian law.

15. The Monitor, Affiliated Professionals, Canadian Representatives and Canadian Professionals shall not be required to seek approval of their retention in the U.S. Court. Additionally, the Monitor, Affiliated Professionals, Canadian Representatives and Canadian Professionals:

(a) shall be compensated for their services solely in accordance with the CCAA and other applicable Canadian law or orders of the Canadian Court; and

(b) shall not be required to seek approval of their compensation in the U.S. Court.

16. The Monitor and any Affiliated Professionals and their officers, directors, employees, counsel and agents, wherever located, shall be entitled to the same protections and

immunities in the United States as those granted to them under the CCAA Order. In particular, except as otherwise provided in any subsequent order entered in the Canadian Proceedings, the Monitor and its Affiliated Professionals shall incur no liability or obligations as a result of the CCAA Order, the appointment of the Monitor or carrying out of the provisions of the CCAA Order by the Monitor or its Affiliated Professionals, except any such liability arising from actions of the Monitor or its Affiliated Professionals constituting gross negligence or wilful misconduct.

17. Any U.S. Representative appointed in the U.S. Proceedings and any examiner or trustee appointed in accordance with section 1104 of the Bankruptcy Code, shall be subject to the sole and exclusive jurisdiction of the U.S. Court with respect to all matters, including:

(a) their tenure in office;

(b) their retention and compensation;

(c) their liability, if any, to any person or entity, including the 360 U.S. Group and any third parties, in connection with the Insolvency Proceedings; and

(d) the hearing and determination of any other matters relating to them arising in the U.S. Proceedings under the Bankruptcy Code or other applicable laws of the United States.

18. The U.S. Representatives shall not be required to seek approval of their retention in the Canadian Court. Additionally, the U.S. Representatives:

(a) shall be compensated for their services solely in accordance with the Bankruptcy Code and other applicable laws of the United States or orders of the U.S. Court; and

(b) shall not be required to seek approval of their compensation in the Canadian Court.

19. Nothing in this Protocol shall be deemed to subject the Monitor to the jurisdiction of the U.S. Court or any court in the United States. To the extent that the Monitor may from time to time utilize the services and expertise of Affiliated Professionals in performing its role as monitor in the Canadian Proceedings, those Affiliated Professionals may include employees of, partners in or other individual affiliated with the Monitor in any jurisdiction including the United States. All services provided by such Affiliated Professionals in connection with the provision of monitoring services to the 360 Group, including services provided by individuals affiliated with the Monitor, shall be billed to the 360 Canada Group by and through the Monitor and shall be subject to the procedures and standards for review and approval of compensation applicable in the Canadian Court under the CCAA, the CCAA Order and any other applicable Canadian law or orders of the Canadian Court, and shall be subject to review and approval solely by the Canadian Court.

Rights to Appear and Be Heard

20. Each of the 360 Group, their creditors and other interested parties in the Insolvency Proceedings, including the Canadian Representatives and the U.S. Representatives, shall have the right and standing to:

(a) appear and be heard in either the U.S. Court or the Canadian Court in the Insolvency Proceedings to the same extent as a creditor and other interested party domiciled in the forum country, but solely to the extent such party is a creditor or other interested party in the forum country, subject to any local rules or regulations generally applicable to all parties appearing in the forum; and

(b) file notices of appearance or other papers with the Clerk of the U.S. Court or the Canadian Court in the Insolvency Proceedings; provided, however, that any appearance or filing may subject a creditor or interested party to the jurisdiction of the Court in which the appearance or filing occurs; provided further, that appearance by the U.S. Committee in the Canadian Proceedings or the Canadian Committee in the U.S. Proceedings, shall not form a basis for personal jurisdiction in Canada over the members of the U.S. Committee or vice versa. Notwithstanding the foregoing, and in accordance with the policies set forth above:

(i) the Canadian Court shall have jurisdiction over the U.S. Representatives and the U.S. Trustee solely with respect to the particular matters as to which the U.S. Representatives or the U.S. Trustee appear before the Canadian Court; and

(ii) the U.S. Court shall have jurisdiction over the Canadian Representatives solely with respect to the particular matters as to which the Canadian Representatives appear before the U.S. Court.

Notice

21. Notice of any motion, application or other pleading or paper filed in one or both of the Insolvency Proceedings and notice of any related hearings or other proceedings mandated by applicable law in connection with the Insolvency Proceedings or the Protocol shall be given by appropriate means (including, where circumstances warrant, by courier, telecopier or other electronic forms of communication) to the following:

(a) to creditors, including Estate Representatives, and other interested parties in accordance with the practice of the jurisdiction where the papers are filed or the proceedings are to occur; and

(b) to the extent not otherwise entitled to receive notice under subpart (a) of this paragraph, to:

(i) the Parent, 1066 West Hastings Street, Vancouver, B.C., Canada, V6E 3X1, attention: Catherine McEachern, Vice-President;

(ii) U.S. Bankruptcy Counsel, Willkie Farr & Gallagher, 787 Seventh Avenue, New York, New York, U.S.A., 10019, attention: Alan J. Lipkin, Esq.; and

(iii) CCAA counsel, Fasken Martineau DuMoulin LLP, 2100 – 1075 West Georgia Street, Vancouver, B.C., V6E 3G2, Canada, attention: Michael A. Fitch, Q.C.;

(iv) the Monitor and its counsel, PricewaterhouseCoopers LLP, 601 West Hastings Street, Vancouver, B.C., V6B 5A5, Canada, attention: David Bowra;

(v) counsel to any statutory committee or any other official appointed in the U.S. Cases or the Canadian Cases; and

(vi) the Office of the United States Trustee, 33 Whitehall Street, 21st Floor, New York, New York, U.S.A., 10004; and such other parties as may be designated by either Court from time to time.

Joint Recognition of Stays of Proceedings Under the Bankruptcy Code and the CCAA

22. In recognition of the importance of the Canadian Stay affecting creditors of the 360 Canada Group, their directors and others, and to the extent appropriate, the U.S. Court shall extend and enforce the Canadian Stay in the United States (to the same extent such stay of proceedings and actions is applicable in Canada) to prevent adverse actions against the 360 Canada Group, their directors and the assets, rights and holdings of the 360 Canada Group in the United States. In implementing the terms of this paragraph, the U.S. Court may consult with the Canadian Court regarding:

(a) the interpretation and application of the Canadian Stay and any orders for the Canadian Court modifying or granting relief from the Canadian Stay; and (b) the enforcement in the United States of the Canadian Stay.

23. In recognition of the importance of the U.S. Stay affecting creditors of the 360 U.S. Group and their assets under section 362 of the Bankruptcy Code for the benefit of the 360 Group and their respective estates and stakeholders, and to the extent appropriate, the Canadian Court shall extend and enforce the U.S. Stay in Canada (to the same extent such stay of proceedings and actions is applicable in the United States) to prevent adverse actions against the assets, rights and holdings of the 360 U.S. Group in Canada. In implementing the terms of this paragraph, the Canadian Court may consult with the U.S. Court regarding:

(a) the interpretation and application of the U.S. Stay and any orders of the U.S. Court modifying or granting relief from the U.S. Stay; and

(b) the enforcement in Canada of the U.S. Stay.

24. Nothing contained herein shall affect or limit the 360 Group or other parties' rights to assert the applicability or non-applicability of the U.S. Stay or the Canadian Stay to any particular proceeding, property, asset, activity or other matter, wherever pending or located.

Effectiveness; Modification

25. This Protocol shall become effective only upon its approval by both the U.S. Court and the Canadian Court.

26. This Protocol may not be supplemented, modified, terminated or replaced in any manner except by the U.S. Court and the Canadian Court. Notice of any legal proceeding to supplement, modify, terminate or replace this Protocol shall be given in accordance with the notice provision contained in this Protocol.

Procedure for Resolving Disputes Under the Protocol

27. Disputes relating to the terms, intent or application of this Protocol may be addressed by interested parties to either the U.S. Court, the Canadian Court or both Courts upon notice as set forth above. Where an issue is addressed to only one Court, in rendering a determination in any such dispute, such Court:

(a) shall consult with the other Court; and

(b) may, in its sole discretion, either:

    (i) render a binding decisions after such consultation;

(ii) defer to the determination of the other Court by transferring the matter, in whole or in part, to the other Court; or

(iii) seek a joint hearing of both Courts.

28. Notwithstanding the foregoing, each Court in making a determination shall have regard to the independence, comity or inherent jurisdiction of the other Court established under existing law.

Foreign Proceedings

29. To the extent that Foreign Proceedings are initiated, all persons affected hereby shall to the greatest extent possible, and provided that all creditors in such Foreign Proceedings are treated equally irrespective of their place of domicile, implement the procedures contemplated hereby in any Foreign Proceedings and be governed to the greatest extent possible by the purpose and policies of this Protocol in dealings related to the Foreign Proceedings.

30. If the Canadian Court enters an order approving a protocol with the courts of jurisdiction other than the U.S. Court, the U.S. Court shall honour such protocol to the extent permitted by the laws and treaties of the United States and consistent with the principles of comity and cooperation.

31. If the U.S. Court enters an order approving a protocol with the courts of a jurisdiction other than the Canadian Court, the Canadian Court shall honour such protocol to the extent permitted by the laws and treaties of Canada and consistent with the principles of comity and cooperation.

Preservation of Rights

32. Neither the terms of this Protocol nor any actions taken under the terms of this Protocol shall prejudice or affect the powers, rights, claims and defenses of the 360 Group and their estates, the Estate Representatives, the U.S. Trustee or any of the 360 Group creditors or equity holders under applicable law, including the Bankruptcy Code and the CCAA.

33. This Protocol shall be binding on and inure to the benefit of the parties hereto and their respective successors, assigns, representatives, heirs, executors, administrators, trustees (including any trustees of the 360 Group under chapters 7 or 11 of the *Bankruptcy Code*), and receivers, receiver-managers, trustees or custodians appointed under Canadian law, as the case may be.

34. Nothing contained herein shall alter the obligations of any number of the 360 U.S. Group to pay fees due under 28 U.S.C. § 1930(a)(6) based upon all disbursements made by U.S. Debtors in any jurisdictions.

APPENDIX "A"

The following terms shall have the following definitions:

(a) "Affiliated Professionals" means any person or corporation in any manner related to the Monitor who provides professionals services in furtherance of the Insolvency Proceedings, the restructuring and reorganization of the 360 Group or any member thereof or who provides any professional service in the normal course of the business of any member of the 360 Group;

(b) "Bankruptcy Code" means Title 11 of the United States Code, 11 U.S.C. § 101 et. seq.;

(c) "Canadian Court" means the Supreme Court of British Columbia which is seized of the Canadian Proceedings and any Court which considers an appeal therefrom;

(d) "Canadian Proceedings" shall mean those proceedings commenced under the CCAA in the Canadian Court in the Supreme Court of British Columbia, Vancouver Registry;

(e) "Canadian Professionals" shall mean any person or corporation retained by any of the Monitor, the 360 Group, or the Canadian Committees as approved by the Court who provides services of a professional nature in furtherance of the Canadian Proceedings or the restructuring or reorganization contemplated by the Canadian Proceedings;

(f) "Canadian Committees" shall mean any person, corporation or group appointed in the Canadian Proceedings to represent the interests of any one or more group of creditors or other interested parties;

(g) "Canadian Representatives" shall mean the Monitor, the Affiliated Professionals, the Canadian Committees and the Canadian Professionals;

(h) "Canadian Stay" means the stay of proceedings contained in the CCAA Order as it may be amended from time to time;

(i) "CCAA" means the Companies' Creditors Arrangement Act R.S.C. 1985, c. C-36 as amended from time to time;

(j) "CCAA Order" means that Order made in the Canadian Proceedings dated June 28, 2001 and any other orders or consequential orders that vary, amend or alter the CCAA Order;

(k) "Court" means any court wherever located wherein proceedings are taken so as to facilitate the object of the restructuring and reorganization of the 360 Group.

(l) "Estate Representatives" means the U.S. Representatives and the Canadian Representatives;

(m) "Foreign Proceedings" means any proceedings brought in countries other than the United States or Canada for the purposes of effecting a restructuring and reorganization of the business and affairs of any member of the 360 Group;

(n) "Insolvency Proceedings" means the Canadian Proceedings and the U.S. Proceedings and any other Foreign Proceedings that may be required for the reorganization and restructuring of the 360 Group;

(o) "Monitor" means PricewaterhouseCoopers Inc. appointed pursuant to the CCAA Order to monitor the affairs of certain members of the 360 Group;

(p) "Parent" means 360networks inc.;

(q) "Protocol" means this Cross-Border Insolvency Protocol as amended from time to time;

(r) "360 Group" means those companies listed in Schedule "A" hereto and includes the Parent, 360 Canada Group and 360 U.S. Group;

(s) "360 Canada Group" means those companies listed in Schedule A-1;

(t) "360 U.S. Group" means those companies listed in Schedule A-2;

(u) "U.S. Committee" means that committee appointed under the Bankruptcy Code to represent the interests of creditors or other parties in the U.S. Proceeding;

(v) "U.S. Court" means the United States Bankruptcy Court for the Southern District of New York and any Court which hears an appeal therefrom;

(w) "U.S. Proceeding" means that proceeding commenced in the U.S. Bankruptcy Court for the Southern District of New York by the 360 U.S. Group;

(x) "U.S. Professional" means any person or corporation retained pursuant to Sections 327 or 1104 of the Bankruptcy Code the U.S. Proceedings;

(y) "U.S. Representatives" means the U.S. Committee and the U.S. Professionals;

(z) "U.S. Stay" means that automatic stay of proceedings arising in the U.S. Proceedings or that applies under the Bankruptcy Code or as may be ordered or amended by the U.S. Court; and

(aa) "U.S. Trustee" means the United States Trustee in the U.S. Proceedings.

APPENDIX 10

SUPERIOR COURT OF JUSTICE

COMMERCIAL LIST

PROTOCOL CONCERNING COURT-TO-COURT COMMUNICATIONS IN CROSS BORDER CASES

The Commercial List has approved the adoption of the *Guidelines Applicable to Court-to-Court Communications in Cross Border Cases* ("Guidelines"), prepared by the American Law Institute, for matters on the Commercial List. The Guidelines have already been applied to international insolvency cases on the Commercial List. It is expected that these Guidelines will facilitate co-operative procedures for insolvency proceedings and other types of commercial disputes involving cross-border proceedings, where court-to-court communications might facilitate in harmonizing proceedings to help ensure consistent results and increase efficiency.

The Guidelines will only be applied in specific cases, following adequate notice to the parties.

Although the Guidelines were prepared for court-to-court communications as between Canada and the United States, the Commercial List endorses their application in court-to-court communications between Canada and other countries, and as between Ontario and the other provinces and territories.

Counsel and/or the parties should ensure that any issues concerning the confidentiality of materials to be transmitted by the Commercial List to another jurisdiction, including the deemed undertaking rule, Rule 30.1 of the Rules of Civil Procedure, be addressed when consideration is given by the court to the transmittal of evidentiary or written materials from the Commercial List to another court. The Guidelines are to apply only in a manner that is consistent with the Rules of Civil Procedure and the practice in this jurisdiction.

The Commercial List confirms, as noted in the Guidelines, that the Guidelines are not meant to be static, but are meant to be adapted and modified to fit the circumstances of individual cases, and to change and evolve as experience is gained from working with them.

A copy of the Guidelines may also be obtained from the Commercial List Office at 393 University Avenue, 10th Floor, Toronto, Ontario M5G 1E6, Telephone 416-327-5043, Fax 416-327-6228.

April 4, 2004

THE AMERICAN LAW INSTITUTE

TRANSNATIONAL INSOLVENCY: COOPERATION AMONG THE NAFTA COUNTRIES
PRINCIPLES OF COOPERATION AMONG THE NAFTA COUNTRIES
Guidelines Applicable to Court-to-Court Communications in Cross-Border Cases

As Adopted and Promulgated
BY
THE AMERICAN LAW INSTITUTE
AT WASHINGTON, D.C.
May 16, 2000

The Executive Office
The American Law Institute
4025 Chestnut Street
Philadelphia, Pennsylvania 19104-3099
Telephone: (215) 243-1600 ● Telecopier: (215) 243-1636
E-mail: ali@ali.org ● Website: http://www.ali.org

Guidelines
Applicable to Court-to-Court Communications in Cross-Border Cases

Introduction:

One of the most essential elements of cooperation in cross-border cases is communication among the administrating authorities of the countries involved. Because of the importance of the courts in insolvency and reorganization proceedings, it is even more essential that the supervising courts be able to coordinate their activities to assure the maximum available benefit for the stakeholders of financially troubled enterprises. These Guidelines are intended to enhance coordination and harmonization of insolvency proceedings that involve more than one country through communications among the jurisdictions involved. Communications by judges directly with judges or administrators in a foreign country, however, raise issues of credibility and proper procedures. The context alone is likely to create concern in litigants unless the process is transparent and clearly fair. Thus, communication among courts in cross-border cases is both more important and more sensitive than in domestic cases. These Guidelines encourage such communications while channeling them through transparent procedures. The Guidelines are meant to permit rapid cooperation in a developing insolvency case while ensuring due process to all concerned. The Guidelines at this time contemplate application only between Canada and the United States because of the very different rules governing communications with and among courts in Mexico. Nonetheless, a Mexican Court might choose to adopt some or all of these Guidelines for communications by a sindico with foreign administrators or courts.

A Court intending to employ the Guidelines — in whole or part, with or without modifications — should adopt them formally before applying them. A Court may wish to make its adoption of the Guidelines contingent upon, or temporary until, their adoption by other courts concerned in the matter. The adopting Court may want to make adoption or continuance conditional upon adoption of the Guidelines by the other Court in a substantially similar form, to ensure that judges, counsel, and parties are not subject to different standards of conduct.

The Guidelines should be adopted following such notice to the parties and counsel as would be given under local procedures with regard to any important procedural decision under similar circumstances. If communication with other courts is urgently needed, the local procedures, including notice requirements, that are used in urgent or emergency situations should be employed, including, if appropriate, an initial period of effectiveness, followed by further consideration of the Guidelines at a later time.

Questions about the parties entitled to such notice (for example, all parties or representative parties or representative counsel) and the nature of the court's consideration of any objections (for example, with or without a hearing) are governed by the Rules of Procedure in each jurisdiction and are not addressed in the Guidelines.

The Guidelines are not meant to be static, but are meant to be adapted and modified to fit the circumstances of individual cases and to change and evolve as the international insolvency community gains experience from working with them. They are to apply only in a manner that is consistent with local procedures and local ethical requirements. They do not address the details of notice and procedure that depend upon the law and practice in each jurisdiction. However, the Guidelines represent approaches that are likely to be highly useful in achieving efficient and just resolutions of cross-border insolvency issues. Their use, with such modifications and under such circumstances as may be appropriate in a particular case, is therefore recommended.

Guideline 1

Except in circumstances of urgency, prior to a communication with another Court, the Court should be satisfied that such a communication is consistent with all applicable Rules of Procedure in its country. Where a Court intends to apply these Guidelines (in whole or in part and with or without modifications), the Guidelines to be employed should, wherever possible, be formally adopted before they are applied. Coordination of Guidelines between courts is desirable and officials of both courts may communicate in accordance with Guideline 8(d) with regard to the application and implementation of the Guidelines.

Guideline 2

A Court may communicate with another Court in connection with matters relating to proceedings before it for the purposes of coordinating and harmonizing proceedings before it with those in the other jurisdiction.

Guideline 3

A Court may communicate with an Insolvency Administrator in another jurisdiction or an authorized Representative of the Court in that jurisdiction in connection with the coordination and harmonization of the proceedings before it with the proceedings in the other jurisdiction.

Guideline 4

A Court may permit a duly authorized Insolvency Administrator to communicate with a foreign Court directly, subject to the approval of the foreign Court, or through an Insolvency Administrator in the other jurisdiction or through an authorized Representative of the foreign Court on such terms as the Court considers appropriate.

Guideline 5

A Court may receive communications from a foreign Court or from an authorized Representative of the foreign Court or from a foreign Insolvency Administrator and should respond directly if the communication is from a foreign Court (subject to Guideline 7 in the case of two-way communications) and may respond directly or through an authorized Representative of the Court or through a duly authorized Insolvency Administrator if the communication is from a foreign Insolvency Administrator, subject to local rules concerning ex parte communications.

Guideline 6

Communications from a Court to another Court may take place by or through the Court:

(a) Sending or transmitting copies of formal orders, judgments, opinions, reasons for decision, endorsements, transcripts of proceedings, or other documents directly to the other Court and providing advance notice to counsel for affected parties in such manner as the Court considers appropriate;

(b) Directing counsel or a foreign or domestic Insolvency Administrator to transmit or deliver copies of documents, pleadings, affidavits, factums, briefs, or other documents that are filed or to be filed with the Court to the other Court in such fashion as may be appropriate and providing advance notice to counsel for affected parties in such manner as the Court considers appropriate;

(c) Participating in two-way communications with the other Court by telephone or video conference call or other electronic means, in which case Guideline 7 should apply.

Guideline 7

In the event of communications between the Courts in accordance with Guidelines 2 and 5 by means of telephone or video conference call or other electronic means, unless otherwise directed by either of the two Courts:

(a) Counsel for all affected parties should be entitled to participate in person during the communication and advance notice of the communication should be given to all parties in accordance with the Rules of Procedure applicable in each Court;

(b) The communication between the Courts should be recorded and may be transcribed. A written transcript may be prepared from a recording of the communication which, with the approval of both Courts, should be treated as an official transcript of the communication;

(c) Copies of any recording of the communication, of any transcript of the communication prepared pursuant to any Direction of either Court, and of any official transcript prepared from a recording should be filed as part of the record in the proceedings and made available to counsel for all parties in both Courts subject to such Directions as to confidentiality as the Courts may consider appropriate; and

(d) The time and place for communications between the Courts should be to the satisfaction of both Courts. Personnel other than Judges in each Court may communicate fully with each other to establish appropriate arrangements for the communication without the necessity for participation by counsel unless otherwise ordered by either of the Courts.

Guideline 8

In the event of communications between the Court and an authorized Representative of the foreign Court or a foreign Insolvency Administrator in accordance with Guidelines 3 and 5 by means of telephone or video conference call or other electronic means, unless otherwise directed by the Court:

(a) Counsel for all affected parties should be entitled to participate in person during the communication and advance notice of the communication should be given to all parties in accordance with the Rules of Procedure applicable in each Court;

(b) The communication should be recorded and may be transcribed. A written transcript may be prepared from a recording of the communication which, with the approval of the Court, can be treated as an official transcript of the communication;

(c) Copies of any recording of the communication, of any transcript of the communication prepared pursuant to any Direction of the Court, and of any official transcript prepared from a recording should be filed as part of the record in the proceedings and made available to the other Court and to counsel for all parties in both Courts subject to such Directions as to confidentiality as the Court may consider appropriate; and

(d) The time and place for the communication should be to the satisfaction of the Court. Personnel of the Court other than Judges may communicate fully with the authorized Representative of the foreign Court or the foreign Insolvency Administrator to establish appropriate arrangements for the communication without the necessity for participation by counsel unless otherwise ordered by the Court.

Guideline 9

A Court may conduct a joint hearing with another Court. In connection with any such joint hearing, the following should apply, unless otherwise ordered or unless otherwise provided in any previously approved Protocol applicable to such joint hearing:

(a) Each Court should be able to simultaneously hear the proceedings in the other Court.

(b) Evidentiary or written materials filed or to be filed in one Court should, in accordance with the Directions of that Court, be transmitted to the other Court or made available electronically in a publicly accessible system in advance of the hearing. Transmittal of such material to the other Court or its public availability in an electronic system should not subject the party filing the material in one Court to the jurisdiction of the other Court.

(c) Submissions or applications by the representative of any party should be made only to the Court in which the representative making the submissions is appearing unless the representative is specifically given permission by the other Court to make submissions to it.

(d) Subject to Guideline 7(b), the Court should be entitled to communicate with the other Court in advance of a joint hearing, with or without counsel being present, to establish Guidelines for the orderly making of submissions and rendering of decisions by the Courts, and to coordinate and resolve any procedural, administrative, or preliminary matters relating to the joint hearing.

(e) Subject to Guideline 7(b), the Court, subsequent to the joint hearing, should be entitled to communicate with the other Court, with or without counsel present, for the purpose of determining whether coordinated orders could be made by both Courts and to coordinate and resolve any procedural or nonsubstantive matters relating to the joint hearing.

Guideline 10

The Court should, except upon proper objection on valid grounds and then only to the extent of such objection, recognize and accept as authentic the provisions of statutes, statutory or administrative regulations, and rules of court of general application applicable to the proceedings in the other jurisdiction without the need for further proof or exemplification thereof.

Guideline 11

The Court should, except upon proper objection on valid grounds and then only to the extent of such objection, accept that Orders made in the proceedings in the other jurisdiction were duly and properly made or entered on or about their respective dates and accept that such Orders require no further proof or exemplification for purposes of the proceedings before it, subject to all such proper reservations as in the opinion of the Court are appropriate regarding proceedings by way of appeal or review that are actually pending in respect of any such Orders.

Guideline 12

The Court may coordinate proceedings before it with proceedings in another jurisdiction by establishing a Service List that may include parties that are entitled to receive notice of proceedings before the Court in the other jurisdiction ("Non-Resident Parties"). All notices, applications, motions, and other materials served for purposes of the proceedings before the Court may be ordered to also be provided to or served on the Non-Resident Parties by making such materials available electronically in a publicly accessible system or by facsimile transmission, certified or registered mail or delivery by courier, or in such other manner as may be directed by the Court in accordance with the procedures applicable in the Court.

Guideline 13

The Court may issue an Order or issue Directions permitting the foreign Insolvency Administrator or a representative of creditors in the proceedings in the other jurisdiction or an authorized Representative of the Court in the other jurisdiction to appear and be heard by the Court without thereby becoming subject to the jurisdiction of the Court.

Guideline 14

The Court may direct that any stay of proceedings affecting the parties before it shall, subject to further order of the Court, not apply to applications or motions brought by such parties before the other Court or that relief be granted to permit such parties to bring such applications or motions before the other Court on such terms and conditions as it considers appropriate. Court-to-Court communications in accordance with Guidelines 6 and 7 hereof may take place if an application or motion brought before the Court affects or might affect issues or proceedings in the Court in the other jurisdiction.

Guideline 15

A Court may communicate with a Court in another jurisdiction or with an authorized Representative of such Court in the manner prescribed by these Guidelines for purposes of coordinating and harmonizing proceedings before it with proceedings in the other jurisdiction regardless of the form of the proceedings before it or before the other Court wherever there is commonality among the issues and/or the parties in the proceedings. The Court should, absent compelling reasons to the contrary, so communicate with the Court in the other jurisdiction where the interests of justice so require.

Guideline 16

Directions issued by the Court under these Guidelines are subject to such amendments, modifications, and extensions as may be considered appropriate by the Court for the purposes described above and to reflect the changes and developments from time to time in the proceedings before it and before the other Court. Any Directions may be supplemented, modified, and restated from time to time and such modifications, amendments, and restatements should become effective upon being accepted by both Courts. If either Court intends to supplement, change, or abrogate Directions issued under these Guidelines in the absence of joint approval by both Courts, the Court should give the other Courts involved reasonable notice of its intention to do so.

Guideline 17

Arrangements contemplated under these Guidelines do not constitute a compromise or waiver by the Court of any powers, responsibilities, or authority and do not constitute a substantive determination of any matter in controversy before the Court or before the other Court nor a waiver by any of the parties of any of their substantive rights and claims or a diminution of the effect of any of the Orders made by the Court or the other Court.

INDEX